W9-BMK-503

American Women Writers

A Critical Reference Guide
from Colonial Times to the Present

*A Critical
Reference Guide
from Colonial Times
to the Present*

ABRIDGED EDITION
IN TWO VOLUMES
VOLUME 1: A TO L

AMERICAN WOMEN WRITERS

Langdon Lynne Faust

Editor

Frederick Ungar Publishing Co.
New York

Library of Congress Cataloging in Publication Data
Main entry under title:

American women writers.

  Includes bibliographies.
    1. American literature—Women authors—History and
criticism.   2. Women authors, American—Biography.
3. American literature—Women authors—Bibliography.
I. Faust, Langdon Lynne.
PS147.A42 1983   810'.9'9287   82-40286
ISBN 0-8044-6164-3 (pbk. : v. 1)

Preface

This two-volume edition of *American Women Writers* is an abridgment of the pioneering four-volume set that owes its publication to the growing interest in women's studies. The positive response of readers and critics to the original work (edited by Lina Mainiero and myself and published from 1979 to 1982) has been most gratifying. As the voluminous original is largely a reference work for libraries, however, there is a need for an edition more readily within the reach of the individual while still serving the interests of both scholar and general reader.

An important purpose of *American Women Writers* has been to present neglected authors of merit and assess them in the light of modern interest in women's position in American society. Many articles herein reflect the difficulties of practicing the craft of writing in a society that puts special obstacles in the path of women's literary ambition. Very few books by women appeared in the eighteenth century. Of these, most were devotional, many were published posthumously, and almost all carried an apology for the impropriety of presenting a woman's views to the public. But by the mid-nineteenth century women not only made up a majority of the reading public but, in spite of all obstacles, were responsible for a significant number of the nation's best sellers. With the rapid expansion of the periodical market, women became contributors and editors. They produced a wide range of fiction and nonfiction, children's stories, inspirational literature, scholarly works, journalism, and temperance and suffrage propaganda.

Of the more than one thousand biocritical articles in the original edition of *American Women Writers*, some four hundred have been selected for this abridgment. They include the more important writers and those whose works have some particular historical significance. Coverage of a range of writers with the greatest variety of style, subject, and genre has been maintained. Here are novelists, short-story writers, and poets, women who wrote for Broadway and the little-theater movement, for movies (silent and talking), for radio and television. It is altogether a record of a very considerable achievement.

Authors are listed under the names used by the Library of Congress. Although this is not the perfect solution to the vexing problem of what names to use for women who changed them when they married—there is probably no perfect solution—it does mean that usage here is coordinated with that of most libraries. The index includes cross-references for other names the women used. Each article is headed by data on birth, ancestry, and marriage. There is a brief summary of the writer's life and a description and evaluation of her major works, followed by a list of published books and a secondary bibliography.

The contributors—all trained scholars—have updated and revised articles wherever necessary. Some few articles have also been added. The continuing commitment of the contributors to the project has made this abridged edition much more than simply a shorter version of the earlier work.

LLF

Contributors to the Abridged Edition

Allen, Suzanne
  Caroline Gordon
  Laura Keane Zametkin
    Hobson
  Lillian Smith

Anderson, Celia Catlett
  Cornelia Lynde Meigs

Anderson, Nancy G.
  Dorothy Scarborough

Armeny, Susan
  Lavinia Lloyd Dock

Armitage, Shelley
  Ina Donna Coolbrith
  Anne Ellis

Bach, Peggy
  Evelyn Scott

Bakerman, Jane S.
  Dorothea Frances Canfield
    Fisher
  Margaret Millar
  May Sarton
  Gene Stratton-Porter
  Mary Alsop Sture-Vasa
  Dorothy Uhnak
  Jessamyn West

Bannan, Helen M.
  Elizabeth Bacon Custer
  Elaine Goodale Eastman
  Helen Maria Fiske Hunt
    Jackson
  Elizabeth Gertrude Levin
    Stern

Barbour, Paula L.
  Jane Auer Bowles

Baruch, Elaine Hoffman
  Susan Sontag

Baytop, Adrianne
  Margaret Walker
  Phillis Wheatley

Beasley, Maurine
  Mary E. Clemmer Ames
  Kate Field

Benardete, Jane
  Abby Morton Diaz
  Mary Abigail Dodge
  Lydia Howard Huntley
    Sigourney

Ben-Merre, Diana
  Helen McCloy

Berke, Jacqueline
Harriet Stratemeyer Adams
Eleanor Hodgman Porter

Berry, Linda S.
Georgia Douglas Camp
Johnson

Bienstock, Beverly Gray
Anita Loos
Cornelia Otis Skinner

Bird, Christiane
Harriet Mulford Stone
Lothrop

Bittker, Anne S.
Mary Margaret McBride

Bixler, Phyllis
Frances Eliza Hodgson Burnett

Blair, Karen J.
Jane Cunningham Croly

Bordin, Ruth
Elizabeth Margaret Chandler

Breitsprecher, Nancy
Zona Gale

Bremer, Sidney H.
Elia Wilkinson Peattie
Edith Franklin Wyatt

Brett, Sally
Bernice Kelly Harris
Edith Summers Kelley
Ida Minerva Tarbell

Brown, Lynda W.
Caroline Lee Whiting Hentz
Anne Newport Royall

Buchanan, Harriette Cuttino
Josephine Lyons Scott Pinckney
Lizette Woodworth Reese

Bucknall, Barbara J.
Pearl Sydenstricker Buck
Ursula K. LeGuin
Phyllis McGinley
Hannah Whitall Smith

Burns, Lois
Shirley Jackson

Byers, Inzer
Annie Heloise Abel
Catherine Drinker Bowen
Carrie Lane Chapman Catt
Frances Manwaring Caulkins
Angelina Emily Grimké
Sarah Moore Grimké
Martha Joanna Reade Nash
Lamb
Alma Lutz
Margaret Bayard Smith

Carnes, Valerie
Janet Flanner

Carr, Pat
Flannery O'Connor

Carroll, Linda A.
Jean Craighead George

Clark, Susan L.
Mignon Good Eberhart

Cleveland, Carol
Patricia Highsmith

Cohn, Jan
Mary Roberts Rinehart

Cook, Martha E.
Annie Fellows Johnston
Katherine Sherwood Bonner
McDowell
Mary Noailles Murfree

Cook, Sylvia
Olive Tilford Dargan
Grace Lumpkin

Coultrap-McQuin, Susan
Catharine Read Arnold
Williams

Cowell, Pattie
Bathsheba Bowers
Annis Boudinot Stockton

Crabbe, Katharyn F.
Jane Andrews

Cutler, Evelyn S.
Rose Cecil O'Neill

Dame, Enid
Edna St. Vincent Millay

Davidson, Cathy N.
Laura Jean Libbey
Tabitha Gilman Tenney

Davis, Thadious M.
Anna Julia Haywood Cooper
Mary Evelyn Moore Davis
Shirley Graham
Rhoda Elizabeth Waterman
White

Deegan, Mary Jo
Sophonisba Preston
Breckinridge
Helen Merrell Lynd

DeMarr, Mary Jean
Charlotte Armstrong
Doris Miles Disney
Janet Ayer Fairbank
Rachel Lyman Field
Agnes Newton Keith
Alice Caldwell Hegan Rice
Mari Sandoz
Anya Seton
Ruth Suckow
Agnes Sligh Turnbull
Carolyn Wells

Deming, Caren J.
Elaine Sterne Carrington

Denniston, Dorothy L.
Paule Marshall

Donovan, Josephine
Louise Imogen Guiney
Sarah Orne Jewett
Lucy Larcom
Celia Laighton Thaxter

Eliasberg, Ann Pringle
Dorothy Thompson

Estess, Sybil
Elizabeth Bishop

Etheridge, Billie W.
Abigail Smith Adams
Mercy Otis Warren

Evans, Elizabeth
Helen MacInnes Highet
Anne Tyler
Eudora Welty

Ewell, Barbara C.
Eliza Jane Poitevent
Nicholson

Faust, Langdon
Frances Elizabeth Caroline
Willard

Ferguson, Mary Anne
Sally Benson
Doris Betts
Tess Slesinger

Fleenor, Juliann E.
Catharine Esther Beecher
Emily Chubbuck Judson
Margaret Sanger

Fowler, Lois
Frances Dana Barker Gage
Ida Husted Harper

Franklin, Phyllis
Judith Sargent Murray
Elsie Worthington Clews
Parsons

Frazer, Winifred
Dorothy Day

Freibert, Lucy M.
Jessica Nelson North
MacDonald

Friedman, Ellen G.
Anna Hempstead Branch
Joyce Carol Oates

Gabbard, Lucina P.
Clare Boothe Luce

Gartner, Carol B.
Rachel Louise Carson
Mary Putnam Jacobi
Myra Kelly

Gaskill, Gayle
Jean Collins Kerr

Giles, Jane
Catharine Maria Sedgwick

Ginsberg, Elaine K.
Amelia Jenks Bloomer
Maria Susanna Cummins
Hannah Webster Foster
Betty Wehner Smith
Emma Dorothy Eliza Nevitte
Southworth

Gladstein, Mimi R.
Ayn Rand

Goldman, Maureen
Esther Edwards Burr

Gorsky, Susan R.
Djuna Barnes

Gowing, S. Julia
Rebecca Harding Davis

Graham, Theodora R.
Louise Bogan
Josephine Miles
Harriet Monroe

Grant, Mary H.
Julia Ward Howe

Greene, Dana
Sophia Hume
Lucretia Coffin Mott

Greyson, Laura
Hannah Arendt

Groben, Anne R.
Ella Wheeler Wilcox

Guin, Sandra Carlin
Louella Oettinger Parsons

Hamblen, Abigail Ann
Margaret Wade Campbell
Deland
Mary Eleanor Wilkins
Freeman

Hardesty, Nancy A.
Phoebe Worrall Palmer
Elizabeth Cady Stanton
Emma Hart Willard

Hardy, Willene S.
Mary Therese McCarthy

Healey, Claire
Hilda Doolittle
Amy Lowell

Helbig, Alethea K.
Lucretia Peabody Hale
Madeleine L'Engle

Henderson, Katherine
Joan Didion

Hill, Vicki Lynn
Bessie Breuer
Helen Hamilton Gardener
Theresa Serber Malkiel
Dorothy Myra Page
Marie Van Vorst
Mary Heaton Vorse
Helen Maria Winslow

Hobbs, Glenda
Harriette Louisa Simpson
Arnow

Hoeveler, Diane Long
Babette Deutsch
Jessica Mitford
Frances Jane Crosby Van
Alstyne

Holdstein, Deborah H.
Mae West

Hornstein, Jacqueline
Sarah Symmes Fiske
Sarah Parsons Moorhead
Sarah Wentworth Apthorp
Morton
Sarah Osborn

Jane Turell
Elizabeth White

Howard, Lillie
Fannie Cook

Hughson, Lois
Mary Ritter Beard
Barbara Tuchman

Johnson, Claudia D.
Olive Logan

Johnson, Lee Ann
Mary Hallock Foote

Johnson, Robin
Marianne Craig Moore

Jones, Judith P.
Eleanor Clark

Kahn, Miriam
Ruth Fulton Benedict
Margaret Mead

Karp, Sheema Hamdani
Adrienne Cecile Rich

Kaufman, Janet E.
Eliza Frances Andrews
Elizabeth Avery Meriwether
Katharine Prescott Wormeley

Keeshen, Kathleen Kearney
Marguerite Higgins

Kern, Donna Casella
Frances Fuller Victor

Kessler, Carol Farley
Elizabeth Stuart Phelps
Elizabeth Stuart Phelps Ward

Kimball, Gayle
Harriet Elizabeth Beecher
Stowe

King, Margaret J.
Emily Price Post
Mary Elizabeth Wilson
Sherwood

Knapp, Bettina L.
Anaïs Nin

Koengeter, L. W.
Maria Gowen Brooks
Hannah Mather Crocker
Margaretta V. Bleeker
Faugeres
Rose Wilder Lane

Kohlstedt, Sally Gregory
Anna Botsford Comstock
Almira Hart Lincoln Phelps

Koon, Helene
Anna Cora Mowatt Ritchie
Sally Sayward Barrell Wood

Kouidis, Virginia M.
Mina Loy

Krieg, Joann Peck
Mary Baker Glover Eddy

Kuznets, Lois R.
Esther Forbes

Lamping, Marilyn
Ida B. Wells Barnett
Pauline Elizabeth Hopkins

Loeb, Helen
Inez Haynes Irwin

Londré, Felicia Hardison
Agnes De Mille
Anne Crawford Flexner
Rose Franken
Marguerite Merington
Lillian Mortimer
Martha Morton
Josephina Niggli

McCarthy, Joanne
Kay Boyle
Betty Bard MacDonald
Kathleen Thompson Norris

McClure, Charlotte S.
Gertrude Franklin Horn
Atherton

McDannell, M. Colleen
Ellen Gould Harmon White

McFadden-Gerber, Margaret
Sally Carrighar
Wilma Dykeman
Josephine Winslow Johnson

Edythe M. McGovern
Susan Glaspell
Lorraine Hansberry
Charlotte Shapiro Zolotow

MacPike, Loralee
Elizabeth Hardwick
Emily Kimbrough

Madsen, Carol Cornwall
Emmeline Blanche Woodward
Wells

Maida, Patricia D.
Lillian O'Donnell

Mainiero, Lina
Willa Sibert Cather

Maio, Kathleen L.
Anna Katharine Green Rohlfs
Metta Victoria Fuller Victor

Margolis, Tina
Rochelle Owens

Masel-Walters, Lynne
Inez Haynes Irwin
Miriam Florence Folline
Leslie

Masteller, Jean Carwile
Annie Nathan Meyer

Matherne, Beverly M.
Alice Gerstenberg

Mayer, Elsie F.
Anne Morrow Lindbergh

Menger, Lucy
Jane Roberts

Mitchell, Sally
Cora Miranda Baggerly Older
Rose Porter

Moe, Phyllis
Helen Stuart Campbell
Eliza Lee Cabot Follen
Sarah Chauncey Woolsey

Mollenkott, Virginia Ramey
Grace Livingston Hill Lutz
Marjorie Hope Nicolson

Morris, Linda A.
Marietta Holley
Frances Miriam Berry
Whitcher

Mortimer, Gail
Katherine Anne Porter

Mossberg, Barbara Antonina
Clarke
Sylvia Plath
Genevieve Taggard

Moynihan, Ruth Barnes
Abigail Scott Duniway

Mussell, Kay
Phyllis Ayame Whitney

Nance, Guin A.
Elizabeth Spencer

Neils, Patricia Langhals
Emily Hahn

Newman, Anne
Julia Mood Peterkin
Amélie Rives Troubetzkoy

Nichols, Kathleen L.
Miriam Coles Harris
Susanna Haswell Rowson
Anne Sexton

Norman, Marion
Lucretia Maria Davidson
Margaret Miller Davidson

Orsagh, Jacqueline E.
Martha Gellhorn

Payne, Alma J.
Louisa May Alcott

Petersen, Margaret
Emily Dickinson
Janet Lewis

Pettis, Joyce
Zora Neale Hurston

Phillips, Elizabeth
Elizabeth Fries Lummis Ellet
Jean Garrigue
Estelle Anna Robinson Lewis
Frances Sargent Locke Osgood
Mabel Loomis Todd
Sarah Helen Power Whitman

Piercy, Josephine K.
Anne Dudley Bradstreet

Pogel, Nancy
Constance Mayfield Rourke

Poland, Helene Dwyer
Susanne Katherina Knauth
Langer

Pringle, Mary Beth
Charlotte Perkins Stetson
Gilman

Puk, Francine Shapiro
Dorothy Rothschild Parker

Rayson, Ann
Ann Lane Petry

Richmond, Velma Bourgeois
  *Frances Parkinson Wheeler
    Keyes*
  Agnes Repplier

Roberts, Audrey
  *Caroline Matilda Stansbury
    Kirkland*

Roberts, Bette B.
  Lydia Maria Francis Child

Roberts, Elizabeth
  Eliza Ann Youmans

Rogers, Katharine M.
  Lillian Hellman

Rowe, Anne
  Elizabeth Madox Roberts
  Constance Fenimore Woolson

Rudnick, Lois P.
  Mabel Ganson Dodge Luhan

Ryan, Rosalie Tutela
  *Jane Erminia Starkweather
    Locke*

Schleuning, Neala Yount
  Meridel Le Sueur

Schoen, Carol B.
  Hannah Adams
  Emma Lazarus
  Penina Moise

Schull, Elinor
  Adela Rogers St. Johns

Schwartz, Helen J.
  Elizabeth Meriwether Gilmer

Seaton, Beverly
  Mary Hartwell Catherwood
  Gladys Bagg Taber
  Susan Bogert Warner
  Kate Douglas Smith Wiggin
  Laura Ingalls Wilder
  Mabel Osgood Wright

Shakir, Evelyn
  Ednah Dow Littlehale Cheney

Sharistanian, Janet
  Elizabeth Janeway
  Helen Waite Papashvily

Sherman, Sarah Way
  Sarah Knowles Bolton
  Alice Brown
  Rose Terry Cooke
  Louise Chandler Moulton
  Mary Alicia Owen

Shinn, Thelma J.
  Margaret Ayer Barnes
  Kate O'Flaherty Chopin
  Martha Finley
  Shirley Ann Grau
  *Harriet Elizabeth Prescott
    Spofford*

Shortreed, Vivian H.
  Elizabeth Oakes Prince Smith
  Jane Grey Cannon Swisshelm

Skaggs, Peggy
  Helen Adams Keller
  Catherine Marshall

Slaughter, Jane
   Elizabeth Gurley Flynn

Smelstor, Marjorie
   Frances Anne Kemble

Smith, Susan Sutton
   Adelaide Crapsey
   Caroline Wells Healey Dall
   Harriet Farley
   Eliza Ware Rotch Farrar
   Caroline Howard Gilman
   Sarah Jane Clarke Lippincott
   Sarah Margaret Fuller Ossoli
   Harriet Jane Hanson Robinson
   Phoebe Atwood Taylor
   Mary Virginia Hawes Terhune
   Jean Webster

Snipes, Katherine
   Laura Riding Jackson
   Carson Smith McCullers

Sprague, Rosemary
   Sara Teasdale

Springer, Marlene
   Edith Newbold Jones Wharton

Sproat, Elaine
   Lola Ridge

Stanford, Ann
   Sarah Kemble Knight
   May Swenson

Staples, Katherine
   Alma Sioux Scarberry

Stauffer, Helen
   Bess Streeter Aldrich
   Bertha Muzzy Sinclair

Steele, Karen B.
   Elizabeth Wormeley Latimer
   Mary Traill Spence Lowell
     Putnam

Stein, Karen F.
   Alice Ruth Moore Dunbar
     Nelson
   Elinor Hoyt Wylie

Stinson, Peggy
   Jane Addams
   Agnes Smedley
   Anzia Yezierska

Swidler, Arlene Anderson
   Aline Murray Kilmer
   Sister Madeleva

Sylvander, Carolyn Wedin
   Jesse Redmon Fauset
   Mary White Ovington

Szymanski, Karen
   Eliza Woodson Burhans
     Farnham

Tebbe, Jennifer L.
   Elizabeth Cochrane
   Rheta Childe Dorr
   Anne O'Hare McCormick
   Anna Louise Strong

Terris, Virginia R.
   Lilian Whiting

Thiébaux, Marcelle
  Faith Baldwin Cuthrell
  Julia Caroline Ripley Dorr
  Ellen Anderson Gholson
    Glasgow
  Marjorie Kinnan Rawlings

Thomas, Gwendolyn
  Pauli Murray

Thompson, Dorothea Mosley
  Mary Simmerson Cunningham
    Logan

Townsend, Janis
  Mildred Aldrich
  Gertrude Stein

Treckel, Paula A.
  Alice Morse Earle
  Lucy Maynard Salmon
  Eliza Roxy Snow Smith

Turner, Alberta
  Barbara Howes
  Denise Levertov
  Muriel Rukeyser

Uffen, Ellen Serlen
  Fannie Hurst

Wahlstrom, Billie J.
  Alice Cary
  Betty Friedan

Walker, Cynthia L.
  Edna Ferber

Wall, Cheryl A.
  Gwendolyn Brooks
  Frances Ellen Watkins
    Harper

Ward, Jean M.
  Ella Rhodes Higginson

Werden, Frieda L.
  Kate Millett

White, Barbara A.
  Lillie Devereux Blake
  Sarah Josepha Buell Hale
  Sara Payson Willis Parton

Wright, Catherine Morris
  Mary Mapes Dodge

Yee, Carole Zonis
  Leane Zugsmith

Yongue, Patricia Lee
  Zoë Akins

Zilboorg, Caroline
  Charlotte Ann Fillebrown
    Jerauld

Abbreviations of Reference Works

AA   American Authors, 1600–1900: A Biographical Dictionary of American Literature (Eds. S. J. Kunitz and H. Haycraft, 1938).

AW   American Women: Fifteen-Hundred Biographies with Over 1,400 Portraits (2 vols., Eds. F. E. Willard and M. A. Livermore, 1897).

CA   Contemporary Authors: A Bio-Bibliographical Guide to Current Authors and Their Works (various editors, 1962–present).

CAL   Cyclopaedia of American Literature, Embracing Personal and Critical Notices of Authors and Selections from Their Writings (2 vols., Eds. E. A. Duyckinck and G. L. Duyckinck, 1866).

CB   Current Biography: Who's News and Why (Eds. M. Block, 1940–1943; A. Rothe, 1944–1953; M. D. Candee, 1954–1958; C. Moritz, 1959–present).

DAB   Dictionary of American Biography (10 vols., Eds. A. Johnson and D. Malone; 5 suppls., Eds. E. T. James and J. A. Garraty; 1927–1977).

FPA   The Female Poets of America (Ed. R. W. Griswold, 1849).

HWS   History of Woman Suffrage (Vols. 1–3, Eds. E. C. Stanton, S. B. Anthony, and M. J. Gage; Vol. 4, Eds. S. B. Anthony and I. H. Harper; Vols. 5 and 6, Ed. I. H. Harper; 1881–1922).

LSL   Library of Southern Literature, Compiled under the Direct Supervision of Southern Men of Letters (16 vols., Eds. E. A. Alderman and J. C. Harris; Suppl., Eds. E. A. Alderman, C. A. Smith, and J. C. Metcalf, reprinted 1970).

NAW   Notable American Women, 1607–1950: A Biographical Dictionary (3 vols., Eds. E. T. James, J. W. James, and P. S. Boyer, 1971).

NCAB   National Cyclopedia of American Biography: Being the History of the United States As Illustrated in the Lives of the Founders, Builders, and Defenders of the Republic, and of the Men and Women Who Are Doing the Work and Moulding the Thought of the Present Time (various editors, Vols. 1–57, 1892–1976; Vols. A–M, Permanent Series, 1930–1978).

20thCA *Twentieth Century Authors: A Biographical Dictionary of Modern Literature* (Eds. S. J. Kunitz and H. Haycraft, 1942).

20thCAS *Twentieth Century Authors, First Supplement: A Biographical Dictionary of Modern Literature* (Eds. S. J. Kunitz and V. Colby, 1955).

WA *World Authors, 1950–1970: A Companion Volume to Twentieth Century Authors* (Ed. J. Wakeman, 1975).

Abbreviations of Periodicals

In the bibliographies, periodicals have been abbreviated in conformity with the Modern Language Association master list of abbreviations. Newspapers and magazines not in that list are abbreviated as follows:

AHR   *American Historical Review*
CathW   *Catholic World*
CSM   *Christian Science Monitor*
EngElemR   *English Elementary Review*
JSocHis   *Journal of Social History*
KR   *Kirkus Review*
NewR   *New Republic*
NYHT   *New York Herald Tribune*
NYHTB   *New York Herald Tribune Books*
NYT   *New York Times*
NYTMag   *New York Times Magazine*
NYTBR   *New York Times Book Review*
PW   *Publisher's Weekly*
SatEvePost   *Saturday Evening Post*
ScribM   *Scribner's Magazine*
VV   *Village Voice*
WallStJ   *Wall Street Journal*
WLB   *Wilson Library Bulletin*
WrD   *Writer's Digest*
WSCL   *Wisconsin Studies in Contemporary Literature*

American Women Writers

*A Critical Reference Guide
from Colonial Times to the Present*

Annie Heloise Abel

B. *18 Feb. 1873, Fernhurst, Sussex, England; d. 14 March 1947, Aberdeen, Washington*
D. *of George and Amelia Anne Hogben Abel; m. George Cockburn Henderson, 1922*

A.'s family emigrated to Salina, Kansas, in 1884. She attained her literary prominence as an authority on American Indian history. Her master's thesis was "Indian Reservations in Kansas and the Extinguishment of Their Title" (1902). Her doctoral dissertation, "The History of Events Resulting in Indian Consolidation West of the Mississippi," won the American Historical Association's Justin Winsor Prize in 1906 and was published in the *Annual Report* of that year.

A.'s major work was the three-volume study, *The Slaveholding Indians*. The first volume was *The American Indian as Slaveholder and Secessionist: An Omitted Chapter in the Diplomatic History of the Confederacy* (1915). In A.'s view, though there was slaveholding among Indian tribes, only the Choctaw and Chickasaw were drawn to the Confederacy because of concern about slavery. The South, out of its own needs, notably strategic concern for territorial solidarity, offered a number of concessions. Most significant perhaps were Confederate guarantees of criminal and civil rights. The South also offered to give Indians control of their own trade, but that offer was later rescinded. Through General Albert Pike, the Confederacy made its approaches to the western tribes, and his wartime disaffection with the Confederacy over its betrayal of promises to the Indians would prove costly to the South.

Despite Southern concessions, A. noted, the Indians "actually fought on both sides and for the same motives and impulses as whites." In her view, it was the failure of the U.S. government to provide the promised protection for the Southern Indians which led them to ally with the Confederacy. From first to last, she maintained, military conditions and events determined political ones.

In the next two volumes, *The American Indian as Participant in the*

Civil War (1919) and *The American Indian under Reconstruction* (1925), A. traced the tragic consequences of Indian involvement in the sectional strife.

Throughout her work A. proves to be both an effective researcher and a perceptive scholar who wrote with sympathy about problems the Indians encountered. Although occasionally she wrote in a paternalistic or romantic tone, she is a sympathetic but essentially objective historian. Her English background, she noted, freed her from sectional attachments in dealing with Civil War issues. And she could likewise appraise with detachment the conflict between Indian claims and American expansionist urges. Her work is marked with a sense of the tragedy which befell the Indians, but that sense did not obscure her judgment. If, in her final view, the fate of the Indians was determined by white greed and power, she recognized also the part which the Indians' "inability to learn from experience" played in the final outcome. The breadth of her research and her capacity for informed, detached judgment gave her work its strength and power.

WORKS: *Brief Guide to Points of Historical Interest in Baltimore City* (1908). *Proposals for an Indian State, 1778–1878* (1909). *The Official Correspondence of James S. Calhoun* (edited by Abel, 1915). *The American Indian as Slaveholder and Secessionist* (1915). *A New Lewis and Clark Map* (1916). *The American Indian as Participant in the Civil War* (1919). *The American Indian under Reconstruction* (1925). *A Sidelight on Anglo-American Relations, 1839–1858* (edited by Abel, with F. J. Klingsberg, 1927). *Chardon's Journal at Fort Clark, 1834–39* (edited by Abel, 1932). *Tabeau's Narrative of Loisel's Expedition to the Upper Missouri* (edited by Abel, 1939).

BIBLIOGRAPHY: For articles in reference works, see: *NAW* (article by F. Prucha).
   Other references: *AHR* (July 1947). *Mississippi Valley Historical Review* (March 1916; March 1920). *Yale University Obituary Record of Graduates* (1946–47).

INZER BYERS

Abigail Smith Adams

B. 11 Nov. 1744, Weymouth, Massachusetts; d. 28 Oct. 1818, Quincy,
  Massachusetts
D. of William and Elizabeth Quincy Smith; m. John Adams, 1764

Due to her poor health, A.'s formal education was virtually non-existent. Fortunately, however, she was surrounded by literate adults who guided her studies, which ranged from Plato, Locke, and Burke to the Bible. A. bore five children in the first eight years of her marriage to John Adams, who became the second U.S. president in 1797. Her son John Quincy was the sixth president.

A.'s claim to literary fame rests upon the hundreds of letters picturing her times in warmly human terms. John was her favorite correspondent, but she wrote extensively to her large family and to a wide circle beyond, including such intellectuals as Mercy Otis Warren and Thomas Jefferson.

In *New Letters of Abigail Adams* (1947), editor Stewart Mitchell printed her correspondence to her older sister, Mary Cranch. To Mary more than anyone else, A. wrote of "women's concerns"—smallpox and fevers, incompetent servants, inflation, poor food, bad weather, and the deplorable state the White House was in when she arrived to become its first mistress.

Mitchell's publication corrects the bowdlerized portrait of A. rendered by her Victorian grandson, Charles Francis Adams. His *Letters of Mrs. Adams* (2 vols., 1840–41) and *Familiar Letters of John Adams and His Wife Abigail Adams during the Revolution* (1876) not only censor her passionate declarations of love to John, but also delete much from her personal accounts of pregnancies and childbirth, the dysentery epidemic of 1775, and smallpox inoculations.

The Book of Abigail and John is limited to what its editors consider the best letters of A. and her husband. In them, A.'s affectionate nature is expressed freely. Her loneliness and pride in herself and in her husband is described, too: "I miss my partner, and find myself uneaquuil [*sic*] to the cares which fall upon me; . . . I hope in time to have the Reputation of being as good a Farmeress as my partner has of being a good Statesman."

A. never hesitated to address herself to political matters. Two issues which drew strong reaction from her were slavery and women's rights. Writing to John in 1774, she wished "most sincerely there was not a slave in the province." Concerning women's rights, A. wrote early in 1776 the letter for which she is most famous: "[A]nd by the way in the new Code of Laws which I suppose it will be necessary for you to make I desire you would Remember the Ladies, and be more generous to them than your ancestors." Undaunted by John's reply denying her petition and charging her with being "saucy," she retorted, "I can not say that I think you very generous to the Ladies, for whilst you are proclaiming peace and good will to Men, Emancipating all Nations, you insist upon retaining absolute power over Wives."

Never dull, always animated, A.'s letters are more like conversations than compositions. For the most part, her style is easy and natural. Her spelling is phonetic, underscoring the verbal nature of her writing, and her punctuation follows natural pauses rather than written conventions. Her letters tell us how it felt to live through the American Revolution and what it was like to be a New England Puritan in Europe in the late eighteenth century. More than that, however, they help us understand the creative force we call the "Puritan ethic."

WORKS: *Letters of Mrs. Adams, the Wife of John Adams* (Ed. C. F. Adams, 2 vols., 1840–41). *Familiar Letters of John Adams and His Wife Abigail Adams during the Revolution* (Ed. C. F. Adams, 1876). *New Letters of Abigail Adams, 1788–1801* (Ed. S. Mitchell, 1947). *Adams Family Correspondence* (Eds. L. H. Butterfield et al., 4 vols., 1963–73). *The Book of Abigail and John* (Eds. L. H. Butterfield et al., 1975).

BIBLIOGRAPHY: Bobbe, D., *Abigail Adams, the Second First Lady* (1929). Bradford, G., *Portraits of American Women* (1919). Gordon, L., *From Lady Washington to Mrs. Cleveland* (1889). Ketcham, R. L., in *"Remember the Ladies": New Perspectives on Women in American History*, Ed. C. V. R. George (1975). Minningerode, M., *Some American Ladies: Seven Informal Biographies* (1926). Richards, L. E., *Abigail Adams and Her Times* (1936). Shepherd, J., *The Adams Chronicles: Four Generations of Greatness* (1975). Stone, I., *Those Who Love* (1965). Whitney, J., *Abigail Adams* (1949).

Other references: *ScribM* (Jan. 1930).

BILLIE W. ETHERIDGE

Hannah Adams

B. 2 Oct. 1755, Medfield, Massachusetts; d. 15 Dec. 1831, Brookline,
  Massachusetts
D. of Thomas and Eleanor Clark Adams

The second of five children, A. was considered too frail to attend public school and was educated at home. Discovering that she was unable to
support herself at needlework, A. undertook a literary career. Although
excessively modest and timid, she was the first and for many years the
only woman permitted to use the Boston Atheneum. Her learning was
prodigious. While her books were successful, poor business arrangements
limited the income she derived from them.

The research into religious sects that A. had begun for her own edifica-
tion became, in 1784, her first published volume, *Alphabetical Compendium of the Various Sects Which Have Appeared from the Beginning
of the Christian Era to the Present Day.* In its objectivity, it represented
a major improvement over existing works on the subject, and although it
contains some misinformation due to inaccurate sources, the scope of its
coverage is impressive. Edited and retitled for later editions, it includes a
dictionary listing of the separate Christian sects, a survey of the beliefs
of non-Christian groups, and a geographical breakdown of world reli-
gions.

For her *Summary History of New England* (1799), A. undertook
serious primary research, delving into state archives and old newspapers,
causing serious injury to her eyesight. The material, which covers events
from the sailing of the *Mayflower* through the adoption of the federal
Constitution, is presented in a clear, straightforward manner with occasional attempts to recreate particularly affecting scenes such as the farewell of the Pilgrims from Holland.

The *Abridgement of the History of New England for the Use of
Young People* (1807) involved a protracted controversy with Dr. Jedidiah
Morse over unfair competition, eventually resolved in A.'s favor. In revising her *History*, A. edited it for greater smoothness and clarity, but
simplified neither the language nor the thought. She added a paragraph
at the end of each chapter to point up the moral lesson to be learned
from the event.

While working on the *Abridgement*, A. published *The Truth and Ex-*

cellence of the Christian Religion Exhibited (1804), surveying the support which laymen had given to their religion since the 17th c. Divided into two parts, it first presents brief biographies of sixty men, showing how their lives exemplified the Christian spirit. The second part provides excerpts listed under various kinds of "Evidence in Favor of Revealed Religion." Most of the material was drawn from the writings of those covered in the first section, but it also includes selections by the Marchioness de Dillery, Hannah More, and a Mrs. West.

The History of the Jews from the Destruction of Jerusalem to the Present Time (1812) represented one of the first attempts to relate their story sympathetically, a story which A. described as a "tedious succession of oppression and persecution." Written to encourage efforts to convert the Jews, her discussion of the early period stresses its substantiation of "our Savior's prediction" of their fate. Not completely free from bias, A. nevertheless carefully recorded the confiscatory taxes, the mass murders, and the expulsions suffered by the Jews.

A. was probably the first professional woman writer in America, pursuing her career despite the knowledge that the "penalties and discouragements attending authors in general fall upon women with double weight." Although most discussions of A. adopt her own designation of herself as a "compiler," she was, in fact, a fine historian whose meticulous research included examination of primary materials when available, extraordinarily wide reading of secondary sources, and a remarkable objectivity. Her histories are no longer relevant, but her contributions to historiography deserve attention.

WORKS: *Alphabetical Compendium of the Various Sects Which Have Appeared from the Beginning of the Christian Era to the Present Day* (1784). *Summary History of New England* (1799). *The Truth and Excellence of the Christian Religion Exhibited* (1804). *Abridgement of the History of New England for the Use of Young People* (1807). *The History of the Jews from the Destruction of Jerusalem to the Present Time* (1812). *A Narrative of the Controversy between the Rev. Jedidiah Morse, D.D., and the Author* (1814). *A Concise Account of the London Society for Promoting Christianity Amongst the Jews* (1816). *Letters on the Gospels* (1824). *Memoir of Hannah Adams* (Ed. J. Tuckerman, 1832).

BIBLIOGRAPHY: Brooks, V. W., *The Flowering of New England* (1936).
   Other references: *The Dedham Historical Register* (July 1896). *The New England Galaxy* (Spring 1971). *New England Magazine* (May 1894).

CAROL B. SCHOEN

Harriet Stratemeyer Adams

B. *3 Dec. 1892, Newark, New Jersey; d. 27 March 1982, Pottersville,*
New Jersey
Writes under: Victor Appleton II, May Hollis Barton, Franklin W. Dixon,
Laura Lee Hope, Carolyn Keene, Ann Sheldon, Helen Louise Thorndyke
D. of Edward and Magdalene Van Camp Stratemeyer; m. Russell Vroom
Adams, 1915

Better known under a variety of pen names, A. may well be the most prolific woman writer of all time. Author of the perennially popular Nancy Drew mysteries for young girls and the equally popular Hardy Boys and Tom Swift, Jr., series for young boys, she has also written numerous volumes in the Bobbsey Twins, Honey Bunch, and Dana Girls series. All of these, along with the famous Rover boys, were originated by her father who founded the Stratemeyer Syndicate in 1901. A "writing factory" located in Maplewood, New Jersey, it still turns out the most successful series books ever written for American youngsters roughly eight to fourteen years of age. The Hardy Boys and Nancy Drew series alone sell sixteen million copies a year.

When he died in 1930, Stratemeyer left to his daughters, Harriet and Edna, the job of keeping up the seventeen sets of series then in print. Edna remained in the business for twelve years; Harriet still remains a senior partner, working with three junior partners to update earlier titles to create new volumes. A. herself has written 179 volumes and shows no signs of slowing down. She has written all fifty-five titles in the Nancy Drew series, including rewrites of the first three originated by her father: the young sleuth's blue roadster with running boards had to be replaced, along with outdated hair styles and various dialects which the modern reader would find offensive.

Characters produced by the Stratemeyer Factory are either good or bad because, A. maintains, mixed characters don't interest children. Plots are spun according to a strict formula guaranteed to satisfy adolescent fantasy: action and suspense packed into twenty cliff-hanging chapters. Only eighteen years of age, Nancy Drew is omniscient and omnipotent, solving mysteries that baffle adults, professional detectives, and the well-intentioned police who, however hard they try, are never as quick-thinking and fast-acting as Nancy.

A 1914 graduate of Wellesley College, an English major with deep interests in religion, music, science, and archeology (her favorite Nancy Drew book, *The Clue in the Crossword Cipher*, 1967, is based on "astounding" archeological discoveries among the Inca ruins), A. is an active alumna and a 1978 winner of the Alumnae Achievement Award. Wellesley's motto, "Non Ministrari Sed Ministrare" (not to be ministered unto but to minister), has been A.'s own guiding principle and the lesson she hopes to teach young readers who gather in schools and libraries all over the country to hear her speak. "Don't be a gimme, gimme kind of person," she tells them in an amusingly loose translation of the Latin. A. has endowed a chair at Wellesley to be known as the Harriet Stratemeyer Adams Professor in Juvenile Literature.

A. travels widely (South America, Hawaii, Africa, the Orient), using the foreign settings to provide "authentic backgrounds" for her stories, especially for the Nancy Drews. Indeed, Nancy—whom she regards as "a third lovely daughter" (in addition to her two real-life daughters)— is rarely out of A.'s thoughts when she takes a trip.

A.'s books have been translated into more than a dozen languages and, although considered nonliterary, they are now staples in most children's libraries.

WORKS: The Nancy Drew Mystery Series (as Carolyn Keene; 56 books, 1930–78). The Barton Books for Girls Series (as May Hollis Barton; 15 books, 1931–50). The Dana Girls Series (as Carolyn Keene; 32 books, 1934–78). The Hardy Boys Series (as Franklin W. Dixon; 20 books, 1934–73). The Tom Swift Series (as Victor Appleton II; 21 books, 1935–72). The Bobbsey Twin Series (as Laura Lee Hope; 15 books, 1940–67). The Honey Bunch Series (as Helen Louise Thorndyke; 7 books, 1945–55). The Linda Craig Series (as Ann Sheldon; 4 books, 1960–66).

BIBLIOGRAPHY: Keene, C., in *The Great Detectives*, Ed. O. Penzler (1978). Prager, A., *Rascals at Large; or, The Clue in the Old Nostalgia* (1971).
For articles in reference works, see: *CA* (1968).

JACQUELINE BERKE

Jane Addams

B. 6 Sept. 1860, Cedarville, Illinois; d. 21 May 1935, Chicago, Illinois
D. of John and Sarah Weber Addams

A. was born into a prominent northwestern Illinois family headed by a father who had served with Abraham Lincoln in the state legislature. Her mother died when A. was two, and A. tried to model herself after her highly-respected father. She attended the Rockford Female Seminary and, for one year, Woman's Medical College in Philadelphia. She never married; the closest emotional ties over her lifetime were to her father and to a few women friends.

A.'s name is most often associated with Hull House, the renowned settlement she founded in 1889 in the immigrant slums of Chicago. Her experiences there formed the basis for her efforts, carried out on a local, national, and international scale, for social reform. She devoted herself to such causes as child-labor legislation, woman suffrage, educational reform, and world peace. She helped found the Women's International League for Peace and Freedom (WILPF) and served as its president until her death. In 1931, she was corecipient of the Nobel Peace Prize. A. wrote ten books, countless articles, and lectured extensively, presenting to a wide audience her conviction that citizens of the new urban-industrial age must move beyond individualism toward a new social ethic.

Her first book, *Democracy and Social Ethics* (1902), is a perceptive analysis of the new industrial American society peopled by masses of immigrants and urban poor. In six essays adapted from earlier articles and lectures, A. suggests that changes in industrial and household relations, in politics and education and organized charity, and in ways of understanding the role of women will be necessary if true democracy is to be extended successfully into the new age. Her view that women's political and social role should be expanded so that women could become caretakers of the well-being and morality not just of their families but of society at large is typical of the viewpoint known as social feminism.

Newer Ideals of Peace (1907) continues and expands A.'s analysis, suggesting that as a social ethic of morality is put into practice, the need for war will disappear. *The Spirit of Youth and the City Streets* (1909),

A.'s own favorite among her books, and *A New Conscience and an Ancient Evil* (1912), a study of prostitution, are pioneering contributions to the field of urban sociology.

A.'s best-known work is *Twenty Years at Hull-House* (1910), the classic autobiography she published at age fifty. The book describes Hull House and its cultural, educational, political, and humanitarian activities, but its broader focus is the education of A. herself. She was indebted to the thought or moral example of such diverse figures as John Ruskin, Abraham Lincoln, Leo Tolstoy, her friend John Dewey, and to the founders of the settlement house in London known as Toynbee Hall. But she also learned from the ideas and problems of her immigrant neighbors, for she viewed Hull House not as a charitable mission to the downtrodden but as a forum where diverse nationalities and social classes could interact for the betterment of all.

Like all autobiography, *Twenty Years at Hull-House* is selective and stylized in its presentation of events. A. writes lucidly and sometimes movingly, enlivening her narrative with anecdotal accounts of the people and situations she met in her Hull House work. She adopts the persona of a seeker, rather than a dispenser, of enlightenment, but she writes with moral earnestness and with a naive optimism that justice and peace will be made to prevail.

During the next two decades, A. passed for a time beyond liberal social reform to positions which many regarded as radical and even seditious. She was a pacifist during World War I, an internationalist in the isolationist 1920s, a supporter of civil liberties when the prevailing mood was suppressive of dissent. A. discusses her peace efforts, and the condemnation and self-doubt she suffered because of her unpopular views, in *Peace and Bread in Time of War* (1922), and in *The Second Twenty Years at Hull-House* (1930) . The latter book is a disjointed but still interesting account of A.'s continuing reform activities and of her view of the postwar years. It includes one of A.'s favorite pieces: an analysis of the appeal to women of the rumor, spread widely in 1913, that a devil baby resided at Hull House.

Even before her death, A. had become a legendary figure. Unfortunately, the image of her which survives is that of the do-gooder—of Saint Jane, the lady in long skirts who helped the poor. But A. was a social reformer of far-ranging breadth and influence, a gifted writer, and a first-rate intellect. She was not so much an original thinker as a perceptive observer of the society around her, and an able synthesizer and popularizer of the ideas of the leading social theorists of her time. A.'s work and writing helped make possible the liberal reforms of the Progressive Era and of the New Deal and helped arouse the social conscience of two generations of Americans.

WORKS: *Democracy and Social Ethics* (1902). *Newer Ideals of Peace* (1907). *The Spirit of Youth and the City Streets* (1909). *Twenty Years at Hull-House, with Autobiographical Notes* (1910). *A New Conscience and an Ancient Evil* (1912). *The Women at The Hague* (with E. Balch and A. Hamilton, 1915). *The Long Road of Woman's Memory* (1916). *Peace and Bread in Time of War* (1922). *The Second Twenty Years at Hull-House, September 1909 to September 1929, with a Record of a Growing World Consciousness* (1930). *The Excellent Becomes the Permanent* (1932). *My Friend, Julia Lathrop* (1935). *Jane Addams: A Centennial Reader* (Ed. E. C. Johnson, 1960). *The Social Thought of Jane Addams* (Ed. C. Lasch, 1965).

BIBLIOGRAPHY: Commager, H. S., Foreword to *Twenty Years at Hull-House* by Jane Addams (1961). Davis, A. F., *American Heroine: The Life and Legend of Jane Addams* (1973). Farrell, J. C., *Beloved Lady: A History of Jane Addams's Ideas on Reform and Peace* (1967). Lasch, C., *The New Radicalism in America (1899–1963): The Intellectual as a Social Type* (1965). Lasch, C., Introduction to *The Social Thought of Jane Addams* (1965). Levine, D., *Jane Addams and the Liberal Tradition* (1971). Linn, J. W., *Jane Addams: A Biography* (1935). Scott, A. F., Introduction to *Democracy and Social Ethics* by Jane Addams (1964).

For articles in reference works, see: *DAB. NAW* (article by A. F. Scott). *NCAB.*

Other references: *Commentary* (July 1961). *Daedalus* 93 (Spring 1964). *JSocHis* 5 (Winter 1971–72). *JHI* 22 April–June 1961).

PEGGY STINSON

Zoë Akins

B. *30 Oct. 1886, Humansville, Illinois; d. 29 Oct. 1958, Los Angeles, California*
D. *of Thomas J. and Elizabeth Green Akins; m. Hugo C. Rumbold, 1932*

A. grew up and went to school in Illinois and Missouri. She expressed an early interest in the theater and acting. When she left St. Louis for New York in 1909—with romantic dreams of going on stage and with the determination and pluck for which she was always admired—she encountered her first defeat: she was told she had no acting talent. A. decided, however, to stay in New York and write plays. When she submitted poetry to *McClure's* magazine, the managing editor, Willa Cather, who was to become a lifelong friend and correspondent, rejected the poetry but told her, prophetically, that she should write for the stage.

Although A.'s first published book was a volume of poetry, *Interpretations* (1911), and although she eventually wrote a novel, *Forever Young* (1941), she is best known for her original dramas, comedies, screenplays, and adaptations. She began to generate attention in 1916 with her vers libre drama, *The Magical City*. She went on to write *Déclassée* (1919), perhaps the best original play of that year. A.'s high comedies, like *Papa* (1913) and *Greatness: A Comedy* (1921) demonstrate continued sophistication and even greatness. She later turned her art, however, to the more popular situation comedies, which, on the whole, do not possess the dramatic quality of her early original work. Her sharp wit and sense of irony, especially, were quite lost in the shift from high to situation comedy. A. won the 1935 Pulitzer Prize for drama for *The Old Maid*, an adaptation of a novella by another of her literary friends, Edith Wharton.

While it is true that A.'s writing is uneven and occasionally suffers from what Mielech calls "romantic excesses" associated with postwar American drama, and while many of her otherwise attractive protagonists periodically engage in a rhetoric that is uncharacteristic or platitudinous, much of her excellence has gone unappreciated. Some of her efforts at characterization have been misconstrued as overindulgence or a lapse in realism. A.'s significance, it seems, lies in her extremely sharp and sympathetic understanding of human foibles in general and of female folly and frustration in particular.

In a play like *Daddy's Gone A-Hunting* (1921), for example, A. insightfully portrays the all-too-common situation of a woman blindly committed to fidelity to a confused husband who psychologically abuses her and who manipulates and keeps her with him largely through the guilt he—as well as society—stirs up in her. When she finally rejects his "open marriage" ideas and leaves him, she flees to another, kinder man who "keeps" her sexually and financially, but whom she refuses to marry because she will not get a divorce. Although the play is recognized for its unorthodox focus on the troubled quest for personal freedom, it is more powerful for its quiet repudiation of woman's considerable dependence on man and for its unhappy admission that women like Edith—most women for that matter—find the world "unsafe" when their traditional sources of security are taken from them. Neither Edith's initial decision to remain true to her adulterous husband nor her later decision to live with Greenough in the face of society's censure is completely admirable according to A. Her keen irony underscores Edith's appalling lack of personal identity and purposiveness, and the reader experiences her horror when she realizes that she cannot expect men or children to provide meaning and identity for her.

In general, A.'s plays—whether serious dramas or high comedies—emphasize the distortions in values, attitudes, and manners which society promulgates. She is simultaneously both amused and disturbed by the often pathetic efforts of her dramatic characters to extricate themselves from the web of social behavior patterns and thinking that they cannot really understand.

A. is probably not a great playwright, but she is surely worthy of more notice and exposure than she has been receiving.

WORKS: (Most of A.'s plays were never published as books.) *Interpretations* (1911). *Papa: An Amorality in Three Acts* (1913). *Cake upon the Waters* (1919). *The Old Maid* by E. Wharton (dramatization by Akins, 1935). *The Little Miracle* (1936). *The Hills Grow Smaller* (1937). *Mrs. January and Mr. Ex* (1944; alternate title, *Plans for Tomorrow*).

BIBLIOGRAPHY: Meilech, R. A., "The Plays of Zoë Akins Rumbold" (Diss., Ohio State Univ., 1974).

Other references: *American Mercury* (May 1928). *SatR* (11 May 1935). *WLB* (June 1935).

PATRICIA LEE YONGUE

Louisa May Alcott

B. 29 Nov. 1832, Germantown, Pennsylvania; d. 6 March 1888, Boston, Massachusetts
Wrote under: L.M.A., Louisa May Alcott, A. M. Barnard, Flora Fairfield, A.M.
D. of Amos Bronson and Abba May Alcott

A. was the daughter of Bronson Alcott, the high priest of Transcendentalism, friend and admirer of Emerson and Thoreau. Although the early years of her life were marked by poverty and uncertainty, as her father sought to establish his "perfect school," they were rewarding years. She had little institutionalized education, but her father taught her under his advanced educational theories. Her love of drama gave her an awareness of the melodramatic and sensational in everyday life. Her attempts to augment the family income by teaching, sewing, working as a servant, and acting as a companion provided the raw material for her own creative works.

Flower Fables (1855), a collection of imaginative fantasies for children, was the first book published under A.'s own name. Earlier, her poems had been published under the pseudonym Flora Fairfield, and scattered throughout her career were "necessity tales," sometimes lurid and sensational, also published pseudonymously. With *Hospital Sketches* (1863) and *Little Women* (1868), A. became an institution, a center of public attention. She wrote on contemporary issues such as suffrage, temperance, prison reform, and child labor.

The positive critical reception of *Hospital Sketches*, which is based on A.'s brief career as a Civil War nurse, convinced its author that success lay in portraying real life rather than flights of fancy. The experiences of "Tribulation Periwinkle" rank with Whitman's poetic record in the pictures of suffering gallantly borne and the compassion of those who served as nurses.

Throughout her career, A. produced autobiographical poems, essays, and stories. "Thoreau's Flute" (1863) reflects her hours spent at Walden Pond; "Transcendental Wild Oats" (1873) provides a frank, humorous-pathetic account of her family's abortive Utopia (Fruitlands); and "Ralph Waldo Emerson" (1882) pays tribute to the guardian angel of the Alcott family.

Little Women was an instant success, with multiple editions and translations in more than thirty languages. The simple everyday events and small crises of Jo, Meg, Beth, and Amy, and the warmth of the family life provided by "Marmee" and Mr. March, along with the friendship of Laurie, Mr. Laurence, and the sharp-tongued Aunt March have influenced every generation since 1868. Although Jo's marriage to Professor Bhaer disappointed many readers who hoped she would marry Laurie and disapproved of his eventual marriage to Amy, the Bhaer family soon developed its own personality.

In *Little Men* (1871) and *Jo's Boys* (1886), A. not only gave Jo two boys of her own but provided a whole school of boys and girls of all ages, races, and levels of wealth, who were loved and educated on the estate bequeathed by Aunt March. The freedom of the learning environment is reminiscent of Amos Bronson Alcott's avant-garde philosophy; the lessons of love and duty taught to the March girls are transmitted to all. The readers' interest in the destinies of the twelve boys who lived at Plumfield led A. to write *Jo's Boys*, set ten years later than *Little Men*.

Although the destinies of all the characters who peopled *Little Men* are traced in *Jo's Boys*, the changes which fifteen years brought in the author herself are evident in the ending of the book. Despite the pleas of young readers, Dan's imprisonment as the result of killing a man, even by accident, shuts him off from marrying Bess, the exquisite daughter of Amy and Laurie. Nan, Meg's daughter, defends her position as a new woman and pursues her career as a doctor, while Bess becomes an artist and Josie an actress, before they become wives.

Lesser known but equally delightful are *Eight Cousins* (1875) and *Rose in Bloom* (1876), which trace the adventures of Rose and her seven cousins, adding more memorable portraits to A.'s gallery and providing the author with many opportunities to comment upon the silliness of values and customs of Victorian society.

The critical reception of A.'s works during her lifetime varied greatly but was generally favorable. Throughout much of the 20th-c. she has been widely known only as the author of *Little Women*, but her honesty, realism, and reluctance to overmoralize continue to win her new readers and critical attention.

WORKS: *Flower Fables* (1855). *Hospital Sketches* (1863). *Moods* (1865). *Morning-Glories, and Other Stories* (1868). *Kitty's Class Day* (1868). *Aunt Kipp* (1868). *Psyche's Art* (1868). *Three Proverb Stories* (1868). *Little Women, or Meg, Jo, Beth and Amy* (1868). *Little Women*, Part Second (1869). *An Old-Fashioned Girl* (1870). *Little Men: Life at Plumfield with Jo's Boys* (1871). *My Boys: Aunt Jo's Scrap-Bag, I* (1872). *Shawl-Straps: Aunt Jo's Scrap-Bag, II* (1872). *Work: A Story of Experience* (1873). *Cupid and Chow-Chow: Aunt Jo's Scrap-Bag, III* (1874). *Eight Cousins; or, The Aunt-Hill* (1875). *Silver Pitchers; and Independence, a Centennial Love Story* (1876). *Rose in Bloom: A Sequel to Eight Cousins* (1876). *A Modern Mephistopheles* (1877). *Under the Lilacs* (1878). *My Girls: Aunt Jo's Scrap-Bag, IV* (1878). *Jack and Jill: A Village Story* (1880). *Proverb Stories* (1882). *An Old-Fashioned Thanksgiving: Aunt Jo's Scrap-Bag, V* (1882). *Lulu's Library, I* (1886). *Jo's Boys and How They Turned Out: A Sequel to Little Men* (1886). *Lulu's Library, II* (1887). *A Garland for Girls* (1888). *Lulu's Library, III* (1889). *Recollections of My Childhood's Days* (1890). *Comic Tragedies Written by Jo and Meg and Acted by the Little Women* (1893). *Behind a Mask: The Unknown Thrillers of Louisa May Alcott* (ed. M. Stern, 1975).

BIBLIOGRAPHY: Anthony, K. S., *Louisa May Alcott* (1936). Bonstelle J., and M. DeForest, eds., *Little Women Letters from the House of Alcott* (1914). Cheney, E., *Louisa May Alcott: Her Life, Letters, and Journals* (1889). Gulliver, L., *Louisa May Alcott: A Bibliography* (1932). Meigs, C. L., *The Story of the Author of Little Women: Invincible Louisa* (1933). Moses, B., *Louisa*

May Alcott, Dreamer and Worker: A Story of Achievement (1909). Papash-vily, H. W., *Louisa May Alcott* (1965). Peare, C. O., *Louisa May Alcott: Her Life* (1954). Stern, M. B., *Louisa May Alcott* (1950). Ullom, J. C., *Louisa May Alcott: A Centennial for 'Little Women'* (1969).

For articles in reference works, see: *Bibliography of American Literature*, Ed. J. N. Blanck (1955).

Other references: *ALR* 1 (Winter 1973). *Bibliographical Society of America Papers* 37 (1943). *NEQ* (June 1943; Dec. 1949). *NYTMag* (Dec. 1964).

ALMA J. PAYNE

Bess Streeter Aldrich

B. 17 Feb. 1881, Cedar Falls, Iowa; d. 3 Aug. 1954, Lincoln, Nebraska
Wrote under: Bess Streeter Aldrich, Margaret Dean Stephens
D. of James Wareham and Mary Anderson Streeter; m. Charles Aldrich, 1907

A.'s grandparents immigrated to frontier Iowa in the 1890s. The families' experiences there became the basis for A.'s most successful novels. After graduating from Iowa State Teachers' College in Cedar Falls in 1901, A. taught for six years. She wrote articles for teachers' magazines and stories for primary-school children. Shortly after her marriage she moved to Elmwood, Nebraska. When her husband, a banker and lawyer, died suddenly in 1925, A. became the sole support of her four children. Writing now became her profession.

In 1930, she became book editor of the *Christian Herald*. She was awarded an Honorary Doctorate of Literature in 1935 from the University of Nebraska, and she was elected to the Nebraska Hall of Fame in 1973.

The Rim of the Prairie (1925), A.'s first novel, is a contemporary story of Nancy, a farm girl living near a small town remarkably similar to Elmwood, Nebraska. Through the recollections of the old people, Aunt Biney and Uncle Jud Moore, A. recounts details of the settling of this part of the country, as civilization and modern farming overtake the wild prairie. The author's knowledge and love of nature, her descriptions of the rolling hills and the flowers of the prairie, are well expressed here, as in all her books.

A Lantern in Her Hand (1928) is a much better work, perhaps because actual events form its basis, several from her family history. The character of Abbie Deal, who moves from Illinois to Iowa in 1854, then marries and homesteads with her husband in Nebraska, is based on her mother. In spite of sorrow, hardship, and lack of opportunity to develop her talents, Abbie has a happy life. The "lantern in her hand" has lighted her children's way. The novel was immensely popular, a bestseller for years. It is probably A.'s best book. Later works sometimes are variations of its theme, setting, and events.

A.'s work is romantic, optimistic, and "wholesome." Her stories usually end happily, her romances join those who should be joined. Some of them are sentimental. Nevertheless, they display certain strengths. Characterization is often excellent, as are her descriptions of nature. The background is always the Midwest, and she describes it precisely and accurately. Although A. is most noted for her stories of the settling of the Midwest, her short stories give fine details of middle-class family life in the midwestern small town of the 1920s and 1930s. Her stories and articles were published in many of the leading periodicals.

A.'s style is not mannered or dated; neither is it remarkably original. The careful attention A. gives to details—dates, clothing styles, food, customs—are strong points, creating a realistic background. The hardships of settling the frontier and of country living, such as the back-breaking labor, particularly for the women, the lack of refinements, the inconvenient kitchens, the bare and ugly houses, are details such as Hamlin Garland often gives. But whereas Garland points out the hopelessness of the unremitting hard labor in fighting poverty, dirt, and squalor, A. affirms life, and her characters find, usually, some reason for happiness, be it through love or belief in honor and duty.

WORKS: *Mother Mason* (1924). *The Rim of the Prairie* (1925). *The Cutters* (1926). *A Lantern in Her Hand* (1928). *A White Bird Flying* (1931). *Miss Bishop* (1933). *Spring Came on Forever* (1935). *The Man Who Caught the Weather* (1936). *Song of Years* (1939). *The Drum Goes Dead* (1941). *The Lieutenant's Lady* (1942). *Journey into Christmas, and Other Stories* (1949). *The Bess Streeter Aldrich Reader* (1950). *A Bess Streeter Aldrich Treasury* (ed. R. S. Aldrich, 1959).

BIBLIOGRAPHY: Aldrich, R., *A Bess Streeter Aldrich Treasury* (1959). Marble, A. R., *A Daughter of Pioneers: Bess Streeter Aldrich and Her Books* (n.d.). Meier, A. M., "Bess Streeter Aldrich: Her Life and Works" (Master's thesis, Kearney State College, 1968). Williams, B. C., *Bess Streeter Aldrich, Novelist* (n.d.).

Other references: *Appleton's Book Chat* (1 Feb. 1930; 21 Nov. 1931). *WLB* (April 1929).

HELEN STAUFFER

Mildred Aldrich

B. 16 Nov. 1853, Providence, Rhode Island; d. 19 Feb. 1928, Huiry, France
Wrote under: Mildred Aldrich, H. Quinn
D. of Edwin and Lucy Ayers Baker Aldrich

A. grew up in Boston. She attended the Hancock School, Girls High School, and trained in the natural sciences at the Lowell Scientific Institute.

A.'s professional career was consistently in the field of journalism. For twelve years, A. was secretary to the manager of the Boston *Home Journal* and a contributor under the pseudonym H. Quinn. She edited *The Mahogany Tree*, a journal of ideas. During 1892 and 1893, A. submitted three substantial pieces on theater to *Arena*. She joined the *Boston Journal* in 1894, and moved the following year to the *Boston Herald*. There she strengthened further her already strong reputation for astute dramatic criticism. Sometime around the turn of the century, but before 1904, A. moved to Paris, where she represented several American theatrical producers and wrote for American magazines. She retired to the French countryside in 1914, when she was sixty-one. Her hilltop home, La Creste, afforded a view of the site of the Battle of the Marne.

A. wrote four firsthand accounts of life in wartime France from La Creste. *A Hilltop on the Marne* (1915), her most successful book, first appeared in the *Atlantic Monthly*. It treats the progress of the battle, the spirit and commitment of both soldiers and villagers. The work's strength derives from the compression of events and A.'s expanding understanding, which the reader shares. *On the Edge of the War Zone* (1917) covers the period September 16, 1914–March 28, 1917, and is more diffuse in its approach. Of special interest are A.'s reports on gas warfare and descriptions of soldiers' wartime entertainments. *The Peak of the Load* (1918) deals with "the waiting months on the hilltop from the entrance of the stars and stripes to the second victory on the Marne." In *When Johnny Comes Marching Home* (1919), A. describes how "the countryside settled down" after the armistice.

Told in a French Garden, August, 1914 (1916) is A.'s sole work of fiction. By a "strange irony of Fate," nine people find themselves in provincial France in the darkest days of the war. To raise their spirits, they follow Boccaccio's example in *The Decameron*, and each relates a story following the day's dinner. Prologues and epilogues frame the stories and reveal the conflicts in values the participants display.

A. also wrote the foreword to *The Letters of Thomasina Atkins (W.A.A.C.) on Active Service* (1918). This volume recounts Atkins's experiences in the British Women's Auxiliary Army Corps stationed "somewhere in France." For her help in swaying American opinion towards entrance into World War I and her assistance to soldiers and refugees, A. was awarded the Legion of Honor by the French government in 1922.

WORKS: *A Hilltop on the Marne* (1915). *Told in a French Garden, August, 1914* (1916). *On the Edge of the War Zone* (1917). *The Peak of the Load* (1918). *When Johnny Comes Marching Home* (1919).

BIBLIOGRAPHY: Stein, G., *The Autobiography of Alice B. Toklas* (1932). Mellow, J. R., *Charmed Circle: Gertrude Stein and Company* (1973).

JANIS TOWNSEND

Mary E. Clemmer Ames

B. 6 May 1831, Utica, New York; d. 18 Aug. 1884, Washington, D.C.
Wrote under: Mary Clemmer Ames, M.C.A., Mary Clemmer
D. of Abraham and Margaret Kneale Clemmer; m. Daniel Ames, 1851;
   m. Edmund Hudson, 1883

The oldest of seven children, A. moved with her family to Westfield, Massachusetts, where she attended the Westfield Academy. Her career began in 1859, when she sent letters from New York City, where she was living temporarily with the poets Alice and Phoebe Cary, to the Utica *Morning Herald* and the Springfield (Massachusetts) *Republican*.

After her marriage to a minister ended, A. began a "Woman's Letter from Washington," for the New York *Independent*. The column continued from 1866 until her death. She also wrote for the Brooklyn *Daily Union* and for the Cincinnati *Commercial*.

A.'s literary significance stems mainly from her column in the influential weekly, the *Independent*. It made her one of the best known of a group of post-Civil War women Washington correspondents, known as "literary ladies." Avoiding social news, she concentrated on political issues, defending the freed Negro and civil rights, and sharply criticizing the excesses of Gilded-Age politics. She moved in the same social circles as leading politicians and used them as news sources.

In spite of her participation in the masculine worlds of both politics and journalism, A. repeatedly told her readers that she modestly shrank from public notice and preferred the domestic scene to the political arena. Asserting her career had been the product of financial necessity, she justified it morally on the grounds that women journalists had a spiritual duty to purify politics, even if their efforts brought them unwelcome personal attention. She did not appear publicly to support woman suffrage, although she did advocate it. Considering suffrage less important than economic gains, she wrote: "Women can live nobly without voting; but they cannot live without bread."

A.'s weekly columns bore the hallmark of popular Victorian literature—excessive sentiment, self-conscious moralizing, and verbosity. Still, they provided an intriguing picture of a woman standing apart from the seamy side of politics and pinpointing politicians guilty of drunkenness and corruption. The books based on her columns—*Outlines of Men, Women and Things* (1873) and *Ten Years in Washington* (1873)—emphasized people and places rather than politics. Part guidebook to the capital, *Ten Years in Washington,* a subscription book reprinted three times, was crammed with historical lore. *Outlines* included descriptions of scenic spots, biographical sketches of literary and theatrical figures, and, more importantly, several essays dealing with relations between the sexes. A. urged men to subscribe to the "pure" moral standards of women and exhorted women to educate themselves. Her most successful work of nonfiction, *A Memorial to Alice and Phoebe Cary*, a gushing tribute to the women who had befriended her, drew critical acclaim in that sentimental era.

Making a virtue of what was obviously a handicap to a Washington correspondent—her sex—she contended that her womanhood gave her the right to comment on political issues to promote reform. Trading on the Victorian myth that women possessed a higher moral sense than do men, she showed that a facile woman writer could make a place for herself by pointing a finger of righteous scorn and indignation at the men who ran the country.

WORKS: *Victoire* (1864). *Eirene, or, A Woman's Right* (1871). *A Memorial to Alice and Phoebe Cary* (1873). *Outlines of Men, Women and Things* (1873). *Ten Years in Washington* (1873). *His Two Wives* (1875). *Memorial Sketch of Elizabeth Emerson Atwater* (1879). *Poems of Life and Nature* (1883).

BIBLIOGRAPHY: Beasley, M. H., *The First Women Washington Correspondents* (George Washington University Studies No. 4, 1976). Beasley, M. H., and S. Silver, *Women in Media: A Documentary Source Book* (1977). Hudson, E., *An American Woman's Life and Work: A Memorial of Mary Clemmer* (1886). Whiting, L., *Our Famous Women* (1884).

For articles in reference works, see: *NAW* (article by J. Cutler Andrews).

Other references: *Arthur's Home Magazine* (Dec. 1884). *The Cottage Hearth* (Feb. 1875). *The Independent* (28 Aug. 1884).

MAURINE BEASLEY

Eliza Frances Andrews

B. 10 Aug. 1840, Washington, Georgia; d. 21 Jan. 1931, Rome, Georgia
Wrote under: Elzey Hay
D. of Garnett and Annulet Ball Andrews

A. was born at Haywood, the plantation home of her parents. The family was moderately wealthy by southern standards, owning about two hundred slaves. A. attended the Washington Seminary for Girls and graduated in the first class from the LaGrange Female College in 1857.

When Georgia seceded from the Union in January 1861, A.'s father achieved notoriety for his uncompromising opposition to secession and his subsequent refusal to support the new Confederacy. Although he permitted three of his sons to join the Confederate army, he did not tolerate the secessionist views of his daughters, which led to many family arguments.

In December 1864, A. began her diary, published as *The War-time Journal of a Georgia Girl* (1908), with an account of a trip to visit her sister near Albany, Georgia. A. and a younger sister had to travel over rough, partially destroyed roads, with the ever-present fear of ambush by Sherman's men. Once at their sister's, however, the two girls enjoyed a round of visits and parties, strangely gay for a time of political and military disintegration. A.'s fine eye for detail gives the reader a fascinating portrait of social life in the rural Confederacy. Occasionally she lapses into girlish concerns, reporting all the compliments she received on her appearance, but her natural skepticism always rescues her and the diary from silliness. In March 1865, A. returned to Washington, Georgia, to witness the fall of the Confederacy. There she met Jefferson Davis on his flight from his pursuers.

After her father's death in 1873, A. began teaching school. She served as principal of the Girl's High School in Yazoo City, Mississippi, later became principal of a girl's seminary in Washington, Georgia, and from 1885 to 1896 taught French and literature at the Wesleyan Female College in Macon, Georgia. A. then returned home to Washington to teach botany in the public high school. After her retirement from teaching, she published two textbooks on botany.

A.'s literary career began in 1865 with an article on Reconstruction in Georgia published in the New York *World*. A second article on women's life and fashions appeared in *Godey's Lady's Book* the following year.

Her first novel, *A Family Secret* (1876), quickly became a bestseller. This mystery, set in the immediate postwar South, revolves around the romance between Audley Malvern and Ruth Hartleur and their attempts to discover the secret of Ruth's parents and the unusual ring she wears. It is filled with such typical 19th-c. literary conventions as a ghost in a graveyard and mistaken identities. The last chapter is called "Everybody Gets Married and Lives Happy Forever After." Two other novels were equally popular.

WORKS: *A Family Secret* (1876). *A Mere Adventurer* (1879). *Prince Hal; or, the Romance of a Rich Young Man* (1882). *Botany All the Year Round; a Practical Textbook for Schools* (1903). *Seven Great Battles of the Army of Northern Virginia: A Program of Study and Entertainment* (1906). *The Wartime Journal of a Georgia Girl* (1908). *A Practical Course in Botany, With Especial Reference to Its Bearings on Agriculture, Economics, and Sanitation* (1911).

The papers of Eliza Frances Andrews are in the Garnett Andrews Papers, Southern Historical Collection, University of North Carolina Library, Chapel Hill, North Carolina.

BIBLIOGRAPHY: Coulter, E. M., *Travels in the Confederate States* (1948). Hart, B. S., *Georgia Writers* (1929). King, S. B., Jr., ed., *The Wartime Journal of a Georgia Girl* (1960).

For articles in reference works, see: *AW*. *Living Writers of the South*, Ed. M. T. Tardy (1872). *NAW* (article by J. Patton).

JANET E. KAUFMAN

Jane Andrews

B. 1 Dec. 1833, Newburyport, Massachusetts; d. 15 July 1887, Newburyport,
Massachusetts
D. of John and Margaret Demmon Rand Andrews

A. was born and raised in the midst of the vigorous nationalism of
mid-19th-c. New England. She inherited from her family a spirit of intellectual concern and benevolence which, taken together with a broad outlook, led her to become one of the earliest proponents of internationalism
in education. A.'s school friends at the Putnam Free School at Newburyport and the State Normal School at West Newton, Massachusetts,
included a sister-in-law of education reformer Horace Mann. Mann persuaded A. that she would find the kind of education she wanted at his new
college, Antioch, where, subsequently, she was the first student to register.
However, the onset of a neurological disorder described as "spinal affection" cut short her education in the middle of the first year and left her
an invalid for the next six years. Nonetheless, Mann's influence reinforced
her commitment to belief in one's responsibility to society, a commitment
that influenced the direction of the teaching and writing she practiced
during the remainder of her life.

In 1860, sufficiently recovered from her illness to work, A. founded a
primary school in her home. This school, characterized by advanced educational methods including experiments, plays, games, and stories, was
extremely successful and continued to be A.'s life for the next twenty-
five years. In her school she cultivated observation, individual responsibility, and creative expression in the hope of molding responsible citizens
for life in a society where all people were equal.

A.'s first book, *Seven Little Sisters Who Live on the Round Ball That
Floats in the Air* (1861), grew out of stories she created to supplement
the geography lessons in her school. Each story focuses on a little girl
in a different culture and emphasizes that although the external circumstances of life are very different for each child, each is happy and is
one of God's family. The same motive held for the sequel, *Each and
All: Seven Little Sisters Prove Their Sisterhood* (1877) and for a historical counterpart, *Ten Boys Who Lived on the Road From Long Ago to
Now* (1886), which traces "our race from its Aryan sources to the
present." Through these books, all of which emphasize the kinship of

children throughout the world, A. hoped to offset the effect of books like Peter Parley's, in which children from other lands were characteristically made to look strange and unlike the children for whom the books were intended. The books also provided an alternative morality to that of the McGuffey readers which depicted virtue as being of personal rather than of social concern.

WORKS: *The Seven Little Sisters Who Live on the Round Ball That Floats in the Air* (1861). *Each and All: Seven Little Sisters Prove Their Sisterhood* (1877). *Geographical Plays for Young Folks at Home and School* (1880). *The Child's Health Primer* (1885). *Ten Boys Who Lived on the Road from Long Ago to Now* (1886). *Only A Year and What It Brought* (1888). *The Stories Mother Nature Told Her Children* (1889). *The Stories of My Four Friends* (1900).

BIBLIOGRAPHY: Green, N. K., *A Forgotten Chapter in American Education: Jane Andrews of Newburyport* (1961). Hopkins, L. P., Foreword to *Seven Little Sisters Who Live on the Round Ball That Floates in the Air* by J. Andrews (1897). Spofford, H. P., *A Little Book of Friends* (1916).
 Other references: *EngElemR* (May 1936).

KATHARYN F. CRABBE

Hannah Arendt

B. 14 Oct. 1906, Hanover, Germany; d. 4 Dec. 1975, New York City
D. of Paul and Martha Cohn Arendt; m. Heinrich Bleucher, 1940

The only child of nonreligious, German-Jewish parents, A. received her formal education in Germany. She studied philosophy under Karl Jaspers at Heidelberg and took her doctorate in 1928, after completing a dissertation on St. Augustine. When the Nazis came to power in 1933, she fled to France, and then emigrated to the United States. A. made her greatest mark on the American academic community. An innovative and forceful political theorist, she taught at various universities across the country.

 A.'s best-known work, *The Origins of Totalitarianism* (1951, 1958), deals with the rise of totalitarianism in Germany and Russia. It offers a description of the fundamental structure of a totalitarian regime and presents an account of social and political conditions—such as the growth of imperialism and anti-Semitism—on which they were built. Above all, A.

attributed the success of totalitarian movements to what she called "organized loneliness." Loneliness, for A., is not merely solitude; it is a condition in which individuals have lost contact with the world as well as with one another. Worldless people do not understand themselves as belonging to the world because they no longer have the ability to add anything of their own to that world. Without a world shared between them, such people lack a "common sense"; they cannot differentiate between reality and fiction—and are easily manipulated by the logic of totalitarian ideology.

In *The Human Condition* (1958), A. considers the meaning of free political action in terms of a distinction between private and public realms. In *On Revolution* (1963), she analyzes the character of revolutionary movements in the modern age.

In 1961, A. went to Jerusalem for *The New Yorker* magazine to cover the trial of Adolf Eichmann. Her report, which appeared first as a series of articles and then as *Eichmann in Jerusalem* (1963), aroused considerable and bitter controversy. A. shocked her readers by asserting that while Eichmann's behavior had been monstrous, his character was not. What struck A. most about the Nazi war criminal was his banality. *The Life of the Mind* (1977), suggests that Eichmann's ability to commit monstrous crimes was related to his lack of thought. The capacity to judge between good and evil, in other words, is related to thought. In *Thinking*, the first volume of this two-part posthumously published work, A. maintained a distinction between reason and intellect, thinking and knowing. It is through thinking that human beings attempt to satisfy their quest for meaning.

To some, A. was an elitist who cared little about the suffering masses around the world. To others, her sensitive writings on political action and the public arena, authority, tradition, violence, and truth provide insight into some of the most perplexing dilemmas of the modern era. It is in the nature of political theory to challenge old ways of thinking and to force its audience to think about political things from a new perspective. In the spirit of this tradition, A. may be controversial and frustrating, but she is never dull.

WORKS: *Der Liebesbegriff bei Augustin* (1930). *Rahel Varnhagen: The Life of a Jewess* (1947). *The Origins of Totalitarianism* (1951; rev. ed., 1958). *Between Past and Future* (1954; rev. ed., 1968). *The Human Condition* (1958). *On Revolution* (1963). *Eichmann in Jerusalem* (1963; rev. ed., 1965). *Men in Dark Times* (1968). *On Violence* (1969). *Crises of the Republic* (1969). *Rahel Varnhagen: The Life of a Jewish Woman* (1974). *The Life of the Mind* (2 vols., 1977).

BIBLIOGRAPHY: Canovan, M., *The Political Thought of Hannah Arendt* (1974).

Other references: *NewR* (15 June 1963; 21 Oct. 1978; 12 April 1980). *NYRB* (26 Oct. 1978). *NYTRB* (19 May 1963; 28 May 1978). *Political Theory* (May 1977; Nov. 1979; Aug. 1980). *Review of Politics* 15 (Jan. 1953). *SocR* 44 (Spring 1977).

LAURA GREYSON

Charlotte Armstrong

B. 2 May 1905, Vulcan, Michigan; d. 18 July 1969, Glendale, California
Wrote under: Charlotte Armstrong, Jo Valentine
D. of Frank Hall and Clara Pascoe Armstrong; m. Jack Lewi, 1928

Having begun as poet (several poems appeared in *The New Yorker*) and playwright (two plays ran briefly on Broadway), A. soon turned to writing suspense novels, her first three being conventional detective stories. The detective, MacDougal ("Mac") Duff is a former history professor who has discovered he prefers real-life puzzles to academic ones. In *Lay On, Mac Duff!* (1942), and in *The Case of the Weird Sisters* (1943), he is the conventional outsider who solves other people's mysteries and then moves on. In *The Innocent Flower* (1945), however, he becomes involved with a divorcee and her six children; with his commitment to them, A.'s use of him ends.

A number of A.'s stories are inverted mysteries in which the identity of the criminal is revealed early. In other novels, suspense is created by a race against time. Sometimes, terror is evoked when an innocent person is trapped in an enclosed space with several people, at least one of whom poses a threat. *The Case of the Weird Sisters*, a Mac Duff mystery, falls into this group, as does *The Albatross* (1957), in which, ironically, the threatening characters are invited into the home of the victims. Variants are *The Girl with a Secret* (1959), *The Witch's House* (1963), and *The Turret Room* (1965).

Another novel of particular interest is *A Little Less Than Kind* (1963), the Hamlet story reset in contemporary California. Using the Shakespearean situation, A. examines motivations and relationships, and although her denouement is quite different from Shakespeare's, it develops logically from the situation and characters. *A Dram of Poison* (1956), despite its serious central situation, is a comic novel, with an unlikely set of characters uniting in a common purpose and discovering in the process much that is admirable in each other.

Along with family relationships, A. was especially interested in children and old people. A recurring motif in her work is that of an innocent child thought responsible for a death. Concern over the impact of the accusation on the child leads others to seek out the truth, and an adult murderer is unmasked (*The Innocent Flower*, 1945, and *The Mark of the Hand*, 1963).

A recurrent theme in A.'s novels is that of our responsibility toward one another. Characters are shown involving themselves in others' problems because they know that if they do not help, no one else will. The title character in *The One-Faced Girl* (1963) defines "good guys" as those who "don't want other people hurt. They feel it, themselves. So if any one is in pain or trouble, then they not only *want* to help, they are obliged. They just about *have* to." This concept underlies much of A.'s fiction; combined with her skill in handling complex plots and her interest in motivation and character, it helps to account for the consistent popularity her work has had.

WORKS: *Ring Around Elizabeth, a Comedy in Three Acts* (1942). *Lay On, Mac Duff!* (1942). *The Case of the Weird Sisters* (1943). *The Innocent Flower: A MacDougal Duff Mystery* (1945). *The Unsuspected* (1946). *The Chocolate Cobweb* (1948). *Mischief* (1950). *The Black-Eyed Stranger* (1951). *Catch-As-Catch-Can* (1952). *The Trouble in Thor* (1953). *The Better to Eat You* (1954). *Walk out on Death* (1954). *The Dream Walker* (1955). *Murder's Nest* (1955). *Alibi for Murder* (1956). *A Dram of Poison* (1956). *The Albatross* (1957). *Duo: The Girl with a Secret and Incident at a Corner* (1959). *The Seventeen Widows of Sans Souci* (1959). *Something Blue* (1959). *The Mark of the Hand and Then Came Two Women* (1963). *A Little Less Than Kind* (1963). *The One-Faced Girl* (1963). *The Witch's House* (1963). *The Turret Room* (1965). *Dream of Fair Woman* (1966). *The Gift Shop* (1966). *I See You* (1966). *Lemon in the Basket* (1967). *The Balloon Man* (1968). *Seven Seats to the Moon* (1969). *The Protege* (1970).

BIBLIOGRAPHY: Cromie, A., Prefaces to *The Charlotte Armstrong Reader* (1970), *The Charlotte Armstrong Treasury* (1972), and *The Charlotte Armstrong Festival* (1975).

Other references: *NYHTB* (13 Sept. 1959). *NYTBR* (25 June 1950; 15 July 1951; 28 March 1954; 16 Jan. 1955; 5 Aug. 1956; 10 Nov. 1957; 12 April 1959; 10 Nov. 1963; 11 April 1965; 7 May 1967; 29 Oct. 1967).

MARY JEAN DeMARR

Harriette Louisa Simpson Arnow

B. 7 July 1908, Wayne County, Kentucky
Writes under: H. Arnow, Harriette Arnow, Harriette Simpson Arnow,
  Harriette Simpson, H. L. Simpson
D. of Elias and Mollie Jane Denney Simpson; m. Harold Arnow, 1939

A.'s best fiction is rooted in Kentucky, her native ground. With both parents descendants of original Kentucky settlers, A. grew up hearing family stories dating from the American Revolution. These kindled the child's desire to write fiction and tell stories herself. She attended Berea College for two years, taught school for a year, then studied at the University of Louisville, where she received a B.S. degree in 1930. In an act her family viewed as scandalous, A. quit her job in 1934 and moved to a furnished room in downtown Cincinnati near the city library, resolving to read "the great novels" and to write. She supported herself with odd jobs and worked for the Federal Writers' Project. After her marriage to newspaperman Arnow, A. moved with him to a farm in southern Kentucky. They settled in their current Ann Arbor home in 1950.

A. received national attention in 1935 with two short stories published in little magazines. Both demonstrate her skill at characterization and at depicting shocking violence. In 1936, she published the novel *Mountain Path*. It is based on A.'s experience of boarding with a hill family in a remote Kentucky hollow and teaching in a one-room schoolhouse; her year there was her first prolonged stay with the people who were to become the primary subjects of her fiction.

"The Washerwoman's Day," published in *Southern Review* (Winter, 1936), is A.'s best and most anthologized short story. She movingly depicts the self-righteousness and the arrogance church members feel toward the "poor white trash" who violate their notions of decency. This story anticipates A.'s fuller treatment of narrow piousness in *Hunter's Horn* (1949) and *The Dollmaker* (1954).

Hunter's Horn, A.'s second novel, was a critically acclaimed bestseller. The story of a hill farmer's obsessive chase after an elusive red fox, *Hunter's Horn* dramatizes the cost of a compulsion as maniacal and as mythic as Ahab's stalking of Moby Dick.

A.'s third novel, *The Dollmaker* (1954) is a masterwork and another bestseller. Gertie Nevels, the hulking heroine who tries to preserve her integrity and her family's unity after their migration from the Kentucky mills to a wartime housing project in Detroit, is A.'s most arresting character. The novel won A. the Friends of American Literature Award and was voted best novel of the year in the *Saturday Review*'s national critics' poll.

Two social histories are the result of twenty years of research on the settlers of southern Kentucky and northern Tennesee from 1780 to 1803. *Seedtime on the Cumberland* (1960) and *Flowering of the Cumberland* (1963), containing vivid reenactments of the settlers' everyday crises, are often as gripping as A.'s best fiction.

A. most recent novels lack the full-bodied characters and narrative drive that propel her earlier work.

Although A.'s work is now enjoying a reassessment, it has still not achieved the stature her talent merits. Too often writers whose work is firmly rooted in one locale are relegated to a minor status by the term "regional," which can suggest a limited appeal.

Far outdistancing other writers treating hill people from the southern Appalachian region, A. is the first and only American novelist to describe them with fidelity and justice and to place them in a setting that is authentic to the last detail. But A. does more than evoke an area no other writer has captured. Like Twain and Faulkner, she creates a private world whose inhabitants face dilemmas reaching beyond geographical boundaries. Her best fiction depicts the conflict between an individual conscience and society—whether it be family, community, or the wider world. If A.'s novels at times need streamlining, they contain worlds as palpable and as real as the reader's own. If her hardy combatants fail to achieve their goals, they nonetheless take responsibility for the outcome of their lives, and endure.

WORKS: *Mountain Path* (1936). *Hunter's Horn* (1949). *The Dollmaker* (1954). *Seedtime on the Cumberland* (1960). *Flowering of the Cumberland* (1963). *The Weedkiller's Daughter* (1970). *The Kentucky Trace: A Novel of the American Revolution* (1974). *Old Burnside* (1977).

BIBLIOGRAPHY: Eckley, W., *Harriette Arnow* (1974). Hobbs, G., "Harriette Arnow's Literary Journey: From the Parish to the World" (Ph.D. diss., Harvard Univ., 1975). Hobbs, G., in *GR* 4 (Winter 1979). Oates, J. C., Afterword to *The Dollmaker* by Harriette Arnow (1972).

Other references: *KCN* 2 (Fall 1976). *Nation* (31 Jan. 1976). *NYHTB* (6 Sept. 1936).

GLENDA HOBBS

Gertrude Franklin Horn Atherton

B. *30 Oct. 1857, San Francisco, California; d. 15 June 1948, San Francisco*
Wrote under: Asmodeus, Gertrude Atherton, Frank Lin
D. of Thomas and Gertrude Franklin Horn; m. George H. Bowen Atherton,
1876

The daughter of a Yankee businessman from California and of a southern belle, A. spent the first thirty years of her life in and around San Francisco, a city whose history and destiny she utilized as subject and background for her favorite character, a new western woman. She sporadically attended private schools, eloped at seventeen with a suitor of her mother's, bore two children, and rebelled against the conventions of domestic life. Only after the death of her husband did she begin her serious writing career in New York in 1888.

Her first significant novel was *Patience Sparhawk and Her Times* (1897), published in London where her novels at first attracted more critical attention than in the U.S. This novel introduces the new western woman, who in three subsequent novels symbolizes the evolution of Western civilization at the turn of the century. In *Patience Sparhawk and Her Times*, A. offers, from the point of view of an aspiring western woman an ironic appraisal of American self-reliance and society in the 1890s. Through her characterization of the heroine as an idealistic, self-reliant, but passionate woman, born into lowly, isolated circumstances in California, A. narrates a romantic-realistic and psychological version of the 19th-c. argument over the effect of heredity and environment on the development of the individual.

In *American Wives and English Husbands* (1898), A.'s independent-spirited heroine, Lee Tarleton, proud of her Creole heritage and aristocratic California upbringing, is confronted with the "solid fact" of English tradition and convention, personified by Cecil Maundrell, scion of a landed English family, whom she marries and who expects her to become his second self. Their marriage tests the past and present values of the two civilizations in regard to the relationship between man and woman and to the perpetuation of the race. In this novel and also in *The Doomswoman* (1893), *The Californians* (1898), and *Ancestors* (1907),

A. penetrates the facade of civilization that organizes the basic relationship between man and woman and between individuals and nature. She
displayed a continually ironic stance toward the argument on heredity
and environment by labeling as a "fool's paradise" an individual's excessive and illusory dependence on either inherited characteristics or a given
environment as a path to happiness. Her independent and self-conflicted
heroine challenges the assumption that a woman unthinkingly accepts a
passive, procreative function as a definition of herself and of the relationship between herself and nature and between herself and civilization.

A. enacted her criticism of Howells's "dull" realism by a call for
originality and imagination in American literature. From Hippolyte Taine,
she borrowed the technique of lifting a type of character out of the
commonplace conditions to which he or she was apparently doomed and
transferring him or her to an environment, replete with change and opportunity, where latent potentialities could be developed.

From her first novel to her last, A.'s genius lies in her ability to tell
exciting stories about worthy characters, even though her style and form
do not always succeed by current critical standards.

WORKS: *What Dreams May Come* (1888). *Hermia Suydam* (1889). *Los
Cerritos, A Romance of the Modern Time* (1890). *A Question of Time* (1891).
The Doomswoman (1893). *Before the Gringo Came* (1894, enlarged in *The
Splendid Idle Forties*, 1902). *A Whirl Asunder* (1895). *Patience Sparhawk and
Her Times* (1897). *His Fortunate Grace* (1897). *The Californians* (1898).
American Wives and English Husbands (1898). *A Daughter of the Vine*
(1899). *Senator North* (1900). *The Aristocrats* (1901). *The Conqueror* (1902).
A Few of Hamilton's Letters (1903). *Mrs. Pendleton's Four-in-Hand* (1903).
Rulers of Kings (1904). *The Bell in the Fog, and Other Stories* (1905). *The
Traveling Thirds* (1905). *Rezánov* (1906). *Ancestors* (1907). *The Gorgeous
Isle* (1908). *Tower of Ivory* (1910). *Julia France and Her Times* (1912).
Perch of the Devil (1914). *California, an Intimate History* (1914). *Mrs. Bal-
fame* (1916). *Life in the War Zone* (1916). *The Living Present* (1917). *The
White Morning* (1918). *The Avalanche* (1919). *Transplanted* (1919). *The
Sisters-in-Law* (1921). *Sleeping Fires* (1922). *Black Oxen* (1923). *The Crystal
Cup* (1925). *The Immortal Marriage* (1927). *The Jealous Gods* (1928). *Dido,
Queen of Hearts* (1929). *The Sophisticates* (1931). *Adventures of a Novelist*
(1932). *The Foghorn* (1934). *Golden Peacock* (1936). *Rezánov and Doña
Concha* (1937). *Can Women Be Gentlemen?* (1938). *The House of Lee* (1940).
The Horn of Life (1942). *Golden Gate Country* (1945). *My San Francisco*
(1946).

BIBLIOGRAPHY: Courtney, W. L., *The Feminine Note in Fiction* (1904).
Jackson, J. H., *Gertrude Atherton* (1940). Knight, G. C., *The Strenuous Age
in American Literature* (1954). McClure, C. S., *Gertrude Atherton* (Boise
State Univ. Western Writers Series, 1976). Parker, G. T., *William Dean*

Howells: Realism and Feminism (Harvard English Studies, 1973). Starr, K., *Americans and the California Dream, 1850–1915* (1973). Underwood, J. C., *Literature and Insurgency* (1914).

Other references: *ALR* 9 (Spring 1976). *The American West* (July 1974). *The Bookman* (July 1929). *CHSQ* 55 (Fall 1976). *SJS* 1 (1975).

CHARLOTTE S. McCLURE

Djuna Barnes

B. *12 June 1892, Cornwall-on-Hudson, New York; d. 18 June 1982,*
  New York City
D. *of Wald and Elizabeth Chappell Barnes*

B. began her career as a journalist. A longtime resident of Europe, her stories, poems, and plays reflect the life and attitudes of the post-World War I Paris expatriates.

B. is best known for *Nightwood* (1936). Using symbolism and a surrealistic atmosphere B. presents a group of American expatriates, living in fashionable 1890s-style decadence, who reveal the abnormality of their world and their individual psychological natures through their words and their interactions. In his introduction to the novel, T. S. Eliot highly praises its gothic qualities, its insistence on horror and doom. He compares B.'s work to Elizabethan tragedy, not only for its themes and motifs but also for its technical brilliance in wit, characterization, and language. Eliot is not wrong in his assessment of the mood of the novel, but his exaggerated praise for *Nightwood* has led to a questionable evaluation of B.'s work.

B.'s stories are peopled by characters whose thoughts and behavior reveal the strange workings of twisted, obsessed minds. The characters with whom the reader is led to sympathize embrace life in all its ambiguities and possibilities. Such a character is Madame von Bartmann in "Aller et Retour," a woman whose advice to the daughter she has not seen for seven years might be B.'s advice to her characters: "think everything" and "do everything," not just for the sake of experience but to gain self-knowledge. The mother is sufficiently selfish to feel relief when her daughter responds by announcing her engagement. Since her daughter will be sheltered by a traditional, protective husband, Madame von Bartmann is saved from responsibility. The reader is led to scorn such characters as the daughter, while feeling sorry for them. They function as foils for the mysterious, even macabre characters in whom B.'s interest lies.

Imagery and word choice intensify the ambiguous horror which marks most of B.'s stories. Dark nights, evenings at dusk, dust, decay, and illness are prevalent. Death, whether from old age, illness, or from sudden unexplained violence, is a repeated symbol. The prevailing atmosphere of decay and quiet brutality makes death seem inevitable.

These motifs and devices are typified in "Spillway," the title story in the 1962 collection. Julie Anspacher returns home to her husband with a child he knew nothing about. Years earlier she had been told she would die from tuberculosis: for five years she lived on in a sanitorium, and had a child, daughter of a fellow patient. Julie's lover is dead, her child has weak lungs, and Julie's own death is near. The child is clearly symbolic of what Julie terms "death perpetuating itself." Julie explains her affair by saying that she and her lover knew they would endanger anyone who was not already dying from tuberculosis. But the child's existence causes Julie's husband to shoot himself, so that Julie's prophecy is ironically fulfilled. This story is typical of B.'s work, in its nearly humorless presentation of sickness and death, frustrated lives filled with tension, and strained sexuality tinged with the grotesque or the violent.

B.'s work is limited in scope, with a few motifs and themes used repeatedly. It is difficult to identify with her characters because of the hyperbolic presentation. Yet there is power in B.'s language and images, and in her ability to evoke an atmosphere of tension and psychological unease. Her work has influenced writers ranging from Isak Dinesen and John Hawkes to Anaïs Nin, who, in her diary, praises B.'s poetic insight and language.

WORKS: *The Book of Repulsive Women* (1915). *A Book* (1923). *Ryder* (1928). *A Night Among the Horses* (rev. and enlarged ed. of *A Book*, 1929). *Nightwood* (1936). *The Antiphon* (1958). *Selected Works* (1962).

BIBLIOGRAPHY: Baxter, C., "A Self-Consuming Light: Nightwood and the Crisis of Modernism," *JML* 3. Johnsen, W. A., "Modern Women Novelists: Nightwood and the Novel of Sensibility," *BuR* 21. Moers, E., *Literary Women* (1976).

SUSAN R. GORSKY

Margaret Ayer Barnes

B. 8 April 1886, Chicago, Illinois; d. 26 Oct. 1967, Cambridge, Massachusetts
D. of Benjamin F. and Janet Hopkins Ayer; m. Cecil Barnes, 1910

Descended on both sides from colonial English families who settled in America in the middle 1600s, B. attended the University School for Girls in Chicago and majored in English and philosophy at Bryn Mawr College, where she was influenced by the feminist president, M. Carey Thomas. While raising three sons, she appeared in performances of the Aldis Players in Lake Forest, Illinois, and of the North Shore Theater in Winnetka, Illinois. Her stories, published by the *Pictorial Review*, were later collected and published in book form as *Prevailing Winds* (1928). B. wrote three plays (two in collaboration with Edward Sheldon, a dramatist and personal friend) and five novels, winning the Pulitzer Prize in 1931 for *Years of Grace* (1930). After the publication of her last novel, *Wisdom's Gate* (1938), B. returned to writing occasional short stories and lecturing.

Prevailing Winds shows evidence of the skills that would bring her critical acclaim, but the narrow focus that would cause her ultimate neglect by most literary critics can also be seen. From her theatrical experience she had learned to define character through conversations. Her careful observations of character, however, were limited to the upper-middle-class society of Chicago in the first third of the 20th c.

Distracted by the element of social history in B.'s fiction, many critics overlooked important underlying themes. Feminism, a major theme which grew out of her education at Bryn Mawr, appeared in early short stories through the portrayals of Martha Cavendish in "The Dinner Party" and of Kate Dalton in "Perpetual Care." Both are women prominent in Chicago society who have chosen marriage and socially conventional lives, but each is confronted with a situation that leads her to question those choices and seek an opportunity to break with convention. Each resolves that the choice has come too late: Martha has learned to live in her thoughts and let the world go as it will; Kate in the end settles for memories to avoid upsetting her children by changing her life.

Most of the women in B.'s novels follow the examples of these two women, but in each succeeding novel they seem less satisfied with the choice. In *Years of Grace*, which traces the life of Jane Ward Carver to the eve of the Great Depression, Jane abandons early adherence to the feminist principles instilled in her at Bryn Mawr and elects to fill the traditional roles of wife and mother. Already before her marriage, she had admitted she lacked the courage of her convictions: "She who thinks and runs away, lives to think another day. . . . I don't act at all. . . . I just drift." When she is offered an opportunity to defy convention and marry Jimmy Trent, she chooses to remain with her responsibilities. Only when her daughter Cicily breaks the pattern by divorcing her husband to marry Albert Lancaster, does Jane wonder if her "struggle to live with dignity and decency and decorum" had been a worthy goal.

Olivia Van Tyne Ottendorf in *Westward Passage* (1931) temporarily accepts her second chance at an artistic life with Nick Allen, but soon returns gratefully to her husband and the limited society she had known. She has been educated only for such a role, and the reader recognizes her, as the critic Lloyd C. Taylor, Jr., points out, as "a victim of an intricately structured social system that securely, if deceptively, deprives the woman of any training that does not contribute to the creation of the lady and the socialite."

B. resolves her interest in feminist themes in her final novel, *Wisdom's Gate*. She returns to the Carver family of *Years of Grace* and chronicles Cicily's life after her marriage to Albert Lancaster. Cicily has broken the pattern of her past, and although she does not achieve greater fulfillment, she gains uncompromising clarity. The topics of divorce and adultery are examined objectively and honestly. While lacking the unity and scope of B.'s earlier novels, *Wisdom's Gate* portrays a marriage based on the honesty of a woman who has the courage of her convictions.

WORKS: *Prevailing Winds* (1928). *Age of Innocence* (1928). *Jenny* (with E. Shelton, 1929). *Dishonored Lady* (with E. Shelton, 1930). *Years of Grace* (1930). *Westward Passage* (1931). *Within This Present* (1933). *Edna His Wife* (1935). *Wisdom's Gate* (1938).

BIBLIOGRAPHY: Barnes, E. W., *The Man Who Lived Twice: The Biography of Edward Sheldon* (1956). Lawrence, M., *The School of Femininity* (1936). Stuckey, W. J., *The Pulitzer Prize Novels: A Critical Backward Look* (1966). Taylor, L. C., Jr., *Margaret Ayer Barnes* (1974). Wagenknecht, E. C., *Chicago* (1964).

Other references: *North American Review* (Jan. 1934).

THELMA J. SHINN

Ida B. Wells Barnett

B. 16 July 1862, Holly Springs, Mississippi; d. 25 March 1931, Chicago, Illinois
Wrote under: Ida B. Wells Barnett, Ida B. Wells, Iola
D. of Jim and Elizabeth Warrenton Wells; m. Ferdinand L. Barnett, 1895

Born six months before the Emancipation Proclamation to parents who were slaves, B. was the oldest of eight children. In 1878, when a yellow-fever epidemic raged, she was left an orphan and became the head of her family. She attended Shaw University and became a teacher in a nearby county school at an early age.

B.'s first public denunciation of discrimination came when she sued the Chesapeake and Ohio Railroad Company over its refusal to allow her to ride in a first-class coach. She won her case in 1884, but her elation was short-lived when the Supreme Court of Tennessee overturned the verdict in 1887.

B. taught for seven years in the public schools in Memphis while also writing articles for local religious weeklies. Eventually she became the editor and part-owner of the *Free Speech and Headlight*. When her articles protesting the conditions in the black schools led to her dismissal from her teaching position, she became a full-time journalist.

On 9 March 1892, three young black men were lynched in Memphis, and B.'s vehement editorial outcry led to the destruction of her offices by the irate white citizens of Memphis. Her absence from the city at the time of the incident probably saved her from bodily harm.

Writing in New York for the *New York Age*, B. continued her polemics against lynchings. Her articles were compiled in pamphlet form and published in October 1892 as *Southern Horrors*.

Finding little support for her antilynching crusade in America, B. journeyed to England in 1893. Here she found the English audience and press more attentive and sympathetic to her pleas.

A Red Record: Tabulated Statistics and Alleged Causes of Lynchings in the United States, 1892–1893–1894, based on figures printed in the *Chicago Tribune*, was published in 1895 when B. arrived back in America. In 1909, she was a featured speaker at the National Negro Conference. From this group emerged the National Association for the Advancement of Colored People, of which she is listed as a founder, though she was never an active member. B. established the Negro Fellowship

League in 1910 to aid needy blacks in finding shelter, food, and employment. She became the first woman probation officer in Chicago, and also organized the Alpha Suffrage Club in 1914 to encourage black women to use their new voting rights.

Intolerant, impudent, impatient, indomitable, and indefatigable are all words that come to mind when reading *Crusade for Justice*, B.'s autobiography, begun in 1928 and edited and published by her daughter, Alfreda M. Duster, in 1970. Intolerant she was—of both whites and blacks who refused to support her crusade, and of those in the ministry, in journalism, and in public office who spoke and acted in a less than honest way. Impudent—for daring to challenge a railroad company in the courts, for daring to rebuke in print black ministers whose private lives were not impeccable, for daring to approach two presidents of the United States, McKinley and Wilson, with the problems of black people.

Crusade for Justice reveals B. as devoted almost equally to her crusade against lynching and to her role as a mother to her children. In her children's early childhood days she withdrew from her most active participation in public affairs, though she had at one time taken her first-born infant with her on a lecture tour so that she might still nurse him. Her interest in children was evidenced by her agitation for a kindergarten for black children similar to Jane Addams's Hull House, which led to a friendship with Miss Addams.

Born a slave, yet an outspoken advocate of human rights, B. has earned her place as one of the foremost early black feminists.

WORKS: *Southern Horrors: Lynch Law in All Its Phases* (1892). *The Reason Why the Colored American Is Not in the World's Columbian Exposition—The Afro-American's Contribution to Columbian Literature* (1893). *A Red Record: Tabulated Statistics and Alleged Causes of Lynchings in the United States, 1892–1893–1894* (1895). *Mob Rule in New Orleans: Robert Charles and His Fight to the Death* (1900). *On Lynchings; Southern Horrors; A Red Record; Mob Rule in New Orleans* (1969). *Crusade for Justice: The Autobiography of Ida B. Wells* (Ed. A. M. Duster, 1970).

Ida B. Wells Barnett's unpublished diary and letters are in the possession of her daughter, Alfreda M. Duster.

BIBLIOGRAPHY: Aptheker, H., ed., *A Documentary History of the Negro People in the United States* (1969). Bontemps, A., and J. Conroy, *They Seek a City* (1945). Dann, M. E., ed., *The Black Press, 1827–1890: The Quest for National Identity* (1971). Lerner, G., ed., *Black Women in White America: A Documentary History* (1972). Loewenberg, B. J., and R. Bogin, eds., *Black Women in Nineteenth-Century American Life: Their Words, Their Thoughts, Their Feelings* (1976).

MARILYN LAMPING

Mary Ritter Beard

B. 5 Aug. 1876, Indianapolis, Indiana; d. 14 Aug. 1958, Phoenix, Arizona
D. of Eli Foster and Marassa Lockwood Ritter; m. Charles Austin Beard, 1900

Educated at De Pauw University, then a rather conservative Methodist institution, B. received her Ph.D. in 1897. She spent her early married years in England in the circle around Ruskin Hall, a center for new economic thought, then moved to New York City and studied at Columbia University, where her husband, the most vital intellectual influence in her life, was to join the faculty.

B.'s earliest books, *American Citizenship* (1914, in collaboration with her husband), *Woman's Work in Municipalities* (1915), and *A Short History of the American Labor Movement* (1920), reflect her lifelong interests: labor, sociology, and women's studies.

The books she wrote with her husband in the 1920s and 1930s, both the school texts and the enormously successful four-volume *The Rise of American Civilization* (1927–1942), were highly influential. The first two volumes of *The Rise of American Civilization* were the product of two decades of Progressive intellectual attack on the formalism of 19th-c. American historical writing, which tended to see American institutions in an ideal, abstract way. The particular economic interpretation of the Revolution which pitted agrarian democrats against capitalist aristocrats, and the view of the Civil War as a second revolution, were widely accepted until after World War II, when Charles A. Beard came under attack for viewing earlier American history from the perspective of the Progressive fight for reform against an entrenched capitalism. Indeed, the Beards modified their economic determinism in the 1940s and gave greater play to the force of ideas and ideals than they had before. But their most significant contribution was their salutory reminder that ideals do not exist outside of social contexts.

While the great collaborative effort with her husband has now largely entered the realm of intellectual history, B.'s pioneering work in women's studies, notably in *On Understanding Women* (1931) and *Woman as Force in History* (1946), remains generative today. Encouraged by the nascent field of anthropology, which was producing work showing woman as the originator of agriculture and the domestic arts, B. studied social realities as disparate as woman's legal status in England and woman's contribution to Pythagorean philosophy in ancient Greece, in order to discover her true status and achievement. Such a vision was obscured, she argued, not only by male bias and social mythology, but by feminists who themselves promulgated a false view of women as a subject sex. The fullest and most important treatment of these views appears in *Woman as Force in History*.

The questions she raises there remain with us, but her answers are sometimes problematic. While her argument against the idea of "equality" as the touchstone for woman's relation to man points out the difficulties it engenders, the argument remains inconclusive. Nor does the book resolve a contradiction in her view of women's contribution. While B. sometimes seems to be saying that women are a peculiarly civilizing force, at other times she seems to be saying only that they have been more of a force both for good and for bad than we have realized. Still, the book leaves us two important lines of thought: one is the definition of woman's just role. B. believed that the early imitation of men by feminists was in part a function of the individualism of 19th-c. America, and that as society moved toward more collectivist forms, alternatives for women would emerge. The other line of thought is that history is not simply the account of the politician, the banker, and the general. Until history describes events on the level of domestic economy and family relationship as well, woman's true force, B. believes, will not be understood, nor will the true causes and effects of history.

WORKS: *American Citizenship* (with C. A. Beard, 1914). *Woman's Work in Municipalities* (1915). *A Short History of the American Labor Movement* (1920). *A History of the United States* (with C. A. Beard, 1921). *The Rise of American Civilization* (Vols. 1 and 2, with C. A. Beard, 1927). *The American Labor Movement: A Short History* (1931). *On Understanding Women* (1931). *America Through Women's Eyes* (ed. by Beard, 1933). *A Changing Political Economy As It Affects Women* (1934). *Laughing Their Way* (ed. by Beard with M. B. Bruere, 1934). *The Making of American Civilization* (with C. A. Beard, 1937). *America in Mid Passage* (Vol. 3, *The Rise of American Civilization*, with C. A. Beard, 1939). *The American Spirit: A Study of the Idea of Civilization in the United States* (Vol. 4, *The Rise of American Civilization*, with C. A. Beard, 1942). *A Basic History of the United States* (with C. A. Beard, 1944). *Woman as Force in History: A Study in Traditions and Realities* (1946). *The Force of Women in Japanese History* (1953). *The Making of Charles A. Beard* (1955).

BIBLIOGRAPHY: Carroll, B. A., *Liberating Women's History: Theoretical and Critical Essays* (1976). Hofstadter, R., *The Progressive Historians* (1968).
Other references: *NewR* (1946). *NYT* (27 Dec. 1931). *PolSciQ* (Sept. 1927).

LOIS HUGHSON

Catharine Esther Beecher

B. 6 Sept. 1800, East Hampton, New York; d. 12 May 1878, Elvira, New York
D. of Lyman and Roxanne Foote Beecher

Sister of Harriet Beecher Stowe, B. was an educator and writer who attempted to expand the domestic power of women. Following the death of her mother, B., age sixteen and the eldest of thirteen children, assumed the family and household responsibilities.

After the death of her fiancé, Alexander Metcalf Fisher, B. established the Hartford Female Seminary in May 1823 with the money inherited from him. She also organized the Western Female Institute in Cincinnati (1832–1837) and the Ladies' Society for Promoting Education in the West, and helped to establish three female colleges (in Burlington, Iowa, in Quincy, Illinois, and in Milwaukee, Wisconsin).

Although B. left the Hartford Female Seminary in 1831, it was considered one of the most significant advances made in early-19th-c. education for women. It marked B.'s first attempt to redefine a new relationship with American culture for herself and for other women.

The author of over thirty books, B. expanded the sentimental view of women as saintly and moral creatures, complements of their immoral and competitive mates. She maintained that the American woman had difficult and peculiar duties which derived mainly from the crudeness and disorder of an expanding nation. She asserted in *Letters to the People on Health and Happiness* (1855) that "it is obvious that Providence designed that the chief responsibility of *sustaining the family state*, in all its sacred and varied relations and duties should rest mainly on the female sex."

B.'s most popular volumes were *A Treatise on Domestic Economy* (1841) and *Domestic Receipts* (1846), written for the use of young wives. *The American Woman's Home* (1869), written with her sister, provides a wide range of advice for home management.

In *The Elements of Mental and Moral Philosophy* (1831), B. asserted that woman was the moral guardian of her culture. Common sense must be used to determine morality, and personal conscience must dominate over doctrine. This position moved theology to social grounds and placed B. in direct conflict with her father, the Reverend Lyman Beecher, a Calvinist.

The major characteristic of B.'s Christianity, however, was passivity, not social activity. She spoke against active abolitionism, asserting in *An Essay on Slavery* (1837) that "Christianity is a system of *persuasion*, tending, by kind and gentle influence, to make men *willing* to leave their sins." B. maintained that women had a proper place, a proper sphere, and that place was out of politics and within the home, influencing men through quiet, proper petition and through the education of their children.

As might be expected, B. was an avid opponent of woman's suffrage, attempting instead to expand the woman's base of power in the home. Although she advocated democracy, she did not feel that it led to women's active participation in politics and to furthering social change. Instead she asserted that there was a social order based on age, health, and the most important distinction, gender.

B. is a transitional figure whose writings influenced women to move from a state of subordination to one in which they attempted to secure a greater role in their changing, shifting society. She was confronted by a competitive society in which men aggressively sought wealth and position, and she perceived this activity as unworthy of women. Women, unlike men, could effect change only by influence and passivity. Aggression and force were male prerogatives.

B.'s solution was to create a quiet eye of the storm and to call it the American Home. There women could rule supreme and men could return for moral refreshment and rest. In this quiet haven, the American Home, B. placed her sentimentalized version of the American woman. She herself never married.

WORKS: *Suggestions Respecting Improvements in Education* (1829). *The Elements of Mental and Moral Philosophy* (1831). *Arithmetic Simplified* (1832). *Primary Geography* (1833). *The Lyceum Arithmetic* (1835). *An Essay on the Education of Female Teachers* (1835). *Lectures on the Difficulty of Religion* (1836). *An Essay on Slavery* (1837). *The Moral Instructor* (1838). *A Treatise on Domestic Economy* (1841). *Letters to Persons Who Are Engaged in Domestic Service* (1842). *The Duty of American Women to Their Country* (1845). *Domestic Receipts* (1846). *Truths Stranger Than Fiction* (1850). *The True Remedy for the Wrongs of Women* (1852). *Letters to the People on Health and Happiness* (1855). *Physiology and Calisthenics* (1856). *Common Sense Applied to Religion* (1857). *Calisthenic Exercises* (1860). *An Appeal to the People* (1860). *Religious Training of Children in the School* (1864). *The American Woman's Home* (with H. B. Stowe; 1869). *Principles of Domestic Science* (with H. B. Stowe; 1870). *Woman Suffrage and Woman's Profession* (1871). *Work for All, and Other Tales* (1871). *Woman's Profession as Mother and Educator* (1872). *Miss B.'s Housekeeper and Healthkeeper* (1873). *The New Housekeeper's Manual* (1873). *Educational Reminiscences and Suggestions* (1874).

BIBLIOGRAPHY: Cross, B. M., *The Educated Woman in America* (1965). Douglas, A., *The Feminization of American Culture* (1977). Harveson, E. M., *Catharine Esther Beecher* (1932). Sklar, K. K., *Catharine Beecher: A Study in American Domesticity* (1973). Woody, T., *A History of Women's Education in the United States* (1966).

Other references: *AQ* 18 (Summer 1966). *Civil War History* 17 (June 1971).

JULIANN E. FLEENOR

Ruth Fulton Benedict

B. 5 June 1887, New York City; d. 17 Sept. 1948, New York City
Wrote under: Ruth Benedict, Anne Singleton
D. of Frederick Samuel and Beatrice Joanna Shattuck Fulton; m. Stanley
Rossiter Benedict, 1914

B.'s father, a surgeon and cancer researcher, died before she was two, leaving her mother to bring up B. and her younger sister on their maternal grandparents' farm in central New York. An attack of measles when she was a child left B. partially deaf, an infirmity from which she suffered personally and professionally throughout her life.

An outstanding student, B. won a scholarship to Vassar College, where she graduated Phi Beta Kappa in 1909. She became disillusioned with her marriage early, especially when the longed-for children never came. When her desire for a job of her own met with her husband's discouragement, she slowly withdrew from him. In 1919, B. enrolled in the New School for Social Research, where she studied anthropology under Elsie Clews Parsons and Alexander Goldenweiser. From there she went to Columbia and received her doctorate under Franz Boas in 1923. She started teaching there that year. Her dissertation, *The Concept of the Guardian Spirit in North America*, about American Indian religion, was published in 1923. Her early fieldwork was done among several American Indian tribes.

Throughout these early years of anthropological apprenticeship, B. remained a sensitive and solitary person, expressing her inner battles with loneliness and the painful relationship with her husband in verse, some of which she published in *Poetry* and *Nation* under the pseudonym of Anne Singleton. In 1930, she and Stanley separated, and at that time

Boas appointed her assistant professor at Columbia. Soon thereafter, her depressions lifted, the need for Anne Singleton faded, and slowly the separate lives she led became fused together in her work.

In 1934, *Patterns of Culture*, her most famous book, was published. It has since been translated into fourteen languages and is still regarded as one of the best introductions to anthropology. Combining problems of psychology and the individual with those of anthropology and culture, she evolved a theory which stated that culture was not only the condition within which personality developed, but was itself a "personality writ large." All culture, she postulated, is structured into patterns which impose a harmony upon the disparate components of life; for any one culture there is a dominant pattern, an overriding cultural temperament.

During the war years, B. became more interested in humanism and published several books about racism.

From 1943 to 1945, B. worked in Washington in the Office of War Information, concentrating on Rumania, Thailand, and Japan. This led to her pioneering work with literate informants from urban centers and a new shift in anthropology to the analysis of complex modern societies. B.'s most gracefully and cogently written book is *The Chrysanthemum and the Sword* (1946). Using an intensive analysis of interviews and literary material, it concerns itself with themes in Japanese culture, stressing primarily those that have to do with reciprocal relations between people. She deals with the hierarchical organization of Japanese life, portrays the structure of obligations to emperor, family, and self, and examines the strong sense of shame so dominant in the culture. The underlying humanist message of the book is that the only way Japan could be reintegrated into the world is by using the favorable Japanese patterns of culture as the building blocks rather than by imposing European values from without. The book had a tremendous impact in the U.S. In 1947, following its great success, the Office of Naval Research gave Columbia University an extensive grant to establish under B.'s direction a program of "Research in Contemporary Cultures," the most ambitious program of anthropological research the U.S. had yet seen.

After Boas's death in 1942, B. was the leading American anthropologist as well as the first American woman to become a prominent social scientist and leader in her profession. Her great contribution was her integration of the idea of patterns, which she slowly pieced together in her own life and applied to her work. In so doing, she gave her profession a theoretical orientation at a time when science for the first time was trying to deal with total cultures. B.'s critics accuse her of never having written a full ethnography and of having done fieldwork either among people living in disintegrating cultures or among literate informants from cultures far away. Some have criticized her patterns as overly simplistic. However, her deafness, shyness, and childhood traumas that cut her personal life off from others were probably not only responsible for her anthropological weaknesses, but are possibly what gave her both the ability to view cultures at a distance and the tolerance for deviance that led to her very great contributions.

WORKS: *The Concept of the Guardian Spirit in North America* (1923). *Tales of the Cochiti Indians* (1931). *Patterns of Culture* (1934). *Zuni Mythology* (2 vols., 1935). *Race: Science and Politics* (1940). *The Races of Mankind* (with G. Weltfish, 1943). *The Chrysanthemum and the Sword: Patterns of Japanese Culture* (1946). *Rumanian Culture and Behavior* (1946). *Thai Culture and Behavior* (1946). *An Anthropologist at Work: Writings of Ruth Benedict* (Ed. M. Mead, 1959).

BIBLIOGRAPHY: Mead, M., ed., *An Anthropologist at Work* (1949). Mead, M., *Ruth Benedict* (1974).
For articles in reference works, see: *NAW* (article by D. Fleming). *NCAB*.
Other references: *AA* (51, 1949; 59, 1957). *Minzokugaku Kenkyu* 14 (Japanese Journal of Ethnology, 1949). *Ruth Fulton Benedict: A Memorial* (Viking Fund, 1949). *UTQ* 18 (1949).

MIRIAM KAHN

Sally Benson

B. 3 Sept. 1900, St. Louis, Missouri; d. 21 July 1972, Woodland Hills, California
D. of Alonzo Redway and Anna Prophater Smith; m. Reynolds Benson, 1919

After B.'s family moved to New York City, she attended the Horace Mann School, started working at seventeen, married at nineteen, had a daughter, and later divorced her husband. She wrote newspaper interviews and movie reviews and in 1929 contributed the first of her 108 stories to *The New Yorker*. B. also edited a volume of myths and wrote mystery reviews for *The New Yorker* and more than twenty screenplays.

People Are Fascinating (1936) includes almost all the stories B. had published in *The New Yorker* and four from the *American Mercury*.

"The Overcoat" and "Suite 2049" were O. Henry prize stories for 1935 and 1936. The title story offers an ironic perspective on the volume: a woman dramatist reads drama into mundane lives. B. reveals the mediocrity of self-deluded and self-indulgent characters but is compassionate about their attempts to deal with their own mediocrity, with poverty and aging, with meaningless lives.

In *Emily* (1938), B. writes somewhat longer stories that allow for character development and elicit compassion for those caught in dilemmas, particularly those of growing up. "Professional Housewife" scathingly reveals the emptiness of that role, as well as that of a door-to-door salesman. When scattered in *The New Yorker* these stories seem witty; in this collection they seem depressing.

Despite libraries' classification, *Junior Miss* (1941) is not a children's book. Each story humorously shows a young girl's attempt to learn about herself and the world; collectively, the stories reveal the human condition. B.'s light touch does not hide the seriousness of Judy's problems and the inadequacies of most adult strategies for coping with them. The dramatization by Jerome Chodorov and Joseph Fields (1942) achieved success by hardening the delicacy gained by B.'s stream-of-consciousness technique; it has the "rounded ends" and "climaxes" B. disliked, and creates a popular stereotype. Readers of the stories will perceive *Junior Miss* as a rare account of female rites of passage.

Meet Me in St. Louis (1942) is a collection of twelve stories, dealing with family life, based on B.'s sister's diary of their family at the time of the World's Fair in St. Louis at the turn of the century. It was made into a popular movie starring Judy Garland.

B.'s stories are "slices of life" in which characters, through stream-of-consciousness or dialogue, reveal foolish pretenses; swift narration and irony preclude sentimentality but sometimes result in cruel revelations. Cumulatively her women are stereotypes of frivolous, stupid, and wasteful upper-middle-class New Yorkers. But B. also described the male self-deception and use of power that compel women to utilize manipulative strategies. Her portraits of young girls reveal the anguish of their socialization.

WORKS: *People Are Fascinating* (1936). *Emily* (1938). *Stories of the Gods and Heroes* (1940). *Junior Miss* (1941). *Meet Me in St. Louis* (1942). *Women and Children FIRST* (1943).

BIBLIOGRAPHY: *Writers and Writing* (22 July 1972). *NYT* (22 July 1972).
MARY ANNE FERGUSON

Doris Betts

B. 4 June 1932, Statesville, North Carolina
D. of William Elmore and Mary Ellen Freeze Waugh; m. Lowry Matthews
  Betts, 1952

Since winning a *Mademoiselle* award in 1953, B. has published seven volumes of fiction. She has been a journalist, a college teacher (at the University of North Carolina, Chapel Hill, and elsewhere), and an active citizen of her town and state (Sanford, North Carolina) on whose history two of her novels focus. She has won several awards and a Guggenheim Fellowship (1958–59).

The Gentle Insurrection, and Other Stories (1954), though published when the author was twenty-two, shows mature understanding of human powers and limitations. In the title story, the daughter of a sharecropper, out of both fear and family loyalty, rejects her chance to escape with a lover; other stories show characters coping with handicaps, poverty, aging, and racial discrimination. There is no sentimentality; a chain-gang, murder, maternal rejection, patriarchal ruthlessness, bitter sexual frustration are dispassionately presented. B.'s characteristic use of interior monologue for ironic self-revelation, her concern for morality and religion, her use of animal symbols, and her humor are all already apparent.

In *The Astronomer, and Other Stories* (1966), the title story is a novella whose central character, a working-class widower, tries to fill his life by pursuing astronomy but finds he cannot fill the emptiness without involvement with other people. B.'s increased control of her medium is evident in the economy with which several lives are simultaneously revealed. In the other stories in this collection, B. succinctly portrays people who deal with life the best they can but not always effectively.

Though excellent in characterization, B.'s first three novels lack the deftness and sure ironic voice of the short stories. *Tall Houses in Winter* (1957), B.'s first novel, is overplotted and melodramatic, and only somewhat redeemed by convincing character portrayal. *The Scarlet Thread* (1964), a historical novel, is noteworthy primarily for its vivid scenes and biblical symbolism. *The River to Pickle Beach* (1972) skillfully uses symbols of nature to make this novel a powerful affirmation of life.

With *Beasts of the Southern Wild, and Other Stories* (1973) and

Heading West (1981), B. moves from the category of Southern regionalist into the mainstream of American literature. An assured ironic voice convincingly tells fantastic, comic adventures as characters leave home on journies of self-discovery and female heroes become paradigms of modern psychological and religious search for ultimate meanings.

B.'s characters, often grotesque, gain dignity from confronting loneliness, family and racial tensions, aging, and death. She achieves rare authenticity about women through detailing graphically the birth process, the emotional effects of abortion, hysterectomy, and childlessness. B.'s discussions of the aesthetics of writing reflect her award-winning teaching.

WORKS: *The Gentle Insurrection, and Other Stories* (1954). *Tall Houses in Winter* (1957). *The Scarlet Thread* (1964). *The Astronomer, and Other Stories* (1966). *The River to Pickle Beach* (1972). *Beasts of the Southern Wild, and Other Stories* (1966). *Heading West* (1981).

BIBLIOGRAPHY: Wolf, G., in *Kite-flying and Other Irrational Acts: Conversations with Twelve Southern Writers*, Ed. J. Carr (1972).

Other references: Chapel Hill *Weekly* (3 May 1972). *Red Clay Reader* (1970). *The Sanford* (5 Dec. 1974).

MARY ANNE FERGUSON

Elizabeth Bishop

B. 8 Feb. 1911, Worcester, Massachusetts; d. 6 Oct. 1979, Boston, Massachusetts
D. of William Thomas and Gertrude Bulmer Bishop

When B. was eight-months old, her father died suddenly, and her mother subsequently suffered a nervous collapse from which she never recovered. B. was taken first to live with her maternal grandparents in Nova Scotia, where her grandfather owned a tannery and farmed, and at age six to live with her paternal grandparents in Worcester, Massachusetts, so that she could be educated in the U.S.

At Vassar College, she and several other young women, among them Mary McCarthy, began a magazine, the *Conspirito*, which rivaled the more traditional *Vassar Review*. After the two publications were amalgamated, however, B. was a regular contributor to the review. The best of her pieces written during these years was a short story, "In Prison," which appeared in the *Partisan Review* in 1938. The year before she graduated (1934), B. met Marianne Moore, who encouraged her to write rather than attend medical school, as she had intended. Moore became a lifelong friend.

B.'s adult life was nearly nomadic, and travel became a central metaphor in her work. She lived and traveled in England, Europe, North Africa, and South America. She lived in Brazil for fifteen years.

B.'s first book of poetry, *North and South* (1946), includes the well-known poems "Florida," "The Map," "The Fish," "The Man-Moth," "The Unbeliever," and "A Miracle for Breakfast." The book was widely acclaimed by critics, who especially praised B.'s descriptive acumen, her reticence, and her subtle ability to metamorphose her encounters with simple objects or scenes into extraordinarily profound imaginative experiences.

North and South; A Cold Spring (1955) won the Pulitzer Prize for poetry in 1956. It was not as widely acclaimed as her first, but it contains several fine new poems. Among them are "Cape Breton," "Over 2000 Illustrations and a Complete Concordance," and "The Bight." In "At the Fishhouses," her characteristic process of "looking once more" and her tendency toward total immersion enable her to reach a final understanding of the meaning of the primordial element—the sea—which supports the fishhouses. The epistemology that she reveals in the last six lines in this poem (and in "Cape Breton," as well) is intriguing. For B. the nature of reality is always to be imagined, it can never be known. Nor would an encounter with the "real," were it possible, necessarily be a desirable experience.

Many critics consider *Questions of Travel* (1965) B.'s best book. It contains many poems, such as "Arrival at Santos," "Manuelzinho," "Brazil, January 1, 1502," "The Burglar of Babylon," and the title poem, about Brazilian people and B.'s experiences in Brazil. In "Questions of Travel," she finds her initial experience of the interior of Brazil so demanding that she begins to wonder if she should ever have come to this place, or if it would not have been better merely to stay at home where the scenery is familiar, comfortable, and safe. By the end of the poem, however, B. appears to discover her own resolution to her questions. She must witness all of the strangeness that she can. Indeed, the corpus of B.'s work seems to imply that if one is to be a perceptive tourist, a sensitive person, or an imaginative artist, one must be constantly vulnerable to every new and strange horizon to which one is exposed.

The Complete Poems (published in 1969) won the National Book Award that year. In 1976, Bishop was awarded the Neustadt International

Prize for Literature from *World Literature Today*.

Since her first book, B. has been hailed as a virtuoso of descriptive poetry, one who has learned from Marianne Moore and from the imagists. Yet her work differs significantly from those who may have influenced her. For B. an image, a phenomenon, is never merely "remarkable." She does not merely record or describe; she is not simply a descriptive poet. Many critics have neglected to realize that for B., re-presentation is a process by which the artist may discover subjectively. B. is mimetic in the sense of giving accurate perceptions of particular realities. She appears to know, however, that to represent is never simply to copy. Any abstract knowledge for B. comes by way of some concrete acknowledgment of the given world. Yet she combines acknowledgment with imaginative leaps, and the knowledge which results changes constantly. Everything in B.'s world is always open to question, revision, and reinterpretation.

WORKS: *North and South* (1946). *North and South; A Cold Spring* (1955). *The Diary of Helen Morley* (translated by Bishop, 1957). *Brazil* (*Life* World Library Series, 1962). *Questions of Travel* (1965). *The Burglar of Babylon* (1968). *The Complete Poems* (1969). *An Anthology of Twentieth-Century Brazilian Poetry* (edited and translated by Bishop, with E. Brasil, 1972). *Geography III* (1976).

BIBLIOGRAPHY: Jarrell, R., *Poetry and the Age* (1972). Jarrell, R., *Third Book of Criticism* (1963). Kalstone, D., *Five Temperaments* (1977). Moore, M., "Archaically New," *Trial Balances* (1935); and "Senhora Helena," *A Marianne Moore Reader* (1961).

Other references: *Nation* (28 Sept. 1946). *NewR* (5 Feb. 1977). *NYTBR* (1 June 1969). *Ploughshares* (2, 1975; 3, 1976). *PR* (Spring 1970). *Salmagundi* (Summer–Fall 1974). *SoR* (Autumn 1977). *SR* (Summer 1947). *WLT* (Winter 1977).

SYBIL ESTESS

Lillie Devereux Blake

B. 12 Aug. 1833, Raleigh, North Carolina; d. 30 Dec. 1913, Englewood,
  New Jersey
Wrote under: Lillie Devereux Blake, Lillie Devereux Umsted
D. of George and Sarah Johnson Devereux; m. Frank Umsted, 1855;
  m. Grenfill Blake, 1866

B. was born into a distinguished southern family. When her father died in 1837, her mother moved to New Haven, Connecticut, where B. attended a girls' school and received private tutoring in the Yale undergraduate course. Mother and daughter were very close and remained so throughout their lives.

When B. "came out" at age seventeen, she became renowned for her beauty and led a strenuous social life. In her writings she often refers to this period of her life, noting that she was taught to regard social success as the only worthwhile goal for a woman. "I was always a belle, flattered and fêted. I only wonder that I was not entirely ruined by an ordeal that would be pretty certain to turn the head of a fairly well-balanced man." She portrays in her fiction, which includes several novels and novellas and hundreds of short stories, many young women enfeebled by flattery, enforced idleness, and what she calls "false education."

In 1869, B. became involved in the women's rights movement, to which she devoted the rest of her life and most of her subsequent writings. From 1879 to 1890 she was president of the New York State Woman Suffrage Association and from 1886 to 1900 president of the New York City Woman Suffrage League. She was an excellent speaker, and her writings on women's rights are remarkable for their wit and humor; they are often in the form of satire or parable.

B. ran for president of the National American Woman Suffrage Association (NAWSA) in 1900, but was forced to withdraw in favor of Susan B. Anthony's choice, Carrie Chapman Catt. B.'s philosophy and approach differed from Anthony's in several respects. She was often true to her aristocratic background, expressing concern that suffrage workers be well-dressed, well-behaved "ladies," and she inaugurated such events as the Pilgrim Mothers' Dinners, held annually at the Waldorf-Astoria. More importantly, she believed that suffrage was only one means of improving women's status. As chair of NAWSA's Committee on Legislative Advice, she advocated campaigning to secure legislation favorable to women and agitating for the appointment of women to new positions (e.g., school trustees, factory inspectors, physicians in mental hospitals, and police matrons). She was instrumental in achieving many of these gains in New York State.

Although she avoids the worst excesses of the sentimental fiction of the times, B. writes much to the general pattern. Spirited young women develop fatal fascinations for evil Lovelace types in her stories and may or may not be saved by their honorable suitors; young lovers are separated, reunited, and then part forever when they discover they are siblings.

In B.'s early writings, characters who espouse feminist sentiments are punished. For instance, in *Southwold* (1859), the protagonist, when rejected by a man she loves, becomes embittered and "bold and even unfeminine" in her opinions. She shocks other characters by not taking every word of the Bible literally and by claiming that Christianity has harmed women's status. The book ends with her suicide. Interestingly enough, B. later was to espouse the opinions her protagonist had expressed. "Dogmatic theology, founded on masculine interpretation of the Bible," was the subject of attack in her *Woman's Place To-Day* (1883), a series of lectures delivered in response to a misogynist theologian. B. was also one of the contributors to Elizabeth Cady Stanton's controversial *Woman's Bible* (1895).

B.'s last novel, *Fettered for Life; or, Lord and Master* (1874), is a feminist work in which wife abuse, unjust marriage laws, discrimination in employment, and lack of educational opportunities for women are illustrated and discussed by the characters. Female friendships are strong in the novel, and the "hero," a successful reporter who frequently rescues the female characters, turns out to be a woman in disguise. When she adopted male attire, she found that "my limbs were free; I could move untrammelled, and my actions were free; I could go about unquestioned. No man insulted me, and when I asked for work, I was not offered outrage."

WORKS: *Southwold* (1859). *Rockford; or, Sunshine and Storm* (1863). *Forced Vows; or, A Revengeful Woman's Fate* (1870). *Fettered for Life; or, Lord and Master* (1874). *Woman's Place To-Day* (1883). *A Daring Experiment and Other Stories* (1892).

BIBLIOGRAPHY: Blake, K. D., and M. L. Wallace, *Champion of Women: The Life of Lillie Devereux Blake* (1943).

For articles in reference works, see *HWS. NAW* (article by W. R. Taylor).

BARBARA A. WHITE

Amelia Jenks Bloomer

B. 27 May 1818, Homer, New York; d. 30 Dec. 1894, Council Bluffs, Iowa
D. of Ananias and Lucy Webb Jenks; m. Dexter C. Bloomer, 1840

B.'s parents were natives of Rhode Island. She received only a few years' schooling at the district school in Courtland County, New York, but was evidently well enough educated to teach in another school when she was seventeen years old.

Her husband, a lawyer and editor of the *Seneca County Courier*, encouraged her to contribute articles on social, political, and moral subjects to his paper. She also began to take an active part in the temperance movement, writing frequently for the *Water Bucket*, an organ of the temperance society of Seneca Falls, New York. She attended the first meeting on women's rights held in Seneca Falls in 1848 but did not actively participate. In 1849 she began the publication of a periodical called the *Lily*, writing on such subjects as temperance, education, unjust marriage laws, and woman suffrage. By 1853, the *Lily* had a circulation of four thousand subscribers. It was the first newspaper owned, edited, and controlled by a woman and devoted solely to the interests of women.

Through the *Lily* B. met Elizabeth Cady Stanton and Susan B. Anthony. She also met Elizabeth Smith Miller, a cousin of Mrs. Stanton, who was the first to wear the short skirt and full Turkish trousers that came to be known as "bloomers." Several of the women adopted the costume, finding it more comfortable, more sanitary, and better adapted to the active life they were leading than the corsets and voluminous skirts that were the fashion. They ceased wearing the costume only when they discovered that their attire was distracting from the message of women's rights.

In 1852 B. began lecturing on temperance and women's rights, never speaking extemporaneously but always carefully writing out and delivering her speeches from manuscript. The following year her husband purchased an interest in the *Western Home Visitor* and the Bloomers moved to Mount Vernon, Ohio. She continued publishing the *Lily*, served as assistant editor of the *Western Home Visitor*, a literary weekly with a fairly large circulation, and lectured occasionally. Early in 1855, when her husband decided to relocate in Council Bluffs, Iowa, it was necessary to cease publication of the *Lily*, but she did not discontinue writing and speaking on behalf of temperance and women's rights. She was instrumental in organizing the Iowa Woman's State Suffrage Society and worked zealously for her church and community.

As a writer B. produced prose that was graceful, clear, and often infused with passion. Her early writings were devoted to temperance, imploring women to unite in that cause. Warning all those who supported it not to relax their vigilance, she wrote in one early essay: "Those who feel most secure will find to their dismay that the viper has only been crushed for a time, and will rise again upon his victim with a firmer and more deadly grasp than before." In starting her journal she made it clear in her first editorial that "it is woman that speaks through the *Lily*. . . . Like the beautiful flower from which it derives its name, we shall strive to make the *Lily* the emblem of 'sweetness and purity'; and may heaven smile upon our attempt to advocate the great cause of Temperance reform!"

Always a woman of strong opinions on almost every subject, she introduced herself to the readers of the *Western Home Visitor* by saying: "What I have been in the past, I expect to be in the future,—an uncompromising opponent of wrong and oppression in every form, and a sustainer of the right and the true, with whatever it may be connected." The causes B. advocated included employment and education for women. The failure to educate women for meaningful occupations she considered a serious wrong and insisted that "parents do a great injustice to their daughters when they doom them to a life of idleness or, what is worse, to a life of frivolity and fashionable dissipation."

B.'s lecture on suffrage, written originally in 1852 and delivered and revised many times through the years, is perhaps one of the finest examples of the clear, forceful, and logical arguments presented in that cause. She ends this stirring speech by calling woman's admission to the ballot box "the crowning right to which she is justly entitled" and states that "when woman shall be thus recognized as an equal partner with man in the universe of God—equal in rights and duties—then will she for the first time, in truth, become what her Creator designed her to be, a helpmeet for man. With her mind and body fully developed, imbued with a full sense of her responsibilities, and living in the conscientious discharge of each and all of them, she will be fitted to share with her brother in all of the duties of life; to aid and counsel him in his hours of trial; and to rejoice with him in the triumph of every good word and work."

It is indeed unfortunate that B.'s skill as a writer is overshadowed by the association of her name with a short-lived and ridiculed experiment in female attire.

WORKS: *Life and Writings of Amelia Bloomer* (Ed. D. C. Bloomer, 1895).

BIBLIOGRAPHY: For articles in reference works, see: *Appleton's Cyclopedia of American Biography*, Eds. J. G. Wilson and J. Fiske (1888). *AW. DAB.*

ELAINE K. GINSBERG

Louise Bogan

B. 11 Aug. 1897, Livermore Falls, Maine; d. 4 Feb. 1970, New York City
D. of Daniel Joseph and Mary Helen Shields Bogan; m. Curt Alexander, 1916;
m. Raymond Holden, 1925

B. was educated at Mount St. Mary's Academy, Manchester, New Hampshire, the Boston Girls' Latin School, and for a year at Boston University. Her first husband, an army officer, died in 1920, shortly after the birth of their daughter, B.'s only child. Her second husband was a poet and, from 1929 to 1932, managing editor of *The New Yorker*; the couple was divorced in 1937. For most of B.'s adult life her home was New York City.

Reluctant to offer details about her personal life, B. valued privacy and close friendships. Published letters to Edmund Wilson, Rolfe Humphries, Morton Zabel, Theodore Roethke, May Sarton, and others reveal a warm, witty, spontaneous side of B., not often evident in her poetry. They also refer to recoveries from nervous breakdowns in 1931 and 1933, as well as to the severe difficulties she experienced in the mid-1930s supporting herself by writing.

Besides poetry, B. wrote some fiction and collaborated in translations from German and French. Two volumes of her criticism consist mainly of articles and reviews from *Nation*, *Poetry*, *Scribner's*, *Atlantic Monthly*, and *The New Yorker*, for which she was a regular reviewer of poetry from March 1931 to December 1968.

While B. advocated primarily formal poetry—in Eliot's words, "verse as speech" and "verse as song"—her critical judgment was far from orthodox. She opposed women's attempts to imitate "a man's rougher conduct" in life and art, observing that there were no authentic women Surrealists, since Surrealism's "frequent harsh eroticism, its shock tactics, and its coarse way with language, comes hard to women writers, whose basic creative impulses usually involve tenderness and affection." The younger women poets she praised were, in following Marianne Moore, "close but detached observers of the facts of nature," able to "display a woman's talent for dealing intensely and imaginatively with the concrete."

B. received many awards for her poetry, among them the Bollinger Prize. The qualities most frequently cited in her poetry are those her friend Leonie Adams notes in a 1954 review of the *Collected Poems*: firmness diction and tone, concision of phrase, and concentrated singleness of effect. Allen Tate, Ford Madox Ford, and Theodore Roethke compared her lyrics to those of the Elizabethan metaphysical mode. Abjuring free verse and experimental forms, B. worked in consciously controlled lyric form with a restraint and precision which contained passionate feeling. "Minor art," she wrote, "needs to be hard, condensed and durable." A few critics of her work have found that control scrupulous to the point of limitation and perhaps the result of unwillingness to reveal herself entirely. There is a clear distancing of poet from subject in the early works of *Dark Summer* (1929); and in all but a few poems B. objectifies responses to experience and ideas through the use of third person or of a persona.

B.'s greatest skill lies in metric variation and in rendering descriptions in taut language whose sound values are brilliant yet seemingly effortless as in "Night," "Song for the Last Act," "Animal, Vegetable, and Mineral," "Roman Fountain," "After the Persian." The subject matter of B.'s poetry includes love, loss, grief, mutability, the struggle of the free mind, marriage, and dream. There is no mention of the city or society; settings and imagery are drawn from nature—the country or sea, seasons and storms.

There is also a recurrent interest in women: struggling to maintain a free mind and independent being ("Sonnet," "The Romantic," "For a Marriage," "Betrothed"); failing to imagine and risk ("Women"); breaking into fury and madness ("The Sleeping Fury," "Evening in the Sanitarium"); experiencing love and surviving its endings ("Men Loved Wholly Beyond Wisdom," "Fifteenth Farewell," "My Voice Not being Proud," "Portrait"). Adrienne Rich has justly called attention to "the sense of mask, of code, of body-mind division, of the 'sleeping fury' beneath the praised, severe, lyrical mode."

WORKS: *Body of this Death* (1923). *Dark Summer* (1929). *The Sleeping Fury* (1937). *Poems and New Poems* (1941). *Achievement in American Poetry, 1900–1950* (1951). *Collected Poems, 1923–1952* (1954). *Selected Criticism* (1955). *The Glass Bees* by Ernst Juenger (translated by Bogan, 1961).

Elective Affinities by Goethe (translated by Bogan, 1963). *The Journal of Jules Renard* (translated by Bogan, with E. Roget, 1964). *The Golden Journey: Poems for Young People* (edited by Bogan, with W. J. Smith, 1965). *The Blue Estuaries: Poems, 1923–1968* (1968). *A Poet's Alphabet: Reflections on the Literary Art and Vocation* (Eds. R. Phelps and R. Limmer, 1970). *The Sorrows of Young Werther* by Goethe (translated by Bogan, 1971). *Novella* by Goethe (translated by Bogan, 1971). *What the Woman Lived: Selected Letters of Louise Bogan, 1920–70* (Ed. R. Limmer, 1973).

BIBLIOGRAPHY: Bowles, G. L., "Suppression and Expression in Poetry by American Women: Louise Bogan, Denise Levertov, and Adrienne Rich" (Ph. D. diss., Univ. of California at Berkeley, 1976). Smith, W. J., *Louise Bogan: A Woman's Words* (1971).

Other references: *BB* 33 (1976). *ChiR* 8 (Fall 1954). *IowaR* 1 (1970). *MAQR* 67 (Aug. 1960). *TCL* 23 (May 1977).

THEODORA R. GRAHAM

Sarah Knowles Bolton

B. 15 Sept. 1841, Farmington, Connecticut; d. 21 Feb. 1916, Cleveland, Ohio
Wrote under: Sarah Knowles Bolton, Sarah Knowles
D. of John Segar and Elizabeth Miller Knowles; m. Charles Edward Bolton, 1866

B. traced her ancestry to the New England colonists. After her father's death in 1852, she moved with her mother to an uncle's house in Hartford, Connecticut. There B. met Harriet Beecher Stowe and Lydia Sigourney, both lasting influences.

B.'s poetry appeared in the *Waverly Magazine* when she was fifteen. Following her graduation from the Hartford Female Seminary in 1860, she taught in Natchez, Mississippi. However, the outbreak of the Civil War sent her home to keep school in Meriden, Connecticut. Her first book, *Orlean Lamar, and Other Poems* (1864), published when she was twenty-three, received mixed reviews. *Wellesley* (1865), a novel about the Hungarian patriot Kossuth, was serialized in the *Literary Recorder* a year later. She published several other books of didactic and sentimental poetry and fiction. In 1866, B. and her husband settled in Cleveland, Ohio, where they became deeply involved in the temperance movement. In her writings, she supported temperance, woman suffrage, and higher education.

Charles Bolton lost his real estate business in the financial panic of 1873. Their struggle to repay his debts spurred B.'s developing career as a journalist and author. From 1878 to 1881, she served as an editor of the Boston paper, the *Congregationalist*. While accompanying her husband on business trips to England in 1878 and 1881, she investigated women's higher education and factory working conditions. In 1883, she presented her findings on British labor relations in an influential paper delivered before the American Social Science Foundation.

While B.'s books shed light on 19th-c. reform movements and the rise of popular education, they are perhaps most valuable to students of women's history. In *Some Successful Women* (1888), *Famous Leaders among Women* (1895), and other collections, B. demonstrates that a woman can win self-respect and worldly fame through intelligence and hard work. Like the fictional Horatio Alger stories, these biographies stress the importance of education, discipline, and self-reliance. According to them, the rapidly changing modern world offers many opportunities for the self-made woman, and stands to benefit from her humanizing influence.

Yet, B.'s work reveals the strain of reconciling traditional female roles with ambition and leadership. In presenting individual women as models, she carefully balances their "masculine" achievements with "feminine" qualities: self-sacrifice, piety, sympathy. Mary Livermore's career, for example, "illustrates the work a woman may do in the world, and still retain the truest womanliness." Helen Hunt Jackson will be remembered because "she forgot self and devoted her strength to the cause of others."

However, B.'s championship of intellectual training, economic independence, and assertive roles for women is much more vigorous than her dutiful nods to the "cult of true womanhood." Her deeper feelings about woman's proper role appear in her portrayal of male/female relations. While convention requires her repudiation of George Eliot's unmarried living arrangement with George Henry Lewes, B. goes on to present a laudatory portrait of their relationship, noting especially Lewes's support of George Eliot's career. Her study of the Brownings also stresses their equality and mutual respect: "Their marriage was an ideal one. Both had a grand purpose in life. Neither individual was merged in the other." B.'s treatment of women who preferred to remain single is equally sympathetic.

B. encouraged young women to take themselves—their minds and their ambitions—seriously. While she showed that women could achieve success in fields such as medicine, literature, education, art, and politics, she also reassured her audience that "true" womanliness and professionalism were compatible. Men, she argued, preferred educated, independent women—it was a "libel" on the sex to think otherwise. Although B.'s skills as a publicist may have gained the upper hand, her optimistic vision bolstered feminine resolve. Her biographies of strong, fully realized women gave American girls crucial models on which to pattern their lives.

WORKS: *Orlean Lamar, and Other Poems* (1864). *Wellesley* (1865). *The Present Problem* (1874). *Facts and Songs for the People. Prepared Specially for Use in the Blaine and Logan Campaign* (1884). *How Success Is Won* (1885). *Lives of Poor Boys Who Became Famous* (1885). *Lives of Girls Who Became Famous* (1886). *Social Studies in England* (1886). *Stories from Life* (1886). *Famous American Authors* (1887). *From Heart and Nature* (with C. K. Bolton, (1887). *Famous American Statesmen* (1888). *Some Successful Women* (1888). *Famous Men of Science* (1889). *Ralph Waldo Emerson* (1889). *Famous English Authors of the Nineteenth-Century* (1890). *Famous European Artists* (1890). *Famous English Statesmen of Queen Victoria's Reign* (1891). *Famous Types of Womanhood* (1892). *Famous Voyagers and Explorers* (1893). *Famous Leaders among Men* (1894). *Famous Leader among Women* (1895). *The Inevitable, and Other Poems* (1895). *Nuggets; or, Secrets of Great Success* (with F. T. Wallace, 1895). *Famous Givers and Their Gifts* (1896). *The Story of Douglas* (1898). *Every-day Living* (1900). *Our Devoted Friend the Dog* (1902). *Charles E. Bolton: A Memorial Sketch* (1907). *Sarah K. Bolton: Pages from an Intimate Autobiography* (Ed. C. K. Bolton, 1923). *What to Read and How to Write* (n.d.).

BIBLIOGRAPHY: Bolton, C. K., *The Boltons in Old and New England* (1890).
    For articles in reference works, see: *AW. NCAB.*

SARAH WAY SHERMAN

Catherine Drinker Bowen

B. 1 Jan. 1897, Haverford, Pennsylvania; d. 1 Nov. 1973, Haverford, Pennsylvania
D. of Henry Sturgis and Aimee Beaux Drinker; m. Ezra Bowen, 1919

Although B. began her career as a writer of fiction, including a novel, *Rufus Starbuck's Wife* (1932), she early chose the role of biographer.

Music gave a central focus for B.'s early biographical works, *Beloved Friend: The Story of Tchaikowsky and Nadejda von Meck* (1937) and *Free Artist: The Story of Anton and Nicholas Rubinstein* (1939). The first work involves interweaving letters by the composer and his patron into a biographical narrative, the second portrays the Rubinsteins' interaction with the musical and political world of late tsarist Russia. In these works, B. early revealed her skill in characterization.

In the 1940s, B. found a new biographical focus: men of law and their role in the development of free government. From this concern came three biographies. *Yankee from Olympus: Justice Holmes and His Family* (1944), is a three-generational study, reaching back for the "roots that permitted so splendid a flowering" in Holmes's own life. In her portrait of Holmes as legal pioneer, judicial dissenter, and man of ideas and passion, B. impressively achieves her aim "to bring Justice Holmes out of legal terms into human terms."

In *John Adams and the American Revolution* (1950), B. concentrates on the lawyer as political leader. She stresses Adam's commitment to British constitutional principles and his growing disillusionment with British practices, and she depicts with force and clarity his role in the colonies' developing independence.

With *The Lion and the Throne: The Life and Times of Sir Edward Coke, 1552–1634* (1957), B. turned to the English roots of American constitutionalism. Her account centers on Coke's transformation from chief prosecutor for the Crown to ardent champion of the House of Commons and the Petition of Right. Her portrait of this "difficult but impressive man" gives full due to the complexity of his nature and his role as jurist and legal authority.

Her last work was *The Most Dangerous Man in America: Scenes from the Life of Benjamin Franklin* (1974). In this account of five periods of Franklin's life, B. traces his change from adherent to critic of Great Britain and explored the complexities of his personality and roles. The book is also a personal document, including reflective essays that indicate her own affirmative response to this Englightenment man.

B. wrote several works on biographical writing itself, including *Adventures of a Biographer* (1959), a series of informal essays, and *Biography: The Craft and the Calling* (1969), a study of biographical problems and techniques. B. also wrote *Friends and Fiddlers* (1935), informal, anecdotal essays on chamber music by amateurs, and *Family Portraits* (1970), a history of the Drinker family.

B. took the narrative approach to biography, focusing both on the individual personality and the age itself. The intricacies of personal development concerned her most, rather than the critical exploration of historical issues. In her early work, B. often utilized fictional devices, such as transposing letters and diary entries into conversation. With the Coke biography, however, she abandoned such techniques, relying henceforth on a skilled use of documents and mastery of detail to convey the sense of reality.

WORKS: *The Story of an Oak Tree* (1924). *A History of Lehigh University* (1924). *Rufus Starbuck's Wife* (1932). *Friends and Fiddlers* (with B. von Meck, 1935). *Beloved Friend: The Story of Tchaikowsky and Nadejda von Meck* (1937). *Free Artist: The Story of Anton and Nicholas Rubinstein* (1939). *Yankee from Olympus: Justice Holmes and His Family* (1944). *John Adams and the American Revolution* (1950). *The Writing of Biography* (1951). *The Lion and the Throne: The Life and Times of Sir Edward Coke, 1552–1634* (1957). *The Biographer Looks for News* (1958). *Adventures of a Biographer* (1959). *The Nature of the Artist* (1961). *The Historian* (1963). *Francis Bacon: The Temper of a Man* (1963). *Miracle at Philadelphia: The Story of the Constitutional Convention, May to September, 1787* (1966). *Biography: The Craft and the Calling* (1969). *Family Portrait* (1970). *The Most Dangerous Man in America: Scenes from the Life of Benjamin Franklin* (1974).

BIBLIOGRAPHY: *AHR* (Oct. 1957). *Atlantic* (July 1957). *NewR* (29 May 1944; 2 Nov. 1974). *NYT* (18 June 1950; 23 June 1963; 20 Nov. 1966). *SatR* (11 June 1950).

INZER BYERS

Bathsheba Bowers

B. ca. 1672, Massachusetts; d. 1718, South Carolina
D. of Benanuel and Elizabeth Dunster Bowers

Noted for its eccentricity, B.'s life has attracted more attention than her writing. She was born to English Quakers who settled in Charlestown. Though they endured the Puritan persecution of Quakers themselves, the Bowers sent their daughters to Philadelphia to escape it.

B. remained single all her life, building a small house, which became known as "Bathsheba's Bower," at the corner of Little Dock and Second Streets. Furnishing her home with books, a table, and little else, she became a gardener, a vegetarian, and, according to her niece Ann Bolton, as much of a recluse "as if she had lived in a Cave under Ground or on the top of a high mountain." Although B. was a Quaker by profession, Bolton's diary reports that she was "so Wild in her Notions it was hard to find out of what religion she really was of. She read her Bible much but I think sometimes to no better purpose than to afford matter for dispute in w[hich] she was always positive." B. eventually became a Quaker preacher, taking her ministry to South Carolina.

Though records exist today for only a single volume, B. is said to have written a number of books: B., in fact, spoke of her "Works" in the plural. B.'s extant volume, *An Alarm Sounded to Prepare the Inhabitants of the World to Meet the Lord in the Way of His Judgments* (1709), used the conventions of spiritual autobiography to trace her life as a seemingly endless series of fears to be overcome. Making an analogy between herself and Job, B. outlined a progression of divinely ordained tests which served to place her in a special relationship with God. One by one, B. conquered her terrors of death, of hell, of her own strong pride, of writing and publishing, of preaching, even of nudity. Her spiritual progress toward a kind of self-control dictated by God is presented in *An Alarm* as an example that others may follow.

Interestingly, B. perceived her most difficult task to be the struggle against her own ambition, her "chief evil" and "very potent Enemy." Paradoxically, she viewed the publication of *An Alarm* as a triumph over that personal ambition. Though presenting her life to the public as an example for emulation may seem an act of pride, B. emphasized the "Scorn and Ridicule" her audacity would bring: " 'tis best known to my self how long I labored under a reluctancy, and how very unwilling I was to appear in print at all; for it was, indeed, a secret terror to me to think of making a contemptible appearance in the world. . . ." Response to *An Alarm* went unrecorded, but readers today may be interested in B.'s use of a conventional spiritual autobiography for her unconventional activities in writing, publishing, and preaching.

WORKS: *An Alarm Sounded to Prepare the Inhabitants of the World to Meet the Lord in the Way of His Judgments* (1709).

BIBLIOGRAPHY: Cowell, P., *Women Poets in Pre-Revolutionary America, 1650–1775* (1981). Paige, L. R., *History of Cambridge, Massachusetts, 1630–1877* (1877). Watson, J. F., *Annals of Philadelphia, and Pennsylvania, in the Olden Times . . .* (1905).

Other references: *PMHB* 3 (1978).

PATTIE COWELL

Jane Auer Bowles

B. 22 Feb. 1917, New York City; d. 4 May 1973, Malaga, Spain
D. of Sydney and Clair Stajer Auer; m. Paul Bowles, 1938

After attending public schools in Long Island, B. was tutored by a French professor in Switzerland. In 1935 she finished *Le Phaeton hypocrite*, a novel in French which was never published and which has disappeared. After 1938 she and her husband lived in Central America, Europe, Mexico, and New York City. From 1947 they spent most of their time in Tangier, Morocco.

B. finished her only novel, *Two Serious Ladies*, in 1941, and from 1944 to 1953 was engaged in writing and revising her only full-length play, *In the Summer House*, ultimately produced in New York City in 1953 by the Playwrights' Company.

Most of the short stories which constitute the remainder of B.'s works were written during the 1940s. According to Paul Bowles, B. became hypercritical of her writing in the 1950s. In 1957 she suffered a cerebral hemorrhage which deprived her of her ability to read and write. Her health worsened slowly, and she died in 1973, in Malaga, Spain.

All of B.'s stories are about women and their attempts at independence; male characters are seldom important, even as blocking characters. When B.'s women characters cannot find themselves, it is other women who are holding them back. The essential B. plot presents a woman who seeks to break away from tradition and find new adventures in the outside world, and a second woman—sister, companion, lover—who tries to keep her at home within the old habits of dependence.

In *Two Serious Ladies*, (1943), Christina Goering tries to earn salvation by leaving her home and her female companion to challenge the hated outside world. There she takes up with a series of increasingly menacing male strangers, the last of whom abandons her. The second serious lady is Frieda Copperfield, who leaves her husband for a prostitute named Pacifica, who ultimately forces Frieda to share her with a young man. The promiscuity, bisexuality, and sadomasochism in this novel are seldom erotic, but tend instead to illustrate the hidden horror in human relationships, most of which consist of greedy individual truth-seekers bouncing their needs off each other.

It is the relationship between sisters that B. examines in her best short

story, "Camp Cataract," part of the collection *Plain Pleasures* (1966).
Harriet leaves her sisters every year to stay at Camp Cataract, in hopes
that she can get used to the outside world and ultimately leave home
permanently. Her sister Sadie tries to convince her that "you don't grow
rich in spirit by widening your circle but by tending your own." When
Sadie panics and comes after Harriet, Sadie realizes that it is she who is
going on that journey from home, not Harriet. Sadie is perhaps the
only Bowles character who gets to the end of her search for herself,
but that quest ends in her death. Rather than emerging free from her
clinging sister, Harriet appears to exchange her for an aggressively dependent friend.

B. introduced almost the same plot in overtly lesbian form in her
unfinished story "Going to Massachusetts," which appears with other
fragments from B.'s notebooks in a posthumous collection called *Feminine Wiles* (1976).

Through her constant resetting of these pairs of warring women, B.
presents a full picture of the female psyche and the extremes to which
the personality is driven by the pressures of modern society. Her representative woman tries to realize her potential within a world that tells
her to be chaste, experienced, loyal to her family, supportive of her
man, and independent. B. describes this fragmented world and its absurd
expectations in a style which is eccentric, and sometimes almost surrealistic. Characters form attachments and abandon each other rapidly and
unreasonably; they speak their minds to each other with a frankness
which the reader does not expect in the middle- to upper-class world
that B. portrays. These sudden twists force the reader to share in the
sense of menace and confusion that the freedom-seeking Bowles heroine
feels in her relationship to the world.

WORKS: *Two Serious Ladies* (1943). *Plain Pleasures* (1966). *Collected
Works of Jane Bowles* (1966). *Feminine Wiles* (1976).

BIBLIOGRAPHY: For articles in reference works, see: *WA*.

Other references: *Life* (16 Dec. 1966). *Mlle* (Dec. 1966). *Novel* (1968). *SatR*
(14 Jan. 1967).

PAULA L. BARBOUR

Kay Boyle

B. *19 Feb. 1902, St. Paul, Minnesota*
D. *of Howard P. and Katharine Evans Boyle; m. Richard Brault, 1922;*
 m. Laurence Vail, 1931; m. Joseph von Franckenstein, 1943

B. studied music and architecture before marrying a French engineering student and moving to his home in Brittany. The marriage had crumbled by 1926, but B. remained in Europe until after the fall of France in 1941.

In 1946, B. returned to Europe as a foreign correspondent for *The New Yorker*, while her third husband served with the War Department in occupied Germany. She later taught at various American universities and has been professor of English at San Francisco State since 1963. She received Guggenheim Fellowships in 1934 and 1961, and the O. Henry Prize for best short story in 1935 ("The White Horses of Vienna") and 1941 ("Defeat").

B.'s settings are frequently European. Her novel, *Plagued by the Nightingale* (1931), is loosely based upon a summer with her Breton relatives. At first, the novel was praised as a sensitive treatment of an American abroad, but today it has taken on new interest as the story of a young couple who decide not to have children (because of hereditary disease) and are bitterly opposed by their rigid, provincial family.

B.'s acute awareness of European social and political conditions is revealed in "The White Horses of Horses of Vienna," where swastika fires bloom at night on the Austrian mountains, prefiguring Nazi domination; the Lippizaners (the famed white stallions) symbolize a lost nobility; and a tamed fox foreshadows the savage future.

Two of B.'s finest novellas are "The Crazy Hunter" (1940) and "The Bridegroom's Body" (1940). "The Crazy Hunter" is a horse that is suddenly struck blind, but its young owner refuses to allow it to be destroyed. B. carefully works through the blindness-sight motif, interweaving it with complex relationships between a weak father, a strong-willed mother, and a budding daughter. "The Bridegroom's Body" dwells on the fatal attraction and isolation of love.

Fascinated by "the subtlety in human relations," B. is often concerned with political issues, which she has always met fearlessly; for B., "silence is not a position." Her book, *The Smoking Mountain: Stories of Germany during the Occupation* (1951), has been called "the finest interpretation of that place and time . . . written in English." Though B. clearly does not sympathize with the Nazis, she exhibits compassion for a proud and defeated people. Perhaps her best-known novel is *Generation without Farewell* (1960), written from the viewpoint of a German journalist who identifies with the Americans and rejects his own countrymen, only to discover that he really belongs to neither world.

Although B. began as a poet, her prose is far more skillful than her verse. Her novels, always technically well-constructed, often contain brilliant passages. Her strongest prose form is the novella. Here she can create a single, sustained theme, and embroider and enrich upon it.

B. is at her best when writing about highly complex human beings caught in political, social or psychological turmoil, struggling to maintain identity and balance. Her outrage at the violation of human dignity is carefully muted, revealed rather than preached. She writes with consummate skill and passionate sincerity, and is recognized as a major novella writer in American fiction.

WORKS: *Wedding Day, and Other Stories* (1929). *Plagued by the Nightingale* (1931). *Year before Last* (1932). *The First Lover, and Other Stories* (1933). *Gentlemen, I Address You Privately* (1933). *My Next Bride* (1934). *Death of a Man* (1936). *The White Horses of Vienna, and Other Stories* (1936). *Monday Night* (1938). *A Glad Day* (1938). *The Youngest Camel* (1939). *The Crazy Hunter* (1940). *Primer for Combat* (1942). *Avalanche* (1944). *American Citizen* (1944). *A Frenchman Must Die* (1946). *Thirty Stories* (1946). *1939* (1948). *His Human Majesty* (1949). *The Smoking Mountain: Stories of Germany during the Occupation* (1951). *The Seagull on the Step* (1955). *Three Short Novels* (1958). *Generation without Farewell* (1960). *Breaking the Silence: Why a Mother Tells Her Son about the Nazi Era* (1962). *Collected Poems* (1962). *Nothing Ever Breaks Except the Heart* (1966). *Pinky, the Cat Who Liked to Sleep* (1966). *The Autobiography of Emanuel Carnevali* (1967). *Being Geniuses Together: 1920–1930* (with R. McAlmon, 1968). *Pinky in Persia* (1968). *The Long Walk at San Francisco State, and Other Essays* (1970). *Testament for My Students, and Other Poems* (1970). *The Underground Woman* (1975). *Fifty Stories* (1980).

BIBLIOGRAPHY: Gado, F., "Kay Boyle: From the Aesthetics of Exile to the Polemics of Return" (Ph.D. diss., Duke Univ., 1968). Jackson, B. K., "The Achievement of Kay Boyle" (Ph.D. diss., Univ. of Florida, 1968). Madden, C. F., ed., *Talks with Authors* (1968). Moore, H. T., *Age of the Modern, and Other Literary Essays* (1971). Tooker, D., and R. Hofheins, *Fiction: Interviews with Northern California Novelists* (1976).

Other references: *CE* 15 (Nov. 1953). *Crit* 7 (1965). *KenR* 22 (Spring 1960). *NYT* (10 July 1966).

JOANNE McCARTHY

Anne Dudley Bradstreet

B. *1612, Northampton, England; d. 16 Sept. 1672, Andover, Massachusetts*
Wrote under: A Gentlewoman in those parts; A Gentlewoman in New-England
D. of Thomas and Dorothy Yorke Dudley; m. Simon Bradstreet, 1628

B.'s youth was spent in England. She had the advantage of living in the household of the Earl of Lincoln, where her father was trusted steward and friend of the earl. Dudley, called by B. "A magazine of history," believed in the education of his daughter. She had complete access to the excellent library of the earl. Here, too, she learned to know and love another protégé of the earl, Simon Bradstreet, whom she married two years before the Dudleys and the Bradstreets sailed on the *Arbella* for Massachusetts Bay in 1630. B.'s father was governor of Massachusetts, and her husband succeeded him when B. was no longer alive.

B. was the first British-American to have a volume of poetry published, and at a time when the Puritan woman's place was in the home. Governor Winthrop, in 1645, was certain that the wife of the Governor of Hartford had lost her wits because she "gave herself wholly to reading and writing . . . if she had attended her household affairs and such as belong to women and not gone out of her way and calling to meddle in such things as are proper for men, whose minds are stronger, etc., she had kept her wits and might have improved them usefully and honorably in the place God had set her."

But B. did write poems which would not have seen the light of day had not an admiring brother-in-law, with family connivance, carried them off to England and had them published under the astonishing title of *The Tenth Muse Lately Sprung up in America* (1650).

As was becoming to a Puritan woman, B.'s first poetry was about biblical themes. Her models were Du Bartas's *Divine Weeks and Works* (1605), a widely read account of the creation, and Sir Walter Raleigh's *History of the World* (1614), a popular book that began with the creation and continued the history of mankind to show God's divine purpose in human events. The first 174 pages of *The Tenth Muse* consist of quaternions—"The Foure Elements," "The Foure Humors of Man's Constitution," "The Foure Ages of Man," "The Foure Monarchies"—all written in closed couplets, all slavishly imitative of Du Bartas. Following the "four times four poems" is "A Dialogue between Old England and New, concerning the present troubles, Anno 1642," which is original in content and bold in her political concern.

B. was not pleased with her poems in print. She set about revising her first poetry, and she continued writing anew, this time with freedom and originality in thought and structure. The second (American) edition, with these changes and additions, appeared in 1678, six years after her death. It is upon these new poems—religious meditations, domestic poems, love poems, and elegies upon lost members of her family—that her reputation as a poet of excellence rests.

The most highly regarded poem of all is "Contemplations," composed of thirty-three stanzas, skillfully wrought, each stanza an entity, yet all interrelated and all expressing the poet's recognition of God in nature, a subject so rare that it did not find its fruition until the Romantic period. An equally remarkable poem in the second edition is "The Flesh and the Spirit," which S. E. Morison called "One of the best expressions in English literature of the conflict described by St. Paul in the eighth chapter of his Epistle to the Romans."

In 1867, John Harvard Ellis edited a complete edition of B.'s work. There is a brief but moving autobiography, revealing the spiritual doubts of a good Puritan woman. Her "Meditations" were short prose pieces showing the influence of the aphoristic essays of Bacon, emblems similar to those of Quarles, and spiritual commentaries like the Psalms, Proverbs, and Ecclesiastes.

The estimate of B.'s later poetry has grown with the years. Moses Coit Tyler and John Harvard Ellis were two scholars who recognized her worth (in the 19th c.). Conrad Aiken was the first to include her in his anthology of American literature; Samuel Eliot Morison, the distinguished historian, pronounced her the best American woman poet before Emily Dickinson.

WORKS: The Tenth Muse Lately Sprung up in America (1650; 2nd ed., 1678). The Works of Anne Bradstreet, in Prose and Verse (Ed. J. H. Ellis, 1867). The Tenth Muse (Ed. J. K. Piercy, 1965). The Works of Anne Bradstreet (Ed. J. Hensley, 1967).

The papers of Anne Bradstreet are at Houghton Library, Harvard University.

BIBLIOGRAPHY: Berryman, J., Homage to Mistress B. (1956). Fuess, C. M., Andover, Symbol of New England (1959). Morison, S. E., Builders of the Bay Colony (1930). Phillips, E., "Women among the Moderns Eminent for Poetry," Theatrum Poetarum (1675). Piercy, J. K., Anne Bradstreet (1965). Tyler, M. C., A History of American Literature during the Colonial Period (1897). White, M. W., Anne Bradstreet, the Tenth Muse (1971).

JOSEPHINE K. PIERCY

Anna Hempstead Branch

B. *18 March 1875, New London, Connecticut; d. 8 Sept. 1937, New London, Connecticut*
D. *of John Locke and Mary Lydia Bolles Branch*

B., the younger of two children, was born in Hempstead House at New London, Connecticut, where her mother's family, the Hempsteads, had lived since 1640. Her father was a New York lawyer; her mother wrote popular children's stories and poems. Following B.'s graduation from Smith College in 1897, she studied dramaturgy at the American Academy of Dramatic Arts in New York, training which is reflected in her numerous verse plays and dramatic monologues.

B. was connected with a number of philanthropic, social work, and art organizations, but most of her time was divided between the Christodora House, a Lower-East-Side settlement house, and Hempstead House, where she lived with her mother. At Christodora, B. established and directed the activities of the Poet's Guild, an association organized to bring poetry to the neighborhood, especially the children, but which also provided occasions for such poets as Edwin Arlington Robinson, Vachel Lindsay, Robert Frost, Carl Sandburg, Sara Teasdale, Ridgely Torrence, Margaret Widdemer, and B. herself to read and discuss poetry.

B.'s poems have a variety of subjects and settings, but even those poems with apparently secular subjects are tinged with a religious and mystical apprehension. In B.'s eclectic first volume, *Heart of the Road* (1901), many of the poems are "road" poems in which the road symbolizes transience. The dramatic monologue "The Keeper of the Halfway House," for instance, depicts an ironically dependent relationship between the transient and the permanent. An innkeeper, a priestly figure who points "the way" to travelers, sits beside a vacant chair, knowing someone will come and fill it and then move on. In this volume, the reader is struck by a haunting precision of some of B.'s lines and by her ability to sustain a mood.

B.'s second volume, *The Shoes That Danced* (1905), contains a strange mixture of settings (e.g., fairyland, New York City, a monastery) and of characters (e.g., Watteau, shop girls, a Puritan minister). Although in sections of the volume B. indulges in greeting-card sentiments, the title verse drama is intriguing and suggestive.

Along with some masterful poems expressing metaphysical doubt and some unexceptional reworkings of great Romantic poems ("Selene" of Keats's "Endymion" and "The Wedding Feast" of Coleridge's "The Rime of the Ancient Mariner"), *Rose of the Wind* (1910) contains B.'s longest and most famous work, "Nimrod," a Miltonic epic named after the Babylonian king. Although it was highly regarded by B.'s contemporaries, the diction now seems strained and the imagery imitative.

B.'s most satisfying volume is *Sonnets from a Lock Box* (1929). In the title sequence of thirty-eight sonnets, B. sheds her personae and speaks in the first person. The sequence is distinguished from some of B.'s earlier work by its directness of expression and originality. It moves from a portrayal of various types of entrapment and enslavement to a search for a means of escape. B. seeks liberation in mystical systems, invoking alchemy, astrology, cabalistic symbolism, numerology, and "Holy Logic." Yet B. intimates that the problem and the solution are secondary to the poetry, the "music," that they inspire.

Although B.'s poetry is at times derivative and contains a large population of fairies, kings, clouds, shepherds, along with the archaic diction appropriate to such a poetic population. B. had a genuine gift and an authentic voice. Her deepest subjects are language and what is to her its truest expression, poetry—"the changeless reflection of the changing dream." For B., words are divine manifestations that not only create, order and give meaning to reality, but that are the very stuff of life: "I say that words are men and when we spell/ In alphabets we deal with living things."

In her time, B. was compared to Robert Browning, Christina Rossetti, and the metaphysical poets. E. A. Robinson and other contemporaries regarded B. as a major figure, repeatedly including her name in discussions of poets of the day. Although she was not as successful as were Blake and Yeats in universalizing a private mystical system, she holds a secure place among the minor poets of the United States.

WORKS: *Heart of the Road* (1901). *The Shoes That Danced* (1905). *Rose of the Wind* (1910). *A Christmas Miracle and God Bless this House* (1925). *Bubble Blower's House* (1926). *Sonnets from a Lock Box* (1929). *Last Poems of Anna Hempstead Branch* (Ed. R. Torrence, 1944).

BIBLIOGRAPHY: Bolles, J. D., *Father Was an Editor* (1940). Cary, R., *The Early Reception of E. A. Robinson: The First Twenty Years* (1974). Widdemer, M., *Golden Friends I Had* (1964).

For articles in reference works, see *NAW* (article by J. T. Baird, Jr.). *20th CA.*

Other references: *NYT* (9 Sept. 1937).

ELLEN G. FRIEDMAN

Sophonisba Preston Breckinridge

B. 1 April 1866, Lexington, Kentucky; d. 30 July 1948, Chicago, Illinois
D. of William Campbell Preston and Issa Desha Breckinridge

Born of a respected, intellectual family, B. graduated from Wellesley College in 1888 but experienced a period of uncertainty characteristic of educated women at this time, who were seen as anomalies with few career opportunities available to them. B. taught high school in Washington, D.C., until 1894, when she returned to her father's home and law office. By 1895, being the first woman successfully to pass Kentucky's bar exams, B. decided to return to school because she could not obtain legal clients. Thus began a lifelong career at the University of Chicago. In 1901 B. earned a Ph.D. in political science and in 1904 a J.D. Simultaneously she worked as an assistant dean of women, and as a faculty member, first in the household administration and later in the social services administration departments.

In 1907, B. moved into Hull House, the social settlement, together with a graduate-school friend, Edith Abbott, and lived there intermittently until 1920. At age forty-one, she turned her life and career fully to the study of social welfare and change.

Women's rights soon emerged as a central concern in her writing and everyday life. She became vice-president of the National American Woman Suffrage Association in 1911, and as a lawyer she helped draft bills regulating women's wages and hours of employment. She was also an active member of the National Trade Women's League, the Women's League, the Women's City Club of Chicago, the American Association of University Women, and the Women's International League for Peace and Freedom.

New Homes for Old (1921) is a fascinating account of difficulties encountered by immigrant women in American society. Chapters on altered family relationships, housecleaning, saving and spending money, and child care provide information on the dramatic changes in everyday life facing the foreign-born housewife. Organizations established to help mitigate the stress created by these situations are discussed, presenting a historical view of social services in this area.

B. and Abbott, as pioneers in social work education, wrote a remarkable series of six books—they each wrote three—which contain selected documents and case records on a variety of social problems. These "texts" helped establish the case-work method of study and reporting in social work and provided a vivid account of individual lives as they were affected by social change, legislation, and public agencies.

Public Welfare Administration in the United States (1927), B.'s first contribution to this series, notes early (1601) origins of legislation and institutions concerning the destitute and mentally ill. Subsequent changes and the resulting hodge-podge of control and disorder, a legacy to today's welfare state, are noted in legal precedents and in statements made by leading authorities of the day in agency management and administration. In the revised edition (1938), the expanding but still chaotic role of the federal government is noted.

Marriage and the Civic Rights of Women (1932) discusses the relationship between marital status and citizenship. A key legislation reviewed is the Cable Act of 1922: for the first time American women could retain their citizenship when marrying an alien. This book is an astute combination of law, social relations, and women's rights. The terseness and clarity of the text, the comprehensive work done by women internationally, the case studies of foreign-born women in America, make this an early classic on the legal status of women and the social barriers they encountered in obtaining citizenship rights.

Any student and scholar of women's role in society from 1890–1933 will find *Women in the Twentieth Century: A Study of their Political, Social and Economic Activities* (1933) a must on their reading lists. The growth of women's participation in life outside the home emerged from women's clubs, increased access to institutions for higher education, the suffrage movement, and concern with the political arena. Data is given on income and the distribution of women in various occupations, with a number of tables providing an invaluable baseline for assessing changes or stability in income, and distribution in occupations over time. Since this historical period is remarkable for its relatively high proportion of women professionals, the chapters discussing professional and near-professional women, women's earnings, and women in business offer factual information that gives a uniquely comparative, historical base to issues still vital to women today.

As a woman completely dedicated to social equality, B.'s life was deeply enmeshed with those of other women who were associated with Hull House: Jane Addams, Julia Lathrop, Grace Abbott, and Edith Abbott. Reading and evaluating B.'s writings, one must consider them as products of her contacts with this group, with other intellectuals, such as

Marion Talbot, and with her students. Her contributions to education and social reform attest to her success as a dedicated and intelligent scholar and educator.

WORKS: *Administration of Justice in Kentucky* (1901). *Legal Tender* (1903). *The Modern Household* (with M. Talbot, 1912). *The Child in the City* (1912). *The Delinquent Child and the Home* (with E. Abbott, 1912). *Truancy and Non-attendance in the Chicago Schools: A Study of the Social Aspects of the Compulsory Education and Child Labor Legislation of Illinois* (with E. Abbot, 1917). *New Homes for Old* (1921). *Madeline McDowell Breckinridge* (1921). *Family Welfare Work* (1924). *Public Welfare Administration in the United States* (1927; rev. ed. 1938). *Marriage and the Civic Rights of Women* (1932). *Women in the Twentieth Century: A Study of Their Political, Social, and Economic Activities* (1933). *Social Work and the Courts* (1934). *The Tenements of Chicago, 1908–1935* (with E. Abbott, 1936). *The Illinois Poor Law and Its Administration* (1939).

BIBLIOGRAPHY: For articles in reference works, see: *DAB. NAW* (article by C. Lasch). *NCAB.*

Other references: *SSR* (Dec. 48; March 1949; Sept. 1949).

MARY JO DEEGAN

Bessie Breuer

B. *19 Oct. 1893, Cleveland, Ohio*
D. *of Samuel Aaron and Julia Bindley Freedman; m. Mr. Breuer; m. Carl Kahler; m. Henry Varnum Poor, 1925*

After graduating from the Missouri State University School of Journalism. B. worked for several years as a newspaper reporter, first for the St. Louis *Times* and subsequently for the New York *Tribune*, where she was editor of the women's department and, briefly, Sunday editor. After staff work for the American Red Cross publicity department, *Ladies' Home Journal*, and *Harper's*, she went to France where her friendships with Kay Boyle and Laurence Vail encouraged her to turn her attention toward fiction writing. She wrote for such periodicals as *World's Work*, *Pictorial Review* (often in collaboration with Henry Ford), *House Beautiful*, *The New Yorker*, and *Mademoiselle* until the 1960s.

B.'s early publications often centered on the significance and implications of post-suffrage feminism. One of these articles, "Feminism's Awkward Age" (*Harper's*, April 1925), a discussion of the difficulty the modern woman faces in attempting to integrate personal and sexual needs with vocational and political goals, provides an excellent introduction to concerns which were crucial in B.'s later fiction. She often concentrates on the fate of women who flounder in endless introspection, unsatisfying jobs, and painful relationships; women who lack either the consolations of a conventional identity or a mass movement in which to submerge themselves. B.'s fiction is sexually explicit and unsparing in its delineation of her heroine's confusion. These tendencies, as well as her experimental style, caused the critical reception of her novel to be frequently negative.

B.'s first novel, *Memory of Love* (1934), is written in the voice of a married man as he remembers an affair he had years before with a woman separated from her husband. For the narrator, a man who prides himself on his sexual exploits, this woman is unexpectedly captivating. Alternating between equally intense moments of attraction and repulsion, the narrative recounts their passionate, tempestuous affair. Finally, the protagonist is forced to abandon this woman when his wealthy parents threaten to cut off his income unless he returns to his socially more prestigious wife. The novel seems to stand as B.'s commentary on the extreme vulnerability of the sexually active "new" woman.

B.'s most successful novel, *The Daughter* (1938), is the story of a young woman, Katy, and her divorced mother. Living on an income provided by Katy's prominent father (with the stipulation that no acknowledgment of the connection be made public), the two women drift from one second-rate resort to another. The mother enjoys a series of casual affairs while the daughter retreats more deeply into a carefully constructed aesthetic artifice of classical music and contemporary poetry. Most of the action takes place in a west coast of Florida hotel where the daughter has her first affair. Lacking her mother's resiliency, this purely physical involvement almost destroys the girl. She attempts suicide.

In addition to its remarkable characterization of Katy, *The Daughter* is memorable because of B.'s repeated juxtaposition of the aimless resort world of her characters and the wider panorama of world events. If her characters do not care, B. seems to, and insistently reminds her readers of the sociopolitical background against which her novel is set. Only Katy has any sense of the significance of this wider world. The best that she can do, however, is to fantasize that in a different place, with a different personality, she too could have been a Jane Addams or a La Pasionaria.

Joanna Trask, the heroine of B.'s *The Actress* (1955), seems at first to be a continuation of the passive, introspective, and excessively vulnerable heroines typical of B.'s early fiction. But the novel traces Joanna's gradual development, a process characterized by B. as a movement toward assuming responsibility for her own actions and control over her own fate. She becomes more active than acted upon and, for the first time in B.'s fiction, sexual experience is viewed as necessary and healthy. The novel ends with the optimistic assertion that Joanna will not only combine a career and a family, but do it well.

B.'s fiction will strike the modern reader as unexpectedly contemporary, in part because of B.'s innovative narrative techniques and her interest in the relationship between woman's sexual and social identities. B. is an often fascinating writer who deserves more serious attention than she has yet received.

WORKS: *Memory of Love* (1934). *The Daughter* (1938). *The Bracelet of Wavia Lea, and Other Stories* (1947). *Sundown Beach* (1948; produced by E. Kazan, 1948). *The Actress* (1955). *Take Care of My Roses* (1961).

BIBLIOGRAPHY: Blake, F., *The Strike in the American Novel* (1972). Hill, V., "Strategy and Breadth: The Socialist-Feminist in American Fiction" (Ph.D. diss., State Univ. of New York at Buffalo, 1979).

For articles in reference works, see: *American Women*, Ed. D. Howes (1939). *20thCA.*

Other references: *CW* (24 Sept. 1948). *NewR* (20 Sept. 1948). *NY* (18 Sept. 1948). *Newsweek* (20 Sept. 1948). *SatR* (16 April 1938; 28 Dec. 1946; 17 Jan. 1949). *Theatre Arts* (Jan. 1949). *WLB* (Oct. 1938).

VICKI LYNN HILL

Gwendolyn Brooks

B. 7 June 1917, Topeka, Kansas
D. of David and Keziah Wims Brooks; m. Henry Blakely, 1939

B. attended public schools in Chicago and was graduated from Wilson Junior College in 1936. A poetry workshop at Chicago's South Side Community Art Center in the early 1940s introduced B. to the rigors of poetic technique; her extraordinary talent was soon recognized. In 1945 her first volume, *A Street in Bronzeville*, appeared. A plethora of prizes quickly followed: grants from the American Academy of Arts and Letters and the National Academy of Arts and Letters, two Guggenheim Fellowships, and, in 1950, the Pulitzer Prize for poetry. She was the first black poet so honored. A similar kind of recognition was hers when in 1968 she was named poet-laureate of Illinois.

In addition to numerous honorary degrees, B. achieved an unusual distinction when in 1971 black poets of all ages contributed to a volume, *To Gwen with Love.* The presence of so many young writers was, in part, a response to a shift in B.'s political stance. From a rather apolitical integrationist in the 1940s, she became in the 1960s a strong advocate of black consciousness. This process of change is described in B.'s autobiography, *Report from Part One* (1972).

In *A Street in Bronzeville* B. penned memorable vignettes of the residents of "Bronzeville," the black neighborhood of Chicago. Significantly, although the characters in these poems are poor, the emphasis is not on their material poverty but on their struggle to sustain their spiritual and aesthetic well-being. In "The Sundays of Satin-Legs Smith," a narrative poem which is a marvel of technical proficiency, the protagonist draws on his considerable imaginative powers to create a world on Sundays which contrasts sharply to the drudgery of his workdays. The poem celebrates Smith's resourcefulness, his sensuality, and his keen aesthetic sense; yet it reveals the lack of substance underneath the style.

Annie Allen (1949), awarded the Pulitzer Prize, is her most experimental work. Its subject is akin to her earlier poems: a young black girl comes of age, hoping to live out the drama and romance she fantasies. But the poverty and powerlessness which she kept at bay in her girlhood threaten her womanhood.

B.'s only novel, *Maud Martha* (1953), illumines the life of a young black woman who must ward off continual, often petty, assaults to her human dignity. *Maud Martha* was one of the first novels to portray a black girl's coming of age.

Written at the height of the civil-rights struggle, *The Bean Eaters* (1960) contains more topical poems than B.'s earlier books; her subjects include lynching and Emmett Till, school integration and Little Rock, and the violence accompanying the arrival of a black family in an all-white neighborhood.

The epic title poem of *In the Mecca* (1968) brilliantly captures the mood of disillusionment and defiance of urban America in the 1960s. It is B.'s most richly textured poem. In her typical fashion, she combines formal eloquence and ordinary speech, and they are perfectly fused. B. employs various forms, but free verse and blank verse predominate. Visually rich as well, the poem projects razor-sharp images and a gallery of memorable and diverse characters. It is a tour de force.

B. was the first black American woman to achieve critical recognition as a poet. Observers have noted influences on her work as diverse as T. S. Eliot and Robert Frost, Langston Hughes and Wallace Stevens. Stylistically, she often remolds traditional verse forms such as the ballad and the sonnet to suit her poetic purposes; she also employs modern forms brilliantly. Philosophically, she is a humanist, particularly concerned with exploring the strengths and travails of black women in her work. By any reckoning, hers is one of the major voices of 20th-c. American poetry.

WORKS: *A Street in Bronzeville* (1945). *Annie Allen* (1949). *Maud Martha* (1953). *Bronzeville Boys and Girls* (1956). *The Bean Eaters* (1960). *Selected Poems* (1963). *In the Mecca* (1968). *Riot* (1968). *Family Pictures* (1970). *The World of Gwendolyn Brooks* (1971). *A Broadside Treasury, 1965–1970* (edited by Brooks, 1971). *Jump Bad: A Chicago Anthology* (edited by Brooks, 1971). *Aloneness* (1971). *Report from Part One* (1972). *The Tiger Who Wore White Gloves* (1974). *Beckonings* (1975).

BIBLIOGRAPHY: Jaffe, D., in *The Black American Writer*, Ed. C. W. E. Bigsby (1969). Juhasz, S., *Naked and Fiery Forms: Modern American Poetry by Women—A New Tradition* (1976). Kent, G., *Blackness and the Adventure of Western Culture* (1972). Miller, R. B., *Langston Hughes and Gwendolyn Brooks: A Reference Guide* (1978). Spillers, H., in *Shakespeare's Sisters: Feminist Essays on Women Poets*, Eds. S. Gilbert and S. Gubar (1979).
  Other references: *Black Scholar* 3 (Summer 1972). *Black World* (June 1973). *CLAJ* (Dec. 1962; Dec. 1963; Sept. 1972; Sept. 1973). *ConL* 12 (Winter 1970). *SBL* 4 (Autumn 1973).

CHERYL A. WALL

Maria Gowen Brooks

B. c. *1794, Medford, Massachusetts; d. 11 Nov. 1845, Mantanzas, Cuba*
Wrote under: Maria del Occidente
D. of William and Eleanor Cutter Gowen; m. John Brooks, 1810

When Maria was orphaned in her childhood, she came under the protection of John Brooks, a Boston merchant. In 1810, the fifty-year-old merchant married his fifteen-year-old ward. The marriage was evidently an unhappy one, and she threw herself into her studies. Maria's dissatisfaction with her marriage was exacerbated when John suffered financial losses and moved the family to backwater Portland, Maine. There she met the Canadian officer who became her romantic fixation. John died in 1823, and Maria moved to Cuba where relatives owned coffee plantations. On a subsequent visit to Canada, she became engaged to the Canadian officer, but they were estranged through a series of misunderstandings. Maria attempted suicide twice. In 1826 she began a correspondence with the British poet laureate Robert Southey. After trips to England and Europe, Maria returned to Cuba, where she died of a tropical fever.

In 1820 some of B.'s poetry was published in a volume titled *Judith, Esther, and Other Poems, by a Lover of the Fine Arts*. The personae in these poems are all female. In "Judith" and "Esther," B. deals with the psychological aspects of the trials of these biblical heroines. "The Butterfly" presents an analogue to relationships between the sexes: a poet is too wrapped up in his own concerns to save an exquisite butterfly from the flame. The frank but almost naive "Written after passing an evening with E. W. R. A******, Esq., who has the finest person I ever saw" warmly describes the physical charms of the Canadian officer with whom B. had fallen in love.

In 1833, Robert Southey supervised publication of *Zophiel; or, The Bride of Seven*, which tells the story of a fallen angel's love for a mortal woman. In it, B. was not afraid to include many passionate and "forbidden" scenes, or to describe vividly human physical beauty. *Zophiel* is "dense" in the manner of Milton and contains full and learned notes on Middle-Eastern history, sorcery, and biblical tradition, with many literary, botanical, cultural, and geographical references, as in the work of Yeats and Eliot. Deeply scholarly in one sense, its actual expression is similar to the sensuality of Keats's *Eve of St. Agnes* and Coleridge's symbolistic uncanniness in *Christabel*.

In 1838, B.'s *Idomen; or, The Vale of Yumuri* was published serially in the Boston *Saturday Evening Gazette*. Several publishers refused the fictionalized autobiography as "too elevated to sell," so B. published it privately in New York in 1843. Idomen, the heroine, is "formed in every nerve for the refinements of pleasure," although her real life is a round of "duties" and "wearisome employments." For B., virtuous passion is a sign of intellectual and emotional consciousness.

The almost hallucinatory clarity of *Idomen*'s imagery heightens the impression that many of its images and scenes must be interpreted symbolically, even as archetypes. The Edenic myth is everywhere apparent—in the idyllic Cuban scenes, but also in the celestially majestic frozen glory of the rivers and mountains of Canada. Idomen herself seems a pattern of the human soul. Caught in a dull marriage as the soul is caught in the mortal body, she yearns for the Ideal Absolute as personified by Ethelwald, a character based on B.'s Canadian officer. Yet Idomen cannot have Ethelwald in this world, for some mysterious inability to communicate with him intervenes even after she is freed by the death of her husband. This is one manifestation of a continuing theme of psychic or supernatural fates or impulses which leads to an exploration of suicidal tendencies and the hypersensitive imagination. Idomen acts out the Christ-like cycle of death, resurrection, and ascension, although such an allegory may have been unconscious on B.'s part. It is as a psychological novel of considerable subtlety that *Idomen* will capture the modern imagination.

It can hardly be explained why B. is not better known and studied. Her work is good, at times great, but she was too large for her assigned role in the social and intellectual world of her time. In this and in the continued lack of recognition of her worth, she is an archetype of the early American woman writer.

WORKS: *Judith, Esther, and Other Poems, by a Lover of the Fine Arts* (1820). *Zophiel; or, The Bride of Seven* (1833). *Idomen; or, The Vale of Yumuri* (1843).

The papers of Maria Gowen Brooks are in the Boston Public Library, Yale University Library, and the Library of Congress.

BIBLIOGRAPHY: Grannis, R., *An American Friend of Southey* (1913). Griswold, R., *Southern Literary Messenger* (1913). Gustafson, Z., Introduction to *Zophiel* by M. G. Brooks (1978). Southey, R., *The Doctor* (1834).

For articles in reference works, see: *Appleton's Cyclopedia of American Biography* (1888). *CAL. DAB. NAW* (article by T. G. Varner).

Other references: *American Collector* (Aug. 1926). *Graham's Magazine* (Aug. 1848). Medford *Historical Register* (Oct. 1899).

L. W. KOENGETER

Alice Brown

B. 5 Dec. 1857, Hampton Falls, New Hampshire; d. 21 June 1948, Boston, Massachusetts
Wrote under: Alice Brown, Martin Redfield
D. of Levi and Elizabeth Lucas Brown

After graduating from Robinson Female Seminary, B. taught school in New England, but soon decided on a literary career. She wrote for the *Christian Register*, then joined the staff of *The Youth's Companion* in 1885.

In Boston, B. belonged to a group of young Bohemian artists led by the poet Louise Imogen Guiney. The collaborations of the two close friends included a biography of Robert Louis Stevenson (1896) and the founding of the Women's Rest Tour Association. During these years B. wrote in support of women's rights and prison-reform movements.

An advocate of American involvement in World War I, she often commented on politics, criticizing the direction of modern life. In her later years, her passion for privacy and religious mysticism carried her further from the mainstream. Highly praised as late as the 1920s, B.'s work was virtually forgotten by the time of her death.

During a career that spanned seven decades, B. wrote in almost every genre, including criticism, biography, and sketches. She considered herself primarily a poet, but the Victorian idealism and strained diction of her verse has not aged well.

B.'s greatest public recognition came to her as a dramatist. In 1914, amid much publicity, she won the $10,000 Winthrop Ames prize for the best play submitted by an American author. Her entry, *Children of Earth* (1915), later opened on Broadway to mixed reviews and a short run. B.'s one-act plays, often adapted from her stories, were more successful.

B.'s fiction is now considered her best work, particularly her early local-color stories. *Meadow-Grass* made her literary reputation in 1895; *Tiverton Tales* confirmed it in 1899. Both consist of loosely connected sketches portraying the fictional village of Tiverton, a farming community close to the sea and modeled after Hampton Falls. These and subsequent stories were compared favorably to the work of Sarah Orne Jewett and Mary Wilkins Freeman. Although B.'s portraits of spinsters and rebellious wives (especially in "A Day Off" and "The Other Mrs. Dill") are as fine in their way as Freeman's, her good-natured humor, idealism, and careful craftsmanship bring her closer to Jewett's more pastoral regionalism.

However, B.'s work can stand easily without such comparisons. Described as a "little masterpiece," "Farmer Eli's Vacation" demonstrates B.'s gentle irony, control of plot, and psychological acuity. Having dreamed all his life of seeing the ocean, only six miles from his pastures, Eli makes the journey at last. The vision is more than he can bear; "He faced [the sea] as a soul might face Almighty Greatness, only to be stricken blind thereafter." Leaving his family camping by the shore, Eli hurries home gratefully to his cows and barns, the world he knows and loves best. "Local color" is too narrow a category for this fine story.

As public interest in regional writing waned at the turn of the century, B. experimented with other genres. Unlike many local colorists, she made the transition successfully. Between 1900 and 1920, she published over 130 stories in prominent magazines. In these short pieces and her many novels, B. attempts more urban settings and sophisticated characters. Her themes concern the strain of reconciling city and country, the industrial future with the values of the agrarian past.

Critical opinion of this later work is mixed. B.'s growing skill as a story-teller and firmer control of structure have been noted by one critic, who observed, however, that she mistakenly adopted an elaborate figurative style beyond her powers. Only when she returned to her New England characters, with their earthy straightforward dialect, did she regain the grace and authenticity of her early work. Although such novels as *Old Crow* (1922) and *John Winterbourne's Family* (1910) achieve a greater philosophical and psychological depth than the more charming local-color stories, B.'s artistry could not keep pace with her ambition; her characters, puppetlike, mouth lofty ideas instead of embodying them.

A devoted artist, B.'s local-color stories hold their own against the more famous work of Jewett and Freeman and represent a distinctive contribution to the genre. Through a synthesis of symbolic and realistic representation, her work conveys an essentially romantic pastoralism. B.'s sentimentality is, however, offset by knowing humor; her idealism is expressed with subtlety. Fresh, evocative, and lovingly detailed, her sketches of country life show a disciplined literary craft. Her New Englanders speak and act with authenticity; their dilemmas are universal, their resolutions sometimes wise and always human.

WORKS: *Stratford-by-the-Sea* (1884). *The Fools of Nature* (1887). *Three Heroines of New England Romance* (with L. I. Guiney and H. P. Spofford, 1894). *Meadow-Grass: Tales of New England Life* (1895). *Robert Louis Stevenson* (with L. I. Guiney, 1896). *The Rose of Hope* (1896). *By Oak and Thorn* (1896). *Women of Colonial and Revolutionary Times—Mercy Otis Warren* (1896). *The Road to Castalay* (1896). *The Day of His Youth* (1897). *Tiverton Tales* (1899). *King's End* (1901). *Margaret Warrener* (1901). *Judgement* (1903). *The Mannerings* (1903). *The Merrylinks* (1903). *High Noon* (1904). *The County Road* (1906). *The Court of Love* (1906). Chap. XI of *The Whole Family* (a novel by twelve authors, 1908). *Rose MacLeod* (1908). *The Story of Thryza* (1909). *Country Neighbors* (1910). *John Winterbourne's Family* (1910). *The One-Footed Fairy* (1911). *My Love and I* (1912). *The Secret of the Clan: A Story for Girls* (1912). *Robin Hood's Barn* (1913). *Vanishing Points* (1913). *Joint Owners in Spain: A Comedy in One Act* (1914). *Children of Earth: A Play of New England* (1915). *The Prisoner* (1916). *Bromley Neighborhood* (1917). *The Flying Teuton, and Other Stories* (1918). *The*

Loving Cup: A Play in One Act (1918). *The Black Drop* (1919). *Homespun and Gold* (1920). *The Wind between the Worlds* (1920). *Louise Imogen Guiney* (1921). *One-Act Plays* (1921). *Old Crow* (1922). *Ellen Prior* (1923). *Charles Lamb: A Play* (1924). *The Mysteries of Ann* (1925). *Dear Old Templeton* (1927). *The Golden Ball* (1929). *The Marriage Feast: A Fantasy* (1931). *The Diary of a Dryad* (1932). *The Kingdom in the Sky* (1932). *Jeremy Hamblin* (1934). *The Willoughbys* (1935). *Fable and Song* (1939). *Pilgrim's Progress* (1944).

BIBLIOGRAPHY: Langill, E. D., "Alice Brown: A Critical Study" (Ph.D. diss., Univ. of Wisconsin, 1975). Overton, G., *The Women Who Make Our Novels* (1922). Pattee, F. L., *The New American Literature, 1890–1930* (1930). Toth, S. A., "More than Local Color: A Reappraisal of Rose Terry Cooke, Mary Wilkins Freeman, and Alice Brown" (Ph.D. diss., Univ. of Minnesota, 1969). Walker, D., *Alice Brown* (1974). Westbrook, P., *Acres of Flint: Writers of Rural New England* (1951). Williams, B., *Our Short Story Writers* (1920). Williams, Sister M., "The Pastoral in New England Local Color: Celia Thaxter, Sarah Orne Jewett, and Alice Brown" (Ph.D. diss., Stanford Univ., 1972).

Other references: *ALR* 2 (Spring 1972). *Atlantic* (July 1906). *Book Buyer* (Nov. 1896). *WS* 1 (1972).

SARAH WAY SHERMAN

Pearl Sydenstricker Buck

B. 26 June 1892, Hillsboro, West Virginia; d. 6 March 1973, Danby, Vermont
Wrote under: Pearl S. Buck, John Sedges
D. of Absalom and Caroline Stulting Sydenstricker; m. John Lossing Buck, 1917; m. Richard J. Walsh, 1935

The daughter of American missionaries who took her to China at the age of three months, B. grew up in close contact with the Chinese and had no intention of ever leaving China except for periods of study, at Randolph-Macon Women's College and Cornell University. Twentieth-century struggles, however, destroyed traditional China and made it impossible for her to continue living there. In 1932, she returned to the U.S. She divorced her husband and, in 1935, married her publisher, Richard J. Walsh. B.'s original incentive to earn money by writing had been her realization, in 1928, that her daughter was retarded. She also raised nine adopted Asian children and supported many philanthropic organizations.

Throughout her career, beginning with her first book, *East Wind: West Wind* (1930), B. wrote to explain China to the West, although she also wrote about other Asian countries and the U.S.

The Good Earth (1931), acknowledged as B.'s best work, is the story of Chinese peasants—Wang Lung, a farmer, and O-Lan, the slave girl he marries. It became a worldwide bestseller and won B. the Pulitzer Prize in 1931 and the Howells Medal of the American Academy of Arts and Letters in 1935. *Sons* (1932) and *A House Divided* (1935) carry the saga of Wang Lung's family through two more generations. The novel on which B. was working at her death, "Red Earth," was to have told the story of the modern descendents of Wang Lung.

Among B.'s lesser-known novels are several of particular interest. *Pavilion of Women* (1946) tells how a Chinese lady finds fulfillment in a spiritual love for an Italian priest. *Peony* (1948) presents the assimilation of the Chinese Jews. *Imperial Woman* (1956) tells the story of Tzu Hsi, who was dowager empress of China when B. was a child.

B. wrote biographies of her mother, *The Exile*, and of her father, *Fighting Angel* (both published in 1936). Her portraits of her parents are fresh, vivid, and true. She describes her father and his evangelical fervor with tenderness, understanding, and an admiration that is not lessened by a touch of humor. The same qualities appear in her portrait of her mother, along with a fellow feeling of sympathy for the trials her mother had to endure. B.'s mother deeply felt the loss of a child who succumbed to tropical disease—and felt almost as deeply her husband's refusal to treat her as an equal. *The Child Who Never Grew* (1950) tells the story of B.'s own retarded daughter.

B.'s obituary in the *New York Times* said that by 1972 she had published more than eighty-five novels and collections of short stories and essays and that more than twenty-five volumes still awaited publication. She has always been popular with the general public. Her simple style, her feeling for traditional values, and her skill in writing on universal themes account for her appeal. Her Confucian tutor had taught her to consider the novel a form of popular entertainment, unworthy of the scholar, and she wished to be popular because she liked ordinary people. In 1938, B. received the Nobel Prize "for rich and genuine portrayals of Chinese life and for masterpieces of biography."

SELECTED WORKS: *East Wind: West Wind* (1930). *The Good Earth* (1931). *Sons* (1932). *The Young Revolutionist* (1932). *The First Wife, and Other Stories* (1933). *Far and Near* (1934; pub. as *Twenty-seven Stories*, 1943). *The Mother* (1934). *A House Divided* (1935). *The Exile* (1936). *Fight-*

ing Angel (1936). This Proud Heart (1938). Of Men and Women (1941). American Unity and Asia (1942). Dragon Seed (1942). The Promise (1943). What America Means to Me (1943). Portrait of a Marriage (1945). Pavilion of Women (1946). The Big Wave (1947). Peony (alternative title, The Bond Maid, 1948). Kinfolk (1949). The Child Who Never Grew (1950). God's Men (1951). The Hidden Flower (1952). Come, My Beloved (1953). Imperial Woman (1956). Command the Morning (1959). A Bridge for Passing (1962). The Time Is Noon (1966). Pearl Buck's America (1971). The Goddess Abides (1972). Words of Love (1974). Secrets of the Heart (1976).

BIBLIOGRAPHY: Doyle, P. A., Pearl S. Buck (1965). Harris, T. E., Pearl S. Buck: A Biography (2 vols., 1969–71). Spencer, C., The Exile's Daughter: A Biography of Pearl S. Buck (1944). Van Gelder, R., Writers and Writing (1946).

BARBARA J. BUCKNALL

Frances Eliza Hodgson Burnett

B. 24 Nov. 1849, Manchester, England; d. 29 Oct. 1924, Plandome, New York
D. of Edwin and Eliza Boond Hodgson; m. Swan Moses Burnett, 1875;
  m. Stephen Townsend, 1900

B., the middle of five children, lived until she was sixteen in Manchester, England. A dame school she attended there provided her only formal education. In 1865, after her businessman father died, the family joined a relative in Knoxville, Tennessee, where financial need prompted B. to sell her first story, published when she was nineteen. In 1873, she married an eye specialist, with whom she had two sons. B.'s writing proved a major means of the young family's support. Her success as a writer of popular fiction made her a celebrity and allowed her family to enjoy an expensive international life-style. In 1898, B. and her husband were divorced. From 1900 to 1907 she was marrid to Stephen Townsend, whose theatrical aspirations she had been championing since 1889 in London, while she was overseeing the stage production of her stories.

B.'s career was productive as well as long. Her fifty-five titles include five bestsellers, and thirteen of her stories and novels were adapted for the stage in England or America. After her first story was published in Godey's Lady's Book in 1868, B. wrote formulaic love stories for fashionable magazines before graduating to novels. Several of these, novels of working-class and political life such as *That Lass o' Lowries* (1877), *Louisiana* (1880), and *Through One Administration* (1883), gained her critical recognition as a serious artist. American reviewers compared her work favorably with that of George Eliot and placed her in the front rank of young American fiction writers.

Little Lord Fauntleroy (1886), based on her son Vivian, established B.'s reputation as a popular writer. Intended primarily for children, the book became a bestseller and was soon translated into more than a dozen languages. B.'s stage version was popular in England and France as well as in America. In 1921, Mary Pickford starred in a film version.

After this success, B. wrote more books for children, two of which continue to find an appreciative audience: *A Little Princess* (1905), which was made into a 1939 film starring Shirley Temple, and *The Secret Garden* (1911), a pastoral novel considered a juvenile classic.

The books that found their way onto annual lists of bestsellers, however, were novels of fashionable social life written for adults: *A Lady of Quality* (1896), the story of a strong-willed woman in early 18th-c. England; *The Shuttle* (1907), a novel about an Anglo-American marriage; *T. Tembarom* (1913), a Horatio-Alger type sequel to *The Shuttle*; and *The Head of the House of Coombe* (1922), a portrayal of social life in London before World War I.

B.'s life and writing were characterized by tensions between the serious artist and the popular writer, the independent woman and the self-sacrificing wife and mother. While she was laboring over a 512-page portrayal of Anglo-American relationships (*The Shuttle*), she would shock her readers with a heroine who has been reared as a boy and later kills her lover with a riding whip (*A Lady of Quality*), then dash off a novella about a woman who, through self-abasing humility, wins the hand of a wealthy nobleman (*The Making of a Marchioness*, 1901).

B.'s recent biographer, Ann Thwaite, suggests that B.'s first bestseller changed her from a talented realist comparable to Elizabeth Gaskell into a pen-driving machine turning out inferior romances. But it can also be argued that B. excelled when she stayed close to the fairy tale, as in her best-known children's works, or when her tensions as artist and woman were allowed to inform and discipline her work, as in *The Making of a Marchioness*, which contains within the literary context of a romantic Cinderella tale a scathing portrayal of women's plight in the Edwardian marriage market.

WORKS: *Dolly* (1877, reprinted as *Vagabondia*, 1883). *Pretty Polly Pemberton* (1877). *Surly Tim* (1877). *That Lass o'Lowries* (1877; dramatization, 1878).

Theo (1877). *Earlier Stories, First and Second Series* (1878). *Kathleen* (1878). *Miss Crespigny* (1878). *Our Neighbor Opposite* (1878). *A Quiet Life* (1878). *The Tide on the Moaning Bar* (1878). *Haworth's* (1879). *Jarl's Daughter* (1879). *Natalie* (1879). *Louisiana* (1880). *Esmeralda* (1881). *A Fair Barbarian* (1881). *Through One Administration* (1883). *Little Lord Fauntleroy* (1886). *Editha's Burglar* (1888; dramatization, *Nixie*, 1890). *The Fortunes of Philippa Fairfax* (1888; dramatization, *Phyllis*, 1889). *The Real Little Lord Fauntleroy* (1888). *Sara Crewe* (1888). *A Woman's Will; or, Miss Defarge* (1888). *The Pretty Sister of José* (1889; dramatization, 1903). *Little Saint Elizabeth* (1890). *The Drury Lane Boys' Club* (1892). *Giovanni and the Other* (1892). *The Showman's Daughter* (1892). *The One I Knew the Best of All* (1893). *Piccino, and Other Child Stories* (1894). *The Two Little Pilgrims' Progress* (1895). *A Lady of Quality* (1896; dramatization, 1897). *The First Gentleman of Europe* (1897). *His Grace of Osmonde* (1897). *In Connection with the De Willoughby Claim* (1899; dramatization, *That Man and I*, 1904). *The Making of a Marchioness* (1901). *The Methods of Lady Walderhurst* (1901). *In the Closed Room* (1905). *A Little Princess* (1905; produced 1902). *The Dawn of a To-morrow* (1906; produced 1909). *Racketty Packetty House* (1906; produced 1912). *The Troubles of Queen Silver-Bell* (1906). *The Cozy Lion* (1907). *The Shuttle* (1907). *The Good Wolf* (1908). *The Spring Cleaning* (1908). *Barty Crusoe and His Man Saturday* (1909). *The Land of the Blue Flower* (1909). *The Secret Garden* (1911). *My Robin* (1912). *T. Tembarom* (1913). *The Lost Prince* (1915). *Little Hunchback Zia* (1916). *The White Peope* (1917). *The Head of the House of Coombe* (1922). *Robin* (1922). *In the Garden* (1925).

BIBLIOGRAPHY: Burnett, C. B., *Happily Ever After* (1969). Burnett, V., *The Romantick Lady* (1927). Laski, M., *Mrs. Ewing, Mrs. Molesworth, and Mrs. Hodgson Burnett* (1950). Thwaite, A., *Waiting for the Party: The Life of Frances Hodgson Burnett* (1974).

Other references: *American Literary Realism* 8 (Winter 1975). *ChildL* 7 (1978). *CE* 41 (April 1980).

PHYLLIS BIXLER

Esther Edwards Burr

B. *1732, Northampton, Massachusetts; d. April 1758, Princeton, New Jersey*
D. *of Jonathan and Sarah Pierrepont Edwards; m. Aaron Burr, 1752*

B. was the third of eleven children of Sarah Pierrepont and the prominent minister, Jonathan Edwards. At the age of twenty she married Aaron Burr, pastor of the Presbyterian church at Newark, New Jersey, and later a founder and second president of Princeton College. At twenty-six years of age, B., having been widowed a year, died from the results of an innoculation against the small pox.

In 1754, B. began a journal of her daily life and exchanged it periodically with one kept by her friend, Sarah Prince, of Boston. B.'s journal is valuable for the views it gives of the Puritan woman's life in the mid-18th c. and for the insights it contains into how Puritan values and habits of mind helped a woman to understand and evaluate the world that she lived in.

The dominant themes of the journal are the loneliness and hardship of everyday existence which are only made endurable by the knowledge of God's providential guidance of human affairs. For example, when her second child was born, B. was entirely alone, but her faith in God helped her to meet the ordeal: "I felt very gloomy when I found I was actually in labour to think that I was, as it were, destitute of earthly friends—no mother, no husband, and none of my particular friends that belong to the town . . . only my dear God was all of these relations to me." On another occasion she was visiting her father in Stockbridge, Massachusetts, where the community was expecting an Indian attack. She had a momentary crisis of faith: "I want to be made willing to die in any way God pleases, but I am not willing to be butchered by a barbarous enemy nor can't make myself willing." Ultimately she trusted in Providence and prayed for survival: the Indians never attacked.

In the Puritan manner the journal records events large and small— for God's will was manifest in every activity of life. Thus, the journal tells of visitations to the sick, attendance at sermons, entertainment of the governor's wife with "cakes" on militia day, the depradations of the French and the Indians, the political maneuverings of the Newark community, the circumstances of the religious revival of the mid-1750s, and the problems of moving to Princeton and of establishing the college —all given with frank, moral assessments of what B. thinks of the behavior of her contemporaries. Her commentary on the protestations of the local government as it prepared to meet the threatened advance of the French and the Indians is typical: "I am perplexed about our publick affairs, the Men say (tho not Mr. Burr, he is not of that sort) that women have no business to concern themselves about 'em but to trust to those that know better and be content to be destroyed—because they did all for the best—Indeed, if I was convinced that our great men did as they really thought was for the Glory of God and the good of the country, it would go a great ways to make me easy."

As a result of this personal evaluation of the events and interests of her time, B.'s journal has a warm, emotional quality which makes the incidents of the past come alive. She is frank and explicit, never falsely sentimental or literary. Like the preachers she heard regularly, B. kept to the plain style, proudly asserting that the "busy housewife" had no time to be "literary." The journal is, then, a moving story of a woman's growth to maturity within the Puritan tradition of provincial America.

WORKS: *Esther Burr's Journal* (Ed. J. Rankin, 1902), an untrustworthy edition containing many pages that appear to be fabrications.

The papers of Esther Edwards Burr are at Yale University, Andover-Newton Theological School (Newton, Massachusetts), and Princeton College.

BIBLIOGRAPHY: Axtell, J., *A School Upon a Hill* (1974). Cott, N., *The Bonds of Womanhood: Woman's Sphere in New England, 1780–1835* (1977). Other references: *NEQ* 3 (1930).

MAUREEN GOLDMAN

Helen Stuart Campbell

B. *4 July 1839, Lockport, New York; d. 22 July 1918, Dedham, Massachusetts*
Wrote under: Helen C. Weeks, Campbell Wheaton
D. *of Homer H. and Jane E. Campbell Stuart; m. Grenville Mellen Weeks, 1860*

Under her married name, C. wrote five children's books as well as many stories in *Riverside Magazine* and *Our Young Folks*. After 1877, C. adopted her mother's maiden name (Campbell) and she wrote works mainly for an adult audience: novels, magazine articles, cookbooks, studies of poverty and women workers. Experience as a teacher in cooking schools qualified C. to become household editor of *Our Continent* (1882–84).

From 1894 to 1912 C. was closely associated with Charlotte Perkins Gilman. They coedited *Impress* in San Francisco and worked in Unity Settlement in Chicago. Eventually C. lived with the Gilmans in New York. During this period she lectured on home economics at the University of Wisconsin in 1895, and at Kansas State Agricultural College in 1897 and 1898. Her final years were spent in Massachusetts.

The Ainslee Series, consisting of *Grandpa's House* (1868), *The Ains-*

lee Stories (1868), *White and Red* (1869), and *Four and What They Did* (1871) reveal C.'s ability to create troublesome, lively children who tumble from one misadventure to another as they explore their New England or midwestern surroundings. The liveliest and most amusing are Ainslee, five-year-old hero of the second book, and Sinny, his black friend. Although no more than a collection of stories, this book is unified by its temporal frame and by the background of New England village life. While Harry in *White and Red* is hardly an interesting hero, the account of his journey and the description of Indian characters and customs in Red Lake capture the imagination and make the tale a valuable portrait of the American past. *Six Sinners* (1877), a boarding-school story written under the name Campbell Wheaton, lacks the freshness of C.'s earlier work, but maintains her characteristic flashes of humor.

His Grandmothers (1877), which marks C.'s transition from juveniles to the adult novel, is a light-hearted sketch of a household turned upside down by a flint-hearted New England grandmother. It stands in lively contrast to C.'s subsequent novels, which often (to the detriment of the fiction) attempt to treat such social themes as the role of heredity, the economic plight of women, the relation of diet to disease, the greed and corruption of postwar America.

Mrs. Herndon's Income (1886), C.'s most important novel, has too many characters and a poorly constructed plot, manipulated to suit the author's moral vision. It is partially redeemed, however, by the comic presence of Amanda Briggs and by the realistic description of New York slums. *Miss Melinda's Opportunity* (1886) uses a smaller canvas and a simpler plot, but is equally didactic. For the modern reader the interest lies less in the scheme for cooperative housekeeping than in the characterization of Miss Melinda and the evocation of New York in the Gilded Age.

C.'s reform writing, as Robert Bremner points out, places her in the company of propagandists "who hoped to alter conditions by rousing the conscience of the nation." *The Problem of the Poor* (1882) and *Darkness and Daylight* (1891) describe life in New York's slums and McAuley's Water Street Mission. *Prisoners of Poverty* (1887) attacks the exploitation of women in New York sweatshops and department stores, employing case histories to illustrate the effects of starvation wages. *Prisoners of Poverty Abroad* (1889) feebly echoes its predecessor in a superficial survey of women workers in Europe. Less emotional than the earlier studies and buttressed by statistics, *Women Wage-Earners* (1893), which received an award from the American Economic Association, treats the plight of women factory workers across America, condemning low wages, long hours, and poor sanitation. C. concludes by recommending the organization of women's labor clubs and the appointment of women inspectors, as well as higher wages and a shorter working week.

As a fiction writer, C. was a minor figure, memorable only for the local color and abundant humor of her children's stories. Her role as reformer, however, was more significant. C.'s studies of women wage-earners stirred the conscience of her age and led to the formation of consumers' leagues in the 1890s, which monitored retail stores to assure fair labor practices.

WORKS: *Grandpa's House* (1868). *The Ainslee Stories* (1868). *An American Family in Paris* (1869). *White and Red: A Narrative of Life among the Northwest Indians* (1869). *Four and What They Did* (1871). *Six Sinners or School Days in Bantam Valley* (1877). *His Grandmothers* (1877). *Unto the Third and Fourth Generation* (1880). *The Easiest Way in Housekeeping and Cooking* (1881). *Patty Pearson's Boy: A Tale of Two Generations* (1881). *The Housekeeper's Year Book* (1882). *The Problem of the Poor* (1882). *Under Green Apple Boughs* (1882). *A Sylvan City or Quaint Corners in Philadelphia* (with others, 1883). *The American Girl's Home Book of Work and Play* (1883). *The What-To-Do Club: A Story for Girls* (1885). *Good Dinners for Every Day in the Year* (1886). *Mrs. Herndon's Income* (1886). *Miss Melinda's Opportunity* (1886). *Prisoners of Poverty* (1887). *Roger Berkeley's Probation* (1888). *Prisoners of Poverty Abroad* (1889). *Darkness and Daylight* (with T. Knox and T. Byrnes, 1891). *Anne Bradstreet and Her Time* (1891). *Some Passages in the Practice of Dr. Martha Scarborough* (1893). *Women Wage-Earners* (1893). *In Foreign Kitchens* (1893). *Household Economics* (1896). *The Heart of It: A Series of Extracts from the Power of Silence and The Perfect Whole* (edited by H. Campbell, with K. Westendorf, 1897).

BIBLIOGRAPHY: Bremner, R. H., *From the Depths: The Discovery of Poverty in the U.S.* (1956). Darling, F. L., *The Rise of Children's Book Reviewing in America, 1865–1881* (1968). Gilman, C. P., *The Living of Charlotte Perkins Gilman* (1935). Taylor, W. F., *The Economic Novel in America* (1942). Wright, Lyle H., *American Fiction, 1876–1900* (1966).

For articles in reference works, see: *Literary Writings in America: A Bibliography* (1977). *NAW* (article by R. Paulson).

PHYLLIS MOE

Sally Carrighar

B. *ca. 1905, Cleveland, Ohio*
D. *of George Thomas Beard and Perle Avis Harden Wagner*

In *Home to the Wilderness* (1973), C. tells a sad story. Partially disfigured at birth by a high-forceps delivery, she was abhorrent to her mother, who once attempted to strangle her. The psychotic woman, loathing even her daughter's touch, sought to deprive C. of all love and openly urged her to commit suicide. C. was rescued from utter wretchedness by her father's devotion, her own remarkable determination, and the supportive atmosphere of Wellesley College. She tried various artistic careers: pianist, dancer, and film production assistant, only to have her mother repeatedly snatch success from her. While undergoing psychoanalysis, C. attempted to establish herself as a fictionalist, failed, and "abandoned words." Convalescing in San Francisco from depression and heart disease, she began feeding the birds outside her window. The birds became fellow-creatures; a mouse nesting inside her radio actually sang to her, and in a revelation she understood her vocation: nature writing. Words need not be abandoned, only the bizarre human world of madness, violence, greed.

After seven years of study, C. published *One Day on Beetle Rock* (1944), a narrative treating the interaction of various species in a Sierra Nevada habitat. C. discovered that she could portray this interaction effectively by adopting in successive chapters the point of view of specific organisms and describing how a dramatic natural event (e.g., a flash flood) affects them. To present the "consciousness" of a female mosquito is of course risky, for the writer appears to be anthropomorphizing nature. But the literary strategy of *Beetle Rock* proved itself in *One Day at Teton Marsh* (1947), about the Grand Tetons; *Icebound Summer* (1953), about the north coast of Alaska; and *The Twilight Seas* (1975), about the blue whales.

These objective narratives, in which the narrator never speaks in her own voice, are only a portion of C.'s corpus. Her personal writings give a good introduction to the land and people of northern Alaska. *Moonlight at Midday* (1958) narrates her adventures researching *Icebound Summer* in the tiny village of Unalakleet; it examines Eskimo life, both the traditional ways and the changes wrought by the white man. *Wild Voice of the North* (1959) is the story of her husky, Bobo, whom she rescued and cared for while living and writing in Nome. C. has worked in other genres as well: a play, *As Far as They Go* (1956), celebrates Alaskan history and pioneer life. An historical novel, *The Glass Dove* (1962), portrays a young girl whose farm home in southern Ohio becomes a station on the Underground Railroad.

Wild Heritage (1965) is C.'s most ambitious work. It synthesizes much of the pioneering work in the field of ethology and includes many of C.'s own observations from her years in various wildernesses. The work treats life experiences which humans share with animals: parenthood, sex, aggressiveness, and play. She is especially concerned with what tendencies of animals are learned. In reporting her observations, she uses the technique of her nature narratives, dramatizing the behavior of a single individual of the species.

But one finally returns to C.'s autobiography, *Home to the Wilderness* (1973), for her most deeply felt writing, for her observations that man's morality originates in nature, for her comments about females as naturalists. Nature was C.'s healer and vocation; she could approach it with naive joy, reverence, and awe. But she also knew it as a scientist who relies only on objective observation. That C. successfully combined these two modes of cognition is perhaps her greatest achievement.

WORKS: *Exploring Marin* (1941). *One Day on Beetle Rock* (1944). *One Day at Teton Marsh* (1947). *Prey of the Arctic* (1951). *Icebound Summer* (1953). *As Far as They Go* (1956). *Moonlight at Midday* (1958). *Wild Voice of the North* (1959). *The Glass Dove* (1962). *Wild Heritage* (1965). *Home to the Wilderness* (1973). *The Twilight Seas* (1975).

BIBLIOGRAPHY: NYHTBR (28 Sept. 1947; 19 July 1953). NYT (10 Dec. 1944). NYTBR (28 March 1965). San Francisco Chronicle (25 Sept. 1947). SatR (20 March 1965). SatRL (24 Feb. 1945). Weekly Book Review (26 Nov. 1944).

MARGARET McFADDEN-GERBER

Elaine Sterne Carrington

B. 1892, New York City; d. 4 May 1958, New York City
Wrote under: Elaine Sterne Carrington, John Ray, Elaine Sterne
D. of Theodore and Mary Louise Henriques Sterne; m. George Dart
   Carrington, 1920

While growing up in New York City, C.'s earliest ambition was to become a musical comedy star. Instead, she became the most prolific writer of radio serials. She also wrote short stories, plays, and songs.

At eighteen, C. sold her first story, "King of the Christmas Feast," to St. Nicholas magazine. At nineteen, she won the first prize in a scenario-writing contest sponsored by the New York Evening Sun in cooperation with Vitagraph for a script entitled Sins of the Mothers. Two more prizes that year—one in a New York Morning Telegraph scenario contest and another in a Collier's magazine short story contest —launched C.'s professional career. Nightstick, a play written under the name of John Ray, was lengthened and produced as a film under the title Alibi (1929).

Like the plays, C.'s stories concern courtship, marriage, and child rearing. Plots based on secret engagements, elopements, hopeless love between people of different classes, and friction between child and stepparent are common. The central characters generally are of the middle class—wives who "like to gossip," storekeepers whose shops are "clean as a whistle," young women with "milk-white skin" and "ash-blond hair," and steady young men who like to do "the deciding."

Ten of C.'s short stories are collected in a volume entitled All Things Considered (1939). The sentimentality of the stories is redeemed by some incisive and devastating portraits in situations critics have deemed worthy of Evelyn Waugh or John Collier. C.'s fondness for ambiguity caused some reviewers to find "a streak of sharp satire running under the gloss." A cool, sparse style allows the characters occasionally to break free of humdrum plots.

C. moved to radio scriptwriting with her first series, Red Adams (1932), later renamed Red Davis. The series starred Burgess Meredith as Davis, a "supposedly typical, happy-go-lucky, middle-class teen-ager, who lived in the supposedly typical small town of Oak Park." C. drew the plots from her own experiences as a wife and mother, incorporating (in her words) "all the pangs of adolescence from both the children's and parents' points of view."

Under the sponsorship of Proctor & Gamble, the program was renamed *Forever Young,* and then *Pepper Young's Family* (1936–1956). The setting became the town of Elmwood, and Red Davis became Pepper. What began as a comedy had emerged as a thoroughgoing soap opera. In 1938 it was on the air at three different hours every day and was carried by both the NBC and CBS networks.

Rosemary (1944–1955) was, as the show's opening announcement proclaimed, "dedicated to all the women of today." Each episode began with "This is *your* story—this is *you.*" The serial told the story of the Dawson family and centered upon Rosemary Dawson's marriage to Bill Roberts. A young working woman at the begining, Rosemary quickly became the woman of domestic experience, the wife and mother endowed with the goodness and kindness required of soap opera heroines. C.'s intense patriotism (she also wrote scripts for the U.S. Treasury Department) manifested itself in appeals to listeners to buy war bonds. In addition, C.'s characters urged each other to buy Easter Seals, to help returning prisoners of war, or to support some other worthy cause.

Acknowledged as the originator of the radio soap opera, C. established a simple principle for plots that often were complex: "the life of a middle-class family and the bringing up of children in an understanding way." This principle led C. to focus on youthful characters, complete with current slang, a focus which television soap operas of the 1970s have reestablished. The "understanding way" of bringing up children involved humor, which was often present in C.'s scripts. Plots—in which illogic was not uncommon—were always subordinate to characters. In C.'s words, "The story must be written about people you come to know and like and believe in. What happens to them is of secondary importance. Once characters are firmly established and entrenched in the hearts of listeners, the latter will have to tune in to find out what becomes of the characters because of what they feel for them." For over twenty years C. succeeded in creating characters that evoked such loyalty from listeners. Without question, the "Queen of the Soapers," as C. was known, had earned her title.

WORKS: *Alibi* (film, released 1929). *Five Minutes from the Station: A Comedy of Life that Comes Close to Being a Tragedy* (1930). *All Things Considered* (1939). *Red Adams* (radio drama, 1932; later entitled *Red Davis;* later entitled *Forever Young;* later entitled *Pepper Young's Family,* 1936–1956). *When a Girl Marries* (radio drama, 1939–1956). *Rosemary* (radio drama, 1944–1955). *Follow Your Heart* (TV drama, 1953).

BIBLIOGRAPHY: Edmondson, M., and D. Rounds, *From Mary Noble to Mary Hartman: The Complete Soap Opera Book* (1976).

For articles in reference works, see: *CB* (1940).

Other references: *NYHT* (19 Nov. 1939). *New York Post* (25 Jan. 1940). *NYT* (12 Nov. 1939; 11 Feb. 1940; 5 May 1958). *Newsweek* (20 Oct. 1941; 3 May 1954). *The Parents' Magazine* (June 1942). *Time* (26 Aug. 1946). *Variety* (8 May 1940; 16 June 1943).

CAREN J. DEMING

Rachel Louise Carson

B. 27 May 1907, Springdale, Pennsylvania; d. 14 April 1964, Silver Spring, Maryland
D. of Robert Warden and Maria McLean Carson

C. shared her mother's love of nature and books. Publication of stories in *St. Nicholas* magazine when she was ten enhanced C.'s determination to be a writer. She discovered biology at college and zoology at Johns Hopkins University (M.S. 1932).

In 1936, C. took a civil service job with the Fisheries Bureau, where by 1947 she was editor-in-chief for the U.S. Fish and Wildlife Service. In 1937, *Atlantic Monthly* published "Undersea," based on a rejected radio script C. had written for the bureau. *Under the Sea-Wind* (1941) was published just before Pearl Harbor. Reviews were excellent but sales poor, until it was reissued in 1952 and joined her huge success, *The Sea Around Us* (1951), on the bestseller list.

In *The Sea Around Us*, C. provides an intensive look at the secrets beneath the sea's deceptive surface, employing history and geology as well as marine biology. "Mother Sea" covers the development of the sea and its islands; "The Restless Sea" deals with wind, water, and tides; and "Man and the Sea about Him" completes the global picture by interweaving human relationships. While utilizing the major wartime advances made in oceanography, C. never lost sight of the deeper significance of such strides, nor of the normal limitations of nontechnical readers. Her thorough detail and precise work reflect consultation with no less than one thousand printed sources, voluminous correspondence, and frequent discussions with oceanographers around the world.

The Sea Around Us received the National Book Award and the John Burroughs Medal. It remained on the bestseller list for eighty-six weeks and was translated into thirty-two languages.

The Edge of the Sea (1955) began as "a popular guide" to the seashore to make people realize the beach is "more than a place to get sunburned," but evolved into an ambitious study of ecological relationships. She saw it as a biological counterpart to the physical descriptions of *The Sea Around Us*, an exploration of the transition zone between land and sea where evolution can actually be seen taking place.

C. completed *Silent Spring* (1962) as she endured the combined effects of cancer, sinus problems, heart disease, and arthritis, and while caring for the young great-nephew she adopted when his mother died in 1957. The death of C.'s mother, always her close companion, in 1958 caused her great suffering. Her mother, C. wrote to a friend, "more than anyone else I know, embodied Albert Schweitzer's 'reverence for life.' "

A book about death which exalts life, *Silent Spring* sparked international controversy when it proved to the public how much harm resulted from thoughtless and uncontrolled use of pesticides. Although the chemical industry fomented personal attacks on her as an "hysterical woman" and issued propaganda to undercut her facts, C.'s work was vindicated by the 1963 report of the President's Science Advisory Committee.

Silent Spring opens with a stark, shocking fable of one composite town's "silent spring" after pesticides have poisoned the environment, destroying not only insects, but the birds which feed on them. She then marshalls massive documentation of the effects organic pesticides have already produced, not only on birds, but on human beings as well. The book closes with a temperate consideration of the future use of pesticides, and of all man's tamperings with his surroundings. She was careful to search out and include feasible alternatives, such as using biological controls as a partial replacement for chemical spraying.

C. was a scientist, perceptive, meticulous, accurate; an artistic writer, concerned with cadences, images, the need to enlighten yet delight; a philosopher, always seeking the lucid pattern beneath seemingly complex and unmanageable details; and a mystic, aware of the spirit that she felt animated all life.

WORKS: *Under the Sea-Wind: A Naturalist's Picture of Ocean Life* (1941). *The Sea Around Us* (1951). *The Edge of the Sea* (1955). *Silent Spring* (1962). *The Sea* (1964). *The Sense of Wonder* (1965). *The Rocky Coast* (1971).

BIBLIOGRAPHY: Brooks, P., *The House of Life: Rachel Carson at Work* (1972). Brooks, P., *Speaking for Nature: How Literary Naturalists from Henry Thoreau to Rachel Carson Have Stamped America* (1980). Gartner, C. B., *Rachel Carson* (1982). Graham, F., Jr., *Since Silent Spring* (1979). Sterling, P., *Sea and Earth: The Life of Rachel Carson* (1970). Whorton, J., et al., *Before Silent Spring: Pesticides and Public Health in Pre-DDT America* (1974).

For articles in reference works, see: *Current Biography* (1951; 1964). Other references: *American Forests* (July 1970). *SatR* (16 May 1964).

CAROL B. GARTNER

Alice Cary

B. 26 April 1820, Mount Healthy, Ohio; d. 12 Feb. 1871, New York City
Wrote under: Alice Carey, Alice Cary, Patty Lee
D. of Robert and Elizabeth Jessup Cary

Growing up in what was then considered the Far West—around Cincinnati, Ohio—C. found educational opportunities limited to those offered by a small country school, from which she was removed altogether quite early. Remarkably, with neither education, books, literary friends, nor encouragement, C. and her sister Phoebe developed and sustained their literary talents. Both sisters began to publish first in western and then in eastern newspapers and journals.

In 1850, C. moved to New York, where Rufus W. Griswold praised her work in his *Female Poets of America*. It was also admired by other writers, including Edgar Allan Poe and Whittier, whose poem "The Singer" is about her. Phoebe joined C. in 1851, and by 1856 both women had well-established literary reputations. Their home in New York City became the center of a literary salon that for fifteen years met each Sunday.

C. was a firm believer in abolition and women's rights, although many of her poems show woman's noblest role to be that of wife and mother. Despite her illness—C. suffered for years with tuberculosis, the disease that had killed her mother and two sisters by the time she was fifteen and would eventually kill her—and her self-imposed rigorous writing schedule, she served as the first president of the first women's club in America, which is now known as Sorosis.

A prolific writer, C. authored five volumes of poetry, several novels, and several books of sketches and short stories. Although generally too didactic for modern sensibilities, her poetry was better than that of most of her contemporaries.

The most interesting personae of C.'s poetry are the women. A recurring figure is that of the unmarried but pregnant woman. This figure in "Morna" and later in "No Ring" is "not mother, wife, nor bride." Seduced and abandoned, she dies of a broken heart. Consistently, C. urges understanding, offers poverty as both explanation and excuse, and stands quietly on the woman's side. A second figure is the strong woman, who although she looks happily upon marriage, retains her own identity. Such a woman is found in "The Bridal Veil," in *Ballads, Lyrics, and Hymns* (1866).

It is in C.'s prose, however, that the modern reader would be most interested. *Clovernook* (1852, later appearing in five pirated editions printed in England), *Clovernook Children* (1855), and *Pictures of Country Life* (1859) taken together make a significant contribution to our understanding of early western community life. The sketches are not romantic; they depict lives that were deprived, hard, and marked by early deaths.

There is ample material for study in C.'s prose, especially for those interested in the folklore of women. Material incidental to the story lines gives fascinating glimpses into a world in which, as Aunt Caty in *Clovernook Children* tells us, "widders [are] sometimes better off than wives," and in which an unmarried woman of twenty-five is a local tragedy. These stories are simple but satisfying, and especially remarkable for their vivid portrayal of life in the West.

WORKS: *Poems of Alice and Phoebe Cary* (1950). *Clovernook; or, Recollections of Our Neighborhood in the West* (1st series, 1852; 2nd series, 1853). *Hagar: A Story for Today* (1852). *Lyra, and Other Poems* (1852). *Clovernook Children* (1855). *Poems* (1855). *Married, Not Mated; or, How They Lived at Woodside and Throckmorton Hall* (1856). *Adopted Daughter, and Other Tales* (1859). *The Josephine Gallery* (edited by Cary, with P. Cary, 1859). *Pictures of Country Life* (1859). *Ballads, Lyrics, and Hymns* (1866). *The Bishop's Son* (1867). *Snow-Berries: A Book for Young Folks* (1867). *A Lover's Diary* (1868). *The Born Thrall* (1871). *The Last Poems of Alice and Phoebe Cary* (Ed. M. C. Ames, 1873). *Ballads for Little Folks* (Ed. M. C. Ames, 1874). *The Poetical Works of Alice and Phoebe Cary; with a Memorial of Their Lives* (Ed. M. C. Ames, 1877).

BIBLIOGRAPHY: Ames, M. C., *A Memorial to Alice and Phoebe Cary, with Some of Their Later Poems* (1873). Derby, J., *Fifty Years among Authors, Books, and Publishers* (1884). Venable, W. H., *Beginnings of Literary Culture in the Ohio Valley* (1891).

For articles in reference works, see: *AW. CAL. FPA. NAW* (article by M. W. Langworthy). *NCAB.*

BILLIE J. WAHLSTROM

Willa Sibert Cather

B. 7 Dec. 1873, Gore, Virginia; d. 24 April 1947, New York City
Wrote under: Willa Cather, Willa Sibert Cather
D. of Charles Fectigue and Virginia Boak Cather

C., the first of seven children, was raised on a farm in the hills of northern Virginia. In 1883, her family moved to the Nebraska frontier and, in 1884, to Red Cloud, a "bitter, dead little western town," where C. lived for the next six years. She began publishing short stories while attending the University of Nebraska in Lincoln (B.A. 1895).

From 1896 to 1906, C. lived in Pittsburgh, Pennsylvania, working first at the *Home Magazine* and the *Daily Leader* and then as a high-school teacher. She published a volume of poetry and one of short stories while she was in Pittsburgh.

In 1906, C. joined the staff of *McClure's* magazine in New York City; she became managing editor in 1909. In 1911, after finishing her first novel, *Alexander's Bridge* (1912), she left *McClure's* to concentrate on her writing. In the following years, she began to write about the people of the Nebraska frontier of her childhood.

O Pioneers! (1913) and *My Ántonia* (1918) are lyric novels of the land and of the lives of strong women on the Nebraska frontier. *My Antonia*, C.'s most widely read novel, is told by Jim Burden, Antonia's childhood friend, who looks back on their past from the perspective of a successful but unhappy eastern lawyer. He sees Antonia as the apotheosis of the pioneer woman who conquered the land and as a personification of eternal values.

The novels written after WWI reflect C.'s increasing concern about the materialism and spiritual aridity of the technological 20th c.

The least distinguished of these—*One of Ours* (1922)—was awarded a Pulitzer Prize. A novel of World War I, it tells the story of Claude Wheeler, a young man who has spent a dreary life on a Nebraska farm and has a brief experience of beauty and fulfillment in France before he is killed in action.

A Lost Lady (1923), set at the end of the era of transcontinental railroad expansion, is the story of Marian Forrester, the beautiful, young wife of a man who had been a dynamic railroad builder in the days of the conquest of the West. As her husband's health and fortunes fail, Mrs. Forrester's world is restricted to Sweet Water, a small railway-junction town.

The novel describes the disillusionment of the narrator, an idealistic young man and a devoted family friend, with Mrs. Forrester's accommodation to materialistic society.

This slender book is surely one of the high points of American fiction. C.'s unaffected, powerful, and lucid style is the result of her untiring struggle for, as she formulated it herself, the correct and appropriate word, which makes possible "the gift of inner empathy."

The Professor's House (1925) also contrasts the contemporary materialistic world with a more ideal world in harmonious relation with nature. Professor St. Peter does, in the end, reach some understanding of how he can survive in his family's world of money and status, but the center of the novel is "Tom Outland's Story," an account of the discovery of the ruins of cliff dwellings in the Southwest.

My Mortal Enemy (1926), a short novel that has not been well-received by all critics, is about the mystery of character. Myra Henshawe, marrying against the wishes of her rich uncle, has given up wealth and the Roman Catholicism in which she was raised for love, which has proved distinctly unsatisfying. She experiences deep conflict not only with her husband but with her own sharply divided character. Myra has many bad qualities—she is arrogant, jealous, and greedy—but she strongly desires immortality and wholeness.

C.'s most mysterious work derives its impact from what remains unsaid, from the depths that seem constantly to be assaulting the cool surface. Religion, Myra comes to believe, "is different from everything else; *because in religion seeking is finding.*" Through a variety of images, C. suggests that Myra's sin was to have sought and found false gods, the most deceitful of which is romantic love. By rejecting the Roman Catholicism of her childhood and the position she was born to, she has lost herself. C. does full justice to the compelling lure of eros, which continues to exert its power over Myra and Nellie Birdseye, the narrator of the story.

Death Comes for the Archbishop (1927), based on the lives of Jean Baptiste Lamy and Joseph Machebeuf, is the chronicle of two 19th-c. French priests assigned to set up an apostolic vicariate in New Mexico Territory. Within a framework similar to a picaresque novel, C. includes biographical sketches, stories of miracles and legends of saints, and description of the Southwestern landscape. *Shadows on the Rock* (1931), set in 17th-c. Quebec, is another novel about the Catholic faith in the New World.

In her last years, C. published two novels—not among her best—two volumes of short stories—one of them, *Obscure Destinies* (1932), contains two excellent stories—and a collection of critical essays—*Not under Forty*

(1936). The last title reflects C.'s claim that she was not writing for the younger generation who, she believed, could not share or understand her values.

The more closely one looks at C.'s works in the context of her life, the more clearly one sees that C. was always writing about herself. "Life began for me when I ceased to admire and began to remember," she said. This reserved woman, who went to unusual lengths to maintain privacy, was driven by an inexorable need to give form to and reveal, albeit indirectly, her inner self. Some of the power in her works surely comes from this tension—the romantic confessional temperament writing in the classical restrained mode.

It is C.'s lot to be America's least comprehended major novelist. Wallace Stevens said about her that "we have nothing better than she is." But the particularity of her genius is elusive, and comments about C.'s work often focus on its less central aspects.

On C.'s style, there is little dissent—her prose is of the highest quality, variously described as classical, restrained, wonderfully transparent. C. wrote language of a kind that is not indigenous to American letters, yet the nature of her genius was such that the prose sounds impeccably American.

C.'s lyrical and profound evocations of nature in its many forms are not surpassed in American letters, and she is one of the few American writers who can take her place among the great European writers who have gloriously pictured the natural world.

C. has, as could not be otherwise, been recognized as a religious writer. It was Henry Steele Commager who wrote: "And all her novels and stories . . . were animated by a single great theme, as they were graced by a single felicitous style. The theme was that of the supremacy of moral and spiritual over material values, the ever recurrent but inexhaustible theme of gaining the whole world and losing one's soul." C. may have been a mystic who saw this world as a prism of God.

Many critics of the 1920s considered her to be the best American writer of her day. C.'s rank is more qualified today, but the tide has started to turn, and C.'s work is apparently to be revived with vigor and enthusiasm.

WORKS: *April Twilights* (1903; enlarged ed., 1923). *The Troll Garden* (1905). *Alexander's Bridge* (1912). *O Pioneers!* (1913). *The Song of the Lark* (1915). *My Ántonia* (1918). *Youth and the Bright Medusa* (1920). *One of Ours* (1922). *A Lost Lady* (1923). *The Professor's House* (1925). *My Mortal Enemy* (1926). *Death Comes for the Archbishop* (1927). *Shadows on the Rock* (1931). *Obscure Destinies* (1932). *Lucy Gayheart* (1935). *Not under Forty*

(1936). *Sapphira and the Slave Girl* (1940). *The Old Beauty, and Others* (1948). *On Writing* (1949). *Writings from Willa Cather's Campus Years* (Ed. J. R. Shively, 1950). *Willa Cather in Europe: Her Own Story of the First Journey* (Ed. G. N. Kates, 1956). *Early Stories* (Ed. M. R. Bennett, 1957). *Willa Cather's Collected Short Fiction, 1892–1912* (Ed. M. R. Bennett, 1965). *The Kingdom of Art: Willa Cather's First Principles and Critical Statements, 1893 to 1896* (Ed. B. Slote, 1966). *The World and the Parish: Willa Cather's Articles and Reviews, 1893–1902* (Ed. W. M. Curtin, 1970). *Uncle Valentine, and Other Stories* (Ed. B. Slote, 1973).

BIBLIOGRAPHY: Auchincloss, L., *Pioneers and Caretakers: A Study of Nine American Women Writers* (1965). Bennett, M., *The World of Willa Cather* (1961). Bloom, E. A., and L. D. Bloom, *Willa Cather's Gift of Sympathy* (1964). Brown, E. K., and L. Edel, *Willa Cather: A Critical Biography* (1953). Commager, H. S., *The American Mind* (1950). Daiches, D., *Willa Cather: A Critical Introduction* (1951). Edel, L., *Willa Cather: The Paradox of Success* (1960). Lewis, E., *Willa Cather Living* (1953). McFarland, D. T., *Willa Cather* (1972). Murphy, J. J., ed., *Five Essays on Willa Cather* (1974). Randall, J. H., III, *The Landscape and the Looking Glass: Willa Cather's Search for Value* (1960). Rapin, R., *Willa Cather* (1930). Schroeter, J., ed., *Willa Cather and Her Critics* (1967). Sergeant, E. S., *Willa Cather: A Memoir* (1963). Slote, B., and V. Faulkner, eds., *The Art of Willa Cather* (1974). Stouck, D., *Willa Cather's Imagination* (1975). Trilling, L., *After the Genteel Tradition* (1964). Van Ghent, D., *Willa Cather* (Univ. of Minnesota Pamphlets on American Writers, No. 36, 1964). Woodress, J., *Willa Cather: Her Life and Art* (1970).

LINA MAINIERO

Mary Hartwell Catherwood

B. *16 Dec. 1847, Luray, Ohio; d. 26 Dec. 1902, Chicago, Illinois*
Wrote under: Mary Hartwell Catherwood, Mary Hartwell
D. *of Marcus and Phoebe Thompson Hartwell; m. James Catherwood, 1877*

After graduation in 1868 from Granville Female College, Granville, Ohio, C. taught in Ohio and Illinois before she was able to support herself by writing. Her early work combines strands of critical realism and melodrama. She published many short stories and long serials in magazines such as the *Atlantic* and *Lippincott's*.

Historians of American fiction suggest that C.'s importance lies in her having been the first novelist to write popular romantic historical novels, forecasting the best-selling genre at the turn of the century. C. was the first woman novelist born west of the Alleghenies and the first woman novelist to be a college graduate. As a writer, however, she is much more important today because of her works of critical realism and her pioneering regional material. Her two early novels, *A Woman in Armor* (1857) and *Craque-o-Doom* (1881), contain tantilizing hints of the social realist she might have become. *A Woman in Armor*, despite its melodramatic plot, has a detailed if satiric description of the town in which the action is set, Little Boston, and a faintly feminist theme.

C.'s major literary achievement as a regional realist can be found in her short stories, three volumes of which are still in print. Her relentless portrayal of various Midwest towns, from Ohio to Indiana and Illinois, attests to her craftsmanship. Surrounded by the beauty of nature and the seasons, her towns are dreary cultural wastelands peopled with squalid characters who, however, often illustrate such basic qualities of human nature as parental love. Except for "The Spirit of an Illinois Town," her most realistic stories are not collected and can only be found in periodicals. When C. abandoned realism, however, she did not leave the short story behind. In fact, she was one of the few writers who tried to use the materials of historical romance in the short-story form.

In 1889, with the publication of *The Romance of Dollard*, an historical romance based on the work of Francis Parkman, C. took a new direction. From then until her death, she wrote romantic historical fiction, using the French settlement of the West and Canada as background. While remaining in the Midwest (in 1886 she helped found the Western Association of Writers), she turned her back on realistic treatment of midwestern material. At her famous confrontation with Hamlin Garland at the Chicago World's Fair of 1893, she argued for "the aristocratic in literature."

C.'s most popular novel, *Lazarre* (1901), is based on the claims of Eleazar Williams (1789–1858) that he was the lost dauphin of France. The novel is well written and exciting, with violence, dramatic scenes such as a visit to Napoleon, traditional American characters such as Johnny Appleseed, and a romantic ending in which Lazarre gives up the throne of France for the woman he loves and the freedom of the western plains. Otis Skinner dramatized *Lazarre* in 1902 and the play had a successful if not spectacular run.

C. has a remarkable record of "firsts" to her name, and her early work is worth reading. It is ironic that perhaps her career as a serious writer was betrayed by her disdain for those prairie villages that she so realistically portrayed. "The aristocratic in literature" has lost its charms for the modern reader, who eagerly looks for evidence of just such provincial experience as C. (and her characters) longed to escape.

WORKS: *A Woman in Armor* (1875). *The Dogberry Bunch* (1879). *Craque-o-Doom* (1881). *Rocky Fork* (1882). *Old Caravan Days* (1884). *The Secrets at Roseladies* (1888). *The Romance of Dollard* (1889). *The Story of Tonty* (1890). *The Lady of Fort St. John* (1891). *Old Kaskaskia* (1893). *The White Islander* (1893). *The Chase of St. Castin, and Other Stories* (1894). *The Days of Jeanne d'Arc* (1897). *The Spirit of an Illinois Town* (1897). *Bony and Ban: The Story of a Printing Venture* (1898). *Heroes of the Middle West: French* (1898). *Mackinac, and Other Lake Stories* (1899). *The Queen of the Swamp, and Other Plain Americans* (1899). *Spanish Peggy* (1899). *Lazarre* (1901; dramatization by O. Skinner, 1902).

BIBLIOGRAPHY: Dondore, D. A., *The Prairie and the Making of America* (1926). Garland, H., *Roadside Meetings* (1931). Price, R., "A Critical Biography of Mary Hartwell Catherwood" (Ph.D. diss., Ohio State Univ., 1943). Wilson, M. E., *Biography of Mary Hartwell Catherwood* (1904).
    For articles in reference works, see: *DAB. NAW* (article by R. Price).
    Other references: *AL* 17 (1945). *Bulletin of Cincinnati Historical Society* (1964). *Michigan Historical Magazine* 30 (1946).

                                                         BEVERLY SEATON

Carrie Lane Chapman Catt

B. 9 Jan. 1859, Ripon, Wisconsin; d. 9 March 1947, New Rochelle, New York
D. of Lucius and Maria Clinton Lane; m. Leo Chapman, 1885; m. George
    William Catt, 1890

A key architect of the woman-suffrage victory in 1920, C. was essentially an activist-lecturer rather than a writer. In 1917, she edited her first book, *Woman Suffrage by Federal Constitutional Amendment*, a series of six essays, four of which C. wrote herself. Here she analyzes briefly the political obstacles women face and focuses on the practical reasons why the federal amendment route seemed the only truly feasible one. She discussed the problems of fraud women encountered in seeking state suffrage amendments and the causes of failure of the three 1916 referenda. She concluded with a chapter countering objections to the federal amendment.

Woman Suffrage and Politics (1923), which C. wrote with Nettie Rogers Shuler immediately after the 1920 victory, is her major work. She gives primary attention not to the history of the woman-suffrage drive itself, nor even to her own role in devising the final winning strategy. Rather, she deals with the question of why that victory had been so long delayed. C. contends that the delay was not caused by hostile or indifferent public opinion; instead, it was the result of political maneuvering, the "buying and selling of American politics."

Apart from these two books, C.'s other publications were generally speeches later issued as pamphlets. Prior to 1920, woman suffrage dominated her concern; later, her major cause became world peace. One of the most significant suffrage pamphlets was *The Winning Strategy*, a 1916 speech in which C. presented her blueprint for the final victory campaign: a double effort for state enfranchisement and the federal amendment.

The thrust of her concern as proponent of world peace is seen in *The Status Today of War vs. Peace* (1928). She defined two great causes of war as being first, the dependence on "war preparedness as the way to peace" and second, economic colonialism with its underlying racism. The hope for peace she found in antiwar treaties between civilized nations and in an educated public opinion in which women must play a key part.

C.'s writings generally reflect the cool, logical style that hallmarked her political action. She avoids rhetorical flashes, relying instead on perceptive analysis and the weight of historical evidence. She saw suffrage as an evolutionary step, the logical outcome of an earlier commitment to democracy.

Though generally objective in her writings, C. in *Woman Suffrage and Politics* often spoke as a partisan deeply wounded in the political struggle. The cost of the long-delayed victory for many women, she argued, was disillusionment with political parties. It is perhaps a mark of the cost of that struggle to herself that after 1920 her major cause was the nonpartisan one, world peace.

WORKS: *Woman Suffrage and Its Basic Argument* (Interurban Woman Suffrage Series, no. 2, 1907). *Woman Suffrage and the Home* (Interurban Woman Suffrage Series, no. 4, 1907). *A Bit of History* (Interurban Woman Suffrage Series, no. 5, 1908). *Perhaps* (ca. 1910). *Do You Know?* (1912). *Woman Suffrage* (1913). *Feminism and Suffrage* (1914). *The Winning Strategy* (1916). *Address to the Congress of the United States* (1917). *Woman Suffrage by Federal Constitutional Amendment* (ed. by Catt, 1917). *Objections to the Federal Amendment* (1919). *Woman Suffrage and Politics* (with N. R. Shuler,

1923). *The Status Today of War vs. Peace* (1928). *Then and Now* (1939). *Who Can Answer?* (1939).

BIBLIOGRAPHY: Peck, M. G., *Carrie Chapman Catt* (1944). *HWS.*
Other references: *American Political Science Review* (Aug. 1923). *NYT* (13 May 1923).

INZER BYERS

Frances Manwaring Caulkins

B. *26 April 1795, New London, Connecticut; d. 3 Feb. 1869, New London, Connecticut*
D. *of Joshua and Fanny Manwaring Caulkins*

C. centered her literary attention on two radically different areas of concern: the religious education of young people and local history. She began her work in the 1830s writing for the American Tract Society, which published a wide range of her work over the next thirty years, including religious and educational books for children.

C.'s major achievements as a writer, however, came in the area of local history. She wrote first *The History of Norwich, Connecticut, from Its Settlement in 1660 to January, 1845.* A second, revised edition carried the history to 1866. She also wrote *The History of New London, Connecticut* (1852), with a second edition continuing to 1860.

In the early sections of both works, C. deals with the local Indian tribes, their leadership conflicts, and their relationships with the new English settlers. In her view, "the providence of God" had prepared the way for peaceable settlement, for the tribes, weakened by conflict, eagerly sought new allies. Her perspective on the Indians is sympathetic, although at times condescending, and she stresses their dependent qualities. She underscores what she sees as the paternalistic concern of Norwich leaders for the Indians.

C. stresses the early religious focus of town life, the decline of fervor in the late 17th c., and the impact of the 18th-c. Great Awakening. She stresses the work of Tennent, Davenport, and Whitefield, citing the positive impact of revivalism as well as the problems of church division and separatism. She also notes the role in New London of the Rogerene sect, typical of religious extremists in their "determination to be persecuted."

While her primary focus is on political and religious history, C. also has a sound grasp of local, social, and economic history. She notes the close hold on town leadership by descendants of the early town fathers; not until the end of the 18th c. was there substantial expansion in the Norwich leadership ranks.

Of the two histories, that of New London has the more localized view, stressing personalities and incidents often of purely local concern. In both histories, C. takes the view that events of local history "illustrate classes of men and ages of time." She writes with ease; her tone is at times romantic. While she does not escape totally the self-congratulatory notes of the native, she does attempt to evaluate events within a broader historical perspective.

Though the material differs sharply, there is a common denominator in her two types of writing. Both in her writing for the American Tract Society and in her histories, C. has in mind young people and their concerns. A sense of God's providence informs both types of works and she seeks to arouse through history "a more affectionate sympathy for your ancestors."

WORKS: *The Child's Hymn Book* (1835). *Children of the Bible: As Examples and as Warnings* (1842). *The History of Norwich, Connecticut, from Its Settlement in 1660 to January, 1845* (1845; rev. ed. 1866). *The Tract Primer* (ca. 1848). *Memoir of the Rev. William Adams, of Dedham, Mass., and of the Rev. Eliphalet Adams, of New London, Conn., and Their Descendants, with the Journal of William Adams, 1666–1682* (1849). *Bride Brook: A Legend of New London, Connecticut* (1852). *The History of New London, Connecticut* (1852; rev. ed. 1860). *Eve and Her Daughters of Holy Writ; or, Women of the Bible* (1861). *Ye Antient Buriall Place of New London, Connecticut* (1899). *The Stone Records of Groton* (Ed. E. S. Gilman, 1903).

BIBLIOGRAPHY: Haven, H. P., "Memoir," in *History of Norwich* (1874). Trumbull, H. C., *A Model Superintendent: A Sketch of the Life . . . of Henry P. Haven* (1880). Wilcox, G. B., *In Memoriam, Miss Frances Manwaring Caulkins* (1869).

For articles in reference works, see: *NAW* (article by M. Freiberg).

Other references: New London County Historical Society Records (1890–94).

INZER BYERS

Elizabeth Margaret Chandler

B. 24 Dec. 1807, Wilmington, Delaware; d. 2 Nov. 1834, Tecumseh, Michigan
D. of Thomas and Margaret Evans Chandler

The youngest child and only daughter of a prosperous Quaker farmer of English stock, C. lost her mother in infancy, was orphaned at nine, and was raised by her grandmother and three Quaker aunts in Philadelphia. She attended Quaker schools until only twelve or thirteen and was an avid reader all her life. At an early age she showed her talents as a poet: at nine she produced a poem called "Reflections on a Thunder Gust," at sixteen she began to publish a few poems in the public press. At eighteen "The Slave Ship" brought her a prize from the editors of *Casket*, in which it was published.

Benjamin Lundy, the antislavery publisher, noticed "The Slave Ship" and reprinted it in the *Genius of Universal Emancipation*. Lundy recruited C. as a regular contributor, and two years later she became the editor of "The Female Repository," the women's department of his paper. C. moved with her brother to the Michigan frontier in 1830, but continued as editor of the *Genius*'s women's department until her death, despite Lundy's complaints about the difficulties of regular communication with a forest outpost.

C. was the first American woman author to make slavery the principal theme of her writing. Half of her published poems and essays dealt with slavery, African life, the emancipation movement, or the American Indian. "The Slave Ship" employed a poignant theme which she used repeatedly: the wrenching despair and horror experienced by proud and independent Africans snatched from their native shores and transported in chains to the Americas and lifelong slavery.

In "The Afric's Dream" she shows the fettered slave remembering his former home where he lay under his own banana tree: "My own bright stream was at my feet, / And how I laughed to lave, / My burning lip and cheek and brow, / In that delicious wave!" C. showed amazing empathy with the black slave of whom she could have had no direct knowledge.

Most of her poems have strong rhythms as well as vivid imagery. Frequently they were sung as hymns at antislavery meetings, or recited as dramatic presentations.

In her essays C. emphasized the contradiction between slavery and the Declaration of Independence, the degrading effect of slavery on master as well as slave, and the need to destroy the economic base of slavery by refusing to use products which were produced by slave labor. In a series of lively pieces, "Letters to Isabel," published in the *Genius*, C. berates an imaginary friend for hesitating to forego the pound cakes and ice creams made with slave-produced sugar, for "devotion to the cause of justice and mercy."

C. was also an early believer in the need for women to champion humane causes. In her essay "To the Ladies of the United States," which appeared in *Genius*, she chided women for deceiving themselves when they protested that they had no power to ameliorate the horrors of slavery: "American women! Your power is sufficient for its extinction! And, oh! by every sympathy most holy to the breast of women, are ye called upon for exertion of that potency."

WORKS: *Essays, Philanthropic and Moral* (1836). *The Poetical Works of Elizabeth Margaret Chandler* (1836).

BIBLIOGRAPHY: Clark, G., *The Liberty Minstrel* (1844). Lundy, B., in *The Poetical Works of Elizabeth Chandler* (1836).

For articles in reference works, see: *DAB. FPA. NAW* (article by S. Lintner). *Woman's Record*, S. J. Hale (1853).

Other references: *MichH* (Dec. 1955).

RUTH BORDIN

Ednah Dow Littlehale Cheney

B. 27 June 1824, Boston, Massachusetts; d. 19 Nov. 1904, Boston, Massachusetts
D. of Sargent Smith and Ednah Parker Dow Littlehale; m. Seth Wells
  Cheney, 1853

Writer, activist, and self-proclaimed jack-of-all-trades, C. was the third daughter of a New England family of comfortable means and liberal sentiments. The independent spirit she displayed as a child found a home when, as a very young woman, C. came under the influence of transcendentalists Theodore Parker, Bronson Alcott, and, above all, Margaret Fuller.

As ardent an abolitionist as her mentors, C. led the way after the Civil War in recruiting Boston teachers for freedmen's schools in the South. But for most of her eighty years, her energies as a reformer were devoted primarily to improving the educational, occupational, and political opportunities available to women.

In 1853, C. married portrait artist Seth Wells Cheney. His death five years later left her with an infant daughter who herself died at the age of twenty-six.

For all her reform activities, C. thought of herself first as a writer. Three of her early books, *Faithful to the Light* (1871), *Sally Williams* (1874), and *Child of the Tide* (1874), are better-than-average children's fiction. Though marred by the besetting sins of the period and the genre—sentimentality, didacticism, and unlikely coincidence—they are absorbing stories which often correct conventional sexist stereotypes.

In 1875, C. published the "Memoir of [surgeon] Susan Dimock," first of several elegies written in tribute to family, friends, and colleagues. The finest, clearly a labor of love, is the sketch of her idol, Margaret Fuller, included in the 1902 volume, *Reminiscences*. Rich in anecdote and personal reminiscence, it shows C. at her sensible, insightful, generous best.

C.'s skills as a biographer again show to advantage in the *Journals of Louisa May Alcott* (1889), which she edited and extensively annotated. Later biographers are indebted to this fine work not only because it includes some journal entries now lost in the original, but because C. does not shrink from presenting the author of *Little Women* "without disguise." Alcott's passionate dissatisfactions are laid bare, as is the compulsive self-denial that embittered her life. Feminist interpretation, however appropriate it might seem, enters only indirectly, perhaps because of C.'s desire to lay no blame, especially on Bronson Alcott.

But *Nora's Return* (1890), a nondramatic sequel to Ibsen's *Doll's House*, is avowedly feminist. It is also outrageously simplistic, contrived, and, inadvertently, very funny.

The delightful opening of C.'s last major work, *Reminiscences* (1902), recalls a time when Boston was all but an island, town criers called out descriptions of lost children, and Election Day was celebrated with oysters, lobster, and baked beans on the Common. Personally revealing detail abounds—C. staying awake in church by pricking her finger and writing in blood in her prayer book, C. being asked to leave a Beacon Hill school because of her "bad influence on the other girls." Later sections of the autobiography, however, are flat and strangely impersonal.

Colleagues like Julia Ward Howe attributed much of C.'s success as a reformer to her judiciousness, calm disposition, and broad-mindedness. The same qualities illuminate her writing, which is consistently lucid, unpretentious, and humane. Much of it deserves notice today only as social history, but her children's fiction still entertains, and her biographies of Alcott, Fuller, and parts of *Reminiscences* hold their own as literature. At moments, C. achieved the kind of originality that sometimes blossoms out of diligent research and honest, compassionate reporting.

WORKS: *Handbook for American Citizens* (1866). *Patience* (1870). *Faithful to the Light* (1871). *Social Games* (1871). *Sally Williams* (1874). *Child of the Tide* (1874). *Memoir of Susan Dimock* (1875). *Memoir of Seth Wells Cheney* (1881). *Gleanings in the Field of Art* (1881). *Memoir of John Cheney, Engraver* (1888). *Memoir of Margaret Swan Cheney* (1889). *Journals of Louisa May Alcott* (1889). *Nora's Return* (1890). *Stories of Olden Times* (1890). *Memoirs of Lucretia Crocker and Abby W. May* (1893). *Life of Christian Daniel Rauch* (1893). *Reminiscences* (1902).

The letters of Ednah Cheney are at the Boston Public Library, the Massachusetts Historical Society, Smith College, and the Schlesinger Library, Radcliffe College.

BIBLIOGRAPHY: For articles in reference works, see *AW. NAW* (article by S. Ingerbritsen). *Representative Women of New England*, Ed. Howe, J. W. (1904).

Other references: *Memorial Meeting of the New England Women's Club* (1905). *Women's Journal* (26 Nov. 1904).

EVELYN SHAKIR

Lydia Maria Francis Child

B. *11 Feb. 1802, Medford, Massachusetts; d. 20 Oct. 1880, Wayland, Massachusetts*
Wrote under : L. Maria Child, Mrs. Child
D. *of David Convers and Susanna Rand Francis; m. David Lee Child, 1828*

C. was the youngest of six children born to a prosperous baker and real-estate broker and his wife. At twelve C. lost her mother and lived with her sister Mary and her husband. On her eighteenth birthday, announcing her independence, she moved to Watertown, Massachusetts, to stay with her brother Convers Francis, a Unitarian minister. She opened a girls' school and startled parents by encouraging her pupils' independent spirit. C.'s literary work included light romances, domestic books for women and children, and historical tracts advocating the rights of black slaves, Indians, and women.

Hobomok (1824), C.'s early attempt to write an American romance, presents the Indian as a noble savage, and makes a plea for tolerance. *The Rebels* (1825) portrays the tensions leading up to the Revolution. In 1826 C. began the *Juvenile Miscellany*, the first periodical for children in the U.S., which ran successfully for eight years. With the wide reception of her practical guide, *The Frugal Housewife* (1829), C. became well known and respected as a literary figure in New England.

This reputation was dashed almost overnight with the publication of *An Appeal in Favor of That Class of Americans Called Africans* in 1833. In her preface to this historical antislavery document, C. wrote: "I am fully aware of the unpopularity of the task I have undertaken; but though I *expect* ridicule and censure, it is not in my nature to *fear* them." C. not only suffered financial ruin and social ostracism, but was forced to end her *Juvenile Miscellany*.

C.'s constant and selfless devotion to abolitionism was supported by her husband David Lee Child, a founder of the New England Anti-Slavery Society in 1832. In addition to writing many pamphlets in support of the cause, financing slave biographies, such as *Incidents in the Life of a Slave Girl* (1861), and editing the *National Anti-Slavery Standard* from 1841 to 1849, C., along with her husband, sheltered fugitive slaves at their residence in Wayland, Massachusetts. Her courageous zeal persisted late into her career when she published the *Freedmen's Book* (1865), the profits of which she donated to the Freedmen's Aid Association. Used as a text in schools for freed slaves, the book stressed the importance of moral principles, good health, neatness, thrift, and politeness, citing black heroes as inspiring examples.

C.'s approach to reform was well thought out and literary. Her documents combined strong argument, carefully researched analysis, and sincere compassion. These faculties are also evident in her feminist works. For a Ladies Library series she wrote biographies of exemplary women and a *History of the Condition of Women in Various Ages and Nations* (1835), in which she argued for female equality.

Best acknowledged as an abolitionist writer, C.'s versatility with feminist tracts, historical romances, and domestic books for women and children points to the principal motive behind all of her work: that of educating her readers and helping them to adopt a moral and humane way of life. She appealed to the young in her *Flowers to Children* (1844, 1846, 1855), which contains the famous "Boy's Thanksgiving" poem beginning with "Over the river and through the woods/ To grandfather's house we go." She addressed the elderly in *Looking toward Sunset* (1864), a miscellaneous collection designed to give "some words of consolation and cheer to my companions on the way," which was applauded by Whittier and Bryant. Even in her romances, she incorporated her ideas on social reform: feminism in *Philothea* (1836) and anti-slavery in *The Romance of the Republic* (1837). Hers was a lifelong commitment to humanitarian values.

WORKS: *Hobomok: A Tale of Early Times* (1824). *The Rebels; or, Boston before the Revolution* (1825). *The Juvenile Souvenir* (1828). *The First Settlers of New England; or, Conquest of the Pequods, Naragansets, and Pokanokets. As Related by a Mother to Her Children* (1829). *The Frugal Housewife* (1829; later editions, The American Frugal Housewife). *The Colonel: A Collection of Miscellaneous Pieces, Written at Various Times* (1831). *The Girl's Own Book* (1831). *The Mother's Book* (1831). *Biographies of Lady Russel and Madam Guion* (1832). *Biographies of Madame de Stael and Madame Roland* (1832). *An Appeal in Behalf of that Class of Americans Called Africans* (1833). *Biographies of Good Wives* (1833). *The Oasis* (edited by Child, with contributions by Child et al., 1834). *History of the Condition of Women in Various Ages and Nations* (2 vols., 1835). *The Anti-Slavery Catechism* (1836). *The Evils of Slavery and the Curse of Slavery* (1836). *Philothea: A Romance* (1836). *The Family Nurse* (1837). *Authentic Narratives of American Slavery* (edited by Child, 1838). *The Anti-Slavery Almanac* (1843). *Letters from New York* (2 vols., 1843–45). *Flowers for Children* (3 vols., 1844–46). *Fact and Fiction* (1846). *Isaac T. Hopper: A True Life* (1853). *New Flowers for Children* (1855). *The Progress of Religious Ideas through Successive Ages* (3 vols., 1855). *Autumnal Leaves: Tales and Sketches in Prose and Rhyme* (1856). *Correspondence between L. M. Child and Gov. Wise and Mrs. Wise (of Virginia)* (1860). *The Duty of Disobedience to the Fugitive Slave Act: An Appeal to the Legislators of Massachusetts* (1860). *The Patriarchal Institution, Described by Members of its Own Family* (1860). *The Right Way the Safe Way, Proved by Emancipation in the West Indies and Elsewhere* (1860). *Incidents in the Life of a Slave Girl* by H. Jacobs (edited by Child, 1861). *The Freedmen's Book* (1865). *A Romance of the Republic* (1867). *Looking towards Sunset: From Sources New and Old, Original and Selected* (1868). *An Appeal for the Indians* (1868).

BIBLIOGRAPHY: Baer, H. G., *The Heart Is Like Heaven: The Life of Lydia Maria Child* (1964).
For articles in reference works, see: *CAL. DAB. Female Prose Writers of*

America, J. S. Hart (1852). *NAW* (article by L. Filler). *NCAB*. *Woman's Record*, S. J. Hale (1853).

BETTE B. ROBERTS

Kate O'Flaherty Chopin

B. 8 Feb. 1851, St. Louis, Missouri; d. 22 Aug. 1904, St. Louis, Missouri
D. of Thomas and Eliza Faris O'Flaherty; m. Oscar Chopin, 1870

Descended on her mother's side from the French and Creole elite of St. Louis and on her father's side from Irish newcomers, C., after her father's death in 1855, was raised in a household dominated by three generations of widowed women. She moved with her husband to New Orleans, where she bore five sons in ten years. The family then settled in Cloutiersville in the Natchitoches Parish, the setting of many of her best stories. C's husband died in 1882, and she then returned to her mother's home in St. Louis to begin a new life as a writer.

Despite its pedestrian style, C.'s first novel, *At Fault* (1890), is notable for antiromantic characters and an absence of moralizing. The first American novel to treat divorce amorally, it tells of a young widow's attempts to apply the morality she has been taught to life itself. When she learns that her suitor had divorced a weak, alcoholic wife in the past, she insists that he return to mend the damage he had done. The subsequent remarriage proves destructive to everyone involved, ultimately leading to the wife's death. Our heroine must admit that it was she who was "at fault," learning that "there is rottenness and evil in the world, masquerading as right and morality."

Allowing her characters to live "in the world" produced the bold realism of the short stories collected in Chopin's next two books, *Bayou Folk* (1894) and *A Night in Acadie* (1897). These stories, many of them published earlier in magazines, established her reputation as a local colorist because of her vivid recreations of the lives and language of Creoles and Acadians in Louisiana. Both collections further explore the theme of nature versus civilization, and they also show an increasing concern with women's quest for self-fulfillment.

C.'s exploration of this women's quest began with her first published stories. In "Wiser Than a God" Paula Van Stolz chooses a career over a marriage which could have provided love and economic security, but then succeeds both in becoming a famous pianist and in gaining the love of her music professor.

C.'s women, however, are not biologically free. In her highly praised masterpiece, "Desiree's Baby," C. tells of a woman who drowns herself and her baby when her husband inaccurately suspects her of having the black blood that manifested itself in their child.

Biology is also the key to understanding Edna's fate in *The Awakening* (1899). Edna, strongest and most controversial of C.'s heroines, has immersed herself in an empty marriage and a confusing maternity. Awakening to a sense of herself through her exposure to the more natural Creole society and through the attentions of Robert LeBrun, she chooses to express herself artistically and sensually despite social and personal repercussions. But although Edna walks away from her marriage and from her children, she cannot escape the biological reality of motherhood. Neither can she achieve her artistic goals, because the artist in C.'s novel can only gain her career at the expense of both her social and her sensual self. Edna chooses to save the self she has discovered, but she must do so at the cost of the life she owes her children. As she walks to the beach to join herself with the eternal flux of Nature symbolized by the sea, "the children appeared before her like antagonists who had overcome her; who had overpowered and sought to drag her into the soul's slavery for the rest of her days. But she knew a way to elude them." The hostile reception of this novel seems to have silenced its author, who thereafter wrote only ten more stories, mostly for young people.

C.'s superb psychological insight, especially into the lives of her women, her vivid descriptions of Creole and Acadian life, and her deepfelt concern with human relationships and social institutions will preserve her reputation long after the initial excitement of her rediscovery by contemporary critics has passed.

WORKS: *At Fault* (1890). *Bayou Folk* (1894). *A Night in Acadie* (1897). *The Awakening* (1899). *The Complete Works of Kate Chopin* (Ed. P. Seyersted, 2 vols, 1969).

BIBLIOGRAPHY: Leary, L., *Southern Excursions: Essays on Mark Twain and Others* (1971). Seyersted, P., *Kate Chopin: A Critical Biography* (1969). Springer, M., *Edith Wharton and Kate Chopin: A Reference Guide* (1976).

For articles in reference works, see: *DAB. NAW* (article by S. Nissenbaum). *NCAB.*

Other references: *ALR 8* (1975). *AQ* 25 (1973). *BB* 32 (1975). *DAI* 36 (1975). *Kate Chopin Newsletter. LaS* 14 (1975). *MarkhamR* 3 (1968). *SoR* 11 (1975).

THELMA J. SHINN

Eleanor Clark

B. 6 July 1913, Los Angeles, California
D. of Frederick Huntington and Eleanor Phelps Clark; m. Robert Penn
   Warren, 1952

Although born in California, C. grew up in Roxbury, Connecticut, and describes herself as an "unregenerate Yankee." She attended a one-room country school in Roxbury, convent schools in Europe, and then Rosemary Hall. After her graduation from Vassar in 1934, she wrote essays and reviews for a number of periodicals including the *Partisan Review*, the *Kenyon Review*, the *New Republic*, and the *Nation*. Her writing has continued to show the control and conciseness which the essay demands. From 1936 to 1939, C. was a member of the editorial staff of W. W. Norton; in 1937, she edited with Horace Gregory a collection of works by young writers called *New Letters in America*. It included her first published short story.

After the publication of her first novel, *The Bitter Box* (1946), C. received grants from the Guggenheim Foundation and an award from the National Institute of Arts and Letters. *The Bitter Box*, a heavily symbolic novel, deals with the acceptance of life as it is and the possibility of redemption through love and suffering. C. carefully manipulates point of view, balancing surrealism and stream of consciousness with a commentary by an objective narrator who is more interested in ideas than events.

In 1952, C. finished the first of her unusual "travel" books produced during long periods abroad, *Rome and a Villa*. Although it is concerned with setting, the book's effect is meditative rather than descriptive. It reveals a keen awareness of atmosphere and the passing of time. C.'s observations are not limited to place but encompass the political, literary, and personal as well. Katherine Anne Porter has said that *Rome and a Villa* is "autobiographical in the best sense" because it reflects the impact of the outer world upon the inner.

For her next book, *The Oysters of Locmariaquer* (1964), C. was awarded the National Book Award for nonfiction. *Oysters*, too, is a book about a place, and it too belongs to a unique genre. It combines the techniques of the essay and the novel to portray life in a little town on the northwest coast of France which nurtures and produces most of the world's oysters.

Eyes, Etc. A Memoir (1977), like so much that C. has written, belongs in a class of its own. It is a moving but never sentimental account of a brief period in her life, shortly after she learned that she was rapidly going blind. *Eyes* tells of the author's angry and always realistic response to "the event," her "affliction." But the book is also an opinionated and wry commentary on contemporary life, especially on our melodramatic and simplistic methods of coping with frustration and disaster. Against this background are woven the events of the *Iliad* and the *Odyssey*. C. constantly contrasts Homer's tough-minded portrayal of suffering and heroism with feeble modern attempts to cope with life. The book contains the familiar themes of past and present, renewal, suffering, and survival. Her style is even more cryptic than usual, due, perhaps, to the circumstances under which she now writes.

WORKS: *New Letters in America* (edited by Clark, with H. Gregory, 1937). *Dark Wedding* by Ramón José Sender (translated by Clark, 1943). *The Bitter Box* (1946). *Rome and a Villa* (1952). *Song of Roland* (adaptation by Clark, 1960). *The Oysters of Locmariaquer* (1964). *Baldur's Gate* (1970). *Dr. Heart: A Novella, and Other Stories* (1974). *Eyes, Etc.: A Memoir* (1977).

BIBLIOGRAPHY: *CW* (13 June 1952). *Ms.* (Nov. 1977). *The Nation* (27 April 1946). *NYRB* (30 July 1964). *SatR* (29 Oct. 1977).

JUDITH P. JONES

Elizabeth Cochrane

B. 5 May 1865, Cochran's Mills, Pennsylvania; d. 27 Jan. 1922, New York City
Wrote under: Nellie Bly
D. of Michael and Mary Jane Cochran; m. Robert L. Seaman, 1895

C. spent her youth in a small milltown; her education, except for one year in a local boarding school, was directed by her father, a lawyer and mill owner. After his death, C. moved to Pittsburgh with her mother and sought work for their support. She worked for the Pittsburgh *Dispatch* before moving to New York at twenty where she won a job with Joseph Pulitzer's New York *World*. She worked there until 1895. C.'s husband was an industrialist and a New York socialite. After his death in 1910, she controlled his failing business interests through 1919, and then, returning to journalism, she worked on the New York *Journal* until her death in 1922.

Ten Days in a Mad-house (1887) contains stories written for the *World*, an article about Blackwell's Island Insane Asylum, sketches on servant girls' experiences at employment agencies, and a piece on shop girls working in a paper box factory.

The story of Blackwell's Island, pronounced by the *World* to be "an immense sensation everywhere," established C. as a journalist in New York. She pretended insanity in order to "chronicle" the "simple tale of life in an asylum." She illustrates conditions and treatment of patients by describing her own experiences and the experiences of women she met. Her narrative, written in unadorned prose, is a dramatic and realistic account. Although this and other stories appeared under sensational head-lines—"Behind Asylum Bars" or "Nellie Bly as a White Slave"—her ex-posé journalism, in both content and style, is an early manifestation of the Progressive era's muckraking journalism.

Six Months in Mexico (1888), C.'s most thoughtful and stylistically pleasing (although often repetitive) book, is an examination of national character and an exposé of corruption and exploitative social conditions. C. went to Mexico in late 1886, at a time when few other American journalists were providing the public with first-hand information about their neighboring country. While the book indicates C.'s sensitivity to unjust social conditions, especially for women and the native Indian population, and provides a record of the responses of an American middle-class woman toward a culture both alien and "beautiful" to her, it is occasionally condescending in tone.

C. received the widest attention for a stunt: she broke the record of Jules Verne's fictional hero Phineas Fogg by traveling around the world in seventy-two days. Chronicling her journey in *Nellie Bly's Book: Around the World in Seventy-two Days* (1890), C. presents herself as a "free American girl" encountering diverse cultures, all exciting and ex-otic, but none measuring up to the American way of life. She provides colorful descriptions of peoples and customs while maintaining the sus-pense of her race against time. From San Francisco to New York, C. was met with extraordinary public adulation; her journey was celebrated in song and dance; toys, clothing, and games carried her name. C.'s story of "Nellie Bly's stunt" and the public response to it are material for a case study of the rapidly changing relationship between the press and the popular mind in the late 19th c.

WORKS: *Ten Days in a Mad-House; or, Nellie Bly's Experience on Blackwell's Island* (1887). *Six Months in Mexico* (1888). *Nellie Bly's Book: Around the World in Seventy-two Days* (1890).

BIBLIOGRAPHY: Marzolf, M., *Up From the Footnote: A History of Women Journalists* (1977). Noble, I., *Nellie Bly: First Woman Reporter* (1956). Quillan, J., *Nellie Bly* (produced 1946). Rittenhouse, M., *The Amazing Nellie Bly* (1956). Ross, I., *Ladies of the Press* (1936).

For articles in reference works, see *AW. NAW* (article by B. Weisberger). Other references: *The Pittsburgh Press* (8 Jan. 1967; 15 Jan. 1967).

JENNIFER L. TEBBE

Anna Botsford Comstock

B. 1 Sept. 1854, Otto, Cattaraugus County, New York; d. 24 Aug. 1930, Ithaca, New York
Wrote under: Anna Botsford Comstock, Marion Lee
D. of Marvin and Phebe Irish Botsford; m. John Henry Comstock, 1878

While attending Cornell University from 1874 to 1876 C. studied zoology under John Comstock, whom she later married. In 1885 she completed a B.S. degree in natural history and about that time began systematic study of wood engraving with John P. Davis of Cooper Union in New York City. Childless, C. had several overlapping careers which were unplanned, the apparent result of her patient application to tasks which provided income or personal potential. Both her autobiographical account, *The Comstocks of Cornell* (posthumously published in 1953), and reminiscences of Cornell students reflect a determinedly cheerful woman who once observed, "our usual way has ever been to pretend that we like whatever happens."

C. illustrated her husband's college textbooks, *An Introduction to Entomology* (1888) and *A Manual for the Study of Insects* (1894); in the latter she was also credited as "junior author." Her contribution was even more evident in *Insect Life* (1897), a simplified textbook on entomology.

In the 1890s C. became involved in the nature study movement, lecturing and writing leaflets on special natural history topics for classroom use. State support for the Cornell extension programs permitted her unprecedented appointment as assistant professor for the summer session in 1898. After protest by some trustees her rank was changed to lecturer, but in 1913 she was again named assistant professor, and in 1920, professor.

Like other leaders in the nature-study movement, C. insisted that her goal was not to teach scaled-down species hunting or microscopical work but rather "to give pupils an outlook regarding all forms of life and their relationship one to another." Nonetheless, her work is accurate, unlike much natural-history writing of the period, and C. often includes taxonomic terms. *How to Know the Butterflies* (1904), for example, begins with an elementary account of butterfly characteristics, outlines methods for collecting, and then discusses twelve families in detail. Such manuals as *How to Keep Bees* (1905), *The Pet Book* (1914), and *Trees at Leisure* (1916) contain anecdotal and literary materials as well as practical advice.

Much of C.'s own energy was channeled into popular lectures and essays which are romantic without being sentimental and suggest her belief in moral education. *Ways of the Six-footed* (1903) contains ten stories illustrating the social organization of insects, their communication by sound, their use of mimicry as a defense strategy, and other adaptive features. The chapter on ants, bees, and wasps is entitled "The Perfect Socialism." C. did not belabor the analogy here nor ascribe human characteristics to the insects; she did, however, use human experience to describe animal behavior as an educational device.

Many of C.'s essays appeared in *The Chautauquan* and *Country Life in America*. She briefly edited *Boys and Girls* (1903–7), a nature-study magazine, before turning it over to her Cornell colleague Martha Van Rensselaer. For years she contributed to the educational *Nature Study Review* (1906–23), serving as its editor from 1917 until its merger with *Nature Magazine*. Typically, her contributions underscored the value of all life, the importance of understanding nature, and the interrelationship among creatures. Personal anecdote was a prominent feature.

C.'s single most important volume was a compendium of her earlier work consolidated into the 900-page *Handbook of Nature Study* (1911). Not discouraged by the skepticism of her husband and her coworker Liberty Hyde Bailey about the need for such a text, C. provided a teaching guide for elementary teachers dealing with animal life, plant life, and the "earth and sky." The *Handbook* outlined programs for nature study in the classroom and outside, provided review questions, and suggested additional references. Vindication of her initiative came in twenty-four editions and translation into eight languages of the *Handbook*. C.'s text became known as the "nature Bible" because of her sensitive counselling on such topics as children's attitude toward death when dealing with predatory behavior, and because of her concern that living creatures be returned to their natural habitat after study.

Only once did C. attempt to write fiction. *Confessions to a Heathen Idol* (1906), written under the pseudonym Marion Lee, is a romantic fantasy without any reference to C.'s daily work of science.

In 1923 the League of Women Voters named C. one of the twelve greatest women in the United States. Popular yet scholarly in her science writing, she was a key figure in the nature-study movement, and a moving force on the Cornell campus.

WORKS: *Ways of the Six-footed* (1903). *How to Know the Butterflies* (with J. H. Comstock, 1904). *How to Keep Bees* (1905). *Confessions to a Heathen Idol* (1906). *Handbook of Nature Study* (1911). *The Pet Book* (1914). *Trees at Leisure* (1916). *Nature Notebook Series* (1920). *The Comstocks of Cornell* (Eds. G. W. Herriar and R. G. Smith, 1953).

The papers of Anna Botsford Comstock are at the Cornell Collection of Regional History and University Archives, Cornell University.

BIBLIOGRAPHY: For articles in reference works, see: *NAW* (article by K. Jacklin). *NCAB*.

Other references: *Annual Review of Entomology* 21 (1975). *ScM* 62 (1946).
SALLY GREGORY KOHLSTEDT

Fannie Cook

B. 4 Oct. 1893, St. Charles, Missouri; d. 25 Aug. 1949, St. Louis, Missouri
D. of Julius and Jennie Frank; m. Jerome E. Cook, 1915

C. grew up and attended school in St. Louis. She received her B.A. from the University of Missouri in 1914, and her M.A. from Washington University in 1916. Though C. published widely and was a painter of some distinction, she is largely remembered for her novel, *Mrs. Palmer's Honey* (1946), which was judged the most important literary contribution "to the importance of the Negro's place in American life." C. was dedicated to defining and improving the Negro's "place" and that of

COOK, FANNIE □ 123

other oppressed groups. She was a member of the Mayor's Committee on Race Relations, an adviser to the National Association for the Advancement of Colored People, and the 1940 chairperson of the Missouri Committee for Rehabilitation of Sharecroppers.

In 1935, C. won first prize in a *Reader's Digest* contest for new writers. Her short works published between 1940 and 1946 reflect her conviction that unions are the only solution for the ailments of struggling people. In "Killer's Knife Ain't Holy," Ambor, the preacher-protagonist, is asked to choose between the church and the union. He chooses both, aiming to serve his people in every way possible. Whereas he had once preached that black men would achieve their kingdom after death, now that he has joined the union and understood what unionization made possible, he preaches the possibility of kingdom on earth. One must *"organize fer Jesus."* C.'s theme in all her novels is basically the same: the coming of age of the individual and, often by extension, of the group to which he or she belongs. *Boot-Heel Doctor* (1941) and *Mrs. Palmer's Honey* best illustrate this point.

The latter novel was criticized for its labor propaganda. One reviewer for *The New Yorker* said that what started as a "quietly perceptive study of a very lovable Negro girl" abruptly shifts to "a sort of labor tract with characters are not so important as people as they are as espousers of the cause for democracy, unionization, justice for all."

Though the master-servant relationship is clearly upheld and therefore seemingly sanctioned in C.'s works, it should be pointed out that the black maids, or their male counterparts working in the factories and the fields, somehow appear to be more capable than their white "charges." They are always "looking after" their white employers as though they needed "tending to" as much as the cooking and cleaning. In fact, it is to C.'s credit that she endows her maids, whether they are serving blacks or whites, with so much dignity that, like them, we too pity those who must be cared for and we become convinced that the white world would be in dire straits without the input of blacks.

C. always renders reality as she sees it, but always manages to suggest that reality can be changed, that it must be improved upon. She writes simply, lovingly, using regional dialects and regional prejudices and shortcomings to convey verisimilitude. Her main characters are "big people spiritually who are lesser people in society." They are always neighborly, always engaging, gently nudging themselves, even when not fully developed as characters, into the reader's life for keeps.

WORKS: *The Hill Grows Steeper* (1938). *Boot-Heel Doctor* (1941). *Mrs.*

Palmer's Honey (1946). *Storm Against the Wall* (1948). *The Long Bridge* (1949).

BIBLIOGRAPHY: For articles in reference works, see: *American Novelists of Today*, Ed. H. R. Warfel (1951). *CB* (1946; 1949).
    Other references: *NYT* (26 Aug. 1949). *PW* (23 Feb. 1946; 17 Sept. 1949). *WLB* (10 Oct. 1949).

LILLIE HOWARD

Rose Terry Cooke

B. 17 Feb. 1827, Hartford, Connecticut; d. 18 July 1892, Pittsfield, Massachusetts
Wrote under: Rose Terry Cooke, Rose Terry
D. of Henry Wadsworth and Anne Wright Hurlburt Terry; m. Rollin H. Cooke, 1873

Born into an old New England family, C. at sixteen graduated from the Hartford Female Seminary. Following her conversion that year, she became a lifelong member of the Congregational church. To support herself, she taught school. In 1848, a legacy gave C. leisure to write. Although she considered herself primarily a poet, she is remembered mainly as a local colorist and short-story writer.

C.'s published works include two volumes of poetry, a novel, children's stories, religious sketches, and more than a hundred short stories. Her verse now seems conventional and spiritless. Only her short stories endure.

For almost forty years C.'s fiction appeared in prominent magazines, where it had a decisive impact on the development of regional or local-color writing. Although the local colorists she influenced soon overshadowed her, Van Wyck Brooks felt that some of C.'s tales were never surpassed by later authors.

Rich in realistic detail and shrewd social observation, C.'s stories re-create rural New England before and during the 19th-c. migration to cities and prairies. C. knew the regional mind as it was shaped by Calvinism and hard work, bleak landscapes, and scanty resources. Although she could treat her characters with broad Yankee humor, she took their "controversies with Providence" seriously and reviewed their eccentric behavior with the sympathetic but critical eye of the insider.

Domestic scenes, rendered lovingly, dominate C.'s fiction. Critical of women's rights activists, she often reminds readers that a woman's place is in her home, under the "headship" of a good husband. However, in "Mrs. Flint's Married Experience," a miserly deacon works his wife nearly to death, grudging her even food and clothing; C.'s repudiation of the patriarchy which supports him is compelling. In "How Celia Changed Her Mind" and "Polly Mariner, Tailoress," C. characterizes outspoken and self-determined spinsters with evident sympathy. Although many of C.'s stories are too didactic, the best probe the Puritan psyche with considerable sophistication.

C.'s respect for Calvinism's moral seriousness is reflected in her careful analysis of character and motivation. Nevertheless, she criticizes the Puritan tradition's legalism and emotional repression and argues that its "sour sublimity" should be sweetened with mercy and human love, the Christian nurture of social bonds.

C.'s importance as an innovator is increasingly clear. A major influence on local-color writing, C. turned the dialect story to serious themes and gained it a place in respectable literary magaznies. Her portrayal of spinsters, deacons, handymen, and farm women opened new possibilities for the representation of everyday life. C. smoothed the transition from the sentimental romances of the 1850s to the realism of William Dean Howells—a role evidenced by C.'s style, which swings from florid romantic rhetoric to vernacular dialect and concrete historical detail. Although her tales are loosely structured and occasionally plotless, their focus on character is a hallmark of the modern short story. Read primarily for her impact on later writers, and for her depiction of a lost time and place, C. offers a significant handful of stories valuable in their own right.

WORKS: Poems (1861). Groton Massacre Centennial Poem (1881). Somebody's Neighbors (1881). A Lay Preacher (1884). Root-Bound, and Other Sketches (1885). No (1886). The Sphinx's Children (1886). The Deacon's Week (1887). The Deacon's Week. And What Deacon Baxter Said (1887). Happy Dodd (1887). The Old Garden (1888). Poems (1888). Steadfast, the Story of a Saint and a Sinner (1889). Polly and Dolly, and Other Stories (1890). Huckleberries Gathered from New England Hills (1891). Little Foxes (1904).

BIBLIOGRAPHY: Brooks, V. W., New England: Indian Summer (1940). Downey, J., "A Biographical and Critical Study of Rose Terry Cooke" (Ph.D. diss., Univ. of Ottawa, 1956). Jobes, K. T., "The Resolution of Solitude: A Study of Four Writers of the New England Decline" (Ph.D. diss., Yale Univ.,

1961). Martin, J., *Harvests of Change: American Literature 1865–1914* (1967). Patee, F. L., *The Development of the American Short Story* (1923). Spofford, H. P., *A Little Book of Friends* (1916). Toth, S. A., "More Than Local Color: A Reappraisal of Rose Terry Cooke, Mary Wilkins Freeman, and Alice Brown" (Ph.D. diss., Univ. of Minnesota, 1969).

Other references: *BB* 21 (1955). *KCN* 2 (1976). *WS* 1 (1972).

SARAH WAY SHERMAN

Ina Donna Coolbrith

B. 10 March 1842, Nauvoo, Illinois; d. 29 Feb. 1928, San Francisco, California
Given name: Josephine D. Smith
D. of Don Carlos and Agnes Coolbrith Smith; m. Robert B. Carsley, 1859

C. was four months old when her father died and with his death, C.'s mother moved the family to St. Louis, Missouri, where she married printer William Pickett. In 1849, two years after the gold rush began, Pickett took his wife and children to California. They settled in Los Angeles where C. spent her early teens and twenties. At eleven, she began writing verses and publishing in the local paper, the Los Angeles *Star. The California Home Journal* also printed many of her early poems.

After a disappointing marriage to Robert Carsley, a partner in the Salamander Iron Works, C. divorced her husband and moved to San Francisco. Here she broke all associations with her unpleasant past and adopted her pseudonym, Ina Donna Coolbrith. Soon her writings attained a local reputation, and when, in 1868, Bret Harte founded the *Overland Monthly*, he named her as one of the co-editors. Primarily a poet, she did write reviews on occasion. C. wrote for the *Californian, Harper's Weekly, Century, Scribner's* and other magazines and became a close associate and friend of Mark Twain, Ambrose Bierce, and Joaquin Miller. With George Stoddard and Bret Harte, she was said to complete the "Golden Gate Trinity" of authors. In 1915, C. was named poet laureate of California by a World Congress of Authors.

Despite C.'s rich personal history, she wrote little of her poetry from autobiographical or topical experiences. An early poem about the ambush of Sheriff Barton, written when she was sixteen and published in the Los Angeles *Star*, is a rare exception to her later sentimental lyrics. Of C.'s mature work, done primarily for the *Overland Monthly* and her books, only four poems refer to her personal past: "Retrospect," "Fragment of an Unfinished Poem," "Unrest," and "A Mother's Grief."

"Fragment of an Unfinished Poem" (*Poetry of the Pacific*, 1867) illustrates the unfortunately brief retrospective period when C. molded a sensuous perception of her disillusioning past: "The soft star closes to the golden days/ I dreamed away, in that far, tropic clime,/ Wherein Love's blossom budded, bloomed and died." In "Unrest" C.'s topic is her failed marriage; the poet "cannot sleep" for the "mourning memory/ Her dream domains." She searches for hopes that have perished on "ruined footpaths" and "by the grave of Love" kneels and "sheds no tear." No doubt C. could make such resolves by forging a new identity in San Francisco where she kept her past a secret, even from close friends. Yet a poem like "A Mother's Grief" (*Outcroppings*, 1866), which mourns the loss of an infant, perhaps Robert Carsley's child, hint that the wounds were permanent.

Because of her reticence on subjects of her past, C.'s "Blossom Time," her second published poem in the *Overland Monthly*, is viewed as typical of the majority of her work in theme and style. It celebrates the coming of spring. What was a personal passion in the autobiographical poems becomes a wistful sadness mixed with love of nature.

When evaluating the writing of C., one must remember the established literary tastes that influenced the poetry of the period and the attitudes that conditioned women writers. There is a strength in C.'s imagery which takes her beyond the sentimental lyricists of her day. As G. Stoddard said of her work: "She has no superior among the female poets of her own land, and scarcely an equal. Her poems are singularly sympathetic; I know of none more palpably spontaneous. The minor key predominates; but, there are a few lark-like carols suffused with the 'unpremeditated art' of heavenly inspiration."

WORKS: *A Perfect Day, and Other Poems* (1881). *The Singer by the Sea* (1894). *Songs from the Golden Gate* (1896).

BIBLIOGRAPHY: Rhodehamel, J., and R. Wood, *Ina Coolbrith, Librarian and Laureate of California* (1973). Walker, F., *San Francisco's Literary Frontier* (1939). Walker, F., *A Literary History of Southern California* (1950).

Other references: *Pacific Historian*, 17 (1973). *Westward* Vol. 1, No. 4 (1928).

SHELLEY ARMITAGE

Anna Julia Haywood Cooper

B. 10 Aug. 1858, Raleigh, North Carolina; d. 27 Feb. 1964, Washington, D.C.
D. of George Washington and Hanna Stanley Haywood; m. George A. C.
  Cooper, 1877

Born a slave in Wake County, North Carolina, C. began her remarkable career at the age of six when she entered St. Augustine's Normal and Collegiate Institute (an Episcopalian school) in Raleigh. There she became a "Pupil Teacher" when only nine years old. From that time until her death at age 105, C. dedicated her life to teaching. The education of others and herself defined the pattern of C.'s career. In 1881, C. enrolled at Oberlin College in Ohio, where she received both a B.A. (1884) and an M.A. (1887). During her matriculation, she continued to teach, holding a position at the college preparatory, Oberlin Academy. In 1884, she returned to the South and to her alma mater, St. Augustine's, as an instructor of Latin, Greek, and mathematics. St. Augustine's became the springboard for C.'s career as a writer.

From 1901 to 1906, C. was principal of the "M" Street (later Dunbar) High School in Washington, D.C. She received a doctorate from the Sorbonne University in Paris in 1925, at a time when few women, especially black women, held a doctorate. C. was sixty-seven. Two books in French are the result of her graduate research at the Sorbonne.

Her first book, *A Voice from the South by a Black Woman of the South* (1892), is a collection of essays, treatises, and reflections, based upon keen feminist insights and heightened racial awareness, which resulted from C.'s own experiences. Her literary reputation rests primarily upon this pioneering volume.

The preface, "Our Raison d'Etre," announces that C. has raised her voice as a black woman who "can more sensibly realize and more accurately tell the weight and the fret" of black life in the South. Her objective is to present the woman's point of view, the "other side" by one who "lives there," and who is "sensitive . . . to social atmospheric conditions." C.'s emphasis emerges out of an awareness that just as whites "were not to blame if they cannot *quite* put themselves in the dark man's place, neither should the dark man be wholly expected fully and adequately to reproduce the exact Voice of the Black Woman." Her vision is clear, intelligent, and forceful.

C.'s essays are not merely impassioned pleas by a woman for the equitable treatment of her race. Thoughtful and scholarly, her work evidences a comprehensive understanding of the position of women in America. Written in an energetic yet graceful prose, her essays are as engaging as they are persuasive. They constitute a significant contribution to the cultural and intellectual history of women and blacks in the U.S. It is fortunate that her collection, reprinted in 1969, is available to contemporary readers.

C. had a lengthy career that she depicted as a conscious attempt to rectify the "one muffled strain in the Silent South," the voice of blacks. She believed that the black woman, in particular, had been "mute." C.'s life and work provided a voice for the "hitherto voiceless black woman of America."

WORKS: *A Voice from the South by a Black Woman of the South* (1892). *L'Attitude de la France à l'égard de l'esclavage pendant la révolution* (1925). *Le Pèlerinage de Charlemagne: Voyage à Jérusalem et à Constantinople* (1925). *Legislative Measures Concerning Slavery in the United States* (1942). *Equality of Races and the Democratic Movement* (1945). *The Life and Writings of the Grimké Family* (1951). *The Third Step* (n.d.).

The papers of Anna Julia Cooper are at the Moorland–Spingarn Research Center, Howard University.

BIBLIOGRAPHY: Bogin, R., and B. J. Lowenberg, *Black Women in Nineteenth-Century American Life* (1976). Harley, S., in *The Afro-American Woman: Struggles and Images*, Eds. S. Harley and R. Terborg-Penn (1978). Lerner, G., ed., *Black Women in White America: A Documentary History* (1972). Majors, M. A., *Noted Negro Women: Their Triumphs and Activities* (1893).

For articles in reference works, see: *Afro-American Encyclopedia*, Ed. J. T. Haley (1976).

Other references: *Baltimore Afro-American* (14 March 1964). *The Parent-Teacher Journal* (May 1930).

THADIOUS M. DAVIS

Adelaide Crapsey

B. 9 Sept. 1878, Brooklyn, New York; d. 8 Oct. 1914, Rochester, New York
D. of Algernon Sidney and Adelaide Trowbridge Crapsey

C. was taken to Rochester in 1879 when her father became rector of St. Andrew's Church. In 1893 C. and her sister Emily were sent to Kemper Hall, an Episcopal boarding school in Kenosha, Wisconsin. After graduation from Vassar in 1901, C. spent one year at home in Rochester and then returned to Kemper Hall to teach history and literature. Around 1903 C. first began to suffer from the fatigue that was a symptom of her fatal disease. From 1906 to 1908 she served as instructor of literature and history at a preparatory school in Stamford, Connecticut. Failing health caused C. to give up teaching, however, and in December 1908 she went to Europe, living in Rome, London, and Kent. In London C. continued her work on the "application of phonetics to metrical problems." In 1911 C. returned to America and began work immediately as an instructor in poetics at Smith College. From September 1913 to August 1914 C. underwent treatment for her tuberculosis in a private nursing home at Saranac Lake, New York. After returning to her family's home in Rochester she suddenly grew worse and died.

C. had long been experimenting with poetic forms. She filled her commonplace book with poems by W. S. Landor, T. L. Beddoes, Oscar Wilde, and Lionel Johnson. Many of her poems show the influence of these and earlier poets, even as they exhibit her own reticence, humor, and interest in experiments in sound and form. Although her consciousness of contemporary poetic and artistic developments is important, it is also essential to recognize the role of C.'s own informed craftsmanship and studies in metrics in shaping her poetry, which shows affinities with the Georgian and Imagist movements.

The cinquain, a five-line poetic form invented and named by C., is "built on stresses, one for the first line, two for the second, three for the third, four for the fourth, with a drop back to one for the fifth line. In the poet's opinion this made the most condensed metrical form in English that would hold together as a complete unit." Although the cinquain is built of stresses rather than syllables, it resembles such Japanese forms as the *haiku* and *tanka* in its brevity and in its juxtaposition of images. C.'s finest cinquains, including "Amaze," "Niagara," "Roma Aeterna," and "Snow," involve a superposition of ideas or intersection between the eternal and the momentary, the motionless and the moving. These qualities, and the distinctive compression of C.'s best work, have led Louis Untermeyer to describe C. as an "unconscious Imagist" and Yvor Winters to state that C. "achieves more effectively than did most of the Imagists the aims of Imagism."

C.'s unfinished work on prosody, on which she worked so hard while in England and at Smith, was published after her death with a preface by Esther Lowenthal. *A Study in English Metrics* (1918) divides English poets into three classes according to the proportions of monosyllabic, dissyllabic, and polysyllabic words used.

The reticence and firm control characteristic of her finest poems marked C.'s own conduct. Her letters to her family and friends provide a rare opportunity to study a person always private and elusive, although never reclusive or withdrawn until her health had been seriously impaired. Her letters from Saranac Lake show her fighting bravely and humorously what she herself knew to be a losing battle; "vital, vivid, and detailed," they "seldom fail to convey an extremely alert intelligence and a sensitivity to what she perceived was going on in the intellectual world."

WORKS: *Verse* (1915). *A Study in English Metrics* (1918). *The Complete Poems and Collected Letters of Adelaide Crapsey* (Ed. S. S. Smith, 1977).

BIBLIOGRAPHY: Bragdon, C., *Merely Players* (1929). Bragdon, C., *More Lives Than One* (1938). Crapsey, A. S., *The Last of the Heretics* (1924). O'Connor, M. E., "Adelaide Crapsey: A Biographical Study" (M.A. thesis, Notre Dame Univ., 1931). Osborn, M. E., *Adelaide Crapsey* (1933). Smith, S. S., *The Complete Poems and Collected Letters of Adelaide Crapsey* (1977). Winters, Y., *Forms of Discovery* (1967). Winters, Y., *In Defense of Reason* (1947).

Other references: *Adam: International Review* (1970). *TLS* (5 May 1978). *Univ. of Osaka College of Commerce Festschrift* (n.d.). *Vassar Miscellany* (1915).

SUSAN SUTTON SMITH

Hannah Mather Crocker

B. 27 June 1752, Boston, Massachusetts; d. 11 July 1829, Roxbury,
    Massachusetts
Wrote under: A Lady of Boston
D. of Samuel and Hannah Hutchinson Mather; m. Joseph Crocker, 1779

With Cotton and Increase Mather her great-grandfather and grandfather, C. has claims to a particular sort of American blue blood. Her husband was a captain in the Continental army and a Harvard graduate. It was not until after her children were grown that C. turned to writing and more public concerns. "When child-rearing duties are past," she said, "this is a fully ripe season" for older women to deliver their "well-digested thoughts for the improvement of the rising generation." C.'s initial publication, *A Series of Letters on Free Masonry* (1815), was written to support her old friends, the Society of Free Masons, when they came under attack in 1810 for carousing in Boston lodges. In the year before her marriage, C. had organized a number of her friends into a female Mason society. C. not only defended the Masons in her treatise, but took the revolutionary position of encouraging women to "promote science and literature" in formal societies, as more suitable to their dignity than those frivolous activities ordinarily thought appropriate for female leisure.

The next year, in *The School of Reform; or, The Seaman's Safe Pilot to the Cape of Good Hope* (1816), C. extends an enthusiastic but occasionally graceless exhortation to seamen against drinking. C.'s *Observations on the Real Rights of Women, with their appropriate duties, agreeable to Scripture, reason and common sense* was published by subscription in 1818. C. is clearly familiar with the foremost feminist thinking of her day and she dedicates her *Real Rights of Women* to Hannah More, an eminent English evangelical writer. C. even praises Mary Wollstonecraft as "a woman of great energy and a very independent mind," although she does "not coincide with her opinion respecting the total independence of the female sex."

Using Christian justice as her basis, C. uncompromisingly insists that men and women have equal powers and faculties. Women's minds are equal to the tasks of the statesman, lawyer, or minister, and only "local circumstances and domestic cares" have prevented them from being as productive as men. But C. makes concessions to what she considers social reality and political necessity: "For the interest of their country, or in the cause of humanity, we shall strictly adhere to the principle and the impropriety of females ever trespassing on masculine ground: as it is morally incorrect, and physically improper."

Women's roles lie in the training of men, and in the teaching of peace and virtue. They must be the psychological counselors who "convince by reason and persuasion," who are "calm and serene" under all crises, and who "soothe and alleviate the anxious cares of men." "Right" takes on the meaning of duty and obligation. "Every female" has the "right" to cover the faults of those around her with the "mantle of meek charity." Women have "rights" to be virtuous, loving, religious, and sympathetic, and thus support and improve human society.

Harmonious relations between the sexes are the basis not only of family life, but the greatness of the nation as well. C. maintains that it was the "mutual virtue, energy, and fortitude of the sexes" that accomplished the American Revolution, and insists that their proper union will preserve it.

The title *Observations on the Real Rights of Women* (1818) is a misnomer. It is, rather, a commonplace book generally imparting advice on the sensible and Christian conduct of life. As a consistent discussion of women's particular issues, it is certainly a failure.

C. was a natural patriot and reformer, and her sincere convictions of the efficacy of human will and energy in solving problems is in the best American tradition. It is her great energy and force of character that appears through the occasionally clumsy form of her writing to convince us of her essential genius as a person, if not as a writer.

WORKS: *A Series of Letters on Free Masonry* (1815). *The School of Reform; or, The Seaman's Safe Pilot to the Cape of Good Hope* (1816). *Observations on the Real Rights of Women, with their appropriate duties, agreeable to Scripture, reason and common sense* (1818).

The papers of Hannah Mather Crocker are at the Massachusetts Historic and Genealogical Society.

BIBLIOGRAPHY: Hill, B., ed., *The Diary of Isaiah Thomas, 1805–1828* (1909).

For articles in reference works, see: *DAB. NAW* (article by J. James).

Other references: *New York Historical Magazine* (March 1965; May 1865).

L. W. KOENGETER

Jane Cunningham Croly

B. *19 Dec. 1829, Market Harborough, Leicestershire, England; d. 23 Dec. 1901, New York City*
Wrote under: *Jennie June, Mrs. J. C. Croly*
D. *of Joseph and Jane Cunningham; m. David Goodman Croly, 1856*

C.'s father's Unitarianism was ill-received by his English neighbors and in 1841 the family moved to Poughkeepsie and then to Wappinger's Falls, New York. C. studied at home, taught district school, kept house for her older brother, a Congregationalist minister, and wrote a popular semimonthly newspaper for his congregation. In 1855, she moved to New York City and began her career as a professional journalist. Unable to win employment as a regular staff member of a city newspaper because she was a woman, C. was assigned to write a regular column on fashion for ladies. In 1857, she became one of the earliest syndicated woman columnists, and was carried in newspapers in New York, New Orleans, Richmond, Baltimore, and Louisville.

In 1856, C. married an Irish immigrant on the staff of the New York *Herald*. In 1859, he bought, edited, and published the Rockford *Daily News* in Illinois, where C.'s official duty was to write a column entitled "Gossip with and for Ladies." C.'s first child, Minnie, was born before the Crolys moved back to New York in 1860 to work on the *World*, where C. wrote the woman's column from 1862 to 1872. In addition to newspaper work, C. contributed to *Graham's Magazine, Frank Leslie's Weekly,* and *Demorest's Monthly Magazine,* coediting the latter for many years. She produced a popular cookbook, several sewing manuals, and three collections of her newspaper columns. She supported the family with her writing and by teaching journalism when her husband, due to illness, left newspaper work in 1875.

C. developed an interest in the woman's club movement of her day. She became an influential member of many clubs, including the Woman's Endowment Cattle Company, the Association for the Advancement of Women, the Women's Press Club of New York, the Association for the Advancement of Medical Education for Women, and, most important, a founder of the literary club, Sorosis. Later in life, C. edited clubwomen's magazines and wrote organizational histories.

C.'s collected articles, like *Jennie Juneiana* (1864), provide vignettes of the domestic world, some as harmless as descriptions of Christmas day and patchwork quilts, but others filled with anger at male arrogance and thoughtlessness. Husbands who opened their wives' mail, fussed about meals, and demanded pristine households when they themselves were shamefully careless, won her scorn. C. also found fault with women, describing them as "hidden under clouds of dyspepsia, nervousness, overeating, personal neglect, personal abuse, vanity, deceit, treachery, fibbing, equivocation, and a hundred other signs of equal magnitude." For all her criticism, however, C. felt women had a special potential to become loving, loyal, morally superior, sensitive, perfect beings.

C.'s observations enabled her to define the sources of women's short-comings. She considered education for girls in the ornamental arts to be useless, a restriction keeping them from the path of perfection. C. also faulted woman's behavior, clothing, and ambitions. Instead, she advocated devotion to home duties, declaring that they prepared women to extend their superior influence beyond family life to identify and rectify injustice. Use of domestic handbooks like her own would minimize household duties and allow women to enter the clubs where they would broaden their education, confidence, friendships, and abilities to analyze and solve social problems.

C.'s brand of women's rights, less shocking than the radical and militant woman suffrage movement, won greater numbers of supporters. The club magazines C. edited won adherents for her movement, and in speech as Sorosis' presiding officer, she alluded to the success of her writing and club activity: "We shall live . . . to see the Woman's Club the conservator of public morals, the uprooter of social evils, the defender of women against women as well as against men, the preserver of the sanctities of domestic life, the synonym of the brave, true, and noble in women."

C.'s *History of the Woman's Club Movement in America* (1898) is further testimony to the appeal of her analysis and solution to women's oppression in the nineteenth century. The work is a staggering 1190-page reference work, with entries describing one thousand clubs—a careful compendium of their programs, leaders, and histories, C.'s introduction is an ambitious and early work in women's history, looking back as far as 5th-c. monasticism for precedents to women's organizations. C.'s modesty, however, caused her to minimize her own contribution to the movement of women's club development.

SELECTED WORKS: *Jennie Juneiana: Talks on Women's Topics* (1864). *Jennie June's American Cookery Book* (1866). *For Better or Worse* (1875). *Knitting and Crochet* (1885). *Needle Work* (1885). *Sorosis: Its Origin and*

History (1886). *Thrown on Her Own Resources* (1891). *The History of the Woman's Club Movement in America* (1898). *Memories of Jane Cunningham Croly* (1904).

The papers of Jane Cunningham Croly are at the Arthur and Elizabeth B. Schlesinger Library, Radcliffe College; in the Sorosis Papers, Sophia Smith Collection, Smith College Library; and in the Caroline M. Severance Papers, Huntington Library, San Marino, California.

BIBLIOGRAPHY: Blair, Karen J., "The Clubwoman as Feminist: The Woman's Culture Club Movement in the U.S., 1868–1914" (Ph.D. diss., State Univ. of New York at Buffalo, 1976). Forcey, C., *The Crossroads of Liberalism* (1961). Wells, M., *Unity in Diversity: The History of the General Federation of Women's Clubs* (1953). Winant, M. D., *A Century of Sorosis, 1868–1968* (1968). Wingate, C. F., *Views and Interviews on Journalism* (1875). Wood, M. I., *The History of the General Federation of Women's Clubs* (1912).

For articles in reference works, see: *AW. DAB. Daughters of America*, P. A. Hanaford (1883). *NAW* (article by E. Schlesinger). *NCAB.*

Other references: *Demorest's Monthly Magazine* (Jan. 1871). *Journalism Quarterly* (Spring 1963). *New York History* (Oct. 1961). *NYT* (24 Dec. 1901). *Woman's Journal* (4 Jan. 1902; 11 Jan. 1902).

KAREN J. BLAIR

Maria Susanna Cummins

B. *9 April 1827, Salem, Massachusetts; d. 1 Oct. 1866, Dorchester, Massachusetts*
D. *of David and Mehitable Cave Cummins*

Both of C.'s parents were descendants of prominent New England families. The Cummins family (the name was originally spelled with a "g") can trace their roots to Isaac Cummings, a Scottish immigrant who settled in Ipswich shortly before 1638.

C.'s father, a man of cultivated taste, made certain that she received a classical education, and he encouraged his daughter's writing talents. After her father's death she lived quietly in Dorchester, devoting the rest of her life to her writing and to church work.

C.'s first novel, *The Lamplighter*, was published in Boston in 1854 and shortly afterward in London. It was the most talked about novel of the year and an immediate best seller. The average sale during the first two months after publication was five thousand copies a week; by the end of the first year it had sold seventy thousand. Her second novel, *Mabel Vaughan* (1857), was not so popular, but in 1858 both novels were selected for publication by the Leipzig-based Tauchnitz Library of British and American Authors, an indication of her international fame.

C.'s novels are filled with pious sentiments and moral formulae, typical of the genre, called "folk fiction" by some, which led to Hawthorne's comment in 1855 that "America is now wholly given over to a d——d mob of scribbling women. . . ." Specifically he asked, "What is the mystery of these innumerable editions of *The Lamplighter?*"

The success of *Lamplighter* is no mystery at all. Relying liberally on Dickens and the Brontë sisters, it tells the story of an abandoned and mistreated orphan, Gerty, befriended by a kindly old lamplighter (aptly named Trueman Flint) and then by a wealthy young blind woman, Emily Graham, who becomes her patron and teacher. The story recounts Gerty's transformation from a ragged, ignorant orphan into a self-reliant and virtuous young woman, "the image of female goodness and purity." By the novel's end Gerty has found her long-lost father (who turns out to be Emily Graham's stepbrother and former lover) and will marry her childhood sweetheart, now a successful businessman.

C.'s second novel, *Mabel Vaughan* (1857), features a heroine who is not a poor orphan waif but who is nevertheless the victim of a series of calamities. Once a pampered child of fashion, she finds herself left nearly penniless and charged with the care of two incorrigible nephews, a melancholic father, and an alcoholic brother. A great part of this novel is set in the West and the reader is introduced to some interesting pioneer characters as well as, in the city scenes, such stock characters as a dying orphan who exemplifies piety and submissiveness to God's will.

Both of these novels relied upon the best-selling formula of the sentimental-domestic novel for their appeal: the plots feature calamities, sudden reversals of fortune, long-lost relatives, and the reform of profligates; the central characters are young women who grow in strength and piety throughout the novel, enabling them to accomplish the gentle subjugation and reform of rogues, alcoholics, and conscienceless men.

El Fureidis (1860), C.'s third novel, is a story of Palestine and Syria, and her fourth, *Haunted Hearts* (1864), is a rather pedestrian sentimental tale. Neither of these approached *Lamplighter* in popular appeal.

WORKS: *The Lamplighter* (1854). *Mabel Vaughan* (1857). *El Fureidis* (1860). *Haunted Hearts* (1864).

BIBLIOGRAPHY: Hart, J. D., *The Popular Book* (1950). Koch, D. A., Introduction to *The Lamplighter* by M. S. Cummins (1968). Mott, F. L., *Golden Multitudes* (1947).

For articles in reference works, see: *AA. DAB. NAW* (article by O. E. Winslow).

ELAINE K. GINSBERG

Elizabeth Bacon Custer

B. 8 April 1842, Monroe, Michigan; d. 4 April 1933, New York City
Wrote under: Elizabeth B. Custer, Elizabeth Bacon Custer
D. of Daniel S. and Sophia Page Bacon; m. George Armstrong Custer, 1864

The only surviving child of a prominent Michigan judge, C. spent the five years between her mother's death in 1854 and her father's remarriage in boarding schools and with relatives. Returning to Monroe, C. became close to her stepmother, and graduated as valedictorian from Boyd's Seminary in 1862. The following winter C. met Captain George Armstrong Custer, then visiting Monroe on leave from Civil War duty. Overcoming parental opposition to C.'s involvement with a soldier, they courted by mail and married in 1864.

C. accompanied her husband to the Virginia front, where he became a major general. His postwar military career took C. to posts in Texas, Kansas, Kentucky, and Dakota Territory, where she learned of his fatal "last stand."

Although C.'s life extended fifty-seven years beyond her husband's, she kept her marriage vows, fulfilling what she believed were her "responsibilities" as "the widow of a national hero" by writing and lecturing.

C. wrote to perpetuate her husband's memory, scrupulously avoiding army political disputes by focusing on the domestic aspects of frontier cavalry life. Her first book, *Boots and Saddles* (1885), describes C.'s life in Dakota with General Custer from 1873 to 1876. C. emphasizes the closeness within and among army couples as both result of and defense against wilderness isolation. Although she tried to appear "plucky," C. expresses her overwhelming fear of Indians and often gives thanks that, as a woman, she was not required to be brave. Women were, however, required to wait; C. compellingly presents the shared anxiety of wives left at Fort Lincoln while husbands fought and died at Little Big Horn.

The enthusiastic reception of her first book led C. to write her reminiscences of earlier campaigns. In *Tenting on the Plains* (1887), C. describes her experiences following General Custer in Kansas and Texas from 1865 to 1867. Insects, illness, and scorpions dominate C.'s recollections of the march to Texas, and her Kansas memories include prairie fire, flood, and cholera. Racism pervades her accounts of blacks in Reconstruction Texas, Mexican mule drivers, and American Indians; class bias colors her portraits of those who attained officers' positions through war service rather than West Point. She alludes to postwar dissension in the ranks, but ends her book before the court-martial and suspension that interrupted her husband's career.

In *Following the Guidon* (1890), C. picks up the story when her husband returned to duty in Kansas in 1868 to join the campaign that culminated in the Battle of Washita. C. vividly recalls her fearful visits with captured Indians and tribal peace council delegates, while glorifying her husband's honest treatment of those he helped defeat. She also explains how constantly menacing rattlesnakes and Indians impair enjoyment of recreational hunting, riding, and horse and mule racing. Her posthumously published letters to husband and family reveal the pampered, pious, and principled aspects of her personality.

C.'s works provide important insights into one woman's attempt to redefine "lady" to fit the regimen of cavalry life. The closeness she depicts among army wives balances the traditional emphasis on military male bonding. While marred by prejudice, self-deprecation, and repetition, and intentionally incomplete by avoidance of controversy, C.'s writings are lively and lucid accounts of an unusual female life style.

WORKS: *Boots and Saddles, or Life in Dakota with General Custer* (1885). *Tenting on the Plains, or General Custer in Kansas and Texas* (1887). *Following the Guidon* (1890). *General Custer at the Battle of Little Big Horn, June 25, 1876* (1897). *The Boy General: Story of the Life of Major-General George A. Custer* (ed. by M. E. Burt, 1901). *The Custer Story: The Life and Intimate Letters of General George A. Custer and His Wife Elizabeth* (ed. M. Merington, 1950).

BIBLIOGRAPHY: Frost, L. A., *General Custer's Libbie* (1976). Stewart, J. R., introduction to E.B.C.'s *Boots and Saddles* (1961 ed.).

For articles in reference works, see: *American Women*, F. E. Willard and M. A. Livermore, eds. (1897).

Other references: *Collier's* (29 Jan. 1927). *Harper's* (Jan. 1891). *Nation* (30 April 1885). *NYT* (11 May 1888; 5 April 1933). *Psychohistory Review* (Fall 1980). *Winner's* (30 June 1935).

HELEN M. BANNAN

Faith Baldwin Cuthrell

B. 1 Oct. 1893, New Rochelle, New York; d. 18 March 1978, Norwalk,
  Connecticut
Wrote under: Faith Baldwin, Faith B. Cuthrell
D. of Stephen C. and Edith Hervey Finch Baldwin; m. Hugh H. Cuthrell, 1920

C. spent a fashionable girlhood in Manhattan and Brooklyn Heights.
She could read at three and at six was writing a drama, "The Deserted
Wife." She first published verse in her teens, prose in her twenties. C.'s
books, stories, poems, and articles appeared steadily from 1921 to 1977,
bringing her enormous popular and financial success. Many of her novels
were made into films. She was a founder and faculty member of the
Famous Writers School in Westport, Connecticut.

C.'s family history emerges in *The American Family* (1935), based on
her grandfather's diaries. Tobias Condit takes his wife to China in the
1860s to work as a missionary. Their son is sent to America to be educated, returning to China as a doctor. The sequel, *The Puritan Strain*
(1935), centers on Dr. Condit's daughter Elizabeth.

Courtship and marriage with their attendant joys and crises are C.'s
favored themes. Her first novel, *Mavis of Green Hill* (1921), shows the
maturing of a childlike bride, once an invalid, into a passionate wife.
Something Special (1940) explores the threats to a union of fourteen
years. Satisfactory resolutions are always brought about. C.'s novels are
usually told from the woman's viewpoint and reveal an intimate group
of women's problems.

Salient problems are the work women do and its relation to love
and marriage. C.'s heroines are secretaries, hostesses, nurses, actresses,
real estate brokers. They sell bonds and securities, design dresses, and run
beauty salons. *White Collar Girl* (1933) speaks of the wasted talent of
girls from affluent families who stay in their hometowns to wrap up
fudge in the Goodie Shoppe. *Private Duty* (1935) describes the working
girl's lot, the long days, the social life crammed into after-hours, the
little sleep. Rich girls might work for pleasure: "To be a working girl
and socially secure gave one a certain cachet. Working without the social
security made all the difference." *Career by Proxy* (1939) queries

whether a wealthy girl ought to work, thus taking employment from one who needs it. In *Hotel Hostess* (1938), an unsympathetic male supposes women usually work for frivolous reasons, or because they are "exhibitionists."

Conflict between career and marriage is a frequent theme. C.'s suitors and husbands generally regard the woman's work as unnecessary, or inimical to their mutual happiness. C. writes searchingly of the emotion on both sides. Most often C.'s heroines vainly strive to keep both marriage and career going, finally abandoning the career. In *Self-Made Woman* (1939) the clash is acute, the resolution uneasy. The wife capitulates to her dominant, sexually magnetic husband with "an awareness of defeat."

C.'s nonfiction, following her husband's death, includes the inspirational, semiautobiographical *Face Toward the Spring* (1956) and *Many Windows: Seasons of the Heart* (1958). From July 1958 to December 1965 she wrote the monthly feature "The Open Door" for *Woman's Day* magazine, which she expanded to produce *Testament of Trust* (1960), *Harvest of Hope* (1962), *Living by Faith* (1964), and *Evening Star* (1966). Reflective and discursive, these "almanac books" follow the year's cycle. C. shares her thoughts on the seasonal activities and weather, on gardens and rooms, on love, sorrow, books, travel, memories, prayer, and people.

Among C.'s last works are the six Little Oxford novels: *Any Village* (1971), *No Bed of Roses* (1973), *Time and the Hour* (1974), *New Girl in Town* (1975), *Thursday's Child* (1976), and *Adam's Eden* (1977). Seasons are breathtakingly beautiful in this suburban town, a "collage" of Westchester, Connecticut, and Long Island. Life is friendly and comfortable. A cast of characters reappears; new people pass through or settle, usually the heirs, relatives, or friends of the inhabitants. The principal action is the forming of a marriage, or an adjustment to marriage of a sympathetic young pair (maturer lovers marry or remarry offstage), who will in subsequent novels have already started a family and become part of the backdrop for the next set of lovers.

C. produced highly professional popular fiction, skillfully plotted, swift-paced, and entertaining. She captures the accents of daily speech, from plain talk to breezy dialogue. Her characters are middle- and upper-class Americans, living in Manhattan penthouses, luxurious country estates, and suburban communities. C. explores matters of concern to women— work, money, love, marriage, motherhood, divorce, dignified age. Her heroines are self-possessed women of mettle, some quietly independent, others spitfires. Individuals, couples, families, and neighbors resolve their difficulties. C.'s inspirational works praise the seasons, the pleasures of books, dwellings, and precious objects, and the importance of solitude and friendship alike.

WORKS: *Mavis of Green Hill* (1921). *Laurel of Stonystream* (1923). *Magic and Mary Rose* (1924). *Sign Posts* (1924). *Thresholds* (1925). *Those Difficult Years* (1925). *Three Women* (1926). *Departing Wings* (1927). *Rosalie's Career* (1928). *Betty* (1928). *Alimony* (1928). *The Incredible Year* (1929). *Garden Oats* (1929). *Broadway Interlude* (1929, with Achmed Adullah). *Judy: A Story of Divine Corners* (1930). *Make-Believe* (1930). *The Office Wife* (1930). *Babs: A Story of Divine Corners* (1931). *Skyscraper* (1931; film version, 1932). *Today's Virtue* (1931). *Mary Lou: A Story of Divine Corners* (1931). *Self-Made Woman* (1932). *Week-End Marriage* (1932, with Achmed Adullah; film version, 1933). *Girl on the Make* (1932). *District Nurse* (1932). *Myra: A Story of Divine Corners* (1932). *White Collar Girl* (1933). *Beauty* (1933; film version, 1933). *Love's a Puzzle* (1933). *Innocent Bystander* (1934). *Within a Year* (1934). *Wife vs. Secretary* (1934). *Honor Bound* (1934). *American Family* (1935). *The Puritan Strain* (1935). *The Moon's Our Home* (1936; film version, 1936). *Men are Such Fools!* (1936; film version, 1938). *Private Duty* (1936). *Girls of Divine Corners* (1936). *Omnibus: Alimony; The Office Wife; Skyscraper* (1936). *The Heart Has Wings* (1937). *That Man Is Mine* (1937). *Twenty-Four Hours a Day* (1937). *Manhattan Nights* (1937). *Hotel Hostess* (1938). *Enchanted Oasis* (1938). *Rich Girl, Poor Girl* (1938). *White Magic* (1939). *Station Wagon Set* (1939). *The High Road* (1939). *Career by Proxy* (1939). *Letty and the Law* (1940). *Medical Center* (1940). *Picnic Adventures* (1940). *Rehearsal for Love* (1940). *Something Special* (1940). *Temporary Address: Reno* (1941). *And New Stars Burn* (1941). *The Heart Remembers* (1941). *Blue Horizons* (1942). *Breath of Life* (1942). *Five Women in Three Novels* (1942). . . . *The Rest of My Life With You* (1942). *You Can't Escape* (1943). *Washington, USA* (1943). *Change of Heart* (1944). *He Married a Doctor* (1944). *Romance Book* (1944). *A Job for Jenny* (1945). *Second Romance Book* (1945). *Arizona Star* (1945). *No Private Heaven* (1946). *Woman on Her Way* (1946). *Give Love the Air* (1947). *Sleeping Beauty* (1947). *They Who Love* (1948). *Marry for Money* (1948). *The Golden Shoestring* (1949). *Look Out for Liza* (1950). *The Whole Armor* (1951). *The Juniper Tree* (1952). *Widow's Walk* (1954). *Face Toward the Spring* (1956). *Three Faces of Love* (1957). *Many Windows* (1958). *Blaze of Sunlight* (1959). *Testament of Trust* (1960). *Harvest of Hope* (1962). *The West Wind* (1962). *The Lonely Man* (1964). *Living by Faith* (1964). *There Is a Season* (1966). *Evening Star* (1966). *The Velvet Hammer* (1969). *Take What You Want* (1970). *Any Village* (1971). *One More Time* (1972). *No Bed of Roses* (1973). *Time and the Hour* (1974). *New Girl in Town* (1975). *Thursday's Child* (1976). *Adam's Eden* (1977).

BIBLIOGRAPHY: Cooper, P., *Faith Baldwin's American Family* (1938). Van Gelder, R., *Writers and Writing* (1946).

For articles in reference works, see: *CA* (1969). *20thCA*. *20th CAS*.

Other references: *CSMMag* (11 Jan. 1947). *Colliers* (27 May 1944). *Cosmopolitan* (Aug. 1959). *Good Housekeeping* (Oct. 1943). *NRTA Journal* (Sept.–Oct. 1975). *NY Post* (2 Sept. 1972). *NYT* (25 Oct. 1973; 20 March 1978). *Pictorial Review* (Dec. 1935). *SatEvePost* (14 March 1936). *SatRL* (11 April 1936; 29 April 1939). *Time* (8 July 1935). *Writer* (May 1940).

MARCELLE THIÉBAUX

Caroline Wells Healey Dall

B. 22 June 1822, Boston, Massachusetts; d. 17 Dec. 1912, Washington, D.C.
D. of Mark and Caroline Foster Healey; m. Charles Henry Appleton Dall, 1844

Daughter of a prosperous Boston merchant who had "desired a son" and was "determined I should supply the place of one," D. received a thorough education and was devoted to her father until her desire to spend her life in charitable and religious work conflicted with her father's desire that she pursue a literary career. Her marriage to Reverend Dall produced a son and a daughter but the union was not happy. In 1855 he went as a Unitarian missionary to India, where he remained, except for occasional visits, until his death in 1886.

D. helped Pauline Wright Davis organize the woman's rights convention in Boston in 1855, and she organized and delivered one of the principal addresses at the 1859 New England woman's rights convention, also in Boston. She was one of the founders of the American Social Science Association.

Essays and Sketches (1849) collects D.'s early essays on moral and religious subjects, which had been published in newspapers and periodicals since she was thirteen. In *The Liberty Bell* (1847), another collection of her writings, she holds, in contrast to her later writings and actions, that political activity for women is "utterly incompatible with the more previous and positive duties of the nursery and the fireside." A series of nine lectures, delivered between 1859 and 1862, was described in the New York *Evening Post* as "the most eloquent and forcible statement of the Woman's Question which has been made."

D. calls for the removal of educational and legal barriers so that each human being can fully develop, and insists on woman's right to work and her right to receive equal pay for equal work. D.'s convincing historical analysis, well supplied with examples, shows that women have "since the beginning of civilization" shared the hardest and most unwholesome work, that they have always been the worst paid, and that their efforts to find "new avenues of labor" (e.g., efforts to train women as watchmakers) have often been met "by the selfish opposition of man." She feels that such opposition will be overcome and that all the work woman asks for "will inevitably be given."

A consistent advocate of coeducation and higher education for women, D. responded to Dr. Edward H. Clarke's book *Sex in Education* (1873), in which he claimed that women's health could not withstand the strain of a college education. Her review affirms her belief that no "greater difference of capacity, whether physical or psychical, *will be* found between man and woman than *is* found between man and man," that a proper coeducational system will make possible the fullest development of both sexes, and that "whatever danger menaces the health of America, it cannot, thus far, have sprung from the overeducation of her women." She calls upon women, "contented in ignominious dependence, restless even to insanity from the need of healthy employment and the perversion of their instincts, and confessedly looking to marriage for salvation," to "make thorough preparation for trades or professions" and to abide by the consequences of their resolutions.

D. was, in later years, a prolific writer of obituary tributes, devotional pamphlets, genealogical studies, and quasihistorical works.

SELECTED WORKS: *Essays and Sketches* (1849). *What We Really Know about Shakespeare* (1855). *Woman's Right to Labor; or, Low Wages and Hard Work* (1860). *A Practical Illustration of "Woman's Right to Labor"; or, A Letter from Marie E. Zakrzewska* (edited by Dall, 1860). *Historical Pictures Retouched* (1860). *Woman's Rights under the Law* (1861). *The College, the Market, and the Court* (1867). *Patty Gray's Journey: From Boston to Baltimore* (1869). *Patty Gray's Journey: From Baltimore to Washington* (1870). *On the Way; or, Patty at Mount Vernon* (1870). *Sex and Education* (1874). *The Romance of the Association* (1875). *My First Holiday* (1881). *The Life of Dr. Anandabai Joshee* (1888). *Margaret and Her Friends* (1895). *Alongside* (1902).

BIBLIOGRAPHY: Buell, L., *Literary Transcendentalism* (1973). Riegel, R. E., *American Feminists* (1963).

For articles in reference works, see: *HWS. NAW* (article by S. Nissenbaum).

Other references: *HLB* 22 (Oct. 1974). *NEQ* (March 1969).

SUSAN SUTTON SMITH

Olive Tilford Dargan

B. *1869, Grayson County, Kentucky; d. 22 Jan. 1968, Asheville, North Carolina*
Wrote under: Fielding Burke, Olive Tilford Dargan
D. of Elisha Francis and Rebecca Day Tilford; m. Pegram Dargan

Raised in Kentucky and Missouri in an academic family, D. was educated at George Peabody College for Teachers in Nashville, and later at Radcliffe College, where she met her future husband, Pegram Dargan. She began her writing career as a poet and lyrical dramatist living in New York, but, following her husband's death by drowning in 1915, she returned to Kentucky and wrote about the southern mountain people. Her literary approach ranged from bemused local-color anecdotes written during the 1920s to angry Marxist novels written during the Depression. Throughout her long life, D. published social fiction under the pseudonym Fielding Burke while using her real name for poetry and local-color stories.

D.'s early lyrical dramas give some clues to the intensely political nature of her mature fiction. *The Mortal Gods* (1912), though archaic in form and remote in setting, is nevertheless a powerful study of the oppression of the working class in modern industrial society. In her collection of plays, *The Flutter of the Gold Leaf* (1922), D. explores conflicting emotional and intellectual loyalties, and the different impulses created by personal and public roles. The plays were not well received by critics.

D.'s more conventional poetry was treated admiringly. The sonnet collection, *The Cycle's Rim* (1916) was described by one reviewer as "in a class with Elizabeth Barrett Browning's *Sonnets from the Portuguese.*"

The extent of D.'s left-wing intellectual leanings becomes apparent in *Highland Annals* (1925), a collection of short stories about the poor-white inhabitants of the southern mountains. Although these sketches exhibit many of the traditional features of southern local-color writing—tall tales, extravagant humor, rhapsodic appreciation of nature, quaintness of language and custom—they also note the ominous threat of the exploitative cotton-mill and the vulnerability of the poor-white woman who suffers both for her class and for her sex.

A bloody strike among hitherto docile workers in a textile mill in Gastonia, North Carolina, in 1929 gave D. the ideal setting for her first novel. *Call Home the Heart* (1932) is about the predicament of Ishma, a southern poor white woman who is torn between her love for her husband, family, and mountain life, and an overwhelming desire to seek freedom from the obligations they heap upon her. But when Ishma deserts her family for an urban, industrial life with a lover, she only finds a new set of duties. She discovers the poor worker trapped by the cruel paternalism of the textile factories, and she slowly educates herself in the intricacies of Marxist socialism until she is ready to participate fully in strike organization. However, just when Ishma's intellectual principles appear to have triumphed, she flees back to her husband and family, driven by ancient prejudices against the black workers who embrace her, and drawn by her yearning for a husband's love and the tranquil beauty of the mountains. Many critics applauded what they called the novel's final "retreat into art" after Marxist and feminist "propaganda." However, D. leaves no doubt that Ishma's retreat, though passionate and consoling, is a failure of principle—a step backward from the new consciousness she seemed to be approaching. The novel implies that there can be no reconciliation of pleasure and principle, that one must always be subordinate to the other.

D. returned to the predicament of Ishma in her second proletarian novel, *A Stone Came Rolling* (1935). Here the heroine achieves the triumph of principle, but only at the cost of the death of her beloved husband. She returns to dedicate her energy to revolutionary activities with a new sense of the danger of a wasted life. Though D.'s novels show a clear Marxist emphasis, their power lies in their sensitivity to the circumstances of an intellectual and passionate woman who discovers that personal happiness is the price demanded by both the traditional feminine role and the revolutionary feminist one.

After the 1930s, D., like most other leftward-leaning American writers, retreated from extreme ideological concerns. She returned to anecdotal fiction of the mountain people in *From My Highest Hill* (1941) and to a liberal treatment of labor warfare among organizing mine workers in *Sons of the Stranger* (1947). However, it is in the earlier novels of political engagement that D. produced her finest and most original work.

WORKS: *Path Flower, and Other Verses* (1904). *Semiramis, and Other Plays* (1904). *Lords and Lovers, and Other Dramas* (1906). *The Mortal Gods, and Other Plays* (1912). *The Cycle's Rim* (1916). *The Flutter of the Gold Leaf, and Other Plays* (with F. Peterson, 1922). *Lute and Furrow* (1922). *Highland*

Annals (1925). *Call Home the Heart* (1932). *A Stone Came Rolling* (1935). *From My Highest Hill: Carolina Mountain Folks* (1941). *Sons of the Stranger* (1947). *The Spotted Hawk* (1958). *Innocent Bigamy, and Other Stories* (1962).

BIBLIOGRAPHY: Polsky, T., *North Carolina Authors: A Selective Handbook* (1952). Rideout, W. B., *The Radical Novel in the U.S. 1900–1954: Some Interrelations of Literature and Society* (1956).

Other references: *Nation* (8 Jan. 1936). *NewR* (29 Jan. 1936). *NYTBR* (15 Dec. 1935). *North Carolina Librarian* (Spring 1960). *SatRL* (16 April 1932).

SYLVIA COOK

Lucretia Maria Davidson

B. 27 Sept. 1808, Plattsburg, New York; d. 27 Aug. 1825, Plattsburg, New York
D. of Oliver and Margaret Miller Davidson

D. received her early schooling at home and later was sent to Troy Female Academy. Her health, already delicate, was further undermined by the school's excessively ambitious curriculum and the virtual absence of outdoor exercise. After three months at another school, Miss Gilbert's Albany Academy, D. returned home to die, not quite seventeen years old.

Restricted by her inexperience, D. sensibly drew her writing subject matter either from her daily life or from her studies. From history, biblical and national, came "David and Jonathon," "Ruth's Answer to Naomi," the prose "Columbus," and the spirited "Vermont Cadets"; from the classroom, the humorous "Week before Examination" which was deservedly popular with her schoolmates; from her brief but poignant personal encounters with suffering, mental and physical, poems like "Headache" and "Fears of Death." These latter, especially, have the ring of sincerity, transcending her usual level of stock images and poetic diction.

Amir Khan, and Other Poems, selected by her mother and with a biographical introduction by the artist and inventor Samuel Morse, was published in 1829. Copies were sent by Morse to a number of leading writers. In his covering letter to Robert Southey, the poet laureate of England, Morse invited comparison with other youthful prodigies such as Chatterton and White, of "this new genuis which sprang up and bloomed in the wilderness, assumed the female form and wore the features of exquisite beauty and perished in the bloom." Southey's response was an eleven-page review in the prestigious *London Quarterly* (1829), the conclusion of which, Poe protested, was "twice as strong as was necessary to establish her fame in England-fearing America." Within thirty years, no less than fifteen editions appeared on both sides of the Atlantic, all but the first preceded by the biographical sketch by Catharine Sedgwick. A German translation was published in 1844, and an Italian edition in 1906.

Edgar Allan Poe, in a review challenging Southey's encomium, argues that we must "distinguish that which, in our heart is love of [her] worth, from that which, in our intellect, is appreciation of [her] poetic ability; with the former, as critic, we have nothing to do." "This distinction," he adds, "would have spared us much twaddle on the part of commentators." This distinction is one very difficult to make, however, in the case of D. She wrote before there was enough American poetry to form a standard and died before her own poetic skills and critical powers could be properly developed.

WORKS: *Amir Khan, and Other Poems* (Ed. M. Davidson, 1829). *Poetical Remains of the Late Lucretia Maria Davidson* (Ed. M. Davidson, 1846; rev. eds., 1857 and 1860). *Poems by Lucretia Maria Davidson* (Ed. M. O. Davidson, 1871).

BIBLIOGRAPHY: Brooks, V. W., *The World of Washington Irving* (1944). Curry, K., ed., *New Letters of Robert Southey* (1965). Dewey, M. E., *Life and Letters of Catharine Sedgwick* (1871). Mabee, C., *Samuel Morse: The American Leonard* (1944).

MARION NORMAN

Margaret Miller Davidson

B. 26 March 1823, Plattsburg, New York; d. 25 Nov. 1838, Saratoga, New York
D. of Oliver and Margaret Miller Davidson

D. received the best education at home from her chronically ill mother. Anxious to assume the family poetic mantle bequeathed her by her dying sister Lucretia, she eagerly absorbed the ideas, tastes, and moral and religious standards of her mother toward whom she formed an exceptionally close attachment. Frequent extended vacations and changes of residence proved unable to arrest D.'s fatal tuberculosis. She died at fifteen.

Mrs. Davidson who, three years earlier when negotiating for a new edition of Lucretia's poetry, had introduced her younger daughter to Washington Irving, now provided him with all that remained of Margaret's poems. She also gave him copious memoranda which he used, often verbatim, for his biographical introduction to D.'s *Poetical Remains* (1841). A second edition was called for in the same year, one each in London and Philadelphia the following year, and by 1864, there were twenty editions in all.

D.'s poems, as is hardly surprising, reflect two main influences: Lucretia, whom she idolized and emulated as far as she could, and her mother, whom she reflected so completely that it is difficult to determine if there was anything of her own. D.'s poems are, on the whole, longer than most of her sister's, written in quatrains rather than rhyming couplets and express stronger religious faith and devotion. Many deal with her various homes and the flowers, trees, rivers, and mountains surrounding them. Despite her mother's disapproval of extensive memorizations, echoes (perhaps unconscious) of Cowper, Thomson, and Scott constantly recur. Among D.'s better efforts are the paraphrases of the twenty-third and forty-second psalms, the "Hymn of the Fire-Worshippers," and "The Destruction of Sodom and Gomorrah"; but these are clearly inferior to Lucretia's handling of similar biblical material.

D.'s mother inadvertently did her a disservice in exposing to the public juvenile verse that should have been reserved for the uncritical eyes of family and close friends. D. was surprisingly popular for the quarter century after her death, but today one is apt to dismiss her as a faint echo of her more promising older sister.

WORKS: *Biographical and Poetical Remains of the Late Margaret Miller Davidson* (Ed. W. Irving, 1841).

BIBLIOGRAPHY: Griswold, R., *Female Poets of America* (1848). May, C., *The American Female Poets* (1848). Poe, E. A., *Complete Works*, Harrison, J., ed. (1902).

MARION NORMAN

Mary Evelyn Moore Davis

B. 12 April 1852, Talladage, Alabama; d. 1 Jan. 1909, New Orleans, Louisiana
Wrote under: Mrs. M. E. M. Davis, Mollie Moore Davis, Mollie Evelyn Moore
  Davis, Mollie E. Moore
D. of John and Marian Lucy Crutchfield Moore; m. Thomas Edward Davis,
  1874

An only daughter in a family of nine children, D. grew up in rural Alabama and on a plantation near San Marcos, Texas, which later provided rich material for her poetry and fiction. In 1860 her first poems appeared in the local newspaper, the *Tyler* (Texas) *Reporter*. Between 1861 and 1865, her poetry, inspired by the Civil War, was printed in the *Reporter* and a number of southern newspapers. During the 1880s, D. turned increasingly to the writing of fiction for publication in national literary magazines.

D.'s more popular poems typify her musical, energetic versification and skillful handling of rhyme. A number of poems after 1869 suggests a shift in D.'s interests from short lyrics to narratives and monologues, such as "The Golden Rose," "The Ball (A True Incident)," and "Eleanor to Arthur," which is possibly autobiographical.

In War Times at La Rose Blanche (1888), her first book of prose and her best-known work, is a semiautobiographical story sequence, which now, however, appears superficial. *Under the Man-Fig* (1895), D.'s first and most fully realized novel, is a southwestern tale of mystery and romance that reveals her fascination with the past. The intricate plot, characteristic of all her novels, involves a wide spectrum of characters spanning several generations and every social class in a small Texas town. The work is most effective in its deft use of regional dialect, historical detail, and humorous characters.

An Elephant's Track, and Other Stories (1897) serves as a sampler of D.'s work in short fiction, in which she is technically at her best. This volume contains fifteen stories depicting rural Texas folk, Louisiana Creoles, and plantation blacks. Among the more memorable are "A Bamboula" and "The Love Stranche," which delve into the mysterious world of voodoo, and "At La Glorieuse" and "The Soul of Rose Dédé," which treat ghosts as an everyday reality. D.'s achievement in the stories lies in her subtle handling of regional settings, faithful rendering of rural mores, and vivid delineation of the different socioeconomic levels of southern society.

The Wire Cutters (1899), a novel set primarily in a rural Texas community, is reminiscent of the work of Charles Dickens in its ingenious plot complications and numerous secret identities. This work contains D.'s most controversial subjects—divorce and physical abuse in marriage—and her most complex characterizations, particularly of women who, though entangled in some stock situations, emerge convincingly as strong individuals. Concerned with the struggle against the fencing in of pasture lands and water sources, *The Wire Cutters* reflects D.'s interest in Texas history.

New Orleans Creole society inspired two of D.'s major works, *The Little Chevalier* (1903), a historical novel regarded as her best, and *The Price of Silence* (1907), her most popular novel. Set in the French Louisiana territory of the mid-18th c., *The Little Chevalier* is an adventure story of intrigue and love on a grand scale. It realistically depicts the manners and milieu of the early Creoles. *The Price of Silence* focuses on a Creole family in contemporary New Orleans whose surviving matriarch guards a family secret. D. effectively portrays the attitudes, activities, and speech of the upper-class French Creoles, but her treatment of the theme of miscegenation is weak in conception and execution.

Equally adept at portraying Texas or Louisiana, plantation or city, D. is exact in locating her work in time, and faithful to contemporary conditions of dress, travel, worship, and entertainment. She has a discerning eye for visual details and paints accurate pictures of background scenes, natural landscapes, and physical appearance of characters, though her tendency is toward the more appealing details. Although her painstaking attention to exteriors does not compensate for her avoidance of much that is beneath the surface in human beings and in personal interactions, D. is an engaging storyteller whose romances and adventures consistently hold the reader's attention.

WORKS: *Minding the Gap, and Other Poems* (1867). *Poems by Mollie E. Moore* (1869). *In War Times at La Rose Blanche* (1888). *Under the Man-Fig* (1895). *A Christmas Masque of Saint Roch, Père Dagobert, and Throwing the Wanga* (1896). *An Elephant's Track, and Other Stories* (1897). *Under Six Flags: The Story of Texas* (1897). *The Wire Cutters* (1899). *The Queen's Garden* (1900). *Jaconetta: Her Love* (1901). *The Mistress of Odd Corner* (1902). *The Yellow Apples* (with P. Stapleton, 1902). *A Bunch of Roses, and Other Parlor Plays* (1903). *The Little Chevalier* (1903). *A Bunch of Roses* (1907). *Christmas Boxes* (1907). *A Dress Rehearsal* (1907). *The New System* (1907). *The Price of Silence* (1907). *Queen Anne Cottages* (1907). *The Moons of Balcanca* (1908). *Selected Poems* (Ed. G. King, 1927).

BIBLIOGRAPHY: Wilkenson, C., "The Broadening Stream: The Life and Literary Career of Mary Evelyn Moore Davis" (Ph.D. diss., Univ. of Illinois, 1947).

For articles in reference works, see: *DAB. The Living Writers of the South*, Ed. J. W. Davidson (1896). *LSL. NAW* (article by C. Wilkenson).

Other references: *LaS* (Summer 1962).

THADIOUS M. DAVIS

Rebecca Harding Davis

B. 24 June, 1831, Washington, Pennsylvania; d. 29 Sept. 1910, Mt. Kisco, New York
D. of Richard W. and Rachel Leet Wilson Harding; m. Lemuel Clarke Davis, 1863

D.'s uneventful and comfortable childhood was spent first in Big Spring, Alabama, and later in Wheeling, Virginia, (now West Virginia) where she lived until her marriage. The eldest of five children, she was tutored privately at home, but her education was, for the most part, acquired by means of her own extensive reading. She relates in *Bits of Gossip* (1904) that at the age of twelve she was profoundly moved by Nathanial Hawthorne's *Twice-Told Tales* in which "the commonplace folk and things which I saw every day took on a sudden mystery and charm." Encouraged by her parents, she began to write at an early age, although it was not until the publication of "Life in the Iron Mills" (*Atlantic Monthly*, April, 1861) that she gained any real recognition.

In 1862, D. visited her publisher in Boston, Massachusetts, and became acquainted with the intellectual coterie in Concord which included Bronson Alcott, Louisa May Alcott, George Ticknor, Nathanial Hawthorne, Ralph Waldo Emerson, and their disciples. D.'s charming portrayal in *Bits of Gossip* of this famous group reveals a great deal of sensitivity and insight.

After her marrige D. settled with her husband in Philadelphia and, in keeping with her beliefs concerning the true vocation of women, devoted herself to her home and family. Her feelings are expressed most strongly in *Pro Aris et Focis—A Plea for Our Altars and Hearths* (1870), where she earnestly asserts that "the highest female intellect finds its greatest delight, in contemplating and admiring the representative men of genius." By way of further explanation she maintains that the female brain "is not capable of such sustained and continuous mental exertion as man's."

Her convictions did not, however, entirely inhibit her own career, and in 1869 she became a contributing editor to the New York *Herald Tribune*. She also continued to publish; essays, articles, and stories appeared in major adult and juvenile periodicals. After her husband's death in 1904, D. applied herself almost entirely to the career of her well-known son, the novelist and journalist Richard Harding Davis.

It is D.'s early work which is most worthy of attention, especially the remarkable "Life in the Iron Mills," a portrayal of Wheeling mill workers as she observed them. It is harsh and unflinching in its realism. Eschewing the romanticism of many of her contemporaries, D. presents a bleak picture of the degrading existence imposed by poverty and hard labor. So powerful is the depiction that at the time many believed it to have been written by a man. Later the same year, *Atlantic* published "A Story for To-day" (published in book form as *Margret Howth*, 1862), followed in the next year by "John Lamar" and "David Gaunt," both of which present the grim horrors of the Civil War. D. never acceded to the popular glorification of war as a patriotic deity but warned, in Bits of Gossip, that "the garments of the deity are filthy and that some of her influences debase and befoul a people."

In what is by far her finest novel, *Waiting for the Verdict* (1868), D. deals with the tragic aftermath of the Civil War, particularly the race problems it engendered. Despite the fact that the work is marred by melodrama, it displays an extraordinary sensitivity to its subject.

It is regrettable that D.'s later work does not fulfill its early promise. Her style increasingly lapses into the sentimental and melodramatic tendencies of the time, becoming more appropriate for the romantic potboilers she often contributed to *Peterson's* magazine. Nevertheless, the significance of D.'s early work to the development of American realism cannot be overestimated. "Life in the Iron Mills," in particular, deserves recognition as a landmark in the history of American literature.

WORKS: *Margret Howth* (1862). *Dallas Galbraith* (1868). *Waiting for the Verdict* (1868). *Pro Aris et Focis—A Plea for Our Altars and Hearths* (1870). *Berrytown* (1872). *John Andross* (1874). *Kitty's Choice* (1874). *A Law Unto Herself* (1878). *Natasqua* (1886). *Kent Hampden* (1892). *Silhouettes of American Life* (1892). *Doctor Warrick's Daughters* (1896). *Frances Waldeaux* (1897). *Bits of Gossip* (1904).

BIBLIOGRAPHY: Downey, F., *Richard Harding Davis: His Day* (1933). Langford, G., *The Richard Harding Davis Years* (1961). Quinn, A. H., *American Fiction* (1936). Sheaffer, H. W., "Rebecca Harding Davis, Pioneer Realist" (Ph.D. diss., Univ. of Pennsylvania, 1947). Wann, L., *The Rise of Realism* (1942). Wyman, M., "Women in the American Realistic Novel" (Ph.D. diss., Radcliffe College, 1950).

For articles in reference works, see: *AA. DAB. NAW* (article by M. Wyman Langworthy). *NCAB.*

Other references: *American* 3 (4 March 1882). *NYT* (30 Sept. 1910).

S. JULIA GOWING

Dorothy Day

B. 8 Nov. 1897, Bath Beach, New York; d. 29 Nov. 1980, New York City
D. of John and Grace Satterlee Day; common-law husband Forster Battingham

As an eight-year-old, D. first experienced that "sweetness of faith" in a Methodist Sunday school that later caused her to become a devout Roman Catholic. After the San Francisco earthquake, which destroyed the newspaper plant for which D.'s father worked, the family moved to Chicago, where D. spent her girlhood years. She studied for two years at the University of Illinois at Urbana, where she further developed her interest in socialism, begun in high school.

At age eighteen, D. began a serious journalistic career as a reporter for the socialist *New York Call.* Later she wrote for Max Eastman's revolutionary publication, *The Masses.* After the suppression of *The Masses* by the government, D. went to Washington with a group of militant suffragists, who were arrested and sentenced to thirty days in prison. This was the first of a number of imprisonments which D. underwent throughout the years for her activism in the causes of peace and justice.

During 1918, D. came to know the Provincetown Players and talked long hours with Eugene O'Neill about religion and death as they walked the streets or "sat out the nights in taverns, in waterfront back rooms."

With five thousand dollars for the movie-rights to her novel, *The Eleventh Virgin* (1924), D. bought a small bungalow on Raritan Bay, Staten Island. There she had a daughter by her common-law husband, Forster Battingham, an anarchist, who parted with her when she later had the child baptised in the Catholic Church. In *From Union Square to Rome* (1938) she tells the story of her conversion, and in her autobiography, *The Long Loneliness* (1952), of her struggle against Catholic priests whose vision did not extend beyond their parish.

Like many other writers in the 1920s, D. spent some fruitless months on a screen-writing assignment in Hollywood, thereafter going with her daughter, Tamar, to Mexico City, where she supported herself by writing articles about the life of the people for *Commonweal*. Back in New York, she met Peter Maurin, whose ideas dominated the rest of her life. He encouraged her to start a paper for the workingman, extolling "personalist action" and using love as a means of changing institutions to enable each individual to lead a full life. In Union Square on May 1, 1933, a day of massive celebration of Russian and world-wide communism, D. heroically hawked the first issue of *The Catholic Worker*, a four-page tabloid-size paper, which urged social Christian action in place of the Marxist communism of *The Daily Worker*. For almost half a century, she continued to publish every month this liberal voice of the Catholic church.

Among the many charitable farms and houses of refuge for the poor and homeless which she helped found are the Maryfarm Retreat House, Newburgh, New York; St. Joseph's House of Hospitality, New York City; Peter Maurin Farm, Pleasant Plains, Staten Island; Maryfarm, Easton, Pennsylvania; Chrystie Street House, New York City; and the Tivoli Farm Retreat on the Hudson. *The Catholic Worker* offices on Mott Street have also served as soup kitchen for the hungry. This tough-minded but gentle-hearted woman, who seemed a saint to wanderers lacking food and shelter, has been the inspiration for numerous Worker Groups, where friendship as well as food is shared.

WORKS: *The Eleventh Virgin* (1924). *From Union Square to Rome* (1938). *House of Hospitality* (1939). *On Pilgrimage* (1948). *The Long Loneliness* (1952). *I Remember Peter Maurin* (1958). *Thérèse* (1960). *Loaves and Fishes* (1963). *On Pilgrimage: The Sixties* (1972).

BIBLIOGRAPHY: Coles, R., *A Spectacle unto the World: The Catholic Worker Movement* (1973). Hennacy, A., *Autobiography of a Catholic Anarchist* (1945). Hennacy, A., *The Book of Ammon* (1970). Maurin, P., *Catholic Radicalism: Phrased Essays for the Green Revolution* (1949). Miller, W. D., *A Harsh and Dreadful Love: Dorothy Day and the Catholic Worker Movement* (1973). O'Brien, D. J., *American Catholics and Social Reform: The New Deal Years* (1968). Sheehan, A., *Peter Maurin: Gay Believer* (1959).

Other references: *The Catholic Worker* (1933 to present). *NY* (4 Oct. 1952; 11 Oct. 1952). *NYRB* (28 Jan. 1971).

WINIFRED FRAZER

Margaret Wade Campbell Deland

B. *28 Feb. 1857, Allegheny, Pennsylvania; d. 13 Jan. 1945, Boston, Massachusetts*
Given name: Margaretta Campbell
D. of Sample and Margaretta Wade Campbell; m. Lorin F. Deland, 1880

D. was educated in private schools before entering Cooper Union, in New York City, for a course in drawing and design. After graduation, she was appointed assistant instructor at Girls' Normal School (now Hunter College.)

D.'s first novel, *John Ward, Preacher* (1888), is a story of religious doubt and adamant orthodoxy. D. had been brought up a strict Presbyterian, but in the years following her marriage she found herself painfully questioning her earlier religious attitudes. She finally left her family's denomination and, with her husband, was confirmed in the Episcopal church. It was many years, however, before she was at peace with her convictions, and *John Ward, Preacher* was the result of her own soul-searching. It made her suddenly famous, for it was much discussed, and often angrily denounced as wicked and immoral.

D. followed this first novel with a steady output of fiction so popular that she became one of the best-known writers of her day. Four honorary doctorates were awarded her, and, in 1926, she was one of the first women elected to membership in the National Institute of Arts and Letters.

"Essentially a novelist of character," as one writer calls her, D. created a group of likable men, women, and children who appear time after time in her various novels and short stories. These are inhabitants of a small town, "Old Chester," which was modelled on Manchester, where she grew up. Dominating the Old Chester scene is the all-wise, all-compassionate Dr. Lavendar, Rector of St. Michael's Church. The plots are concerned with sin and its expiation, self-sacrifice, maternal love, pride, and oddly assorted marriages. Through them all runs a strong current of religion, for D.'s people conceive of a deity who is intensely personal. Also apparent is a delightful appreciation of nature—the shifting seasons, flowers, hills, rivers.

Though D.'s fiction is definitely dated, it is extremely useful to any student seeking to understand the values and mores of a bygone era. Further, while its faint gloss of sentimentality, its assertions regarding extramarital relations, and its firm insistence on the need for renouncing "sin" may seem quaint and unreal to the modern reader, D.'s work does portray the timeless qualities of personal integrity, devotion, and courage.

WORKS: *The Old Garden* (1886). *John Ward, Preacher* (1888). *A Summer Day* (1889). *Philip and His Wife* (1890). *Sidney: The Story of a Child* (1892). *The Wisdom of Fools* (1894). *Mr. Tommy Dove and Other Stories* (1897). *Old Chester Tales* (1899). *Dr. Lavendar's People* (1903). *The Common Way* (1904). *The Awakening of Helena Richie* (1906). *An Encore* (1907). *The Iron Woman* (1911). *The Voice* (1912). *Partners* (1913). *The Hands of Esau* (1914). *Around Old Chester* (1915). *The Rising Tide* (1916). *The Vehement Flame* (1922). *New Friends in Old Chester* (1924). *The Kays* (1926). *Captain Archer's Daughter* (1932). *Old Chester Days* (1935). *If This Be I* (1935). *Golden Yesterdays* (1941).

BIBLIOGRAPHY: Dodd, L. H., *Celebrities at Our Hearthside* (1959). Overton, G., *The Women Who Make Our Novels* (1928). Williams, B. C., *Our Short Story Writers* (1920).

For articles in reference works, see: *NAW* (article by J. Levenson). *NCAB*. *20th CA*.

Other references: *NYT* (14 Jan. 1945).

ABIGAIL ANN HAMBLEN

Agnes De Mille

B. 1905, New York City
D. of William C. and Anna George De Mille; m. Walter Prude, 1943

D.'s mother was the daughter of political economist Henry George. Her father was a successful playwright, but after an unexpected flop on Broadway he went west to join his younger brother, Cecil B. De Mille, and became a movie director.

D.'s first book, *Dance to the Piper* (1951), begins with her family's move from New York City to Hollywood in 1914, covers her difficult years of struggle to become a dancer and to launch a career, and culminates with her first two solid choreographic successes, *Rodeo* (1942) and *Oklahoma!* (1943). The book ranges from child's-eye sketches of personalities who frequented the De Mille household, such as Geraldine Farrar, Ruth St. Denis, Elinor Glyn, and Charlie Chaplin, to more detailed portraits of those who affected D.'s dance career—Martha Graham, Argentina, Marie Rambert, Antony Tudor, Lucia Chase.

Enthusiasm and honesty are the keynotes of D.'s literary style. Her greatest enthusiasm is for other accomplished artists, and her most brutal honesty concerns her own limitations. At fifteen, she says, "I considered my body a shame, a trap and a betrayal. But I could break it. I was a dancer." She is absolutely forthright in her advice on careers in dance, with constructive suggestions for dance teachers and critics, in *To a Young Dancer* (1962). In several of her books, she discusses how the development of professional dance, like the development of female consciousness, has been retarded by social, religious, and economic restraints.

Lizzie Borden: A Dance of Death (1968) is a book-length study of the creation of her 1948 folk ballet, *Fall River Legend*. D.'s historical research was meticulous, as it was for her earlier, illustrated *Book of the Dance* (1963). After a careful exploration of the scene of Lizzie Borden's crime, D. conducts the reader through her own transformation of historical fact into dance-drama. Accidents, personality clashes, and economic obstacles make of the creative process itself a taut, suspenseful narrative. In her *Russian Journals* (1970), D. recalls the stunned appreciation of Soviet audiences for this ballet when it was performed by American Ballet Theater on its USSR tour.

Where the Wings Grow (1978) covers the earliest period in D.'s life, before she had any serious thought of becoming a dancer. In this childhood memoir of summers at Merriewold, in Sullivan County, New York, D. evokes a turn-of-the-century way of life innocent of indoor plumbing and refrigeration, with home remedies, Irish-Catholic house servants, lemonade, and embroidery on the verandah, and ladies—like her mother—who prided themselves on their sheltered, genteel public image, even though it masked a great deal of anguished drudgery. This book is a landmark in D.'s literary career, because its lyricism and passion and the interest it sustains depend not at all upon the author's reputation as a dancer and choreographer.

Long recognized for her energetic contributions to American dance theater, D. is now respected as a serious and prolific writer as well. Five of her ten books are autobiographical; the others, like most of her magazine articles and speaking engagements, deal more specifically with dance as an artistic and social form of expression. D. is much in demand as a speaker, for she displays in person, as in her writing, a very engaging zeal and wit.

WORKS: *Dance to the Piper* (1951). *And Promenade Home* (1956). *To a Young Dancer* (1962). *The Book of the Dance* (1963). *Lizzie Borden: A Dance of Death* (1968). *Russian Journals* (1970). *Speak to Me, Dance with Me* (1973). *American Ballet Theatre, 35th Anniversary Gala* (with L. Chase, 1975). *Where the Wings Grow* (1978). *America Dances* (1980). *Reprieve: A Memoir* (1981).

BIBLIOGRAPHY: For articles in reference works, see: *CB* (1943). *Notable Names in the American Theatre*, Eds. J. T. White et al. (1976).
   Other references: *Dance Magazine* (Oct. 1971; Sept. 1973; Nov. 1974; June 1974). *NYTBR* (13 Jan. 1952; 12 Oct. 1968).

FELICIA HARDISON LONDRÉ

Babette Deutsch

B. *22 Sept. 1895, New York City; d. 13 Nov. 1982, New York City*
D. *of Michael and Melanie Fisher Deutsch; m. Avrahm Yarmolinsky, 1921*

Of German descent, D. grew up in New York City, where she received her B.A. from Barnard College in 1917. Although best known as a poet, D. has published novels, translations, literary criticism, and children's books.

In 1919, D. published her first volume of poems, *Banners*, whose title piece celebrates the Russian Revolution as "new freedoms, and new slavery." *Honey out of the Rock* (1925), D.'s second book, contains a number of short imagistic poems, biblically inspired ballads, and poems to her son. Both volumes display the influence of imagism, Japanese haiku, and Greek and Jewish culture.

Considered by some critics to be D.'s best work, *Epistle to Prometheus* (1930), is a letter written by a contemporary to the Greek god. It is a survey of man's history, beginning with his creation and tracing the Promethean spirit as it has inspired humanity in 5th-c. Greece, 18th-c. France, and 20th-c. Russia.

D.'s final three volumes of poetry, *One Part Love* (1939), *Take Them,*

Stranger (1944), and *Animal, Vegetable, and Mineral* (1954), all reveal her rage at the destruction of World War II. In "To Napoleon" she asks, "But who will cut the growth/ That gnaws at Europe now?" D.'s poetry has been collected in two volumes: *Collected Poems, 1919–62* (1963) and *Coming of Age: New and Selected Poems* (1959).

As a novelist, D. began her career with *A Brittle Heaven* (1926), a thinly veiled autobiography about a young woman's youth, education, and marriage. The novel reveals the major conflicts facing a woman struggling to define herself both as a professional writer, and a wife and mother. D.'s second novel, *In Such a Night* (1927), is essentially a series of character sketches showing the influence of Virginia Woolf's stream-of-consciousness technique in *Mrs. Dalloway*. D.'s other novels are *Mask of Silenus* (1933), a historical novel based on Socrates' life, and *Rogue's Legacy* (1942), a tale patterned after the life of the French poet, François Villon.

D.'s critical writings are concerned with the correlation between modern poetry and modern society. *Potable Gold: Some Notes on Poetry and This Age* (1929) discusses the influence of technology on poetry and the poet's relationship to his public. *This Modern Poetry* (1935) and *Poetry in Our Time* (1952) both analyze major poetic figures and study the interrelationship between poet and politics. According to D., the modern poet must "create a myth beyond the power of man" and therefore be a "true revolutionary."

WORKS: *Banners* (1919). *Honey out of the Rock* (1925). *A Brittle Heaven* (1926). *In Such a Night* (1927). *Potable Gold: Some Notes on Poetry and This Age* (1929). *Fire for the Night* (1930). *Epistle to Prometheus* (1930). *Mask of Silenus* (1933). *This Modern Poetry* (1935). *One Part Love* (1939). *Rogue's Legacy* (1942). *Take Them, Stranger* (1944). *Poetry in Our Time* (1952). *Animal, Vegetable, Mineral* (1954). *Poetry Handbook: A Dictionary of Terms* (1956). *Coming of Age: New and Selected Poems* (1959). *Collected Poems, 1919–62* (1963).

BIBLIOGRAPHY: For articles in reference works, see *CA* (1977).

Other references: *NYHTB* (12 July 1959). *Poetry* (1964). *SatR* (25 July 1959). *TLS* (18 June 1964). *VQR* (1964).

DIANE LONG HOEVELER

Abby Morton Diaz

B. 22 Nov. 1821, Plymouth, Massachusetts; d. 1 April 1904, Belmont, Massachusetts
Given name: Abigail Morton
D. of Ichabod and Patty Weston Morton; m. Manuel Diaz, 1845

Christened Abigail, known as Abby, D. was the only daughter of Ichabod Morton, a shipbuilder, liberal Unitarian, and social reformer. In 1842 he took his family to the Transcendental utopian community, Brook Farm, where D. remained until 1847, teaching in the Association's infant school. She later taught school in Plymouth and began writing. In May 1861, her first story appeared in the *Atlantic Monthly*, and she eventually published in many leading juvenile and domestic magazines of the day. D. was a founder and, from 1881 to 1892, president of the Women's Educational and Industrial Union of Boston which she saw as a "sisterhood" allying urban women of means with country girls seeking work in the city. In the 1880s and 1890s D. traveled widely, organizing women's unions and lecturing at women's clubs. She was active in the woman-suffrage movement which she saw as an outgrowth of the abolition of slavery. In her later years she became interested in Christian Science and published articles on religious subjects.

D.'s best, and most successful, juvenile fiction is *The William Henry Letters* (1870), first published in 1867 in the magazine *Our Young Folks*. Epistolary in form, it recounts the adventures of a mischievous red-headed boy raised by his loving grandmother. Overall the *Letters* sentimentally evoke family life and simple fun in an idealized New England village. Theodore Roosevelt in his *Autobiography* (1913) described this book, one of his favorites, as a "good healthy" story, "teaching manliness, decency and good conduct."

Two sequels were popular: *William Henry and His Friends* (1871) and *Lucy Maria* (1874). The latter, apparently loosely autobiographical, concerns a girl who took up "school-keeping with too much self-confidence" and soon concluded that it is a "very solemn thing" to give "even one life its first direction." Lucy Maria wants to do "heart-teaching," rather than head-teaching; like D. at Brook Farm, she takes her students into the woods to interest them in "flowers, trees, insects

—all natural objects." On woman suffrage, Lucy Maria, again like D. at this time, disclaims personal interest in the vote (except on "some neighborhood affair" such as the "location of a schoolhouse") but feels that other women should have the vote if they want it, as suffrage is a natural right.

D.'s interest in improving home life and the instruction of young children is evinced in several of her most effective books: *The Schoolmaster's Trunk* (1874), *A Domestic Problem* (1875), *Bybury to Beacon Street* (1887), *Only a Flock of Women* (1893). These novels are set in small towns that have little social life. Isolated and repressive, they are half-way stations between the old-fashioned village and the modern city. Families struggle to maintain "decent" standards and parents wear themselves out with work. To reform these conditions, D. proposes various domestic economies, simplifying women's chores so that they may devote more time to their children and to self-improvement. Men, she feels, should share household tasks, so that they may appreciate the difficulty of women's work. The community should meet convivially to discuss its problems.

Through more than twenty years, D. was a prolific author of juvenile stories and essays. These consistently reflect her affection for children and a charming delight in games and pastimes. The volumes of domestic advice are pleasantly stated, chatty, down-to-earth. Many of the household reforms D. suggests have since been accomplished by labor-saving machinery, but her comments testify to the physical difficulty of farm and village life for women a century ago. D.'s early exposure to Transcendental or Emersonian idealism is evident to the end of her life in her views of children, education, and the prospect of moral improvement.

WORKS: *The Entertaining Story of King Bronde, His Lily and His Rosebud* (1869). *The William Henry Letters* (1870). *William Henry and His Friends* (1871). *Lucy Maria* (1874). *The Schoolmaster's Trunk* (1874). *A Domestic Problem* (1875). *A Storybook for the Children* (1875). *Neighborhood Talks, As Reported By Mr. Codding* (1876). *Birds of Prey* (with N. A. Calkins, 1878). *Cat Family* (with N. A. Calkins, 1878). *The Jimmyjohns, and Other Stories* (1878). *Scratching Birds* (with N. A. Calkins, 1878). *Swimming Birds* (with N. A. Calkins, 1878). *Wading Birds* (with N. A. Calkins, 1878). *Brave Little Goose-girl: Little Stories for Little Folks* (1880). *Christmas Morning* (1880). *Merry Christmas* (1880). *Molasses Candy* (1880). *Simple Traveller* (1880). *The Story of Boxberry* (1880). *King Grimalkin and Pussyanna* (1881). *Polly Cologne* (1881). *Chronicles of the Stimpcett Family and Others* (1882). *Spirit As Power* (1886). *The Law of Perfection* (1886). *Bybury to Beacon Street* (1887). *The John Spicer Lectures* (1887). *Leaves of Healing* (1887). *Conventions during the Anti-Slavery Agitation* (1889). *In the Strength of the Lord* (1889). *Mother*

Goose's Christmas Party (1891). *Only a Flock of Women* (1893). *The Law of Perfection* (1895). *The Religious Training of Children* (1895). *The Flatiron and the Red Cloak* (1901). *"Those People from Skyton," and Nine Other Stories* (1906).

BIBLIOGRAPHY: Codman, J. T., *Brook Farm* (1884). Croly, J. C., *History of the Women's Club Movement in America* (1898). Donham, S. A., "History of the Women's Educational and Industrial Union" (Diss., Radcliffe College, 1955). Swift, L., *Brook Farm* (1900).

For articles in reference works, see: *AW. NAW* (article by J. Benardete). Other references: *Women's Journal* (14 April 1904).

JANE BENARDETE

Emily Dickinson

B. 10 Dec. 1830, Amherst, Massachusetts; d. 15 May 1886, Amherst, Massachusetts
D. of Edward and Emily Norcross Dickinson

D. was one of three children. Her older brother and younger sister were always her closest companions. Her father—a Massachusetts judge, member of the state legislature, a U.S. congressman, and an exemplar of the Puritan ethic of industry and public service—was "too busy with his briefs" to notice his children. Her mother appears to have been an equally remote parent, a semi-invalid for much of her children's lives, and, in D.'s view, a failure as a mother. D. once wrote a friend, "I never had a mother."

D. attended Amherst Academy and was sent for a year to Mount Holyoke Female Seminary. Except for occasional visits to neighboring cities and a trip with her father to Washington, D.C., she did not leave her birthplace again. By her thirtieth year she had withdrawn even from the life of Amherst. To the townspeople she became a legendary figure, an eccentric spinster who dressed always in white, rarely received a visitor, and refused to venture beyond the family house and garden.

Found in her room after her death was a manuscript, in the style of homemade pamphlets, of almost nine hundred poems, only seven of which she had published. All were short lyrics, often no more than a quatrain or two; almost all were untitled and undated; some were unfinished; some appeared in variant versions. The labor of collecting additional manuscripts and of publishing selections of her verse was undertaken first by family and friends, none of whom suspected their actual value. The first *Poems by Emily Dickinson* appeared four years after her death, to mainly hostile reviews. Periodically, as new poems, originally sent to friends, were discovered, new collections followed. In this century the number of poems has continued to increase; more than 650 were published for the first time as late as 1945. The authoritative text of all known poems, numbering almost 1800, is the three-volume edition by Thomas H. Johnson, which appeared in 1955. (The poems cited below are identified by their numbers in the Johnson edition.)

The subjects of D.'s poetry are, broadly, the subjects of lyric tradition: love, nature, death, and God. Her religious attitudes, in all their bewildering variety, permeate the bulk of her verse. In some of these religious poems she is seemingly the orthodox believer, "Given in marriage unto Thee" (317). More often she acknowledges herself the disbeliever whom "Christ omitted," observing of her exclusion that "The abdication of belief/ Makes the behavior small" (1551). Characteristically, she is both doubter and quester, probing the mysteries of death, immortality, and eternity, appropriating biblical sources of Calvinist theology, but preferring to question on her own terms—"Infinitude, hadst thou no face/ That I might look on Thee?" (564).

Death was a common theme in D.'s poetry. In one of her most famous poems, "Because I could not stop for Death" (712), death appears personified, and with the eerie "civility" of a gentleman caller, escorts her to her grave: "The carriage held but just ourselves/ And Immortality."

D.'s love poems are also usually about parting, separation, and loss. They support the biographical evidence that she suffered from a secret and hopeless love that explains her years of seclusion. The identity of the man has not been established. Circumstantial evidence suggests Charles Wadsworth, a married minister with whom she corresponded for many years. Other candidates have been suggested.

The most impassioned poems are the "renunciation" and "bridal" poems of the 1860s, in which earthly separation is a prelude to spiritual reunion in heaven. In these, the theological doctrines of Divine Election and the Marriage Covenant are applied to a spiritual "contract" with a temporal groom. The subject is sometimes handled with an ingenuity reminiscent of John Donne, as in "I cannot live with you" (640).

Many of D.'s nature poems are slight, whimsical exercises describing the particulars available in her own garden—a caterpillar, a garden snake, a robin, or butterfly. Their charm is in their metaphorical exactitude. A snake becomes a "whip-lash,/ Unbraiding in the sun" (986). In its larger aspects, nature may be responsive to her moods, but it never becomes the surrogate divinity of Emersonian transcendentalism. It remains remote, a "haunted house" from which man is excluded, an ominous reminder of transiency and human isolation.

The strengths, as well as the strangeness, of D.'s poetry derive in large measure from her Puritan heritage. She saw, as she said, "New Englandly." In the waning years of Puritanism, life remained for her a spiritual drama. She lived the drama, and she recorded it with the terseness of her native idiom. She did not translate the terms of the conflict simplistically into those of good and evil—evil did not interest her—but into the shifting oppositions of doubt and belief, of the known and the unknowable. Even her major themes—denial and renunciation—were the themes of the Puritan pulpit, enacted in the rigorous lives and otherworldliness of her ancestors. Her favorite verse forms were the short lines and stanza patterns of the hymnal.

D. is noted for the technical irregularities that aroused the scorn of some of her 19th-c. reviewers—and caused drastic revisions by early editors: off-rhymes, broken meters, curious punctuation, and ungrammatical phrasing. These are given less importance by the less conventional-minded critics of today. The flaws rarely obtrude on her better poetry, and when they do, they hardly outweigh its virtues. At her best, she is a skillful prosodist, who adapted rhyme and meter to her purposes, achieving emotional shadings unobtainable by conventional means. Her elliptical grammar remains troublesome. It adds to an already highly abbreviated style the mark of mannerism, of private note-taking. Ivor Winters's assessment that she is "one of the greatest poets of our language" has stood.

WORKS: *Poems of Emily Dickinson* (Eds. M. L. Todd and T. W. Higginson, 1890; second series, 1891; third series, Ed. M. L. Todd., 1896). *The Single Hound* (Ed. M. D. Bianchi, 1914). *The Complete Poems of Emily Dickinson* (Eds. M. D. Bianchi and A. L. Hampson, 1924). *Further Poems of Emily Dickinson* (Eds. M. Bianchi and A. L. Hampson, 1929). *The Poems of Emily Dickinson* (Eds. M. D. Bianchi and A. L. Hampson, 1930). *Unpublished Poems of Emily Dickinson* (Eds. M. D. Bianchi and A. L. Hampson, 1935). *Poems by Emily Dickinson* (Eds. M. D. Bianchi and A. L. Hampson, 1937). *Ancestors' Brocades: The Literary Debut of Emily Dickinson* (Ed. M. T. Bingham, 1945). *Bolts of Melody: New Poems of Emily Dickinson* (Eds. M. L. Todd and M. T. Bingham, 1945). *The Poems of Emily Dickinson* (Ed. T. H. Johnson, 3 vols., 1955). *The Letters of Emily Dickinson* (Eds. T. H. Johnson and T. Ward, 3 vols., 1958). *The Years and Hours of Emily Dickinson* (Ed. J. Leyda, 2 vols., 1960). *Final Harvest: Emily Dickinson's Poems* (Ed. T. H. Johnson, 1961).

BIBLIOGRAPHY: Anderson, C. F., *Emily Dickinson's Poetry: Stairway of Surprise* (1960). Blackmur, R. P., *Language as Gesture* (1952). Cambon, G., in *Transcendentalism and Its Legacy*, Eds. M. Simon and T. H. Parsons (1966). Chase, R., *Emily Dickinson* (1951). Cunningham, J. V., *Collected Essays* (1976). Donoghue, D., *Emily Dickinson* (Univ. of Minnesota Pamphlets on American Writers No. 81, 1969). Frye, N., *Fables of Identity* (1963). Gelpi, J., *Emily Dickinson: The Mind of the Poet* (1965). Griffith, C., *The Long Shadow: Emily Dickinson's Tragic Poetry* (1964). Higgins, D., *Portrait of Emily Dickinson: The Poet and Her Prose* (1967). Pearce, R. H., *The Continuity of American Poetry* (1961). Sewall, R. B., *The Life of Emily Dickinson* (1974). Tate, A., *Collected Essays* (1959). Ward, T., *The Capsule of the Mind: Chapters in the Life of Emily Dickinson* (1961). Winters, Y., *Maule's Curse* (1938).
Other references: *Perspectives USA* (Spring 1956).

MARGARET PETERSON

Joan Didion

B. 5 Dec. 1934, Sacramento, California
D. of Frank Reese and Eduene Jerrett Didion; m. John Gregory Dunne, 1964

D. was graduated from the University of California at Berkeley with a B.A. in English in 1956, and in that same year became an associate feature editor with *Vogue* magazine in New York City. She remained at *Vogue* until 1963, the year in which she published her first novel, *Run River*, set in Sacramento in the 1940s. Between 1963 and 1969 D. wrote essays and feature articles for *Vogue*, the *National Review*, *Harper's*, *Holiday*, and, most regularly, the *Saturday Evening Post*. D. has written several screenplays with her husband.

Slouching towards Bethlehem (1968) is a collection of essays which had been published previously, the majority in the *Saturday Evening Post*. In reading them together, however, one sees that they make a powerful statement about American society in the 1960s. The title essay describes the variety of young people D. met in 1967 when she spent some time in Haight-Ashbury. It is a vivid narrative, a recording of actual dialogue which conveys the pathetic naiveté of the "flower children," drifting through drug-filled days, their lives circumscribed by a few vague ideas rendered only in pale and repetitious platitudes. The other essays which comprise the first section of the collection, entitled "Life Styles in the Golden Land," are companion pieces to the title essay in that they either dramatize a desperation for immediate gratification or recall with nostalgia the old American values of courage, self-sufficiency, and privacy. In all of these essays California emerges as the last frontier of American idealism, the place where people act out their largely vain hopes for peace, for community, for eternal romance.

D. has all the qualities of a brilliant essayist. Her themes are clear, her anecdotes dramatic, her style swift and crisp. In addition to their merit as models of prose style, her essays increase our understanding of her fiction. "Notes from a Native Daughter" narrates the history of the Sacramento Valley, and "Los Angeles Notebook" depicts that city as one of impersonal tensions, while providing sketches of the barren relationships that we find in *Play It as It Lays* (1970).

In 1972 D. alienated many feminists with an essay in the *New York Times Book Review* that attacked feminists for their tendency to become obsessed with trivia. The essay makes explicit a view of women that is pervasive in her fiction; women share, she believes, a "sense of living one's deepest life underwater, that dark involvement with blood and birth and death." In the same essay D. attacked narrow feminist interpretations of literature, expressing the view that, since the writer is committed to the "exploration of moral distinctions and ambiguities," all political interpretations of literature must of necessity represent a distortion.

Ironically, there is much in D.'s fiction to appeal to the true feminist. All three of her novels concern the experience of women—their relationships with men, with their parents and children, and with each other.

D.'s deepest concern, however, is with the illusions on which people build their lives, illusions made necessary by the death of old values and the absence of viable new ones. Her novels dramatize the consequences of social, economic, and political change that occurs so rapidly as to produce disorder in individual lives, in families, and, ultimately, in whole societies.

The novel *Play It as It Lays* is a biting portrayal of a world in which people use each other to gain success, recognition, or sensual pleasure. Because men possess most of the power, women are especially likely to be victims. As narrator of the novel, D. is unobtrusive, completely neutral; she simply presents Maria's thoughts and actions. As a consequence of her technique, the reader is not sure of her attitude towards her central character. Some reviewers of the novel considered Maria the victim of a brutal society; others considered her malevolent. The truth lies somewhere between these extreme interpretations. As a child-woman, Maria was far too fragile for the society in which she lived; however, through her passivity she participated in her own exploitation, so that her breakdown became, in effect, a self-confirming prophecy.

In her recent novel, *A Book of Common Prayer* (1977), D. employs as narrator the strongest female character found in her fiction. This is D.'s most ambitious novel in several respects. It has the most complex narrative structure: since the narrator met Charlotte Douglas late in both their lives, she must convincingly reconstruct all of the previous action involving her. It also has the most complex cast of characters, four of whom—Charlotte, Grace, and Charlotte's two husbands—are fully developed, and the most complex setting, with scenes in San Francisco, New York City, and several southern cities, all interlaced with scenes in Boca Grande, a fictitious Central American country which D. renders as convincing as any of the other locales.

In these last two novels D. has refined a style which is tight and colloquial, stripped of any expansive descriptions or explanations. The strength of her fiction resides in this dramatic style, which she uses to bring the reader close to the events and characters and to render complex, often ironic, relationships through pure dialogue. Writing now at the height of her powers, D. can be looked to for significant future contributions to American fiction.

WORKS: *Run River* (1963). *Slouching towards Bethlehem* (1968). *Play It as It Lays* (1970). *A Book of Common Prayer* (1977). *The White Album* (1979).

BIBLIOGRAPHY: *Commentary* (July 1977). *Harper's* (Dec. 1971). *Ms.* (Jan. 1973). *NYTBR* (3 April 1977).

KATHERINE HENDERSON

Doris Miles Disney

B. 22 Dec. 1907, Glastonbury, Connecticut; d. 8 March 1976, Fredericksburg, Virginia
D. of Edward Lucas Hart and Elizabeth Anne Malone Miles; m. George J. Disney, 1936

D. was a prolific, versatile writer of mystery and suspense; she has been praised for never repeating herself and skillfully varying her approaches. She created three detectives; each is a fully realized and distinct character. Jim O'Neill, a county detective; Jefferson DiMarco, an insurance claim adjuster, the most famous; and David Madden, a U.S. postal inspector.

In D.'s fiction, suspense evolves from both plot and character. Her characters are rounded and consistently portrayed, their relationships and motivations often creating complex plots. She was particularly adept at characterizing children. For example, Jenny, an eight-year-old girl in *Don't Go into the Woods Today* (1974), and Sandy, a seven-year-old boy recuperating from rheumatic fever in *Heavy, Heavy Hangs* (1952), are sometimes cranky, frequently confused by the grown-up world, occasionally disobedient, but often charming and always believable.

D. began with true mysteries, in which the criminal's identity is withheld until the climax (see, for example, *A Compound for Death*, 1943, and *Murder on a Tangent*, 1945, both Jim O'Neill mysteries). *Dark Road* (1946), a Jeff DiMarco story, is an inverted mystery, in which the murderer's identity and motivation are revealed early. Hazel Clements causes her husband's death because of her desire to be reunited with an old lover. Her greed and ambition are clearly shown, but so is the awful background which helps explain her. At the end, the question of responsibility is paramount, her lover recognizing that he has been her unwitting accomplice.

For several novels D. turned to the past. *At Some Forgotten Door* (1966), a variation on gothic romance, has a partly predictable plot but builds suspense gradually, as the heroine fits together clues which help her understand both her origins and her present danger. Both mysteries are clarified in a powerful climactic scene. *Dark Lady* (1960) blends past and present. A young professor rents a cottage in which the wife of a gifted young writer had been murdered seventy-five years earlier. Becoming obsessed with the writer's beautiful sister-in-law, he solves the old mystery and learns to see his own present more clearly.

D.'s novels are consistently interesting and readable. The originality of her plots, the effectiveness of her characterizations, and her skill in controlling tone make her a leader among mystery writers. In addition, her ability to show how victims sometimes precipitate their fates and how the commission of a crime affects the criminal gives her work a depth often lacking in this genre.

WORKS: *A Compound for Death* (1943). *Murder on a Tangent* (1945). *Dark Road* (1946). *Who Rides a Tiger* (1946). *Appointment at Nine* (1947). *Enduring Old Charms* (1947). *Testimony by Silence* (1948). *That Which Is Crooked*

(1948). *Count the Ways* (1949). *Family Skeleton* (1949). *Fire at Will* (1950). *Look Back on Murder* (1951). *Straw Man* (1951). *Heavy, Heavy Hangs* (1952). *Do unto Others* (1953). *Prescription: Murder* (1953). *The Last Straw* (1954). *Room for Murder* (1955). *Trick or Treat* (1955). *Unappointed Rounds* (1956). *Method in Madness* (1957). *My Neighbor's Wife* (1957). *Black Mail* (1958). *Did She Fall or Was She Pushed?* (1959). *No Next of Kin* (1959). *Dark Lady* (1960). *Mrs. Meeker's Money* (1961). *Find the Woman* (1962). *Should Auld Acquaintance* (1962). *Here Lies . . .* (1963). *The Departure of Mr. Gaudette* (1964). *The Hospitality of the House* (1964). *Shadow of a Man* (1965). *At Some Forgotten Door* (1966). *The Magic Grandfather* (1966). *Night of Clear Choice* (1967). *Money for the Taking* (1968). *Voice from the Grave* (1968). *Two Little Children and How They Grew* (1969). *Do Not Fold, Spindle, or Mutilate* (1970). *The Chandler Policy* (1971). *Three's a Crowd* (1971). *The Day Miss Bessie Lewis Disappeared* (1972). *Only Couples Need Apply* (1973). *Don't Go into the Woods Today* (1974). *Cry for Help* (1975). *Winifred* (1976).

BIBLIOGRAPHY: *LJ* (15 May 1966). *NYHTB* (31 Oct. 1948; 21 Oct. 1951). *NYTBR* (13 Jan. 1946; 22 May 1949; 15 Dec. 1968). *WLB* (June 1954).

MARY JEAN DeMARR

Lavinia Lloyd Dock

B. *26 Feb. 1858, Harrisburg, Pennsylvania; d. 17 April 1956, Chambersburg, Pennsylvania*
D. *of Gilliard and Lavinia Bombaugh Dock*

D. was one of six children of a well-to-do family long settled in central Pennsylvania. Nurtured on a sense of elite responsibility, D., her botanist sister Mira, and physician brother George all had careers in which they tried to harness trained expertise to civic purposes, from conservation to sex education.

D. attended private schools and in 1886 graduated from the training school for nurses at Bellevue Hospital in New York. In the late 1880s, after working as a visiting nurse, she began to pursue an administrative and teaching career. A decade later she became a member of the all-female "family" at the Henry Street Settlement in New York and a devoted friend of its founder, Lillian D. Wald. D. recalled that at Henry Street, her home for nearly twenty years, she "began to think." Already a feminist, she became a supporter of the labor movement and a socialist.

D. was an activist who wrote to encourage the professionalization of nursing, the emancipation of women, and the reform of American industrial society. From 1900 to 1923, she edited departments in the *American Journal of Nursing* (which she helped to found) and, from 1905 to 1908, in *Charities and the Commons*. Her career as a nurse, reformer, and writer ended soon after 1922 when she retired to care for an invalid sister.

In the 1890s, as the first successful attempts to unite nurses nationally began, D. advocated organization in speeches and magazine articles. *Short Papers on Nursing Subjects* (1900) shows that at Henry Street D. had learned to hope organization would awaken nurses' social consciences as well as their aspirations to professional status. The book's most important essay, "Ethics—or a Code of Ethics?," influenced by the pragmatism of Henry Street–supporter John Dewey, argues that neither a written code nor the self-interested advice physicians gave nurses could nourish a living ethical sense. This could develop only as nurses participated in self-governing associations and learned democratic social responsibility (as members of women's club did) and solidarity (as members of trade unions did).

In *Hygiene and Morality* (1910), D.'s contribution to the movement against prostitution and for sex education, the themes of women's autonomy and social mission temporarily eclipse the theme of organization. D. argues that the "discoveries and teachings of science" confirm "personal and civic morality." Vice is not only a moral evil which enslaves women but a menace to public health. Like tuberculosis, then the target of a lively campaign, it must be vanquished by teaching individuals to shun contagion and by rooting out social conditions where disease flourished. Prostitution, which "fosters" venereal disease, results from the economic vulnerability and, ultimately, the "political and legal inferiority" of women. The book culminates in the argument that enfranchising women would prevent prostitution and disease by helping women earn honest livings and creating a voting bloc in favor of laws protecting women and children.

In her most ambitious work D. fuses the themes which had preoccupied her since the 1890s. Mary Adelaide Nutting, the coauthor of the four-volume *History of Nursing* (1907–12), had conceived and mapped out the project. But it was D. who did most of the writing and interpreted nursing history as a record of women's efforts to govern themselves and serve society. Because training-school courses used a shortened version (published by D. and Isabel Stewart in 1920) and the authors of other nursing history textbooks appropriated its arrangement, ideas, omissions, and distortions, the *History* helped shape the professional self-image of many 20th-c. American nurses.

Like *Hygiene and Morality*, the *History of Nursing* argues that freeing women necessarily benefits society. D.'s hopes for the emancipation of women and the remaking of American society rest on the belief shared by Wald, Jane Addams, an other feminists that women's special nature destines them for redeeming social roles. D. believes that motherliness defines women, but insists that women can and must express that motherliness actively and outside the home. Her vocabulary displays her assumption that women are by nature active and beneficent.

D.'s writings are propaganda. Although scrupulous about specific facts, she evades topics she dislikes and feels no obligation to understand or present adversaries' viewpoints. Her books and articles are therefore not always dependable guides to the events they describe. But, although they emphasize feminist goals which other nurses left implicit in their programs, they offer insight into the minds of the founders of modern American nursing. The verve, the conviction, and even the lack of balance in D.'s writings also place them among the most vivid and personal expressions of American feminism.

WORKS: *Text-book of Materia Medica for Nurses* (1890). *Short Papers on Nursing Subjects* (1900). *A History of Nursing* (4 vols., with M. Nutting, 1907–12). *Hygiene and Morality: A Manual for Nurses and Others* (1910). *A Short History of Nursing* (with I. Stewart, 1920). *History of American Red Cross Nursing* (with S. Pickett, C. Noyes, et al., 1922).

There is material by and about D. in the papers of Lillian D. Wald at the New York Public Library and Butler Library, Columbia University; in the papers of M. Adelaide Nutting at Teachers College, Columbia University; and in the Dock family papers at the Pennsylvania Historical and Museum Commission, Harrisburg, Pennsylvania.

BIBLIOGRAPHY: Dock, L. L., "Self-Portrait," *Nursing Outlook* 25 (Jan. 1977).

Other references: *American Journal of Nursing* (July 1907; Sept. 1910; Feb. 1956; June 1956). *Nursing Outlook* 17 (June 1969). *NYT* (18 April 1956). *Survey* 24 (20 Aug. 1910).

SUSAN ARMENY

Mary Abigail Dodge

B. 31 March 1833, Hamilton, Massachusetts; d. 17 Aug. 1896, Hamilton,
  Massachusetts
Wrote under: Gail Hamilton
D. of James Brown and Hannah Stanwood Dodge

D. spent her early adult years teaching and, in 1858, she became governess to the children of Gamaliel Bailey, editor of the antislavery *National Era* in Washington, D.C. With his help she established herself as a writer. From 1865 to 1867 she was an editor of *Our Young Folks*. After 1871 she spent much of each year in Washington in the home of Congressman James G. Blaine, whose wife was D.'s first cousin. Blaine was Speaker of the House and a frequent presidential hopeful. In his household D. met politicians, writers, and numerous famous persons of the day. In these years she wrote on political issues, especially civil service reform.

The literary style of Gail Hamilton is characteristically lively, opinionated, and often argumentative. Several of her books are feminist in tone. D. often proclaims her personal and professional independence and encourages a similar spirit in others. *Country Living and Country Thinking* (1861), based upon D.'s experience as a woman running her family's farm, urges women to consider careers other than marriage, and especially to consider writing, despite the "fine, subtle, impalpable, but real" prejudice against "female writers." The economic argument for independence appears again in *Woman's Worth and Worthlessness* (1872), in which D. notes that a woman is not "supported" by a man "when she works as hard in the house as he does out of it."

For many years D. was closely associated with Blaine: she worked with him on his *Twenty Years of Congress* (1884–86) and many believed that she also drafted his speeches. Her biography of Blaine, undertaken as a tribute, is eulogistic and nonanalytical. Her verse, collected and published posthumously by her sister H. Augusta Dodge, in *Chips, Fragments, and Vestiges* (1902), is derivative.

D.'s most characteristic theme, derived from her own experience as a writer, is the need to train woman for spiritual and economic independence. Given her insistence on the need for independence, it seems ironic that D.'s own career, as well as her social contacts, depended to a great degree upon her association with Blaine, and that much of her work for him cannot be recognized as independent from that framework.

WORKS: *Country Living and Country Thinking* (1861). *Courage!* (1862). *Gala Days* (1863). *A Call to My Countrywomen* (1863). *Stumbling-Blocks* (1864). *A New Atmosphere* (1865). *Scientific Farming* (1865). *Skirmishes and Sketches* (1865). *Red Letter Days in Applethorpe* (1866). *Summer Rest* (1866). *Wool Gathering* (1868). *Woman's Wrong* (1868). *Memorial to Mrs. Hannah Stanwood Dodge* (1869). *A Battle of the Books* (1870). *Little Folk Life* (1872). *Woman's Worth and Worthlessness* (1872). *Child World* (1873). *Twelve Miles from a Lemon* (1874). *Nursery Noonings* (1875). *Sermons to the Clergy* (1876). *First Love Is Best* (1877). *What Think Ye of Christ* (1877). *Our Common School System* (1880). *Divine Guidance* (1881). *The Spent Bullet* (1882). *The Insuppressible Book* (1885). *A Washington Bible Class* (1891). *English Kings in a Nutshell* (1893). *Biography of James G. Blaine* (1893). *X-Rays* (1896). *Gail Hamilton's Life in Letters* (Ed. H. A. Dodge, 1901). *Chips, Fragments, and Vestiges* (Ed. H. A. Dodge, 1902).

BIBLIOGRAPHY: Beale, H. S., ed., *Letters of Mrs. James G. Blaine* (1908). Dodge, M. A., *Memorial to Mrs. Hannah Stanwood Dodge* (1869). Spofford, H. R., *A Little Book of Friends* (1916). Tryon, W. S., *Parnassus Corner: A Life of James T. Fields* (1963).

For articles in reference works, see: *AW. NAW* (article by M. W. Langworthy).

JANE BENARDETE

Mary Mapes Dodge

B. *26 Jan. 1830, New York City; d. 21 Aug. 1905, Onteora Park, New York*
D. *of James Jay and Sophia Furman Mapes; m. William Dodge, 1851*

D.'s family moved often, finally settling in Irvington, New Jersey, where, on a large farm, overlooking Staten Island and Manhattan, her father conducted horticultural experiments and edited a magazine called *The Working Farmer*. When D. rejoined her family at the farm after the death of her husband, her father started her writing for his magazine in order to occupy her time and assuage her grief. D. also began telling stories to her two young sons.

As a result of her boys' interest in the Dutch sport of skating, which was just becoming popular in the U.S., and her frequent visits with a Dutch family who told her stories of Holland, D. wrote *Hans Brinker; or, The Silver Skates*, which has been translated into many languages is still a bestseller after more than a hundred years.

From 1865 on, D. helped to edit a magazine called *Hearth and Home*, until asked by Roswell Smith of the Century Company to start a children's magazine for them. So in 1873, D. became the editor of *St. Nicholas*, the greatest children's magazine of all time. *Hans Brinker* and *St. Nicholas* established D.'s top-notch reputation, but she also produced a number of other books.

St. Nicholas set a new and lasting pattern for children's literature: Kipling wrote *The Jungle Books* and Frances Hodgson Burnett *Little Lord Fauntleroy* (1886) for the magazine. Other top authors, among them Robert Louis Stevenson, Samuel Clemens, Alfred Tennyson, eager to be published in this vital periodical, also sent D. their work. Many reputations were made in these pages. *St. Nicholas* was still thriving when, at age seventy-five, D. died at her summer residence in Onteora Park, New York.

WORKS: *Irvington Stories* (1864). *Hans Brinker: or, The Silver Skates* (1865). *A Few Friends and How They Amused Themselves* (1869). *Rhymes and Jingles* (1874). *Theophilus and Others* (1876). *Along the Way* (1879). *Donald and Dorothy* (1883). *Baby World* (1884). *The Land of Pluck* (1894). *When Life Is Young* (1894).

BIBLIOGRAPHY: For articles in reference works, see: *AW. DAB. NAW* (article by H. S. Commager). *NCAB.*

Other references: *Century* (Nov. 1905). *Critic* (Oct. 1905). *Current Literature* (Oct. 1905). *NYT* (22 Aug. 1905). *St. Nicholas* (Oct. 1905).

CATHERINE MORRIS WRIGHT

Hilda Doolittle

B. 10 Sept. 1886, Bethlehem, Pennsylvania; d. 27 Sept. 1961, Zurich, Switzerland
Wrote under: H. D.
D. of Charles L. and Helen Wolle Doolittle; m. Richard Aldington, 1915

D. was the daughter of a professor of astronomy and the granddaughter of the principal of a local Moravian seminary, who was a descendant of a member of the original 18th-c. mystical order knows as the Unitas Fratrum, or Moravian Brotherhood. Since the founding of the order, the concept of *Unitas Fratrum* has been identified with "the Mystery which lay at the center of the world." Young D. participated in Moravian religious exercises and rituals, all of which had a profound effect upon her. In *Tribute to Angels* (1945), more than forty years after her childhood experiences, she returned to the enigmatic "Mystery," the essence of Moravian belief, describing it as "the point in the spectrum/where all light becomes one/ . . . as we were told as children."

Educated chiefly in private schools, D. spent a year and a half at Bryn Mawr, withdrawing in 1906 due to a "slight breakdown." She became engaged briefly to Ezra Pound, who encouraged her to pursue her classical studies and to continue to write serious poetry. Soon after, D. left for London to begin the life of an expatriate, and rarely returned to America.

In 1913, D. married the British poet Richard Aldington. Later (1917) she assumed the editorship of *The Egoist*, while she earnestly pursued her career as a poet. The period between 1915 and 1920 was filled with personal crisis: a miscarriage in 1915, the death of her older brother in combat in 1918, separation from Aldington (final divorce in 1938), and the death of her father in 1919. In 1919, D. found herself essentially alone, seriously ill, and pregnant. She wrote from her flat in war-torn London: "Death! Death is all around us!" The foregoing events precipitated a severe breakdown, and D. eventually sought the help of Sigmund Freud, whom she refers to as the "blameless physician" in her brilliant psychobiography, *Tribute to Freud*, published in 1956.

Following World War I, D. wrote thirteen volumes of poetry, along with translations, essays, dramas, film criticism, and novels. When her *Collected Poems*, the volume that established her reputation, was published in 1925, many of the vital experiences that tempered her writing had occurred.

The early tightly honed, discrete Imagist poems are familiar to most readers. In them with clarity, precision, and control, D. described pear trees with "flower-tufts/thick on the branch"; sea poppies "spilled near the shrub pines/to bleach on the boulders"; or grapes "red-purple/their berries dripping/with wine." D.'s final, major modern poetic sequences, *Helen in Egypt* (1961), is less well known. Throughout her work, however, from the slender Imagist verse to the final monumental poetic sequence, D. was in search of what she dimly defined as "a myth, the one reality." This would permit her not only to articulate her emotions but would also allow her the freedom to create an "organizing structure" in which she could function as both a woman and an artist.

D. ingeniously shaped the classical world to her own temperament, weaving and reweaving the legends of the past into modern form, emulating myth in order to gain a sense of the spiritual, the timeless. For D., events, emotions, experiences, became continuations of a simpler, more structured mythic past, which she found more manageable than the immediate, chaotic contemporary scene. As she developed her skills, D. was able to transfer mythic patterns from one culture to another, as reflected in her wide-ranging vision of Woman throughout the ages, which is included in *Tribute to Angels*. More notably, however, in *The Walls Do Not Fall* (1944), she comfortably mingles classical allusions with observations of the shell-shocked, bombed-out, devastation of London: "there as here, ruin opens/the tomb, the temple . . . /the shrine lies open to the sky/the rain falls . . . /sand drifts, eternity endures." Typically D. emphasizes once again her concept of identity and self-possession in the lines: ". . . living within/you beget, self-out-of-self/ . . . that pearl-of-great-price."

The search for "a myth, the one reality" was successfully achieved by means of the pervasive, legendary figure of Helen in D.'s last major work. In the earlier Imagist poem, "Helen," the heroine, a wan maiden with "still eyes in (a) white face" is clouded with subtle ambiguities—she is the Helen Greece could love "only if she were laid/white ash amid funereal cypresses." In *Helen in Egypt*, the mature, intelligent, confident Helen struggles for self-definition following the cataclysmic Trojan War. With "things remembered forgotten/remembered again," Helen assembles and reassembles her thoughts and emotions and resolves: "I *must* fight for Helena." In this long poem D. artfully weaves and reweaves the mythic pattern until the legendary figure of Helen (the

Woman who will not now be denied) achieves her identity: "I am awake/ . . . I *see* things clearly at last,/ the old pictures are really there."

With *Helen in Egypt*, D. herself achieves self-definition, and brings to a close her search for an identity, "the one reality," for which she had been striving all her life.

D.'s work transcends the limitations of the Imagist movement, for which she allegedly was not only the inspiration but, together with Ezra Pound and Richard Aldington, also a formulator of its principles. Currently she is, and justifiably so, identified as a modern. Norman Holmes Pearson, D.'s literary executor, contends that D. is in "the very center of the modern poetic movement . . . and will increasingly be recognized" when her audience not only learns how to read her poetry but becomes familiar with classical mythology.

WORKS: *Sea Garden* (1916). *Hymen* (1921). *Heliodora, and Other Poems* (1924). *Collected Poems* (1925). *Palimpsest* (1926). *Hippolytos Temporizes: A Play in Three Acts* (1927). *Hedylus* (1928). *Red Roses for Bronze* (1931). *The Walls Do Not Fall* (1944). *Tribute to Angels* (1945). *The Flowering of the Rod* (1946). *By Avon River* (1949). *Tribute to Freud* (1956). *Selected Poems of H. D.* (1957). *Hermetic Definition* (1958). *Bid Me to Live* (1960). *Helen in Egypt* (1961). *End to Torment: A Memoir of Ezra Pound* (Eds. N. H. Pearson and M. King, 1979).

BIBLIOGRAPHY: Coffman, S. K., *Imagism: A Chapter for the History of Modern Poetry* (1951). Hughes, G., *Imagism and the Imagists* (1931). Mearns, H., *Hilda Doolittle* (The Pamphlet Poets, 1926). Monroe, H., *Poets and Their Art* (1932). Quinn, V., *Hilda Doolittle* (1968). Swann, T. B., *The Classical World of Hilda Doolittle* (1962). Waggoner, H. H., *American Poets: From the Puritans to the Present* (1968).
    Other references: *ConL* 10 (Autumn 1969). *Poetry* (June 1962).

                                                                    CLAIRE HEALEY

Julia Caroline Ripley Dorr

B. *13 Feb. 1825, Charleston, South Carolina; d. 18 Jan. 1913, Rutland, Vermont*
Wrote under: Julia C. R. Dorr, Caroline Thomas
D. *of William Y. and Zulma De Lacy Thomas Ripley; m. Seneca M. Dorr, 1847*

D.'s mother's family fled from Santo Domingo to the U.S. during a slave uprising. Her father was a bank president, and she spent most of her formative years in Vermont receiving her education there at Middlebury seminary. D. enjoyed the friendship of R. W. Emerson, Edmund Clarence Stedman, and Oliver Wendell Holmes, among others. She was a founder of the Rutland Library, and received a Litt.D. from Middlebury College in Vermont.

D.'s first novels, *Farmingdale* (1854), *Lanmere* (1856), and *Sibyl Huntington* (1869), deal with young women living in New England villages who are subject to a grinding routine of home chores. These novels are noteworthy for their realistic depiction of family bitterness and the round of household activities: tubs filled with laundry, milk pans to be scalded, rag rugs to be pieced, work baskets piled with mending. Each novel contains pointed discussions on books, learning, literature, and libraries, offered as the heroines' reprieve from woman's toil.

Expiation (1873) views domestic tragedy from the stance of a neighborly female narrator who is middle-aged, tranquil, unmarried. The plot involves hereditary insanity, its concealment by a young wife, an adolescent son's attempt to kill his mother, a coffin that yields up its supposed corpse. Gothic horrors come to light amidst the beauties of the Vermont countryside, descriptions of which D. excells in: the riot of green, the meadows and uplands, brawling trout streams, the barefoot boy and the singing thrush, wild roses and honeysuckles under a sapphire sky.

D.'s poetry appeared in newspapers and magazines such as *Scribner's, Harper's, Atlantic Monthly*, and *Sartain's Union Magazine of Literature and Art*. Her poems were anthologized in Emerson's *Parnassus* (1874), and Stedman's *An American Anthology* (1900). D. experimented with a variety of forms—narratives, dramatic monologues, patriotic and war verses, historic celebrations, sonnets, hymns, and ballads.

D.'s travel books are companionable, anecdotal, and historically informative. *Bermuda* appeared in 1884. *The Flower of England's Face; sketches of English Travel* (1895) takes the reader from Wales to Scotland with a long stop at Haworth to collect firsthand reminiscences about the Brontës. *A Cathedral Pilgrimage* (1896) revels in rustic gardens, chapels, spires, "ruined arches, forsaken courts open to all the sky, and columns ivy-grown and lichen clad." It imaginatively recreates medieval life and recounts legends of martyrs and warriors.

Despite D.'s dislike of suffering women poets as expressed in *Farmingdale*, she was unable to keep the lachrymose strain out of her own last works. Her poetic diction includes the formalized lyrical utterance of her shorter poems, as well as the colloquial forthrightness of her dramatic monologues. The same chatty directness is evident in her books of travel and advice, and recalls the vigor of her early domestic novels. Her interest in family problems arising from cruelty, pride, or error enters into her narrative poems. Like many women poets of her time, she tended to give them exotic, medieval, Germanic, or oriental settings; however, the regional locales of her New England fiction bestow a more enduring value on her portrayals of family life.

WORKS: *Farmingdale* (1854). *Lanmere* (1856). *Sibyl Huntington* (1869). *Poems* (1872). *Bride and Bridegroom* (1873). *Expiation* (1873). *Friar Anselmo and Other Poems* (1875). *Bermuda. An Idyl of the Summer Islands* (1884). *Afternoon Songs* (1885). *Poems* (1892). *The Fallow Field* (1893). *"The Flower of England's Face": Sketches of English Travel* (1895). *A Cathedral Pilgrimage* (1896). *In Kings' Houses: A Romance of the Days of Queen Anne* (1898). *Afterglow* (1900). *Poems, Complete* (1901). *Beyond the Sunset, Latest Poems* (1909). *Last Poems* (1913). *W. Y. R. A Book of Remembrance* (n.d.).

BIBLIOGRAPHY: Baym, N., *Woman's Fiction: A Guide to Novels by and about Women in America, 1820–1870* (1978). Carleton, H., *Genealogy and Family History of Vermont* (1903). Crockett, W. H., *Vermont the Green Mountain State* (1921). Morse, J. J., ed., *Life and Letters of Oliver Wendell Holmes* ('1896). Ripley, H. W., *Genealogy of a Part of the Ripley Family* (1867). Stedman, L., and G. M. Gould, eds., *Life and Letters of E. C. Stedman* (1910). Thiébaux, M., in *Theory and Practice of Feminist Literary Criticism*, Eds. G. Mora and K. S. Van Hooft (1982).

For articles in reference works, see: *AA. AW. DAB.*

MARCELLE THIÉBAUX

Rheta Childe Dorr

B. 2 Nov. 1866, Omaha, Nebraska; d. 8 Aug. 1948, New Britain, Pennsylvania
Given name: Reta Louise Childe
D. of Edward and Lucie Childe; m. John Pixley Dorr, 1892

The daughter of Episcopalian parents, D. joined the National Woman Suffrage Association at twelve, attended the University of Nebraska for one year, and enrolled at the Art Students' League in New York City in 1890. She took her first reporting job on the New York *Evening Post* and was a muckraker at *Everybody's Magazine* and *Hampton's* from 1907 to 1912. Briefly a member of the Socialist Party, she became active in the Republican Party in 1916. A militant suffragist, she edited the *Suffragist*, and from 1913 to 1916 was a member of the Heterodoxy, an early feminist discussion group. As a foreign correspondent she covered the Pankhursts' suffrage struggle in England, the Russian Revolution, World War I, and Mussolini's march into Rome.

D. was the author of several books, most of which (aside from her autobiography) consist of materials she previously published in newspapers and magazines. As an autobiography, *A Woman of Fifty* (1924) represents both a highly successful creative act and a "self-revelation." Illustrating the traditional effort of an American intellectual to relate personal experience to the pattern of cultural change, D. sketched a political journey—one which led from a progressive vision of cooperative millenialism to a conservative faith in a "sane, practical democracy," with the "Great War" acting as the important transforming experience. However, D. was firm in her commitment to feminism; the chronological narrative revolves around her own early awakening to feminism, and her struggle as a journalist to support herself and her son. Throughout her lifetime, D. worked to bring others from a perception of women as a "ladies' aid society to the human race" to an affirmation of their "breaking into the human race" with "full freedom."

In *What Eight Million Woman Want* (1910), D. dealt with "woman's invasion of industry" as a permanent factor in the American economy, carefully employing data obtained from reporting on all social classes of women in Europe and America. Having investigated various employments by working as a laundress, seamstress, department store clerk, and assembly-line worker, D. sympathetically revealed the "intimate lives of the factory workers in order to tell their story as they would tell it themselves if they had a chance." She also emphasized the social-reform activities of educated middle-class women's organizations, concluding that the fulfillment of their demands for women's economic, social, and political freedom was in the best interest of a democratic society. D. reiterated these beliefs in *Susan B. Anthony* (1928), a witty and sympathetic biography and history of women's life in America which dramatically situated Anthony within the social context of the post-Civil War era.

D. was a war correspondent from 1917 to 1918. *Inside the Russian Revolution* (1917) condemned Bolshevik politics and marked her break with New York socialist friends. Interpreting events in terms of "excesses" of an "unruly, unreasoning, sanguinary mob" intent on disengaging from the "Great war," D. recommended a large dose of American economic aid and the "help and guidance" of strong leaders with pragmatic republican values. D. ably captured the feeling of a country at war in her description of the July Revolution and the "women's batallion of death"; but *Inside the Russian Revolution* was marred by its strong ethnocentric bias.

D. was among the first journalists to report "hard news" about all classes of women, and she was among the best of the muckracking journalists. While her war correspondence was not consistently outstanding, she was among only a few women who obtained western-front reporting assignments during World War I. Her autobiography must be considered not only an "extraordinarily revealing" document but also a provocative commentary on American culture.

WORKS: *What Eight Million Women Want* (1910). *Inside the Russian Revolution* (1917). *A Soldier's Mother in France* (1918). *A Woman of Fifty* (1924). *Susan B. Anthony: The Woman Who Changed the Mind of a Nation* (1928). *Drink: Coercion or Control?* (1929).

BIBLIOGRAPHY: Banner, L. W., *Woman in Modern America: A Brief History* (1974). Filler, L., *Crusaders for American Liberalism* (1939). Marzolf, M., *Up from the Footnote: A History of Women Journalists* (1977). Ross, I., *Ladies of the Press* (1936).

For articles in reference works, see: *NAW* (article by L. Filler).

Other references: *Bookman* (11 March 1911). *Books* (21 Oct. 1928).

JENNIFER L. TEBBE

Abigail Scott Duniway

B. 22 Oct. 1834, Groveland, Illinois; d. 11 Oct. 1915, Portland, Oregon
D. of John Tucker and Ann Roelofson Scott; m. Benjamin C. Duniway, 1853

The second daughter among twelve children, D. grew up on the Illinois frontier. At seventeen, she accompanied her family on the overland trail to Oregon, keeping a journal of their 1852 crossing which is one of the best of the genre. Her mother and baby brother died of cholera on the way, and the family arrived virtually destitute in Oregon.

D.'s first novel, *Captain Gray's Company* (1859), is a fictionalized account of her wagon trail journey to Oregon and her early life in an Oregon town. It reveals as much about its author and her attitudes as about her milieu. Agrarian as well as feminist in principle, D. was writing for "the world's workers, the stay and strength of our land," and hoped her book would "be instrumental in causing the sterner to look more to the welfare of the weakest of the . . . weaker sex." More realistic than many other women's novels of the time, the book was nevertheless criticized by D.'s political and religious opponents for being too romantic. It remains of interest for its pervasive wit and its historical detail.

Between May 1871 and January 1887, D. published and edited a weekly newspaper called the *New Northwest*. It advocated both women's rights and human rights and circulated throughout the Pacific Northwest and to women in other parts of the country. Its lively style, strong opinions, revelations of political and social scandals, and fervent advocacy of legal reforms and woman suffrage made it a particularly influential and controversial publication. In it D. also serialized sixteen more of her own novels. These were essentially polemical, featuring strong, mistreated female heroines who suffer numerous adversities and finally triumph over refined ladies and antisuffragist enemies. Though flawed as literature, the stories include extraordinary details of frontier family life and social relationships. Many passages show a fine gift for writing dialogue and humor.

D. also lectured extensively, bringing her message to isolated women and men with fervor and courage. Each year she averaged two hundred lectures, and traveled three thousand miles by steamboat, mud-wagon, stagecoach, horseback, and railroad. She lectured her way across the country six times and became vice-president of the National Woman Suffrage Association in 1884. D.'s "editorial correspondence" now constitutes a unique historical record of the people and places she saw.

Though D. almost succeeded in winning woman suffrage in Oregon and Washington during the 1880s, the closing of the frontier led to changes which delayed it for another generation. From 1887 until her death, D. continued to write and lecture, publishing in the *Portland Oregonian,* the *Pacific Empire* (which she edited), and the *Coming Century*. When woman suffrage was declared in 1912, she wrote the official proclamation of victory and became the first woman voter in Oregon.

D.'s ambition and achievement as a writer was undoubtedly affected by her lack of formal education. Her historical role is more significant than her literary achievements because she never had the leisure, economic means, or intention to write for art's sake. Nevertheless, the quality of D.'s vigorously amusing polemics is worthy evidence of her strong convictions and forceful, talented personality.

WORKS: *Captain Gray's Company; or, Crossing the Plains and Living in Oregon* (1859). *My Musing* (1875). *David and Anna Matson* (1876). *From the West to the West: Across the Plains to Oregon* (1905). *Path Breaking* (1914).

BIBLIOGRAPHY: Bandow, G. R., "In Pursuit of a Purpose: Abigail Scott Duniway and the *New Northwest*" (M.A. thesis, Univ. of Oregon, 1973). Capell, L., "Biography of Abigail Scott Duniway" (M.A. thesis, Univ. of Oregon, 1934). Morrison, D. N., *Ladies Were Not Expected: Abigail Scott Duniway and Women's Rights* (1977). Moynihan, R. B., *Circuit Rider for Women: Abigail Scott Duniway of Oregon* (forthcoming, 1983). Roberts, L. M., "Suffragist of the New West: Abigail Scott Duniway and the Development of the Oregon Woman Suffrage Movement" (B.A. thesis, Reed College, 1969). Richey, E., *Eminent Women of the West* (1975). Ross, N. W., *Westward the Women* (1944). Smith, H. K., *The Presumptuous Dreamers* (1974).

RUTH BARNES MOYNIHAN

Wilma Dykeman

B. 20 May 1920, Asheville, North Carolina
Wrote under: Wilma Dykeman, Wilma Dykeman Stokely
D. of Willard Jerome and Bonnie Cushman Cole Dykeman; m. James R. Stokely, Jr., 1940

D.'s works betray a twofold love of southern Appalachia: the fervid love of an immigrant for the new land, and the comfortable, well-rooted love of one whose forebearers have shaped a region's history. Her father came from New York state but married into a long-established Asheville family, thus partially removing the "newcomer" stigma. After graduating from Northwestern University, D. returned home to marry poet-writer James Stokely. They remained in Appalachia, writing, teaching, raising a family, and lecturing. Stokely died in 1977. D. continues her work, living now in the village of Newport, Tennessee.

The South—but most especially the Appalachian South—is D.'s subject. Her novels, biographies, histories, and regional landscapes explore such themes as the mountain woman's unique social role, technology and "progress" as threats to mountain environments, the interconnectedness of blacks and whites, the crucial impact of Protestantism. D.'s first work, *The French Broad* (1955), nicely showcases her talent for social history. The French Broad River rises in the mountains of Transylvania County, North Carolina, changes directions through the region several times, and finally joins the Holston to form the Tennessee River at Knoxville. A river study, says D., is the best kind of travel book, for it enables one to get the feel of the region. *The French Broad* is structured both chronologically and thematically; central figures of the region's past and present are detailed, as anecdotes illuminate such topics as the divisiveness of the Civil War, Appalachian religiosity, the fashionable watering places of the 19th c., or the prototypical mountain midwife.

D.'s other social histories combine the same informality and personal engagement. The 1957 book, *Neither Black nor White*, written with James Stokely, responded to the Brown school desegregation decision of 1954. It tried to understand "the many Souths" and "discover, record and interpret a republic of the human mind." For its contribution to race relations, the book received the Hillman award. D. and Stokely later produced *The Border States* (1968), and in 1975 D.'s bicentennial history of Tennessee appeared. The book depicts that state's three geographical regions and shows how Tennessee remains in many ways a frontier area.

D.'s storytelling knack is apparent in her three novels, all of which explore regional themes. Centering on the character of Lydia McQueen, *The Tall Woman* (1962) portrays the special functions that mountain women performed during the Civil War and Reconstruction. *The Far Family* (1966) delineates the mountain woman's importance in preserving tradition and family; sociologically, her role resembles both that of the heroically strong black woman and the southern plantation wife. *Return the Innocent Earth* (1973) explores the impact of industrial development on the region.

D.'s three biographies manifest her talent for social history and strong characterization. *Seeds of Southern Change* (1962), also written with Stokely, traces the life of Will Alexander (1884–1956), a southern white liberal who, as director of the "Commission on Interracial Cooperation," and later as chief of Roosevelt's Farm Security Administration, did as much as any one person to direct the South toward economic and racial justice. *Prophet of Plenty* (1966) explores the life and work of W. D. Weatherford (1875–1970), a champion of Appalachia whose fund-raising work at Berea College gave it national renown.

Edna Rankin McKinnon is the subject of D.'s third biography, *Too Many People, Too Little Love* (1974). The younger sister of Jeannette Rankin, the first woman elected to Congress, Edna began lobbying in Washington in 1936 for birth control and then worked in Appalachia and around the world, establishing birth control and family planning clinics. D. says that Edna's story interested her because it combined the three most important issues of the 20th c.—the population explosion, the changing status of women, and the necessity for world peace.

D., not often given a careful reading because of her "regionalism," deserves a wider critical audience. She uses an easy and flowing style, perfectly suited to the anecdotal character of much of her work. She excels in describing folkways and vividly captures mountain speech. Her themes—though regional at base—are in the best sense universal human concerns.

WORKS: *The French Broad* (1955). *Neither Black nor White* (with J. Stokely, 1957). *Seeds of Southern Change: The Life of Will Alexander* (with J. Stokely, 1962). *The Tall Woman* (1962). *The Far Family* (1966). *Prophet of Plenty: the First Ninety Years of W. D. Weatherford* (1966). *The Border States: Kentucky, North Carolina, Tennessee, Virginia, West Virginia* (with J. Stokely, 1968). *Look to This Day* (1968). *Return the Innocent Earth* (1973). *Southern Appalachian Books: An Annotated Selected Bibliography* (1973). *Too Many People, Too Little Love—Edna Rankin McKinnon: Pioneer for Birth Control* (1974). *Tennessee, a Bicentennial History* (1975).

BIBLIOGRAPHY: *Chicago Sunday Tribune* (29 July 1962). *CSM* (5 May 1955). *NYHTB* (1 May 1955). *NYTBR* (1 July 1962; 3 June 1973; 8 Sept. 1974). *SatEvePost* (April 1974).

MARGARET McFADDEN-GERBER

Alice Morse Earle

B. 27 April 1851, Worcester, Massachusetts; d. 16 Feb. 1911, Hempstead, Long Island, New York
Given name: Mary Alice Morse
D. of Edwin and Abigail Mason Clary Morse; m. Henry Earle, 1874

E., antiquarian and social historian, was a descendant of men important in the history of New England and Massachusetts. She was educated at Worcester High School and at Dr. Gannett's boarding school in Boston. After her marriage E. moved to Brooklyn Heights and remained there her entire life. Her early life was devoted to her husband and the care of her four children, with little thought to a career in writing or history. After the death of her husband E. traveled extensively through Europe with her sister. It was about this time that family members, particularly her father, began urging her to write professionally.

The publication of *The Sabbath in Puritan New England* (1891) marked the beginning of E.'s writing career, and during the next twelve years she wrote, edited, and contributed to the publication of seventeen books and over thirty articles describing various aspects of early American history. All of E.'s works deal with the human, domestic side of American history. Utilizing primary source materials—wills, letters, journals, newspapers, court records—E. pieced together an accurate picture of what everyday life was like in colonial America.

E. had a particular interest in the role played by women in early America. All of her books contain a great deal of information on the economic and social activities of women in families and their respective communities. In *The Diary of Anna Green Winslow, a Boston School Girl of 1771* (1894) and *Margaret Winthrop* (1895) E. views her subjects as representative women of their times, and utilizes them as focal points for discussing the everyday lives, duties, and responsibilities of women in the colonial era.

Colonial Dames and Good Wives (1895) deals with the roles played by women in America from first settlement to the American Revolution. Primarily devoted to investigation of the women of New England, E. also makes reference to notable women who lived in the middle and southern colonies. As a general work on the history of women in America, it is a valuable and informative book even today.

The most widely read and referred to book written by E., *Home Life in Colonial Days* (1898) is an informative and entertaining account of daily life. Starting with an account of the kinds of homes lived in by the early settlers and how they were constructed, E. devotes chapters to the histories of such subjects as the lighting, food, drink, clothing, and gardens of the first settlers of America.

E. considered *Two Centuries of Costume in America, 1620–1820* (two volumes, 1902) her finest work. In the many years since its publication, no other work of its accuracy and detail has appeared. With her extensive knowledge of the life-styles and activities of early Americans, E. offers a stimulating discussion of the significance of the costumes worn by the colonists with respect to their lives.

E.'s articles and books were widely read and appreciated by her contemporaries. Celebration of the Revolutionary centennial in 1876 had reawakened popular interest in early American history. This popular interest demanded a new kind of historical literature devoted to the life of American society and E.'s books and articles found a welcoming audience. She never sacrificed her scholarship and historical integrity to meet the demands of her public, however. Her research was always of the highest quality, and she shared an interest in unearthing historical truths with professionally trained historians. Although her books are sometimes repetitive (possibly because she was so prolific), they are, with few exceptions, valuable and still enjoy popularity today.

WORKS: *The Sabbath in Puritan New England* (1891). *China Collecting in America* (1892). *Customs and Fashions of Old New England* (1893). *Costume of Colonial Times* (1894). *Diary of Anna Green Winslow, a Boston School Girl of 1771* (edited by Earle, 1904). *Colonial Dames and Good Wives* (1895). *Margaret Winthrop* (1895). *Colonial Days in Old New York* (1896). *Curious Punishments of Bygone Days* (1896). *Historic New York* (1897). *Chap Book Essays* (1897). *Home Life in Colonial Days* (1898). *In Old Narragansett: Romances and Realities* (1898). *Child Life in Colonial Days* (1899). *Stage Coach and Tavern Days* (1900). *Old Time Gardens* (1901). *Sun Dials and Roses of Yesterday* (1902). *Two Centuries of Costume in America, 1620–1820* (2 vols., 1903).

The papers of Alice Morse Earle are in the Sophia Smith Collection, Smith College, Massachusetts.

BIBLIOGRAPHY: For articles in reference works, see: *DAB. NAW* (article by W. Garrett).

Other references: *NYT* (18 Feb. 1911). *NYHT* (18 Feb. 1911). *Old Time New England* (Jan. 1947). Worcester (Mass.) *Telegram* (18 Feb. 1911).

PAULA A. TRECKEL

Elaine Goodale Eastman

B. *9 Oct. 1863, Mount Washington, Massachusetts; d. 22 Dec. 1953, Hadley, Massachusetts*
Wrote under: Elaine Goodale Eastman, Elaine Goodale
D. *of Henry Sterling and Dora Hill Read Goodale; m. Charles A. Eastman, 1891*

For her first eighteen years, E.'s world was Sky Farm, the Goodales' Berkshire homestead. There she learned about literature from her mother, about nature from her father, and started combining these lessons in poetry at the age of seven. In 1883, after the single year of boarding school that family finances allowed, E. began teaching Indian students at Hampton Institute in Virginia. Visiting Dakota convinced E. that reservation schools would accelerate Indian assimilation, and she established a government day school among the Sioux in 1886. Her teaching success earned her appointment in 1890 as Supervisor of Education in the

Dakotas. In 1891 E. married Santee Sioux Dr. Charles A. Eastman (Ohiyesa), and resigned her position, dedicating herself to her husband and his people.

Thirty years of marriage brought E. six children, and frequent relocations due to her husband's fluctuating career. E. attempted to augment her family income by writing, editing Carlisle Indian School's newspaper and her husband's works, arranging his lectures, and running a summer camp. Financial tension, editorial resentment, and her husband's rumored infidelity ended E.'s marriage in 1921, although both kept their separation secret. E. returned to the Berkshires, continuing to write until shortly before her death at ninety.

E.'s literary career began early, when three volumes of poetry she and her younger sister Dora had written for family gatherings were published and enthusiastically received. E.'s development of death and rejuvenation themes, her love imagery, and her deft use of language and rhyme belie her youth. In *Journal of a Farmer's Daughter* (1881), she romantically celebrates in prose and poetry and annual cycle of rural life. Nearly fifty years later, E. collected her subsequently published verse in *The Voice at Eve* (1930), which reflects the broadened interests and insight of her maturity. Her dominant themes include woman as giver, the painful joy of loving, the noble vanishing Indian, and intercultural understanding.

When E. embraced the cause of Indian education, she moved from poetry to polemics, writing many articles and pamphlets urging establishment of reservation day schools and Protestant missions. Although she admitted that all could learn "Some Lessons from Barbarism" (1890) regarding women's dress, equality, and generosity, she constantly emphasized the goal of assimilating the Indians into American culture. *Pratt: The Red Man's Moses* (1935) is a biography of the founder of Carlisle Indian School, the federal government's first boarding school for Indians. E. praises General Richard Henry Pratt's efforts (although she voices her preference for day schools) and condemns policies contrary to the assimilationist philosophy that she and Pratt shared.

Consistent with this emphasis, E. appraised the value of Native American oral traditions narrowly, as stories for children. With her husband, she published two collections of Sioux tales, and she simplified folklore selected from various anthropological collections in *Indian Legends Retold* (1919). She also wrote several works of sentimental prose fiction for children.

E.'s only adult novel, *Hundred Maples* (1935), focuses upon Ellen

Strong who, regretting her early marriage, wanders in search of herself. She eventually accepts her complicated ties to family, and to the Vermont landscape hallowed by her foremothers. *Sister to the Sioux* (1978) is a posthumously published autobiography.

E.'s writings provide much insight into the ambiguities of intercultural relations and of the female sacrifice of career for motherhood. E.'s inability to reconcile both her sincere regard for the Sioux with her ethnocentrism and her need for self-expression within her marriage describes one woman's experience of the eternal conflict between ideals and reality.

WORKS: *Apple Blossoms: Verses of Two Children* (with D. R. Goodale, 1878). *In Berkshire with the Wild Flowers* (with D. R. Goodale, 1879). *All Round the Year: Verses from Sky Farm* (with D. R. Goodale, 1881). *Journal of a Farmer's Daughter* (1881). *The Coming of the Birds* (1883). *Wigwam Evenings: Sioux Folktales Retold* (with C. A. Eastman, 1909). *Smoky Day's Wigwam Evenings: Indian Stories Retold* (with C. A. Eastman, 1910). *Little Brother o' Dreams* (1910). *Yellow Star: A Story of East and West* (1911). *The Eagle and the Star: American Indian Pageant Play in Three Acts* (ca. 1916). *Indian Legends Retold* (1919). *The Luck of Oldacres* (1928). *The Voice at Eve* (1930). *Hundred Maples* (1935). *Pratt: The Red Man's Moses* (1935). *Sister to the Sioux: The Memoirs of Elaine Goodale Eastman, 1885-91* (Ed. K. Graber, 1978).

BIBLIOGRAPHY: Wilson, R., "Dr. Charles Alexander Eastman (Ohiyesa), Santee Sioux" (Ph.D. diss., Univ. of New Mexico, 1977).

For articles in reference works, see: *NCAB. The Twentieth Century Biographical Dictionary of Notable Americans*, Ed. R. Johnson (1904).

Other references: *Atlantic* (Aug. 1928). *Mississippi Valley Historical Review* (March 1936). *NYT* (23 Dec. 1953). *NYTBR* (26 May 1935).

HELEN M. BANNAN

Mignon Good Eberhart

B. 6 June 1899, Lincoln, Nebraska
D. of William Thomas and Margaret Hill Good; m. Alanson C. Eberhart, 1923; m. John Hazen Perry, 1946; m. Alanson C. Eberhart, 1948

E. attended Nebraska Wesleyan University and received a Litt. D. from that same institution in 1935. Although she published plays (*Eight*

O'Clock Tuesday, 1941, with Robert Wallsten; *320 College Avenue*, 1938, with Frederick Ballard) and short stories during the first half of her career, E. later wrote only novels of suspense, for which the Mystery Writers of America awarded her their Grand Master Award in 1971.

Several of E.'s novels, such as *The Cup, the Blade, or the Gun* (1961) and *Family Fortune* (1976), both set during the Civil War, and *Enemy in the House* (1962), set during the American Revolution, are historical. The majority of her novels, however, are contemporary in setting. Most are set in the U.S. or the West Indies and, particularly during WWII, display considerable patriotism. Often her novels feature some sort of inclement weather as a commentary to the human conflicts. E.'s style is leisurely, with dialogue that serves to reiterate rather than advance the plot; these techniques not only increase the atmosphere of suspense that is her trademark, but also buy time for character development.

E.'s main characters are women, who find antagonists in jealous female rivals or relatives and show respect to older women. With only one exception (*Another Man's Murder*, 1957), E.'s novels are told from a female character's point of view and the murderers are usually male. Her heroines are primarily cast in the roles of marriageable young women suddenly confronted with love triangles. They may work for a living (*The White Dress*, 1945; *Danger Money*, 1974) but they rarely hold positions of power.

E.'s heroines are not always virginal but they are always passive. They are often married to older men who physically abuse them (*Speak No Evil*, 1941; *Woman on the Roof*, 1963) or to men who practice a type of psychic torture (*Fair Warning*, 1936). Sometimes the husband exercises crippling control even in his absence (*Message from Hong Kong*, 1969; *The Unknown Quantity*, 1953; *Never Look Back*, 1950). Invariably, these husbands become the victims of murder, and the progress to their various deaths goes hand in hand with awakening on the part of their wives. The path to a newfound consciousness in a married E. heroine is twofold: the woman initially learns to understand and reject her present subordinate position to her husband, but in the second stage of the process she voluntarily begins to rely upon another man —generally younger and always more physically attractive than her spouse. This man usually becomes her husband at the conclusion of the novel.

In the characters of Susan Dare in *The Cases of Susan Dare* (1934) and Nurse Sarah Keate in *The Patient in Room 18* (1929), however, E.

develops a different type of female protagonist, a woman who relies more on her brains than on her ability to be attractive to a man. Moreover, Dare and Keate are not humorless creatures; unlike their confused counterparts in the other novels, they have a feel for the good joke, for the lucidrous situation, and for comedy in tragedy.

While E.'s novels lack the compassion of those of Charlotte Armstrong, the plotting of those of Agatha Christie, or the lively literacy and profundity of those of Dorothy L. Sayers, Margery Allingham, or Ngaio Marsh, they offer a blend of mystery, suspense, and romance not found in the works of those other authors, and they appeal to a different audience.

WORKS: *The Patient in Room 18* (1929). *While the Patient Slept* (1930). *The Mystery of Hunting's End* (1930). *From This Dark Stairway* (1931). *Murder by an Aristocrat* (1932). *The Dark Garden* (1933). *The White Cockatoo* (1933). *Murder of My Patient* (1934). *The Cases of Susan Dare* (1934). *The House on the Roof* (1935). *Fair Warning* (1936). *Danger in the Dark* (1936). *The Pattern* (1937). *320 College Avenue* (with F. Ballard, 1938). *The Glass Slipper* (1938). *Hasty Wedding* (1938). *The Chiffon Scarf* (1939). *The Hangman's Whip* (1940). *Eight O'Clock Tuesday* (with R. Wallsten, 1941). *With This Ring* (1941). *Speak No Evil* (1941). *Wolf in Man's Clothing* (1942). *Unidentified Woman* (1943). *The Man Next Door* (1943). *Sisters* (1943). *Escape the Night* (1944). *The White Dress* (1945). *Wings of Fear* (1945). *Five Passengers from Lisbon* (1946). *Another Woman's House* (1947). *House of Storm* (1949). *Hunt with the Hounds* (1950). *Never Look Back* (1950). *Dead Men's Plans* (1952). *The Unknown Quantity* (1953). *Man Missing* (1954). *Post Mark Murder* (1956). *Another Man's Murder* (1957). *Melora* (1959). *Jury of One* (1960). *The Cup, the Blade, or the Gun* (1961). *Enemy in the House* (1962). *Run Scared* (1963). *Call after Midnight* (1964). *R.S.V.P. Murder* (1965). *Witness at Large* (1966). *Woman on the Roof* (1968). *Message from Hong Kong* (1969). *El Rancho Rio* (1970). *Two Little Rich Girls* (1971). *Murder in Waiting* (1973). *Danger Money* (1974). *Family Fortune* (1976).

BIBLIOGRAPHY: Haycraft, H., *Murder for Pleasure: The Life and Times of the Detective Story* (1941).

For articles in reference works, see: *20thCA*.

Other references: *PW* (16 Sept. 1974).

SUSAN L. CLARK

Mary Baker Glover Eddy

B. *16 July 1821, Bow, New Hampshire; d. 3 Dec. 1910, Chestnut Hill, Massachusetts*

D. *of Mark and Abigail Ambrose Baker; m. George Washington Glover, 1843; m. Daniel Patterson, 1853; m. Asa Gilbert Eddy, 1877*

Founder of the Christian Science movement and of the Church of Christ, Scientist, E. was originally a member of the Congregational church. In 1862 she received treatment for a nervous ailment from Phineas P. Quimby, noted Massachusetts practitioner of "animal magnetism," and became interested in mind cure. In 1866 E. sustained a serious spinal injury from which she recovered through what she later described as the total conviction that her life was in God and God was Life.

In the same year her husband deserted E. and for the next three years she lived with various friends and relatives. In 1870 she wrote a textbook, *The Science of Man*, and began teaching in Lynn, Massachusetts. In 1875 she published the first edition of *Science and Health*, and organized the Christian Science Association in 1876. The year 1879 saw the establishment of the Church of Christ, Scientist, and 1881 the chartering of the Massachusetts Metaphysical College. Both were dissolved in 1889 in preparation for the founding in Boston of the Mother Church in September 1892. By 1900 a network of six hundred churches existed, and Christian Science was no longer a sect but an organized religion.

Known chiefly for its emphasis on psychical healing, Christian Science embraces a full theology. Though E. firmly professed herself and her religion to be Christian, orthodox Christianity rejected both. Basic to Christian Science is the doctrine that God is All, Life, and Mind. Since God is Spirit, the only manifestation of life is in Spirit, not in matter. Matter, sin, pain, and death are all erroneous concepts, part of the great error, the belief in evil. Healing, then, is an important part of overcoming the error involved in the belief in the ills of the flesh.

Christian Science rejects all anthropomorphic and personal ideas associated with God. E.'s identification of Christian Science as the Holy Comforter linked it to that aspect of God which she saw as feminine. At one point in the evolution of *Science and Health* she went so far as to speak of God as "She," but the reference was dropped from succeeding editions.

E. recognized the power of the written word in disseminating doctrine. In her life there were close to four hundred editions of *Science and Health* published. The monthly *Christian Science Journal* began in 1883, in 1898 the weekly *Christian Science Sentinel* appeared, and in 1908 the daily newspaper, the *Christian Science Monitor*, was established. The *Monitor* is one of the most respected among international newspapers.

At one time the object of severe criticism and ridicule (see Mark Twain's *Christian Science*, 1907), Christian Science is now a recognized part of the religious institution in America, a denomination whose members maintain more than twenty-five hundred churches. E. served as pastor of the Mother Church in Boston for many years, and never relinquished leadership of the movement until her death. Her *Manual of the Mother Church* (1895) still provides the framework of government for the churches, and *Science and Health* remains the religion's basic text. Thus E.'s imprint on Christian Science is as strong now as it was when she founded it.

WORKS: *The Science of Man* (1870). *Science and Health* (1875). *Christian Healing* (1880). *The People's God* (1883). *Historical Sketch of Metaphysical Healing* (1885). *Defence of Christian Science* (1885). *Christian Science: No and Yes* (1887). *Rudiments and Rules of Divine Science* (1887). *Unity of Good and Unreality of Evil* (1888). *Retrospection and Introspection* (1891). *The Manual of the Mother Church* (1895). *Miscellaneous Writings* (1896). *The First Church of Christ, Scientist, and Miscellany* (1913). *Science and Health with Key to the Scriptures* (1910).

BIBLIOGRAPHY: Gottschalk, S., *The Emergence of Christian Science in American Religious Life* (1973). Milmine, G., *The Life of Mary Baker Glover Eddy and the History of Christian Science* (1909). Orcutt, W. D., *Mary Baker Eddy and Her Books* (1913). Peel, R., *Mary Baker Eddy: The Years of Discovery* (1966), *Mary Baker Eddy: The Years of Trial* (1971), *Mary Baker Eddy: The Years of Authority*.

JOANN PECK KRIEG

Elizabeth Fries Lummis Ellet

B. Oct. 1812 (?), Sodus Point, New York; d. 3 June 1877, New York City
D. of William Nixon and Sarah Maxwell Lummis; m. William Henry Ellet,
   ca. 1835

Overlooked in traditional chronicles of military and political events, E. is the first historian of American women. She is important also as an early social historian. E.'s first significant work was *The Women of the American Revolution* in two volumes (1848), supplemented by a third volume (1850) and by the *Domestic History of the American Revolution* (1850). (The two original volumes were reprinted in 1974 as *The Eminent and Heroic Women in America.*)

Noting a dearth of sources, fragmentary anecdotes, meager correspondence and documents, the distortions of reminiscences, and other scholarly handicaps, E. also observed that "women's sphere is secluded" and "in very few instances does her personal history, even though she may fill a conspicuous position, afford sufficient incident . . . and salient points for description," in contrast to the actions of men. Her work, then, is primarily episodic; and the methodology of it a result of the limitations she recognized.

Scrupulous in the use of reliable accounts, E. provides contexts and settings for the remarkably varied activities of women in the "heroic age of the republic." While she concentrates on the wives, sisters, mothers, and daughters whose existence was devoted to the men fighting the War of American Independence and forming a new nation, E. also presents many remarkable instances of the independent exploits of women.

Achieving success with the histories, E. further explored the lives of American women by writing three books that obviously reflect the range and vigor of a developing country: *Pioneer Women of the West* (1852), *The Queens of American Society* (1867), and *The Court Circles of the Republic* (1869). Having grown up on the Lake Ontario frontier and having lived in both the South and the North, E. took a broad, liberal view of regional and human diversities.

The thesis of *Court Circles* is that "a fair idea" of a political administration can be gained from the fashionable life and everyday habits of a president and those who surround him. Consequently, E. describes the attitudes, practices, and influence of successive social circles from Washington to Grant. Antics and the ambience of entertainments, conversations and orations, balls, teas, weddings, funerals, and inaugurals suggest differences in the character and spirit of the nation's leaders. Perhaps the best written of E.'s books, *Court Circles* is based on letters, journals, and gossip. The style is bold and easy. There are good moments: one president has his butcher to dinner, another a country merchant; the black servant of an American foreign minister speaks French or German or Russian so that guests will feel at home; a president's wife reports that Charles Dickens looked bored when he visited her, and she preferred the company of Washington Irving; two suffragists argue on the street about whether women should wear pantaloons. It is ironic that E. is often remembered as a gossip; she was expert at putting together true stories for the historical record.

WORKS: *Euphemio of Messina* by S. Pellico (trans. by Ellet, 1834). *Poems, Translated and Original* (1835). *Rambles about the Country* (1847). *The Women of the American Revolution* (3 vols., 1848–50). *Family Pictures from the Bible* (1849). *Domestic History of the American Revolution* (1850). *Pioneer Women of the West* (1852). *Summer Rambles in the West* (1853). *The Practical Housekeeper* (1857). *Women Artists in All Ages* (1859). *The Queens of American Society* (1867). *The Court Circles of the Republic* (1869).

BIBLIOGRAPHY: Bayless, J., *Rufus Wilmot Griswold* (1943). Beard, C. and M., *The Rise of American Civilization* (1927). Moss, S. P., *Poe's Literary Battles* (1963). Poe, E. A., "Autography," in *The Complete Works of Poe*, (Vol. 15, Virginia ed., 1902).

For articles in reference works, see: *CAL. NAW* (article by A. Lutz).
ELIZABETH PHILLIPS

Anne Ellis

B. 1875, Missouri; d. Aug. 1938, Denver, Colorado
D. of Albert Laurence and Rachel Sweareangen Heister; m. G. Fleming, 1895; m. Herbert Ellis, 1901

When still a child, E. traveled with her family behind an oxen team to Silver Cliff, Colorado. As E. remembers: "I went up the gulch at the age of six and came down at the age of sixteen." When she came down, a seasoned veteran of life in Colorado's mining towns, it was with the first batch of experience that would make her a writer.

Soon after the family's move from Missouri, E.'s father left his wife for a job in Buffalo and never came back. One of E.'s earliest memories is of the abject poverty which drove her mother to take one of her pieced quilts door to door trying to trade it for food. In 1882, her mother married a miner, and the family moved to Bonanza. Here, though never free of want, they survived the ups and downs of the mining business chiefly through her mother's ingenuity as a cook and seamstress. Miners (with names like "Si Dore" and "Picnic Jim"), fancy women, cliff-climbing, first love, a first milk cow, dances, tales of women's rights, and dresses made of cabin curtains—all these filled E.'s life and later her writings. Though school consisted primarily of home mastery of a fifth-grade reader, E. remarked that "when one cannot read, one thinks a lot."

Shortly after her mother's death in 1893, E. married and moved to a new mine, the Only Chance, to stake a claim. Living from hand to mouth most of these years, E. spent much of her spare time writing. In 1938, her friends rallied to pay for the necessary clothes and travelling expenses when she received a telegram invitation to appear at the University of Colorado to receive an honorary Master of Letters degree. At that time she had published her three autobiographical works—*The Life of an Ordinary Woman* (1929), *Plain Anne Ellis* (1931), and *Sunshine Preferred* (1934).

The Life of An Ordinary Woman gives valuable first-hand description and analysis of the mining West. It focuses on the variety of characters and activities characteristic to a mining town: "A New Mine," "The Baby's First Bed," "Theatricals," "Seeing a Prize Fight," "Cripple Creek Troubles," "The First Telephone." In *Plain Anne Ellis*, E. details house-building, contracting with the government to travel with and cook for a telephone gang, sheep shearing, race relations, Indian maneuvers, county politics, and equal-rights conventions. *Sunshine Preferred*, though not as interesting as E.'s earlier works, nevertheless offers a rare insight into sanitariums of the 1920s and 1930s and a few glimpses of life in Albuquerque and Santa Fe, New Mexico.

One of the most refreshing rewards of reading E.'s books is the abundant humor that characterizes her style. She also has a talent for putting herself in perspective, which greatly enhances the psychological insight that her works provide. E.'s observations are often straightforward accounts of an active mind and a vibrant body for whom the

Victorian mores of her era fell by the wayside. Of her political experiences, she writes: "These men, who were supposed to be my friends, tried to make it hell for me; but I, who recognize no hell, was neither worried, frightened nor disturbed; in fact, I rather enjoyed it; holding the whip hand was for me a new experience." It's no surprise that this is the same woman of whom Irene McKeehan, professor of English at the University of Colorado, said: "Out of hardships and limitations she had made comedy and tragedy, touching the commonplace with the magic of interest, transmuting ordinary life into literaature."

WORKS: *The Life of An Ordinary Woman* (1929). *Plain Anne Ellis* (1931). *Sunshine Preferred* (1934).

BIBLIOGRAPHY: *NYT* (30 Aug. 1931; 19 Aug. 1934). *NYTBR* (29 Sept. 1929). *The Colorado Quarterly* (Summer 1955).

SHELLEY ARMITAGE

Janet Ayer Fairbank

B. 7 June 1878, Chicago, Illinois; d. 28 Dec. 1951, Wauwautosa, Wisconsin
D. of Benjamin F. and Janet Hopkins Ayer; m. Kellogg Fairbank, 1900

The older sister of novelist Margaret Ayer Barnes, F. was educated in private schools and attended the University of Chicago.

A dedicated worker for woman suffrage, F. was a member of the executive committee of the Democratic National Committee (1919–20), served as Illinois Democratic national committeewoman (1924–28), and was a delegate to the Democratic national convention (1932). During World War I she was a member of the Woman's National Liberty Loan Committee and of the Illinois Committee of the Woman's Division of the Council for National Defense. Before World War II, she was a national officer of the America First Committee, and in 1940 she campaigned for Willkie. F.'s most notable philanthropic activity was her twenty-four years on the board of the Chicago Lying-in Hospital, including service as its president.

Three of F.'s novels form a trilogy. *The Cortlandts of Washington Square* (1922) introduces Ann Byrne, ten-year-old ward of a wealthy New Yorker, and follows her growing up in the years prior to and during the Civil War. The novel concludes with her marriage to Peter Smith, a young worker from Chicago who promises they will be "partners." *The Smiths* (1925), set in Chicago, stretches from the Civil War almost to World War I. It is the story of a marriage: Ann's shattering discovery that to Peter being "partners" does not mean involving her in his business; the birth and rearing of children; and Peter's growth in wealth and status. Throughout, Ann's increasing strength and wisdom parallel the rise of the city. *Rich Man, Poor Man* (1936) centers on Ann's grandson, Hendricks Smith, and his wife, Barbara, tracing their involvement in Roosevelt's Progressive Party, World War I, and the suffragist movement. Though sometimes described as a "suffrage novel," the book does not depict that movement very fully, and the portrayal of Barbara, the suffragist, is not completely sympathetic. F.'s interest was in character delineation, not in propaganda.

Her two other novels of note both bear thematic relationships with the trilogy. *The Lions' Den* (1930), a political novel, has as its protagonist an idealistic young Wisconsin congressman. His disillusionment, partial corruption, and eventual courageous behavior when tested make up the substance of the novel. *The Bright Land* (1932), perhaps F.'s finest novel, tells the life story of Abby-Delight Flagg, child of New England Puritans, brought up in a world where women face hard work and, all too often, early death in childbirth. Partly to escape her dour father, she elopes, and the second half of the novel tells of her married life in Galena, Illinois, during its years first as a boom town and then in decline. Like Ann Smith, Abby-Delight grows in strength and wisdom, but she has more humor and is less idealized than Ann.

Once popular, F.'s fiction is neglected now. Her favored Illinois settings during the 19th and 20th centuries are objectively presented, and her characters, particularly her women, are sharply and believably delineated. The novels move at a leisurely pace, sometimes with little action, although F. occasionally attempted even battle scenes. In *The Cortlandts of Washington Square*, her impressionistic presentation, from the point of view of a young woman caught up in it, of the Battle of Gettysburg is gripping. Her studies of historical trends and political issues are serious and perceptive. Although the quantity is not great, the quality of her work is high; her claim upon our attention is greater than has been recognized in recent times.

WORKS: *At Home* (1910). *In Town, & Other Conversations* (1910). *Three Days More* (1910). *Report of National Woman's Liberty Loan Committee for the Victory Loan Campaign, April 21st to May 10th, 1919* (compiled by Fairbank, 1920). *The Cortlandts of Washington Square* (1922). *The Smiths* (1925).

Idle Hands (1927). *The Lions' Den* (1930). *The Bright Land* (1932). *The Alleged Great-Aunt* by H. K. Webster (completed by Fairbank, with M. A. Barnes, 1935). *Rich Man, Poor Man* (1936).

BIBLIOGRAPHY: For articles in reference works, see: *NCAB*, 39. *20thCA*. *20thCAS*.

Other references: *Literary Digest International Book Review* (Sept. 1925). *NYTBR* (15 Oct. 1922; 28 June 1925; 7 Dec. 1930). *SatR* (7 Jan. 1933; 12 Dec. 1936).

MARY JEAN DeMARR

Harriet Farley

B. ca. 18 Feb. 1813, Claremont, New Hampshire; d. 12 Nov. 1907,
 New York City
D. of Stephen and Lucy Saunders Farley; m. John Intaglio Donlevy, 1854

The sixth of ten children of a Congregational minister and his wife, who became "harmlessly insane" after bearing the ten children, F. began contributing to her family's support when she was fourteen. After plaiting straw for hats, binding shoes, and engaging in other home manufactures, she made a brief and unrewarding attempt to teach and then went to work in the Lowell textile mills in 1837. In Lowell, as the autobiographical "Letters from Susan" show, she felt free to attend lectures, sample different churches, and join an improvement circle. In spite of the thirteen-hour working day and the crowded corporation boardinghouse, she felt that the work offered the best economic rewards for women and didn't require "very violent exertion, as much of our farm work does."

When the two products of the improvement circles, the *Lowell Offering* and the *Operatives Magazine*, were bought by a local Whig newspaper in 1842 and combined under the name of the *Lowell Offering*, F. and Harriott Curtis, assisted by Harriet Lees, became editors and, later, owners.

Under attack from Sarah G. Bagley and others, F. denied that her magazine was supported by the corporations, but F.'s father and brother both received help from mill-owner Amos Lawrence, and the Hamilton

Company bought up $1,000 worth of back numbers during the *Lowell Offering*'s last year.

Determinedly genteel and noncontroversial, the *Lowell Offering* lost its audience as the ten-hour movement gained in strength, and its appeal waned even further when the well-written labor paper, the *Voice of Industry*, appeared in Lowell in October 1845. The *Offering* ceased publication in December, but after the failure of the ten-hour movement in 1847, it was revived as the *New England Offering*, with F. as both editor and publisher. Her efforts, however, again proved unsuccessful with the operatives. After the failure of the *Offering* in 1850, F. moved to New York City, where she became a contributor to *Godey's Lady's Book*. After her marriage, F. gave up her writing, of which her husband did not approve.

F.'s avowed intention in the publications she edited was to bring a little "cheer" into the lives of female operatives, and the literary nature of the magazines was, she thought, above sordid issues. Her first signed editorial said of the operatives: "We should like to influence them as moral and rational beings. . . . Our field is a wide one. . . . With wages, board, etc., we have nothing to do—these depend on circumstances over which we have no control." F. assumed that her readers were too lady-like to press for reforms by surrounding "City Hall in a mob, but, if wronged, would seek redress in some less exceptionable manner."

F.'s essays and stories, though sometimes self-consciously literary and "tiresomely inspirational," often provide insights into the lives and aspirations of the female factory workers. Her most interesting sketches, because most realistic and closely based on her own experience, are the "Letters from Susan," which appeared in the 1844 numbers of the *Lowell Offering*. "Susan" gives her first impressions of Lowell, of the crowding and noise as well as the economic and intellectual independence. Such stories as "The Sister" and "Evening before Pay-Day" use factory and boardinghouse backgrounds for sentimental homilies of self-sacrificing sisters or daughters.

F.'s poetry, like most of the poetry in her magazines, is undistinguished: Lacking true details, it is more removed than her other writing from the real experience of the workers' lives.

WORKS: *Shells from the Strand of the Sea of Genius* (1847). *Operatives Reply to . . . Jere. Clemens* (1850). *Happy Nights at Hazel Nook; or, Cottage Stories* (1854). *Fancy's Frolics; or, Christmas Stories Told in a Happy Home in New England* (1880).

BIBLIOGRAPHY: Eisler, B., *The Lowell Offering: Writings by New England Mill Women* (1977). Foner, P. S., *The Factory Girls* (1977). Josephson, H., *The Golden Threads: New England's Mill Girls and Magnates* (1949). Robinson, H. H., *Loom and Spindle; or, Life among the Early Mill Girls* (1898).

For articles in reference works, see: *AA. CAL. DAB*, III, 2. *NAW* (article by G. R. Taylor). *NCAB*, 11.

SUSAN SUTTON SMITH

Eliza Woodson Burhans Farnham

B. *17 Nov. 1815, Rensselaerville, New York; d. 15 Dec. 1864, New York City*
Wrote under: Eliza W. Farnham
D. of Cornelius and Mary Wood Burhans; m. Thomas Jefferson Farnham, 1836;
m. William Fitzpatrick, 1852

While her first husband was away on exploring expeditions in the Far West, F. developed her interests in reform. Her most controversial work was at Sing Sing prison where, as matron from 1844 to 1848, she revolutionized the treatment of female prisoners through her phrenological approach to the problem of rehabilitation. She resigned after frequent conflicts with conservative staff members who denounced her environmentalism and determinism. In California, where she went in 1849 to settle her first husband's estate, she visited and criticized San Quentin prison and lectured on various subjects. In 1858, she addressed the New York Women's Rights Convention on her theory of female biological and moral superiority. During the Civil War, she became involved in the Women's Loyal National League, which sought a constitutional amendment abolishing slavery. She also nursed the wounded at Gettysburg.

F.'s writing shows the independence of mind, the curiosity, and the strength that she exhibited in her life. *Life in Prairie Land* (1846) is a vivid account of her experiences in Illinois. The account of her life in the West, *California, In-Doors and Out* (1856), is colorful and compelling. The reader is drawn into the world of California after the Gold Rush, when a woman's appearance brought crowds of gaping men to the street. In this very fluid, primitive society, F. bought her own ranch, built her own house, and traveled on horseback unchaperoned. The last part of the book, which describes and evaluates California society and culture, tends to be moralistic, although F.'s analysis of the particular problems of women in frontier society is penetrating.

Eliza Woodson (1864) is an autobiographical novel treating F.'s life as a foster child in a home where she was treated as a household drudge and denied the benefits of a formal education. The fictional heroine reflects F.'s own character as a tough, determined individual who works hard to achieve her goals, overcoming all obstacles. Clearly, F.'s independence of thought and her interest in biological evolution originated in her childhood.

Woman and Her Era (1864), F.'s major work, argues that women are not only morally superior to men but biologically superior as well. Her position is based on the following syllogism: "Life is exalted in proportion to its Organic and Functional complexity; Woman's Organism is more complex and her totality of Function larger than those of any other being inhabiting our earth; Therefore her position in the scale of Life is the most exalted, the Sovereign One." Reproductive functions, commonly cited to demonstrate female inferiority, are used in F.'s philosophy to place woman far above the male.

The same idea dominates *The Ideal Attained* (1865). This novel's heroine, Eleanora Bromfield, is an ideal, superior woman who tests and transforms the hero, Colonel Anderson, until he is a worthy mate who combines masculine strength with the nobility of womanhood and is ever ready to sacrifice himself to the needs of the feminine, maternal principle.

In a society that defined the true woman as submissive, pure, and weak, F. forged her own definitions of female selfhood and lived by her own standards. Both her theory and practice (sometimes contradictory) provided alternatives for women unsatisfied with the narrow lives laid out for them by their culture.

WORKS: *Life in Prairie Land* (1846). *Rationale of Crime* by M. Sampson (introduction by Farnham, 1846). *California, In-Doors and Out; or, How We Farm, Mine, and Live Generally in the Golden State* (1856). *My Early Days* (1859; rev. ed., *Eliza Woodson; or, The Early Days of One of the World's Workers*, 1864). *Woman and Her Era* (1864). *The Ideal Attained; Being the Story of Two Steadfast Souls, and How They Won Their Happiness and Lost It Not* (1865).

BIBLIOGRAPHY: Davies, J. D., *Phrenology, Fad and Science* (1955). Kirby, G. B., *Years of Experience* (1887). Lewis, W., *From Newgate to Dannemora: The Rise of the Penitentiary in New York, 1796–1848* (1965). Mount Pleasant State Prison, *Annual Report of the Inspectors* (1846). Prison Association of

New York, *First, Second,* and *Third Reports* (1845, 1846, 1847) and *First Report of the Female Department* (1845). Woodward, H. B., *The Bold Women* (1953).

For articles in reference works, see: *AA. CAL. DAB,* III, 2. *HWS,* I. *NAW* (article by W. D. Lewis). *NCAB,* 4.

Other references: *Atlantic* (Sept. 1864). New York *Tribune* (16 Dec. 1864). *NYT* (18 Dec. 1864).

KAREN SZYMANSKI

Eliza Ware Rotch Farrar

B. 12 July 1791, Dunkirk, France; d. 22 April 1870, Springfield, Massachusetts
Wrote under: Eliza Farrar
D. of Benjamin and Elizabeth Barker Rotch; m. John Farrar, 1828

Daughter and granddaughter of Nantucket Quakers who had emigrated to France to establish a tax-free whaling port, F. went with her family to England during the Reign of Terror. At her father's estate near Milford Haven she received an excellent education and grew up among eminent European and American visitors. When her father lost his fortune in 1819, she went to live with her grandparents in New Bedford, Massachusetts. Disowned as too liberal by the Quaker meeting there, she became a Unitarian. Except for trips to England to visit her parents, she spent the rest of her life in Massachusetts.

In her "Address to Parents" at the beginning of *The Children's Robinson Crusoe* (1830), F. praises Defoe's work for its "spirit" and "naturalness": "It seems to be exactly what it purports to be, the narrative of a profane, ill-educated, runaway apprentice of the 17th c." F. then asks, "Can such a tale, though perfect in itself, be suited to children who have been carefully guarded from all profaneness, vulgarity, and superstition?" Her version of Crusoe is accordingly cleansed of such faults as his "disobedience to his parents, and his inordinate love of adventure" and endowed with qualities parents would wish their children to admire and cultivate: "industry, perseverance, resignation to the will of God." To increase the utility of her hero's adventures, F. adds "as much information about domestic arts as could well be interwoven with the story" and makes Friday into a native "of a mild, affectionate, and tractable nature."

F. presented another proper hero to be emulated by children in *The Story of the Life of Lafayette as Told by a Father to His Children* (1831). Henry Moreton tells his father that he wishes he lived in the days of Alexander or Caesar and could see these great men; his father takes issue with Henry's idea of these men as great, and reminds him that he has seen on Boston Common "one of the most extraordinary men that ever lived!" Again, the hero's life acquires value as an example and lesson, but his actions are generally left to speak for themselves without intrusive moralizing. The tale takes seventeen evenings. Stirring events are briskly and clearly related, the moral intent doesn't interfere with the often exciting story and interesting anecdotes, and many vignettes of Moreton family life provide humor.

A manual of advice, *The Young Lady's Friend* (1836), was F.'s most important work, widely popular in England and America and reprinted as late as 1880. F. addresses her work to middle-class girls who have finished school. It opens with a brisk chapter of warning to those who assume that their intellectual life ends when they leave the schoolroom and a second chapter "On the Improvement of Time." It closes with a chapter on "Mental Culture" and impressive lists of books for a "course of reading" on history, biography, and travel. In between, she holds to an essentially conservative view of "woman's peculiar calling," but emphasizes practical details of behavior and treats these with gentle amusement and, above all, common sense.

The Young Lady's Friend provides valuable insight into the activities and preoccupations of the 19th-c. American middle class. *Recollections of Seventy Years* (1865), F.'s last book, furnishes fascinating glimpses of life in England and France between 1783 and 1819. Her method is anecdotal, and many of her lively anecdotes seem, in themselves, to furnish enough material for entire novels. F. cared for her invalid husband for fourteen years before his death in 1853. These are the tales she told to enliven his sickroom. They remain beguiling entertainment today.

WORKS: *The Children's Robinson Crusoe* (1830). *The Story of the Life of Lafayette as Told by a Father to His Children* (1831). *John Howard* (1833). *The Youth's Letter-Writer* (1834). *The Young Lady's Friend* (1836). *Recollections of Seventy Years* (1865).

BIBLIOGRAPHY: Carson, G., *The Polite Americans* (1966). Hopkins, V. C., *Prodigal Puritan: A Life of Delia Bacon* (1959). Lynes, R. J., *The Domesticated Americans* (1963). Schlesinger, E. B., "Two Early Harvard Wives: E. F. and Eliza Follen," *NEQ* (June 1965).

For articles in reference works, see: *The Female Prose Writers of America, with Portraits, Biographical Notices, and Specimens of Their Writing*, J. S. Hart (1852). *NAW* (article by E. B. Schlesinger). *NCAB*, 13.

SUSAN SUTTON SMITH

Margaretta V. Bleecker Faugeres

B. 11 Oct. 1771, Tomanick, New York; d. 14 Jan. 1801, Brooklyn, New York
Wrote under: Margaretta V. Faugeres
D. of John J. and Ann Eliza Schuyler Bleecker; m. Peter Faugeres, 1792

F. was an heiress to both the wealth and the intellectual traditions of two of the most respected families in New York. Against her father's wishes, she married a French physician, Peter Faugeres. Called an "infidel," Faugeres was actually a member of the popular Jacobin circles. F. was an enthusiastic supporter of what she took to be the new millenium of human freedom; her choice of Bastille Day as marriage day shows the whole bent of her alliance. She was marrying a movement rather than a man. Unfortunately, her husband abused her and quickly ran through the fortune left to her by her father. F. and her infant daughter were reduced to living in a granary for some time in 1796. Faugeres died of yellow fever in 1798, and F. thereafter supported herself by teaching school in New Brunswick, New Jersey, and Brooklyn, New York. Broken in health and spirit, she was only twenty-nine years old when she died.

The majority of F.'s work was produced before she was twenty. In 1793, F. prepared *The Posthumous Works of Ann Eliza Bleecker*, a collection of her mother's work supplemented with F.'s own poetry and prose, including an affecting "Memoir." After 1795, she wrote some pieces for the *New York Monthly Magazine* and the *American Museum* and, in 1797, published "The Ghost of John Young," but her literary output was hampered by her family problems.

Her tendency towards sentimental melancholy, the sadness sincere, is expressed in highly artificial language in the early poems included in *The Posthumous Works*. Although rendered fairly obscure by an abundance of private references, her poetic language is very formal, with few naturalist touches. There is an excessive use of the infelicitous neoclassical poetical devices: "fleecy tribe" is substituted for sheep, birds are the "feather'd choir," personifications are overabundant. The unhappy and short life of her mother, acting upon an immature imagination, to which the pose of melancholy seemed the height of human delicacy, contributed to the themes that would now seem morbid for an eighteen-year-old girl.

Supplementing these sad strains are several lively patriotic poems. F. was genuinely convinced of the noble renewal of human liberty embodied by the American and French revolutions. In her long topographical poem, "The Hudson" (1793), one of the few pieces in which she employs natural description, F.'s primary purpose is to give an account of the political history of the Hudson River during the American Revolution.

In 1795 she offered *Belisarius: A Tragedy* to the John Street Theatre. It was refused, but published by subscription that same year. Written simply and tastefully in blank verse, the message of pacifism, antimaterialism, and the vanity of power is extraordinary for the times. In a clear analogy with French politics, Belisarius is the just man caught between corrupt courtiers on the one hand, and heartless and cruel revolutionists on the other. Belisarius represents uncompromising human values. The play quietly exposes the vanity of fame and pomp and maintains the sacredness of ordinary human life.

The further development of F.'s maturity of mind and political opinion can be seen in "The Ghost of John Young," a monody opposing capital punishment, "shewing how inconsistent sanguinary Laws are, in a Country which boasts of her Freedom and Happiness."

F. appears to have been an extraordinarily fair and good woman, "a favorite among her literary acquaintances" whose life of early genius and promise so quickly disintegrated into ruin. Her political idealism is typical of many talented women of this era; so is the personal tragedy that prevented many of them, F. included, from living long enough to develop maturity of literary judgment and production.

WORKS: *The Posthumous Works of Ann Eliza Bleecker in Prose and Verse. To Which Is Added, a Collection of Essays, Prose and Poetical, by Margaretta V. Faugeres* (1793). *Belisarius: A Tragedy* (1795).

BIBLIOGRAPHY: For articles in reference works, see: *Biographie Universelle*, M. Michaud (1855). *CAL* (article on Ann Eliza Bleecker, 1877). *FPA. NAW* (article on Ann Eliza Bleecker by L. Leary). *Nouvelle Biographie Generale*, J. C. F. Hoefer (1958).

L. W. KOENGETER

Jessie Redmon Fauset

B. *27 April 1882, Camden County, New Jersey; d. 30 April 1961, Philadelphia,*
Pennsylvania
D. *of Redmon and Annie Seamon Fauset; m. Herbert Harris, 1929*

F. was the youngest of seven children born to an African Methodist
Episcopal minister in Philadelphia. F.'s family was poor, but her father's
black church position and interest in books and art kept the family
"working, aspiring, and discussing." The children were educated as much
as biases would permit. With opportunities nearer to home shut off
because of her race, F., the first black woman at Cornell University,
graduated Phi Beta Kappa and spent many years teaching French at an
all-black high school in Washington, D.C.

Correspondence from 1903 with W. E. B. DuBois, the black sociolo-
gist, led F. to early involvement with the National Association for the
Advancement of Colored People. In 1919, DuBois persuaded her to move
to New York City to work with *The Crisis*, of which he was the editor.
As its literary editor from 1919 to 1926, F. discovered and published
Langston Hughes, Countee Cullen, Jean Toomer, Claude McKay, and
other "Harlem Renaissance" writers. She also published her own work,
held and attended innumerable literary soirees with black and white
writers, and traveled abroad with DuBois's Pan-African conferences. F.
edited and did most of the writing for the *Brownies' Book*, a delightful
monthly magazine for black children.

F. also contributed to black American literature a large body of her
own creative writing. Her poetry, frequently anthologized, her short
stories, and her essays—which show sensitivity to racism and sexism
worldwide—were published primarily in *The Crisis*, 1912–29, and in the
Brownies' Book, 1920–21. It is for her four novels, however, that F. is
primarily remembered.

There Is Confusion (1924) was written in response to the picture
drawn of black life by a white writer, T. S. Stribling, in *Birthright*. F.
believed that she could more accurately and honestly depict characters
of her own race. Through the story of Joanna Marshall and Peter Bye,
from childhood to marriage, she makes clear her themes and concerns.

History, heredity, and environment impinge on the free will of F.'s characters, and their roles as women and black Americans come close to limiting and defining them.

F.'s second novel, *Plum Bun* (1929), deals with a topic frequent in black literature: Angela Murray, the lighter of two sisters, "passes" for white. Attention by critics to the subject matter of the book has led to their ignoring its formal strengths, which represent a distinct improvement over the writing in F.'s first novel and which make *Plum Bun* the best of her four novels.

The Chinaberry Tree (1931) concentrates in a rather nostalgic way on black home and community life in a small New Jersey village. Formally, it takes Greek mythology and drama as its most immediately recognizable analogue. The comparison with Greek drama is evident, from a tragically inescapable family curse with overtones of incest, to the seasonal pattern of death and rebirth.

F.'s last published novel zeroed in on the ironies of American black life with more directness and less sentimentality than any of her work. In *Comedy: American Style* (1933), race discrimination is internalized in the black characters, particularly in the destructive power of Olivia Carey. Themes have not changed much from F.'s 1924 novel, but what has changed is her willingness to unstintingly depict those who are destroyed by their environments, as well as those who overcome them.

F.'s literary strengths are those of her own character. Intelligence and curiosity are supplemented by kindness, generosity, graciousness, and tolerance. She had no dominating passion, no driving opinions which scattered all else before them. Her books are more exploratory than dogmatic, more searching than protesting. The facts of her life and her time make clear the struggle and hard work which gave her strength.

WORKS: There Is Confusion (1924). *Plum Bun* (1929). *The Chinaberry Tree* (1931). *Comedy: American Style* (1933).

BIBLIOGRAPHY: Aptheker, H., ed., *The Correspondence of W. E. B. DuBois* (1973). Bone, R., *The Negro Novel in America* (1966). Bontemps, A., *The Harlem Renaissance Remembered* (1972). Braithwaite, W., in *The Black Novelist*, Ed. R. Hemenway (1970). Davis, A., *From the Dark Tower: Afro-American Writers, 1900–1960* (1974). Gayle, A., *The Way of the New World: The Black Novel in America* (1976). Huggins, N., *Harlem Renaissance* (1971). Hughes, L., *The Big Sea* (1940). Sylvander, C. W., *J. R. F., Black American Writer* (1980).

For articles in reference works, see: *Black American Writers Past and Present: A Biographical and Bibliographical Dictionary*, T. Rush and A. Myers (1975). *Profiles of Negro Womanhood*, S. Dannett (1966). *20thCA. 20thCAS.*

Other references: *CLAJ* 14 (1971); 17 (1974). *Freedomways* (Winter 1975). *Phylon* (June 1978). *Southern Workman* (May 1932).

CAROLYN WEDIN SYLVANDER

Edna Ferber

B. *15 Aug. 1887, Kalamazoo, Michigan; d. 16 April 1968, New York City*
D. *of Jacob Charles and Julia Neuman Ferber*

F. began her writing career as a newspaper reporter in Appleton, Wisconsin, Milwaukee, and Chicago, but wrote her first novel, *Dawn O'Hara* (1911), during a prolonged illness. She earned sudden success and great popularity with her stories of Emma McChesney, a traveling saleswoman (1913, 1914, 1915).

In 1925, F. won the Pulitzer Prize for *So Big* (1924), her best novel, and a few years later saw her novel *Show Boat* (1926) transformed into a classic American musical. Her love of the theater was further indulged through her successful collaboration with George S. Kaufman, with whom she wrote such popular plays as *Royal Family* (1928), *Dinner at Eight* (1932), and *Stage Door* (1936). *Royal Family* was successfully revived in 1975. F. was seriously disillusioned by World War II; her postwar novels were more idea-laden and contrived, although she remained a popular novelist to her death.

In *So Big*, Selina Peake, the properly raised daughter of a gambler, is forced to make her own way in the world after her father is accidentally killed. She takes a teaching position in High Prairie, a Dutch farming community outside Chicago, and spends the rest of her life there. After the death of her husband, Selina struggles by herself to run their truck farm and to raise her son, Dirk, nicknamed "So Big." Dirk's youth is the counterpoint in every respect of Selina's. Where she cherishes life, he cherishes success; where she reveres beauty, he reveres money. By the novel's end, Dirk is an immensely wealthy, successful, miserable young man.

Show Boat deals with three generations of women—Parthenia Ann Hawks, Magnolia Hawks Ravenal, and Kim Ravenal—but the novel centers on Magnolia, her bizarre childhood on her father's showboat, her idyllic love affair with Gaylord Ravenal, her marital difficulties as she learns that her husband is a confirmed gambler, and her determination to provide for her daughter after Gaylord's desertion. As in many F. novels, the heroine's daughter is not nearly her mother's equal. Also as in most F. novels, there is a subplot concerned with racist attitudes, here about the mulatto showboat actress Julie, whose role was expanded in the musical.

Cimarron (1929) is F.'s most overtly feminist novel. Sabra Venable Cravat moves with her husband Yancey to the recently opened territory of Oklahoma. Despite his many talents, Yancey is impractical and irresponsible and seems unable to stay in one place longer than five years at a time. Thus, in addition to the housework and the raising of her children, Sabra finds herself helping with Yancey's newspaper—the first in Oklahoma—and, on those occasions when Yancey abandons her, running it herself. Yancey is the dreamer; Sabra the doer. She becomes Oklahoma's first U.S. congresswoman.

Clio Dulaine Maroon, the protagonist of *Saratoga Trunk* (1941), is as close as F. ever came to creating an antiheroine. Clio, illegitimate daughter of an established Creole family (the Dulaines) on her father's side and a series of "loose" women (including a free woman of color) on her mother's, returns from France to New Orleans to avenge herself on the Dulaines and to make her fortune by marrying a millionaire. Clio realizes at the last minute that love is more important than money, but luckily Clint Maroon, a Texan adventurer who has been making his fortune among the detested railroad men while Clio tries to marry one of them, can now provide both love and money.

F.'s writing remained untouched by the innovations of her contemporaries. She was neither responsible for any innovations of her own, nor did her own work appreciably evolve in terms of style, content, or structure. Still, her work deserves serious consideration for her treatment of the land, her feminism, and her egalitarianism.

Even when F. writes about the land, her novels are first and foremost about women—strong women, pioneer women, women determined to hold on to the land and to keep their families together. The women always triumph and often survive their men; the visionaries see their dreams come true, and the practical ones see the present inexorably improving toward the future. Although F. is not in the tradition of the great American literary experimenters, she is a solid member of another tradition, that of the celebrators of America.

WORKS: *Dawn O'Hara: The Girl Who Laughed* (1911). *Buttered Side Down*

(1912). *Roast Beef, Medium: The Business Adventures of Emma McChesney* (1913). *Personality Plus: Some Experiences of Emma McChesney and Her Son, Jock* (1914). *Emma McChesney and Co.* (1915). *Fanny Herself* (1917). *Cheerful by Request* (1918). *Half Portions* (1920). *$1200 a Year* (with N. Levy, 1920). *The Girls* (1921). *Gigolo* (1922; film version, 1926). *So Big* (1924; film versions, 1925, 1953). *Eldest* (1925). *Minick* (with G. S. Kaufman, 1925; film versions, 1925, 1932). *Show Boat* (1926; film versions, 1929, 1936, 1951). *Mother Knows Best: A Fiction Book* (1927; film version, 1928). *Royal Family* (with G. S. Kaufman, 1928; film version, 1930). *Cimarron* (1929; film versions, 1931, 1961). *American Beauty* (1931). *Dinner at Eight* (with G. S. Kaufman, 1931; film version, 1933). *They Brought Their Women: A Book of Short Stories* (1933). *Come and Get It* (1935; film version, 1936). *Stage Door* (with G. S. Kaufman, 1936; film version, 1937). *Nobody's in Town* (1938). *A Peculiar Treasure* (1939). *The Land Is Bright* (with G. S. Kaufman, 1941). *Saratoga Trunk* (1941; film version, 1945). *Great Son* (1945). *One Basket: Thirty-One Short Stories* (1947). *Bravo* (with G. S. Kaufman, 1949). *Giant* (1952; film version, 1956). *Ice Palace* (1958; film version, 1960). *A Kind of Magic* (1963).

BIBLIOGRAPHY: Shaughnessy, M. R., *Women and Success in American Society in the Works of E. F.* (1976).

For articles in reference works, see: *CA*, 5–8 (1969); 25–28 (1971). *20thCA. 20thCAS. Wisconsin Writers: Sketches and Studies*, W. A. Titus (1974).

Other references: *BB* 22 (1958). *Chicago Jewish Forum* 13. *MTJ* 13. *NYTBR* (5 Oct. 1952).

CYNTHIA L. WALKER

Kate Field

B. 1 Oct. 1838, St. Louis, Missouri; d. 19 May 1896, Honolulu, Hawaii
Given name: Mary Katherine Keemle Field
D. of Joseph M. and Eliza Riddle Field

The daughter of an actor and newspaper publisher and an actress, F. became the ward of a millionaire uncle, Milton L. Sanford, following her father's death when she was eighteen. The Sanfords financed her education at Lasell Seminary, Auburndale, Massachusetts, and took her to Italy, where she was the darling of Anthony Trollope and other members of the writers' colony in Florence. Her support for the Union in the Civil War caused Sanford, a Southern sympathizer, to change his mind about making her his heir.

To support herself she turned to journalism, writing travel letters for the Springfield (Massachusetts) *Republican* and other newspapers. She lectured on the lyceum circuit, wrote humorous accounts of various journeys to Europe, and undertook a mildly successful theatrical career. She also did commercial publicity. *The Drama of Glass* (n.d.) was a slick advertisement for the Libby Glass Company disguised as a brief "history" of glass-making. Although she received valuable stock for publicizing the newly invented telephone, she lost the proceeds in an unsuccessful dressmaking venture to promote simpler styles.

Desiring a platform for her views, she founded a weekly newspaper, *Kate Field's Washington*, which lasted from 1890 to 1895. She died a year later in Hawaii, where she had gone to regain her health after the newspaper failed.

Genuine gifts of humor and social satire characterize *Hap-Hazard* (1873), a collection of letters from the New York *Tribune* that feature the trials of a lady lecturer and poke fun at both the British monarchy and the nouveau riche American tourists. *Ten Days in Spain* (1875) bristles with her American middle-class prejudices displayed on travels through Spain during a political upheaval.

Kate Field's Washington focused on her own personality and special interests. It featured book reviews, theatrical news, novelettes, and drawing-room comedies, often written by F. herself. Although slight in content, several of her plays were produced. Her kaleidoscopic opinions championed numerous causes: temperance (not abstinence); the right of the rich to conspicuous consumption; cremation; prohibition of Mormon polygamy; international copyrights; the arts; and tariff and civil service reform. She weakly endorsed woman suffrage.

Although F. demonstrated considerable literary talent, her importance lies less in what she wrote than in what she represented—the accomplishments of an intelligent and independent American woman in the late Victorian era. Her significance as a journalist stems from her views on the news, including reform efforts and politics, in an era when it was unusual for a woman to found and run a newspaper.

WORKS: *Adelaide Ristori* (1867). *Pen Photographs of Charles Dickens's Readings* (1868). *Planchette's Diary* (1868). *Mad on Purpose: A Comedy* (1868). *Hap-Hazard* (1873). *Ten Days in Spain* (1875). *Charles Albert Fechter* (1882). *The Drama of Glass* (n.d.).

BIBLIOGRAPHY: Beasley, M. H., *The First Women Washington Correspondents* (George Washington Univ. Studies #4, 1976). Sadlier, M., *Anthony Trollope* (1927). Trollope, A., *An Autobiography* (1883). Whiting, L., *K. F.: A Record* (1899). Woodward, H., *The Bold Women* (1953).

For articles in reference works, see: *DAB*, III, 2. *NAW* (article by David Baldwin). *NCAB*, 6.

Other references: *NYT* (31 May 1896). *Records of the Columbia Historical Society* (1973–74).

MAURINE BEASLEY

Rachel Lyman Field

B. *19 Sept. 1894, New York City; d. 15 March 1942, Beverly Hills, California*
Wrote under: Rachel Field
D. *of Matthew D. and Lucy Atwater Field; m. Arthur S. Pederson, 1935*

Descended from a distinguished family, F. was educated in public schools. She attended Radcliffe College and later wrote synopses for a silent film company.

For about the first two-thirds of F.'s writing career, she was primarily a writer of juvenile literature for children of varying ages. Her one-act plays (many separately published in acting versions) include farces, comedies, serious and poetic dramas, modern reinterpretations of old stories, and nostalgic period pieces. Lacking literary pretension, they are nevertheless stageworthy. F.'s juvenile poems also show her versatility, for she worked in a number of forms and types, but tendencies toward sentimentality and rhythmic monotony lessen their effectiveness.

The best of F.'s work for young people is to be found in three juvenile novels. *Hitty: Her First Hundred Years* (1929) was awarded the Newbery Medal for children's literature. Set in the 19th c., it is the history of a wooden doll, narrated by herself. The parts depicting the Maine F. loved are especially vivid and evocative. *Calico Bush* (1931) covers one year (1743–44) in the life of a French girl indentured to an English family who settle in Maine. Her sense of isolation, both as a foreigner and as a pioneer, is well conveyed, as are the terrors and delights of frontier life.

Hepatica Hawks (1932) has as its protagonist a fifteen-year-old girl who is 6′4″ tall and a member of a freak show. The novel takes her from an early acceptance of her differentness through a period of desperate yearning for friends of her own age and participation in normal society. Eventually she finds a place (as a Wagnerian soprano) where her size is not a hindrance. Told with restraint, the novel movingly conveys its message, that it is all right to be different.

In her last years, F. turned to writing novels for adults. *To See Our-selves* (1937), written with her husband, is a comic Hollywood novel of little significance. More ambitious are two historical novels. *Time out of Mind* (1935), set in Maine, shows the decline of a shipbuilding family as seen by a young woman intimately connected with it. It is a story of family conflict, pitting young against old and artistic against materialistic values. *All This, and Heaven Too* (1938) is F.'s imagina-tive and sympathetic reconstruction of the experiences of a young Frenchwoman who was involved in a celebrated 19th-c. murder trial and later came to the U.S. and married F.'s great-uncle.

Less substantial is *And Now Tomorrow* (1942), the story of a wealthy young woman temporarily afflicted with deafness; it is played out against the contemporary background of the Depression and labor strife. The female protagonists of the three latter novels are all forced by circumstances to find in themselves strength, endurance, and breadth of sympathy and understanding. They learn, in an image F. uses several times, to become trees and not vines.

F.'s work, in many genres, shows her concern for craftsmanship and her broad sympathies. The single most frequently occurring image in her work, the patchwork quilt, is indicative: peculiarly a woman's im-age, it suggests women's creativity, nostalgia for the past, and the crea-tion of something new, beautiful, and useful from old and heteroge-neous materials. F. tended toward sentimentality, and her three major works are all old-fashioned "romantic" novels. Nevertheless, they are mature studies of human relationships and of suffering and growth. These novels, with the best of her work for young people, should secure for her a lasting, if modest, literary reputation.

WORKS: *Six Plays* (1922). *The Pointed People: Verses & Silhouettes* (1924). *An Alphabet for Boys and Girls* (1926). *Eliza and the Elves* (1926). *Taxis and Toadstools: Verses and Decorations* (1926). *A Little Book of Days* (1927). *The Magic Pawnshop: A New Year's Eve Fantasy* (1927). *The Cross-Stitch Heart, and Other One-Act Plays* (1928). *Little Dog Toby* (1928). *Polly Patch-work* (1928). *The White Cat and Other Old French Fairy Tales* by Mme. d'Aulnoy (arranged by Field, 1928). *American Folk and Fairy Tales* (edited by Field, 1929). *Hitty: Her First Hundred Years* (1929). *Pocket-Handkerchief Park* (1929). *A Circus Garland* (1930). *Patchwork Plays* (1930). *Points East: Narratives of New England* (1930). *Calico Bush* (1931). *The Yellow Shop* (1931). *The Bird Began to Sing* (1932). *Hepatica Hawks* (1932). *Fortune's Caravan* by L. Jean-Javal (adapted by Field, 1933). *Just across the Street* (1933). *Branches Green* (1934). *God's Pocket: The Story of Captain Samuel Hadlock, Junior, of Cranberry Isles, Maine* (1934). *Susanna B. and William C.* (1934). *People from Dickens: A Presentation of Leading Characters from the*

Books of Charles Dickens (1935). *Time out of Mind* (1935; film version, 1947). *Fear Is the Thorn* (1936). *To See Ourselves* (with A. Pederson, 1937). *All This, and Heaven Too* (1938; film version, 1940). *All through the Night* (1940). *Ave Maria: An Interpretation from Walt Disney's "Fantasia," Inspired by the Music of Franz Schubert* (1940). *Christmas Time* (1941). *And Now Tomorrow* (1942; film version, 1944). *Prayer for a Child* (1944). *Christmas in London* (1946). *Poems* (1957). *The Rachel Field Story Book* (1958).

BIBLIOGRAPHY: For articles in reference works, see: *CB* (May 1942). *Junior Book of Authors*, Eds. S. J. Kunitz and H. Haycraft (1951). *NAW* (article by C. Meigs). *Newbery Medal Books, 1922–1955*, Eds. B. M. Miller and E. W. Field (1955). *20thCA*. *20thCAS*.

Other references: *NYHTB* (31 May 1942). *NYTBR* (13 Nov. 1932; 7 April 1935; 30 Oct. 1938; 31 May 1942). *SatR* (15 Nov. 1930; 22 Oct. 1938).

MARY JEAN DeMARR

Martha Finley

B. *26 April 1821, Chillicothe, Ohio; d. 30 Jan. 1909, Elkton, Maryland*
Wrote under: *Martha Farquharson, Martha Finley*
D. *of James Brown and Maria Theresa Brown Finley*

Both of F.'s parents, first cousins of Scotch-Irish descent, died before she was twenty-five. F. supported herself by teaching and writing. Beginning in 1856, F. published more than twenty Sunday-school books under the name of Martha Farquharson for the Presbyterian Board of Publication in Philadelphia. (Farquharson is Gaelic for Finley.)

Popular success and financial security came with *Elsie Dinsmore* (1867). The tremendous popularity of this book, both in America and in England, led F. to write a series of juvenile novels exploring the life of her heroine from childhood to old age. In twenty-eight volumes, Elsie captured the religious and feminine devotion of the 19th-c. reading public. By 1876, F. was able to buy her own home in Elkton, Maryland, where she lived out her eighty years comfortably. The Elsie books alone earned her a quarter of a million dollars.

None of F.'s other works can compare in importance with the Elsie Dinsmore series, which has challenged psychologists and literary historians to define its formula of success. Despite what critics have seen as F.'s "amateurish craftsmanship, superficial moralizing, and lame scholarship," despite even the character of the heroine who, in the eyes of one critic, is "a nauseous little prig," Elsie Dinsmore captured the attention of more than twenty-five million readers.

Some of the elements that attracted young readers to the Elsie books are easy to explain: This fairy-tale heroine is a blonde heiress, unjustly mistreated by the relatives who take her in while her father is in Europe and after her beautiful mother has died. Uncompromisingly moral, unfailingly sweet, Elsie reminds us of Cinderella and Snow White. The fundamentalist religious values that emerge in her meditations and the Biblical quotations render the fairy tale acceptable to the Christian society of 19th-c. America.

With Elsie's southern heritage, F. also provided a topical attraction. What could be more glamorous to her predominantly northern audience immediately after the Civil War than the echo of a lost world—the world of plantations and delicate southern ladies such as Elsie's mother had been, the world of black mammies such as "poor old Aunt Chloe," with her heavy dialect and unswerving devotion to young Elsie? In fact, Ruth Suckow goes so far as to suggest that when Elsie saves her southern father, she is really saving the whole South and committing the rebels to the fundamentalist religious values of her creator, F. herself.

The father-daughter theme which permeates the Elsie books has been seen as psychologically excessive. Elsie worships her father, and even though she does marry (a friend of her father's who is himself much older than she), after her husband's death she is once again with her devoted parent. Some have seen this theme as reinforcing the "father knows best" attitude prevalent in Victorian society, but in fact, Elsie gains power over the most powerful person in her life, her own father, by her religious devotion.

One might argue, as Suckow does, that Elsie represents the truth that "a woman craves a master," yet within the religious framework Elsie Dinsmore controls the lives of all around her. The 19th-c. woman could hardly hope to achieve more than Elsie held out to her: beauty, riches, the love of her father, a husband, and children. Best of all, she exemplified victory after victory over the oppressors of the world, even over that all powerful demigod, her father. Only God was more powerful than Elsie Dinsmore—and He was on her side.

WORKS: Cassella; or, The Children of the Valleys (1867). Elsie Dinsmore (1868). Elsie's Holidays (1869). An Old Fashioned Boy (1870). Wanted: A Pedigree (1870). Elsie's Girlhood (1872). Our Fred; or, Seminary Life at Thurston (1874). Elsie's Womanhood (1875). Elsie's Motherhood (1876). Elsie's Children (1877). Mildred Keith (1878). Signing the Contract and What *it Cost* (1878). *Mildred at Roselands* (1879). *Elsie's Widowhood* (1880). *The Thorn in the Nest* (1880). *Mildred and Elsie* (1881). *Grandmother Elsie* (1882). *Mildred's Married Life* (1882). *Elsie's New Relations* (1883). *Elsie at Nantucket* (1884). *Mildred at Home* (1884). *The Two Elsies* (1885). *Elsie's Kith and Kin* (1886). *Mildred's Boys and Girls* (1886). *Elsie's Friends at Woodburn* (1887). *Christmas with Grandma Elsie* (1888). *Elsie and the Raymonds* (1889). *Elsie Yachting with the Raymonds* (1890). *Elsie's Vacation* (1891). *Elsie at Viamede* (1892). *Elsie at Ion* (1893). *The Tragedy of Wild River Valley* (1893). *Elsie at the World's Fair* (1894). *Elsie's Journey on Inland Waters* (1894). *Mildred's New Daughter* (1894). *Elsie at Home* (1897). *Elsie on the Hudson* (1898). *Twiddledetwit: A Fairy Tale* (1898). *Elsie in the South* (1899). *Elsie's Young Folks* (1900). *Elsie's Winter Trip* (1902). *Elsie and Her Loved Ones* (1903). *Elsie and Her Namesakes* (1905).

BIBLIOGRAPHY: Brown, J. E., "The Saga of Elsie Dinsmore," *University of Buffalo Studies* (1945). Ely, W. A., *The Finleys of Bucks* (1902). Suckow, R., "Elsie Dinsmore: A Study of Perfection, or How Fundamentalism Came to Dixie," *Bookman* (Oct. 1927).

For articles in reference works, see: *AA. American Authors*, M. L. Rutherford (1894). *AW. DAB*, III, 2. *Indiana Authors and Their Books, 1816–1916*, Ed. R. E. Banta (1949). *NAW* (article by C. T. Kindilien). *NCAB*, 11. *Ohio Authors and Their Books*, Ed. W. Coyle (article by J. Blanck, 1962).

Other references: Baltimore *Sun* (31 Jan. 1909). *NY* (14 March 1936).

THELMA J. SHINN

Dorothea Frances Canfield Fisher

B. *17 Feb. 1879, Lawrence, Kansas; d. 9 Nov. 1958, Arlington, Vermont*
Wrote under: Dorothy Canfield, Dorothy Canfield Fisher
D. of James Hulme and Flavia Camp Canfield; m. James Redwood Fisher, 1907

After extensive formal education (Ph.B., Ohio State; Ph.D., Columbia; graduate work, Sorbonne), F. and her husband traveled widely, eventually settling in Vermont, home of F.'s ancestors. During World War I, F. did relief work in France, and she remained active in public life throughout her career, serving as secretary of New York's Horace Mann School, as the first woman on the Vermont Board of Education, and on the editorial board of the Book-of-the-Month Club (1926–51).

F.'s interest in education and her love of the U.S. and of Vermont are steadily reflected in her works, which include textbooks, commentaries on education (*A Montessori Mother*, 1912; *The Montessori Manual*, 1913), patriotic reflections (*American Portraits*, 1946; *Our Independence and the Constitution*, 1950), translations (Papini's *Life of Christ*, 1923; Tilgher's *Work*, 1930), Vermont, poetry (*Another Night for America*, 1942), and fiction.

Perhaps F.'s most lastingly popular work, *Understood Betsy* (1917), is the story of a fearful, sickly little girl who, through a change of guardians and environments, becomes an independent, capable child. Written in a pleasant, conversational tone, the book codifies some of F.'s major ideas: the importance of early training, the value of work, the necessity for self-confidence, and the virtues—as she perceived them—of the American heritage.

These ideas, as well as attacks on big business and materialism, are central to *The Bent Twig* (1915), the story of Sylvia and Judith Marshall. Tested sorely, the sisters grow from their experiences, primarily through an awareness of their mother's dictum that if life is to be good, both joys and sorrows must be accepted. In an episode about a mulatto family passing for white, F. makes a plea for racial understanding without glossing over the biases and limitations of the period.

Seasoned Timber (1939) sets F.'s attack on anti-Semitism within the narrative frame of Timothy Hulme's romance in middle age. The relationship between Timothy and his Aunt Lavinia illustrates F.'s realism. Both characters are as capable of self-delusion as they are of self-sacrifice. Flashbacks based upon oral tradition vivify the Vermont setting.

Marriages in transition are a frequent plot device. *The Brimming Cup* (1921) compares and contrasts the marital relationships of Neale and Marise Crittenden and of Gene and Nelly Powers. Both women are mothers, both are clearly at the hub of their families, and both are tempted by attractive, sensual, single men. While the resolution of the Powers' difficulty is melodramatic, Marise's decision that sexual union is valid only when it nourishes personal growth is a convincing presentation of a basic F. theme. Another theme, the importance of woodland reclamation, appears here also, and regional customs are well drawn.

A woman of extraordinary energy, F. was one of the most popular writers of her day and is considered particularly adroit at exploring the drama of everyday life, portraying the inner growth of thoughtful, sensitive characters, and employing skillful variations of the interior monologue.

WORKS: *Emile Augier, Playwright-Moralist-Poet* (1899). *Corneille and Racine in England* (1904). *Elementary Composition* (with G. B. Carpenter, 1906). *Gunhild: A Norwegian American Episode* (1907). *The Secret of Serenity* (1908). *A Montessori Mother* (1912). *The Squirrel Cage* (1912). *The Montessori Manual* (1913). *Mothers and Children* (1914). *The Bent Twig* (1915). *Hillsboro People* (1915). *A Peep into the Educational Future* (1915). *Fellow Captains* (with S. N. Cleghorn, 1916). *The Real Motive* (1916). *Self-Reliance* (1916). *Understood Betsy* (1917; dramatized by S. N. Cleghorn, 1934). *Home Fires in France* (1918). *The Day of Glory* (1919). *The Brimming Cup* (1921). *Rough-Hewn* (1922). *What Grandmother Did Not Know* (1922). *The French School at Middlebury* (1923). *Life of Christ* by G. Papini (translated by Fisher, 1923). *Raw Material* (1923). *The Home-Maker* (1924; film version, 1925). *Made-to-Order Stories* (1925). *Her Son's Wife* (1926). *Why Stop Learning?* (1927). *The Deepening Stream* (1930). *Learn or Perish* (1930). *Work* by A. Tilgher (translated by Fisher, 1930). *Basque People* (1931). *Our Children: A Handbook for Parents* (edited by Fisher, with S. M. Gruenberg, 1932). *Vermont Summer Homes* (1932). *Bonfire* (1933). *Moral Pushing and Pulling* (1933). *Tourists Accommodated* (1934). *Fables for Parents* (1937). *On a Rainy Day* (with S. F. Scott, 1938). *The Election on Academy Hill* (1939). *Seasoned Timber* (1939). *A Family Talks about War* (1940). *Liberty and Union* (with S. N. Cleghorn, 1940). *Nothing Ever Happens and How It Does* (with S. N. Cleghorn, 1940). *In the City, and In the City and on the Farm* (with E. K. Crabtree and L. C. Walker, 1940). *My First Book* (with E. K. Crabtree and L. C. Walker, 1940). *Runaway Toys* (with E. K. Crabtree and L. C. Walker, 1940). *Tell Me a Story* (1940). *To School and Home Again* (with E. K. Crabtree and L. C. Walker, 1940). *Under the Roof* (with E. K. Crabtree and L. C. Walker, 1941). *Under the Sea* (with E. K. Crabtree and L. C. Walker, 1941). *Another Night for America* (1942). *Our Young Folks* (1943). *American Portraits* (1946). *Book-Clubs* (1947). *Highroads and Byroads* (with E. K. Crabtree and L. C. Walker, 1948). *Four-Square* (1949). *Something Old, Something New* (1949). *Our Independence and the Constitution* (1950). *Paul Revere and the Minute Men* (1950). *A Fair World for All* (1952). *Vermont Tradition* (1953). *Dorothy Canfield Fisher on Vermont* (1955). *A Harvest of Stories* (1956). *Memories of Arlington, Vermont* (1957). *And Long Remember* (1959). *Report on Old Age* (n.d.).

BIBLIOGRAPHY: McCallister, L., "D. C. F.: A Critical Study" (Diss., Case Western Reserve Univ., 1969). Yates, E., *Pebble in a Pool* (1958).

   For articles in reference works, see: *NCAB*, 44. *20thCA*. *20thCAS*.

   Other references: *Educational Forum* (Nov. 1950). *SatR* (11 Oct. 1930; 29 Nov. 1958).

JANE S. BAKERMAN

Sarah Symmes Fiske

B. 1652, Charleston, Massachusetts; d. 2 Dec. 1692, Braintree, Massachusetts
D. of William Symmes; m. Moses Fiske, 1671

F. was the granddaughter of the noted minister Zachariah Symmes and the daughter of a justice of the peace for the county of Middlesex. Her mother, whose name is unknown, died when she was very young. Her husband was ordained minister of the Braintree (now Quincy), Massachusetts, congregation. He had a profitable ministry, which included a house and six acres, as well as a substantial yearly income. F. and her husband had fourteen children, which probably contributed to her early death.

F.'s only published work is her spiritual autobiography, a document which she prepared for admission to church membership. *A Confession of Faith; or, A Summary of Divinity* (1704) was written in 1677, when F. was twenty-five years old. The manuscript circulated among her acquaintances for many years after her death, until it was printed. Such posthumous publication was common for works by early American women writers.

Whereas most spiritual autobiographies of the 17th c. express the inner turmoil of the writer in the struggle for salvation, F.'s confession is notable for its impersonal tone and religious erudition. Its highly structured form evidences her familiarity with Ramist logic, the system of reasoning used by the New England Puritans in their theological discourses.

The form and content which F. chose for her confession reflect intense religious study. Each topic she discusses is broken into subtopics or subsets for definition and analysis; then each subset is further analyzed. F.'s topics include the truth of the Bible, God's creation of the natural world, the Fall and its consequences, sin and death, grace and predestination, and the nature of Christ. She also discusses the organization of the church and the significance of the sacraments. She concludes with a brief but striking apocalyptic vision. Puritan historiography—that is, history viewed as God's redemptive scheme—provides the organizing principle for her beliefs, as she discusses events from the beginning of time to the end of the world.

F.'s work is not outstanding for its originality of thought or style.

But the purpose of the document—admission to church membership—precluded creativity. The posthumous publication of her theological discussion and review is important because it indicates an early recognition of women's ability to contribute to religious subjects in an intellectual and educative manner.

WORKS: *A Confession of Faith; or, A Summary of Divinity, Drawn Up, By a Young Gentlewoman* (1704).

BIBLIOGRAPHY: Pierce, F. C., *Fiske and Fisk Family* (1896). Vinton, J. A., *The Symmes Memorial* (1873).

JACQUELINE HORNSTEIN

Janet Flanner

B. *13 March 1892, Indianapolis, Indiana; d. 7 Nov. 1978, New York City*
Wrote under: Janet Flanner, Genêt
D. *of Francis and Mary-Ellen Hockett Flanner*

Born to Quaker parents, F. attended preparatory school in Tudor Hall, Indianapolis, spent a year in Germany with her parents, then entered the University of Chicago in 1912. After being expelled from the university as a "rebellious influence" in the dormitory, she returned to Indianapolis (1916–17) and then went on to New York City, becoming, in her own words, "the first cinema critic ever invented."

A trip to Greece, Crete, Constantinople, and Vienna ended with her settling down in Paris in 1922. Harold Ross, a former New York acquaintance, asked her to write a small "Paris Letter" for a newly conceived magazine called *The New Yorker*. For fourteen years F. wrote all of *The New Yorker*'s Paris letters, and in the 1930s, all of its London letters, under the pseudonym of "Genêt."

When F. returned to the U.S. in 1939, she continued writing her profiles and sketches for *The New Yorker*. After the fall of France, her articles became more overtly political; she also began speaking and writing extensively on France and French culture and politics. She now wrote for *The New Yorker* a more ambitious series (under her own name) on conditions in unoccupied France, on the "bitter civil war of words" between the generations of the two world wars, and on the revival of the Church in the wake of the poverty and deprivation suffered by postwar France.

F.'s books include a novel, *The Cubical City* (1926), which she describes as "really a character sketch and not a novel at all." Three volumes—*An American in Paris* (1940), *Paris Journal, 1944-65* (1966), *Paris Journal, 1965-71* (1971)—comprise the collected *New Yorker* "Paris Letters" and represent, in many ways, the best of F.'s achievement. She invented the formula for her Paris letters: a mixture of incisive epigram, personal and political profiles, and news, mixed with critical reviews of cinema, theater, opera, and gallery openings.

Always it is the characteristic blend of the personal and the political, the temper of the times and the mood of the streets, that marks her writing. The ripening of the mushrooms called *les trompettes de la mort* is detailed no less meticulously than the rise and decline of General de Gaulle's political fortunes. Details become significant in a way that mere reportage is not. Current fashions in the streets and shops, vegetables in the market, holiday celebrations, and even a run of good weather signal, as stock-market reports could not do, France's economic recovery from the war. And the death of Colette, a nationally loved figure, is in F.'s hands more than the occasion for reporting the funeral of a noted author; it is, quite literally, the end of an era in literary and social history. *Paris Journal* exemplifies, at its best, the blend of memoir and reportage, as well as the keen sense of irony, that F. had by then perfected.

WORKS: *The Cubical City* (1926). *Chéri* by Collete (translated by Flanner, 1929). *Maeterlinck and I* by G. Leblanc (translated by Flanner, 1932). *Souvenirs; My Life with Maeterlinck* by G. Leblanc (translated by Flanner, 1932). *An American in Paris: Profile of an Interlude between Two Wars* (1940). *Petain: The Old Man of France* (1944). *Men and Monuments* (1957). *Paris Journal, 1944-65* (Ed. W. Shawn, 1966). *Paris Journal, 1965-71* (Ed. W. Shawn, 1971). *Paris Was Yesterday, 1925-1939* (Ed. I. Drutman, 1972). *London Was Yesterday, 1934-1939* (Ed. I. Drutman, 1975). *Janet Flanner's World: Uncollected Writings, 1932-1975* (Ed. I. Drutman, 1979).

BIBLIOGRAPHY: For articles in reference works, see: *CB* (May 1943). *Indiana Authors and Their Books, 1816-1916*, Ed. R. E. Banta (1949). *WA*.

Other references: *Lost Generation Journal* (Winter 1976). New York *Post* (3 Oct. 1941). New York *World Telegram* (21 Jan. 1941). *Time* (22 April 1940; 9 Nov. 1942).

VALERIE CARNES

Anne Crawford Flexner

B. 27 June 1874, Georgetown, Kentucky; d. 11 Jan. 1955, New York City
D. of Louis G. and Susan Farnum Crawford; m. Abraham Flexner, 1898

After her graduation from Vassar College in 1895, F. supported herself by tutoring for two years in Louisville, Kentucky, until she had saved enough money to go to New York City. There, she attended the theater regulary and began writing plays. After a two-year engagement, she married Flexner, a prominent educator. In his 1940 autobiography, he wrote of their union: "We agreed at the outset of our married life that her interest and work were as sacred as mine; and for over forty years we have tried to respect each other's individuality and that of our two daughters." Encouraged by F., her younger daughter Eleanor Flexner also became a writer and published books on American drama and the woman-suffrage movement in America.

In 1901, Harrison Grey Fiske opened his Manhattan Theater with F.'s first professionally produced play, *Miranda of the Balcony*, which featured Minnie Maddern Fiske in the title role. The *New York Times* review stated that "Mrs. Flexner has written a strong emotional drama of modern style and the audience of last night was quick to recognize its value."

That success enabled F. to obtain the rights to dramatize Alice Hegan Rice's *Mrs. Wiggs of the Cabbage Patch* in 1904. F. took a number of liberties with the original plot in order to sustain a narrative line throughout the three-act play structure, but she preserved all the flavor of the novel in her sprightly, humorous dialogue and characterizations. It became F.'s most frequently performed play.

Aged 26, F.'s last play, was produced in 1936. In the seventeen years since her latest produced play, F. had traveled extensively in Europe with her husband. Her abiding interest in British literature is reflected in this interpretation of the romance of John Keats and Fanny Brawne. The action spans the year between the publication of Keats's *Endymion* and his departure for Italy, where he was to die six months later at age twenty-six. There is an artificial quality to the opening scene in which Keats, Byron, Shelley, Gifford, Lockhart, and Fanny's mother are all brought into the reception room of Keats's publisher. The audience is won over in subsequent scenes, however, by F.'s deft characterization, and by dialogue in which even the incorporation of familiar lines from Keats's poetry is made to sound natural. F. departed from the traditional view of Fanny Brawne by treating her as sensitive and sincere in her love for Keats, even to the point that she spends the night with him on the eve of their separation. The sympathetic interpretation of her character was vindicated by the publication a few months later of Fanny Brawne's letters to Keats's sister.

F.'s plays were audience-pleasers and might be summed up, in the words of one reviewer, as "crisp, clean, wholesome, and refreshing fun." Seven of F.'s plays were produced in New York over a thirty-five-year period. They reveal a variety of interests and a better-than-average talent as a dramatist for the pre-World War I period.

WORKS: *A Man's Woman* (1899). *Miranda of the Balcony* (1901). *Mrs. Wiggs of the Cabbage Patch* (dramatization of the novel by A. H. Rice, 1903). *A Lucky Star* (dramatization of the novel, *The Motor Chaperone*, by C. N. and A. N. Williams, 1909). *The Marriage Game* (1913). *Wanted—An Alibi* (1917). *The Blue Pearl* (1918). *All Soul's Eve* (1920). *Aged 26* (1936).

BIBLIOGRAPHY: Flexner, A., *I Remember: An Autobiography* (1940).
    Other references: *Nation* (2 Jan. 1937). *Theatre Arts Monthly* (Feb. 1937; June 1937).

                                    FELICIA HARDISON LONDRÉ

Elizabeth Gurley Flynn

B. 7 Aug. 1890, Concord, New Hampshire; d. 5 Sept. 1964, Moscow, USSR
D. of Thomas and Elizabeth Gurley Flynn; m. Jack Archibald Jones, 1908

The daughter of first-generation Irish immigrants, F. was raised in an atmosphere of concern for social and political issues. Her parents were both members of the Socialist Party, and her mother was a strong women's rights advocate. When the family moved to the South Bronx, New York, in 1900, F. was introduced to city poverty and to radical political activity. At twelve she won the prize in a Socialist Party debate, and at sixteen gave her first public speech, "What Socialism Will Do for Women," at the Harlem Socialist Club. Later that year she was arrested in New York City (the first of many arrests) for speaking without a public permit.

In 1906, F. joined the Industrial Workers of the World (I.W.W.) and a year later quit school to travel throughout the U.S. as one of the I.W.W.'s most effective speakers and organizers. F. had a son in 1910, and in that same year she separated from her husband (with formal divorce notice in 1920) because she was not prepared to give up her political activity to settle into a more limited domestic life. Both her mother and her sister Kathie provided an important home base for F. and her son after the separation.

During World War I and in the postwar years, as government arrests of radical political leadership increased, F. was the moving force in several labor defense leagues. She became seriously ill in 1927 and for about ten years lived in semiretirement with a friend in Portland, Oregon. Against the advice of her doctor, she returned to the East Coast in 1936, joined the Communist Party of the U.S., became a columnist for the *Daily Worker* in 1937, and in 1938 was elected to the party's national committee. In 1952, she was arrested for subversive activities under the Smith Act and served from January 1955 to May 1957 at the women's prison in Alderson, West Virginia. Upon her release she returned to party activity and was elected national chair in 1959, a post she held until her death while on a visit to the USSR.

All of F.'s writing relates directly to her political activism and focuses on the rights and problems of workers, on the status and corresponding activities of working women, and on civil liberties in general. Underlying all these works is the attempt to acquaint future generations with the historical legacy of the workers' struggle in the U.S. and with the role of working-class leadership in this struggle. Referring to a speech made to the party in 1945, F. noted that it had been "partly biographical, partly confessional, and partly an evaluation of our weaknesses." The perspective expressed in this statement—combined with a continued advocacy of working-class rights and a belief in socialism as the solution to economic, social, and political problems—characterizes all of her writing. F.'s strength as a writer rested on her ability to present ideas with clarity, simplicity, and personal fervor.

In addition to numerous pamphlets, journal and newspaper articles (in *Political Affairs* and *Solidarity*, for example), and regular columns in the *Daily Worker* and *Sunday Worker* from 1937 to 1964, F. also wrote two major works that are primarily autobiographical. *I Speak My Own Piece* (1955, reprinted in 1973 as *The Rebel Girl*, incorporating F.'s own editorial comments) describes her life, her contemporaries, and the events of radical working-class history from 1906 to 1926, using amusing and pertinent anecdotal material. At times the events and people are idealized, in keeping with her purpose to insure that the heroic struggle of those early days would not be lost to history. At the time of her death F. had completed only the notes and outlines for the sequel to this volume, to cover what she called her "second life."

The Alderson Story (1963) details the experiences of F.'s 1952 trial and the following period of imprisonment. It is of more than autobiographical significance because F. tries to record, in a series of prison poems, the voices and emotions of other women with whom she associated in the prison. The book thus becomes a document on women's prison experience in addition to a chapter in her life.

F.'s associates and friends considered her a "great political leader and a great human being." Her ability to express complex issues in simple, unassuming, yet convincing language made her one of the most effective popular leaders of her time. Her autobiographical and political writings are among the best sources available for the history of women's involvement in radical U.S. politics.

WORKS: *Women in the War* (1942). *Women Have a Date with Destiny* (1944). *Women's Place in the Fight for a Better World* (1947). *The Twelve and You* (1948). *The Plot to Gag America* (1950). *Communists and the People* (1953). *I Speak My Own Piece: Autobiography of "The Rebel Girl"* (1955; reprinted as *The Rebel Girl*, 1973). *Horizons of the Future for a Socialist America* (1959). *Freedom Begins at Home* (1961). *The Alderson Story: My Life As a Political Prisoner* (1963). *The McCarran Act: Fact and Fancy* (1963).

The largest collection of Elizabeth Gurley Flynn's writings and personal records is located at the American Institute for Marxist Studies, New York City.

BIBLIOGRAPHY: Dixler, E. J., "The Woman Question: Women and the American Communist Party, 1929–41" (Ph.D. diss., Yale Univ., 1974). Maupin, J., *Labor Heroines: Ten Women Who Led the Struggle* (1974). Wertheimer, B. M., *We Were There: The Story of Working Women in America* (1977).

Other references: *Nation* (17 Feb. 1926). *Political Affairs* (Oct. 1964; Nov. 1964). *Radical America* (Jan.-Feb. 1975).

JANE SLAUGHTER

Eliza Lee Cabot Follen

B. 15 Aug. 1787, Boston, Massachusetts; d. 26 Jan. 1860, Brookline, Massachusetts
Wrote under: Eliza Lee Follen, Mrs. Follen, Mrs. C. T. C. Follen
D. of Samuel and Sally Barrett Cabot; m. Charles Theodore Christian
    Follen, 1828

One of thirteen children, and assured by her family's prominence of a stimulating social and intellectual environment, F. early became a friend and follower of William E. Channing and taught in his Unitarian Sunday school. She married a German political refugee who, from 1830 to 1835, was professor of German literature at Harvard. A son was born in 1830. During the Harvard years the couple became friends of Harriet Martineau and worked actively in the antislavery cause.

Because F. had previously written two works of fiction, edited the *Christian Teachers' Manual*, and composed poems and stories for children, it was natural for her after her husband's death in 1840 to turn to her pen for a livelihood. She edited *Gammer Grethel* (1840), the first American edition of Grimm's fairy tales, and the *Child's Friend*, a juvenile periodical, from 1843 to 1850. In addition to writing a biography of her husband, she composed poetry, plays, and stories for children. Until her death she remained active in the abolition movement, working on committees and writing numerous tracts.

The first and most popular of F.'s stories for children was *The Well-Spent Hour* (1827–28), in which nine-year-old Catherine Nelson learns through benevolence and self-control the meaning of a sermon text: "Let them show their piety at home." Although this didactic tale, suitable for the Sunday-school library, substitutes conversations for action and episodes for plot, its kindly tone and benign view of childhood are winning. *The Birthday* (1832) takes up the history of Catherine just before her fourteenth year, when her father's financial losses force the mother and children to move to a country cottage. The ensuing idyll of family life, which includes stories told during a party, suffers from a contrived plot and the heavy-handed contrast of good and evil so typical of early 19th-c. children's literature.

Simpler in content and more graceful in execution are F.'s short tales, such as *True Stories about Dogs and Cats* (1855), *The Old Garret*

(1855), and *The Pedler of Dust Sticks* (1855), later collected with other tales in the twelve-volume *Twilight Stories* (1858). In *The Old Garret*, where discarded objects—a wig, a musket, a broadsword, a tea kettle—give their biographies, F. adopts the technique, associated with Hans Christian Andersen, of having inanimate objects assume a narrator's role.

Although her children's poetry is now almost forgotten, F. was a pioneer who turned from the harsh, morbid verse characteristic of early 19th-c. American children's poetry to rhymes frankly meant to give more pleasure than instruction. *Little Songs* (1833), reprinted as the final volume of *Twilight Stories*, was intended, she tells us, "to catch something of that good-natured pleasantry and musical nonsense which makes Mother Goose so attractive to children of all ages." Even though the verse in this volume lacks the vigor of traditional nursery rhymes, it is remarkable both for its response to children's tastes and for its gentle vision of childhood.

F.'s adult fiction, *The Skeptic* (1835) and *Sketches of Married Life* (1838), deals ostensibly with marriage. The first work, however, resembles a religious tract both in the account of Alice Grey's efforts to save her husband from the influence of his free-thinking cousin and in F.'s recommendations of Dr. Channing's Unitarian writings. In the second work, a domestic novel, F. creates a heroine who demonstrates, as Helen Papashvily points out, "the marked ability of women in the practical concerns of everyday life."

F.'s *Life of Charles Follen* (1840), for which she traveled to Germany to obtain additional material, is a sympathetic but unsentimental treatment of her husband's life.

A woman of conviction, both in her support of religion and in her opposition to slavery, F. is notable for bringing to American children's literature of the pre-Civil War period a sensitive concern for the feelings and tastes of her young readers.

WORKS: *The Well-Spent Hour* (1827–28). *Selections from the Writings of Fénelon* (edited by Follen, 1829). *Hymns, Songs, and Fables for Children* (1831). *Sequel to "The Well-Spent Hour"; or, The Birthday* (1832). *Words of Truth* (1832). *Little Songs for Little Boys and Girls* (1833). *The Skeptic* (1835). *Sketches of Married Life* (1838). *Hymns and Exercises for the Federal Street Sunday School* (1839). *Nursery Songs* (1839). *Poems* (1839). *Sacred Songs for Sunday Schools, Original and Selected* (1839). *Gammer Grethel; or, German Fairy Tales and Popular Stories* (edited by Follen, 1840). *The Liberty Cap* (1840). *Life of Charles Follen* (1840). *The Works of Charles Follen with a Memoir of His Life* (1841–42). *Made-up Stories* (1855). *The Old Garret* (3 vols., 1855). *The Pedler of Dust Sticks* (1855). *Poems* (1855). *To Mothers in the Free States* (1855). *True Stories about Dogs and Cats* (1855). *Conscience* (1858). *May Morning and New Year's Eve* (1858). *Piccolissima* by A. Montgolfier (translated by Follen, 1858). *Travellers' Stories* (1858). *Twilight Stories* (12 vols., 1858). *What Animals Do and Say* (1858). *Home Dramas for Young People* (compiled by Follen, 1859). *Our Home in the Marsh Land; or, Days of Auld Lang Syne* (1877).

BIBLIOGRAPHY: Meigs, C., *A Critical History of Children's Literature* (1969). Papashvily, H. W., *All the Happy Endings* (1956). Wright, L. H., *American Fiction, 1774–1850* (1969).

For articles in reference works, see: *AA. DAB*, III, 2. *FPA. NAW* (article by E. B. Schlesinger). *NCAB*, 7.

Other references: *ElemEngR* 8 (1931). *NEQ* 38 (1965).

PHYLLIS MOE

Mary Hallock Foote

B. *19 Nov. 1847, Milton, New York; d. 25 June 1938, Hingham, Massachusetts*
D. *of Nathaniel and Anne Burling Hallock; m. Arthur De Wint Foote, 1876*

The youngest child of Quakers, F. was raised on the family farm in the Hudson River valley. After completing her schooling in 1864, she took the step, unusual for a young lady of her era, of enrolling at New York City's Cooper Union to study art. Over the course of three years at Cooper, she prepared herself for a career in black-and-white illustration. Her professional debut came in 1867 with the publication of four of her drawings in A. D. Richardson's *Beyond the Mississippi*.

During the following twenty-five years, F. enjoyed fame as one of the most accomplished of American illustrators. She executed drawings for many of the prominent giftbooks of the period, including Longfellow's *The Skeleton in Armor*, Whittier's *Mabel Martin*, and Hawthorne's *The Scarlet Letter*. Her illustrations were published regularly in *St. Nicholas* and *Century* magazines; "Pictures of the Far West," her most celebrated series, appeared in the latter during 1888–89. By the 1890s, F.'s position as "the dean of women illustrators" was secure, and she was elected to the National Academy of Women Painters and Sculptors.

F.'s success as an illustrator was ultimately eclipsed by her achievements as an author. After her marriage to a civil engineer, she spent much of her life in western mining camps whose picturesque aspects invited literary as well as visual interpretation. Her first attempt at serious prose, "A California Mining Camp," appeared in *Scribner's* in 1878 and highlighted her experiences in New Almaden, California; it was followed by descriptive sketches of other locales where her husband's profession took them. From a stay in Leadville, Colorado, came *The Led-Horse Claim* (1883), F.'s first novel and a modest bestseller.

Between 1883 and 1925, F. published eleven more novels and four volumes of short stories; she also wrote an excellent autobiography and numerous uncollected tales and sketches. Most of her fiction derived from material rooted deeply in her own experience: in particular, the tension between the urbane East and the boisterous West—between the genteel security of the East Coast and the pioneer existence beyond the Rockies—informed her writing. F., approaching her material more sympathetically as her appreciation for the West grew, made the frontier a subject of realistic interest and of romance. As Owen Wister observed, hers was the first voice "lifted to honor the cattle country and not to libel it."

F.'s finest writing came after 1895, once she had retired from professional illustration and had settled comfortably with her husband and three children in Grass Valley, California. Especially noteworthy is *The Desert and the Sown* (1902), a novel inspired in part from F.'s experiences in Idaho between 1884 and 1894. Although the plot covers only the three years between the arrival of Emily Bogardus in Idaho and the death of her estranged husband Adam in New York, the tale spans the family fortunes for three generations. A biblical framework reinforces the story's symbolic reconciliation of East and West, past and present. Two other significant works by F. are *Edith Bonham* (1917) and *The Ground-Swell* (1919). Both are poignant tributes to the past—the former dedicated to the memory of F.'s best friend, Helena Gilder, and the latter designed as a tribute to Agnes Foote, the author's youngest daughter, who died in 1904.

After 1919 F. ceased to publish, although during the 1920s she undertook a project that served as the capstone to her career. Written when she was nearing eighty and had not published for decades, F.'s *Reminiscences* (1972) is a truly distinguished autobiography of interest to historians as well as to literary scholars. From the quiet milldams of Milton to the noisy mining stamps of Leadville, from the frustration and disappointments of Idaho to the comforts and acclaim of the Grass Valley years, this personal account of a genteel Quaker "irretrievably married into the West" makes compelling reading. In 1932 F. returned with

Arthur to the East, living in Hingham, Massachusetts, until her death six years later.

To her 20th-c. successors F. bequeathed a legacy of western fiction which, at its best, provides fresh perspectives, substitutes sensitivity for sentimentality, and strives for fidelity. At a time when the West was still subject to humorous exploitation, F. was the first to achieve the stance of a discerning literary observer, while as a gifted illustrator she also contributed memorable interpretations of the frontier.

WORKS: *The Led-Horse Claim: A Romance of a Mining Camp* (1883). *John Bodewin's Testimony* (1886). *The Last Assembly Ball and The Fate of a Voice* (1889). *The Chosen Valley* (1892). *Coeur d'Alene* (1894). *In Exile, and Other Stories* (1894). *The Cup of Trembling, and Other Stories* (1895). *The Little Fig-Tree Stories* (1899). *The Prodigal* (1900). *The Desert and the Sown* (1902). *A Touch of Sun, and Other Stories* (1903). *The Royal Americans* (1910). *A Picked Company* (1912). *The Valley Road* (1915). *Edith Bonham* (1917). *The Ground-Swell* (1919). *A Victorian Gentlewoman in the Far West: The Reminiscences of Mary Hallock Foote* (Ed. R. W. Paul, 1972).

BIBLIOGRAPHY: Johnson, L. A., *M. H. F.* (1980). Maguire, J. H., *M. H. F.* (Boise State College Western Writers Series #2, 1972). Stegner, W., *Angle of Repose* (1971). Taft, R., *Artists and Illustrators of the Old West, 1850–1900* (1953).

For articles in reference works, see: *AW. DAB*, III, 2. *NAW* (article by T. Wilkens). *NCAB*, 6.

Other references: *Colorado Magazine* (April 1956). *Idaho Yesterdays* (Summer 1976). *Univ. of Wyoming Publications* (15 July 1956). *WAL* (May 1975).

LEE ANN JOHNSON

Esther Forbes

B. 28 June 1891, Westborough, Massachusetts; d. 12 Aug. 1967, Worcester, Massachusetts
D. of William Trowbridge and Harriette Merrifield Forbes; m. Albert Learned Hoskins, 1926

F. was the youngest of five children; her father was a judge, her mother a historian. She graduated from Bradford Academy in 1912 and studied at the University of Wisconsin (1916–18) before serving as a farmhand in Virginia in response to the war effort. Returning to New England, she became an editor from 1920 until her marriage.

During her marriage, F. traveled extensively abroad and continued to write. At the time of her divorce in 1933, she had already made a literary reputation as a historical novelist with *O Genteel Lady!* (1926) and *A Mirror for Witches* (1928). The height of her fame came in the 1940s when she won first the Pulitzer Prize in History for *Paul Revere and the World He Lived In* (1942) and then the Newbery Medal for *Johnny Tremain: A Novel for Young and Old* (1943). F. was the first woman member of the American Antiquarian Society and received seven honorary degrees.

F.'s earliest works are brief and focused upon the development of their heroines, who are of various types and fates. Several of these early novels explore the expression of female sexuality and its psychological connection with the attraction to the demonic in a repressive society that is part of, or heir to, the Puritan tradition. Lanice Bardeen in *O Genteel Lady!* is a sensual and intellectual Boston editor and writer of the late 19th c. who gives up both her passion for a Lawrence-of-Arabia type and for writing in order to marry a staid Harvard professor. In *A Mirror for Witches*, set in the late 17th c., Doll Bilby has a love affair with the "devil" and dies in childbirth, an accused witch, in a Salem prison. The novel is purportedly written by an 18th-c. apologist for the Salem witchcraft trials.

Johnny Tremain is the briefer, focused, and fictionalized outgrowth of *Paul Revere and the World He Lived In,* on which F. and her mother collaborated. Both the life of the real silversmith and the now-famous story of the silversmith's apprentice who adjusts to the handicap of a maimed hand and participates in the Boston revolutionary movement, display F.'s intense interest in the part that individuals, significant or insignificant, play in historical events. Both books clearly owe their immediate inspiration to F.'s concern with the meaning and nature of human freedom in the context of World War II.

Rainbow in the Road (1954), made into a musical in 1969, is F.'s last published work. It is a lyric lament for the unspoiled New England countryside before the coming of the railroad and for the ephemeral popular arts practiced by itinerant artists, "limners" (portrait painters), like its hero, Jude Rebough, and his ballad-making friend, Mr. Sharp. Although she was working on a study of witchcraft at the time of her death, *Rainbow in the Road* seems an appropriate swan song for F. herself, whose own choice of a rather popular art form, the historical novel, helped her to win immediate but perhaps transient recognition.

Even in her nonfiction, F.'s sole analytical thrust is psychological and somewhat Freudian. F. considers personalities and social relationships among personalities, rather than broader social, political, or economic issues. She saves her sharp sense of irony, expressed often in wry comments, for individual foibles and generally accepts learned but conventional interpretations of events. Perhaps only in *A Mirror for Witches*, with its craftily delineated narrator, and in *Johnny Tremain*, where the problems of an adolescent and of a new society reflect upon each other, do her talents as a novelist and a historian mesh artistically enough to transcend the limits of her genre. Here her efforts to depict the human universal in a particular period and place will probably earn her longer-lasting aesthetic esteem.

WORKS: *O Genteel Lady!* (1926). *A Mirror for Witches* (1928). *Miss Marvel* (1935). *Paradise* (1937). *The General's Lady* (1938). *Paul Revere and the World He Lived In* (with H. M. Forbes, 1942). *Johnny Tremain: A Novel for Young and Old* (1943). *The Boston Book* (with A. Griffin, 1947). *The Running of the Tide* (1948). *America's Paul Revere* (with L. Ward, 1948). *Rainbow in the Road* (1954; musical version, 1969).

BIBLIOGRAPHY: For articles in reference works, see: *CA*, 25–28 (1971); *Permanent Series* (1975). *Newbery Medal Books 1922–55*, Eds. B. M. Miller and E. W. Field (1955). *Something about the Author*, Ed. A. Commire (1971). *20thCA. 20thCAS.*

Other references: *LJ* (15 May 1944). *NYT* (13 Aug. 1967).

LOIS R. KUZNETS

Hannah Webster Foster

B. *10 Sept. 1758, Salisbury, Massachusetts; d. 17 April 1840, Montreal, Canada*
Wrote under: A Lady of Massachusetts
D. *of Grant and Hannah Wainwright Webster; m. John Foster, 1785*

Little is known of either F.'s childhood or education, but the numerous historical and literary allusions in her books suggest that she was well-educated for her time and sex. F. is best known for her novel *The Coquette; or, The History of Eliza Wharton* (1797). After the publication of her second book, *The Boarding School; or, Lessons of a Preceptress to Her Pupils* (1798), F. wrote only short articles for newspapers. Upon her husband's death she moved to Montreal to live with two of her five children, two daughters who also wrote.

The Coquette, which is "founded on fact," was based on the life of Elizabeth Whitman of Hartford, Connecticut, a distant cousin of F.'s husband. It is a seduction novel in epistolary form (obviously much influenced by the novels of Samuel Richardson, such as the epistolary seduction novel, *Clarissa Harlowe*) with the typical strengths and weaknesses of this genre. Incidents are reported several times by different people, a technique that reveals character through a comparison of points of view. Many of the letters seem natural and spontaneous. Others, however, suffer from excessive length, didactic digressions, and an overemphasis on sentiment and sensibility.

From the novel's beginning Eliza emerges as a strong-willed young woman delighting in a newly found freedom from her parents and a dull fiancé. She is convincingly indecisive about her two new suitors, the admirable Mr. Boyer, a clergyman, and Major Sanford, who, she is warned, is " a second Lovelace" (the seducer in *Clarissa*).

Sanford, too, is a convincing and complex character. Seduction to Sanford is a game; he sees Eliza as a coquette and determines to "avenge [his] sex by retaliating the mischiefs she meditates." He writes: "If she will play with a lion, let her beware the paw, I say." Sanford is confident of his powers, but his pride is hurt by her friends' warnings against him and by her attraction to Boyer. These make him even more determined to win Eliza, which he does eventually, even though he has, in the meantime, married for money.

Justice appropriate to the seduction-novel genre is meted out to Eliza and Sanford, accompanied by lengthy confessions and moral lectures. The lessons are taught by the characters themselves, however, and their contrition seems real enough, a fact which makes *The Coquette* one of the better American examples of the genre.

The Coquette went through thirteen editions in its first forty years. *The Boarding School* was not so popular. It is dedicated to "the young ladies of America" and demonstrates how a clergyman's widow, Mrs. Williams, educates young girls to fulfill their future roles as well-bred ladies, wives, and mothers.

WORKS: *The Coquette; or, The History of Eliza Wharton* (1797). *The Boarding School; or, Lessons of a Preceptress to Her Pupils* (1798).

BIBLIOGRAPHY: Brown, H. R., *The Sentimental Novel in America, 1789–1860* (1940). Mott, F. L., *Golden Multitudes* (1947). Osborne, W. S., ed., *The Power of Sympathy and The Coquette* (1970). Petter, H., *The Early American Novel* (1971).

For articles in reference works, see: *AA. DAB*, III, 2. *NAW* (article by H. R. Brown).

Other references: *AL* (Nov. 1932).

ELAINE K. GINSBERG

Rose Franken

B. Dec. 1898, Gainesville, Texas
Wrote under: Rose Franken, Margaret Grant, Franken Meloney
D. of Michael and Hannah Younker Lewin; m. Sigmund Walter Anthony
Franken, 1915; m. William Brown Meloney V, 1937

F.'s parents were separated when she was a few years old, and her mother took the four children to New York City to live with F.'s grandparents and several aunts, uncles, and cousins in a large house in Harlem. She attended the Ethical Culture School, but, having failed a sewing course, did not obtain a high-school diploma. At sixteen, she married a prominent oral surgeon ten years her senior. Two weeks later, they learned that he was tubercular. Their first year of marriage was spent in a sanitarium.

To take her mind off constant worrying about her husband's health, F. began writing short stories. After the publication of a novel, *Pattern* (1925), her husband suggested that she try playwrighting. Her first dramatic effort, *Fortnight*, was optioned but never produced or published. Her second play, first presented under the title *Hallam Wives* in a summer 1929 production in Greenwich, Connecticut, later became the very successful *Another Language* (1932).

After Sigmund Franken's death in 1933, F. moved with her three sons to California. She collaborated with her second husband on a number of screenplays. After their marriage, they moved to a Connecticut farm. Using the pen name Franken Meloney, they regularly published novels and magazine serials, to which he contributed the plots and she wrote the dialogue.

Another Language is a comedy-drama about the dangerously self-righteous attitudes of a middle-class family dominated by a possessive matriarch who encourages their tasteless and materialistic instincts. When F. brought the same family back to the stage in 1948 with her sixth and last professionally produced play, *The Hallams*, the characters had not changed.

Beginning with her dramatization of *Claudia* (1941), F. directed all of her own plays. Her second husband produced her third Broadway play, *Outrageous Fortune* (1943), and all subsequent ones. That play departed from her established style by raising questions about such social concerns as homosexuality, the treatment of black servants, marital difficulties in middle age, and anti-Semitism. Despite misgivings about F.'s attempt to handle so many themes in one play, some critics believed it to be her best work for the stage.

Her "Claudia" novels, begun in 1939 as a series of stories for *Redbook* magazine, became the basis for a play, a radio series, and two motion pictures, and they were widely published in translation abroad. It was *Claudia* that made F.'s name familiar to the public for two decades. Beginning with the first days of Claudia's marriage at eighteen to David Naughton, the series of novels chronicles, with humor and sentimental appeal, the gradual maturation of a child-wife. Eternally artless, impulsive, and charming, Claudia comes to grips with such problems as hiring servants, testing her sex appeal, becoming a mother, shopping in a posh dress salon, and coping with her own mother's death. Although the Claudia novels rely heavily upon illness, accidents, and death for the emotional upheavals that lead Claudia toward increasing self-awareness, they are essentially the saga of a blissful marriage.

Referring to her twenty-year involvement with Claudia, F. wrote in her autobiography, *When All Is Said and Done* (1963), that "the sheer technical task of remaining within her consciousness became increasingly onerous and demanding." F., however, was able to draw upon her own notably successful marriages. Her particular skill as a novelist and playwright is the ability to inject sparkle into trivial nuances of everyday life, and to unfold a narrative action largely through dialogue.

WORKS: *Pattern* (1925). *Another Language; a Comedy Drama in Three Acts* (1932). *Mr. Dooley, Jr.; a Comedy for Children* (with J. Lewin, 1932). *Twice Born* (1935). *Call Back Love* (with W. B. Meloney, 1937). *Of Great Riches* (1937). *Claudia* (1939; dramatization by Franken, 1941; screenplay by Franken, 1943). *Claudia and David* (1939; screenplay by Franken, 1946). *Strange Victory* (with W. B. Meloney, 1939). *When Doctors Disagree* (with W. B. Meloney, 1940; dramatization by Franken, 1943). *American Bred* (with W. B. Meloney, 1941). *The Book of Claudia* (containing *Claudia* and *Claudia and David*, 1941). *Another Claudia* (1943). *Outrageous Fortune; a Drama in Three Acts* (1943). *Beloved Stranger* (with W. B. Meloney, 1944). *Soldier's Wife; a Comedy in Three Acts* (1944). *Young Claudia* (1946). *The Hallams; a Play in Three Acts* (1947). *The Marriage of Claudia* (1948). *From Claudia to David* (1950). *The Fragile Years* (also published as *Those Fragile Years; a Claudia Novel*, 1952). *Rendezvous* (English title, *The Quiet Heart*, 1954). *Intimate Story* (1955). *The Antic Years* (1958). *The Complete Book of Claudia* (1958). *Return to Claudia* (1960). *When All Is Said and Done; an Autobiography* (1963). *You're Well Out of a Hospital* (1966).

BIBLIOGRAPHY: Mantle, B., *Contemporary American Playwrights* (1938).
For articles in reference works, see: *American Novelists of Today,* H. R.
Warfel (1951). *CB* (1947). *20thCA. 20thCAS.*
Other references: *NYT* (8 Jan. 1933). *NYTMag* (4 May 1941). *Players Magazine* (Spring 1974).

FELICIA HARDISON LONDRÉ

Mary Eleanor Wilkins Freeman

B. 31 Oct. 1852, Randolph, Massachusetts; d. 15 March 1930, Metuchen,
New Jersey
Wrote under: Mary E. Wilkins Freeman, Mary E. Wilkins
D. of Warren E. and Eleanor Lothrop Wilkins; m. Charles Manning Freeman,
1902

F. was an attractive, rather introspective child. In 1867 her father, a builder, moved his family to Brattleboro, Vermont. F. attended the Brattleboro high school; she also attended Mt. Holyoke Seminary and Mrs. Hosford's Glenwood Seminary in West Brattleboro, for one year each. In 1883 she returned alone to Randolph, her mother, father, and only sister all having died. Here she lived with friends, the Wales family. She did not, however, confine herself to Randolph, but visited friends in the U.S. and traveled in Europe. After her marriage, F. settled in Metuchen, New Jersey. In 1921, F. obtained a legal separation from her husband, who had become an alcoholic requiring institutionalization. The year 1926 brought honors to F.: She was awarded the Howells medal for distinction in fiction by the American Academy of Letters, and she was elected to membership in the National Institute of Arts and Letters.

F. established herself as a children's author in the early 1880s. *Decorative Plaques* (1883) collected, in an ornamental format, twelve of her poems from the children's magazine, *Wide Awake.* In 1882, the first adult story she sold won a prize in a contest sponsored by the Boston *Sunday Budget.* "A Shadow Family" has been lost, but F. said later it was "quite passable as an imitation of Charles Dickens." Winning the contest caused her to concentrate on adult fiction, and her stories began to appear frequently in *Harper's Bazar* and *Harper's Weekly.* F.'s capacity for work was enormous, and in the years that followed she became an exceedingly popular author of both adult and juvenile short stories (including some eerie tales of the supernatural), novels, and poetry for children.

Her best stories and novels are about New England people and deal with several themes characteristic of them: stoical endurance in the face of hopeless poverty and adversity, unshakeable pride, and the fierce flame of Calvinistic religion.

A typical short story is "Calla-Lilies and Hannah," in which a girl, shielding her lover, courageously bears the villagers' reprobation for a theft she has not committed. Another is "A Taste of Honey," in which a young woman denies herself everything in the way of comfort and luxury to pay off a mortgage, even losing her fiancé because of the length of time involved.

Of the novels, *Pembroke* (1894) is F.'s greatest achievement, a novel that deserves to be recognized as an American classic. It is densely peopled, with every facet of the New England character in evidence: greed, parsimony, tenacity of purpose, industriousness, sexuality, fanaticism, unselfishness, even heroism. Symbolism is occasionally employed in a way that has reminded critics of Hawthorne's fiction.

An early play, *Giles Corey, Yeoman* (1893), is based on a true incident in the Salem witchcraft trials. Here F. skillfully tells the story of a farmer and his wife who are put to death; she does it so well that the drama, as she wrote it, may be effectively performed, though it has not often been produced on the stage.

As F. wrote more voluminously and her work appeared constantly in magazines, her style changed. Losing its distinctive New England flavor, it became increasingly elaborate, elegant, and, at times, unbearably precious. Although she continued to use New England locales and characters, she began to write also of prosperous suburban life in New Jersey. In addition, she tried to keep in step with fashions in fiction, writing a historical romance set in Virginia (*The Heart's Highway*, 1900), and a labor novel (*The Portion of Labor*, 1901). Both were embarrassing failures.

F.'s significance lies in those of her stories and novels that show New England life deglamorized. She never wrote anything one could call sordid, but her early work conveys the appalling poverty of remote New England farms and villages, the constriction of the lives there, the suffering, the meanness, and the occasional flashes of real nobility. Granville Hicks has said that "her stories made the record of New England more nearly complete."

WORKS: *Decorative Plaques* (1883). *The Adventures of Ann; Stories of Colonial Times* (1886). *A Humble Romance, and Other Stories* (1887). *A New*

England Nun, and Other Stories (1891). *The Pot of Gold, and Other Stories*
(1892). *Young Lucretia, and Other Stories* (1892). *Giles Corey, Yeoman* (1893).
Jane Field (1893). *Pembroke* (1894). *Comfort Pease and Her Gold Ring* (1895).
Madelon (1896). *Jerome: A Poor Man* (1897). *Once upon a Time, and Other
Child-Verses* (1897). *The People of Our Neighborhood* (1898). *Silence, and
Other Stories* (1898). *In Colonial Times* (1899). *The Jamesons* (1899). *The
Heart's Highway; a Romance of Virginia in the Seventeenth Century* (1900).
The Love of Parson Lord, and Other Stories (1900). *The Portion of Labor*
(1901). *Understudies; Short Stories* (1901). *Six Trees; Short Stories* (1903). *The
Wind in the Rose-Bush, and Other Stories of the Supernatural* (1903). *The
Givers; Short Stories* (1904). *The Debtor* (1905). *By the Light of the Soul*
(1906). *"Doc" Gordon* (1906). *The Shoulders of Atlas* (1908). *The Fair Lavinia,
and Others* (1909). *The Winning Lady, and Others* (1909). *The Green Door*
(1910). *The Butterfly House* (1912). *The Yates Pride; a Romance* (1912). *The
Copy Cat, and Other Stories* (1914). *An Alabaster Box* (with F. M. Kingsley,
1917). *Edgewater People* (1918).

BIBLIOGRAPHY: Foster, E., *M. E. W. F.* (1956). Hamblen, A. A., *The New
England Art of M. E. W. F.* (1966). Hicks, G., *The Great Tradition* (1935).
Pattee, F. L., *The New American Literature* (1930). Pattee, F. L., *Sidelights on
American Literature* (1922). Quinn, A. H., *American Fiction* (1936).

For articles in reference works, see: *DAB*, IV, 1. *NAW* (article by E. Foster).
NCAB, 9. *20thCA.*

Other references: *Atlantic* (May 1899).

ABIGAIL ANN HAMBLEN

Betty Friedan

B. 4 Feb. 1921, Peoria, Illinois
D. of Harry and Miriam Horowitz Goldstein; m. Carl Friedan, 1947

One of three children of parents who encouraged neither her reading
nor her feminism, F. attributed her later awareness of oppression partly
to being Jewish. In high school F. founded a literary magazine and
graduated as class valedictorian. At Smith College she studied psychology
with noted Gestalt psychologist Kurt Koffka and graduated in 1942
summa cum laude. After winning her second research fellowship at the
University of California at Berkeley, she realized that to go on would
commit her to a doctorate and a career as a psychologist. She gave in to
what she called the pressure of the feminine mystique, gave up Berkeley
for a nonprofessional job in New York City, and soon married and began
raising her three children.

By the mid-1950s F. was deeply dissatisfied with her life. Approaching the resulting crisis thoughtfully, she began to wonder if other women shared her dissatisfaction. Through a questionnaire sent to her Smith College classmates, she discovered that her ailment was widespread and began several years of research which culminated in *The Feminine Mystique* (1963). She analyzed the post–World War II pressures that forced promising young women out of the colleges and into the suburbs to raise children. The book's impact has been widespread. It was excerpted in *McCall's, Saturday Review*, and elsewhere; it sold very well in the hardcover edition and has gone through many printings in paperback. Its central thesis is that those forces supposed to be "the chief enemies of prejudice"—that is, education, sociology, psychology, and the media—have, in effect, conned American women into believing that their entire identity and worth could be derived from being wives and mothers.

After publishing *The Feminine Mystique*, F. began actively to campaign against the feminine mystique in its variety of guises. She founded NOW, the National Organization for Women, in 1966. Attacked since its start by more radical women's groups who felt that it was too middle-class, too hierarchically structured, and too conservative in its aims, NOW became and has remained the largest and most visible feminist organization in the U.S. Since leaving the presidency of NOW in 1970, F. has continued her activism, interspersed with lecturing and teaching at various universities. She wrote a column for *McCall's*, "Betty Friedan's Notebook," and contributed to a wide range of magazines including *Saturday Review, Harper's, New York Times Magazine, Redbook, Ladies' Home Journal*, and *Working Women*.

In 1976, F. published *It Changed My Life: Writings on the Women's Movement*. In a series of essays and open letters, F. assesses the progress of the women's movement and her relationship with it. The book provides a personal as well as a movement history. It points, as well, to what F. sees as a necessary change in the women's liberation movement: it must transcend polarization and become "human liberation."

It is because so many women recognized in F.'s *Feminine Mystique* their own lack of fulfillment as human beings that she is credited with having begun the current women's movement, with having turned the nation's attention to the significance of women's problems. She has urged women to take a risk and attempt to improve the quality of their lives. Hers has been a loud, clear, and important voice, and she has earned her place in the history of the women's movement.

WORKS: *The Feminine Mystique* (1963). *Anatomy of Reading* (Eds. L. L. Hackett and R. Williamson, 1966). *Voices of the New Feminism* (Ed. M. L. Thompson, 1970). *It Changed My Life: Writings on the Women's Movement* (1976).

The papers of Betty Friedan are in the Schlesinger Library of Radcliffe College, Cambridge, Massachusetts.

BIBLIOGRAPHY: Janeway, E., *Man's World, Woman's Place* (1971). Lerner, G., *The Female Experience: An American Documentary* (1977). Ryan, M. P., *Womanhood in America from Colonial Times to the Present* (1975). Sochen, J., *Herstory: A Woman's View of American History* (1974). Sochen, J., *Movers and Shakers: American Women Thinkers and Activists, 1900–1970* (1973).

For articles in reference works, see: CB (Nov. 1970).

BILLIE J. WAHLSTROM

Frances Dana Barker Gage

B. 12 Oct. 1808, Marietta, Ohio; d. 10 Nov. 1880, Greenwich, Connecticut.
Wrote under: Aunt Fanny, F. D. Gage, Frances Gage, Mrs. Frances Dana Gage
D. of Joseph and Elizabeth Dana Barker; m. James L. Gage, 1829

G., whose parents emigrated from New Hampshire to Ohio in 1788, was born on a farm, the fifth daughter and the ninth of ten children. Although her education was limited to that of most rural children in a large, hard-working family, she gained the habit of independence of thought and an interest in reform. Her mother, daughter of an educated New England family, encouraged her to learn as much as she could under the difficult circumstances of frontier life in Ohio; the parents' aid to fugitive slaves underscored their concern with social issues. G. drew from her background a toughness that served her well in life. After her marriage to a lawyer and businessman, she managed to rear eight healthy children while educating herself further, gaining respect as a prolific journalist and writer, and becoming increasingly active in reform.

G.'s concern over slavery extended to the problems of slaves freed during the Civil War. She spent some time during 1862 in a part of South Carolina controlled by the Union; here she worked with freed slaves who needed help in starting new lives. After the war, when she became better known as a journalist, she continued to urge northerners to give aid to the freedmen. Here, as in all her speaking and writing, she drew on her vigorous homely style to make telling points and to make the unfamiliar acceptable. Her impact on audiences was especially dramatic in her appeals for temperance, in which she used case histories to move women to tears and men to new resolutions. Her spontaneous, conversational manner helped her to win her audiences.

These gifts served her well in the women's rights movement. So eloquent was G. at the important Akron Convention (1851), that she unanimously won the election as president of the convention. G.'s reminiscences (in the *National Anti-Slavery Standard*, May 1866) provide the tone and feeling of the dramatic episode in which Sojourner Truth (a former slave, unable to read or write, but a moving speaker) rose to speak at the Akron convention, against the advice of some of the participants. G.'s own language does not lack color as she describes the importance of woman suffrage: she speaks of "war cries," the "advance-guarde," the "rebellion," and in a somewhat less militant tone, "most unwearied actors."

G. also wrote to support her large family. Under the pseudonym of Aunt Fanny (whose real identity was no secret) she wrote letters of advice to women in Amelia Bloomer's *The Lily*, Jane Grey Swisshelm's *The Saturday Visiter*, and other papers, especially feminist ones. Aunt Fanny's words about practical household matters often contained shrewd wit, especially in her reflections on the roles of men and women in daily life. As she counsels her readers on the making of soap, the use of practical clothing, the churning of butter, the efficient use of time, Aunt Fanny amuses herself and them with (often satiric) replies to anti-suffrage male correspondents about female frailty.

For a time G. also served as associate editor of both the Ohio *Cultivator* and *Field Notes*, farmers' weekly papers that disappeared after the Civil War. Later she published several temperance works and, in 1867, a volume of poems—sentimental verse to be sure, but they are accurate descriptions of farm life especially as that life reflects the position of women.

G. stands as one of those active, resourceful 19th-c. women, who—without the formal education of some of her contemporaries, such as Elizabeth Cady Stanton or Susan B. Anthony—succeeded in becoming an influential writer and a force in the women's rights movement. She exerted her influence through work in antislavery, temperance, and women's organizations, but even more through the homely, pithy writing with which she spread her ideas. Her work had perhaps its greatest impact on rural women, with whom she could easily establish rapport because of her similar background.

WORKS: *Christmas Stories* (1849). *The Man in the Well: A Temperance Tale* (1850). *Fanny's Journey* (1866). *Fanny at School* (ca. 1866). *Elsie Magoon; or, The Old Still-House in the Hollow* (1867). *Poems* (1867). *Gertie's Sacrifice; or, Glimpses at Two Lives* (1869). *Steps Upward* (1870).

BIBLIOGRAPHY: Brockett, L. P., and M. C. Vaughn, *Woman's Work in the Civil War* (1867). Hanson, E. R., *Our Woman Workers* (1882).

For articles in reference works, see: *AA. AW. DAB*, IV, 1. *Eminent Women of the Age*, Eds. J. Parton et al. (1869). *HWS*, I, II. *NAW* (article by E. H. Roseboom). *NCAB*, 2. *Ohio Authors and Their Books*, Ed. W. Coyle (1962).

Other references: New York *Tribune* (13 Nov. 1884).

LOIS FOWLER

Zona Gale

B. 26 Aug. 1874, Portage, Wisconsin; d. 27 Dec. 1938, Chicago, Illinois
D. of Charles Franklin and Eliza Beers Gale; m. W. L. Breese, 1928

An only child, G. grew up in the sheltered small-town environment that became the setting for her fiction. She graduated from the University of Wisconsin at Madison in 1895. After working as a journalist in Milwaukee, G. went on to New York in 1900 and began selling stories and poems. She returned permanently to Wisconsin after winning the 1910 *Delineator* short-story prize of two thousand dollars.

A longtime friend of Jane Addams, G. was active with the Women's Peace Party, woman suffrage, La Follette Progressivism, the Wisconsin Dramatic Society, and the growing community-theater movement. Throughout the 1930s, she continued to write fiction and to work for social reform and peace. She saw to the publication and wrote the introduction to *The Living of Charlotte Perkins Gilman* in 1935.

The women in G.'s work are remarkable for the consistency of their development. Calliope Marsh, the leading personality of the Friendship Village stories, was based on G.'s mother and represents the wisdom that G. saw as basic to an ideal maternal model. *Heart's Kindred* (1915) and *A Daughter of the Morning* (1917) are declarations of G.'s own feminist awareness.

Her most successful novel is *Miss Lulu Bett* (1920), an unsentimental look at family and marriage customs. Lulu Bett, family "beast of burden," is shown in rebellion against the life her time and place have thrust upon her: It is a story of growth. There is no overt moralizing to interrupt the flow of the plot. G. adapted this novel herself for the stage, and, in 1921, won the Pulitzer Prize for drama. There was some controversy about the changes G. made in the ending of the play after a trial run, but in a letter to the editor of the New York *Tribune*, G. made it clear she understood the feelings that keep many Lulus locked in their shells for years until a dramatic emotional event sets them free.

G.'s short stories appeared in popular magazines and were then put out in book form; her novels were often serialized before appearing in complete form. She was a regular contributor to magazines, often on feminist topics. Besides adapting some of her other novels for the theater, she wrote a one-act play, *The Neighbors* (1914), which had great success with college and community groups across the country. G. published one book of poetry, *The Secret Way* (1921), which reveals her search for deeper-than-surface reality.

Working from life as she observed it, G. took ordinary occurrences and invested these events with power to affect the inner lives of her characters. G. expressed her own basic philosophy as "life is more than we can ever know it to be." Consequently, some of her work is flawed by too heavy a reliance on mysticism: the stories cannot always sustain the transcendent events within their framework. When G. is successful, however, she touches a response in the reader that rises above the sentimental.

WORKS: *Romance Island* (1906). *The Loves of Pelleas and Etarre* (1907). *Friendship Village* (1908). *Friendship Village Love Stories* (1909). *Mothers to Men* (1911). *Christmas* (1912). *Civic Improvement in the Little Towns* (1913). *When I Was a Little Girl* (1913). *Neighborhood Stories* (1914). *The Neighbors* (1914). *Heart's Kindred* (1915). *A Daughter of the Morning* (1917). *Birth* (1918; dramatization by Gale, *Mister Pitt*, 1925). *Peace in Friendship Village* (1919). *Miss Lulu Bett* (1920; dramatization by Gale, 1921). *The Secret Way* (1921). *Uncle Jimmy* (1922). *What Women Won in Wisconsin* (1922). *Faint Perfume* (1923; dramatization by Gale, 1934). *Preface to a Life* (1926). *Yellow Gentians and Blue* (1927). *Portage, Wisconsin, and Other Essays* (1928). *Borgia* (1929). *Bridal Pond* (1930). *The Clouds* (1932). *Evening Clothes* (1932). *Old Fashioned Tales* (1933). *Papa La Fleur* (1933). *Light Woman* (1937). *Frank Miller of Mission Inn* (1938). *Magna* (1939).

BIBLIOGRAPHY: Derleth, A., *Still Small Voice: The Biography of Z. G.* (1940). Gard, R., *Grassroots Theater: A Search for Regional Arts in America* (1955). Herron, I., *The Small Town in American Literature* (1939). Mac-Dougall, P., *Some Will Be Apples* (film, 1974). Simonson, H. P., *Z. G.* (1962). Sochen, J., *Movers and Shakers: American Women Thinkers and Activists 1900–1970* (1974).

For articles in reference works, see: *DAB*, Suppl. 2. *NAW* (article by W. B. Rideout). *NCAB*, B. *20thCA*.

Other references: *American Magazine* (June 1921). Madison (Wisconsin) *Capital Times* (29–31 May 1974; 3, 4 June 1974).

NANCY BREITSPRECHER

Helen Hamilton Gardener

B. 21 Jan. 1853, Winchester, Virginia; d. 26 July 1925, Washington, D.C.
Given name: Alice Chenoweth
D. of Alfred Griffith and Katherine Peel Chenoweth; m. Charles Selden Smart, 1875; m. Selden Allen Day, 1902

The initial impetus to G.'s public career as an author, freethinker, suffragist, and political lobbyist came from her father, whose abolitionist activities and rejection of formal Episcopalian thought instilled in G. a strong commitment to independent scientific inquiry, sociological analysis, and concomitant activism. G. acknowledged this debt to her father in her last novel, *An Unofficial Patriot* (1894), a slightly fictionalized biography focusing on her father's conversion to the Methodist church and on his Civil War activities.

After an extensive education at various private schools in the Washington, D.C., area and two years of school teaching, G. moved with her husband to New York City, where she studied biology at Columbia University and lectured in sociology at the Brooklyn Institute of Arts and Sciences. In 1884, prompted by her friendship with the prominent agnostic and skeptic, Robert G. Ingersoll, G. gave a series of lectures devoted to the principles of free thought and a discussion of the relationship between heredity and environment.

Her first book-length publication, *Men, Women, and Gods* (1885), contains many of these lectures. It was published under the name Helen Hamilton Gardener, a name that she subsequently adopted in both her personal and professional life. It is not known whether she rejected her given name and her married name to further her assertion of individual independence, to shield her family from the uproar which accompanied many of her publications, or to underscore a growing dissatisfaction with her marriage.

From 1885 to 1890, G. published numerous essays and short stories in a wide variety of periodicals. Many of these pieces were collected in *Pushed by Unseen Hands* (1890) and *A Thoughtless Yes* (1890). In the former, G. describes the scope of her subject matter as "unanalyzed varieties of mental, moral, social, industrial, or other aberrations of what is by courtesy called civilized society." Here, as in all of her writings, G. insists that her readers formulate independent conclusions, conclusions invariably counterposed to their previous passivity.

G. continued this work in two essay collections, *Pulpit, Pew, and Cradle* (1892) and *Facts and Fictions of Life* (1893). Exploring such diverse topics as insurance fraud, penal reform, labor disputes, hypocrisy in religion and philanthropy, the subservient position of women, and tenement living conditions, these two books make G. one of the earliest of the American muckrakers. The most significant and widely discussed of these essays was "Sex in Brain," the result of a fourteen-month biological study conducted to refute the contention of Dr. W. A. Hammond, surgeon general of the U.S., that the brains of men and women are structurally different. G. originally presented the conclusions reached through this research to the International Council of Women in Washington, D.C., in 1888.

During the 1890s, when she served as contributor, associate editor, and, briefly, coeditor of B. F. Flower's reform-oriented magazine, *The Arena*, she was chiefly responsible for the journal's progressive stance on a wide variety of feminist issues.

G.'s two novels, *Is This Your Son, My Lord?* (1891) and *Pray You Sir, Whose Daughter?* (1892), explicitly confront and condemn the sexual double standard. The first of these attacks the hypocritical upbringing of young American men, especially with respect to the emphasis on external respectability rather than moral convictions and independent thought. G.'s condemnation of institutionalized Christianity as abettor of this false social system figures heavily in her argument.

The companion novel, *Pray You Sir, Whose Daughter?*, focuses on the lives of three young women. Here G. writes a strident, but effectively argued denunciation of an attempt by the New York state legislature to lower the age-of-consent law; she also condemns the low wages paid to working women, and attacks the inferior position of women in the marital relationship. The novel is especially significant for its memorable portrait of a "new-woman" heroine, Gertrude Foster.

Although Elizabeth Cady Stanton's prediction that G.'s writings would do for the women's rights movement what Harriet Beecher Stowe's

Uncle Tom's Cabin did for the abolitionist cause was not fulfilled, the two novels were frequently reprinted and were the subject of widespread controversy.

Throughout her long and varied career, G.'s commitment to feminism was a prominent aspect of her self-proclaimed separation from conventional thought and action. Possibly G.'s most significant contribution lay in her attack on the standards of propriety and respectability imposed upon the woman writer. In her essay, "The Immoral Influence of Women in Literature" (*Arena*, February 1890), for example, G. cites the need for an uncensored and distinctly female literary voice.

WORKS: *Men, Women, and Gods, and Other Lectures* (1885). *Pushed by Unseen Hands* (1890). *A Thoughtless Yes* (1890). *Is This Your Son, My Lord?* (1891). *Pray You Sir, Whose Daughter?* (1892). *Pulpit, Pew, and Cradle* (1892). *Facts and Fictions of Life* (1893). *An Unofficial Patriot* (1894; dramatized as *Rev. Griffith Davenport, Circuit Rider,* by J. Herne, 1899).

The papers of Helen Hamilton Chenoweth Gardener are in the Schlesinger Library, Radcliffe College, Cambridge, Massachusetts.

BIBLIOGRAPHY: Flexner, E., *Century of Struggle* (1959). Gordon, L., *Woman's Body, Woman's Right* (1976). *H. H. G. (Alice Chenoweth Day) 1853–1925* (privately printed memorial booklet, 1925). Hill, V. L., "Strategy and Breadth: The Socialist-Feminist in American Fiction" (Diss., SUNY at Buffalo, 1979). Park, M., *Front Door Lobby* (1960). Putnam, S., *400 Years of Freethought* (1894).

For articles in reference works, see: *AW. DAB*, IV, 1; Suppl. 4. *HWS*, IV, V. *NAW* (article by A. Washburn). *NCAB*, 9.

Other references: *American Journal of Physical Anthropology* (Oct.–Dec. 1927). *Arena* (Jan. 1891; June 1892; Dec. 1894). *Business Woman* (Jan. 1923). *Free Thought Magazine* (Jan. 1890; Jan. 1897; March 1901; July 1902). *Independent* (8 Sept. 1892). *Literary World* (13 Aug. 1892; 9 Sept. 1893). *Nation* (16 June 1892). *Woman Citizen* (2 May 1925).

VICKI LYNN HILL

Jean Garrigue

B. *8 Dec. 1914, Evansville, Indiana; d. 27 Dec. 1972, Boston, Massachusetts*
D. *of Allan Colfax and Gertrude Heath Garrigue*

The youngest child of a postal inspector who published short fiction and a mother who was musical, G. spent her childhood in Indiana. She received a B.A. from the University of Chicago (1937) and an M.F.A.

from the University of Iowa (1943). She has taught in many American colleges and universities, and worked as an editor (serving as poetry editor of the *New Leader* from 1965 to 1971) and as a journalist. G. has received many awards.

For G., the Imagists made daring to write poetry possible. One of her earliest aims, she said, was to set to music what the eye brings forth. This disposition helped her to benefit from the examples of strict visual details, as well as to cope with the lack of structural necessity in the verse she first emulated.

In *Thirty-Six Poems, and a Few Songs* (1944), G. is both outside and inside the lucid scene: in the immediacy of the moment sight staggers and consciousness trembles ("With Glaze of Tears"), but the significance of the images balances the poems between an intimate and impersonal tone so that they are not as autobiographical as they are prototypical. The subjects are those of a young poet—the memory of the loss of brilliant innocence, the emptiness of a place in which a vision of a beautiful girl (a stranger) disappeared, questions about identity and love.

In *The Ego and the Centaur* (1947), the landscapes of youth are replaced by configurations for the "centre of the fury in which we live" and more elaborate structures. The poems are characterized by a tension between delicacy of feeling and suppressed rage for the fact that sensations are brutalized. Changes of style signal changes of subject from an exemplum on gaping at the handicapped animals and flightless birds in the false country of the zoo to the obvious satire of "There Is No Anti-Semitism in the Village."

The startling image of *The Monument Rose* (1953) suggests G.'s powerful modesty in relation to what T. S. Eliot calls "the ideal order" of literature's "existing monuments." Open to the full measure of the works of the past, G. says in effect: "Here's one flower." "The Maimed Grasshopper [with three simple eyes] Speaks Up" can be compared to the wit of the metaphysical poets, as she pleads warily for the particular against the universal view. Her virtuosity, neither imitative nor self-insistent, is proof of a mature woman's dedication to keeping language alive, and gives the book its stature.

G.'s work in prose, in the novella *The Animal Hotel* (1966) and in *Chartres and Prose Poems* (1970), although it has the aura of poetry, contributes to the irregular rhythms and colloquial lines that mark an almost radical anonymity of style in *Studies for an Actress, and Other Poems* (1973). The sense of an ending, the dominant death theme, accounts for the austere clarity of "Requiem," "Elegy," or "Movie

Actors Scribbling Letters Very Fast in Crucial Scenes." G. continues to write love poems, some of her best because they are as direct as prose heightened by bare metaphor: "To Speak of My Influences" ("Above all, your eyes") or "The Gift of Summer" ("Once more, my love, once more / I am where you were / When midsummered, you wrote / Outright on my heart").

Sensitive to literary tradition but audaciously independent in the search for new correspondences between the disconnections and discontinuities of the modern period, G. occupied the meeting place between knowledge and imagination, between reality and dream. Possessed of critical intelligence, she knew the truth "in the feeling that comes from seeing" as well as the power of the invisible in the visible. She was consequently both at home in the world and a stranger in it.

WORKS: *Thirty-Six Poems, and a Few Songs* (1944). *The Ego and the Centaur* (1947). *The Monument Rose* (1953). *A Water Walk by Villa d'Este* (1959). *Country Without Maps* (1964). *Marianne Moore* (1965). *The Animal Hotel: A Novella* (1966). *New and Selected Poems* (1967). *Chartres and Prose Poems* (1970). *Translations by American Poets* (edited by Garrigue, 1970). *Studies for an Actress, and Other Poems* (1973). *Love's Aspects: The World's Great Love Poems* (edited by Garrigue, 1975).

BIBLIOGRAPHY: For articles in reference works, see: *CA*, 37–40 (1973). *Indiana Authors and Their Books, 1917–1966*, Ed. D. E. Thompson (1974). *20thCAS*.

Other references: *New Leader* (29 Jan. 1968). *NewR* (2 Nov. 1953). *NYRB* (4 Oct. 1973). *Parnassus* (Winter 1975). *Poetry* (Dec. 1953; May 1960; June 1965; May 1968). *SatR* (19 June 1948). *SR* (Spring 1954). *YR* (Autumn 1973).

ELIZABETH PHILLIPS

Martha Gellhorn

B. *Nov. 1908, St. Louis, Missouri*
Writes under: Martha Gellhorn, Martha Hemingway
D. *of George and Edna Fischel Gellhorn; m. Ernest Hemingway, 1940;*
  m. Thomas Matthews, 1953

The only daughter of a distinguished physician and of a social reformer and suffragist, G. learned that one's purpose in life should consider the well-being of others. Her home environment fostered a profound respect for the individual and a confidence in her own ability to accomplish anything she was willing to work for.

G. left Bryn Mawr after her junior year to become a cub reporter for the Albany *Times Union*, quit after six months, and free-lanced for the St. Louis *Post-Dispatch*, publishing, before the age of twenty-one, an article in the *New Republic*. When *Collier's* published an unsolicited article on the life of Madrid during the Spanish Civil War, adding G.'s name to its masthead, G. knew that she had made herself a war correspondent, won a front-row seat to the history of her time, and wedged a place in a heretofore masculine world. In Spain, G. lived and worked with Ernest Hemingway. They were married in 1940 and divorced in 1945.

G. investigated Czechoslovakia before and after the Munich Pact, reported from Russian-bombed, subzero Finland, analyzed the British defenses in China, stowed away to see the Invasion of Normandy, flew in a Black Widow, and spent V-E Day in Dachau. After the war, she attended the Nuremberg and Eichmann trials, reported on the Six-Day and Vietnam wars. Scarcely returning to the U.S. for more than an extended visit, G. set up temporary residences in Spain, Cuba, Mexico, Italy, Kenya; today she lives and writes in her favored London.

Aiming to enlist support for those struggling to live their lives with decency—the poor in America's Depression, the republicans in Madrid, the refugees in Czechoslovakia, the Jews in Dachau—G. learned quickly to concentrate paragraphs into a few careful details. Rather than philosophize about the absurdity of war, G. utilized the power of image: a mother still walking her son across the street, unaware that the last shellburst had taken his life. G. made her pieces vivid by reordering what she saw into a natural unity, investing statistics with humanity.

Although her journalism appeared almost weekly in American magazines after 1940, G. never lost sight of her goal to write fiction. The autobiographical emphasis of her first novel, *What Mad Pursuit* (1934), continued to mar her fiction until the late 1940s. It was with the publication of *Liana* (1944), a novel about a powerless mulatto woman living on a Caribbean island, that G.'s fiction matured. Although she was still reporting in her black-and-white fashion on the Nazi atrocities, G. shifted in her fiction from a concern with political philosophies and external movements to an exploration of the individual and his or her inner needs.

In 1948, G. published her best work, a World War II novel called *The Wine of Astonishment*. Borrowing from her journalism the details needed to convince her readers of the external action which centers around the Battle of the Bulge, G. wrote about the isolation of the 20th-c. man and his power to break through the self-imposed imprisonment to a richer, more meaningful life. The lesson of responsible action, no longer sentimentalized in an autobiographical protagonist, was dramatically heightened by the encounter of a Jew, who had denied his heritage, with the atrocities of Dachau. The characters lose their hero or villain status and impress as human beings; the craft is careful and effective.

G.'s journalism was constantly applauded, and several of her war articles were collected into the much-praised *Face of War* (1959), but her fiction was received less enthusiastically. The three postwar volumes of short stories which G. chose to collect from many more surfacing in American magazines, however, reveal her fine craft and perception. *The Honeyed Peace* (1953), *Two by Two* (1958), and *Pretty Tales for Tired People* (1965) illustrate G.'s recurring themes of human liberation, the crush of poverty and war on the human psyche, the intensity of human relationships, and the way to invest meaning into otherwise meaningless lives.

G.'s journalism, at its best, functions for those who read it as a kind of conscience. Her fiction, at its peak, serves as a type of mirror, a compelling reflection of humanity and a penetrating glance at ourselves.

WORKS: *What Mad Pursuit* (1934). *The Trouble I've Seen* (1936). *A Stricken Field* (1940). *The Heart of Another* (1941). *Liana* (1944). *Love Goes to Press* (with V. Cowles, 1947). *The Wine of Astonishment* (1948). *The Honeyed Peace* (1953). *Two By Two* (1958). *The Face of War* (1959). *His Own Man* (1961). *Pretty Tales for Tired People* (1965). *Vietnam: A New Kind of War* (1966). *The Lowest Trees Have Tops* (1969). *Travels with Myself and Another* (1978). *The Weather in Africa* (1980).

BIBLIOGRAPHY: Baker, C., *Ernest Hemingway: A Life Story* (1969). Cowles, V., *Looking for Trouble* (1941). Matthews, T. S., *O My America! Notes on a Trip* (1962). Orsagh, J., "A Critical Biography of M. G." (Ph.D. diss., Michigan State Univ., 1978).

For articles in reference works, see: *20thCA. 20thCAS.*

Other references: *Guardian* (5 Oct. 1966). St. Louis *Post-Dispatch* (3 Oct. 1936). *Time* (18 March 1940).

JACQUELINE E. ORSAGH

Jean Craighead George

B. 2 July 1919, Washington, D.C.
Writes under: Jean Craighead, Jean George
D. of Frank and Carolyn Johnson Craighead; m. John L. George, 1944

G., writer, illustrator, and naturalist, attended Pennsylvania State University and edited its literary magazine. During World War II she worked as a reporter for the International News Service (1941–43) and the *Washington Post* and *Times-Herald* (1943–45). She worked as an artist for *Pageant* magazine (1945–46) and as reporter-artist for the Newspaper Enterprise Association (1946–47). G. married a conservationist and ecologist with whom she had three children; they were divorced in 1963.

In the 1960s and 1970s, G. wrote thirty-three books (and illustrated some of them), mostly for children. She also published many articles on nature subjects in *Reader's Digest*, for which she is a roving editor, and in other magazines. An unusual characteristic of G. is that, if at all possible, she lives with the animals she writes about; she reports having raised at least 173 wild pets.

My Side of the Mountain (1959) is the story of adolescent Sam Gribley, who is tired of living with his large family in a cramped city apartment and wants to go live in the Catskills on his great-grandfather's homestead. For thirteen months he does just that. He collects and cooks his own food, makes himself a home inside a tree trunk, and figures out a source of heat for protection against the cold mountain winters. He has a variety of animal friends, including Frightful, a young falcon he trains. The life is difficult and sometimes lonely, but Sam succeeds, and the story is told so realistically and with such detail that it all seems very credible.

The conflicts of adolescence are further explored in *The Summer of the Falcon* (1962), a story that seems to incorporate some of G.'s own biography. It is told through the cycle of a family's return, three summers in a row, to the grandfather's Victorian house in the mountains. The heroine struggles toward self-discipline. In one scene she is able to go ahead and use her wits to complete a cave rescue only after she has admitted her nearly overwhelming fear. Perhaps the ending is too pat, but this is more than outweighed by the book's basic strengths, including fascinating hawk lore.

Julie of the Wolves (1972) is the story of an adolescent Eskimo girl who is befriended by a wolf pack while searching for her lost father and a lost cultural tradition. G. captures the conflict of Eskimo life, the desire on the part of some to retain the old ways of living in harmony with the earth and the desire of others to enjoy some of the luxuries of "civilization"—such as radios, refined foods, alcohol, and high-powered rifles. *Julie of the Wolves,* with its sections of fine naturalistic writing, won the 1973 Newbery Medal and was voted among the ten best children's books of the last two hundred years by members of the Children's Literature Association.

Hook a Fish, Catch a Mountain (1975), like the earlier *Who Really Killed Cock Robin?* (1971), can be termed an ecological mystery, but like many other books by G., it is also a story of an adolescent trying to be accepted as an individual. Again, the protagonist is female, and again she is trying to shake off her lack of experience and her fears in order to become an able and independent outdoorsperson.

G.'s successful mixing of nature stories with novels centering on adolescents and their concerns works to the advantage of both genres. The adolescent concerns of learning to manage physical danger and fear, to take responsibility, to discipline oneself and to become a part of a group, as well as to develop independence, are set against the backdrop of the need for all humans to be aware of the interconnectedness of all the ecosystems of this earth. A deep understanding of nature's harmonies—beautiful and death-causing alike—pervades each of the books. G. is a fine writer who has chosen to write books that are primarily appropriate for young people, but at her best she is equally interesting to adults.

WORKS: *Vulpes, the Red Fox* (with J. L. George, 1948). *Vision, the Mink* (with J. L. George, 1949). *Masked Prowler: The Story of a Racoon* (with J. L. George, 1950). *Meph, the Pet Skunk* (with J. L. George, 1952). *Bubo, the Great Horned Owl* (with J. L. George, 1954). *Dipper of Copper Creek* (with J. L. George, 1956). *The Hole in the Tree* (1957). *Snow Tracks* (1958). *My Side of the Mountain* (1959; film version, 1969). *The Summer of the Falcon* (1962). *Red Robin, Fly Up* (1963). *Gull Number 737* (1964). *Hold Zero* (1966). *Spring Comes to the Ocean* (1966). *The Moon of the Bears* (1967). *The Moon of the Owls* (1967). *The Moon of the Salamanders* (1967). *Coyote in Manhattan* (1968). *The Moon of the Chickarees* (1968). *The Moon of the Fox Pups* (1968). *The Moon of the Monarch Butterflies* (1968). *The Moon of the Mountain Lions* (1968). *The Moon of the Wild Pigs* (1968). *The Moon of the Alligators* (1969). *The Moon of the Deer* (1969). *The Moon of the Gray Wolves* (1969). *The Moon of the Moles* (1969). *The Moon of the Winter Bird* (1969). *All upon a Stone* (1971). *Beastly Inventions* (1971). *Who Really Killed Cock Robin?* (1971). *Wildguide to the Everglades* (1971). *Julie of the Wolves* (1972). *All upon a Sidewalk* (1974). *Walking Wild Westchester* (1974). *Hook a Fish, Catch a Mountain* (1975). *Going to the Sun* (1976). *Dirty Work, Inc.* (1978). *Wentletrap Trap* (1978). *American Walk Book: An Illustrated Guide to the Country's Major Historical and Natural Walking Trails from the Northeast to the Pacific Coast* (1978). *River Rats, Inc.* (1979). *The Wounded Wolf* (1979). *The Cry of the Crow* (1980). *The Grizzley Bear with the Golden Ears* (1981). *Journey Inward* (1982). *The Wild, Wild Cookbook* (1982).

BIBLIOGRAPHY: Huck, C., and D. Kuhn, eds., *Children's Literature in the Elementary School* (1968). Sutherland, Z., and M. H. Arbuthnot, *Children and Books* (1977).

For articles in reference works, see: *Authors of Books for Young People,* Eds. M. E. Ward and D. A. Marquardt (1964). *CA,* 7-8 (1963). *More Junior Authors,* Ed. M. Fuller (1963). *Something About the Author,* Vol. 2, Ed. A. Commire (1971). *Who's Who in Children's Books: A Treasury of the Familiar Characters of Childhood,* M. Fisher (1975).

Other references: *Elementary English* (Oct. 1973). *Horn Book* (Aug. 1973). *WrD* (March 1974).

LINDA A. CARROLL

Alice Gerstenberg

B. 2 Aug. 1885, Chicago, Illinois; d. 28 July 1972, Chicago, Illinois
D. of Erich and Julia Wieschendorff Gerstenberg

G.'s grandparents on both sides of the family were Chicago pioneers. From her father she inherited endurance, and from her mother a love of theater. She attended the Kirkland School in Chicago and Bryn Mawr College.

Before writing plays, G. was interested in writing novels. Her first full-length play, a three-act version of Lewis Carroll's *Alice in Wonderland* and *Through the Looking Glass,* opened in 1915 at both the Fine Arts Theatre and the Booth Theatre in New York. G.'s next play, the one-act *Overtones,* her most original and best-known work, was produced in 1915 by the Washington Square Players at the Bandbox Theatre, New York, under the direction of Edward Goodman. It also played in

London, starring Lily Langtry. In 1922, G. wrote a three-act version of *Overtones* which she directed herself at Powers Theater in Chicago.

In *Overtones* G. created two lines of action to tell the story of Harriet and Margaret. Harriet has married for money and longs for the man she loves, while Margaret has married for love (the same man Harriet, too, had loved) and now longs for money. The surface action of the play, which reveals only the "civilized" selves of these women, is shown in conventional dramatic form, while the action below the surface reveals the subconscious selves of the two women in two characters named Hetty and Maggie. Harriet and Margaret exist in the present in a world as it appears to be; Hetty and Maggie speak of the past and life as they honestly feel them. The two actions placed side by side create not just a conventional conflict between two women, but a compelling irony and a conflict wthin each character, Harriet-Hetty and Margaret-Maggie.

Overtones was heralded as representing a new formula in theater. Today it is still seen as a forerunner of later psychological drama by major playwrights, including Eugene O'Neill, who acknowledged its influence on his work. This same concern for the dramatic "representation" of the subconscious is obvious in *Strange Interlude* (1928) and in *Days Without End* (1932), both of which use masks to draw the conflict between the false outer self and the painfully honest subconscious self.

The Pot Boiler (later titled *Dress Rehearsal*), a comedy about the pretensions of conventional theater, and *Fourteen*, a light satire on the pettiness of high-society dinner parties, along with *Overtones*—all appearing in G.'s second collection, *Ten One-Act Plays* (1921)—are G.'s most popular plays. They have appeared in numerous anthologies of one-act plays and have been produced by little theaters all over the U.S., England, and Australia.

G. was one of the original members of the Chicago Little Theatre, the first little theater in the U.S., which was founded by Maurice Browne in 1912. In 1921, she and Annette Washburne founded the Chicago Junior League Theatre for children. For two years, G. was this theater's director. Using her early model for children's theater, junior leagues have developed in communities all over the country.

G.'s most significant contribution to the little-theater movement is her founding of The Playwright's Theatre of Chicago (1922–45), which was designed to offer the local playwright an opportunity to produce plays. For her work as playwright and producer, G. won the Chicago Foundation for Literature Award in 1938. Her articles on little theater appear in *Townsfolk Magazine, The Little Theatre Monthly,* and *The Drama.* G. has also enjoyed a modest career as an actress.

G.'s characters, mostly women, inhibited by outworn institutions and by their own fears, make choices that lead to honest self-expression. Needing new dramatic forms to express the daring of her unconventional characters, G. took the comic form and gave it not only a variety of structures but a modern psychological dimension as well. G.'s dramaturgy reflects her own vitality as a woman and as a playwright dedicated to a new theater which placed artistic integrity as its highest goal.

WORKS: *A Little World* (1908). *Unquenched Fire* (1912). *Alice in Wonderland* (dramatization of *Alice in Wonderland* and *Through the Looking Glass* by L. Carroll, 1915). *The Conscience of Sarah Platt* (1915). *Ten One-Act Plays* (1921). *Four Plays for Four Women* (1924). *The Land of Don't Want To* by L. Bell (dramatization by Gerstenberg, 1928). *Overtones* (1929). *Comedies All* (1930). *Water Babies* by C. Kingsley (dramatization by Gerstenberg, 1930). *Star Dust* (1931). *When Chicago Was Young* (with H. Clark, 1932). *Glee Plays the Game* (1934). *Within the Hour* (1934). *Find It* (1937). *London Town* (dramatization by Gerstenberg, 1937). *The Queen's Christmas* (1939). *Time for Romance* (with M. Fealy, 1942). *Victory Belles* (with H. Adrian, 1943). *The Hourglass* (1955). *Our Calla* (1956). *On the Beam* (1957). *The Magic of Living* (1969).

BIBLIOGRAPHY: Dean, A., *Comedies All* (1930). Sievers, D., *Freud on Broadway* (1955).

Other references: *NewR* (20 Nov. 1915).

BEVERLY M. MATHERNE

Caroline Howard Gilman

B. *8 Oct. 1794, Boston, Massachusetts; d. 15 Sept. 1888, Washington, D.C.*
Wrote under: Caroline Gilman, Caroline Howard, Clarissa Packard
D. of Samuel and Anna Lillie Howard; m. Samuel Gilman, 1819

G.'s father died when she was two, her mother when she was ten. She had an irregular education, as the family moved from one Boston suburb to another. After her marriage to a Unitarian minister she moved to Charleston, South Carolina. Three of her seven children died in infancy.

In 1832, G. began publication of the *Rose Bud; or, Youth's Gazette,* one of the earliest American magazines for children. Renamed the *Southern Rose-Bud* in 1833 and the *Southern Rose* in 1835, it gradually became a general family magazine before ceasing publication in 1839. Many of G.'s writings appeared first in its pages.

In *Recollections of a Housekeeper* (1834), "Clarissa Packard" gives a brief account of her education and then describes her first years of marriage. Because its first-person narrator is solidly middle-class (Mr. Packard is an attorney), Clarissa Packard's chronicle presents a "case history" of the "disestablishment" of the American woman as described by Ann Douglas in *The Feminization of American Culture*. Her duties as a housekeeper seem to consist largely of training cooks, hired girls, or nursemaids; and the domestic crises of her early marriage usually involve the unexpected departure of one or more of these servants. She emphasizes throughout that she can roast and boil, make puddings and pies, sweep and dust, and she is pleased that her mother has educated her for usefulness: "My mother was proud to say that I could manufacture a frilled shirt in two days, with stitches that required a microscope to detect them." She is busy, however, teaching others to do her cooking, sweeping, and washing. No sooner does she train women than they tire of devoting themselves to her and her family and want to get married and have lives of their own.

Much of the humor in the *Recollections of a Housekeeper* is afforded by the vocabulary and accents of the rustic New Englanders who come to serve and by their inability to grasp the forms (and perhaps the spirit) of such service.

When G. wrote her chronicle of a New England housekeeper, she had already been living in Charleston for many years. The disestablishment of the middle-class housewife and the attitudes towards servants revealed in the first book reach a logical culmination in its companion-piece, *Recollections of a Southern Matron* (1838), which depicts all for the best in that best of all possible worlds, the southern plantation. The first-person narrator of this second book supplies more information on her background and early life, and a romantic plot with a subplot involving a secondary heroine, but the focus is again on scenes of domestic life. G. places great emphasis on the contentment of the slaves (they are always called "servants," but they stay around once they are trained), and she claims their lot is better than that of northern servants and millhands. G.'s letters to her children after the Civil War show her still unchanged in the opinion that slavery had benefited the slaves.

In *The Poetry of Travelling in the United States* (1838), G. sets out to "present something in the same volume which might prove attractive to both the Northern and Southern reader" and "to increase a good sympathy between different portions of the country."

G. also published collections of short stories, poetry (some with her daughter Caroline Howard Jervey), and novels. She prided herself most on her writings for children and young people, but these are now of interest mostly as indications of what Americans of the 1830s thought suitable reading for their children. Her position as a humorous chronicler of middle-class domesticity, North and South—a sort of early Erma Bombeck—became more and more difficult to sustain, as this New England-born Unitarian gave her sympathies to her adopted South.

WORKS: *Recollections of a Housekeeper* (1834). *The Lady's Annual Register and Housewife's Memorandum Book* (1838). *The Poetry of Travelling in the United States* (1838). *Recollections of a Southern Matron* (1838). *Letters of Eliza Wilkinson* (edited by Gilman, 1839). *Tales and Ballads* (1839). *Love's Progress* (1840). *The Rose-Bud Wreath* (1841). *Oracles from the Poets* (1844). *Stories and Poems for Children* (1844). *The Sibyl; or, New Oracles from the Poets* (1849). *Verses of a Life Time* (1849). *A Gift Book of Stories and Poems for Children* (1850). *Oracles for Youth* (1852). *Recollections of a New England Bride and a Southern Matron* (1852). *Record of Inscriptions in the Cemetery and Building of the Unitarian . . . Church . . . Charleston, S.C.* (1860). *Stories and Poems by Mother and Daughter* (with C. H. Jervey, 1872). *The Poetic Fate Book* (1874). *Recollections of the Private Centennial Celebration of the Overthrow of the Tea* (1874). *The Young Fortune Teller* (with C. H. Jervey, 1874).

BIBLIOGRAPHY: Saint-Amand, M. S., *A Balcony in Charleston* (1941).

For articles in reference works, see: *DAB*, Suppl. 1. *The Living Writers of the South*, Ed. J. W. Davidson (1869). *NAW* (article by S. Nissenbaum). *NCAB*, 13. *Women of the South Distinguished in Literature*, Ed. M. Forrest (1861).

Other references: *NCHR* (April 1934). *SAQ* (Jan. 1924).

SUSAN SUTTON SMITH

Charlotte Perkins Stetson Gilman

B. 3 July 1860, Hartford, Connecticut; d. 17 Aug. 1935, Pasadena, California
D. of Frederick Beecher and Mary A. Fritch Perkins; m. Charles Walter
    Stetson, 1884; m. George Houghton Gilman, 1900

G.'s father left the family soon after G. was born. Although he made infrequent visits home and provided meager support for his family, he was largely responsible for G.'s early education, emphasizing reading in the sciences and history. Her only formal education consisted of brief attendance at the Rhode Island School of Design. Like her great-aunt, Harriet Beecher Stowe, G. was a reformer. At an early age, she recognized the plight (particularly the economic servitude) of her mother and many New England housewives. By age twenty-one, she was writing poetry that described the limitations of being female in late-19th-c. New England.

As a teenager, G. was a commercial artist, art teacher, and governess. Ten months after her marriage to Stetson, also an artist, their only daughter was born. G. suffered extreme depression after the birth and made a recuperative trip to California. She moved there in 1888 and divorced Stetson in 1894.

G. did not establish her reputation as a forceful writer and lecturer until the last decade of the century when she published a series of satiric poems in the *Nationalist*. She also began lecturing on a wide variety of topics. For a time she was a member of the National Movement, during which her writing and lectures reflected that group's nationalistic fervor.

In 1893, G. collected about seventy-five poems into a small volume entitled *In This Our World*. G. designed the cover, "based on Olive Screiner's *Three Dreams in a Desert*." The book was first published in England but enjoyed scanty success in the U.S., where, besides G.'s family and friends, William Dean Howells first recognized its greatness. He called G. "the only optimist reformer he ever met." The poems outline G.'s economic and social views and are considered by many to be a classic statement on the women's movement.

Women and Economics, originally titled *Economic Relation of the*

Sexes as a Factor in Social Development, appeared in 1898. This book's arguments in behalf of women's rights arise out of a firm and broad philosophical and historical base. G. calls American society "androcentric" and illustrates how traditionally male values have dominated almost every aspect of American life. It is considered one of the most important works on the women's movement.

Written in 1890 but not published as a separate work until 1899, *The Yellow Wall-Paper* is a fictional though partially autobiographical treatment of a woman artist's nervous breakdown. Having recently given birth, she is forced by her husband and physician to spend the summer in isolation in a Gothic-style country estate. She is forbidden to write, which is the one thing she truly wants to do. The result is the woman's madness, her delusion that another woman is trapped behind the wallpaper in her attic bedroom.

G.'s *Concerning Children* (1900) and *The Home* (1904) expand on arguments originally advanced in *Women and Economics*. Both suggest that children's lives can be stunted instead of enriched by a home in which the mother's sole occupation is housekeeping. G. argues instead for day-care centers where children are well cared for, and where they can continue to explore the "thrilling mystery of life." G. called *The Home* "the most heretical—and the most amusing—of anything I've done."

In 1900, G. married her first cousin, a lawyer from New York. During their honeymoon, G. read him the book she had been writing, *Human Work* (1904). It attempts to make the same claim for work that Cardinal Newman made for knowledge: that it is intrinsically valuable, its own end. According to G., work is both a responsibility and a pleasure. One does it because one is obligated to the human community.

In 1909, G. began a seven-year editorship of her own monthly periodical, the *Forerunner*. Written entirely by G. and containing twenty-one thousand words per issue, G. figured that the *Forerunner* equaled four books a year, of thirty-six thousand words apiece. The periodical contained articles on social and economic issues (invariably about women) and some poetry and fiction. It published two full-length novels by G.: *What Diantha Did* (1910) and *The Crux* (1911). *The Man-Made World* (1911) was also published in *Forerunner*. It juxtaposed male and female values. Women, G. wrote, are peace-loving and concerned with community. Contrarily, the prevailing values in our society are male: aggressiveness, competition, and destructiveness.

His Religion and Hers (1923) was published six years after G. had resigned from the *Forerunner*. In it, G. compares the male conception of the world (a postponement and preparation for the afterlife) with the female (heaven in the present time and place). She directs her argument toward current social considerations, suggesting that if women controlled society, they would place greater emphasis on practical issues: how to live comfortably and peacefully from day to day.

Her autobiography, *The Living of Charlotte Perkins Gilman* (1935), is an excellent source for understanding G.'s life, work, and death. Suffering from cancer and surviving her husband's unexpected death in 1934, G. lived quite peacefully for a time near her daughter in Pasadena, then committed suicide by chloroform. The conclusion of her autobiography is an appropriate epitaph and was part of a letter left to her survivors: "The one predominant duty is to find one's work and do it, and I have striven mightily at that. The religion, the philosophy, set up so early, have seen me through."

WORKS: *In This Our World* (1893). *Women and Economics* (1898). *The Yellow Wall-Paper* (1899). *Concerning Children* (1900). *The Home* (1904). *Human Work* (1904). *What Diantha Did* (1910). *The Crux* (1911). *The Man-Made World* (1911). *Moving the Mountain* (1911). *His Religion and Hers* (1923). *The Living of Charlotte Perkins Gilman: An Autobiography* (1935).

BIBLIOGRAPHY: Dell, F., *Women as World Builders* (1913). Wellington, A., *Women Have Told: Studies in the Feminist Tradition* (1930).

For articles in reference works, see: *DAB*, Suppl. 1. *HWS*, V, VI. *NAW* (article by C. N. Degler). *NCAB*, 13.

Other references: *AQ* (Spring 1956). *Canadian Magazine* (Aug. 1923). *Century Magazine* (Nov. 1923). *Poet-Lore* (Jan.-March 1899).

MARY BETH PRINGLE

Elizabeth Meriwether Gilmer

B. *18 Nov. 1870, Woodstock, Tennessee; d. 16 Dec. 1951, New Orleans, Louisiana*
Wrote under: Dorothy Dix
D. *of William and Maria Winston Meriwether; m. George Gilmer, 1888*

G.'s career as a newspaper columnist and reporter stemmed from her tragic marriage. The daughter of impoverished southern gentry, G. had little formal training and no work experience when, shortly after her marriage, she had to assume financial responsibility for herself and her husband, a victim of an incurable mental disease. Rejecting the idea of divorce, she began working as a woman's-page writer on the New Orleans *Picayune* in 1896. Successful as a columnist and reporter, G. moved to the New York *Evening Journal* in 1901, where she continued her column, "Dorothy Dix Talks," and covered sensational murder trials (usually involving women) and vice investigations. From 1917 until her death, she confined her newspaper writing to her advice column, first for the Wheeler syndicate and from 1923 for the Ledger syndicate.

Between 1912 and 1914, G., a supporter of woman suffrage, wrote three pamphlets on the subject. She also published a number of books of advice, some fictional in technique and southern in setting, like *Mirandy* (1914) and *Mirandy Exhorts* (1922), but mostly drawn from her columns, like *Fables of the Elite* (1902), *Hearts à la Mode* (1915), and *How to Win and Hold a Husband* (1939). In addition, she published travel books describing the customs and problems in the places she visited.

Best known for her column, reaching an estimated sixty-million readers worldwide with sympathy, humor, and common sense, G. dispensed sermonettes on courtship and marriage as well as answers to letters. She advised that women develop a positive self-image and know how to work at a job, but also retain femininity, good nature, and adaptability. Beginning many columns with "Men are a selfish lot," G. accepted the reality of a sexual double standard and advised her readers how to deal with that reality.

Convinced of the healthy and life-enriching power of love, G. nevertheless explained how to achieve that goal with imagery taken from games, hunting, and marketing, with what one reviewer has called "hard-boiled realism that would do credit to a brothel keeper." For example: "A young girl who lets any one boy monopolize her, simply shuts the door in the face of good times and her chances of making a better match." "Few grafts are more profitable than comforting a widower. But remember that fast work is required." And in a "recipe" book for marriage: "All wives should encourage their husbands in dough-making. It keeps them out of mischief and promotes domestic felicity."

Coexistent with the pragmatism, however, is the pride, independence, and self-worth G. advocates for all women. In *Woman's Lack of Pride* (ca. 1912), she writes that women lack sex pride "when they permit themselves to be classed politically with the offscourings of the earth [the criminal, the idiot, the insane]. . . . All of woman's failures are due to her shame of her sex, and she will never succeed until she . . . realizes that . . . she is entitled to stand side by side with man, not to have to trail along in his wake like a humble slave."

Sociologists Robert and Helen Lynd in their sociological study of middle America, *Middletown* (1929), assess G.'s column as the best single available source to represent Middletown's views about marriage, and also as "perhaps the most potent single agency of diffusion from without shaping the habits of thought of Middletown in regard to marriage." G. defined the ideal of love and marriage, acknowledged the reality, and wrote pragmatic advice reflecting but also shaping the behavior and mores of her readers.

WORKS: *Fables of the Elite* (1902). *What's Sauce for the Gander Is Sauce for the Goose* (ca. 1912). *Woman's Lack of Pride* (ca. 1912). *Dorothy Dix on Woman's Ballot* (1914). *Mirandy* (1914). *Hearts à la Mode* (1915). *Mirandy Exhorts* (1922). *My Trip around the World* (1924). *Dorothy Dix, Her Book* (1926). *Mexico* (1934). *How to Win and Hold a Husband* (1939).

BIBLIOGRAPHY: Kane, H. T., *Dear Dorothy Dix* (1952). Lynd, R. S. and H. M. Lynd, *Middletown* (1929).

For articles in reference works, see: *CB* (1940; Feb. 1952). *DAB*, Suppl. 1, 5. Other references: *NYT* (17 Dec. 1951). *Time* (14 Aug. 1939).

HELEN J. SCHWARTZ

Ellen Anderson Gholson Glasgow

B. *22 April 1873, Richmond, Virginia; d. 21 Nov. 1945, Richmond, Virginia*
Wrote under: Ellen Glasgow
D. of Francis Thomas and Anne Jane Gholson Glasgow

G. was the eighth of her parents' ten children. Her father was director of the Tredegar Iron Works, chief armaments factory during the Civil War. His dour Scotch-Irish Calvinist background instilled in her qualities of strength G. was to sum up as a "vein of iron." This phrase and the staunch values it implied occur approvingly in over half her novels; yet she hated her father for his tyranny, his religious severity, his philandering. He was, she wrote, "more patriarchal than paternal." She adored her generous, long-suffering mother, a "perfect flower of the Tidewater" aristocracy. In her autobiography, *The Woman Within* (1954), G. described her own nature as deeply divided between this gentle mother and stern father.

G. acquired her learning at home. She was excused early from a formal education because of shyness and headaches at school. She lived most of her life in Richmond, although she traveled often to Europe, especially in her younger days, and lived in New York for years at a time.

G. held her work and literary reputation uppermost; these compensated for what she called "the long tragedy of my life." An especial burden was her deafness, which assailed her in adolescence and worsened. It isolated her, and plunged her into profound depressions. She consulted psychoanalysts and aurists. Eventually her hearing devices improved, but she never ceased to complain. Allusions in the novels to a "soundless tumult," a "rustling vacancy," apparently grow out of this affliction.

G.'s first two novels, *The Descendant* (1897) and *Phases of an Inferior Planet* (1898), together with *The Wheel of Life* (1906), wrestle with, among other things, the plight of the woman as artist. All are based in New York which, to G., meant intellectual Bohemia. The first two books show obvious signs of her deep reading of Darwin, Nietzsche, Henry George, Mill, Haeckel, Weismann, and other writers on heredity, milieu, class struggle, evolution, and survival. Gradually, the social concerns of these apprenticeship novels would be more skillfully integrated into her Virginia novels; and G.'s successes enabled her to drop the anxious woman artist theme.

With her Virginia novels, G. was breaking new ground. She wished to correct the sentimental picture of "Ole Virginia" perpetrated by romances of plantation life and the glorious defeat of the Civil War. The South suffered from what G. termed "evasive idealism." *The Battle-Ground* (1902) gently satirizes the prewar fable: honey-voiced belles, picturesque Negroes, a crusty old major and an enlightened governor disputing the virtues of slavery by a comfortable library fire. *The Deliverance* (1904) deals with tobacco farming and the moral struggles of a destroyed planter family in the post-Reconstruction period of 1878–90.

In writing about the New South, G. liked to show an underdog hero fighting his way to personal acceptance and public service. This pattern of action is found in several of G.'s novels of Virginia political life. *The Voice of the People* (1900), G.'s first Virginia novel, is one of the earliest fictional treatments of the southern poor white.

G. celebrates Virginia heroines in *Virginia* (1913), *Life and Gabriella* (1916), and *Barren Ground* (1925). One of her best works, *Virginia* traces the dawning self-knowledge—too late—and lifelong disillusionment of a southern woman bred conventionally and decorously to a romantic ideal of marriage.

Of *Barren Ground* and the novels that followed it, G. wrote that this was the work upon which "I like to imagine that I shall stand or fall as a novelist." The novel is among her best, and probably her most renowned. Seduced, pregnant, and abandoned, Dorinda Oakley leaves her Virginia farm home. Fortuitously she miscarries. Upon her return she adjusts her nature to the demands she establishes for her life: to remain aloof from love and all entanglements, to labor unremittingly to control the fertility of the worn and wasted land as it had controlled her parents' lives, and to prosper richly. At the last, as a strong, white-haired woman, Dorinda watches her erstwhile lover die. "For once in Southern fiction," wrote G., "the betrayed woman would become the victor instead of the victim."

Leaving the Virginia countryside, G. comes indoors with her Queensborough (i.e., Richmond) novels of manners: *The Romantic Comedians* (1926), *They Stooped to Folly* (1929), and the somberer *The Sheltered Life* (1932). *The Romantic Comedians* centers on the fatuous, aged, would-be lover, Judge Gamaliel Honeywell, whose "withered heart urgently craves to be green again." The word "happiness" recurs with ironic frequency. G's satiric vision is both classic and fresh in this work whose aphoristic dialogue is reminiscent of theater.

The comic possibilities of youth's encounters with age in a framework of sexual morality are also explored in *They Stooped to Folly*. G. introduces diverse women characters, focusing on the seduced and fallen women of three generations.

As in the other Queensborough novels, the themes of youth and age and the insufficiency of love are pervasive in *The Sheltered Life*, which observes the interaction of three generations of southerners before World War I. Courtly General Archbald reflects on the polite hypocrisies that warped lives in his youth. It is, however, the adherents of a newer morality, the new happiness seekers, who trample on those they love, but don't "mean anything."

Vein of Iron (1935) documents the lives of the Scotch-Irish "good people" of Ironside, a village of the Upper Valley of the James River in Virginia. The surrounding mountains loom as personal presences. G. takes her much-tried heroine Ada Fincastle from girlhood to middle age, from 1901 to 1933. The vision produced by the novel is one of nostalgia and of perpetual accommodation to necessity in the face of futility. In *Vein of Iron*, G. is best when extolling ancestral values, for she saw the future as a dying age.

Despite its being awarded a Pulitzer Prize, a belated consolation for the committee's having passed over *The Sheltered Life*, *In This Our Life* (1941) is a minor achievement. The portrayals of the elderly weary hero and his desperate daughters betray G.'s declining health and her difficulty in coming to grips with the modern world.

G.'s social perspectives and her thirst for realism made her a precursor of writers she failed to appreciate, notably a stylist like Faulkner. She was outspoken about newer writers, whom she characterized as amateurs and illiterates. As she grew older she found it difficult to cast aside the values she had once lightheartedly satirized. She saw the modern world as "distraught, chaotic, grotesque, . . . an age of cruelty without moral indignation, of catastrophe without courage." Her efforts to embrace the young within her artistic vision, even to deal with contemporary argot, turn out shrill and awry. Despite awards and honors during her lifetime, G.'s literary reputation suffered after her death.

G.'s best writing is in the comic spirit. There are fine humorous characterizations, many buried in the subplots of her novels. As an innovator, she rejected the South's codes and genteel fables to write about politics and industry rising up out of the Virginia soil. Race and stock are for her determinants of character in the battle for survival. Work, whether of the grower, the tycoon, or the artist, brings salvation. Manners are both valued and criticized. G. drew her chief inspirations from the land that bred the vein of iron and from the tremors of society. Past and present, the conflict of generations, the uneasy commerce between an older patriciate and the new working classes, mores and wars, ceremony and the fresh winds of change—these were the broad concerns of G.'s writing which she treated with the "blood and irony" she had prescribed for southern fiction.

WORKS: *The Descendant* (1897). *Phases of an Inferior Planet* (1898). *The Voice of the People* (1900). *The Battle-Ground* (1902). *The Freeman, and Other Poems* (1902). *The Deliverance* (1904). *The Wheel of Life* (1906). *The Ancient Law* (1908). *The Romance of a Plain Man* (1909). *The Miller of Old Church* (1911). *Virginia* (1913). *Life and Gabriella* (1916). *The Builders* (with H. W. Anderson, 1919). *One Man in His Time* (1922). *The Shadowy Third, and Other Stories* (1923). *Barren Ground* (1925). *The Romantic Comedians* (1926). *They Stooped to Folly* (1929). *The Old Dominion*

Edition of the Works of Ellen Glasgow (8 vols., 1929–1933). *The Sheltered Life* (1932). *Vein of Iron* (1935). *The Virginia Edition of the Works of Ellen Glasgow* (12 vols., 1938). *In This Our Life* (1941). *A Certain Measure: An Interpretation of Prose Fiction* (1943). *The Woman Within* (1954). *Letters of Ellen Glasgow* (Ed. B. Rouse, 1958). *The Collected Stories of Ellen Glasgow* (Ed. R. K. Meeker, 1963). *Beyond Defeat: An Epilogue to an Era* (Ed. L. Y. Gore, 1966).

BIBLIOGRAPHY: Auchincloss, L., *Pioneers and Caretakers* (1965). Ekman, B., *The End of a Legend: E. G.'s History of Southern Women* (1979). Godbold, E. S., Jr., *E. G. and the Woman Within* (1972). Holman, C. H., *Three Modes of Southern Fiction* (1966). Inge, M. T., ed., *E. G.: Centennial Essays* (1976). Jessup, J. L., *The Faith of Our Feminists: A Study in the Novels of Edith Wharton, E. G., Willa Cather* (1950). Kelly, W. W., *E. G.: A Bibliography* (1964). Kraft, S., *No Castles on Main Street: American Authors and Their Homes* (1979). McDowell, F. P. W., *E. G. and the Ironic Art of Fiction* (1960). Parent, M., *E. G.: Romancière* (1962). Raper, J. R., *Without Shelter: The Early Career of E. G.* (1971). Richards, M. K., *E. G.'s Development As a Novelist* (1971). Rouse, B., *E. G.* (1962). Santas, J. F., *E. G.'s American Dream* (1965). Thiébaux, M., *Ellen Glasgow* (1982).

For articles in reference works, see: *CB* (Jan. 1946). *DAB*, Suppl. 3. *LSL. NAW* (article by M. R. Kaufman). *NCAB*, C. *20thCA. 20thCAS.*

Other references: *Ellen Glasgow Newsletter* (Ashland, Virginia).

MARCELLE THIÉBAUX

Susan Glaspell

B. 1 July 1876, Davenport, Iowa; d. 27 July 1948, Provincetown, Massachusetts
D. of Elmer S. and Alice Keating Glaspell; m. George Cram Cook, 1913;
m. Norman Matson, 1925

G. began her career writing numerous short stories—for popular magazines—in line with the sentimental and escapist mode popular at the time, and two conventional romantic novels. When she met and married her first husband, her life-style and the direction of her work changed radically. Her novel *Fidelity* (1915) is thematically connected to this love affair. With Eugene O'Neill, she and Cook became the founders of and prime contributors to the Provincetown Players, an experimental group begun on Cape Cod in 1915 to provide a place where native drama could develop freely outside the fetters of commercialism. The company, which moved to New York's Greenwich Village (as the Playwrights Theatre) in the fall of 1916, proved to be one of the most important and seminal forces in the history of American theater.

G.'s first one-act play, written with Cook, was part of the Province-town Players' initial season. Her second one-act play, *Trifles*, was pro-duced in 1916 during the second summer season. (G.'s short-story adap-tation of it, "A Jury of Her Peers," appeared in *Best American Short Stories* of 1916). On a bleak Iowa farm, a dour farmer, John Wright, has been found dead in his bed, his own rope around his neck. His wife, Minnie, who never appears onstage, is in custody pending investigation of the murder. The tacit agreement of two women onstage to conceal the telltale evidence of guilt implies that Wright was a man who deserved to die as he did, and their sympathy (with that of the audience) goes to the abused wife. After fifty years, this piece is still deservedly cited as an example of expert craftsmanship.

For the next two seasons G. continued to write, act in, and direct plays. Her first full-length play, *Bernice* (1920), in which again the heroine never appears onstage, was produced in 1919.

G. returned in *The Inheritors* (1921) to a favorite theme: the de-sirability of preserving the best values of pioneer character. The only character who represents the true spirit of her forefathers (the found-ers of a liberal college) and of America itself is the granddaughter Madeline Morton, who goes to jail for the rights of Hindu students protesting British domination of India.

In *The Verge* (1921), G. deals with a "new woman" again. However, Claire Archer is very different from Madeline. Claire is so intent on at-taining her own freedom—an "otherness," she calls it—that she is driven over the edge of sanity when she rejects the past and present (ancestors, husband, and daughter) in hopes of a new future.

G. dramatizes the subject of the artist's life and connection to society in her final two plays, *The Comic Artist* (1928) and *Alison's House* (1930). The latter, dealing with the posthumous disposition of the po-etry of a woman much like Emily Dickinson, was produced at the Civic Repertory Theatre, with Eva LeGallienne playing the role of the niece who favors publication. It won the Pulitzer Prize.

G. had only minor connections with the theater after 1931. She had returned to the novel in 1928 with *Brook Evans*. In *Ambrose Holt and Family* (1931), G. clearly connects the "free woman" of the 20th c. with the best qualities of the pioneer, as in her play *The Inheritors*. This novel and the one that followed, *The Morning Is Near Us* (1939), have phil-osophical depth, but little relevance to the time of the Great Depres-sion. It was not until *Norma Ashe* (1942) and then *Judd Rankin's*

Daughter (1945) that G. took cognizance of failures inherent in mid-western isolationist attitudes, appropriate though they may have been for the original pioneers.

Because her work in the theater was of necessity much more experimental than her work in other genres, G.'s main significance stems from her Provincetown connection, not only as a playwright, but, more importantly, as an innovator instrumental in changing the course of American drama forever. The most striking hallmark of her best writing is her consistent emphasis on the need for human beings to fulfill their highest potential by utilizing what is desirable from the past and applying it with faith and courage to the future. Because she developed a broad humanistic viewpoint, she never became a typical midwestern regionalist in the narrow sense; she eschewed always the 20th-c. provincialism, super-patriotism, and fatuousness that evolved as Main Street, USA.

WORKS: *Glory of the Conquered* (1909). *The Visioning* (1911). *Fidelity* (1915). *Bernice* (with seven one-act plays, 1920). *The Inheritors* (1921). *The Verge* (1921). *The Road to the Temple* (1927). *Brook Evans* (1928). *The Comic Artist* (with N. Matson, 1928). *Fugitive's Return* (1929). *Alison's House* (1930). *Ambrose Holt and Family* (1931). *The Morning Is Near Us* (1939). *Cherished and Shared of Old* (1940). *Norma Ashe* (1942). *Judd Rankin's Daughter* (1945).

BIBLIOGRAPHY: Gelb, A., and B. Gelb, *O'Neill* (1960). Goldberg, I., *Drama of Transition* (1922). Hapgood, H., *A Victorian in a Modern World* (1939). Lewisohn, L., *Expression in America* (1932). Quinn, A. H., *History of American Drama from the Civil War to the Present Day* (1927). Vorse, M. H., *Time and the Town* (1942). Waterman, A. E., *S. G.* (1966).

For articles in reference works, see: *DAB*, Suppl. 4. *NAW* (article by A. E. Waterman). *NCAB*, 15. *20thCA*. *20thCAS*.

Other references: *Arts and Decoration* (June 1931). *Bookman* (Feb. 1918). *Commonweal* (20 May 1931). *Drama* (June 1931). *Independent Woman* (Jan. 1946). *Nation* (3 Nov. 1920; 6 April 1921; 4 April 1923). *NewR* (17 Jan. 1923). *NYT* (12 April 1931; 10 May 1931). *Palimpsest* (Dec. 1930). *Review of Reviews* (June 1909). *SatR* (30 July 1938). *WLB* (Dec. 1928). *Women's Journal* (Aug. 1928; June 1931).

EDYTHE M. McGOVERN

Caroline Gordon

B. 6 Oct. 1895, Merry Mount Farm, Kentucky; d. 11 April 1981, Chiapas,
  Mexico
Writes under: Caroline Gordon, Caroline Tate
D. of James Morris and Nancy Meriwether Gordon; m. Allen Tate, 1924

Born on her mother's ancestral farm in the Kentucky tobacco region near Tennessee, the setting for much of her fiction, G. was tutored by her father until she was ten. She then attended his all-boys classical school. In 1916, she received a B.A. from Bethany College in West Virginia. After teaching high school until 1920, she became a journalist for the *Chattanooga News*. While there she met many of the Agrarians, including Allen Tate.

G. readily identified with the Agrarians' traditional conservative values, favoring a stable, hierarchical society based on Christianity over an urban, technological society. G. became deeply involved in Tate's literary world; both spent much of the late 1920s in Europe on Guggenheim Fellowships. The Tates raised their daughter Nancy at Benfolly Farm, Tennessee, entertaining many artistic visitors.

Although G. and Tate were divorced in 1959, in 1960 they coedited a second edition of their successful and influential *The House of Fiction: An Anthology of the Short Story* (1950, 1960). Both this and G.'s *How to Read a Novel* (1957) adapt many New Critical poetic principles to fiction.

As Ford Madox Ford's literary secretary, G. finished her first novel, *Penhally* (1931), acclaimed by Ford as "the best novel that has been produced in modern America." It chronicles one hundred years of antebellum southern culture by tracing the decline of the Penhally estate and the Llewellyn family. The ancient virtues violently conflict with the inevitability of change.

In *Aleck Maury, Sportsman* (1934), her most popular novel, an old classics teacher, modeled on G.'s father, spends every spare moment hunting and fishing. Maury's ritualistic, almost sacramental devotion to sport allows him a dignity rarely possible in the chaos of the wasteland world which has replaced the Old South. Only the quest for love—apparent in many of G.'s women characters, like Maury's wife Molly—provides a similar dignity.

G.'s fiction of the late 1930s and the 1940s continued to develop her ancestral, regional material; it also reflected a growing emphasis on sophisticated knowledge in contrast to primitive innocence, while religion became a means of confronting the abyss, a terrifying image permeating her fiction.

The literary milieu at Benfolly Farm appears in several works, particularly *The Strange Children* (1951), G.'s first novel after her conversion to Catholicism in 1947. It traces the search for grace in a fallen world. The central intelligence of nine-year-old Lucy Lewis records the despair and materialism of the skeptical intellectual world and the need for an order only religious belief can provide.

The salvation that is possible in *The Strange Children* becomes real in *The Malefactors* (1956). Tom Claibourne, a nonproducing poet, must reevaluate the direction of his life after he leaves his wife Vera for the ambitious and intellectual poet, Cynthia Vail. Through the influence of Catherine Pollard, a symbol of Christian charity, Claibourne discovers that he is bound nowhere unless he can return to his wife. While in her earlier work the classical Greek world subtly patterned G.'s vision, in *The Malefactors* it is the archetypal world of Jungian psychology that prepares for Claibourne's religious conversion, reversing the pattern of action in G.'s fiction from death and destruction to grace.

G.'s worth as a novelist has been too often ignored by critics. She is more frequently identified as coeditor of *The House of Fiction* and as Allen Tate's former wife than as a creative artist in her own right. In addition, because her work is usually set in the South and because of her close association with the Agrarians, critics have tended to dismiss her too easily as a regionalist. Her talent for dealing with religious themes and with the themes of male/female relationships and the possibility of creativity in a wasteland world has been virtually overlooked by critics who miss the broader implications of the South in her fiction. Though G. is presently enjoying a renewal of interest, her novels, particularly *The Strange Children* and *The Malefactors*, have not received the attention they deserve. She is as fine a fiction writer as Robert Penn Warren and Allen Tate and should share equally in the acclaim so often accorded the Agrarians and New Critics as the generators of the Southern Renascence.

WORKS: *Penhally* (1931). *Aleck Maury, Sportsman* (1934). *None Shall Look Back* (1937). *The Garden of Adonis* (1937). *Green Centuries* (1941). *The Women on the Porch* (1944). *The Forest of the South* (1945). *The House of Fiction: An Anthology of the Short Story* (edited by Gordon, with A. Tate,

1950; rev. ed., 1960). *The Strange Children* (1951). *The Malefactors* (1956). *A Good Soldier: A Key to the Novels of Ford Madox Ford* (1957). *How to Read a Novel* (1957). *Old Red, and Other Stories* (1963). *The Glory of Hera* (1972). *The Collected Stories* (1981).

BIBLIOGRAPHY: Golden, R. E., and M. C. Sullivan, *Flannery O'Connor and Caroline Gordon: A Reference Guide* (1977). Landess, T. H., *The Short Fiction of Caroline Gordon: A Critical Symposium* (1972). McDowells, F. P., *Caroline Gordon* (Univ. of Minnesota Pamphlet, 1966). Stuckey, W. J., *Caroline Gordon* (1972).

For articles in reference works, see: *20thCA. 20thCAS.*

Other references: *Crit* (Winter 1956). *Renascence* (Fall 1963). *SR* (Summer 1946; Autumn 1949; Spring 1971).

SUZANNE ALLEN

Shirley Graham

B. 11 Nov. 1907, Evansville, Indiana; d. 27 March 1977, Peking, China
Wrote under: Shirley Graham DuBois, Shirley Graham
D. of David A. and Lizzie Etta Bell Graham; m. Shadrach T. McCanns, 1921;
m. William Edward Burghardt DuBois, 1951

G., a lifelong advocate of human rights, was born on the farm of her great-grandfather, a freed slave and blacksmith who used his home as an Underground Railroad station for runaway slaves. G. and her four brothers grew up in a variety of cities—New Orleans, Colorado Springs, and Spokane—in which their father, an African Episcopal minister, received pastoral assignments. G. married a year after completing high school, but within three years she became a widow with two sons to support.

G. studied music theory and composition at the Sorbonne. While there, she also learned about African music from West African students studying in France. In 1931, G. matriculated at Oberlin College, where she received both the B.A. and M.A. degrees. Her years there marked the beginning of her career as a dramatist and composer. G.'s one-act play, *Coal Dust*, and her three-act comedy, *Elijah's Ravens*, were performed during this period; both had been written in 1930. A music-drama, *Tom-Tom* (1932), was based upon G.'s knowledge of African rhythms; it was later revised into an opera for which G. wrote the libretto and music.

Although she was a successful dramatist, G.'s major literary contribution was made in the field of biography. Her decision to research and record the lives of significant black people was influenced indirectly by her cultural and political activities with the NAACP (National Association for the Advancement of Colored People), which appointed her a national field secretary in 1942, and directly by the death of her son Robert, who, because of his race, was mistreated in an army camp and denied proper hospital care.

G.'s biographies combine history and fiction in celebrating black life during a period of general neglect. They are primarily popular books that recognize the contributions made by blacks to American culture and preserve the history of black achievement for the world. Because G.'s biographies delineate heroic qualities for emulation and seem especially suited for young adults, they have become categorized as "juvenile" literature and have not received the critical attention they deserve.

G. wrote eleven biographies. Among the most successful is *Paul Robeson, Citizen of the World* (1946), which traces the life of the famous singer from his boyhood through his forty-sixth birthday. G. uses the musical patterns of a classical concerto and a modern blues to orchestrate the details of Robeson's life.

In *There Was Once a Slave: The Historic Story of Frederick Douglass* (1947), G. relies on an association between the North Star and liberty as the controlling metaphor for her poignant narrative. *Your Most Humble Servant* (1949), the first book-length treatment of Benjamin Banneker, a late 18th-c. astronomer, mathematician, and surveyor, is G.'s major work on a historical figure.

G. married the famous Harvard-trained social scientist, Dr. W. E. B. DuBois, four days after his eighty-third birthday and on the eve of his indictment as an "agent of a foreign principle." Their marriage culminated a thirty-year friendship during which G. was guided by DuBois's emphasis on "Beauty, Accomplishment, and Dignity" as the criteria of Negro art. Throughout the years of her marriage, G. devoted much of her attention to political work against oppression and to cultural activities for peace. She was also her husband's companion-helpmate on his final project, a massive *Encyclopedia Africana*, yet she did not live in his shadow; she helped to found *Freedomways*, a magazine on the African-American freedom movement, and was selected its first editor. Her last three books, *Gamal Abdel Nasser, Son of the Nile* (1972), *Zulu Heart* (1974), and *Julius K. Nyerere: Teacher of Africa* (1975), reflect G.'s international perspective after a decade of living on the African continent.

His Day Is Marching On: A Memoir of W. E. B. DuBois (1971) is essentially G.'s own biography. In it, she emerges as the exemplar of the values and virtues defining the heroic men and women of her biographies. The book is notable for its quiet celebration of love, loyalty, conviction, and courage. Sensitive and vivid in language, G.'s memoir documents a personal experience and outlines a cultural history.

WORKS: *Coal Dust* (1930). *Elijah's Ravens* (1930). *Tom-Tom* (1932). *Little Black Sambo* (1937). *The Swing Mikado* (1938). *I Gotta Home* (1939). *It's Morning* (1940). *Dust to Earth* (1941). *Track Thirteen* (1942). *Dr. George Washington Carver, Scientist* (with G. D. Lipscomb, 1944). *Paul Robeson, Citizen of the World* (1946). *There Was Once a Slave: The Heroic Story of Frederick Douglass* (1947). *The Story of Phillis Wheatley* (1949). *Your Most Humble Servant* (1949). *Jean Baptiste Pointe de Sable, Founder of Chicago* (1953). *The Story of Pocahontas* (1953). *Booker T. Washington: Educator of Hand, Head, and Heart* (1955). *His Day Is Marching On: A Memoir of W. E. B. DuBois* (1971). *Gamal Abdel Nasser, Son of the Nile: A Biography* (1972). *Zulu Heart: A Novel* (1974). *Julius K. Nyerere: Teacher of Africa* (1975).

BIBLIOGRAPHY: Bedini, S. A., *The Life of Benjamin Banneker* (1972). Miller, E., ed., *The Negro in America* (1970).

For articles in reference works, see: *Afro-American Encyclopedia*, Ed. J. T. Haley (1974). *Black American Writers: Bibliographical Essays*, Ed. M. T. Inge (1977). *Black Playwrights, 1823–1977: An Annotated Bibliography of Plays*, Eds. J. V. Hatch and O. Abdullah (1977). *CB* (Oct. 1946). *Negro Almanac*, Ed. H. A. Ploski (1976).

Other references: *Crisis* (Aug. 1932). *NYT* (5 June 1973; 5 April 1977).

THADIOUS M. DAVIS

Shirley Ann Grau

B. 8 July 1929, New Orleans, Louisiana
D. of Adolph Eugene and Katherine Onions Grau; m. James Kern
Feibleman, 1955

Daughter of a dentist, G. describes her family as "ordinary middle class. White. Protestant." However, she also admits that the family members were well enough set financially that they could choose not to work. Her mother was in her middle forties when G. was born, yet she had another daughter even later. G. attended the Booth Academy in Montgomery, Alabama, until she transferred to the Ursuline Academy in New Orleans as a senior. She attended Sophie Newcomb, the "girl's wing" of the all-male Tulane University, where she took many of her classes and met her future husband, a philosophy professor twenty-six years her senior.

They were married in New York City, where G. had moved to pursue her writing career, and live in New Orleans with their four children.

G.'s first collection of short stories, *The Black Prince* (1955), won immediate acclaim and was compared in its importance to J. D. Salinger's *Nine Stories* and to Eudora Welty's *A Curtain of Green*. These stories reveal concerns and characters that would dominate her later fiction. The first of these are her primitives, living—like young Joshua in the story of that name—in tune with nature, sharing its creative violence and heroically, if hopelessly, defying its destructive forces. They also introduce G.'s concern with city-bred southerners locked away from nature and with women trapped between stereotypes of the past and the confusion of the present.

These primitives burst forth in her first novel, *The Hard Blue Sky* (1958), a flawed work but with moments of great power. The Louisiana island fishermen of the novel take on mythic proportions, similar to the Aran Islanders in Synge's plays, owing to G.'s simple and realistic dialogue, her vivid recreation of their daily struggles with nature, and her concentration on their awareness rather than on their innocence.

The modern woman steps forth again in G.'s next novel. Trapped in *The House on Coliseum Street* (1961) is Joan Caillet, who floats into an abortion only to be tossed and torn by its psychological aftermath. The emptiness within reflects the emptiness outside, and Joan's growing awareness of this emptiness, this lack of values within the surviving shell of southern society—perhaps of American society as a whole—leads her to destructive violence. G. seems to argue that unless individuals live in tune with nature, as do her primitives, their violence will destroy rather than recreate the world.

A similar violence is produced by Abigail Tolliver's discovery of hypocrisy in *The Keepers of the House* (1964). This Pulitzer Prize-winning novel combines G.'s primitives with her southern lady and blacks with whites, as she traces the heritage of a family that rises above the prejudices of the stereotypes to assert the integrity of the individual. Abigail has been taught the role of the southern lady, but her grandfather, William Howland, has given her an even more important legacy. The evidence of his love for his black housekeeper Margaret, a hardy primitive reminiscent of the folk-heroine Alberta in "The Black Prince," destroys Abigail's illusions of safety, thus exposing her to the violence of life itself. But William Howland has also provided in his actions an example of humanity which keeps Abigail from being destroyed by her own rebellious violence, which enables her to be born again into a new awareness of life.

G.'s most recent novels, *The Condor Passes* (1971) and *Evidence of Love* (1977), as well as many of the stories from her most recent collection, *The Wind Shifting West* (1973), continue her interest in family and social heritage, but they concentrate more than ever on character studies. Each novel opens with an old man and ends with his death, in between examining the people and experiences of his life. Each also explores the interactions of love and money. The economic security of the central characters allows G. to touch only lightly on the social context except in flashbacks; the characters struggle instead with the complexity of human relationships and of personal identity.

G. displays throughout each novel her consummate skill at manipulating point of view, her unique ability to empathize with each character. Above all, she is a superb storyteller, creating her Louisiana world in rich detail and letting her characters live, speak, and argue for themselves. Although she has been criticized for her traditional style, her symbolic realism, with its roots in the Louisiana bayous of Kate Chopin, still rises far above imitation. Her originality is evident in her consistent philosophy of nature and in her uniquely female imagery, from the caverns of emptiness which haunt Joan in *The House on Coliseum Street* to the vivid description of his own birth offered by Edward Milton Henley as the first scene of *Evidence of Love*.

WORKS: *The Black Prince, and Other Stories* (1955). *The Hard Blue Sky* (1958). *The House on Coliseum Street* (1961). *The Keepers of the House* (1964). *The Condor Passes* (1971). *The Wind Shifting West* (1973). *Evidence of Love* (1977).

BIBLIOGRAPHY: Gossett, L. Y., *Violence in Recent Southern Fiction* (1965). For articles in reference works, see: *CA*, 1–4 (1967). *CB* (1959).
   Other references: *Crit.* (6, 1963; 17, 1975). *Insula: Revista Bibliografica de Ciencias y Letras (Madrid)* (1966). *NewR* (18 April 1964; 24 Nov. 1973). *NYRB* (2 Dec. 1971). *NYTBR* (22 March 1964). *SatR* (21 March 1964). *SR* 70 (1962).

THELMA J. SHINN

Angelina Emily Grimké

B. *20 Feb. 1805, Charleston, South Carolina; d. 26 Oct. 1879, Hyde Park,*
  Massachusetts
Wrote under: *A. E. Grimké, Angelina Grimké, Angelina Grimké Weld*
D. *of John Faucheraud and Mary Smith Grimké; m. Theodore Dwight*
  Weld, 1838

An abolitionist and women's rights pioneer, G. launched her meteoric
career in the abolitionist movement in a letter to William Lloyd Garrison
published in *The Liberator* (1835).

G.'s first pamphlet was *Appeal to Christian Women of the Southern
States* (1836). In the *Appeal* she attacked the traditional religious justi-
fications of slavery and focused instead on the God-given equality of
the slave as human being. The most powerful and original part of the
Appeal was her call to southern women to take action against slavery.
Though women lacked political power, they could free slaves who
were their own property, ameliorate the conditions for other slaves, and
petition legislatures for emancipation. Such actions might lead to fines
or imprisonment; nevertheless, she called women to civil disobedience.
She contended: "If a law commands me to sin, I will break it; if it calls
me to suffer, I will let it take its course unresistingly." G.'s *Appeal* was
the only abolitionist message by a southern woman addressed specifically
to southern women. As such it aroused violent opposition in the South.

G.'s second pamphlet, *An Appeal to the Women of the Nominally Free
States* (1837), stressed women's particular responsibility to their fellow
women in bondage. Female slaves are "our countrywomen . . . our sisters."

Letters to Catharine E. Beecher (1838) came in response to Beecher's
*Essay on Slavery and Abolitionism with Reference to the Duty of Ameri-
can Females* (1837). Beecher had attacked G. both for advocating abolition and for urging women's involvement therein. In the *Letters*, first
published serially in *The Liberator* and *The Emancipator* in 1837, G.
concentrated primarily on a detailed defense of the efficacy of immediate
abolition, but in two letters that deal specifically with the concept of
women's limited sphere, G. developed a strong feminist argument based
on a doctrine of human rights. According to G., "human beings have
rights because they are moral beings." As moral beings, women no less
than men must act publicly on moral issues. As human beings, women

should participate in making all laws concerning their own condition. She saw a new cause emerging out of the abolitionist controversy, a broad drive to reclaim the usurped rights of all disadvantaged persons, including women and slaves.

When she married Theodore Weld, her career as a writer came to an end. She collaborated with him and her sister, Sarah, in compiling *American Slavery As It Is: Testimony of a Thousand Witnesses* (1839). Some speeches and a letter on women's rights were later published. But it is on the three works written between 1836 and 1838 that her reputation rests.

As a writer, G. has a forceful and clean-cut style. Her arguments are lucid and cogent, and she writes with ease and directness. She utilizes 18th-c. reformist ideas to support her arguments, drawing heavily on environmentalist theories to explain the perversion of original equality. She also draws on 18th-c. republican ideology with its stress on the imperative necessity for moral virtue among citizens if the republic is to survive. Above all, however, as a 19th-c. evangelical reformer, she relies on religious arguments. The Bible offered the standard of judgment by which to determine the evils of slavery. It offered the religious-historical role models for women undertaking responsible moral action against slavery. In her religious convictions, G. found the basis for the formulation of the doctrine of human rights. In so doing, she finally fused the two causes with which her private life and her public career became identified, abolition and women's rights.

WORKS: Slavery and the Boston Riot: A Letter to Wm. L. Garrison (1835). Appeal to Christian Women of the Southern States (1836). An Appeal to the Women of the Nominally Free States; Issued by an Anti-Slavery Convention of American Women & Held by Adjournment from the 9th to the 12th of May, 1837 (1837). Letters to Catharine E. Beecher, in Reply to an Essay on Slavery and Abolitionism, Addressed to A. E. Grimké (1838). American Slavery As It Is: Testimony of a Thousand Witnesses (edited by Grimké, with T. Weld and S. M. Grimké, 1839). Letter from Angelina Grimké Weld to the Woman's Rights Convention, Held at Syracuse, September, 1852 (1852).

BIBLIOGRAPHY: Barnes, G. H., and D. L. Dumond, eds., *Letters of Theodore Dwight Weld, Angelina Emily Grimké, and Sarah Grimké,: 1822–1844* (2 vols., 1934). Birney, C., *The Grimké Sisters: Sarah and Angelina Grimké: The First Women Advocates of Abolition and Women's Rights* (1885). Lerner, G., *The Grimké Sisters from South Carolina: Rebels against Slavery* (1967). Lumpkin, K. Du P., *The Emancipation of Angelina Grimké* (1974). Weld, T. D., *In Memory: Angelina Grimké Weld* (1880).

For articles in reference works, see: *HWS*, I. *NAW* (article on Sarah Grimké, by B. L. Fladeland). *NCAB*, 2.

INZER BYERS

Sarah Moore Grimké

B. 26 Nov. 1792, Charleston, South Carolina; d. 23 Dec. 1873, Hyde Park, Massachusetts
D. of John Faucheraud and Mary Smith Grimké

G. made her impact upon American history and literature as an abolitionist and advocate of women's rights. Her first publication was a pamphlet, *An Epistle to the Clergy of the Southern States* (1836). In it, G. stresses the inherent conflict between slavery and Christianity, basing her argument against slavery on the premise that God had created all men equal. Referring to state laws and practices, she effectively demonstrates how the law kept ministers from meeting religious obligations to slaves, and she calls on the southern clergy to act as moral leaders against slavery.

G.'s second publication came out of an antislavery lecture tour of New England in 1837 and 1838. Because G. and her sister Angelina lectured publicly on abolition to both men and women, they were sharply criticized, especially by the Congregationalist Ministerial Association of Massachusetts. G. responded with fifteen letters, first published serially in 1837 in the New England *Spectator* and later collected as a book.

In the *Letters on the Equality of the Sexes* (1838), G. rejects indignantly the contention that women should not speak publicly on moral issues, asserting that as morally responsible individuals, they cannot do otherwise. She further argues that women should themselves become ministers. She went on to develop a full-fledged argument for women's equality. Again, she started with the religious premise. God had created man and woman with equal moral rights and duties. That original equality and responsibility remained unaltered by the Fall. Nor did Christ distinguish between male and female virtues. The biblical message is clear: "Whatever is right for man to do, is right for woman."

After the *Letters*, G. largely withdrew from writing. She collaborated with her sister and brother-in-law in compiling *American Slavery As It Is: Testimony of a Thousand Witnesses* (1839); she wrote occasionally for newspapers and did a translation of Alphonse de Lamartine's *Joan of Arc* (1867).

In explaining women's historical inequality, G. particularly stressed the environmentalist argument. She contrasted the role women in general were allowed to play with the role women in authority showed themselves capable of fulfilling. Especially she denounced the deliberate efforts to "debase and enslave" women's intellect. "All I ask of our brethren is that they take their feet from off our necks and permit us to stand upright." Only then can the validity of male assumptions about women's nature and abilities be tested.

Of the two publications of 1836–38, the *Epistle to the Clergy of the Southern States* is essentially a minor work. It added little to the antislavery argument, and the often turgid style of writing further limited its appeal. The *Letters on the Equality of the Sexes*, on the other hand, is a significant pioneering work written with power and originality. In it her style is forthright and lucid, the tone grave and dispassionate. Her arguments are lit with occasional flashes of ironic humor and anger.

WORKS: *An Epistle to the Clergy of the Southern States* (1836). *Letters on the Equality of the Sexes and the Condition of Woman; Addressed to Mary Parker, President of the Boston Female Anti-Slavery Society* (1838). *American Slavery As It Is: Testimony of a Thousand Witnesses* (edited by Grimké, with T. Weld and A. E. Grimké, 1839). *Joan of Arc: A Biography* by A. de Lamartine (translated by Grimké, 1867).

BIBLIOGRAPHY: See bibliography for Angelina Emily Grimké.

INZER BYERS

Louise Imogen Guiney

B. 7 Jan. 1861, Boston, Massachusetts; d. 2 Nov. 1920, Chipping Camden, England
Wrote under: Louise Imogen Guiney, Roger Holden, P.O.L.
D. of Robert Patrick and Janet Margaret Doyle Guiney

An Irish Roman Catholic and daughter of a Civil War general, G. was something of a literary novelty in late 19th-c. Boston, yet she was warmly received into the by then well-established literary circle of Annie Adams Fields and Sarah Orne Jewett. Fields eventually bequeathed a large portion of her estate to G.

Her health was never excellent. She had a hearing impairment which grew steadily more severe. She collapsed twice from overwork, once in 1896 and again in 1897. These breakdowns were partially precipitated by the hostile reception she received after her appointment as postmistress of Auburndale, Massachusetts, in 1894. A combination of anti-Irish, anti-Catholic, and antifemale sentiment led local citizens to organize a boycott to force her resignation. Later she was employed in the Catalogue Room of the Boston Public Library. G. emigrated to England in 1901 and devoted her later years to scholarly research at Oxford. At the same time, she moved toward a more reclusive life-style, as her religious dedication deepened. Her closest friends included Fred Holland Day, with whom she uncovered some important Keats material, Grace Denslow, and Alice Brown, with whom she traveled abroad. Brown dedicated her *The Road to Castaly* (1896) to G. and wrote her biography. They also collaborated on a book on Robert Louis Stevenson (1896).

G. published her first lyrics under pseudonyms ("P.O.L." and "Roger Holden") in 1880. Her first collection of poems, *Songs at the Start*, appeared in 1884; and her first collection of essays, *Goose-Quill Papers*, in 1885.

She considered *A Roadside Harp* (1893) her best poetical effort, while critics estimate *Patrins: A Collection of Essays* (1897) to include her most important critical work. Especially significant are the essays "On the Rapid versus the Harmless Scholar" and "Wilfull Sadness in Literature," in which she rejects Arnoldian "disinterestedness" as a proper critical attitude. Her collected lyrics, *Happy Endings*, were published in 1909.

G. was also a dedicated biographer and scholar. *Robert Emmet* (1904) is about an Irish nationalist, and *Blessed Edmund Campion* (1908) is about an English Jesuit martyr. She also put forth several important critical editions of relatively minor figures, such as *Katherine Philips, "The Matchless Orinda"* (1904). One volume of her magnum opus of scholarship, an anthology of Catholic poets from Thomas More to Alexander Pope, entitled *Recusant Poets*, was published posthumously in 1938.

G. favored the cavalier rather than the puritan spirit; her letters suggest a lively, engaged personality. In her works, she was attracted to flamboyant gypsy-like women such as Carmen. In 1896, she wrote a critical preface to Merimée's short story. "Martha Hilton," a vivacious Cinderella figure drawn from Portsmouth, New Hampshire, history, was G.'s contribution to *Three Heroines of New England Romance* (1894), which also included sketches by Harriett Prescott Spofford and Alice Brown.

Some consider that G.'s unpublished letters contain her finest writing. Two volumes of her letters were published in 1926. Yet even among her published works the consensus is that her religious lyrics are among the finest American contributions to the genre, and that her criticism contains much that is still of value.

WORKS: *Songs at the Start* (1884). *Goose-Quill Papers* (1885). *Brownies and Bogles* (1887). *Monsieur Henri: A Footnote to French History* (1892). *A Roadside Harp* (1893). *A Little English Gallery* (1894). *Lovers' Saint Ruth's, and Three Other Tales* (1895). *Robert Louis Stevenson* (with A. Brown, 1896). *Three Heroines of New England Romance* (with A. Brown and H. P. Spofford, 1894). *Patrins: A Collection of Essays* (1897). *England and Yesterday* (1898). *The Martyr's Idyl, and Shorter Poems* (1899). *Hurrell Fronde* (1904). *Katherine Philips, "The Matchless Orinda"* (edited by Guiney, 1904). *Robert Emmet* (1904). *Blessed Edmund Campion* (1908). *Happy Endings* (1909; rev. ed., 1927). *Letters* (2 vols., 1926). *Recusant Poets* (1938).

Many of Louise Imogen Guiney's unpublished letters are at the Dinand Library at Holy Cross College, Worcester, Massachusetts, and at the Library of Congress.

BIBLIOGRAPHY: Adorita, Sister M., *Soul Ordained to Fail: Louise Imogen Guiney, 1861–1920* (1962). Brown, A., *Louise Imogen Guiney* (1921). Fairbanks, H. G., *Louise Imogen Guiney: Laureate of the Lost* (1973). Guiney, G. C., *Letters of Louise Imogen Guiney* (1926). Tenison, E. M., *Louise Imogen Guiney: Her Life and Works* (1923).

For articles in reference works, see: *AW. DAB*, IV, 2. *NAW* (article by S. M. Parrish). *NCAB*, 9. *2othCA. 2othCAS*.

JOSEPHINE DONOVAN

Emily Hahn

B. *14 Jan. 1905, St. Louis, Missouri*
D. *of Isaac Newton and Hannah Hahn; m. Charles R. Boxer, 1945*

As a child, H. developed an adventurous spirit and an independent mind. Scorning custom and convention, she became the first woman to enroll in, and earn a degree from, the University of Wisconsin's College of Engineering. She also studied mineralogy at Columbia University, New

York City, and anthropology at Oxford, England. Later, many Americans would be scandalized when H. openly introduced her lovers to her readers.

Her first book, *Seductio ad Absurdum: The Principles and Practices of Seduction; a Beginner's Handbook* (1928), had a mixed reception. Some critics did not find her rules and regulations very interesting or very subtle and others were astonished by the gossipy episodes, but most readers found the book delightfully entertaining. Having begun her writing career, H. took on a wide variety of projects, including documentary reports, histories, novels, biographies, children's books, a guide book, a cookbook, and several autobiographical works.

In 1930, H. began a two-year stay, the first of several, in Africa. She lived with a tribe of Pygmies in the Ituri Forest of the Belgian Congo, where she worked with a doctor at a medical mission. *Congo Solo* (1933) was based on her diary. Although her vocabulary and expression often seem too rough, her informal and amusing style has proved appealing to many readers.

In 1935, H. set off on a world tour. She was to remain in China for nine years, settling in Hong Kong and beginning a career as *The New Yorker*'s China Coast correspondent. Her experiences amidst war and revolution had dramatic effects on her literary career, as well as on her personal life.

H.'s support of Chiang Kai-shek is unmistakable in *China to Me* (1944), a "partial autobiography" in which she recounts the dramatic political events as well as the trivial daily incidents that filled her days in Shanghai, Hong Kong, and Chungking. Although she undoubtedly tried to be objective in the biography *Chiang Kai-shek* (1955), her admiration for her subject resulted in a very defensive account of the corruption in his government and his lack of inspirational leadership.

H. continues to write on diverse topics. *Animal Gardens* (1967) is a history of zoos from the pre-Christian era in China and Egypt to the construction of the Milwaukee Zoo. *Breath of God* (1971) examines world folklore. *Once Upon a Pedestal* (1974) is an account of prominent women in art and literature from colonial times to the present. In *Lorenzo: D. H. Lawrence and the Women Who Loved Him* (1975), she depicts the writer as a neurotic, self-centered genius, to whom a great number of women were eager to dedicate themselves. Like so many of H.'s books, it is intriguing, gossipy, readable, and entertaining.

WORKS: *Seductio ad Absurdum: The Principles and Practices of Seduction;*

a Beginner's Handbook (1928). *Beginners' Luck* (1931). *Congo Solo: Misadventures Two Degrees North* (1933). *With Naked Foot* (1934). *Affair* (1935). *The Soong Sisters* (1941). *Mr. Pan* (1942). *China to Me: A Partial Autobiography* (1944). *Hong Kong Holiday* (1946). *Picture Story of China* (1946). *Raffles of Singapore: A Biography* (1946). *Miss Jill* (1947). *England to Me* (1949). *Purple Passage: A Novel about a Lady Both Famous and Fantastic* (1950). *A Degree of Prudery* (1950). *Francie* (1951). *Love Conquers Nothing: A Glandular History of Civilization* (1952). *Francie Again* (1953). *James Brooke of Sarawak: A Biography of Sir James Brooke* (1953). *Mary, Queen of Scots* (1953). *Meet the British* (1953). *Chiang Kai-shek: An Unauthorized Biography* (1955). *The First Book of India* (1955). *Diamond* (1956). *Francie Comes Home* (1956). *Leonardo da Vinci* (1956). *Kissing Cousins* (1958). *Aboab: First Rabbi of the Americas* (1960). *Around the World with Nelli Bly* (1960). *June Finds a Way* (1960). *Tiger House Party* (1960). *China Only Yesterday, 1850–1950: A Century of Change* (1963). *Indo* (1963). *Africa to Me: Person to Person* (1964). *Animal Gardens* (1967). *Romantic Rebels: An Informal History of Bohemianism in America* (1967). *The Cooking of China* (1968). *Zoos* (1968). *Time and Places* (1970). *Breath of God: A Book about Angels, Demons, Familiars, Elementals, and Spirits* (1971). *Fractured Emerald: Ireland* (1971). *On the Side of the Apes* (1971). *Once Upon a Pedestal* (1974). *Lorenzo: D. H. Lawrence and the Women Who Loved Him* (1975). *Mabel: A Biography of Mabel Dodge Luhan* (1977). *Look Who's Talking* (1978).

BIBLIOGRAPHY: For articles in reference works, see: *Authors of Books for Young People*, Eds. M. E. Ward and D. A. Marquardt (second ed., 1971). *CA*, 1–4 (1967). *CB* (July 1942). *NCAB*, H. *20thCAS*.

PATRICIA LANGHALS NEILS

Lucretia Peabody Hale

B. *2 Sept. 1820, Boston, Massachusetts; d. 12 June 1900, Boston, Massachusetts*
D. *of Nathan and Sarah Preston Everett Hale*

H. came from a distinguished New England literary family. Her mother was a writer; her father, nephew of the famous revolutionary-war patriot, was owner-editor of the Boston *Daily Advertiser*. Among H.'s six brothers and sisters were Edward Everett, Unitarian clergyman, abolitionist, and writer, best known for his short story "A Man Without a Country"; Charles, consul general to Egypt at the time of the opening of the Suez Canal; and Susan, writer and traveler.

H. gained a reputation as a bright student at the highly regarded George B. Emerson School for Young Ladies, the graduates of which had the equivalent of a contemporary Bachelor of Arts degree. There she and four other girls comprised a group called the Pentad, maintaining their friendship for many years. When the Pentad visited one another, H. often made up stories for amusement when they were in bed at night. After her schooling, H. remained at home helping with the housework, sewing, attending cultural events, and writing. The only one of her immediate group never to marry, she became known as Aunt Lucretia to the children of her friends. She often visited their homes, telling stories to their children as she had to their mothers when she and they were children.

A prolific writer, H. began wielding a pen at a very early age, because the Hale children were often called upon to help out with editorials, book reviews, and translations. Although much of her work consisted of editorials and fillers for the journals her brothers published, she wrote texts and Sunday-school books, edited collections of games and needlework, and produced several novels and books of short stories, sometimes in conjunction with other writers. After the death of her father in 1863, H. supported herself by her writings.

Her first venture into fiction, *Margaret Percival in America* (1850), written in collaboration with Edward, was a religious novel that was well received and had modest sales. The first of her independent writings to attract attention was "The Queen of the Red Chessmen" (*Atlantic Monthly*, 1858), a short, fanciful tale in which a strong-willed red chess queen comes alive. A novel, *Six of One by Half a Dozen of the Other* (1872), a six-way collaboration with Harriet Beecher Stowe and Edward, among others, is an amusing comedy of manners.

H.'s claim to literary distinction, though she never knew it, came through her stories about the Peterkin family. The first one, "The Lady Who Put Salt in Her Coffee" (1868), was made up to amuse Meggie, the daughter of H.'s old school friend, Mrs. Lesley. One summer vacation, when Meggie was sick and forced to miss the family fun, H. sat down by her bedside and on the spot created the story about Mrs. Peterkin's problems with her cup of coffee. She later published it in the periodical *Our Young Folks*. Five more Peterkin stories were printed there, and still others followed in *St. Nicholas*, its successor. Some two-dozen stories were first put out in book form in 1880, and 1886 saw a sequel of eight more, *The Last of the Peterkins, with Others of Their Kin*. The stories were called after Mr. Lesley, whose first name was

Peter, his children forming the "kin," while Mrs. Lesley herself was the wise Lady from Philadelphia.

The first significant nonsense done for children in the U.S., the Peterkin stories became immensely popular throughout the nation, not only with children but with adults as well. Their gentle satire on American attitudes and ways tickled the national funny bone and helped people laugh at themselves. The lovable, foolish Peterkins of Boston consisted of Mr. and Mrs. Peterkin; Agamemnon, who had been to college; Elizabeth Eliza; Solomon John; and the three little boys, always nameless, but never without their india rubber boots.

Although the stories reflect the manners and attitudes of their period, in their revelation of character they ring true yet today, and it is upon the droll, whimsical adventures of this winning family of bumblers, still favorites with children, that H.'s reputation as a writer rests.

WORKS: *Margaret Percival in America* (with E. E. Hale, 1850). *Seven Stormy Sundays* (1859). *Struggle for Life* (1861). *The Lord's Supper and Its Observance* (1866). *The Service of Sorrow* (1867). *Six of One by Half a Dozen of the Other* (with E. E. Hale et al., 1872). *The Wolf at the Door* (1877). *Designs in Outline for Art-Needlework* (1879). *More Stitches for Decorative Embroidery* (1879). *Point-Lace: A Guide to Lace-Work* (1879). *The Peterkin Papers* (1880). *The Art of Knitting* (1881). *The Last of the Peterkins, with Others of Their Kin* (1886). *Fagots for the Fireside* (1888). *The New Harry and Lucy* (with E. E. Hale, 1892). *Stories for Children* (1892). *Sunday School Stories* (with B. Whitman, n.d.). *An Uncloseted Skeleton* (with E. L. Bynner, n.d.).

BIBLIOGRAPHY: Hale, E. E., *A New England Boyhood* (1893). Hale, N., Introduction to *The Complete Peterkin Papers* (1960).

For articles in reference works, see: *AA. DAB*, IV, 2. *The Junior Book of Authors*, Eds. S. J. Kunitz and H. Haycraft (1934). *NAW* (article by M. D. Wankmiller). *NCAB*, 5. *The Who's Who of Children's Literature*, Ed. B. Doyle (1968).

Other references: *Horn Book* (Sept.–Oct. 1940; April 1958). *PW* (28 Oct. 1957).

ALETHEA K. HELBIG

Sarah Josepha Buell Hale

B. 24 Oct. 1788, Newport, New Hampshire; d. 30 April 1879, Philadelphia,
   Pennsylvania
Wrote under: Cornelia, Sarah Josepha Hale, Mrs. Hale, A Lady of New
   Hampshire
D. of Gordon and Martha Whittlesey Buell; m. David Hale, 1813

H. was educated at home, in rural New Hampshire, by her mother, who,
H. later said, encouraged her "predilection for literary pursuits," and by
her older brother, who shared his college studies when on vacation from
Dartmouth. H. conducted a private school for children from 1806 until
1813, when she married a lawyer. By her own account, H.'s married
life was a model of domestic bliss. She admired her husband greatly and
spent idyllic evenings with him in reading and study. In 1822, however,
just before the birth of their fifth child, Hale died, leaving H. in financial distress. She soon turned to writing and, with the assistance of her
husband's Masonic friends, published *The Genius of Oblivion* (1823), a
thin volume of poetry.

Although the poems are undistinguished, they contain the seeds of
themes H. was later to develop—the superiority of American character,
the need for higher education for women, and the differing roles of the
sexes (man "rides the wave" and "rules the flame," while woman is the
"star of home"). In addition, the first line of the book, "No mercenary
muse inspires my lay," is H.'s first pronouncement to the world of the
self-image which, as skillful advertiser of herself and her magazines, she
was to promote for the rest of her life: she became a writer only to raise
funds to educate her children.

H.'s career was launched in 1827 with the publication of her first
novel. *Northwood* is usually represented as one of the earliest novels to
contrast American life in the North and South; however, the subtitle,
A Tale of New England, more accurately describes H.'s intent. Southern scenes and characters are introduced, like British ones, to point up
the characteristics of Yankee life.

Despite its flaws *Northwood* was original and became an instant popular success. Its renown brought H. an offer to edit a new magazine,

and the year after the publication of her novel she found herself in Boston, the editor of *Ladies' Magazine.*

Although there had previously been female editors and periodicals for women, *Ladies' Magazine* was the first one of quality and the first to last more than five years. It attracted the attention of Louis Godey, an enterprising publisher who was editing an inferior magazine in Philadelphia. Godey offered to buy out the *Ladies' Magazine* and unite it with his *Lady's Book* under H.'s editorship. H. accepted and began an association which lasted from 1837 until 1877. She edited *Godey's Lady's Book* until she was in her ninetieth year.

Because Godey was able to finance the novel practice of paying contributors, H. could attract better writers, such as Edgar Allan Poe. She also expanded the number of domestic departments begun in *Ladies' Magazine.* In *Godey's* can be found the forerunners of most departments existing in today's home magazines.

Missing from *Godey's* were essays on the political, economic, and religious questions of the day. H.'s advocacy of education for women and other reforms was carried on principally in her editorial columns, for Godey, with an eye on circulation, forbade any controversial articles. Incredibly, the Civil War was never mentioned in *Godey's* pages. The magazine was successful, however, as circulation climbed from 10,000, in 1837, to 150,000, by 1860, an astounding figure for the time. *Godey's* was the arbiter of American taste and manners, and H.'s name became literally a household word.

During her career as editor, H. continued prolifically to produce her own work: fiction, collections of her sketches, recipe books, and household handbooks; she edited gift books, anthologies of verse and letters by women, and works for children. In her *Poems for Our Children* (1830) is "Mary Had a Little Lamb," the poem for which she is best known today, although her authorship of the first stanza has been disputed. H.'s major work is *Woman's Record; or, Sketches of All Distinguished Women from 'The Beginning' till A.D. 1850* (1853). This monumental biographical encyclopedia, still useful today, took her several years to write and contains some 2500 entries.

H. has been criticized for her views on slavery, but *Northwood* and *Liberia* (1853) have also been called antislavery novels. Interpretation of H. thus has varied widely. Some of her biographers claim she was a "militant feminist," others a "true conservative." Actually her philosophy, expressed repeatedly in her works, was internally consistent and explains many seeming contradictions. She believed that God created women morally superior to men. Eve's sin was less than Adam's, as she fell because of desire for spiritual truth and he from sensual appetite. Eve did sin, however, and woman's punishment is to be subordinate to her husband. She is required to work through him, elevating him and transforming his nature in order to save humanity. In America she is particularly to restrain his materialism and greed to save the nation. Woman's sphere is restricted—she must use her influence only in the domestic realm because if she entered public affairs she might be contaminated.

H.'s philosophy also explains the major contradiction in her life. She thought of herself as a reformer and indeed was an energetic and outspoken supporter of many causes. Yet, apart from her advocacy of education for women, the causes for which she labored were essentially trivial ones, such as eliminating the use of "female" as a noun, having Thanksgiving declared a national holiday, and raising money to complete the Bunker Hill Monument. H. wielded tremendous influence and could unite large numbers of women. She used her power to promote, in her words, women's "happiness and usefulness in their Divinely appointed sphere."

SELECTED WORKS: *The Genius of Oblivion* (1823). *Northwood: A Tale of New England* (1827; rev. ed., *Northwood; or, Life North and South: Showing the True Character of Both*, 1852). *Sketches of American Character* (1829). *Poems for Our Children* (1830). *Flora's Interpreter; or, The American Book of Flowers and Sentiments* (edited by Hale, 1832; rev. ed., 1849). *Traits of American Life* (1835). *The Ladies' Wreath* (compiled by Hale, 1837; rev. ed., 1839). *A Complete Dictionary of Poetical Quotations* (1850). *Liberia; or, Mr. Peyton's Experiments* (1853). *Woman's Record; or, Sketches of All Distinguished Women from 'The Beginning' till A.D. 1850* (1853; rev. eds., 1855, 1870). *Manners; or, Happy Homes and Good Society All the Year Round* (1868).

BIBLIOGRAPHY: Entrikin, I. W., *Sarah Josepha Hale and Godey's Lady's Book* (1946). Finley, R. E., *The Lady of Godey's* (1931). Fryatt, N. R., *Sarah Josepha Hale* (1975). *The Story of Mary and Her Little Lamb* (commissioned by H. Ford, 1928). Taylor, W. R., *Cavalier and Yankee* (1961). Wright, R., *Forgotten Ladies* (1928).

For articles in reference works, see: *AA. CAL. DAB*, IV, 2. *FPA. NAW* (article by P. S. Boyer). *NCAB*, 22.

Other references: *Historian* (Feb. 1970). *NEQ* (Jan. 1928).

BARBARA A. WHITE

Lorraine Hansberry

B. 19 May 1930, Chicago, Illinois; d. 12 Jan. 1965, New York City
D. of Carl Augustus and Nannie Perry Hansberry; m. Robert Nemiroff, 1953

Youngest of four children in a prosperous Republican, black family, H. spent two years at the University of Wisconsin, then went to New York City, where she studied African history under W. E. B. DuBois and worked on a radical monthly, *Freedom*, published by Paul Robeson. In her words, her editor there, Louis E. Burnham, taught her that "all racism is rotten, black or white, that everything is political, and that people tend to be indescribably beautiful and uproariously funny," tenets which are themes of her entire oeuvre.

By 1959, she had attained fame as the youngest American and the only black dramatist to win the Best Play of the Year award, for *A Raisin in the Sun* (1959). H. continued to write and work until her untimely death from cancer during the run of *The Sign in Sidney Brustein's Window* (1964). In addition to her dramatic works, essays, and journals, she made a significant contribution to the black movement by writing the text for a photographic journal, *The Movement: A Documentary of a Struggle for Equality* (1964), published shortly before she died.

A landmark in American theater, *A Raisin in the Sun* ran for 530 performances, toured extensively, and has been published and produced in over thirty countries. Its title and theme are based on a poem by Langston Hughes that questions, "What happens to a dream deferred?" The play derives its power from the inevitable conflicts which arise because each member of the Younger family has a different dream, an individual "plan" for escaping the dreary life of the Chicago ghetto in which they live.

H.'s second commercially produced play, *The Sign in Sidney Brustein's Window*, features a white protagonist, an engagé whose statements that he has always been "a fool who believes that death is waste and love is sweet . . ." and that "hurt is desperation and desperation is energy and energy can MOVE things" sound like the playwright's voice verbatim. Criticism by some reviewers on the basis that the characters are merely personifications of conflicting ways to view the world meant early closure, before giving the public a chance to estimate its value. Through herculean efforts—donations and advertisements sponsored by distinguished people in the American theater—it remained open until over eighty thousand people had seen the production. At H.'s death, the sign came down in New York, but the play was successful on tour and has had subsequent productions in a dozen countries, including a particularly distinguished one in Paris with Simone Signoret as translator and producer.

To H., her most important play was *Les Blancs* (1972), an accurate foretelling of what has happened in Africa in terms of black revolution. When produced posthumously (1970), there were cries of antiwhite bias, despite the fact that it deals as fairly with opportunistic blacks as with white capitalists.

In a similar vein, H.'s ninety-minute television drama, *The Drinking Gourd* (1960), commissioned by NBC for the Civil War centennial, was shelved as "too controversial," although many of its scenes are forerunners of those done more recently on television in such plays as *Roots*.

Throughout her life, H. kept diaries, journals, and letters, and wrote many essays for newspapers and magazines. Bits and pieces of these, along with scenes from her plays, are well blended by Robert Nemiroff in *To Be Young, Gifted, and Black* (1969), a two-act drama. It was published as a book with extensive background notes and an introduction by James Baldwin.

This playwright's influence in the theater in terms of black performers, as well as black audiences—who saw themselves truthfully presented onstage for the first time in *A Raisin in the Sun*—was far greater than it might seem from the number of her works. Actually, since her death, there has been a growing interest in this woman whose philosophy was summed up in her address to young black writers. She said: "What I write is not based on the assumption of idyllic possibilities or innocent assessments of the true nature of life, but, rather, on my own personal view that, posing one against the other, I think that the human race does command its own destiny and that that destiny can eventually embrace the stars."

WORKS: *A Raisin in the Sun* (1959; film version, 1960; musical, *Raisin*, 1978). *The Drinking Gourd* (1960). *The Movement: A Documentary of a Struggle for Equality* (1964; English ed., *A Matter of Colour*, 1965). *The Sign in Sidney Brustein's Window* (1964). *To Be Young, Gifted, and Black* (Ed. R. Nemiroff, 1969). *Les Blancs: The Collected Last Plays of Lorraine Hansberry* (Ed. R. Nemiroff, 1972). *Raisin* (1973).

BIBLIOGRAPHY: For articles in reference works, see: *Black Theatre USA*, Ed. J. V. Hatch (1974). *CA*, 25–28 (1971). *CB* (Sept. 1959; Feb. 1965).

Other references: *Ebony* (18 Sept. 1963). *Freedomways* 19 (1979). New York *Amsterdam News* (29 Jan. 1972). *Newsweek* (20 April 1959). *NY* (9 May 1959). *NYT* (29 Nov. 1970). *SatR* (31 Dec. 1966). *Time* (10 Jan. 1969). *Vogue* (June 1959).

EDYTHE M. McGOVERN

Elizabeth Hardwick

B. 27 July 1916, Lexington, Kentucky
D. of Eugene Allen and Mary Ramsay Hardwick; m. Robert Lowell, 1949

H. holds a B.A. and M.A. from the University of Kentucky, Lexington, and did graduate work at Columbia University, New York City. A well-known figure in artistic, literary, and critical circles in New York and Boston, H. has published novels, short stories, critical and belletristic articles and reviews, and an edition of William James's letters. She is the editor of eighteen volumes of *Rediscovered Fiction by American Women* (1977). In 1948 she was awarded a Guggenheim Fellowship in fiction and in 1967 received the George Jean Nathan Award for outstanding drama criticism—the first woman ever to be so honored. Since 1964 H. has been adjunct professor of English literature at Barnard College, New York City. She has one daughter, Harriet, and is divorced from the poet Robert Lowell.

In March 1963, to fill the gap left by a printers' strike in New York City, H. became one of the founding editors of the *New York Review of Books*, for which she remains advisory editor and a frequent contributor. For many years she also wrote essays for the *Partisan Review* and other magazines.

H.'s short stories have appeared in *The New Yorker*, the *Partisan Review*, the *Sewanee Review*, and other magazines; four were chosen for reprinting in *Best American Short Stories*. In all her stories, H. reproduces the vagueness of human thought and motivation, the amorphousness of unexamined experience. Yet the stories demonstrate that the most ordinary human experience is the central core of life. In "The Mysteries of Eleusis" the delinquent girl embarking upon marriage with a soldier she barely knows, on the basis of a "love" she has only heard about, "dimly perceived that all this world was pitifully dependent upon the steady recurrence of the emotion into which she and the boy were drawn," an emotion neither of them can explicitly feel, let alone understand.

The theme of the unknowableness of human experience recurs in H.'s novels, which are less well known than her stories. *The Ghostly Lover* (1945) is a stream-of-consciousness *bildungsroman* of sorts. Marian Coleman is deprived of all emotional sustenance; her parents desert her, and her grandmother, with whom she lives, is virtually autistic. The novel deals with Marian's gradual realization that she alone can provide a connection between experience and emotion that will give meaning to her life.

H.'s second novel, *The Simple Truth* (1955), is somewhat more complex. In it a poor college youth is accused of murdering his rich girlfriend. His trial is presented through the minds of two casual observers —a middle-class, liberal graduate student who views the issue as one of class injustice, and a chemistry professor's wife who considers herself an aesthete. Both believe themselves more enlightened than the masses (i.e., the jury) and are therefore dismayed when the boy is acquitted. H. explores the need of liberals, of whatever persuasion, to consider themselves superior to the masses. Both novels focus on the formlessness of human experience and the difficulty of approaching another's mind. In the end, for H.'s characters, truth remains unknowable and feeling unsayable.

H.'s third novel, *Sleepless Nights* (1979), is a logical extension of her attempt to fix and focus the nature of human experience. Combining autobiography with fiction, the book presents the plotless musings of H. herself as a fictional old woman in a nursing home. The creation of self is explored mainly through the protagonist's perception of others, from the famous Billie Holiday to apparently insignificant maids and laundresses, made significant through naming and describing. Life—of the old woman in the nursing home, of H. in her New York apartment— becomes only what one chooses to remember and re-invent; "fact," says H., "is to me a hindrance to memory." In *Sleepless Nights* H.'s earlier overly diffuse style and her tendency toward reflection rather than action become, at last, explicit tools for defining the genesis and essence of the human individual.

H. is justly famed for her reviews and for her social criticism. It is not, however, always easy to differentiate the two. The attempt to capture the movement of thought which appears in her novels also informs the criticism with the brilliance of dialogue and encourages the reader to participate in the critical act. There is in all H.'s writing a gentility, an aristocracy, a respectful love affair with words and sentences that soothes as do the essays of Virginia Woolf. H.'s intimate concern with the English language is cause for quiet joy.

WORKS: *The Ghostly Lover* (1945). *The Simple Truth* (1955). *Selected Letters of William James* (edited by Hardwick, 1961). *A View of My Own* (1962). *Seduction and Betrayal* (1974). *Rediscovered Fiction by American Women: A Personal Selection* (18 vols., edited by Hardwick, 1977). *Sleepless Nights* (1979).

BIBLIOGRAPHY: For articles in reference works, see: *CA*, 5–8 (1969). *WA*.
    Other references: *Nation* (5 May 1945). *NewR* (14 Feb. 1955). *NYTBR* (29 April 1979).

LORALEE MacPIKE

Frances Ellen Watkins Harper

B. 24 Sept. 1825, Baltimore, Maryland; d. 22 Feb. 1911, Philadelphia,
    Pennsylvania
Wrote under: Frances E. W. Harper, Frances Ellen Watkins
M. Fenton Harper, 1860

H., the author of the first novel published by an Afro-American woman, was the most popular black poet of her day. She was a sought-after lecturer, as well, speaking on behalf of abolitionism, temperance, and women's rights. Born to free parents, H. was orphaned at an early age, then reared and educated by an aunt and uncle active in the antislavery movement. She became self-supporting at age thirteen.

After working at various occupations—including nursemaid, seamstress, and teacher—H. found her true calling on the lecture platform. She gave her first speech in 1854 in New Bedford, Massachusetts; her subject was "The Education and the Elevation of the Colored Race." Few women in the abolitionist movement traveled so widely or spoke to so many audiences.

Apparently no copies of *Forest Leaves* (ca. 1845), an early book of poetry by H., are extant. *Poems on Miscellaneous Subjects* (1854), with an introduction by William Lloyd Garrison, went through some twenty editions by 1874. Her dramatic readings of her verse were highlights of her lectures, and according to William Still, with whom she worked on the Underground Railroad, more than fifty thousand copies of her books were sold.

H. married in 1860; she was the mother of one daughter. After her husband's death in 1864, H. resumed her career as a lecturer.

With the end of the Civil War, H. carried her message of education and moral uplift to the southern states. Here she took the greatest interest in meetings called exclusively for black women, whose needs she felt were more pressing than those of any other class.

H.'s poems are of a piece with her oratory, determinedly propagandistic and emotional. In poems such as "The Slave Auction" and "The Slave Mother," H. presents the horrors of slavery from a female point of view. These poems are unabashedly sentimental, but undeniably effective. Her frequently anthologized poem, "Bury Me in a Free Land," derives its considerable strength both from its powerful theme and its balladlike simplicity. H.'s is very much an oral poetry; it needs to be heard, not merely read. By all accounts, H. herself was an outstanding performer, rendering her lines with dramatic voice and gesture, with sighs and tears. Her stage presence reflected her oratorical skill, but it was clearly derived as well from her profound commitment to the freedom struggle.

The first novel by a black author to depict the Reconstruction, *Iola Leroy; or, Shadows Uplifted* (1892), drew heavily on H.'s experiences in the South after the Civil War. *Iola Leroy* also contains frequent flashbacks to earlier periods and thus embraces the whole of 19th-c. black experience.

The main characters, Iola Leroy and Robert Johnson, are mulattoes whose actions are motivated specifically by their desire to reunite their families after emancipation and generally by their desire to uplift the race. As mulattoes they enjoy certain privileges not shared by other blacks, notably access to education, but they are steadfast in their refusal to set themselves apart from their fellows.

Iola Leroy is not a well-written work; its weaknesses to a large degree are those of the sentimental novel, the literary genre to which it belongs. The plot is often confused and incredible, and the characters overly idealized. The novel is nevertheless valuable for its historical insights, especially its portrayal of the bravery of black soldiers during the war and of the sacrifices made by the black community during Reconstruction. In its Christian humanism and its dedication to the principle of equality, *Iola Leroy* dramatizes the ideals to which H. devoted her life.

WORKS: *Forest Leaves* (ca. 1845). *Poems on Miscellaneous Subjects* (1854). *Moses: A Story of the Nile* (1869). *Sketches of Southern Life* (1872). *Iola Leroy; or, Shadows Uplifted* (1892). *The Martyr of Alabama, and Other Poems* (ca. 1894).

BIBLIOGRAPHY: Lerner, G., *Black Women in White America: A Documentary History* (1973). Montgomery, J. W., *A Comparative Analysis of the Rhetoric of Two Negro Women Orators—Sojourner Truth and Frances Ellen Watkins Harper* (1968). Robinson, W. H., *Early Black American Poets* (1971). Sherman, J., *Invisible Poets: Afro-Americans of Nineteenth Century* (1974). Sillen, S., *Women against Slavery* (1955). Still, W. G., *The Underground Railroad* (1872).

For articles in reference works, see: *Black American Writers Past and Present*, T. G. Rush, C. F. Myers, and E. S. Arato (1975). *NAW* (article by L. Filler).

Other references: *Black World* (Dec. 1972).

CHERYL A. WALL

Ida Husted Harper

B. *18 Feb. 1851, Fairfield, Indiana; d. 14 March 1931, Washington, D.C.*
D. *of John Arthur and Cassandra Stoddard Husted; m. Thomas Winans*
    Harper, 1871

H. was a prolific writer and journalist and an active feminist. A suffragist of international reputation, H. traveled throughout the U.S. and Europe with Susan B. Anthony, who asked her to become her official biographer. She handled publicity for the National American Woman Suffrage Association when Carrie Chapman Catt served as president.

After leaving Indiana University to become principal of a high school in Indiana, H. began her writing career at twenty by sending articles under a male pseudonym to the Terre Haute *Saturday Evening Mail*. Under her own name she then wrote a column, "A Woman's Opinions," for that same newspaper for twelve years. She simultaneously edited weekly discussions of women's activities in the *Locomotive Fireman's Magazine*, the official organ of the union of which her husband was chief counsel. After her divorce in 1890, she joined the staff of the Indian-apolis *News*. From then on she devoted her life to her daughter, to writing, and to her activities in the woman suffrage movement.

Her career in journalism led her from Indiana to New York, where she wrote a column for the New York *Sun* (1899–1903) and, best-known, a woman's page in *Harper's Bazar* (1909–13). She devoted most of this writing to the suffrage movement; her interests, unlike those of An-thony, Elizabeth Cady Stanton, and Lucy Stone, centered on the primary importance of the vote for women. She offers detailed reports about the status of women and their right to vote in countries all over the world. Her insight into international politics gives to her work the standards of accurate social history. In *Harper's Bazar* she reported on working women demanding suffrage, on women as officeholders in states that had the vote, on the deaths of her friends who had "lived for the Movement," and on the joys of seeing her dreams become a reality: "Yes, woman suffrage is becoming fashionable and it is all very amusing to veterans of the cause. They understand fully that, underlying the fashion, are years of hard and persistent work yet ahead before a uni-versal victory."

Her spirit is striking as she writes that "women of today who are not helping in the effort for the franchise do not know the joy they miss . . . so vital, so compelling, so full of the progressive spirit of the age." This same vigor appears in her two volumes of the *History of Woman Suffrage*, that monumental compilation begun by Anthony and Stanton. H. helped Anthony edit Volume Four, and herself edited Vol-umes Five and Six, dealing with state and national activities from 1900 to 1920. While the *History* contains records rather than interpretations of documents, speeches, and state and national activities, it nevertheless forms a coherent pattern of immense value for historians.

H. was Susan B. Anthony's Boswell: to her we owe a detailed study of Anthony's life and activities in two long volumes published in 1898. Dur-ing later life she continued her work on the Anthony biography; Vol-ume Three was published in 1908. The searcher for psychological insight will be disappointed by *The Life and Work of Susan B. Anthony*. Its deepest penetration in explaining Anthony's personality and motivation is through its astute description of Anthony's Quaker family background and of the encouragement in her education given by both parents.

Otherwise, the biography remains largely a chronicle, dull at times and burdened with detail. Stylistically, it belongs to the tradition of sen-timental 19th-c. prose. Yet no historian concerned with Anthony's role in the 19th-c. women's movement can ignore the intimate details of social history in H.'s story: Anthony's role as teacher, her support of both temperance and Amelia Bloomer, her acceptance of hydropathic medicine, and her relationships and correspondence with leaders of social reform, such as Garrison, Stanton, Stone, and Antoinette Brown.

Though close to her daughter, who continued her mother's work in the women's movement, H. remained independent, spending her last years working in the headquarters of the American Association of University Women in Washington, D.C. Using her journalistic talent to good effect, H. served the suffrage movement well. The extent and variety of her writing is impressive; fourteen large indexed volumes of her writings stand in the Library of Congress.

WORKS: *The Life and Work of Susan B. Anthony* (Vols. 1 and 2, 1898; Vol. 3, 1908). *History of Woman Suffrage* (Vol. 4, edited by Harper, with S. B. Anthony, 1902; Vols. 5 and 6, edited by Harper, 1922).

BIBLIOGRAPHY: Lutz, A., *Susan B. Anthony* (1959).
  For articles in reference works, see: *AW. DAB*, IV, 2. *Indiana Authors and Their Books, 1816–1916*, Ed. R. E. Banta (1949). *NAW* (article by C. J. Phillips). *NCAB*, 25.
  Other references: Indianapolis *News* (16 March 1931). *NYT* (17 March 1931). Terre Haute *Star* (17 March 1931).

LOIS FOWLER

Bernice Kelly Harris

B. 8 Oct. 1893, Mt. Moriah, North Carolina; d. 13 Sept. 1973, Seaboard, North Carolina
Wrote under: Bernice Kelly Harris, Bernice Kelly
D. of William Haywood and Rosa Poole Kelly; m. Herbert Harris, 1926

Born the third of six children in an established farming family, H. spent her childhood and adult years in the coastal plains region that dominated her novels. Like other writers, including Carson McCullers, H.'s first writing efforts were childhood plays performed for family and friends. Her subsequent attempts at poetry and novel writing were short-lived. She attended Meredith College in Raleigh, North Carolina, expressly to train as a teacher of English. After graduation, H. taught for three years at an academy in the foothills of western North Carolina, instructing rural Baptist preachers in the rudiments of grammar. She then took a post with the Seaboard, North Carolina, public schools and remained in Seaboard the rest of her life.

In 1919, a summer-school class introduced H. to folk drama. Although she used her skills in drama primarily for pedagogical purposes, the years 1920 to 1926, when she encouraged students to write and to produce folk plays, provided an intense period of story collection and writing apprenticeship for herself. Her marriage and the obligatory retirement from teaching prompted her to write her own plays rather than to encourage others to write. From 1932 to 1938 she wrote folk drama, drawing from actual people and events in the North Carolina towns around her. Seven of the better plays were published collectively in 1940; almost all were produced at regional drama festivals.

H.'s novels grew out of her feature stories written on a free-lance basis for Raleigh and Norfolk newspapers. Encouraged by her editor, H. began in 1937 the work which became *Purslane*, published by the University of North Carolina Press in 1939. Also in 1939, H. interviewed tenant farmers for four pieces appearing in *These Are Our Lives*, the Federal Writers Project publication.

The nostalgic first novel impressed critics, but H.'s second novel, *Portulaca* (1941), a realistic portrait of the rural and small-town middle class, won even more support from the literary establishment on both sides of the Atlantic. It also necessitated the change to a commercial publisher, since the university press feared such blunt themes would offend southern readers.

All of H.'s novels have related characters and draw from real-life experiences of H. and those she knew. She is the narrator of a region, with a thorough understanding of its people and mores; as such she can be compared to Cather or Faulkner in her ability to evoke time and place—to produce social history in novel form. So skillful is she at delineating character from life that reviewers of her one novel dealing exclusively with black farmers (*Janey Jeems*, 1946) failed to understand that the characters were not white because the depiction did not follow accepted stereotypes. The characters of her seven novels encompass all classes, races, ages, and personalities of the region. The strength of her novels clearly lies in their vivid characterization, which evokes not only a sense of regional identity and folkways but also of dynamic humanity.

WORKS: *Purslane* (1939). *Folk Plays of Eastern Carolina* (1940). *Portulaca* (1941). *Sweet Beulah Land* (1943). *Sage Quarter* (1945). *Janey Jeems* (1946). *Hearthstones* (1948). *Wild Cherry Tree Road* (1951). *A Southern Savory* (1964).

BIBLIOGRAPHY: Walser, R., *B. K. H.: Storyteller of Eastern Carolina* (1955).
For articles in reference works, see: *American Novelists of Today*, Ed. H. Warfel (1951). *CA*, 5–8 (1969); 45–48 (1974). *CB* (1949).
Other references: *WLB* (Jan. 1949).

SALLY BRETT

Miriam Coles Harris

B. *7 July 1834, Glen Cove, New York; d. 23 Jan. 1925, Pau, France*
Wrote under: Author of "Rutledge," Miriam Coles Harris, Mrs. Sidney S. Harris
D. *of Butler and Julia Anne Weeks Coles; m. Sidney S. Harris, 1864*

A descendant of Robert Coles of Suffolk, England, who accompanied John Winthrop to America in 1630, H. attended religious and exclusive private schools in New Jersey and New York City. After writing for periodicals and producing a bestseller at age twenty-six, H. married a New York lawyer, raised two children, and continued to produce popular novels, as well as travel and devotional books. Widowed in 1892, she spent most of her remaining years in Europe.

H.'s first novel, the bestseller *Rutledge* (1860), has been called the "first fully American example" of the gothic romance. It is narrated by the unnamed orphan heroine, a passionately resentful teenager who, in *Jane Eyre* fashion, falls in love with Rutledge, the older brooding hero— her temporary guardian—whose ancestral home hides a dark family secret. After being introduced to fashionable society by her worldly permanent guardian, the rebellious heroine becomes involved in a series of jealous misunderstandings, including a rash engagement to a handsome social climber who turns out to be a murderer and who commits suicide after the heroine hides him in the secret room at the Rutledge estate and he discovers he is Rutledge's illegitimate nephew. A period of penitence completes the education of the humbled heroine, who is finally reunited with the "masterful" Rutledge.

Like *Rutledge*, H.'s other fictions are characterized by psychological studies of negative feminine attitudes, religiously didactic themes, and sensational incidents. Anticipating in some ways the psychological realism of Henry James, H. probes, with surprising honesty, the degrees of hostility, powerlessness, and masochism experienced by an unusual variety of 19th-c. heroines: teenagers in *Rutledge* and in its juvenile counterpart, loosely based on H.'s schoolgirl days, *Louie's Last Term at St. Mary's* (1860); unhappily married heroines in *Frank Warrington* (1863) and *A Perfect Adonis* (1875); a young widowed mother in *Happy-Go-Lucky* (1881); and middle-aged mother-wives in *Phoebe* (1884) and *An Utter Failure* (1891).

H. frequently resolves her plots by transforming her rebellious heroines into self-abnegating women who exemplify the author's religious beliefs about renunciation of self and the world of vanity. Yet H.'s mixed feelings about her humbled heroines can be seen in the conclusion of *A Perfect Adonis:* The new bride asserts, "I can't see what I was created for," to which her bridegroom replies, "I can't either, except to make people want to possess you. To have and to hold you." Then he silences all further questions with an all-absorbing kiss, a romantic conclusion that is immediately undercut by the author's final remark: "It is a blessing that when you are a failure, you can forget it sometimes for a while. But the fact remains the same." Her last novel, *The Tents of Wickedness* (1907), interweaves a love story with a defense of the Roman Catholic Church.

Although melodramatic incident mars portions of her love plots, H.'s use of topical subjects also marks her as a forerunner of realism. *The Sutherlands* (1862) is a proslavery novel, while *Richard Vandermarck* (1871) contains one of the earliest literary portraits of the Wall Street businessman hero. A murder trial, realistically depicted, makes up a major segment of *Happy-Go-Lucky*, which also covers prejudice against Irish immigrants and lower-class poverty. Her last three novels treat daring sexual issues such as premarital sex, resentment of maternal duties, near-adultery, and divorce, as well as other topical subjects such as tenement conditions, racial violence, politics, and alcoholism.

H.'s minor place in literary history has depended solely on her most romantically sensational novel, the best-selling *Rutledge,* but all of her fictions contain perceptive, slightly ironic studies of a particular type of feminine psychology, portraits which, in their own limited ways, contributed to the development of the realistic tradition.

WORKS: *Rutledge* (1860). *Louie's Last Term at St. Mary's* (1860). *The Sutherlands* (1862). *Frank Warrington* (1863). *St. Philips* (1865). *A Rosary for Lent; or, Devotional Readings* (1867). *Roundhearts, and Other Stories* (1867). *Richard Vandermarck* (1871). *Dear Feast Lent: A Series of Devotional Readings* (1874). *A Perfect Adonis* (1875). *Missy* (1880). *Happy-Go-Lucky* (1881). *Phoebe* (1884). *An Utter Failure* (1891). *A Chit of Sixteen, and Other Stories* (1892). *A Corner of Spain* (1898). *The Tents of Wickedness* (1907).

BIBLIOGRAPHY: Baym, N., *Woman's Fiction: A Guide to Novels by and about Women in America* (1978). Cole, F. T., *The Early Genealogies of the Cole Families in America* (1887). Mott, F. L., *Golden Multitudes: The Story of Best Sellers in the United States* (1947).
For articles in reference works, see: *AA. DAB*, IV, 2. *NCAB*, 11.

KATHLEEN L. NICHOLS

Lillian Hellman

B. 20 June 1905, New Orleans, Louisiana
D. of Max and Julia Newhouse Hellman; m. Arthur Kober, 1925

H., an only child, spent her childhood in New York City and New Orleans. After two years at New York University, she took a job with a publisher, where she became acquainted with the literary world and met her future husband. After she and Kober got an amicable divorce, H. lived with Dashiell Hammett, the detective-fiction writer.

H. has published several volumes of distinguished memoirs. *An Unfinished Woman* (1969), which won a National Book Award, is H.'s vivid autobiography, running from her childhood in New Orleans to the death of Hammett in 1960. The whole book is characterized by painstaking honesty, as H. analyzes her rebellions and conflicts, her ambivalent attitudes toward money and the theater, and the tensions of her relationship with Hammett. Often she renders her experience in dramatic dialogues. *Pentimento* (1973) is H.'s reconsideration of certain themes in her life not developed in *An Unfinished Woman*. It consists mostly of portraits, of which the most memorable is that of her beloved girlhood friend "Julia," a passionate anti-Nazi who involved H. in the mission (especially perilous for a Jew) of carrying fifty thousand dollars into Berlin to ransom political prisoners. H.'s innocence, played against the elaborate subterfuges undertaken to safeguard her mission, makes for taut suspense. *Scoundrel Time* (1976) describes H.'s experience of political persecution in the 1950s.

Hammett guided her to the source for her first produced play, *The Children's Hour* (1934), an account of an actual libel suit in 19th-c. Scotland. It tells the story of Karen Wright and Martha Dobie, owners of a successful girls' school, who are ruined by a charge of lesbianism. Extremely successful, partly because of its then-shocking theme, the play ran for 691 performances on Broadway. *The Children's Hour* is a skillfully wrought melodrama deepened by psychological penetration and moral significance.

The Little Foxes (1939) is a gripping drama about the Hubbards of Alabama, who display the greed and driving egotism that H. saw in her mother's family. Ben and Oscar Hubbard and their sister, Regina Giddens, form a partnership with a northern industrialist to set up a profitable cotton factory in their town; but they cannot secure a controlling interest without obtaining money from Regina's husband, Horace, which he refuses to advance because he is disgusted by the Hubbards' ruthless greed. Throughout the play, mastery shifts between the brothers and their sister, depending upon who seems more likely to get control of Horace's money. In the end, Regina gains control by deliberately provoking him into a fatal heart attack.

Because the Hubbards are intended to be human beings as well as monsters of selfishness, H. decided to "look into their family background and find out what it was that made them the nasty people they were." In *Another Part of the Forest* (1947) she went back twenty years to show Ben, Oscar, and Regina as young people dominated by their father, Marcus. H. found humor as well as evil in people like the Hubbards, and made this more obvious in her second play about them.

The Autumn Garden (1951) is unlike H.'s earlier plays in emphasizing character over plot. In a handsome but shabby southern resort hotel, she gathers ten people who lack purpose, joy, and love. H.'s characterization here shows a notable advance in subtlety, as she views her people with more sympathy and less simple judgment.

Perhaps the most obvious characteristic of H.'s writing is her first-rate craftsmanship: the neat plotting of the Hubbard plays, where thrilling melodramatic climaxes are meticulously prepared for, as hints are dropped in the beginning, every one to be picked up by the end; the relief from this suspenseful melodrama through pathos or comedy; the sharp characterization and vividly authentic speeches, which at the same time economically move the plot along.

In her last two original plays—*The Autumn Garden* and *Toys in the Attic* (1960), which both present middle-aged people who come to recognize the bleakness of their lives, but find they cannot change them—

H.'s artistry appears more in character development. She relaxes her tight plotting to give her characters more room to develop, although she unfortunately retains some jarring melodramatic elements. H. is surely right in considering *The Autumn Garden* her finest play.

Well-made and popular as her plays have been, they are all redeemed from commercialism by their strong moral commitment. H. constantly makes the point, equally applicable to private and public affairs, that it is immoral to remain passive when evil is being done. She believes that a clear moral message "is only a mistake when it fails to achieve its purpose, and I would rather make the attempt, and fail, than fail to make the attempt." Only in a few cases, such as the anticlimactic discussion after Martha's death in *The Children's Hour* and the antifascist plays, does the moral message become obtrusive. Generally, it is organically part of her artistic structure and characterization. H.'s works, like her life, have consistently demonstrated responsibility, courage, and integrity.

WORKS: *The Children's Hour* (1934; film versions: *These Three*, 1936, *The Children's Hour*, 1962). *Days to Come* (1936). *The Little Foxes* (1939; film version, 1941; opera, *Regina*, 1949). *Watch on the Rhine* (1941; film version, 1943). *The North Star: A Motion Picture about Some Russian People* (1943). *The Searching Wind* (1944; film version, 1946). *Another Part of the Forest* (1947; film version, 1948). *Montserrat* by E. Roblès (adapted by Hellman, 1950). *The Autumn Garden* (1951). *The Selected Letters of Anton Chekhov* (edited by Hellman, 1955). *The Lark* by J. Anouilh (adapted by Hellman, 1955). *Candide* by Voltaire (dramatization by Hellman, with music by L. Bernstein and lyrics by R. Wilbur, J. LaTouche, and D. Parker, 1957). *Toys in the Attic* (1960; film version, 1963). *My Mother, My Father, and Me* (dramatization of the novel *How Much?* by B. Blechman, 1963). *The Big Knockover: Stories and Short Novels by Dashiell Hammett* (introduction by Hellman, 1966). *An Unfinished Woman: A Memoir* (1969). *Pentimento: A Book of Portraits* (1973; film version, *Julia*, 1977). *Scoundrel Time* (1976). *Maybe: A Story* (1980).

BIBLIOGRAPHY: Heilman, R. B., *The Iceman, the Arsonist, and the Troubled Agent* (1973). Heilman, R. B.. *Tragedy and Melodrama: Versions of Experience* (1968). Holmin, L. R., *The Dramatic Works of Lillian Hellman* (1973). Moody, R., *Lillian Hellman: Playwright* (1972). Triesch, M., *The Lillian Hellman Collection at the University of Texas* (1968).

For articles in reference works, see: *CB* (May 1941; June 1960). *NCAB*, G. *20thCA. 20thCAS.*

Other references: *Contact* III (1959). *Modern Drama* III (1960). *Paris Review* IX (1965).

KATHARINE M. ROGERS

Caroline Lee Whiting Hentz

B. 1 June 1800, Lancaster, Massachusetts; d. 11 Feb. 1856, Marianna, Florida
D. of John and Orpah Danforth Whiting; m. Nicolas Marcellus Hentz, 1824

H. was the eighth and youngest child of an old New England family directly descended from the Reverend Samuel Whiting, who settled in Massachusetts in 1636. Her father served as a colonel in the revolutionary war. Two years after H.'s marriage to a French entomologist, her husband became chairman of modern languages and belles-lettres at the University of North Carolina in Chapel Hill. This move was the first of many the family made following his erratic teaching career. H. bore five children; the oldest son died when he was two years old. In addition to rearing the children, running the household, supervising boarding students, and helping her husband with teaching and insect collecting, H. wrote verse, drama, tales, and novels. Reputedly, she could write easily in the midst of household distractions.

Her first novel, *Lovell's Folly* (1833), was suppressed by her family as "too personal." Some accounts say it was libelous. While in Kentucky, H. wrote a prize-winning play, *DeLara; or, The Moorish Bride* (1843). The five-act drama, set in a Spanish castle during the Moors' conquest of Spain, was produced in Philadelphia and Boston. Of her poems written for special occasions, perhaps the most important one was composed for the visit of Andrew Jackson to Florence, Alabama, in 1836. Her husband read the poem for President Jackson.

Although she began writing as a girl, H. did not become a well-known writer until the Philadelphia *Saturday Courier* serially published a domestic tale in 1844. It was later published in book form as *Aunt Patty's Scrap Bag* (1846). When her husband became chronically ill in the late 1840s, H., out of financial necessity, began the most prolific period of her writing at the age of fifty. Her novel, *Linda; or, The Young Pilot of the Belle Creole* (1850), became a bestseller. Seven more domestic novels and six collections of stories were published in rapid succession. Her books remained popular after her death until the end of the century. Two novels, *Eoline; or, Magnolia Vale* (1852) and *The Planter's Northern Bride* (1854), were reprinted in the 1970s.

While living in Cincinnati, H. knew Harriet Beecher Stowe. Both women belonged to a literary group, the Semi-Colons. Although they might have shared cultural interests, the issue of slavery separated them. H.'s novel, *The Planter's Northern Bride*, was written as an answer to *Uncle Tom's Cabin*. It is proslavery propaganda. In *Marcus Warland* (1852), probably composed before she had read Stowe's work, H. made only a partial defense of slavery, but the later novel is a full-blown counter-statement to abolition.

With other writers of antebellum novels, H. helped to create and perpetuate an image of ideal plantation life. This fictional world of pious belles, gallant gentlemen, and happy slaves appeals so strongly to the popular mind that the myth persists.

WORKS: *Lovell's Folly* (1833). *DeLara; or, The Moorish Bride* (1843). *Aunt Patty's Scrap Bag* (1846). *Mob Cap* (1848). *Linda; or, The Young Pilot of the Belle Creole* (1850). *Rena; or, The Snow Bird* (1851). *Eoline; or, Magnolia Vale* (1852). *Marcus Warland; or, The Long Moss Spring* (1852). *Helen and Arthur; or, Miss Thusa's Spinning Wheel* (1853). *Wild Jack; or, The Stolen Child, and Other Stories* (1853). *The Victim of Excitement* (1853). *The Planter's Northern Bride* (1854). *Robert Graham* (1855). *The Banished Son* (1856). *Courtship and Marriage* (1856). *Ernest Linwood* (1856). *The Lost Daughter* (1857). *Love after Marriage* (1857).

BIBLIOGRAPHY: Ellison, R. C., Introduction to *The Planter's Northern Bride* by C. L. W. Hentz (1970). Papashvily, H. W., *All the Happy Endings* (1956). Williams, B. B., *A Literary History of Alabama: The Nineteenth Century* (1979).

For articles in reference works, see: *AA. CAL. DAB*, IV, 2. *NAW* (article by H. W. Papashvily). *NCAB*, 6. *Ohio Authors and Their Books*, Ed. W. Coyle (1962).

Other references: *AL* 22 (1950). *AlaR* 4 (1951).

LYNDA W. BROWN

Marguerite Higgins

B. 3 Sept. 1920, Hong Kong; d. 3 Jan. 1966, Washington, D.C.
D. of Lawrence Daniel and Marguerite Godard Higgins; m. Stanley Moore, 1942; m. William E. Hall, 1952

H. was born in the British Crown Colony of Hong Kong to a globe-trotting businessman and his French war bride. She was educated in France and later, when the Higgins family returned home to the U.S., she was enrolled in an exclusive private school in Oakland, California. After graduating from the University of California at Berkeley, with honors, in 1940, she went to work as a cub reporter for the local Vallejo *Times-Herald*. She was hired by the *New York Herald Tribune* after receiving her master's degree in New York from Columbia University's Graduate School of Journalism; she worked for the paper for the next twenty-one years.

After three routine years on the *Tribune*, reporting city visitors, suburban fires, and visiting royalty, H. won a coveted spot in the London bureau. Shortly thereafter, she transferred to the Paris bureau—largely because of her proficiency in French—and soon found herself reporting the wartime liberation of Europe. She made the front page regularly and built up a respected name for herself among the most experienced foreign correspondents in the world. She was twenty-five when the *Tribune* named her Berlin bureau chief. Tokyo bureau chief during the Korean War, H. was with the first reporters who made their way into Korea on returning evacuation planes, the only woman correspondent in Korea.

After her remarriage and the birth of two children, H. settled down to a less peripatetic schedule as a roving reporter for the *Tribune* and as a free-lance writer for many periodicals. In the mid-1950s, H. reopened the *Tribune*'s Moscow bureau, and in 1956 she returned to Washington to cover the diplomatic beat. From then on, her competition claimed H. could be counted on to show up wherever a crisis occurred, from the Congo to the Dominican Republic. In 1963, H. resigned to become a syndicated columnist for Long Island's *Newsday*.

H. became increasingly interested in Vietnam as that country opened up into one of the world's most controversial hot spots, and made ten trips to Vietnam. In late 1965, she was air ambulanced home, the victim of leishmaniasis, a disease brought on by the bite of a tropical sandfly, and within six weeks she was dead.

Out of her experiences covering the Korean conflict came *War in Korea: The Report of a Woman Combat Correspondent* (1951), which also appeared in a condensed form in *Woman's Home Companion* in 1951. The book was a bestseller, and H. became an overnight sensation, touring and lecturing throughout the country. In *Report of a Woman Combat Correspondent*, H. recounted her experiences on the front in Korea with a lively style and the sense of adventurous excitement she felt. Although the book tends to provide an unbalanced view of history, reviews were favorable, and it enjoyed a wide readership.

In 1954, she received a Guggenheim Fellowship, allowing her to make a ten-week tour of Russia. Her experiences and reactions to life in Cold

War Russia during the 13,500-mile trek are detailed in *Red Plush and Black Bread*, published in 1956.

H. and her long-time personal friend, the late newsman Peter Lisagor, together wrote and published *Overtime in Heaven: Adventures in the Foreign Service* (1964), a series of behind-the-scenes true stories of ten Foreign Service incidents. A highly entertaining set of adventure vignettes, the series won credits for its carefully researched and documented materials, although one critic noted they had created a "composite portrait of the Foreign Service man who looks suspiciously like a more moral James Bond."

Her Vietnam study, *Our Vietnam Nightmare* (1965), presented her research and conclusions on what was actually happening in Vietnam as a result of U.S. foreign policy and actions, covering the period from the Buddhist revolt and Diem's fall in 1963 to the changing political tactics of the Viet Cong in the summer of 1965. Herman Dinsmore, former *New York Times* international edition editor, called it "superb." He said, "she was not the most popular correspondent for one excellent reason: she was so brilliant she outshone every writer around her, men and women: and, of course, she was industrious, clever, and, of all things, patriotic."

WORKS: *War in Korea: The Report of a Woman Combat Correspondent* (1951). *News Is a Singular Thing* (1955). *Red Plush and Black Bread* (1956). *Jessie Benton Frémont* (1962). *Overtime in Heaven: Adventures in the Foreign Service* (with P. Lisagor, 1964). *Our Vietnam Nightmare* (1965).

BIBLIOGRAPHY: Editors of the Army Times, *American Heroes of Asian Wars* (1968). Fleming, A. M., *Reporters at War* (1970). Forese, A., *American Women Who Scored Firsts* (1958). Jakes, J., *Great War Correspondents* (1967). Kelly, F. K., *Reporters Around the World* (1957).

For articles in reference works, see: *CA*, 5–8 (1969); 25–28 (1971). *CB* (June 1951; Feb. 1966).

Other references: *Life* (2 Oct. 1950). *NYHT* (16 Feb. 1946; 19 Oct. 1950; 8 May 1951). *NYT* (8 May 1951). *Time* (25 Sept. 1950).

KATHLEEN KEARNEY KEESHEN

Ella Rhoads Higginson

B. ca. 1860, Council Grove, Kansas; d. 29 Dec. 1940, Bellingham, Washington
Wrote under: Ella Higginson, Ella Rhoads
D. of Charles and Mary Ann Rhoads; m. Russell Carden Higginson, ca. 1880

In the early 1860s, H.'s family crossed the plains from Kansas to the Grand Ronde Valley of Oregon. In 1870, they moved to Portland and then to a farm eight miles from town. Later they lived in Oregon City, where H. received her few years of education in a public school. The youngest of three children, H. enjoyed freedom from punishments and farm chores. Although the family was poor, their home was filled with good books, visitors, and conversation. Her father's ability as a storyteller and her mother's poetic sensitivity to the beauty of nature enriched H.'s childhood experiences.

At the age of eight, H. wrote her first poem and was encouraged to continue writing by her mother and sister, Carrie Blake Morgan, who later became known as a poet in her own right as the author of *Path of Gold* (1900). Her father and brother laughed at her early poetic attempts, but at fourteen H. published a love poem in the Oregon City paper. At sixteen she joined the newspaper staff to learn everything from typesetting to editorial writing. Early stories were contributed to the *West Shore*, a Portland literary magazine, and to the Salem *Oregon Literary Vidette*.

In 1888, H. moved to Whatcom (now Bellingham), Washington, with her husband. A druggist from New York, he possessed charming "Eastern" manners but, according to H., did not sufficiently encourage or appreciate her literary work. From Bellingham she edited a department entitled "Fact and Fancy for Women" for the weekly *West Shore*. Her first column, in 1890, presented advanced views on the controversial subject of divorce.

For twenty-five years after the demise of the *West Shore* in 1891, H. contributed fiction to national magazines such as *Century*, *Harper's Weekly*, *Cosmopolitan*, *Short Stories*, *The New Peterson*, *McClure's*, and *Collier's*. H.'s stories were collected in several volumes. Her stories of common people of the Far West were praised by the *Overland Monthly* as "unpretentious tales . . . told simply and naturally, yet so vivid and graphic are they, that they charm the reader from the first to the last." The *Outlook* described her as one of the best American short-story writers, while the Chicago *Tribune* noted: "Mrs. Higginson has shown a breadth of treatment and knowledge of the everlasting human verities that equals much of the best work of France."

H.'s poetry appeared in magazines such as *Atlantic*, *Harper's*, and *Scribner's*, and in the columns of many Pacific Coast and eastern newspapers. Two of her most popular poems were "God's Creed" and "Four Leaf Clover." Many of her poems were set to music and performed by singers such as Caruso, McCormack, and Calve. The vivid imagery and singing quality of her poetry were achieved through diligence—she often rewrote a dozen times—and keen observation of nature. Many poems deal with theme of the Pacific Northwest, and several, such as "The Grande Ronde Valley" and "The Evergreen Pine," are specifically about Oregon.

H.'s only published novel, *Mariella, of Out West* (1904), presents a young girl facing a hard frontier farming life, the economic boom of 1888–89, and the proposals of men who represent a variety of social backgrounds. The novel conveys a strong feeling for nature coupled with a sense of piety and spirituality. *Alaska, the Great Country* (1908), H.'s last book, is a combination of guide book, history, and romance.

As a writer of poetry, short stories, travel articles, songs, and one novel, H. achieved prominence in the ranks of Pacific Northwest authors and earned national and international recognition for several of her works. The states of Oregon and Washington both claimed her as a daughter, and she was honored in 1931 as Washington's poet laureate. H. realized her life's ambition based on what she termed "the consuming desire to write." As she explained, "It is the only thing I ever really wanted to do."

WORKS: *A Bunch of Western Clover* (1894). *The Flower That Grew in the Sand* (1896). *The Forest Orchid* (1897). *From the Land of the Snow Pearls* (1897). *When the Birds Go North Again* (1898). *The Voice of April-Land, and Other Poems* (1903). *Mariella, of Out West* (1904). *Alaska, the Great Country* (1908). *The Vanishing Race, and Other Poems* (1911).

The papers of Ella Rhoads Higginson are at the Oregon Historical Society, Portland, Oregon.

BIBLIOGRAPHY: Bright, V., in *With Her Own Wings*, Ed. H. K. Smith (1948). Horner, J. B., *Oregon Literature* (1902). Powers, A., *History of Oregon Literature* (1935). Turnbull, G. S., *History of Oregon Newspapers* (1939).

For articles in reference works, see: *AW*.

JEAN M. WARD

Helen MacInnes Highet

B. 7 Oct. 1907, Glasgow, Scotland
Writes under: Helen MacInnes
D. of Donald and Jessica Cecilia Sutherland McInnes; m. Gilbert Highet, 1932

H. earned an M.A. degree at Glasgow University in 1928 and received her diploma in librarianship from University College, London, in 1931. In 1939, she and her husband, a classics professor, left Oxford and settled in New York City. H. adopted a variant spelling of her family surname under which she has published. In addition to her eighteen novels, H. also has published a clever comic play on Ulysses's return, *Home Is the Hunter* (1964).

Ralph Harper in *The World of the Thriller* suggests that crime in detective stories threatens to destroy a portion of society and in spy stories the threat is that civilization will be undermined. The spy genre in America fully emerged with World War II, and H.'s *Above Suspicion* (1941) and *Assignment in Britanny* (1942)—still two of her best books— used contemporary events of the war and successfully established her reputation as a master of the thriller, as the queen of suspense, and as a popular writer of spy novels. Several of her novels have been made into films, and a new H. title predictably is a bestseller. Her audience extends into numerous countries where translations of her work have appeared.

In a MacInnes spy novel, professional agents abound, but interest usually centers on the amateur—an Oxford don, an architect, an artist, a lawyer, a playwright, a music critic—thrust into international intrigue to confront real dangers which are often serious enough to undermine the social structure. David Mennery in *Snare of the Hunter* (1974), Tom Kelso in *Agent in Place* (1976), and Colin Grant in *Prelude to Terror* (1978) illustrate her continued success in portraying the amateur agent effectively.

After World War II, H.'s subject matter involved data still vital and dangerous after the war; later she moved to complex political plots in which communist forces pose threats to individuals' safety and to the security of nations. Although H. has not moved into the elaborate gimmicks of the James Bond novels, readers nevertheless find sinister enemy agents, coded messages, kidnappings, elaborately planned secret meetings, narrow escapes, chases, betrayals, brutal murders, and love affairs—

devices that have made H.'s novels extremely popular over her writing career of nearly forty years. If the situations in her novels do not lead readers to serious self-examination and profound self-judgment, she does often present a character who is apolitical; who staunchly insists that good be recognized as good, evil as evil; and who acts relentlessly from strong beliefs.

Set throughout the world, H.'s novels reflect her extensive travel and careful research. Most reviewers have noted the convincing locales; others have complained that characters frequently are too good, too bad, or too idealistic. At times, multiple subplots and excessive literary and musical allusions weigh down the main story line. A more serious defect is occasional propaganda, which one reviewer of *Message from Málaga* (1971) saw as so marring her work that it is unreadable because "she seems now less concerned to tell a good story than to make an apologia for the United States, assailed by external enemies, riddled from within."

Nevertheless, H. combines adventure, a patriotic struggle against evil forces, individual heroism, and rewards by love in novels read by millions. *Friends and Lovers* (1947) and *Rest and Be Thankful* (1949), her two novels outside the spy genre, were not particularly successful. Her continued popularity has come from her spy novels, in which genre she is, as one reviewer has noted, "such a pro."

WORKS: *Sexual Life in Ancient Rome* by O. Kiefer (translated by Highet, with G. Highet, 1934). *Friederich Engels: A Biography* by G. Mayer (translated by Highet, with G. Highet, 1936). *Above Suspicion* (1941). *Assignment in Brittany* (1942). *While Still We Live* (1944). *Horizon* (1946). *Friends and Lovers* (1947). *Rest and Be Thankful* (1949). *Neither Five Nor Three* (1951). *I and My True Love* (1953). *Pray for a Brave Heart* (1955). *North from Rome* (1958). *Assignment: Suspense* (1961). *Decision at Delphi* (1961). *The Venetian Affair* (1963). *Home Is the Hunter* (1964). *The Double Image* (1966). *The Salzburg Connection* (1968). *Message from Málaga* (1971). *Snare of the Hunter* (1974). *Agent in Place* (1976). *Prelude to Terror* (1978).

BIBLIOGRAPHY: Breit, H., *The Writer Observed* (1956). Fadiman, C., *The Art of Helen MacInnes* (1971). MacInnes, H., Introduction to *Assignment: Suspense* (1961).

For articles in reference works, see: *CB* (Nov. 1967). *20thCAS.*

Other references: *Counterpoint* (1965). *Film Literature Quarterly*, V (1977).

ELIZABETH EVANS

Patricia Highsmith

B. 19 Jan. 1921, Fort Worth, Texas
Writes under: Patricia Highsmith, Claire Morgan
D. of Jay Bernard and Mary Coates Plangman

Both of H.'s natural parents were artists, as was her stepfather, Stanley Highsmith, whom her mother married when H. was three. By the time H. graduated from Barnard in 1942, she had decided to put her creative energy into writing rather than painting. But she still sees with a painter's eye; the landscapes and cityscapes of her crime novels are cleanly drawn and evocative. By 1949 she was able to travel to Europe, where she eventually settled, first in England, later in France.

It has been recognized for some time, especially in Europe, that H. writes crime novels of great psychological acuity. In 1964, Brigid Brophy ranked her with Georges Simenon, and critical opinion has increasingly confirmed Brophy's judgment. H.'s first novel, *Strangers on a Train* (1950), introduced a plot twist of considerable originality: an innocent, decent man meets a man who is evil, or mad, or both, and through this meeting and the collusion of events, the innocent becomes a murderer. *The Blunderer* (1954) repeats this configuration of main characters and lays heavy emphasis on the power of rumor and sensational publicity in modern society. The court of public opinion convicts Walter Stackhouse of a murder he has twice resisted the temptation to commit.

The Talented Mr. Ripley (1955) won the Mystery Writers of America Scroll and the Grand Prix de Littèrature Policière in 1957. It introduced a genuinely fascinating character, Tom Ripley, who also stars with chilling blandness in two later novels. Rarely has an amoral murderer been so likeable, had such good intentions, projected such pathos. Tom, having met Dickie Greenleaf, a man who has or is everything Tom wants, kills Dickie and then becomes him. Tom wears Dickie's clothes and personality until he has acquired sufficient confidence to reassume his own name. Tom's story is a sort of unholy rite-of-passage.

These three novels introduce the main themes which H.'s sixteen crime novels explore and the central plot device on which she rings a number of variations. Several of H.'s novels revolve around an increasingly compulsive relationship between a good and an evil man.

H. never exploits this device for the same thematic purposes twice. In

The Cry of the Owl (1962), the former mental patient and voyeur turns out to be the beleaguered innocent, and the clean-cut American boy is revealed as a natural killer, waiting for the right combination of circumstances to trigger his violence. In *The Two Faces of January* (1964), which was the Crime Writers of England's novel of the year, and *Those Who Walk Away* (1967), it is the innocent who attach themselves to the guilty and, for their own psychological purposes, haunt them. The main theme of *A Dog's Ransom* (1972) is the breakdown of the social institutions meant to protect the decent from predators.

In Tom Ripley, H. created the first of several characters who unite terrible innocence and terrible guilt in one personality. Vic Van Allen's well-earned reputation for being the most long-suffering of upright citizens protects him long enough to commit murder twice, in *Deep Water* (1957). In *This Sweet Sickness* (1960), when David Kelsey retreats into an imaginary life and personality in order to enjoy the success in love that reality has denied him, he begins a slow deterioration into dangerous madness.

One of H.'s major themes, then, is the ease with which a decent man can cross the line into criminality, or a sane one slip into insanity. In H.'s world, society can be counted on to accelerate these disasters in a variety of ways: by protecting the guilty, harassing the innocent, brutalizing prisoners, enjoying innuendo, wallowing in sensationalism, and tolerating terrorism.

H. should not be approached as a mystery or suspense novelist, since there are very few mysteries and little suspense in her books. In the service of plot, her police frequently behave like idiots and sometimes her protagonists' actions are incomprehensible. Anthony Boucher noted that two of her novels were too long, and it is a charge that could be leveled at many of them. At her best, however, she is a sensitive chronicler of psychological stress and deterioration, and a clear-eyed observer of social tragedy.

WORKS: *Strangers on a Train* (1950; film version, 1951). *The Price of Salt* (1952). *The Blunderer* (1954). *The Talented Mr. Ripley* (1955; film version, *Purple Noon*, 1961). *Deep Water* (1957). *A Game for the Living* (1958). *Miranda the Panda Is on the Veranda* (with D. Sanders, 1958). *This Sweet Sickness* (1960). *The Cry of the Owl* (1962). *The Glass Cell* (1964). *The Two Faces of January* (1964). *The Story-Teller* (English title, *A Suspension of Mercy*, 1965). *Plotting and Writing Suspense Fiction* (1966). *Those Who Walk Away* (1967). *The Tremor of Forgery* (1969). *Ripley Under Ground* (1970). *The Snail Watcher, and Other Stories* (English title, *Eleven*, 1970). *A Dog's Ransom* (1972). *Little Tales of Misogyny* (in German, 1974; in English, 1977). *Ripley's*

Game (1974). *The Animal Lover's Book of Beastly Murder* (1975). *Edith's Diary* (1977). *The Boy Who Followed Ripley* (1980).

BIBLIOGRAPHY: Brophy, B., *Don't Never Forget* (1966).

For articles in reference works, see: *Contemporary Novelists*, Ed. J. Vinson (1976). *WA*.

Other references: *London Magazine* (June 1969; June–July 1972). *TLS* (24 Sept. 1971).

CAROL CLEVELAND

Laura Keane Zametkin Hobson

B. 18 June 1900, New York City
Wrote under: Peter Field, Laura Z. Hobson
D. of Adella Kean and Michael Zametkin; m. Thayer Hobson, 1930

Most of H.'s childhood was spent on Long Island with her mother and father, a Russian émigré. Stefan Ivarin, the hero of her 1964 novel *First Papers*, closely resembles her father, who felt he must earn the right to his naturalization papers as a liberal editor of a Yiddish newspaper and an adamant labor leader. The warm portrait of the Ivarin family is simultaneously accurately detailed and sentimental in its evocation of the lower–East Side life as it moved from the relative calm at the turn of the century to the exciting, overcrowded pre–World War I period.

H.'s background in advertising and publishing greatly influenced her fiction. She worked as an advertising copywriter, as a reporter with the New York *Evening Post*, and, until 1940, as promotion director of *Time*, as well as writing short stories for popular magazines such as *Collier's*, the *Ladies' Home Journal*, *McCall's*, and *Cosmopolitan*. With her husband, H. wrote two westerns. Divorced in 1935, she lived with her adopted sons Michael and Christopher in New York City, where she has continued to contribute to popular magazines and newspapers as well as to publish short fiction throughout her career as a novelist.

H.'s first adult novel written on her own, *The Trespassers* (1943), establishes the liberal tone and controversial subject matter of all of her work. The double plot involves both a love story and a moral stand on the part of a strong, successful woman and a powerful radio tycoon. H. is quite adept at presenting the minutia of the well-to-do New York liberal, including the psychological intricacies of the male/female relationship as the lovers take opposing sides on the issue of the quota system that prevented refugees from immigrating to the U.S. One of the fascinating aspects of H.'s fiction is the consistent appearance of a strong-willed liberal female career woman who endangers her love relationship by supporting a cause—in this case the liberalization of the immigration laws.

Gentleman's Agreement (1947) analyzes the social and economic effects of anti-Semitism by tracing the experience of Phil Green, a Gentile magazine writer, as he pretends he is a Jew to gather material for a series on anti-Semitism. H. dramatizes so sharply the pain caused by anti-Semitism in the lives of Phil Green and those involved in his research that the reader identifies with and understands the subtle permeation of prejudice throughout the American culture, particularly in the liberal eastern establishment. The weakest element of the novel is the formulaic melodrama of the love relationship between Phil Green and Kathy Lacey, his editor's niece.

H.'s most successful novel, *Gentleman's Agreement* sold millions of copies and was translated into many languages. The film version received the New York Film Critics Award and the Academy Award for best picture of 1947. The effects of the notoriety surrounding the literary success, including the Hollywood ordeal, supplied much of the subject matter and insight for H.'s 1951 novel, *The Celebrity*.

H.'s fictional concerns reflect her personal zeal for tolerance and understanding. Her novels are for the most part propaganda novels and suffer artistically from the strength of the message overpowering the style. But H. is an effective storyteller and *Gentleman's Agreement*, though somewhat dated, can still succeed in creating a sharp awareness of the insidiousness and pain of bigotry.

WORKS: *Dry Gulch Adams* (with T. Hobson, 1934). *Outlaws Three* (with T. Hobson, 1934). *A Dog of His Own* (1941). *The Trespassers* (1943). *Gentleman's Agreement* (1947; film version, 1947). *The Other Father* (1950). *The Celebrity* (1951). *First Papers* (1964). *I'm Going to Have a Baby* (1967). *The Tenth Month* (1971). *Consenting Adult* (1975). *Over and Above* (1979).

BIBLIOGRAPHY: For articles in reference works, see: *CA*, 17–20 (1976). *CB* (Sept. 1947). *20thCAS*.

Other references: Chicago *Sun Book-Week* (2 March 1947). *Life* (27 Nov. 1964). *NYHTB* (9 March 1947; 8 Nov. 1964). *SatR* (27 Feb. 1965). *Time* (29 May 1950; 9 Nov. 1953).

SUZANNE ALLEN

Marietta Holley

B. 16 July 1836, Jefferson County, New York; d. 1 March 1926, Jefferson
County, New York
Wrote under: Samantha Allen, Jemyma, Joshia Allen's Wife
D. of John Milton and Mary Taber Holley

The youngest of seven children, H. was born on the family farm where
she lived her entire life. Financial difficulties ended her formal education at fourteen, but she maintained a lifelong fondness for reading. In
the 1870s, she augmented her family's modest income by teaching piano
lessons. Always inordinately shy, she was fifty years old before she left
Jefferson County for the first time. Her shyness eventually prevented
her from accepting invitations to read her work in public or to address
the leading feminist reformers of the day. After the death of her parents, she lived alone with her unmarried sister, Sylphina, who died in
1915. Nothing about her private life reflects the fact that she was a celebrated humorist whose popularity rivaled Mark Twain's.

Although she initially wrote and published poetry under the pseudonym Jemyma, her contributions to the American vernacular-humor tradition began with *My Opinions and Betsey Bobbet's* (1873). H. created
in Samantha Allen, her commonsensical persona, an ideal spokesperson
for her primary theme: women's rights. H. made relatively unpopular
feminist ideas more acceptable by grounding them in the domestic perspective of a farm wife and stepmother. Even Samantha's nom de plume,
Josiah Allen's Wife, served as an ironic comment on women's subordinate social, political, and economic status.

Two antagonists to Samantha's feminism appear in the novel: Josiah
Allen and Betsey Bobbet. Josiah's views are suffused with sentimentality
and male egoism, while Betsey Bobbet, an aging spinster, holds that
woman's only sphere is marriage. Although Betsey soon disappeared
from H.'s work, Josiah continued as a comic foil to Samantha's feminism and common sense.

For her second novel, *Josiah Allen's Wife as a P. A.* [Promiscuous
Advisor] *and P. I.* [Private Investigator]: *Samantha at the Centennial*
(1877), H.'s publisher, Elisha Bliss, supplied her with extensive material
about the Centennial Exposition in Philadelphia. Thus began the practice
that became characteristic of H.'s humor; she wrote realistic descriptions

of places she never visited in person. The travel motif gave Samantha increased opportunity to expound upon a variety of feminist issues, in-including women's right to privacy, and to celebrate the wide range of talents displayed in the Woman's Pavillion at the Exposition.

In *My Wayward Pardner; or, My Trials with Josiah, America, the Widow Bump, and etcetery* (1880), inspired by an open letter from the women of Utah to the women of the U.S., H. responded to another contemporary issue, polygamy. She dramatized the abuses of polygamy by having Josiah, under the influence of a Mormon deacon, flirt with a widow. Although we never seriously believe Josiah will take a second wife, H. came perilously close to destroying the strong family unit that served as the basis for Samantha's domestic feminism.

H.'s fourth novel, *Sweet Cicely* (1885), dramatized the plight of women who married intemperate men. The novel was influenced by H.'s correspondence with Frances Willard, head of the Women's Christian Temperance Union, and it echoed the sentimental tone of temperance tracts. Because it dealt extensively with women's legal status, it was a great favorite of the feminist leaders; Susan B. Anthony wrote H. to tell her of the pleasure the novel gave her. It was not, however, a popular success.

In contrast, her next novel, *Samantha at Saratoga; or, Racin' after Fashion* (1887), was H.'s most popular work. It features Samantha and Josiah vacationing at the country's most fashionable resort, Saratoga. There H. attacks, through humor, society's preoccupation with the genteel values that were antithetical to her goals of full political and economic equality for women.

Between 1887 and 1914, H. wrote fourteen more humorous novels that addressed a variety of social issues, ranging from women's role in the Methodist church to American foreign policy. None of these, however, enjoyed the success of *Samantha at Saratoga*, and in many the quality of her humor declined. Nonetheless, H. made important contributions to the American vernacular-humor tradition and to the feminist movement. No other humorist made the opponents of feminism the targets of her humor, and no other feminist used humor as her primary weapon for furthering the women's rights movement. She gave to American literature one of its strongest and most eloquent heroines of the 19th c., and she was influential in making feminist principles acceptable to a wide audience of women.

WORKS: *My Opinions and Betsey Bobbet's: Designed As a Beacon Light, to Guide Women to Life, Liberty, and the Pursuit of Happiness, but Which May*

Be Read by Members of the Sterner Sect, without Injury to Themselves or the Book. (1873). *Joshia Allen's Wife as a P. A. and P. I.: Samantha at the Centennial. Designed As a Bright and Shining Light, to Pierce the Fogs of Error and Injustice That Surround Society and Josiah, and to Bring More Clearly to View the Path That Leads Straight on to Virtue and Happiness* (1877). *Betsey Bobbet: A Drama* (1880). *The Lament of the Mormon Wife: A Poem* (1880). *My Wayward Pardner; or, My Trials with Josiah, America, the Widow Bump, and etcetery* (1880). *Miss Richard's Boy, and Other Stories* (1883). *Sweet Cicely; or, Josiah Allen As a Politician* (1885). *Miss Jones' Quilting* (1887). *Poems* (1887). *Samantha at Saratoga; or, Racin' after Fashion* (1887). *Samantha Among the Brethren* (1890). *The Widder Doodle's Courtship, and Other Sketches* (1890). *Samantha on the Race Problem* (1892). *Tirzah Ann's Summer Trip, and Other Sketches* (1892). *Samantha at the World's Fair* (1893). *Samantha Among the Colored Folks* (1894). *Josiah's Alarm, and Abel Perry's Funeral* (1895). *Samantha in Europe* (1895). *Samantha at the St. Louis Exposition* (1904). *Around the World with Josiah Allen's Wife* (1905). *Samantha vs. Josiah: Being the Story of a Borrowed Automobile and What Came of It* (1906). *Samantha on Children's Rights* (1909). *Josiah's Secret: A Play* (1910). *Samantha at Coney Island and a Thousand Other Islands* (1911). *Samantha on the Woman Question* (1913). *Josiah Allen on the Woman Question* (1914).

BIBLIOGRAPHY: Blair, W., *Horse Sense in American Humor: From Benjamin Franklin to Ogden Nash* (1962). Blyley, K. G., "M. H." (Ph.D. diss., Univ. of Pittsburgh, 1936). Curry, J. A., "Women As Subjects and Writers of Nineteenth-Century American Humor" (Ph.D. diss., Univ. of Michigan, 1975). Morris, L. A. "Women Vernacular Humorists in Nineteenth-Century America: Ann Stephens, Frances Whitcher, and M. H." (Ph.D. diss., Univ. of California, Berkeley, 1978).

For articles in reference works, see: *AA. AW. DAB*, V, 1. *NAW* (article by M. Langworthy). *NCAB*, 9.

Other references: *Critic* (Jan. 1905).

LINDA A. MORRIS

Pauline Elizabeth Hopkins

B. *1895, Portland, Maine; d. 23 Aug. 1930, Cambridge, Massachusetts*
Wrote under: *Sarah A. Allen (?), Pauline Elizabeth Hopkins*
D. of *William A. and Sarah A. Allen Hopkins (?)*

H. was educated in the public schools of Boston. Before she was graduated from the Girls' High School she had won a prize of ten dollars in gold, offered by the Congregational Publishing Society of Boston, for the best essay on "The Evils of Intemperance and Their Remedies." Initially she aspired to be a playwright and in 1879 wrote the musical drama *Slaves' Escape; or, The Underground Railroad*, also known as *Peculiar Sam*. Another play, *One Scene from the Drama of Early Days*, based on the biblical story of Daniel, was also written in this period.

From 1892 to 1895, she worked as a stenographer and eventually won a civil service appointment to the Bureau of Statistics on the Massachusetts Decennial Census, where she worked from 1895 to 1899. In May 1900, she resumed her literary career with a short story in the inaugural issue of *The Colored American Magazine*.

By May of 1903, she had become the literary editor of the magazine and contributed many short stories and essays, one series of twelve biographical articles on "Famous Men of the Negro Race," and another series on "Famous Women of the Negro Race." Two of her novels, *Winona: A Tale of Negro Life in the South and Southwest* and *Of One Blood; or, The Hidden Self*, were serialized in the magazine in 1902. Another serialized novel, *Hagar's Daughter*, was apparently also written by H., under the pen name Sarah A. Allen.

Because of ill health, H. left *The Colored American*, which had moved to New York, in 1904, and returned to the stenographic profession, this time at the Massachusetts Institute of Technology. Her only literary endeavor after this was a series of articles, "Dark Races of the Twentieth Century," which appeared in *The Voice of the Negro* from December 1904 through July 1905.

Contending Forces (1900), H.'s only novel published in book form, is a romance written in the typical genteel style common at the turn of the century. The plot centers on four young people in Boston who fall in love and, in spite of calamities, tragedies, and a complicated series of events, end up happily married and in possession of a lost family fortune. The "contending forces" in the novel are those problems and injustices which Afro-Americans encountered both in the North and in the South after the Civil War, such as the lack of political power, the difficulty in obtaining jobs, and, most serious, the lynchings which were such a common occurrence in the South. In her frequently didactic style she refers often to the inevitable, and desirable, mixing of the races through marriage. Mysticism and other psychic phenomena are important in the novel, existing concurrently with staunch, traditional Christianity. In the preface she speaks of herself as "one of the proscribed race" and frequently uses the terms "inferior" and "superior" when referring to the black race and the white race, respectively.

The serialized novels and numerous short stories share a similar style and subject matter; almost all have a strong mystical element, and many deal with interracial love and marriage. Many of her essays are biographical with an obvious didactic tone, and she invarably points out that perseverance and hard work have resulted in the various individuals' success. In an essay in *The Colored American* of June 1900, she advocates limited suffrage for women.

As one of the first black women writers H. has a secure niche among the "Talented Tenth" of the Negro race, as W. E. B. DuBois designates the Afro-American middle class of his day. Hers were not explicitly novels of protest, of which there were none at the turn of the century. She writes only of the black middle class and its problems. Her descriptive prose is often excessively florid, and when writing in dialect she falls short of authentic reproduction. Nonetheless, she occupies a unique place in the Afro-American literary heritage as a woman who did no less herself than what she expected of her readers.

WORKS: *Contending Forces: A Romance Illustrative of Negro Life North and South* (1900).

The papers of Pauline Elizabeth Hopkins are at Fisk University Library, Nashville, Tennessee.

BIBLIOGRAPHY: Bone, R., *The Negro Novel in America* (1965). Gloster, H., *Negro Voices in American Fiction* (1948). Loggins, V., *The Negro Author: His Development in America to 1900* (1964).

For articles in reference works, see: *Black American Writers Past and Present*, T. G. Rush, C. F. Myers, and E. S. Arata (1975).

Other references: *The Colored American Magazine* (Jan. 1901). *Phylon* (Spring 1972).

MARILYN LAMPING

Julia Ward Howe

B. 27 May 1819, New York City; d. 17 Oct. 1910, Newport, Rhode Island
D. of Samuel and Julia Rush Cutler Ward; m. Samuel Gridley Howe, 1843

H. was born into a wealthy New York City family. A combination of tutors and private schools provided H. with an excellent education in literature and the Romance languages. She later taught herself German and studied the German philosophers. During her sheltered childhood and youth, her only vent for her emotions was the writing of religious poetry. H.'s life of seclusion ended when she married Howe, the director of the Perkins Institute for the Blind. She bore six children in sixteen years.

Throughout the 1850s and 1860s, H. struggled to establish a literary career despite her husband's disapproval. She felt required to publish her first book of verse, *Passion Flowers* (1854), anonymously. The poems, regular in meter and rhyme, vary in theme and purpose. *Passion Flowers* contains a number of powerful emotional poems with themes of conflict, disappointment, and inadequacy. Although some of the poems in *Words for the Hour* (1857) continue to reflect H.'s inner turmoil and unhappiness, most of the verses are conventional in tone. *Words for the Hour* introduces what was to become H.'s primary poetic form: commemorative verses designed to celebrate a public event or notable personality. *Later Lyrics* (1866) contains a combination of sentimental, conventional, and public verse. H.'s final book of poetry, *From Sunset Ridge* (1898), reprints some of her early poems in addition to publishing new commemorative verse.

Other writing ventures included articles for the abolitionist newspaper *Commonwealth*, a brief stint as editor of *Northern Lights*, two travel books, travel letters to the New York *Tribune*, two wordy and unsuccessful plays, and a series of philosophical essays designed to be read as parlor lectures. H.'s one substantial literary success was the publication of her "Battle Hymn of the Republic," in the *Atlantic Monthly* (February 1862). The poem gained increasing popularity as the century progressed, but H.'s publishers forced her to recognize that the audience for her poetry was dwindling. By 1870, H. was casting around for other ways to express herself.

In 1868, H. embarked on two new projects which departed dramatically from the literary-salonière image which she had cherished for so long. She helped found the new American Woman Suffrage Association. She was an officer of the AWSA and its successor, the National American Woman Suffrage Association, for forty-one years. H. also helped found the New England Woman's Club and served as its president for thirty-eight years.

H.'s feminist theory pervaded her lectures, articles, and even her occasional sermons. It was an articulate blend of conventional notions about women's natural domesticity and moral superiority with more radical views concerning women's spiritual and intellectual equality with men. She saw traditional femininity as a power base which women should strengthen by broader education and work experience. As a means to these ends, she advocated a better distribution of power within the family and the state, opportunities for higher education for women, support for working women, and access to the professions. H. believed that America would achieve the glory to which she aspired during the 19th c. only when women had received the opportunities and respect they deserved.

As her sermons and lectures gained renown, H. came to see herself as a guardian of American virtue. Two of her published lectures—*Modern Society* (1881) and *Is Polite Society Polite?* (1895)—reflect her convictions concerning the manners and morals of the New England elite, combined with a new emphasis on woman's role in maintaining these values.

When, in the 1890s, old age limited H.'s mobility, she began a new career as an essayist for popular and religious magazines. She wrote about everything from "The Joys of Motherhood" to "Lynch Law in the South." The exposure which these publications provided built up a new, gratifying reputation for H. as "Queen of America" and "America's Grand Old Lady."

Although H.'s writings for public consumption were enormous, very few of them were published by a commercial establishment. The small fraction of her work which was published is not her best writing. The reams of articles and lectures which were never published, however, contain lively images and vigorous, convincing arguments. H.'s major contribution was her ability to galvanize thousands of women into cooperative action on behalf of their sex. Her flair for "finding the right word," as she put it, helped improve the status of women for generations, long after her poems and plays were forgotten.

WORKS: *Passion Flowers* (1854). *Words for the Hour* (1857). *The World's Own* (1857). *A Trip to Cuba* (1860). *Later Lyrics* (1866). *From the Oak to the Olive* (1868). *Sex and Education* (edited by Howe, 1874). *Memoir of Dr. Samuel Gridley Howe* (1876). *Modern Society* (1881). *Margaret Fuller, Marchessa Ossoli* (1883). *Is Polite Society Polite?; and Other Essays* (1895). *From Sunset Ridge; Poems, Old and New* (1898). *Reminiscences, 1819–1899* (1899). *Sketches of Representative Women of New England* (edited by Howe, 1904). *At Sunset* (1910).

The papers of Julia Ward Howe are at the Schlesinger Library, Radcliffe College; the Houghton Library, Harvard University; and the Library of Congress.

BIBLIOGRAPHY: Clifford, D., *Mine Eyes Have Seen the Glory: A Biography of Julia Ward Howe* (1979). Elliott, M., *The Eleventh Hour in the Life of Julia Ward Howe* (1911). Hall, F., *The Story of the "Battle Hymn of the*

Republic" (1916). Mead, E., *Julia Ward Howe's Peace Crusade* (1910). Richards L., and M. Elliott, *Julia Ward Howe, 1819–1910* (1915). Richards, L., *Two Noble Lives: Samuel Gridley Howe and Julia Ward Howe* (1911). Tharp, L., *Three Saints and a Sinner* (1956).

For articles in reference works, see: *AA. AW. CAL. DAB,* V, 1. *FPA. NAW* (article by P. S. Boyer). *NCAB,* 1.

MARY H. GRANT

Barbara Howes

B. *1 May 1914,* New York City
D. *of Osborne and Mildred Cox Howes; m. William Jay Smith, 1947*

After graduating from Bennington College, Vermont, H. lived in Italy, England, France, and Haiti; she now lives in North Pownal, Vermont, and frequently visits the West Indies. She has two sons and is divorced. H. is the recipient of many fellowships and awards. Her professional activities have been literary rather than academic; she was editor of *Chimera* magazine from 1943 to 1947.

In her essay in *Poets on Poetry,* H. discusses the poets who have influenced her, her interest in translation and in adapting Old French and other literary forms to contemporary concerns, her purpose in writing, the importance in her work of domestic subject matter and of place, and her distrust of the "snarling little ego," her aversion to writers who "give in to violence and spite."

The constants in H.'s poetry are a detached, restrained tone which carries considerable tight-lipped intensity; an intellectual concern with physical and human nature and with the patterns and principles which underlie and relate their behavior; and a technique which is flexible, controlled, and relatively traditional. Unlike so many contemporary postmodernist poets, she does not write social protest about the women's movement or the Vietnam war, and she is neither confessional nor surrealistic. Also unlike them, she manipulates rather than abandons conventional prosody.

H. chooses many traditional subjects, such as still-life; mythological personages; *objets d'art;* specific persons ("To W. H. Auden on His Fiftieth Birthday"), places ("On a Bougainvillaea Vine at the Summer

Palace," "Views of Oxford Colleges"), and occasions; and nature interpreted by and for civilization: a deer in hunting season "dropped like a monument," a dead toucan described as "a beak with a panache / chucked like an old shell back to the Caribbean."

H.'s most insistent theme is that unrestricted emotion blinds and imprisons if allowed to dominate either life or art. In "The New Leda," H. speaks of the woman dedicated to the god, whether Zeus or Christ: "Her / limbo holds her like a fly in amber, / Beyond the reach of life." In "For an Old Friend" she imagines the friend thinking, "This hullabaloo about life / is not my forte"; in "Radar and Unmarked Cars," she writes ". . . our / Radar / Will hold us True: / We need / Love / At a constant speed." Her aesthetic credo matches the personal one in "Portrait of the Artist": "For dear life some do / Many a hard thing, / Train the meticulous mind / Upon meaning, seek / And find, and yet discard / All that is not of reality's tough rind / . . . To be / Ascetic for life's sake, / Honest and passionate."

The effect of this personal and aesthetic credo on her work is both her poems' strength and their weakness. In a poem like "Still-life: New England" the tone of restrained disgust and assumed indifference is deliberately and successfully used to create horror, the ironic opposite of indifference. But when, in "Dream of a Good Day," H. puts all the action of the poem into conventional romantic dreams of sailing and discovering (i.e., making a poem), which are quite separate from reality, and then uses only the last line to state but not to experience reality ("Then in the colloquial evening to come back to love"), the poem suffers because the honesty is there without the passion.

Yet it is passion which makes her such a disciplined craftsperson. H. speaks of the need to train the eye to notice and the ear to listen, to recognize the necessity of form ("language must have discipline to have meaning"), and to distinguish between the forms of art and journalism. It is this disciplined passion which enables her to make her poetry "a way of life, not just an avocation," a way in which "one orders and deepens one's experience, and learns to understand what is happening in oneself and in others."

Overall, H.'s poetry strongly continues the "Apollonian" strain of Eliot, Stevens, and Wilbur, rather than the "Dionysian" strain of Whitman and Williams. But though she has not quite Eliot's dramatic compression, nor Stevens's mercurial imagination, nor Wilbur's classical balance, her depth of perception, firm ironic tone, and technical control make her a worthy member of their company.

WORKS: *The Undersea Farmer* (1948). *In the Cold Country: Poems* (1954). *Light and Dark: Poems* (1959). *23 Modern Stories* (edited by Howes, 1963). *From the Green Antilles: Writings of the Caribbean* (edited by Howes, 1966). *Looking Up at Leaves* (1966). *The Sea-Green Horse: Short Stories for Young People* (edited by Howes, with G. J. Smith, 1970). *The Blue Garden* (1972). *The Eye of the Heart: Stories from Latin America* (edited by Howes, 1973). *A Private Signal: Poems New and Selected* (1977).

The papers of Barbara Howes are at the Yale University Library, New Haven, Connecticut.

BIBLIOGRAPHY: Bogan, L., *Selected Criticism* (1955). Friedman, N., *Contemporary Poets* (1975). Nemerov, H., ed., *Poets on Poetry* (1966). Untermeyer, L., ed., *Modern American Poetry* (1962).

For articles in reference works, see: *CA*, 9–12 (1974). *Contemporary Poets*, Eds. J. Vinson and D. L. Kirkpatrick (1975). *WA*.

Other references: *Choice* (April 1978). *NYHTB* (15 Nov. 1959). *NYT* (4 April 1954). *SatR* (19 March 1949). *TLS* (10 Feb. 1978).

ALBERTA TURNER

Sophia Hume

B. *1702, Charleston, South Carolina; d. 26 Jan. 1774, London, England*
D. *of Henry and Susanna Bayley Wigington; m. Robert Hume, 1721*

Born to a prosperous landowning family, H. was raised in the Anglican tradition of her father and educated for a life of elegance in high society. She married a lawyer and prominent citizen of Charleston; they had two children. After her husband's death in 1737 and a series of illnesses, she became increasingly preoccupied with religion and the necessity to convert to Quakerism, the religious tradition of her mother and maternal grandmother Mary Fisher (ca. 1623–1698). She subsequently moved to England and joined the Society of Friends.

In 1747, H. returned to Charleston, where in a series of public meetings she reproached the inhabitants for their sinful lives and called them to a life of simplicity as exemplified in Quakerism. In order to spread her concern for their salvation, she published, with the help of fellow Quakers in Philadelphia, *An Exhortation to the Inhabitants of the Province of South Carolina* (1748). This forcefully written but poorly organized appeal admonished Charlestonians to repent, to give up their diversionary, prideful, and ostentatious lives, and to seek good forms of recreation, live simply, and dress modestly. She made a special plea that females cease neglecting their children in their quest for diversion.

Returning to England, H. became a Quaker minister and wrote *A Caution to Such As Observe Days and Times* (1763). In this piece she warned formal Christians, those who "observe days and times," that God may bring them suffering as He did the Jews in order that they learn that His power was in the heart and not the world.

In an attempt to reform the Society of Friends and help stave off the decline in membership, H. published *Extracts from Divers, Antient Testimonies* (1766), a collection of early Quaker writings. In her introduction addressed to ministers, elders, and members of the Society, she urged them not to conform to the ways of the world but to become the "foundation for the church of Christ." In 1767, H. went back to Charleston in an attempt to revive Quakerism there. Unsuccessful, she returned to England, where she died in 1774.

The principal theme of H.'s writing is the call to repentance and nonworldliness which she found exemplified in Quaker life. Through rejection of worldly pleasures one came to enjoy the fruits of the spirit —joy, love, and peace—the highest of all pleasures. The rewards of simplicity, the universality of God's grace, and the indwelling of the Holy Spirit in each person are emphasized in her work. While she maintained a very traditional attitude toward woman's role, her Christian belief spurred her to write and speak publicly in defense of religion.

WORKS: *An Exhortation to the Inhabitants of the Province of South Carolina, to Bring Their Deeds to the Light of Christ, in Their Own Consciences* (1748). *A Caution to Such As Observe Days and Times. To Which Is Added, An Address to Magistrates, Parents, Mistresses of Families etc.* (1763). *Extracts from Divers, Antient Testimonies* (1766). *The Justly Celebrated Mrs. Sophia Hume's Advice* (1769).

BIBLIOGRAPHY: Bowden, J., *The History of the Society of Friends in America*, Vol. I (1850). Woolman, J., *The Journal and Essays of John Woolman*, Ed. A. M. Gummere (1922).

For articles in reference works, see: *NAW* (article by S. V. James).

DANA GREENE

Fannie Hurst

B. 18 Oct. 1889, Hamilton, Ohio; d. 23 Feb. 1968, New York City
D. of Samuel and Rose Koppel Hurst; m. Jacques S. Danielson, 1915

H., daughter of American-born Jews of German descent, was raised and educated in St. Louis, Missouri (B.A. 1909, Washington University). In 1910, eager to observe the working people of whom and for whom she wrote, H. moved to New York City. There she took assorted jobs as saleswoman, actress, and waitress, and started bombarding publications with her fiction. Her marriage to a Russian-born pianist, in which they both pursued separate careers, endured successfully until her husband's death in 1952.

H. became an established writer while still in her twenties. She began as a short-story writer, but she is best remembered for her best-selling novels, especially *Back Street* (1931) and *Imitation of Life* (1933). Her works have been widely translated, and many became successful films.

Back Street is about the beautiful Ray Schmidt, who is mistress to a married man and for over twenty years is confined to the "back streets" of his life. After her lover's death, Ray spends her last few years penniless at a European spa, surviving on the few francs winners at the casino throw to her; she dies alone in her room.

The novel's enormous popularity was due largely to two factors: It appeared during the Depression, when escapist entertainment was assured a large following, and it deals with the especially titillating subject of sex, which H. handles most cleverly. She avoids graphic description, knowing that the lack of it would afford greater excitement for her audience and, therefore, greater readership for her. Although we remain uncertain why the selfish and immature lover is even attractive to the lovely Ray, this is calculated; we are not meant to focus on the relationship, but on Ray, her feelings and responses. She is dominated, used, and ultimately destroyed, yet throughout the reader, perhaps recalling similar trials, identifies and empathizes profoundly.

In Imitation of Life, Beatrice Fay Chipley, widowed mother of a young daughter, sells maple syrup door-to-door with the help of Delilah, a black woman who also has an infant daughter. Beatrice becomes one of the most prominent businesswomen in America, but the novel ends with her realization that she must continue to live an "imitation of life" without a man to love.

Imitation of Life, in rough outline, is a woman's version of the timeless rags-to-riches American success story. But the specific type of irony evident at the conclusion, as well as its stereotyped characterization of the black "mammy" figure, places it solidly in its time. Feminists would be outraged at its underlying philosophy—that, regardless of professional achievements, life must be worthless without what Delilah terms "manlovin'." H.'s audience, however, was attracted by the novel's sympathetic—today we would call it "sentimental"—depiction of the heroine; by its handling of the touchy matter of race relations; and by its "bittersweetness," still one of the recognizable marks of the popular novelist.

In her time, H. was very popular with readers and was scarcely taken seriously by critics. Today she retains our interest primarily because her works are accurate gauges of her contemporary audience's beliefs.

WORKS: *Just around the Corner* (1914). *Every Soul Hath Its Song* (1916). *Land of the Free* (1917). *Gaslight Sonatas* (1918). *Humoresque* (1919). *Back Pay* (1921). *Star Dust* (1921). *The Vertical City* (1922). *Lummox* (1923). *Appassionata* (1926). *Mannequin* (1926). *Song of Life* (1927). *A President Is Born* (1928). *Five and Ten* (1929). *Procession* (1929). *Back Street* (1931; film versions, 1932, 1941, 1961). *Imitation of Life* (1933; film versions, 1934, 1959). *Anitra's Dance* (1934). *No Food with My Meals* (1935). *Great Laughter* (1936). *Hands of Veronica* (1937). *We Are Ten* (1937). *Lonely Parade* (1942). *Hallelujah* (1944). *Any Woman* (1950). *The Man with One Head* (1953). *Anatomy of Me* (1958). *Family!* (1959). *God Must Be Sad* (1961). *Fool—Be Still* (1964).

BIBLIOGRAPHY: For articles in reference works, see: *CA*, 25–28 (1971). *NCAB*, E. *Ohio Authors and Their Books*, Ed. W. Coyle (1962). *20thCA*. *20thCAS*.

Other references: *Arts and Decoration* (Nov. 1935). *Bookman* (May 1929; Aug. 1931). *Mentor* (April 1928). *NYTBR* (25 Jan. 1942). *SatR* (Oct. 1937).

ELLEN SERLEN UFFEN

Zora Neale Hurston

B. 7 Jan. 1901, Eatonville, Florida; d. 28 Jan. 1960, Saint Lucie County, Florida
D. of John and Lucy Hurston

Born in the first incorporated black town in America, H. was the only writer in the 1920s and 1930s from a southern background who evaluated her southern exposure, realized the richness of her racial heritage, and built her fiction on it. At age nine, H. lost nearly all of her childhood security when her mother died, and she had to live from relative to relative, deprived of formal schooling, drifting through several domestic jobs.

Supporting herself, H. completed two years at Morgan College in Baltimore and enrolled at Howard University, where her first short fiction was published in a literary journal there. She moved to New York, became secretary to the popular novelist Fannie Hurst, and earned a scholarship to Barnard College, where she studied anthropology under Franz Boas. When she graduated in 1928, Dr. Boas had arranged a fellowship for H. to go south to collect folklore. The result of this southern expedition was *Mules and Men* (1935). Throughout the 1920s H. had continued to write short fiction which had been published in *Opportunity*. Her best efforts were "Spunk," "Sweat," and "The Gilded Six-Bits."

H.'s first novel, *Jonah's Gourd Vine* (1934), a narrative loosely based on the lives of her parents, chronicles the life of John Pearson, an itinerant preacher. Incorporating her knowledge of folklore into her fiction, H. depicts John's second wife as a character reliant on conjure to speed the first wife to an early death and to snare the protagonist quickly into marriage, a marriage which crumbles once he discovers the conjure tactics.

H. is lauded for her utilization of folklore, the ripeness and realism of black dialect, the poetic sermon, and the distinct racial flavor of *Jonah's Gourd Vine*. However, critics have faulted plot construction, characterization, and dialogue. Additionally, much of the criticism of H.'s fiction is the result of her choice of setting—Eatonville, Florida, a black town. H.'s critics accuse her of neglecting to confront the problems of racism which constituted a daily issue in the livelihood of blacks in the 1930s and 1940s. H. writes in her autobiography that what she wanted to write was a story about a man, but from what she had read and heard,

"Negroes were supposed to write about the Race problem. My interest lies in what makes a man or woman do such-and-so regardless of his color."

H.'s second novel, *Their Eyes Were Watching God* (1937), also set in Eatonville, is frequently acclaimed her best novel. It is the story of Janie, a young black woman who searches for happiness, self-realization, and love; she is a woman who refuses to settle for less than her own realistic appraisal of what love should be. After the death of her second husband, when Janie is forty years old, she marries a man much younger than she, who is unpretentiously one of the "folk," who loves and wants her without imposing restrictions on her. In the Florida Everglades where Janie and Teacake move after their marriage, they experience a few years of happiness working in the fields together, and Janie is serenely content being a part of the folk culture. Somewhat melodramatically, the novel ends, after a hurricane destroys the Everglades community and Teacake is bitten by a mad dog. Jane is forced to shoot and to kill Teacake because, mentally deranged by rabies, he tries to kill her. The characterization of Janie is excellent, and plot structure, depiction of the folk culture, and the use of black dialect are all equally fine.

H.'s last novel, *Seraph on the Suwanee* (1948), the only one in which a southern white woman is the protagonist, has received little critical attention. Nevertheless, Arvay Henson is the second of H.'s fully delineated protagonists. More than any other woman in H.'s fiction, Arvay offers a psychologically complete view of the complex entanglement of forces which impinge on the southern rural woman and make her life, both externally and internally, a continuous struggle.

From the early autobiographical story, "Drenched in Light" (1924), to her last novel, H. based her fiction on personal experience. The inclusion of folk elements gives a uniquely southern flavor to character and setting. As a writer who had grown up in the South, H. recognized the aesthetics of that particular setting and culture and utilized them as no other black writer of the 1920s or 1930s did.

WORKS: *Jonah's Gourd Vine* (1934). *Mules and Men* (1935). *Their Eyes Were Watching God* (1937). *Tell My Horse* (1938). *Moses, Man of the Mountain* (1939). *Dust Tracks on a Dirt Road* (1942). *Seraph on the Suwanee* (1948).

BIBLIOGRAPHY: Bone, R., *The Negro Novel in America* (1958). Hemenway, R., *Zora Neale Hurston: A Literary Biography* (1977). Huggins, N., *Harlem Renaissance* (1971). Hughes, L., *The Big Sea* (1940). Turner, D., *In a Minor Chord* (1971). Young, J., *Black Writers of the Thirties* (1973).

For articles in reference works, see: *CB* (May 1942; April 1960). *20thCA.*
20thCAS.

Other references: *Black World* (Aug. 1972). *NYHTB* (22 Nov. 1943).
NYT (2 Feb. 1960). *SBL* (Winter 1974).

JOYCE PETTIS

Inez Haynes Irwin

B. *2 March 1873, Rio de Janeiro, Brazil; d. 30 Sept. 1970*
D. *of Gideon and Emma Jane Hopkins Haynes; m. Rufus Hamilton Gillmore,*
1897; m. William Henry Irwin, 1916

I. was educated in Boston schools and attended Radcliffe College from
1897 to 1900. At the turn of the century, Radcliffe was a center of suffragist sentiment. Determined to extend this feeling to college alumnae, I.
and Maud Wood Park founded the Massachusetts College Equal Suffrage
Association in 1900. This group expanded into the National College Equal
Suffrage League, an active force in the enfranchisement campaign.

I.'s other feminist activities centered around the more radical wing of
the suffrage movement, the National Woman's Party. Lead by Alice Paul
and Lucy Burns, the party was patterned after the British suffrage movement in its militancy and political tactics. I. was a member of the party's
advisory council; she wrote for the party's publications and was the
party's biographer. *The Story of the Woman's Party* (1921) is flawed by
its lack of objectivity and the failure to mention the other wing of the
suffrage movement, but it is the only record of the party's activities,
other than the stories repeated in I.'s more ambitious work on the history of American women, *Angels and Amazons* (1933).

I.'s first fictional work was published in *Everybody's* in 1904. She then
became a regular contributor to British and American magazines and devoted herself to writing short stories and novels. Other than her feminist
chronicles, I.'s only digressions from these genres occurred during World
War I. Having become the wife of newspaperman Will Irwin after the
death of Gillmore, I. visited the European fronts with her husband. Her
accounts of these visits were printed in the magazines of three countries.

"The Spring Flight" was the O. Henry Memorial Award first-prize
winner in 1924, a puzzling choice, for the story is a quasi-biographical
sketch of William Shakespeare trying to overcome writer's block before

composing *The Tempest*. It is ironic that I. received the highest acclaim for this story, so far removed from her field of expertise.

After a few ventures with highly sentimentalized and simplistic novels about orphaned children and an idealized brother and sister, I. began writing fiction that addressed the issues with which she is now most often associated—those underlying the suffrage movement. Of her feminist fiction, *The Lady of the Kingdoms* (1917) has been undeservedly forgotten. This long novel presents two young heroines, the beautiful and self-assured Southward and the plain and self-effacing Hester. I. uses both heroines to examine the conventional moralities women have been forced into, as well as the unconventional, even "immoral," ones women have chosen for themselves. Though I. may disapprove of the latter roles, she never condemns the women who choose them.

I. published two books dealing with divorce, *Gideon* (1927) and *Gertrude Haviland's Divorce* (1925). The heroine of the latter work is a fat, dull, sloppy woman who has further alienated her husband by being overly absorbed in her children. The book begins as Gertrude receives her husband's request for a divorce, follows her through mental illness, watches her recover as she realizes she is pregnant, and witnesses her transformation into a woman of resolution, intelligence, self-reliance, and new beauty. Her final triumph occurs when she rejects her husband's offer of remarriage; however, this victory is mitigated by the fact that Gertrude now realizes she loves and will marry another man. Also troubling is the assertion that having a baby is enough to end a woman's suffering, an attitude no doubt affected by I.'s failure to have children of her own.

In the 1930s and 1940s, I. returned to sentimental, descriptive novels and wrote upper-class murder mysteries and moralistic children's books. The strongest indictment that may be made against I. comes from these books, the last she wrote. She had run out of good ideas, and no longer had the ability to write strongly, to state issues clearly, and to imagine vital characters. I. apparently decided that those qualities of authorship she still possessed were good enough for children's books. She was a prolific writer whose finest works came early and whose mediocre later works have so thoroughly reduced her reputation as a writer of adult and children's fiction that she is virtually forgotten in these fields. Between 1917 and 1927, however, she wrote several impressively direct novels about divorce and women's roles.

WORKS: *June Jeopardy* (1908). *Maida's Little Shop* (1910). *Phoebe and Ernest* (1910). *Janey* (1911). *Phoebe, Ernest, and Cupid* (1912). *Angel Island*

(1914). *The Ollivant Orphans* (1915). *The Californians* (1916). *The Lady of the Kingdoms* (1917). *The Happy Years* (1919). *The Native Son* (1919). *Maida's Little House* (1921). *Out of the Air* (1921). *The Story of the Woman's Party* (1921). *Gertrude Haviland's Divorce* (1925). *Maida's Little School* (1926). *Gideon* (1927). *P. D. F. R.* (1928). *Confessions of a Business-man's Wife* (1931). *Family Circle* (1931). *Youth Must Laugh* (1932). *Angels and Amazons* (1933). *Strange Harvest* (1934). *Murder Masquerade* (1935). *The Poison Cross* (1936). *Good Manners for Girls* (1937). *A Body Rolled Downstairs* (1938). *Maida's Little Island* (1939). *Maida's Little Camp* (1940). *Many Murders* (1941). *Maida's Little Village* (1942). *Maida's Little House-boat* (1943). *Maida's Little Theatre* (1946). *The Women Swore Revenge* (1946). *Maida's Little Cabins* (1947). *Maida's Little Zoo* (1949). *Maida's Little Lighthouse* (1951). *Maida's Little Hospital* (n.d.). *Maida's Little Farm* (n.d.). *Maida's Little House Party* (n.d.). *Maida's Little Treasure Hunt* (n.d.). *Maida's Little Tree House* (n.d.).

BIBLIOGRAPHY: For articles in reference works, see: *NCAB, F. 20thCA. 20thCAS.*

LYNNE MASEL-WALTERS
HELEN LOEB

Helen Maria Fiske Hunt Jackson

B. *15 Oct. 1830, Amherst, Massachusetts; d. 12 Aug. 1885, San Francisco, California*
Wrote under: *"H. H.," Saxe Holm, Helen Hunt Jackson, Helen Jackson, "Marah," "No Name," "Rip Van Winkle"*
D. *of Nathan Welby and Deborah Vinal Fiske; m. Edward Bissell Hunt, 1852; m. William Sharpless Jackson, 1875*

The elder and more impetuous of two surviving children of a minister-turned-professor and his devout and educated wife, J. was raised in an atmosphere of learning, piety, and enforced propriety. Although her parents both succumbed to tuberculosis while J. was a teenager, she continued to attend private schools until 1850. J. married then-Lieutenant Hunt and began the restless life of an army wife and mother of two sons, one of whom survived infancy. In 1863 J.'s husband was killed testing his newly invented torpedo. When, two years later, J.'s son died, she turned to writing poetry as an outlet for her grief.

J.'s early poems won her recognition from the influential Thomas Wentworth Higginson; her subsequent prolific periodical publications gathered a wide popular audience and critical praise, even from Emerson. J. supported herself and traveled widely on the profits of her pen. Her generally pious and sentimental treatments of death, love, and nature themes date much of her poetry, but many of her *Verses* (1870) and *Sonnets and Lyrics* (1886) can still be appreciated for their skillful technique and use of language.

J.'s first prose efforts were travel pieces, enriched by her flair for observation of detail in interior decoration and natural scenery. Her descriptions of unconventional people encountered along her way reveal the lingering influence of J.'s narrowly proper upbringing.

While wintering in Colorado Springs in 1873, J. met Jackson, a Quaker banker and railroad promoter, whom she married two years later. J. continued writing and experimented in prose fiction. Her passion for anonymity continued; "Saxe Holm" aroused popular curiosity as the author of two series of J.'s short stories (1874 and 1876), and J. wrote two novels, *Mercy Philbrick's Choice* (1876) and *Hetty's Strange History* (1877), for her publisher's "No Name" series. These works, set in New England, focus upon strong women characters dealing with complications wrought by love, death, family responsibility, and illness. For example, Draxy Miller, a memorable "Saxe Holm" heroine, arranges her sick father's retirement, marries a minister, and takes over his pulpit after his death, all to the approval of the small-town community.

In 1879 J. heard Suzette "Bright Eyes" LaFlesche, an Omaha Indian, describe the wrongs suffered by Native Americans. Aroused by a righteous passion for justice for Indians comparable to abolitionist fervor, J. produced her most memorable works, and abandoned her pseudonyms to speak her mind. In *A Century of Dishonor* (1881), J. also abandoned fiction, writing impassioned history documenting several heinous examples of governmental perfidy practiced upon Indian tribes. J.'s strong indictment of the U.S. government and, by extension, its acquiescent populace, delighted reformers and enraged some critics who believed J.'s lack of objectivity damaged her case.

J. was most appalled by the wrongful treatment inflicted upon California's Mission Indians. She and Abbot Kinney served as official investigators, producing a *Report on the Conditions and Needs of the Mission Indians* (1883). J. was determined to publicize the situation of California's natives and, since government documents reach few, she wrote *Ramona* (1884), a romance involving a half-Indian girl raised on a

Spanish hacienda who elopes with an Indian, and subsequently shares his life as victim of land fraud and prejudice. *Ramona* has enjoyed continuing popularity in over three hundred reprintings, but unfortunately had little real impact upon Indian policy. Perhaps the outrage J. intended to arouse was lost in local color and drowned in tears, the very elements of *Ramona*'s story that have encouraged its frequent retelling in local pageants and national media productions.

Although most modern critics fault J.'s obvious sentimentality, her works are important, both as an index for the taste of her times as well as for their focus upon women who act to determine their destiny. Marriage is not the end of their stories; J. shows them coping with widowhood, poverty, infidelity, and work. The presentation of Native Americans in her works deserves some criticism for its "noble savage" inclination and implications of Indian passivity, but the aim of her writing, to reach and arouse a white audience susceptible to such stereotypes, must be considered in any evaluation. Readers may weep at Ramona's plight, but must still be subconsciously impressed by her strength of purpose.

WORKS: *Bathmendi: A Persian Tale* (1867). *Verses* (1870). *Bits of Travel* (1872). *Bits of Talk about Home Matters* (1873). *Saxe Holm's Stories* (Series 1, 1874). *The Story of Boon* (1874). *Bits of Talk in Verse and Prose for Young Folks* (1876). *Mercy Philbrick's Choice* (1876). *Hetty's Strange History* (1877). *Bits of Travel at Home* (1878). *Nellie's Silver Mine* (1878). *Saxe Holm's Stories* (Series 2, 1878). *Letters from a Cat* (1879). *A Century of Dishonor* (1881). *Mammy Tittleback and Her Family* (1881). *The Training of Children* (1882). *Report on the Conditions and Needs of the Mission Indians* (with A. Kinney, 1883). *Easter Bells* (1884). *Ramona* (1884). *Zeph* (1885). *Glimpses of Three Coasts* (1886). *The Procession of Flowers in Colorado* (1886). *Sonnets and Lyrics* (1886). *Between Whiles* (1887). *My Legacy* (1888). *A Calendar of Sonnets* (1891). *Poems* (1891). *Cat Stories* (1898). *Pansy Billings and Popsy* (1898). *Father Junipero and the Mission Indians* (1902). *Glimpses of California and the Missions* (1902).

Many of the papers of Helen Hunt Jackson are at the Huntington Library, San Marino, California.

BIBLIOGRAPHY: Higginson, T. W., *Contemporaries* (1899). Higginson, T. W., *Short Studies of American Authors* (1906). Odell, R., *H. H. J.* (1939).
For articles in reference works, see: *AA. AW. Appleton's Cyclopaedia of American Biography*, Vol. 3, Eds. J. G. Wilson and J. Fiske (1887). *Authors at Home*, Eds. J. L. and J. B. Gilder (1886). *CAL. DAB*, IX. *Herringshaw's National Library of American Biography*, Vol. 3 (1914). *NAW* (article by T. Wilkins). *Notable Women in History*, Ed. W. J. Abbott (1913). *Twentieth Century Biographical Dictionary of Notable Americans*, Vol. 6, Eds. R. Johnson and J. H. Brown (1904).

Other references: *American Literary Realism* (Summer 1969; Summer 1973). *AL* (Jan. 1931). *American Scholar* (Summer 1941). *Common Ground* (Winter 1946). *NYT* (6 April 1916; 15 May 1928; 7 Oct. 1936). *Southwest Review* (Spring 1959).

HELEN M. BANNAN

Laura Riding Jackson

B. 16 Jan. 1901, New York City
Writes under: Laura Riding Gottschalk, Laura Riding Jackson, Barbara Rich, Laura Riding
D. of Nathaniel S. and Sarah Edersheim Reichenthal; m. Louis Gottschalk, 1920; m. Schuyler Jackson, 1941

J., raised in a nonreligious Jewish household actively espousing socialism, is best known for her strikingly original poetry, although she has also written criticism, novels, and biographical sketches. She attended Cornell University, married Louis Gottschalk (divorced, 1925), then spent thirteen years abroad. She and Robert Graves were companions, establishing the Seizin Press in 1927 in Majorca. In 1939 they came to America, where Laura met and married Schuyler Jackson (poet, farmer, contributing editor of *Time*). For almost thirty years, she and her husband worked on a reference work called the *Dictionary of Exact Meaning*. Jackson died in 1970, however, and the work is still unfinished.

During the dozen years of J.'s association with Robert Graves, the two collaborated on literary criticism and on one odd, satirical novel, *No Decency Left* (1932). *A Survey of Modernist Poetry* (1927) is a perceptive discussion of innovative techniques in poetry, such as those practiced by E. E. Cummings, Ezra Pound, and T. S. Eliot. It analyzes the shortcomings of "temporary fads" such as Imagism and Georgianism and argues that modern experimental poetry, some of which they condemn to an early death, has been influenced by nonrepresentational art. Poets have too often simply abandoned coherent statement, creating abstract arrangements of emotionally laden phrases and sounds.

J. also shared with Graves an interest in the Greco-Roman world and the status of women in ancient times, as evidenced by her novel *A Trojan*

Ending (1937) and her biographical sketches of famous women, *Lives of Wives* (1939).

Most of J.'s poetry is free verse, with a sensitive use of assonance and repetition and relatively little concern for rhyme. Each poem is a different problem, and each seeks to match sound to sense. In this J. has been compared with Gertrude Stein.

Her poetry is often simultaneously playful and serious. Sometimes there is a trace of condescension toward nonpoetic thinking. In the first stanza of "Further Details," for example, the poet, who presumably arrives at the "higher" truth intuitively and holistically, speaks to the analytical, rational pursuer of knowledge: "The reward of curiosity / In such as you / (Statistician of doubt) / Is increased cause of curiosity. / And the punishment thereof, / To be not a cat."

J. is concerned with mental experience more than with sense experience. She favors philosophical subjects—the coexistence of multiplicity and sameness, the mysterious transformations of life and death, the ambiguous relationship between body and mind, the nature of love. Some readers find her poems obscure, but she implies that is the reader's fault, not hers: "Doom is where I am and I want to make this plain because I know there are people to whom it can be plain" (preface to *Poems: A Joking Word*, 1930). She sometimes combines humor with metaphysical fantasy, as in the delightful creation story, "The Quids." Other poems, like the enigmatic "Lucrece and Nara," convey some eerie insight quite beyond rational explanation. In 1943, Robert Graves referred to J. as writing in "the supreme female I, the original Triple Muse, who in her original Olympian mountain was mother of Apollo, *not* his chorus-girl troupe."

Her poetry has never achieved widespread popularity with general readers, but it is an important part of the modern flight from the conventions of 19th-c. romanticism. Her diction shows a deliberate avoidance of traditional sentiments, a bare minimum of imagery and metaphor, a tendency to abstraction. The vocabulary is often deceptively simple, yet the reader must intuit meaning from limited clues. At its worst, this may require sheer guesswork. At its best, it achieves a delicate precision and economy in the expression of complex meanings.

WORKS: *The Close Chaplet* (1926). *Voltaire: A Biographical Fantasy* (1927). *A Survey of Modernist Poetry* (with R. Graves, 1927). *Contemporaries and Snobs* (1928). *Love As Love, Death As Death* (1928). *Poems: A Joking Word* (1930). *Twenty Poems Less* (1930). *Laura and Francesco* (1931). *No Decency Left* (with R. Graves, 1932). *The Life of the Dead* (1933). *Poet: A Lying*

Word (1933). *Four Unposted Letters to Catherine* (1933). *Americans* (1934). *A Trojan Ending* (1937). *Collected Poems* (1938). *Lives of Wives* (1939).

BIBLIOGRAPHY: For articles in reference works, see: *Contemporary American Authors*, F. B. Millet (1944). *20thCA* (under "L. R."). *20thCAS*.
  Other references: *CQ* (Spring 1971). *Poetry* (Aug. 1932, May 1939).

KATHERINE SNIPES

Shirley Jackson

B. *14 Dec. 1919, San Francisco, California; d. 8 Aug. 1965, North Bennington, Vermont*
D. *of Leslie H. and Geraldine Bugbee Jackson; m. Stanley Edgar Hyman, 1940*

Most of J.'s early life was spent in Burlingame, California, which she later used as the setting of her first novel, *The Road through the Wall* (1948). J. was interested in writing from childhood; she won a poetry prize at twelve, and while in high school began to keep a diary which recorded her writing progress.

J. was troubled early in life with a sense of inferiority. Her family moved to Rochester, New York, in 1933, and she attended the University of Rochester but left after a year because of depression. At home she practiced her craft, writing a consistent one thousand words a day. She entered Syracuse University in 1937, publishing in the student literary magazines and founding, with Stanley Hyman, the magazine *The Spectre*. With Hyman, who was to become a noted literary critic, J. had four children while both continued active literary careers.

"The Lottery" (1948) received mixed reactions when it appeared in *The New Yorker*, but many critics believed that this one short story would give J. lasting fame. She regarded her short stories as "tales" in the sense of Hawthorne's usage. J. writes about the hidden evil of the human mind, and her themes often concern evil disguised as good. "The Lottery" is a return to the concept of the Fisher King, the human who must be sacrificed for community good in order that the crops might prosper.

Hangsaman (1951), regarded as one of the best of J.'s early novels, is her first lengthy study of mental disturbance, in this case schizophrenia. The novel deals with the gradual breakdown of a brilliant seventeen-year-old girl, Natalie Waite, who, unable to cope with her first experience away from home at college, creates for herself a friend, Tony, with whom she can feel acceptance. The book comes to an optimistic conclusion, and Natalie will, supposedly, come to more reasonable terms with existence.

Life among the Savages (1953) and *Raising Demons* (1957), two collections of domestic chronicles, and J.'s uncollected articles, mainly from women's magazines, form the humorous side of J.'s work. She wrote realistically and with tongue in cheek of her own and her husband's eccentricities and of the problems of raising four children. Some of the incidents such as "The Night We All Had Grippe" and "Charles" have become classics of domestic humor. The Hymans tended to regard these works as "potboilers," but they give voice to the humorous side of J.'s character.

We Have Always Lived in the Castle (1962) was named one of the year's ten best novels by *Time* magazine. The play production, however, ran only four days on Broadway. The action takes place around the old Blackwood home, in which four people have died of arsenic poisoning. The survivors are Uncle Julian, an invalid, twelve-year-old Mary Katherine (Merricat), and her twenty-two-year-old sister Constance. Constance is tried and acquitted of the crime due to lack of evidence. The novel opens six years after the crime and follows mainly the characterization of Merricat, who turns out to be the murderer. Merricat is another of J.'s delineations of the psychologically unstable personality.

J. develops a broad topic range in her fiction, and her place as a competent and professional storyteller is well established. Her humor can be purely for fun or can run to black humor. She recognizes the existence of human evil with a blitheness that increases rather than decreases the sting. The psychological studies are completely plausible in the reasoning which they depict. J.'s style is sharp and clear; however, the clarity becomes a detriment to the development of a continuing philosophic statement. Her major works lack an essential depth or mystery, but J. will remain an important minor author for her quick, clear glimpses of the dark side of human nature.

WORKS: *The Road through the Wall* (1948). *The Lottery; or, The Adventures of James Harris* (1949). *Hangsaman* (1951). *Life among the Savages* (1953). *The Bird's Nest* (1954). *Witchcraft of Salem Village* (1956). *Raising Demons* (1957). *The Bad Children* (1958). *The Sundial* (1958). *The Haunting of Hill House* (1959). *Special Delivery* (1960). *We Have Always Lived in the Castle* (1962). *Nine Magic Wishes* (1963). *The Magic of Shirley Jackson* (Ed. S. E. Hyman, 1966). *Come Along with Me* (Ed. S. E. Hyman, 1968).

BIBLIOGRAPHY: Aldridge, J. W., *After the Lost Generation: A Critical Study of the Writers of Two Wars* (1958). Friedman, L., *S. J.* (1975). Lyons, J. O., *The College Novel in America* (1962).
For articles in reference works, see: *20thCAS.*
Other references: *Explicator* (March 1954).

LOIS BURNS

Mary Putnam Jacobi

B. 31 Aug. 1842, London, England; d. 10 June 1906, New York City
Wrote under: Mary Putnam Jacobi, Mary Putnam
D. of George Palmer and Victorine Haven Putnam; m. Abraham Jacobi, 1873

The descendant of American Puritan families and the eldest of eleven children, at fifteen J. traveled to the first public high school for girls in Manhattan, where her writing received critical attention. Her story "Found and Lost" was published in the *Atlantic Monthly* when she was seventeen, while another, "Hair Chains," appeared there in 1861. The family expected J. to be a writer, but she tended toward medicine.

In 1863, J. was the first woman to receive a degree from the College of Pharmacy in New York City. Since no male medical school would accept women, J. attended the Female Medical College of Pennsylvania. Believing that only in Paris, where no woman had ever studied medicine, could she find proper training, J. went there and fought to enter the École de Médicine. She supported herself by writing sketches, stories, and even a short novel for the New Orleans *Times,* the New York *Evening Post,* and both *Putnam's* and *Scribner's* magazines. Because she felt that fiction took more from her and left her poorer, she began her prolific medical writing (printed in medical journals and collections) with a series of charming, literate medical letters from Paris.

J. won a bronze medal for her thesis and graduated in 1871. Returning home one of the best-prepared physicians in America, she was ready to teach at the fledgling women's medical school of the New York Infirmary, to practice medicine, and to continue scientific research. J. wrote no more fiction.

J. married a prominent physician and had two children, but continued her profession. In 1896, came the onset of J.'s final illness. Brain tumors had been a subject of her medical writing, and she was the first to diagnose her own condition. Her description of her symptoms, published after her death, is a classic of medical literature.

All but one of J.'s magazine pieces were republished in *Stories and Sketches* (1907). All of the writing is graceful and lucid, with incident and character captured in concrete images. "Found and Lost" is a philosophical adventure story about a German who has found the source of the Nile, but loses it again when an American, seeking to commercialize it, goes with him. The best of this early writing, "Some of the French Leaders," presents incisive portraits of ineffectual politicians. A critic considered it "one of the ablest ever printed in an American magazine," with "intellectual grasp" and "grim and elucidating wit."

The remarkable *Question of Rest for Women during Menstruation* (1877), which won the prestigious Boyleston Prize from Harvard University, reflects classical background, research into medical literature, and questionnaires to women in all walks of life. Prepared with J.'s thorough, commonsense approach and literary flair, it should have forever retired the belief that women must inevitably withdraw from ordinary activity during menstruation. In the excellent historical overview, she points out that only in women have normal functions been considered pathological. Beliefs in temporary insanity, instability, or inability to make decisions during menstruation are demolished. Some of the medical theory is no longer valid, but the conclusions and recommendations are sensible, still pertinent, and thoroughly convincing.

J.'s writings about women's roles began with an article in the *North American Review* (1882), "Shall Women Practice Medicine?" In surveying the history of women in medicine, she notes that it is not an innovation at all. Women practiced freely when medicine was unpaid.

"Common Sense" Applied to Woman Suffrage (1894) combines history, clear dissection of the current situation, and incisive argument. "No one expected the vote to raise women's wages or drastically reform the social order," she wrote, "but what is . . . very seriously demanded, is that women be recognized as human beings." Her letter on "Modern Female Invalidism" (1895) comments: "Too much attention is paid to women as objects" while they remain "insufficiently prepared to act as independent subjects."

Despite her talent for imaginative literature, J. wrote little fiction and stopped entirely before she was thirty. She was a pioneer in medicine, both as a woman and simply as a physician, while successfully combining marriage and a profession and doing humanitarian social work. Commenting on her Paris thesis, a French medical journal noted her "poetic form, which does not detract from the value of the statement." She excelled in clear, incisive writing on controversial topics. The voluminous medical writings are characterized by wit, clarity, and literate style.

WORKS: *De la graisse neutre et de les acides gras* (1871). *Infant Diet* by A. Jacobi (revised, enlarged, and adapted to popular use by Jacobi, 1874). *The Question of Rest for Women during Menstruation* (1877). *The Value of Life: A Reply to Mr. Mallock's Essay, "Is Life Worth Living?"* (1879). *On the Use of the Cold Pack Followed by Massage in the Treatment of Anaemia* (with V. A. White, 1880). *Essays on Hysteria, Brain-Tumor, and Some Other Cases of Nervous Disease* (1888). *Physiological Notes on Primary Education and the Study of Language* (1889). *Uffelman's Manual of Dietetic Hygiene for Children* (edited by Jacobi, 1891). *"Common Sense" Applied to Woman Suffrage* (1894). *Found and Lost* (1894). *From Massachusetts to Turkey* (1896). *Stories and Sketches* (1907). *M. P. J., M.D.: A Pathfinder in Medicine* (1925).

The papers of Mary Putnam Jacobi are at the Schlesinger Library, Radcliffe College, Cambridge, Massachusetts.

BIBLIOGRAPHY: Hume, R. F., *Great Women of Medicine* (1964). Hurd-Mead, K. C., *Medical Women of America* (1933). Irwin, I. H., *Angels and Amazons: A Hundred Years of American Women* (1934). Marks, G., and W. K. Beatty, *Women in White* (1972). *In Memory of Mary Putnam Jacobi* (1907). Putnam, R., ed., *Life and Letters of Mary Putnam Jacobi* (1925). Truax, R., *The Doctors Jacobi* (1952).

For articles in reference works, see: *AW. DAB*, V, 1. *NAW* (article by R. Lubove).

Other references: *Jour. Hist. Med.* (Autumn 1949). *Med. Life* (July 1928).

CAROL B. GARTNER

Elizabeth Janeway

B. 7 Oct. 1913, Brooklyn, New York
D. of Charles H. and Jeanette F. Searle Hall; m. Eliot Janeway, 1938

The daughter of middle-class parents, J. attended Swarthmore College and graduated from Barnard College in 1935. She is married to a well-known economist and author and has two sons. The Janeways live in New York City.

J.'s first novel, *The Walsh Girls* (1943), is a psychological study of two sisters living in a New England town during the Depression. The younger, widow of a German intellectual killed at Dachau, experiences conflicting feelings about her new husband, a businessman, and about the institution of marriage. The elder, both prudish and independent, is committed to remaining single. *The Walsh Girls* is typical of J.'s novels in its focus on a small group, often a family, whose members are struggling with a crisis or through a period of transition, their personal dilemmas and relationships intersecting with events in a carefully delineated social and historical milieu.

For instance, *The Question of Gregory* (1949), set partly in Washington, D.C., and New England, studies the effects of a young man's death in wartime upon his parents and their marriage. *Leaving Home* (1953) follows two young sisters and a brother as they make their way into the world during the years 1933 to 1940. In *The Third Choice* (1959), an elderly and crippled woman, once a reigning beauty, and her niece, who is unable to substitute satisfaction in motherhood for satisfaction in marriage, struggle to salvage the past and come to terms with the present and future.

The strengths of J.'s best novels—*The Walsh Girls, The Question of Gregory*, and *The Third Choice*—are subtle and lucid handling of psychology, clean-cut writing, and precise depiction of milieu. Her treatment of relationships among women is particularly noteworthy. However, her works have sometimes been criticized for lacking a unifying theme or point of view.

Unable to deal with some of the large social issues of the 1960s in the kind of fiction she writes, "in which theme is carried by character," J. turned to nonfiction in her best-known work, *Man's World, Woman's Place: A Study in Social Mythology* (1971). The book, much praised for its clarity and undogmatic thoughtfulness, is based upon wide reading in history, philosophy, and the social sciences, as well as upon considerable personal experience. J.'s focus is the assertion that woman's place is in the home. She treats this from a contemporary perspective, showing that it no longer describes the experience of most women in the U.S., and from a historical one, showing its association with the development of the nuclear family. The book's most important contribution, however, is its scrupulous and well-developed treatment of the ways in which this concept functions as a myth, a complex of feeling, fact, and fantasy that satisfies emotional and social needs despite—and because of—its historical inaccuracy.

Between Myth and Morning: Women Awakening (1974) is a collection of thirteen essays, originally addressed to various audiences, on public and private aspects of women's lives. J. regards the women's movement as "irrevocable" because it is "rooted in reality, and reality has changed formidably." Partly because of this certitude, the book looks toward the future; it also suggests that the most significant aspect of women's past is the notions and limitations that have been applied to them, not the actions of women themselves. Individual essays are good, particularly on the difficulties that both sexes experience in dealing with changes in the relationship between private life and work, but the book as a whole does not represent a new stage in J.'s thinking.

Building on earlier ideas, in *Powers of the Weak* (1980) J. analyzes power as "a process of human interaction" shaped by both weak and strong rather than as "an attribute or possession" of the powerful. Drawing on child development, abnormal psychology, history, myth, and recent political events to show how the development of a sense of power over the practical universe is essential to creativity, how it can be interrupted or thwarted on both individual and group levels, and how it can be manipulated to benefit the few, J. argues that those who accept others' definitions of themselves as powerless instead of withholding legitimacy from their rulers acquiesce in their own subordination. Defining women as a paradigm of the historic condition of being weak, and drawing analogies between their status and those of groups such as children, subjects, slaves, and the physically handicapped, J. exhorts women to dissent, band together, and take risks in order to benefit themselves as individuals and as a group, and more importantly to help establish a regenerated social order.

WORKS: *The Walsh Girls* (1943). *Daisy Kenyon* (1945; film version, 1947). *The Question of Gregory* (1949). *The Vikings* (1951). *Leaving Home* (1953). *The Early Days of Automobiles* (1956). *The Third Choice* (1959). *Angry Kate* (1963). *Accident* (1964). *Ivanov Seven* (1967). *Man's World, Woman's Place: A Study in Social Mythology* (1971). *Between Myth and Morning: Women Awakening* (1974). *Powers of the Weak* (1980).

BIBLIOGRAPHY: For articles in reference works, see: *20thCAS*.
Other references: *Harper's* (Sept. 1971). *MR* 13 (1972). *Nation* (6 Nov. 1943; 2 Aug. 1975). *NewR* (12 Oct. 1974). *NYHTB* (21 Aug. 1941). *NYT* (29 Sept. 1974). *NYTBR* (17 Oct. 1943; 21 Aug. 1941; 3 May 1964; 20 June 1971). *SatR* (31 Oct. 1953). *TLS* (8 April 1960). *YR* 35 (1946).

JANET SHARISTANIAN

Charlotte Ann Fillebrown Jerauld

B. 20 April 1820, Old Cambridge, Massachusetts; d. 2 Aug. 1845, Boston,
  Massachusetts
Wrote under: Charlotte A. Fillebrown, Mrs. Charlotte A. Jerauld
D. of Richard and Charlotte Fillebrown; m. J. W. Jerauld, 1843

The daughter of working-class parents, J. received her education in Boston's common schools. Although she left school at fourteen to work in a bookbindery, she read widely and was familiar with Shakespeare, Spenser, and Milton, while particular favorites were Byron, Scott, and Wordsworth. J. soon began to publish poetry in the Universalist magazine, the *Ladies Repository*, and later her work appeared in the annual *Rose of Sharon*. Not until 1841, however, did she start to publish her prose sketches—the real beginning of her literary life, as her editor Henry Bacon notes.

J. had suffered for most of her life from "a determination of blood to the brain," but it seems likely that complications after the birth of her son (born late in July 1845 and dying on August 1) as well as a severe post-partum depression (Bacon writes that within days of her child's birth she became "a raving maniac") contributed to her early death.

J.'s many letters to her close friend Sarah C. Edgarton Mayo reveal a sharp wit and sensitive eye for detail not often found in her poetry and abundant only in her later prose. This friendship produced dual poetic sequences and provided J. with a confidant for the more personal reflections that were frequently absent from her published writings.

J.'s poetry does not reveal the increasing facility and acuity of her prose, but some of her efforts are clearly tighter and fresher than those of many of her contemporaries. Her subjects, forms, and themes are conventional, but the poems rise above the conventional when she assumes a voice different from her own (as in "The Meccas of Memory"), when she experiments with form ("'No More'" and "Isabel" echo Poe's rhymes and rhythms), or when she adheres to the discipline of a strict form (her sonnets are generally better than her other poems, and those she writes with Mayo on alternate lines of "The Lord's Prayer" are good poems). Thematically, her verse tends to be dull: She stresses heaven as a peaceful home where life's problems are resolved; longs nostalgically for a happy childhood that will never return; and bewails sentimentally life's tragedies—ill-fated lovers, general loss, and the cycles of nature.

J.'s early prose is much like her poetry; however, her later prose, as she moves away from heroines who die young and plots based on series of disasters, reveals a talented writer beginning to find herself. Her final prose sketches comprise two groups of tales—"Lights and Shadows of Woman's Life" and "Chronicles and Sketches of Hazelhurst." In the first group, J. explores different women's lots. In each story the author uses a distinct tone—"Our Minister's Family" is essentially gay; "The Mother's Heart" is grim but relatively unsentimental; "The Irish Daughter-in-Law" is light and witty. J.'s concern with her characters' inner lives dominates these tales. In "The Mother's Heart" she examines the jealous and obsessive personality of Isabel Sommers, who is unable to have a child until her twelfth year of marriage. In "Caroline" the protagonist becomes insane when forced to give up her daughter. J.'s characters also grow more realistic in appearance: Hannah in "The Auld Wife" is rustically attractive if not beautiful by the standards of the 1840s; thus, J. notes her "well-developed figure, which gave ample evidence that it had never suffered from compression or whalebone, or any other bones, save those which Nature had given her." .

The conversational and intimate relationship J.'s narrator creates with the reader pervades the tales of the first group and becomes a unifying element in "Chronicles and Sketches of Hazelhurst." These connected stories prefigure in delicacy and tone Sarah Orne Jewett's *Country of the Pointed Firs*, as J.'s unsentimentally nostalgic speaker invites the reader to join her on a walking tour of the village and "to gossip . . . about people and events, past and present." J.'s final prose suggests that she might have attained a high level of literary artistry.

WORKS: *Poetry and Prose by Mrs. Charlotte A. Jerauld, with a Memoir by Henry Bacon* (1850).

BIBLIOGRAPHY: Douglas, A., *The Feminization of American Culture* (1977). Mayo, S. C. E., *Selections from the Writings of Mrs. Sarah C. Edgarton Mayo, with a Memoir by Her Husband* (1849).

For articles in reference works, see: *Daughters of America*, P. A. Hanaford (1882).

CAROLINE ZILBOORG

Sarah Orne Jewett

B. 3 Sept. 1849, South Berwick, Maine; d. 24 June 1909, South Berwick, Maine
Wrote under: Caroline, A. C. Eliot, Alice Eliot, Sarah Orne Jewett,
  Sarah O. Sweet
D. of Theodore Herman and Frances Perry Jewett

J.'s life and works are rooted in the southern tier of Maine. Her own life was a favored one: Born into relative wealth, J. was educated at Miss Raynes's School and at Berwick Academy in South Berwick. She was, however, a somewhat listless student and later remarked that her real education came from her father, a country physician whom she often accompanied on house calls. He imparted to her his extensive knowledge of nature and of literature, and it was to some extent through these house visits that she came to know so intimately the people of her region.

J. earned success and modest fame as a writer at an early age. When she was eighteen years old, her story "Jenny Garrow's Lovers" was published in a weekly Boston periodical, The Flag of Our Union.

J. was sustained throughout her life by a group of intimate female friends. In her earliest diaries (1867–79) she describes her intense emotional attachment to several young women. Her most important liaison was with Annie Adams Fields of Boston. J. lived part of each year at Fields's Charles Street home, and the two traveled extensively together. Hundreds of letters remain to document the significance of this friendship to J. It seems likely that many of J.'s stories were written at least in part for Fields's amusement.

In her later years J.'s reputation was firmly established. Younger writers sought her advice, which she generously supplied. Her face was one of the few women writers on the "Authors" card deck of the time, which is supposedly where the young Willa Cather learned of J. Some of J.'s most perceptive and poignant advice may be found in her letters to Cather, who later acknowledged the influence of her mentor by dedicating O Pioneers! (1913) to J., noting that in J.'s "beautiful and delicate work there is the perfection that endures." Cather estimated J.'s The Country of the Pointed Firs (1896) as one of three American works guaranteed immortality.

Deephaven (1877), J.'s first book-length collection of stories, deals with a series of experiences and characters met by two young women during a summer vacation on the coast of Maine. The relationship between the two is handled somewhat sentimentally, but the character sketches display J.'s genius for the genre, although she later regarded this work as juvenilia. Contemporary reviews were slight and mixed. Reviews were increasingly favorable for three subsequent story collections.

J.'s first novel, *A Country Doctor* (1884), perhaps her most feminist work, is semiautobiographical. It is a classic *bildungsroman* concerning the growth to maturity of a young woman whose ambition is to become a doctor. The woman faces considerable prejudice and discrimination in her pursuit. Eventually she rejects a suitor and resolves to pursue her career.

A White Heron, and Other Stories (1886) marks the beginning of J.'s mature phase. Her mastery of style and a sophisticated sense of craft are quite evident in several of these stories, including the much-anthologized title story, "Marsh Rosemary," and "The Dulham Ladies."

In the decade following *A White Heron*, J. published several further collections, and J.'s best work is to be found among these. *The Country of the Pointed Firs*, generally considered J.'s masterpiece, is difficult to classify by genre. It is more unified than a collection of sketches but much looser than the traditional novel. Like *Deephaven* it uses the structural device of the relationship between two women, which anchors the character sketches to a continuing narrative event. The power of the work resides in the sense of mysterious personal depth many of the characters seem to possess. The protagonist, Mrs. Almiry Todd, one of J.'s enduring characters (prefiguring in many ways Willa Cather's Ántonia), is the town herbalist. She has a singular capacity for healing spiritual as well as physical ills, and is one of the prime sustainers of a sense of communication and of community among the scattered residents of the coastal settlement. J.'s own extensive knowledge of herbs is seen in this and other works.

The Country of the Pointed Firs includes several vignettes of characters who have lost touch with the mainstream of human relationship. J.'s tone is elegiac. The lament is for these failed lives, and perhaps ultimately, as many critics have suggested, for the general economic and social decline of New England in the latter half of the century. There is, moreover, a sense of the fragility and fleetingness of human bonds, seen in the poignant parting scene between Mrs. Todd and the narrator, a thinly disguised persona for J. But the work is not a tragedy,

nor does it espouse the pessimism and fatalism of contemporary naturalistic novels. Rather, it conveys a sense of celebration, a sense of the
triumph of the human community against the forces of spiritual destruction.

J.'s last major work, a historical novel, *The Tory Lover* (1901), was
by far her most popular (it went into five printings in its first three
months), but it has received the least critical approbation.

J. was writing in the heyday of realism (the critical principles of her
editor at the *Atlantic Monthly*, William Dean Howells, were those of
the realists), but she can be classified as a realist only with qualifications.
In her own critical comments she rejected slice-of-life "objectivity" as an
artistic ideal and insisted that personal point of view was an essential
ingredient of competent fiction. J. wrote about ordinary people with
gentle humor, respect, and compassion. Her mastery of style—her ability
to fuse technique and content with her personality—has ensured that her
work will survive.

WORKS: *Deephaven* (1877). *Play Days* (1878). *Old Friends and New* (1879).
Country By-Ways (1881). *A Country Doctor* (1884). *The Mate of the Day-
light, and Friends Ashore* (1884). *A Marsh Island* (1885). *A White Heron,
and Other Stories* (1886). *The Story of the Normans* (1887). *The King of
Folly Island, and Other People* (1888). *Betty Leicester: A Story for Girls*
(1890). *Strangers and Wayfarers* (1890). *Tales of New England* (1890). *A
Native of Winby, and Other Tales* (1893). *Betty Leicester's Xmas* (1894).
The Life of Nancy (1895). *The Country of the Pointed Firs* (1896). *The
Queen's Twin, and Other Stories* (1899). *The Tory Lover* (1901). *The
Letters of Sarah Orne Jewett* (Ed. A. Fields, 1911). *Verses* (1916). *Sarah Orne
Jewett Letters* (Ed. R. Cary, 1967). *The Uncollected Short Stories of Sarah
Orne Jewett* (Ed. R. Cary, 1971).

BIBLIOGRAPHY: Auchincloss, L., *Pioneers and Caretakers: A Study of Nine
American Women Novelists* (1965). Cary, R., ed., *Appreciation of Sarah Orne
Jewett: Twenty-nine Interpretive Essays* (1973). Cary, R., *Sarah Orne Jewett*
(1962). Frost, J. E., *Sarah Orne Jewett* (1960). Donovan, J., *New England and
Local Color: A Study of Women's Literary Tradition* (1982). Donovan, J.,
Sarah Orne Jewett (1980). Harkins, E. F., and C. H. L. Johnston, *Little Pil-
grimages among the Women Who Have Written Famous Books* (1902). Mat-
thiessen, F. O., *Sarah Orne Jewett* (1929). Nagel, G. L., and J. Nagel, *Sarah
Orne Jewett: A Reference Guide* (1978). Pickett, L. C., *Across My Path:
Memories of People I Have Known* (1916). Richards, L., *Stepping Westward*
(1931). Spofford, H. P., *A Little Book of Friends* (1916). Thorp, M. F., *Sarah
Orne Jewett* (1966). Weber, C. C., and C. J. Weber, *A Bibliography of the
Published Writings of Sarah Orne Jewett* (1949). Westbrook, P. D., *Acres of
Flint: Writers of Rural New England, 1870–1900* (1951). Winslow, H. M.,
Literary Boston of Today (1902).

For articles in reference works, see: *AA. AW. DAB*, V, 2. *NAW* (article by W. Berthoff). *NCAB*, 1.

JOSEPHINE DONOVAN

Georgia Douglas Camp Johnson

B. *10 Sept. 1886, Atlanta, Georgia; d. May 1966, Washington, D.C.*
Wrote Under: Georgia Douglas Johnson, Paul Tremaine
D. *of George and Laura Jackson Camp; m. Henry Lincoln Johnson, 1903*

Little is known about J.'s early childhood or her parents. She studied at Atlanta University (through the Normal program) and Oberlin College, Ohio. In 1909 she moved to Washington, D.C., with her lawyer husband. While living in the capital, J. wrote lyrics, poetry, short stories, and plays. She established the Literary Salon, a weekly Saturday-night meeting place for a burgeoning group of young poets, including many of the Harlem Renaissance writers. J. was active in several literary organizations, the Republican party, the pan-African movement, and human-rights groups connected with the Congregational church. Following her husband's death in 1925, she became a commissioner of conciliation with the Department of Labor (1925–34), held other government positions, remained active in racial and political organizations in New York and Washington, and continued to publish individual poems sporadically.

J. was the first black female to receive national recognition as a poet since Francis Harper, an abolitionist writer. Although her three major volumes were published within a ten-year span, each represents a distinctly different period in her life, flowing from the naive inquiry found in *The Heart of a Woman* (1918), through the pain and deprivation of being black recorded in *Bronze* (1922), to the mature acceptance of grief expressed in *Autumn Love Cycle* (1928). J. received many awards not only for her poetry but for her plays and short stories. Although J.'s literary strength is found in her poetry, her plays and short stories remain significant to the development of black American literature from a literary, as well as from a political and a historical, perspective.

The sixty-two poems in *The Heart of a Woman* are four-, eight-, and twelve-line queries regarding the nature of womanhood. While many of these poems are trite, J. expresses a haunting sensitivity toward women's unfulfilled aspirations in "The Dreams of the Dreamer" and

"Dead Leaves." Although sadness prevails in this volume, J. does not paint a bleak picture of womanhood. She finds solace in nature ("Peace" and "When I am Dead") and fulfillment in requited love ("Mate"). J. apparently believed that women were destined to the life of a voyeur—declaring that they lacked the freedom to express themselves openly, that they lacked the means of fulfilling their dreams, and that only through their lovers could they fully experience life.

Bronze is an energetic expression of the pain, humiliations, and fears of a 1920s black woman. The sixty-five poems in this volume are grouped under nine headings. J.'s greatest literary contribution to an understanding of womanhood and of her era is found in the ten poems in the "Motherhood" section. "Maternity" expresses a mixture of emotions as a child is awaited: pride is coupled with fear that, at worst, the child would be lynched and, at best, rejected by the world. "Black Woman" implies that it is cruel to bring black children into this world.

In *Autumn Love Cycle* an obvious stylistic and thematic maturity is displayed. J.'s dominant theme is the depth of mature love, as expressed in "I Want to Die While You Love Me," "Autumn," and "Afterglow," but there is the fear that lost youth can result in infidelity or in impotency. Many of these poems were probably written during the period when her husband suffered three strokes and eventually died. A dozen of the poems describe her adjustment to life without the physical presence of love.

J., together with other black writers after World War I, was responsible for bringing black poetry out of the bonds of dialect and into the realm of a high art form. The poets of her period eventually were overshadowed by the writers of the Harlem Renaissance, but their importance to the movement should not be underestimated. J.'s significance as both a black and a woman writer cannot be denied.

WORKS: *The Heart of a Woman, and Other Poems* (1918). *Bronze: A Book of Verse* (1922). *Blue Blood* (1927). *Plumes: Folk Tragedy* (1927). *Autumn Love Cycle* (1928).

BIBLIOGRAPHY: Bontemps, A., ed., *American Negro Poetry* (1974). Bontemps, A., *The Harlem Renaissance Remembered* (1972). Johnson, J. W., *The Book of American Negro Poetry* (1922). Locke, A., *The New Negro: An Interpretation* (1968). Mays, B., *The Negro's God As Reflected in His Literature* (1968). White, N., and W. Jackson, eds., *An Anthology of Verse by American Negroes* (1924).

For articles in reference works, see: *Black American Writers Past and Present*, T. G. Rush, C. F. Myers, and E. S. Arata (1975).

Other references: *Crisis* (Dec. 1952). *Journal of Negro History* (July 1972).
LINDA S. BERRY

Josephine Winslow Johnson

B. 20 June 1910, Kirkwood, Missouri
D. of Benjamin and Ethel Franklin Johnson; m. Thurlow Smoot, 1939;
  m. Grant G. Cannon, 1942

J. was reared on a one-hundred-acre farm in south-central Missouri. Reflecting on her mother's lineage, J. has noted the long dominance of franklins, i.e., Anglo-Saxon freeholders, untitled agrarians with a fervent attachment to specific pieces of land. The strength of this passion is intensified in J.

At the age of eight J. wrote a poem to mark the end of the war and glimpsed her vocation as a writer. Her first novel, *Now in November* (1934), brought her the Pulitzer Prize. Another novel—as well as poems and short stories—soon appeared, for in these years, J. says, she "wrote, if not endlessly, then enormously." Her first marriage, to a Labor Relations Board lawyer, only perpetuated her growing sense that (as she said in her autobiography, *Seven Houses: A Memoir of Time and Places*, 1973), "I seemed to be waiting to begin to live." Later, in Grant Cannon she found a partner whose hopeful nature temporarily dispelled her own profound pessimism. With Cannon, an editor of *Farm Quarterly*, she raised three children. His death in 1969 took from her one who, in her words, "made no lifelong truce with despair as I have made."

Although her work covers many decades and genres, the important themes almost all appear in the early fiction. *Now in November* celebrates the land and the self-sufficient farm family even while it deplores the Depression and the tyranny of weather. The work is lit by occasional set pieces of nature description, and by a clear attention to the limited point of view of the narrator, the middle daughter on a small Missouri farm, as she remembers her childhood and her growing understanding of her sister's mental illness.

J.'s second novel, *Jordanstown* (1937), about a small-town newspaperman and community organizer during the Depression, is less successful because the didactic ideology of socialist-realism is too little camouflaged. Still, *Jordanstown* has memorable elements. The later novels, *Wildwood* (1945) and *The Dark Traveler* (1963) are more disappointing; the anguish which is evident in the early fiction is here completely unrelieved.

J.'s short fiction, however, shows that more compact forms better display both her descriptive talents and her facility with surprise endings. "Gedacht," her first published short story, is the best of the *Winter Orchard* (1935) collection. It concerns a World War I veteran who, having lost his sight from poison gas, regains it briefly. J.'s early poetry incorporates the themes of her fiction: social protest, loss of religious faith, love of nature, and the struggle with cynicism.

A publishing hiatus of almost twenty years occurred in J.'s mid-career, and when she resumed publication, some very different genre preferences manifested themselves. She produced essays, memoirs, and diaries instead of fiction. J.'s vision is now quieter, more introspective, more ameliorated by the natural world, although social concerns and pessimism are still there.

Thus, *The Inland Island* (1969), a kind of nature journal in the style of Walden, laments the Vietnam War and promotes the environmental movement in the midst of solitary meditations and exquisite observations on the natural year. With *The Circle of Seasons* (1974), the text for a book of nature photographs, J. reiterates the themes begun in *Now in November*. It is both an ode and an elegy that celebrates and questions: "Will there be any rhythm and difference of season left, any feeling of the great circular flow of living things [for our children]?"

J. has contributed brilliantly to the "proletarian" tradition in American letters. Indeed, one is frequently tempted to rank her with the great shapers of that tradition, London, Sinclair, Norris, and Steinbeck. But J.'s activity displays other dimensions which make her difficult to categorize, for she is also a writer of naturalistic fiction, a didactic poet, a Thoreauvian essayist, and an anguished contemplative decrying militarism and the inhumanity of modern technology. In a time when the often-divided currents of agrarianism, radical trade unionism, conservationism, and militant pacifism seem about to form a curious new merger, J.'s lifelong nurturing of these concerns may prompt a rediscovery of her achievement.

WORKS: *Now in November* (1934). *The Winter Orchard, and Other Stories* (1935). *Unwilling Gypsy* (1936). *Jordanstown* (1937). *Year's End* (1937). *Paulina: The Story of an Apple-Butter Jar* (1939). *Wildwood* (1945). *The Dark Traveler* (1963). *The Sorcerer's Son, and Other Stories* (1965). *The Inland Island* (1969). *Seven Houses: A Memoir of Time and Places* (1973). *The Circle of Seasons* (1974).

The manuscripts and papers of Josephine Winslow Johnson are in the Rare Books Collection at Washington University, St. Louis, Missouri.

BIBLIOGRAPHY: For articles in reference works, see: *CA*, 25–28 (1971). *Contemporary Novelists*, Eds. J. Vinson and D. L. Kirkpatrick (1976). *NCAB*, H. *20thCA*. *20thCAS*.

Other references: *Nation* (21 Aug. 1935). *NYHT* (13 Sept. 1934; 13 Aug. 1935). *NYT* (16 Sept. 1934; 11 April 1937). *NYTBR* (2 March 1969; 13 May 1973). *SatR* (3 April 1937; 15 Feb. 1969).

MARGARET McFADDEN-GERBER

Annie Fellows Johnston

B. 15 May 1863, Evansville, Indiana; d. 5 Oct. 1931, Pewee Valley, Kentucky
D. of Albion and Mary Erskine Fellows; m. William L. Johnston, 1888

J. grew up on a farm outside Evansville, Indiana. Although her father, a Methodist minister, died when she was only two, J. was influenced by him, through his theological books, and by her mother, who had strong ideas about the importance of education for women. J. attended public schools in Evansville and the University of Iowa (for a year). After teaching for several years and working for a time as a private secretary, she married her cousin, a widower. After his death in 1892, J. turned to writing as a career. Eventually, she and her three stepchildren settled in Pewee Valley, Kentucky, which J. fictionalized as Lloydsboro Valley in her popular "Little Colonel" series. In 1899, J.'s stepdaughter Rena died; two years later J. moved to Arizona for her stepson John's health, and then on to Texas, where they lived until his death in 1910.

As a children's author, J. was both prolific, with over forty volumes, and popular—reportedly, at her death her books had sold over a million copies. Some readers today are still familiar with J.'s thirteen-volume "Little Colonel" series, which began with the publication of *The Little Colonel* (1896). Unlike many authors of series books, J. allows her characters to mature. For example, we see Lloyd Sherman first as a five-year-old, impetuous and stubborn, and last as a young married woman, lovely and vivacious. Many people know J.'s most famous character only through David Butler's 1935 Fox film, "The Little Colonel," starring Shirley Temple as Lloyd and Lionel Barrymore as old Colonel Lloyd. The story of the conflict of pretty, spunky Lloyd with her crusty old grandfather, who severed relations with his only daughter, Elizabeth, when she eloped with a Yankee, was a perfect vehicle for Temple's talents.

J.'s work was commercially successful, and her publisher clearly took advantage of the popularity of the "Little Colonel" books. For example, in 1909 the Page Company issued *The Little Colonel's Good Times Book*, with blank pages for a child to record her "good times," as Betty Lewis did in *The Little Colonel's House Party* (1900). Many of the legends and tales in J.'s books were subsequently published as separate volumes, such as *The Legend of the Bleeding Heart* (1907) and *The Road of the Loving Heart* (1922), both of which first appeared in *The Little Colonel's House Party*.

J.'s works have the flaws of many children's books of the late 19th and early 20th centuries. The characters are idealized; the conflicts, resolved too easily; the themes, simplistic and naive. The typical world of J.'s fiction is one of wealth and aristocracy, in which separation of the races and the inferiority of blacks are assumed. But, interestingly, it is a world in which women are not automatically relegated to the life of wife and mother or to unfulfilled spinsterhood. Especially through the experiences of Lloyd Sherman and her friends, J. emphasizes the importance for women of education in academic subjects; likewise, she allows her young women the option of independence, through characters such as unmarried Joyce Ware, pursuing her career as a commercial artist in an apartment in New York.

A strong moral code underlies every work by J. Through legends and tales, some traditional and others original, J. cleverly makes points which her young characters are never allowed to miss. Readers of an earlier, simpler day took these lessons to heart and were inspired to model their lives after Lloyd, Betty, Joyce, and other characters; but contemporary readers in our complex age often find J.'s stories more didactic than inspiring or entertaining.

SELECTED WORKS: *Big Brother* (1894). *Joel: A Boy of Galilee* (1895). *The Little Colonel* (1896). *The Little Colonel's House Party* (1900). *The Little Colonel's Holiday* (1901). *The Little Colonel's Hero* (1902). *The Little Colonel at Boarding School* (1903). *The Little Colonel in Arizona* (1904). *The Little Colonel's Christmas Vacation* (1905). *The Little Colonel: Maid of Honor* (1906). *The Little Colonel's Knight Comes Riding* (1907). *The Little Colonel's Chum: Mary Ware* (1908). *Mary Ware in Texas* (1910). *Mary Ware's Promised Land* (1912). *Miss Santa Claus of the Pullman* (1913). *Georgina of the Rainbows* (1916). *It Was the Road to Jericho* (1919). *The Land of the Little Colonel: Reminiscence and Autobiography* (1929).

BIBLIOGRAPHY: Steele, E., "Mrs. Johnston's *Little Colonel*," in *Challenges in American Culture*, Eds. R. B. Browne, L. N. Landrum, and W. K. Bottoroff (1970).

For articles in reference works, see: *Arizona in Literature: A Collection of the Best Writings of Arizona Authors from Early Spanish Days to the Present Time*, M. G. Boyer (1971). *DAB*, V, 2. *Indiana Authors and Their Books, 1816–1916*, Ed. R. E. Banta (1949). *The Junior Book of Authors*, Eds. S. J. Kunitz and H. Haycraft (1934). *NAW* (article by A. W. Shumaker). *NCAB*, 13. *20thCA*.

Other references: *St. Nicholas* (Dec. 1913).

MARTHA E. COOK

Emily Chubbuck Judson

B. 22 Aug. 1817, Eaton, New York; d. 1 June 1854, Hamilton, New York
Wrote under: Emily Chubbuck, Fanny Forester, Mrs. Emily Judson
D. of Charles and Lavinia Richards Chubbuck; m. Adoniram Judson, 1846

J.'s self-taught skills enabled her to teach in local schools from 1832 to 1840. Enrolled at the Utica Female Seminary for one year, she remained there as a teacher of English composition from 1841 to 1846. She rose from poverty eventually to find fame and wealth with her early children's books. With the income from those books she was able to buy her family a home and to make their lives comfortable. J.'s short life-span of thirty-six years was a full and varied one. Her writing career divides into three clearly defined phases; in each she wrote under a different name.

Publishing under the name Emily Chubbuck, J. wrote several successful children's books between 1841 and 1844. Like other mid–19th-c. writers, J. writes consciously as an American and as a "republican." Her fiction is for young Americans, and all the stories are heavily moralistic and didactic. For example, the stories in *Charles Linn; or, How to Observe the Golden Rule* (1841) have the theme of self-sacrifice.

Publishing under the name of "Fanny Forester," J. wrote stories with a completely different tone, changing from the previously moral tone to one of irony and fancy. The sketches gathered into *Trippings in Author-Land* (1846) reveal a writer enjoying the world she was creating and perhaps enjoying the recreation of herself as Fanny Forester, a character in that world. Two more volumes continued to construct the village of Alderbrook, *Lilias Fane, and Other Tales* (1846) and *Alderbrook* (1846), which contained some of the same tales from *Lilias Fane*. Simplicity and unpretentiousness is praised; village life is uncomplicated and contains a community unknown to the larger, sprawling urban scene.

"Fanny Forester" returned several times to the character "Ida Ravelin," a genius, a poet, an angel (all synonyms in these stories), as she created her vision of the poet who is "not like them" but who can live completely in the ideal. By the time a revised edition (1847) of *Alderbrook* was published, J. wished to suppress "Ida Ravelin" and substitute "Angel's Pilgrimage," a very different story of human greed, murder, and cruelty, in which the angels try to change the world by continuing the holy mission begun by their prototype, Christ. The work published under "Fanny Forester" continued to bring J. money and fame. *Alderbrook* went through at least eleven editions.

The third phase of J.'s career began when she left the imaginary world of Alderbrook and entered into missionary life, marrying the Reverend Judson, who was nearly thirty years her senior, and going to Burma with him and three of his children from his second marriage. In this phase she published a *Memoir of Sarah B. Judson* (1849), her husband's second wife. This volume by its popularity furthered the cause of the missionaries. Printed in both London and New York, it was reprinted several times for a total of over thirty thousand copies. Less popular, *The Kathayan Slave* (1853) is a defense of missionary activity and maintains that the barbarism of the natives of Burma and India can only be alleviated through Christianity.

Her life and work indicate some of the tensions and contradictions inherent in mid–19th-c. America, its commercialism and also its idealism. Perhaps these tensions led her to frame her literary answer to them by assuming three different identities. These three different literary personalities, the didactic Emily Chubbuck, the frivolous and charming Fanny Forester, and the defensive Mrs. Emily Judson, need not coalesce into one personality, although the prevailing opinion is that identity is such a synthesis. In some writers the paradoxes of their cultures cause them to produce ambiguous and morally contradictory works. In others these same paradoxes produce moral absolutism in the writing and ambiguity in the identity of the writer herself. J. was such a writer.

WORKS: *Charles Linn; or, How to Observe the Golden Rule* (1841). *The Great Secret; or, How to Be Happy* (1842). *Allen Lucas: The Self-Made Man*

(1843). *John Frink; or, The Third Commandment Illustrated* (1844). *Alderbrook* (1846). *Lilias Fane, and Other Tales* (1846). *Trippings in Author-Land* (1846). *How to Be Great, Good, and Happy* (including *Allen Lucas; the Self-Made Man, Charles Linn; or, How to Observe the Golden Rule,* and *The Great Secret; or, How to Be Happy,* 1848). *Memoir of Sarah B. Judson* (1849). *A Mound Is in the Graveyard* (ca. 1851). *An Olio of Domestic Verses* (1852). *The Kathayan Slave* (1853). *My Two Sisters* (1854).

BIBLIOGRAPHY: Douglas, A., *The Feminization of American Culture* (1977). Kendrick, A. C., *The Life and Letters of Mrs. Emily Chubbuck Judson* (1860). Pattee, F., *The Feminine Fifties* (1940). Stuart, A. W., *The Lives of Mrs. Ann H. Judson and Mrs. Sarah B. Judson, with a Biographical Sketch of Mrs. Emily Chubbuck Judson* (1851).

For articles in reference works, see: *AA. CAL. DAB*, V, 2. *FPA. NAW* (article by E. E. Lewis). *NCAB*, 3.

JULIANN E. FLEENOR

Agnes Newton Keith

B. 6 July 1901, Oak Park, Illinois
D. of Joseph Gilbert and Grace Goodwillie Newton; m. Henry George
  Keith, 1934

Reared in California, K. graduated from the University of California at Berkeley in 1924. Her brief career with the San Francisco *Examiner* ended when she was brutally attacked by a frenzied drug addict. A prolonged incapacitation, including the loss of eyesight, followed. Surgery eventually restored her to health. Married to an English tropical-forestry expert, she found the materials for her sensitive and evocative books about Asia and Africa in their subsequent travels.

From 1934 to 1952 the Keiths lived in North Borneo. Four books are based on that experience. *Land Below the Wind* (1939), a bride's sunny report on her Eden, examines the life of westerners in an outpost of Empire, describes her experiences there, and characterizes her native friends. Like most of K.'s books, it is illustrated by her own sketches. *Three Came Home* (1947) is the story of imprisonment by the Japanese during World War II. K. and her young son were interned together, her husband in a neighboring camp. Despite its subject, the book is strangely affirmative: she shows brutality and humanity in both jailers and prisoners, stressing that war, not race, has dehumanized them all. Her depiction of the heroism of many prisoners and their Asian friends outside the camp is moving, and throughout she stresses the courage and endurance that enabled them to bring all thirty-four interned children through alive.

White Man Returns (1951) rounds off this series by showing the return to North Borneo after the war; the beginning of the process of rebuilding is central to this book. Similar to *Land Below the Wind* in approach and structure, it lacks the happy idealism of the first book; the war experience had destroyed K.'s Eden. Much later came yet another work based on the Borneo years, this time a novel, *Beloved Exiles* (1972). Only loosely autobiographical, it is less successful than the nonfiction works.

Having retired from his government's service, K.'s husband was, in 1953, prevailed upon to go to the Philippines for the Food and Agriculture Organization of the United Nations. *Bare Feet in the Palace* (1955) resulted. Like her first and third Borneo books, it is a mixture of personal experiences, sketches of people, and information about the society and its history. A central theme is the creation of democracy in Asia; the title refers to the coming of poor natives to the two-hundred-year-old former palace of Spanish governors, now the residence of a democratically elected president.

Children of Allah (1966), K.'s only non-Asian book, tells of their following assignment in Libya. K. used her previously successful formula here, and this work is particularly notable for its studies of Libyan Moslem women in various stages of subservience to and liberation from the veil and all that its wearing implies.

K.'s most recent book, *Before the Blossoms Fall* (1975), must be paired with *Three Came Home*, which had been widely admired in Japan. In 1973 she was sent by the Japan Foundation on a six-week visit to Japan, the goal being that she would write something that would increase understanding between Japan and the U.S. Important themes here are the young, the aged, and women's changing status and attitudes. Like her other books, it is a perceptive and sympathetic study, though K. admits she is unable completely to understand or trust these people, whom she nevertheless loves.

Throughout her career, and hinging on her imprisonment experience, K.'s attitude toward her Asian subjects altered subtly. While she was always sympathetic and even admiring, the earliest book also sometimes seems patronizing, and the idea of the white man's burden is not totally absent. The later books reveal a truer sense of equality and a surer stress on the values of alien cultures, along with a more open admission of inability thoroughly to understand them. All of the works, however, are both informative and absorbing.

WORKS: *Land Below the Wind* (1939). *Three Came Home* (1947; film version, 1949). *White Man Returns* (1951). *Bare Feet in the Palace* (1955). *Children of Allah* (1966). *Beloved Exiles* (1972). *Before the Blossoms Fall* (1975).

BIBLIOGRAPHY: For articles in reference works, see: *CA*, 17–18 (1967). *20thCAS*.

Other references: *Atlantic* (March 1966). *NYHTB* (6 April 1947; 5 Aug. 1951). *NYTBR* (12 Nov. 1939; 26 March 1972). *SatR* (5 April 1947; 13 Dec. 1955).

MARY JEAN DeMARR

Helen Adams Keller

B. *27 June 1880, Tuscumbia, Alabama; d. 1 June 1968, Westport, Connecticut*
Wrote under: Helen Keller, Helen Adams Keller
D. *of Arthur H. and Katherine Adams Keller*

K. was nineteen months old when illness left her deaf and blind. She soon became wild and unmanageable, locked inside a dark, silent world that no humanizing influence seemed able to penetrate.

In the 1890s, almost no hope existed for educating people both deaf and blind, but K.'s parents turned to the Perkins Institution for the Blind in Boston for help. The institution sent Anne Sullivan, a new graduate who had recently had her own sight partially restored, to educate the child to whatever extent proved possible. Undreamed of success followed, and K. eventually, in 1904, earned a B.A. cum laude from Radcliffe College.

K. became friends with many of the world's greatest people, including Alexander Graham Bell, Mark Twain, William Dean Howells, Charlie Chaplin, and Andrew Carnegie. At least nine presidents received her, and a half-dozen of the most prestigious universities in the world bestowed honorary degrees upon her.

From 1924 until her death in 1968, K. was associated with the American Foundation for the Blind, traveling to every state in the U.S. and to every continent in the world, working to enlarge the possibilities for handicapped people.

K.'s first book was *The Story of My Life* (1902), first published serially by the *Ladies' Home Journal*. The book contains, in addition to her early autobiography, her letters from 1887 to 1901, passages from Anne Sullivan's reports about K.'s education, and comments by John Albert Macy.

K. describes the terrible isolation of the blind and deaf mute as a "twofold solitude" in which one can "know little of the . . . affections that grow out of endearing words and actions and companionship." She tells about an incident of unconscious plagiarism, which happened in 1892, and about the fear that grew from that "disgrace," saying that "even now I cannot be quite sure of the boundary line between my ideas and those I find in books. I suppose that is because so many of my impressions come to me through the medium of others' eyes and ears."

Midstream: My Later Life (1929) brings up to date the story of this remarkable woman and her teacher. It also gives the reader a lively picture of life in America during the first three decades of this century.

In *Midstream*, K. seems to delight in using images of sight and sound, perhaps because some critics had questioned the honesty of this aspect of her style. Surely she had experienced in some physical way the scene she describes thus: "Out of the big, red, gaping mouths of the furnaces leaped immense billows of fire." Such vivid sensory images enliven this entire book in a degree that would be noteworthy even in a writer without handicaps.

Teacher: Anne Sullivan Macy (1955) is certainly, as the title page proclaims, "a tribute by the foster-child of her mind." K. memorably describes the incredible difficulties faced by Sullivan in introducing K. to language. Once the child discovered that things have names, her education proceeded with astonishing rapidity. Sullivan is presented as a human being with more than her share of human problems and foibles, but when compared with K.'s earlier clean, concrete writing, the book seems somewhat repetitious and sentimental.

K.'s many other books include poetry (*Double Blossoms*, 1931) and social criticism (*Helen Keller, Her Socialist Years: Writings and Speeches*, 1967). But her best work is found in her autobiographical books.

WORKS: *The Story of My Life* (1902; film version, *Deliverance*, 1918). *Optimism, an Essay* (1903). *The World I Live In* (1908). *The Song of the*

Stone Wall (1910). *Out of the Dark: Essays, Letters, and Addresses on Physical and Social Vision* (1913). *My Religion* (1927). *Midstream: My Later Life* (1929). *We Bereaved* (1929). *Double Blossoms* (1931). *Peace at Eventide* (1932). *Helen Keller in Scotland* (Ed. J. K. Love, 1933). *American Foundation for the Blind, 1923–1938: A Report from Helen Keller to the Blind People of America* (1938). *Journal, 1936–1937* (1938). *Let Us Have Faith* (1940). *Teacher, Anne Sullivan Macy: a Tribute by the Foster-Child of Her Mind* (1955). *Open Door* (1957). *Helen Keller, Her Socialist Years: Writings and Speeches* (Ed. P. S. Foner, 1967).

BIBLIOGRAPHY: Braddy, N., *Anne Sullivan Macy: The Story behind Helen Keller* (1933). Brooks, V. W., *Helen Keller: Sketch for a Portrait* (1956). Gibson, W., *The Miracle Worker: A Play for Television* (1957). Graff, S., and P. A. Graff, *Helen Keller: Toward the Light* (1965). Harrity, R., and J. G. Martin, *The Three Lives of Helen Keller* (1962). Hickok, L. A., *The Touch of Magic* (1961). Peare, C. O., *The Helen Keller Story* (1959). Waite, H. E., *Valiant Companions: Helen Keller and Anne Sullivan Macy* (1959).

For articles in reference works, see: *CB* (Dec. 1942; July 1968). *LSL. NCAB*, 15.

PEGGY SKAGGS

Edith Summers Kelley

B. *1884, Ontario, Canada; d. 1956, Los Gatos, California*
Wrote under: Edith Summers Kelley, Edith Summers
M. *Allan Updegraff, 1908; m. Claude Fred Kelley, 1915*

Like the protagonists of her two novels, K. struggled much of her adult life for financial security and for realization of her dream to be a writer. After taking an honors degree in languages from the University of Toronto, the nineteen-year-old Edith moved to New York and began working on Funk and Wagnall's *Standard Dictionary* project.

In 1906, K. became secretary to Upton Sinclair and part of the staff at Helicon Hall, Sinclair's socialist commune (inspired by Charlotte Perkins Gilman's plans for municipal housing, advanced in 1904). At the Hall she met two other aspiring writers cum janitors, Sinclair Lewis and Alan Updegraff. Both Lewis (to whom she was engaged) and Sinclair remained lifelong correspondents. The marriage to Updegraff produced two children; K. apparently was primary breadwinner as a teacher in the Hell's

Kitchen area of New York City. After her divorce she became the common-law wife of Claude Fred Kelley. The Kelleys pursued a series of mostly unprofitable jobs from 1914 to 1945: tenant tobacco farming in Kentucky; boardinghouse management in New Jersey; alfalfa and chicken ranching, and bootlegging in California. Thus, unlike Sinclair's journalistic fiction, K.'s novels reflect her own experiences and observations as an economically depressed rancher.

In *Weeds* (1923), Judith Pipinger is different from other members of her tenant tobacco-farming community in Kentucky because she is a throwback to purer pioneer stock, an exception to the usual results of inbreeding and poor nutrition. Her early repugnance to traditional female chores and her preference for "man's" (outdoors) work isolate her from the closely knit female subculture. This isolation is underlined by imagery linking Judith with natural (as opposed to societal) objects, and by a character "double," Jabez Moorhouse, an iconoclastic fiddler who shares Judith's intuitive grasp of beauty and meaning in life. With her marriage and subsequent motherhood, Judith is trapped in the very role she has despised; when Moorhouse dies, her death in spirit concludes the novel.

Encouraged by a monetary award from a civil-liberties group, K. began work in 1925 on a second novel, a study of the Imperial Valley in Southern California and "the life it harbors." From 1925 through 1929, K. wrote and revised as her knowledge of California development and the International Workers of the World increased, but *The Devil's Hand* was not published until 1974, eighteen years after her death.

Marriage proves to be a spiritual death for Rhoda Malone, an acknowledgment of defeat which closes *The Devil's Hand*. Tempted by her friend Kate Baxter to leave her passive and orderly life as an office clerk in Philadelphia, Rhoda takes on a partnership with Kate in a California alfalfa farm. Because Rhoda's is the central consciousness through which the story is told, focus is equally on what she sees and who she becomes. Her awareness of the exploitation of people like herself, and the Hindu, Mexican, and Oriental laborers, by rapacious realtors and big landowners gradually intensifies; two male friends serve (as did Moorhouse in *Weeds*) as examples of the individual freedom which Rhoda, as a woman, cannot achieve. Disheartened by the loss of these friends, the drudgery of profitless farming, and her realization that to challenge the economic system is to suffer social and material martyrdom, Rhoda marries the very realtor who initially took advantage of her ignorance.

K. is among several American women writers of the 1920s, such as Josephine Herbst, Frances Newman, Evelyn Scott, and Ruth Suckow, who have been "rediscovered" after being long forgotten or ignored. K. is also emerging as a master of fiction in the Dreiser, Garland, Howells vein. She does not limit her work to tedious cataloguing of realistic detail, but her work is firmly rooted in everyday experience. Although the imagery of her novels underlines the forgotten connection of men and women to nature, her fiction is oriented more toward sociological (even socialist) study; time and again she emphasizes the effect of social environment on individual fate. Thus, the feminist concerns grow naturally out of her realistic approach to life and fiction.

WORKS: *Weeds* (1923). *The Devil's Hand* (1974).

Selected papers of Edith Summers Kelley are in the Special Collections of the Morris Library, Southern Illinois University at Carbondale. Kelley's letters to Sinclair Lewis and to Upton Sinclair are in collections of the Lilly Library, Indiana University.

BIBLIOGRAPHY: Bruccoli, M., Afterword to *The Devil's Hand* (1974) and *Weeds* (1974). Irvin, H., *Women in Kentucky* (1979). Schorer, M., *Sinclair Lewis: An American Life* (1961).

Other references: *Michigan Papers in Women's Studies* (June 1975). *Regionalism and the Female Imagination* III (Spring 1977).

SALLY BRETT

Myra Kelly

B. 26 Aug. 1875, Dublin, Ireland; d. 30 March 1910, Torquay, England
D. of James and Annie Morrogh Kelly; m. Allan Macnaughton, 1905

K. came to New York City with her family when she was a child; they lived on the East Side, where her physician father developed a large practice. Educated first at convent schools, she attended Horace Mann High School and then Teachers College of Columbia University, receiving a diploma in 1899 as a teacher of manual training. Her experience at East-Side Public School 147, where she taught from 1899 to 1901, provided material for her popular stories about "Bailey's Babies."

K.'s long stream of published stories began with the sentimental "A Christmas Present for a Lady," which she had sent to two magazines, thinking both would reject it. When both accepted it, K. had complicated adjustments to make. She told friends later that no manuscript of hers was ever rejected. The story was included in her first book, *Little Citizens: The Humours of School Life* (1904).

Little Citizens caught the attention of Allan Macnaughton, president of Standard Coach Horse Company, who arranged to meet her. They were married in 1905; their one child, a boy, died in infancy. The Macnaughtons lived briefly at Oldchester Village, Orange Mountain, New Jersey, while working to establish a literary colony there.

In her scant thirty-five years, the prolific K. produced not only three books of East-Side stories but popular romantic tales as well. She also wrote essays about educational methods and effects, some of which appeared in collections with her stories. K. died from tuberculosis in England, where she had gone in hope of a cure. Her last books were published posthumously.

Little Citizens is a collection of K.'s earliest stories about the children in Constance Bailey's first-reader class, boys and girls primarily from poor Jewish immigrant families but including the son of the local Irish policeman for contrast and occasional conflict. K. wrote that she was not the model for Constance Bailey. " 'What I aspired to be and was not' Constance Bailey was. Only her mistakes are mine and her very earnest effort."

The stories were intended as educational, but have the charms of novelty and originality, although verisimilitude suffers in both incidents and dialogue. The humor that tempers the message is usually at the immigrant's expense and is often condescending, but it sometimes touches on the teacher's embarrassment as she realizes the limitations of her knowledge or experience.

Wards of Liberty (1907) contains more stories of Miss Bailey's fifty-eight students. There are disruptive influences like the nine-year-old "Boss" who is running his late father's cellar garment shop. K. believed the schools played a crucial role in helping immigrants get along in America, but the Boss's story shows that she recognized the system's limitations. The Boss has previously avoided all schooling and other Americanizing influences, but comes to school when he decides learning to read will bring better-paid work for his shop. Discouraged by the slow pace and unessential busy work, he disappears. His life has no room for childhood activities. He lives in a world the schools could not reach.

Although K. continues to emphasize the fun, under it rages revolt against conditions among the poor.

After several less critically successful novels, K. returned, as her critics hoped she would, to the world of her schoolchildren in *Little Aliens* (1910). There is still humor and pathos but with a deeper understanding of children and the nature of alienation. "Games in Gardens" shows how immigrants can misinterpret the bits of America that filter into their ghetto world, as the children try to don proper costume for track and field events. Miss Bailey takes her share of the satire for her inadequate communication. Whereas earlier K. had saved discussion for her essays, here she explains how natural these misunderstandings are with children "alien to every American custom, and prejudiced by religion and precept against most of them."

Although generally unknown now, K. achieved tremendous popular success, publishing frequently in mass-circulation magazines like *McClure's*. Even President Theodore Roosevelt sent her a letter of appreciation. She exaggerated both characters and incidents, looked for sentiment, and created wry humor always on the verge of pathos, but she was honest in her approach, often touching on serious issues such as the values of Americanization and the clash between immigrant and American traditions. Writing with warmth, sympathy, and as much understanding as she could muster, K. did much to acquaint the reading public with the harsh conditions of ghetto life and to suggest that Americans learn to know their immigrants before thoughtlessly attempting to Americanize them. When she left the narrow area of the East-Side schools, her stories were less well received and less significant.

WORKS: *Little Citizens: The Humours of School Life* (1904). *The Isle of Dreams* (1907). *Wards of Liberty* (1907). *Rosnah* (1908). *The Golden Season* (1909). *Little Aliens* (1910). *New Faces* (1910). *Her Little Young Ladyship* (1911).

BIBLIOGRAPHY: Fine, D. M., *The City, the Immigrant, and American Fiction* (1977). Friedman, L. M., *Pilgrims in a New Land* (1948). Lieberman, E., *The American Short Story: A Study of the Influence of Locality in Its Development* (1912).

For articles in reference works, see: *DAB*, V, 2. *NCAB*, 24.

Other references: *American Mercury* (Feb. 1926). *American Studies* (Spring 1978).

CAROL B. GARTNER

Frances Anne Kemble

B. 27 Nov. 1809, London, England; d. 15 Jan. 1893, London, England
Wrote under: Frances Anne Butler (Miss Fanny Kemble), Mrs. Butler,
  Frances Anne Kemble
D. of Charles and Maria Kemble; m. Pierce Butler, 1834

Born into London's leading theatrical family, K. was an actress who became one of the most articulate Victorian women of letters in both America and England. Daughter of an actor who was also manager of Covent Garden Theatre, K. received all her formal education at boarding schools in France. K.'s first stage performance, as Shakespeare's Juliet at Covent Garden in 1829, was a phenomenal success which transformed her life. K. became the pinup girl of the London stage, enjoying admiration from people in England and the provinces. In 1832 she toured America.

Her marriage to a wealthy Philadelphian initiated a period of emotional upheaval. K. gave up her acting career for marriage, but she never became the model 19th-c. woman. Instead of accepting the role of subservient wife, she demanded equality. Furthermore, instead of accepting and approving of her husband's homeland, she was quite critical of it. The record of her experiences, *Journal of a Residence in America* (1835), publicly announced her negative attitudes, much to the chagrin of her husband. A particularly crucial issue for him, as the owner of large Georgian plantations and hundreds of slaves, was K.'s passionate and outspoken opposition to the "peculiar institution." After the birth of her two daughters, two return visits to England, and numerous attempts to sever her relationship with Butler, K. left her husband and daughters in 1844.

K. returned to England, published a volume of poetry, and resumed her acting career. When Butler filed for divorce in 1848, she came back to America and spent her final years in public readings of Shakespeare, frequent visits to Europe, and, finally, in devoting herself to her lifelong ambition: writing. She wrote more memoirs, a critical work on Shakespeare, poetry, a comedy, and a novel (Henry James noted that not many people published a first novel at the age of 80). She developed friendships with a number of literary figures and died where she was born—in England.

Written twenty-two years before the outbreak of the Civil War and published in the same year that the slaves were emancipated, *Journal of a Residence on a Georgian Plantation, 1838–1839* (1863) describes the condition of the slaves in brutally realistic terms. Among many of the inhuman aspects which K. denounces, the painful life of women slaves is carefully detailed. Decrying their oppressed state of manual labor and continual childbearing, K. speaks of the females' "sorrow-laden existence" and their endurance of sufferings which appeared to be "all in the day's work." The book was well read during K.'s day, although its stark realism was disconcerting to the Victorian readership.

While posterity tends to remember K. as an actress, perhaps her place as a chronicler of the American experience should be reevaluated. Her autobiographical works, especially *Journal of a Residence in America* and *Journal of a Residence on a Georgian Plantation*, have a particular psychological and historical significance as documents that reveal the struggles and challenges facing a 19th-c. woman critical of national and regional narrowness.

The memoirs, bestsellers of their day, also contain keen insights into the enormous changes transforming the nation; K. recognized and evaluated the movement away from Victorian America toward the modern age. Criticized by some reviewers for her "racy" language and for her subjective judgments of particular individuals, K. nonetheless had the rare ability to write vivid and insightful observations of places, people, and historical changes she witnessed. Her journals are neither carefully crafted nor totally consistent pictures of life in early America, but they are rich psychological and cultural documents because of their author's complex personality, interests, and skills of observation. Perhaps Henry James's evaluation is the best assessment of K.: "There was no convenient or handy formula for Mrs. Kemble's genius, and one had to take her career, the juxtaposition of her interests, exactly as one took her disposition, for a remarkably fine cluster of inconsistencies."

WORKS: *Francis the First: A Tragedy in Five Acts* (1832). *Journal of a Residence in America* (1835). *The Star of Seville: A Drama in Five Acts* (1837). *A Year of Consolation* (1837). *Poems* (1844). *Poems* (1859). *Journal of a Residence on a Georgian Plantation, 1838–1839* (1863). *On the Stage* (1863). *Records of a Girlhood* (1878). *Notes upon Some of Shakespeare's Plays* (1882). *Records of a Later Life* (1882). *Poems* (1883). *Adventures of John Timothy Homespun in Switzerland* (1889). *Far Away and Long Ago* (1889).

BIBLIOGRAPHY: Armstrong, M., *Frances Kemble: The Passionate Victorian* (1938). Bobbe, D., *Frances Kemble* (1931). Driver, L., *Frances Kemble* (1933). Gibbs, H., *Yours Affectionately, Fanny* (1947). Marshall, D., *Frances Kemble* (1977). Wister, F. K., *Fanny: The American Kemble* (1972). Wright, C. C. *Frances Kemble and the Lovely Land* (1972).

For articles in reference works, see: *AA. British Authors of the Nineteenth Century*, Ed. S. J. Kunitz (1936). *DAB*, V, 2. *LSL. NAW* (article by H. L. Kleinfield).

MARJORIE SMELSTOR

Jean Collins Kerr

B. *10 July 1923, Scranton, Pennsylvania*
Writes under: Jean Kerr
D. *of Thomas J. and Kitty O'Neill Collins; m. Walter Kerr, 1943*

K. earned an M.A. in theater from the Catholic University, where she met her husband, a dramatics professor who later became the *New York Times* theater critic. K. regards herself principally as a playwright and her essays as a diversion, but it is the latter that have gained vast popularity. The typical style of K.'s plays and essays is the carefully polished imitation of easy conversation.

K. wrote three plays for her husband's direction at the Catholic University. The third, *Jenny Kissed Me* (1948), opened on Broadway, starring the famous comic actor Leo G. Carroll. Collaborating with her husband and the musician Jay Gorney, K. won praise for energy and intelligence in the revue, *Touch and Go* (1949). In the successful Broadway production *John Murray Anderson's Almanac* (1953), K.'s sketch "Don Brown's Body" uses the violent, sexually suggestive style of Mickey Spillane's detective stories to lampoon orchestrated readings of Stephen Vincent Benet's Civil War poem.

In K.'s most successful play, *Mary, Mary* (1961), the title character discovers her true, timid nature through a new admirer's eyes but returns to her first love just before he can divorce her for a less disarming wife. K.'s urbane wit is not only richly decorative but integral to character: Mary antagonizes her husband not with her superior insight into his publishing business but with the hilarious sarcasm that masks her personal insecurity. Mary draws audience sympathy for her clever vulnerability, but she wins her man because she learns to demonstrate sophistication.

K.'s most successful book, *Please Don't Eat the Daisies* (1957), collects fifteen humorous sketches written for popular magazines. Intelligent literary allusion and stylish satire enliven the familiar essay form, making spirited fun of an alert woman's irritations with rambunctious sons, slick-magazine advice, and a celebrated husband. Phrasing motherly boasting as complaints, K. idealizes family affections. She burlesques the distressingly clichéd 1950s prescriptions for glamorous or maternal feminine behavior by opposing them with precise details. In 1965, K. adapted her sketches for a two-season NBC situation comedy about a suburban free-lance writer, a college dramatics professor, and their four sons.

The best pieces in *The Snake Has All the Lines* (1960) portray K. less as a homemaker than as an author revising a play in a rehearsal or growing cynical over mixed critical reviews. Tributes to her determined Irish mother and her awkward Catholic school days show K. learning the value of her generous verbal wit.

In the best essay of her collection *Penny Candy* (1970), K. combines her two personae of a mother and a student of literature to recall her success in bringing her sons to share her love of poetry. Unfortunately, the made-to-order sketches for *Family Circle* and the *Ladies' Home Journal*, which outnumber the more original work, force K. to act the housewife flustered by babytalk, wilting houseplants, cocktail parties, and her weight.

Humorously alert to absurd trivialities, the strong female character who dominates K.'s essays and plays saves herself from selfish insignificance by her own generous instinct. During the thirty years of her writing career, K.'s essays have grown loose and self-revealing while her stage comedies have faced increasingly difficult social issues within constricting dramatic unities. Wary of intimidating her readers, K. rarely mentions the strains her writing and successful marriage place on each other. With merry charm, in the early 1960s, she seemed to synthesize the careers of Larchmont homemaker and Broadway playwright and thus unexpectedly became an American ideal, without being forced to scrutinize the difference between the values she held and those she represented.

WORKS: *The Song of Bernadette* by F. Werfel (dramatization by Kerr, 1944). *Our Hearts Were Young and Gay* by C. O. Skinner and E. Kimbrough (dramatization by Kerr, 1946). *The Big Help* (1947). *Jenny Kissed Me* (1948). *Touch and Go* (with W. Kerr and J. Gorney, 1949). *King of Hearts* (with E. Brooke, 1954; film version, *That Certain Feeling*, 1956). *Please Don't Eat the Daisies* (1957; film version, 1960; television series, 1965–67). *Goldilocks* (with W. Kerr and L. Anderson, 1958). *The Snake Has All the Lines* (1960). *Mary, Mary* (1961; film version, 1963). *Poor Richard* (1964). *Penny Candy* (1970). *Finishing Touches* (1973). *How I Got to Be Perfect* (1978). *Lunch Hour* (1980).

BIBLIOGRAPHY: For articles in reference works, see: *CA*, 5–8 (1969). *CB* (July 1958). *WA*.

Other references: *New York Theatre Critics Reviews* (1946–73). *NYT* (18 Feb. 1973). *SatR* (30 Nov. 1957). *Theatre Arts* (March 1961). *Time* (14 April 1961).

GAYLE GASKILL

Frances Parkinson Wheeler Keyes

B. *21 July 1885, Charlottesville, Virginia; d. 3 July 1970, New Orleans, Louisiana*
Wrote under: *Frances Parkinson Keyes*
D. *of John Henry and Louise Fuller Johnson Wheeler; m. Henry Wilder Keyes, 1904*

An only daughter, K. received but seven years of formal schooling—in Boston, Switzerland, Berlin—as was appropriate for a "gently born girl." Her husband, more than twenty years her senior, with whom she had three sons, was governor of New Hampshire and served three terms in the U.S. Senate. She describes her role as hostess in *Capital Kaleidoscope* (1937).

Always a rapid and omnivorous reader, K. wrote as a child but was not encouraged. She began publishing after her marriage because of desperate financial need. Soon a regular contributor to *Good Housekeeping*, K. was widely known for monthly "Letters from a Senator's Wife," which ran for fourteen years, and for other political analyses. A contributing editor from 1923 to 1936, K. wrote about her world trip in

1925–26 and another to South America in 1929–30. These formative years are described in *All Flags Flying* (1972), an incomplete autobiography published posthumously. K. contributed to other magazines, was editor of the Daughters of the American Revolution *National Historical Magazine* from 1937 to 1939, and was a frequent lecturer.

K.'s fame rests upon her extraordinary career as a best-selling novelist. Her first novel, *The Old Gray Homestead,* was published in 1919. Not until *Honor Bright* (1936) did she have a bestseller, but she was seldom without one throughout the next decades.

In spite of frequent and severe illness and a crippling back injury, K. was a person of great vitality and enthusiasm, many interests, extraordinary dedication to work, and an urgent need for fulfillment. She produced very long and fluent novels that reflected careful and diligent research to ensure correctness of setting and circumstance. She reveled in descriptions of rich foods, elegant clothes, gay parties, and exotic locales. Older civilizations fascinate, but also evidence decay; in her novels promise in the modern world lies in simplicity and hard work.

K. favored accounts of a family's fortunes through several generations. The first novels are set in New England, Washington, and Europe. Perhaps the most lavish is *Crescent Carnival* (1942), sumptuously detailing complex New Orleans traditions through three generations. After its enormous success K. spent her winters in Louisiana and developed a pattern in which she wrote Louisiana books alternatively with other novels. The highly successful *Dinner at Antoine's* (1948) added mystery to her customary romance.

The typical K. heroine is young, beautiful, naive, and in love with an older experienced man who is ennobled by passion for her. Temptations abound, but high principle triumphs, though the rule that a K. heroine is never seduced altered in the later novels. K.'s women are competent, loyal, and stoic in their acceptance of hardships. Some have personal careers, but usually their lives are shaped by marriage, and fulfillment comes in motherhood, woman's triumph for K.

Religion was important to K. Though her family was Congregational, she was attracted to formal ritual and was confirmed at fourteen in the Episcopal church. In *Along a Little Way* (1940) she describes her gradual growth to Catholicism and recent conversion. She wrote about a number of saints' lives and often described religious practice in her novels.

Her novels had a large audience in England and were also translated into several languages. K. received many awards and honorary degrees. Although resigned to not receiving critical acclaim, K. made a strong case for her craft in *The Cost of a Best-Seller* (1950). Admittedly sentimental and often rhetorical, her high romance is strengthened by common sense and diversified incidents. K.'s exposition of political and social circumstances and concern with international relations challenged American provincialism.

WORKS: *The Old Gray Homestead* (1919). *The Career of David Noble* (1921). *Letters from a Senator's Wife* (1924). *Queen Anne's Lace* (1930). *Silver Seas and Golden Cities* (1931). *Lady Blanche Farm: Senator Marlowe's Daughter* (1933). *The Safe Bridge* (1934). *The Happy Wanderer* (1935). *Honor Bright* (1936). *Capital Kaleidoscope* (1937). *Written in Heaven* (1937). *Parts Unknown* (1938). *The Great Tradition* (1939). *Along a Little Way* (1940). *Fielding's Folly* (1940). *The Sublime Shepherdess* (1940). *All That Glitters* (1941). *The Grace of Guadalupe* (1941). *Crescent Carnival* (1942). *Also the Hills* (1943). *The River Road* (1945). *Came a Cavalier* (1947). *Once on Esplanade* (1947). *Dinner at Antoine's* (1948). *All This Is Louisiana* (1950). *The Cost of a Best-Seller* (1950). *Joy Street* (1950). *Therese: Saint of a Little Way* (1950). *Steamboat Gothic* (1952). *Bernadette of Lourdes* (1953). *The Royal Box* (1954). *Frances Parkinson Keyes Cookbook* (1955). *Mother of Our Saviour* (1955). *The Blue Camellia* (1957). *Land of Stones and Saints* (1957). *Victorine* (1958). *Frances Parkinson Keyes Christmas Gift* (1959). *Mother Cabrini: Missionary to the World* (1959). *Station Wagon in Spain* (1959). *The Chess Players* (1960). *Roses in December* (1960). *The Third Mystic of Avila* (1960). *The Rose and the Lily* (1961). *Madame Castel's Lodger* (1962). *The Restless Lady, and Other Stories* (1963). *Three Ways of Love* (1963). *A Treasury of Favorite Poems* (1963). *The Explorer* (1964). *I, the King* (1966). *Tongues of Fire* (1966). *The Heritage* (1968). *All Flags Flying* (1972).

BIBLIOGRAPHY: For articles in reference works, see: *CA*, 5–8 (1969); 25–28 (1971). *Catholic Authors: Contemporary Biographical Sketches, 1930–1947*, Ed. M. Hoehn (1948). *20thCA*. *20thCAS*.

Other references: *CathW* (Jan. 1943). *CSM* (28 Nov. 1950). *NYHTB* (19 Nov. 1939). *NYTBR* (8 Nov. 1936; 8 Nov. 1942; 9 Dec. 1945). *Time* (26 Dec. 1960).

VELMA BOURGEOIS RICHMOND

Aline Murray Kilmer

B. 1 Aug. 1888, Norfolk, Virginia; d. 1 Oct. 1941, Stillwater, New Jersey
Wrote under: Aline Kilmer, Aline Murray
D. of Kenton and Ada Foster Murray; m. Joyce Kilmer, 1908

Among the literary members of K.'s family were her father, an editor; her stepfather, Henry Mills Alden, the editor of *Harper's Magazine;* and her husband, one of the more famous poets of the day and the poetry editor of the *Literary Digest.* Two of her sons were published poets. K. was educated at Rutgers Prep and at the Vail-Deane School in Elizabeth, New Jersey. In 1913, both she and her husband entered the Roman Catholic Church. They were the parents of five children. In 1918, Sgt. Joyce Kilmer of the "Fighting 69th" was killed in action in France.

Although she had published a few poems before her marriage, selling her first poem to *St. Nicholas* magazine at age eleven, K. was always overshadowed by her husband, both professionally and socially. Most critics concede, however, that she was the better poet. After his death her reserve lessened, and she occasionally made lecture tours to help with expenses. She served as vice-president of the Catholic Poetry Society of America. The death of her husband had been preceded by the death of one child from polio and was followed in a few years by the death of another. Both the subject matter and the tone of her work were largely determined by these events and her task of bringing up a family alone.

In *Candles That Burn* (1919) K. presents intensely personal poems, most of them about children, and many of these dealing with the still-raw pain of personal bereavement or the fear of loss. In some of these she is unable to transcend the experience, yet already in this first volume one can occasionally see the note of gentle irony that pervades her best mature poetry.

Vigils (1921) continues K.'s emphasis on personal preoccupations. A mere two strings of her instrument suffice, she writes in "The Harp": "One is for love and one for death. . . . I play on the strings I know." Although the cry of pain reappears in many of these poems, the poet has learned to transmute her material and to choose more evocative imagery. The rhythms have become her own. Literary subjects—the Lady of Shalott and Sappho—appear.

In *The Poor King's Daughter* (1925), K. has perfected her distinctive tone of gentle but unrelieved disillusionment, of irony delicate but never bitter. The intimacy remains, but a reticence disciplines it. The poet has now learned to maintain distance and to detach the poetic process from the experience. In "Favete Linguis" the poet admires the plum tree heavy with blossom but warns: "You lift your lute to celebrate its beauty / And all its petals flutter to the ground." The theme of enforced silence emerges again in the fine poem "Against the Wall." Here the irony of the parent calmly mending armor for the sons' fights, while silently lamenting the emptiness of victory and glory, achieves tragic overtones by K.'s use of conversational language and rhythms.

K.'s prose works include two children's books and *Hunting a Hair Shirt* (1923), a collection of brief personal essays similar in theme and tone to her verse.

WORKS: *Candles That Burn* (1919). *Vigils* (1921). *Hunting a Hair Shirt* (1923). *The Poor King's Daughter, and Other Poems* (1925). *Emmy, Nicky, and Greg* (1927). *A Buttonwood Summer* (1929). *Selected Poems* (1929).

BIBLIOGRAPHY: For articles in reference works, see: *Catholic Authors: Contemporary Biographical Sketches, 1930–1947*, Ed. M. Hoehn (1948). *CB* (Dec. 1941).

Other references: *America* (18 Oct. 1941). *Bookman* (Dec. 1921; May 1925). *CathW* (June 1929). *Commonweal* (17 July 1929; 14 Aug. 1929).

ARLENE ANDERSON SWIDLER

Emily Kimbrough

B. 23 Oct. 1899, Muncie, Indiana
D. of Hal Curry and Charlotte Emily Wiles Kimbrough;
  m. John Wrench, 1926

K. graduated from Bryn Mawr College in 1921, studied at the Sorbonne in Paris, and in 1923 began a career in advertising copywriting for Marshall Field & Co. that was to lead, four years later, to the managing editorship of the *Ladies' Home Journal*, a position she held until 1929.

In 1929 she gave birth to twin daughters; she was divorced after only several years' marriage. By 1934 K.'s articles had begun to appear in various national magazines, including *Country Life, House and Garden, Travel, Readers' Digest,* and *Saturday Review of Literature.* Even a reader of *Parents' Magazine* would have come across her down-to-earth advice about raising twins. By 1968 she had devoted herself to accounts of her frequent travels to Europe and around America.

Emily Kimbrough used to be a household name. "Oh, I LOVED *Our Hearts Were Young and Gay,*" is the inevitable cry of almost anyone old enough to read in 1942. K.'s first and most famous work, written jointly with Cornelia Otis Skinner, was a chronicle of their nineteenth summer, spent in Europe contracting measles on an ocean liner, over-nighting in an unsuspected brothel, lunching at the Ritz in Paris, and generally charming one continent with their exploits and another with the reminiscences of them. K.'s next volume, *We Followed Our Hearts to Hollywood* (1943), describes the summer she and Skinner spent writ-ing a film script for *Our Hearts.*

And it is the amusement and satisfaction that remain with the reader of any of K.'s subsequent books, which followed *Our Hearts Were Young and Gay* in rapid succession. At one time, K.'s travel books were standard guides to England, Italy, Portugal, Greece, France, and Ireland; that they have fallen out of currency is our loss. Full of Miche-lin-type restaurant and hotel lore, news of vistas and sights far beyond the guidebooks, and chatty stories of the people behind the walls and doors forming the boundaries of most tourists' experiences, they were the guiding tour lights of an entire generation. K. does more than re-count the sights seen or merely detail the humorous adventures of four middle-aged women who "no speaka da language"—she takes the reader into the atmosphere of the places she visits, and throughout she pro-vides the reader with the most intimate historical details.

But it is not only for her travel books that K. deserves to be remem-bered. *Through Charley's Door* (1952) is an intimate biography of Mar-shall Field & Co. and takes the reader to the heart of Chicago's venerable department store. Equally good are her stories of her childhood. *How Dear to My Heart* (1944) introduces six-year-old Emily about to begin school. The innocence and imagination of childhood are recreated in this story of her extended family (including Indiana Senator Charles M. Kimbrough), of the birth of her baby brother, and of her growing understanding of the world. In *The Innocents from Indiana* (1950) the eleven-year-old Emily moves from Muncie to Chicago and learns to love the big city in a series of adventures that includes playing catch unawares with Douglas Fairbanks and driving around and around the block in an electric car that cannot be stopped because its clutch is stuck. In *Now and Then* (1972) K. goes back, through her twins' childhood experiences, to more of her own. These delightful, low-key books, reminiscent of James Thurber, should be included among adolescent reading selections, for they reproduce the puzzlement and triumph of a child growing into herself.

K.'s writing has a simplicity and directness that immediately attracts. Her own naive pleasure at what she has seen, heard, and experienced is communicated directly to the reader. Of course, such simplicity dates the travel books; they could hardly be written in these days of jet travel, inflation, and mass education. It is for this reason that K. is an important mid–20th-c. writer, for she manages to reproduce the wonderment of which the American, particularly the sophisticated American matron, is no longer capable.

In addition to a sharp sense of the times, K.'s books present a great deal of information that, even if much of it is dated, provides the sort of rich historical background which is only now being noted in the writings of such regionalists as Jewett and Chopin. K.'s readers can hardly help but experience an otherwise unrecapturable past. Each book ends before we want it to and dances around the edges of our memories. It is little wonder that *Our Hearts Were Young and Gay* remains in print, and beloved, to this day.

WORKS: *Our Hearts Were Young and Gay* (1942). *We Followed Our Hearts to Hollywood* (1943). *How Dear to My Heart* (1944). *The Innocents from Indiana* (1950). *Through Charley's Door* (1952). *Forty Plus and Fancy Free* (1954). *So Near and Yet So Far* (1955). *Water, Water Everywhere* (1956). *And a Right Good Crew* (1958). *Pleasure by the Busload* (1961). *Forever Old, Forever New* (1964). *Floating Island* (1968). *Now and Then* (1972). *Time Enough* (1974). *Better Than Oceans* (1976).

BIBLIOGRAPHY: For articles in reference works, see: *CA*, 17–20 (1976). *CB* (March 1944). *Indiana Authors and Their Books, 1917–1966*, Ed. D. E. Thompson, 1974.

Other references: *Atlantic* (Dec. 1942). *NYTBR* (22 Nov. 1942). *SatR* (11 Dec. 1943).

LORALEE MacPIKE

Caroline Matilda Stansbury Kirkland

B. 11 Jan. 1801, New York City; d. 6 April 1864, New York City
Wrote under: Mrs. Mary Clavers, Caroline M. Stansbury Kirkland, Aminadab Peering
D. of Samuel and Eliza Alexander Stansbury; m. William Kirkland, 1828

K., an eldest child, came from a literary family (her mother was a writer and her great-grandfather was a Tory poet during the American Revolution). In the Quaker school of her aunt Lydia Mott she received an unusually good education for a girl born at the beginning of the 19th c. After her marriage to Kirkland the couple settled in Geneva, New York, where they established a school. In 1835, they crossed overland to Detroit, an already thriving "metropolis" on the edge of the frontier to direct the newly established Detroit female seminary. The land fever and get-rich schemes that were circulating through Detroit engaged their imagination, and two years later they located sixty miles west, in the tiny hamlet of Pinckney.

The pioneering experience was the impetus for K.'s writing career. A New Home—Who'll Follow? (1839), written by K. under the pseudonym "Mrs. Mary Clavers, an Actual Settler," gives her slightly fictionalized account of the early years of a new community on the frontier. Loosely constructed of character sketches, brief essays on events unique to frontier life, tales, and a few mild adventures, the book covers the development of the town from the log cabin to the community. Though K. claims that nothing very adventurous happens, the life she describes is, in fact, eventful and arduous. In her second book, Forest Life (1842), the device of a tour of Michigan allows K. to comment on the developing institutions of the frontier, to generalize on events, and to describe the natural terrain and the process of the transformation of the diverse aspects of pioneer life into a less precarious existence. Integrating her impressions, K. comments on the scene in retrospect and with accumulated insight.

K. returned to the East in 1843, where her husband would have better professional opportunities and their four children (Joseph Kirkland, the

eldest son, later became a well-known novelist) could get proper schooling. After her husband's death in 1846, K. immediately took up his
responsibilities at the *Christian Inquirer,* operated her school for girls,
reviewed for Duyckinck's *Literary World,* and shortly thereafter undertook the editorship of the *Union Magazine of Literature and Art.* In its
earliest days under K.'s leadership the *Union* was considered one of the
best family magazines of its kind.

A New Home—Who'll Follow? brought immediate popularity; *Forest
Life* followed to enthusiastic reviews. Poe thought *Western Clearings*
(1845), a collection of sketches that move toward the short-story form,
the best of all. Though best known for this western writing, K. also
completed a travel book, a biography of Washington, a novel, and three
collections of essays. But the work of the last twenty years of her life
remains unexplored and unevaluated.

Though never identified with the women's rights movement, K.'s introduction to Reid's *A Plea for Women* (1845) appeared three years before the first women's rights convention at Seneca Falls. K. advocated
equal legal and political rights, and was especially bitter on the problem
of women's financial dependence. She was also deeply concerned about
the slavery issue and, by 1856, after completing her Washington biography, wrote a friend, "I am terribly low-spirited about public affairs. I
see nothing but civil war and disunion before us." Though a pacifist, she
supported and worked for the Union.

In the early 1850s, her short stories and essays were brought out as
gift-book collections: *The Evening Book* (1852); *A Book for the Home
Circle* (1853); and *Autumn Hours* (1854). The major topic in each was
the correction and improvement of American manners and morals,
which she managed to urge with sophisticated, disarming simplicity quite
different from the saccharine and somber utilitarianism that characterized most literature on the same topics. In one essay, "Literary Women,"
a spirited defense of women authors, K. with tongue in cheek suggests
that shopkeepers not sell pens to women who write, and that women
should be excluded from school—at least till they are over forty.

At a time when popular literature consisted of moralizing essays on
self-improvement and sentimental tales, K., in contrast, expressed herself
clearly, concisely, and humorously. Her themes, settings, characters, and
moral vision were a realist's. Her range of female characters gives a
more complete picture of the nature and condition of women than can
be derived from the work of the first-ranking American authors of the
period. K. wrote, "It has been thought necessary to dress up and render

conspicuous a certain class of events, while another class, perhaps far more efficient in producing the real features of the age, are unnoticed and forgotten." K., with her realist's perspectives, makes a significant contribution to our own times.

WORKS: *A New Home—Who'll Follow? or, Glimpses of Western Life* (1839). *Forest Life* (1842). *Principles of Morality* by J. Dymond (edited by Kirkland, 1847). *Western Clearings* (1845). *Spenser and the Faery Queen* (edited by Kirkland, 1847). *Holidays Abroad* (1849). *The Book of Home Beauty* (1852). *The Evening Book* (1852). *Garden Walks with the Poets* (1852). *A Book for the Home Circle; or, Familiar Thoughts on Various Topics, Literary, Moral, and Social* (1853). *The Helping Hand* (1853). *Autumn Hours* (1854). *Memoirs of Washington* (1857). *The School-Girl's Garland* (1864). *Patriotic Eloquence* (1866).

BIBLIOGRAPHY: Dondore, D. A., *The Prairie and the Making of Middle America: Four Centuries of Description* (1926). Keyes, L. C., "Caroline Matilda Kirkland: A Pioneer in American Realism" (Ph.D. diss., Harvard Univ., 1935). Osborne, W. S., *Caroline Matilda Kirkland* (1972). Poe, E. A., "The Literati of New York City," *Godey's Lady's Book* (August 1846). Riordan, D. G., "The Concept of Simplicity in the Works of Mrs. Caroline Matilda Kirkland" (Ph.D. diss., Univ. of North Carolina, 1973). Roberts, A. J., "The Letters of Caroline Matilda Kirkland" (Ph.D. diss., Univ. of Wisconsin, 1976).

For articles in reference works, see: *AA. CAL. DAB*, V, 2. *NAW* (article by L. C. Keyes). *NCAB*, 5.

Other references: *MichH* (Sept. 1956; March 1958; Dec. 1961).

AUDREY ROBERTS

Sarah Kemble Knight

B. *19 April 1666, Boston, Massachusetts; d. 25 Sept. 1727, New London,*
   Connecticut
D. *of Thomas and Elizabeth Trerice Kemble; m. Richard Knight, 1689*

When K. was born, her family had already been in New England for a generation. Her husband was by some accounts a shipmaster, though a recent study suggests that he may have been the Richard Knight listed in two records as a publican. Upon her father's death, K. inherited a house on Moon Street, where she maintained a large household, which included her mother, her daughter, and several lodgers, some of whom may have been relatives.

K. herself was active in the copying and witnessing of legal documents and in the settling of estates. She kept a shop in the Moon Street house and is said to have run a writing school, though this has not been verified.

In the fall and winter of 1704–05, in order to settle an estate for one of the relatives in her household, K. traveled on horseback from Boston to New York and back. She was the first woman to accomplish such a feat, securing guides and stopping at various post-houses, inns, and, occasionally, homes in the towns she passed through.

There remains no further record of Richard Knight after 1706. In 1713, when K.'s daughter married, K. sold the Boston house and moved to Norwich and New London, Connecticut. There she speculated in Indian lands, ran several farms, and kept a house of entertainment.

During the journey from Boston to New York, K. kept notes which upon her return she fashioned into a journal. At that time overland travel between the colonies was difficult; there were no main roads, and a traveler had to secure local guides to get from one town or posting place to another. The colonies were separate in government and customs; there were as yet no newspapers; it was only through letters or travelers' tales that colonists learned about events and customs elsewhere. K.'s racy narrative describes the difficulties of travel, the inconveniences of inns, and the people she met, ranging from the governor of Connecticut, with whom she supped, to the poor family who allowed her refuge in their drafty hut. Her perceptive, sharp wit spares no one, not even herself. The narrative is a series of episodes pulled together by the vitality and strength of character of its author.

Brief as it is, and though it remained in manuscript until 1825, the journal is a landmark in our literature for several reasons. Along with the journal of Samuel Sewall, it represents the lay view as opposed to that of the ministers, who until this time dominated American letters. As K.'s account rushes along, she displays several of the types of humor and characters that were to develop as typically American. The pompous judge making a fool of himself, the laconic master of understatement, the country "bumpkin" who later may be seen as Yankee Doodle, and a succession of other tobacco-chewing yokels. Her use of generic names for characters, such as "Bumpkin Simpers," "Joan Tawdry," and "Gaffer," perhaps based on a reading of *Pilgrim's Progress*, presages the use of stereotyped characters in the newspapers soon to be started in England

and America. In one passage where K. is riding at night, she imagines the towers of towns and palaces, displaying a longing for Europe which recurs in much of American literature through Henry James and later expatriates, and her descriptions of the terrors of night resemble the Gothic effects later used by Irving.

Her journal indicates throughout that its author was well-versed in the popular literature of the day. Its prose is interlaced with poems in a variety of current styles; in one poem she uses the kind of couplets in vogue in England but not in America at the time. Altogether her journal represents an early movement toward the satire and other forms that were used throughout the 18th c. and presents an unusual and vivid series of pictures of the ordinary and extraordinary people of New England.

WORKS: *The Journals of Madam Knight, and Rev. Mr. Buckingham* (1825). *The Private Journal of a Journey from Boston to New York in the Year 1704 Kept by Madam Knight* (1865).

BIBLIOGRAPHY: Freiberg, M., Introduction to *The Journal of Madam Knight* (1972). Stanford, A., "Images of Women in Early American Literature," in *What Manner of Woman*, Ed. M. Springer (1977). Winship, G. P., Introduction to *The Journal of Madam Knight* (1920, 1935).
  For articles in reference works, see: *AA. DAB*, V, 2. *NAW* (article by M. Freiberg).
  Other references: *Bostonian Society Publications* 9 (1912). *CLAJ* (March 1964; Dec. 1966). *PBSA* (First quarter, 1964).

ANN STANFORD

Martha Joanna Reade Nash Lamb

B. *12 Aug. 1826, Plainfield, Massachusetts; d. 2 Jan. 1893, New York City*
Wrote under: Aunt Mattie, Mrs. Martha J. Lamb
D. of Arvin and Lucinda Vinton Nash; m. Charles A. Lamb, 1852

L. began her career as a writer of children's stories and a romantic novel. It was, however, as a historian of the city of New York and as an editor

(1883–93) of the *Magazine of American History* that she did her most significant work.

L.'s major publication is her *History of the City of New York*, the first volume appearing in 1877, the second in 1880. The two comprise the history of New York from the era of Hudson's discovery to the inauguration of Washington. After L.'s death, Constance Cary Harrison contributed a brief supplementary volume to the history, *Externals of Modern New York* (1896).

L.'s perspective in the *History of the City of New York* is that of the narrative historian, and she concentrates particularly on political developments. In the Dutch era, she traces with acuity the internal conflicts, giving special stress to the role of Peter Stuyvesant. She discusses with sympathetic insight the efforts of the British to amalgamate peacefully the two communities in the colony of New York. In the 18th-c. history, L. particularly stresses the growing conflict with the British and the city's role in the Revolution and the new nation.

L. also gives some attention to the social history of New York, noting particularly the roles of the emerging major families and their interlocking interests. On the other hand, she does not attempt to deal in any depth with the city's economic development.

L.'s *The Homes of America* (1879) is an account of historic homes, primarily of political leaders, from the early 17th to the mid-19th centuries. For the 19th c., she included residences of artists and writers. The work was not a history of American architecture but rather a descriptive account, including biographical sketches and a number of brief family histories.

As editor of the *Magazine of American History*, L. contributed some fifty signed and many unsigned articles. Her *Wall Street in History* (1883) consists of material that first appeared in three issues (May–July 1883). The book is a lively, well-researched account of three stages of the history of the street: the early Dutch and English developments; its 18th-c. role as "seat of fashion, aristocracy and state government"; and its 19th-c. role as financial center. L.'s account is descriptive rather than analytical, and she deals in very general and positive terms with Wall Street's financial role.

L. also wrote fiction. Her novel *Spicy* (1873) is a romantic mystery, with the recent Chicago fire giving dramatic climax to the work. She also wrote several children's stories, generally moralistic, and edited such publications as *The Christmas Basket* (1882), a collection of poetry.

It was as a narrative historian that L. was most successful. She handled with clarity and balance the broad developments of public life. She had a keen eye for character, and she wrote with a dramatic flair of such events as the Zenger trial. Her style is somewhat stilted at times, but she wrote with ease. Though somewhat discursive and occasionally preoccupied with minute detail, on the whole she developed forcefully and with balanced judgment the major political themes.

L. was a thorough if untrained researcher with a great interest in primary sources. She utilized manuscript collections, public records, private letters, and personal interviews. Accordingly, her historical work has depth and solidity. She wrote primarily for an educated general public. In her *History of New York* she best achieved her goal of combining sound historical scholarship with popular appeal.

WORKS: *Laughing Kittie and Purring Kittie, with Other Little Folks at Robinwood* (1868). *The Playschool Stories for Little Folks* (1869). *Aunt Mattie's Library* (1870). *Drifting Goodward* (1870). *Fun and Profit* (1870). *Spicy* (1873). *History of the City of New York: Its Origin, Rise, and Progress* (2 vols., 1877, 1880). *The Homes of America* (1879). *The Christmas Owl: A Budget of Entertainment* (edited by Lamb, 1881). *The Christmas Basket: Holiday Entertainment* (edited by Lamb, 1882). *Snow and Sunshine: A Story for Boys and Girls* (1882). *Wall Street in History* (1883). *A Guide for Strangers to General Grant's Tomb in Riverside Park* (1886). *Our Country Fifty Years Ago: Some Incidents in Connection with Lafayette's Visit* (1887). *The Washington Inauguration* (1889).

BIBLIOGRAPHY: Lyman, S. E., *Lady Historian: Martha Joanna Lamb* (1969).
For articles in reference works, see: *AA. AW. DAB*, V, 2. *NAW* (article by R. H. Robinson). *NCAB*, 1.
Other references: *Godey's Lady's Book* (Nov. 1887). *NYT* (3 Jan. 1893).

INZER BYERS

Rose Wilder Lane

B. 5 Dec. 1886, De Smet, South Dakota; d. 30 Oct. 1968, Danbury, Connecticut
D. of Almanzo and Laura Ingalls Wilder; m. Gillette Lane, 1909

Unconventional from the first, L. left her parents' Mansfield, Missouri, home to work as a telegraph operator for Western Union. She married a land speculator whose ne'er-do-well behavior soon forced L. to fend for herself as the first woman real-estate agent in California. She was a reporter for the San Francisco *Bulletin* from 1914 to 1918. Written during this period, and indicative of her admiration for American heroes, are *Henry Ford's Own Story* (1917) and *The Making of Herbert Hoover* (1920), both panegyrics to men she considered archetypally American in their resourcefulness and individualism. After formally divorcing her husband, L. worked for the American Red Cross during World War I, primarily in Russia, Turkey, and Albania. *The Peaks of Shala* (1923) is a travelogue of her adventures in Albania.

In the 1920s, her articles and short stories filled the most popular magazines and journals. In 1922, she received the second-place O. Henry best short story of the year award for "Innocence." "Yarbwoman" was included in O'Brien's *The Best Short Stories of 1927*, and her "Old Maid" was singled out for O. Henry honors again in 1933. L. became one of the highest-paid writers in the U.S. "Innocence" and "Yarbwoman" are both set among poor whites of the South. Ironically, L.'s two prize-winning stories have an atypically eerie air. The dark forces are eventually shown to be those cruel and ignorant aspects of human nature that come from within man himself, especially as he is limited by moribund social structures.

Her Ozark novels, *Hill Billy* (1925) and *Cindy* (1928), were followed by her pioneer novels, *Let the Hurricane Roar* (1933) and *Free Land* (1938). In *Let the Hurricane Roar* two young pioneers struggle with the most intolerable conditions of the Dakota frontier, finding at last a sort of sad strength in themselves, even after their most cherished illusions are gone. The novel celebrates the capacity of the individual pioneer. *Free Land* takes a sardonic view of the governmental scheme to settle the frontier by the free grant of land. L.'s portrait of foolish expectations is satirical, but tempered by sympathy for the real sufferings of the naive settlers.

In *Old Home Town* (1935), a collection of stories about women in a midwestern town, L. dissects small-town life. Convention, intolerance, and gossip force the various women characters into unhappy marriages, into shame at being old maids of twenty-six, and even into suicide and murder. In the most overtly feminist story, "Immoral Woman," the lovely and talented Mrs. Sims is unjustly driven from the town by her clod of a husband and by the townspeople, who are held in thrall by the meanness of their accepted mores. She becomes a liberated woman and an internationally famous designer.

Give Me Liberty (1936) began L.'s overtly political career, and her belletristic efforts correspondingly diminished. In *The Discovery of*

Freedom (1943), she maintains that the progress of human civilization is towards "individualistic libertarianism" (with emphasis on private ownership) and individual freedom from coercion by collective society. Her adamant refusal to support New Deal programs such as social security and her opposition to taxation led her into increasingly conservative political company.

L. was editor of the National Economic Council's *Review of Books* from 1945 to 1950, but after some of her more bitter political disputes, she retreated from the public arena, concerning herself with domestic arts, local politics, and behind-the-scenes encouragement of individualistic libertarianism. In 1965, *Woman's Day* magazine called L. out of retirement to serve as their war correspondent in Vietnam. She died suddenly of a heart attack just before a projected trip abroad in 1968.

L. was a woman of varied adventures and several careers, but the greatest proportion of her prolific literary production centered around intensely American life. She wrote in praise of the American capitalist and of the pioneer woman of the American West. In many ways her style is simple, but delightful in its factual detail and portraiture of life from a primarily feminine point of view.

L.'s thought and work resist traditional labels. Brilliant, adventurous, and self-sufficient, she was very opposed to the socialistic idealism that has been historically connected with revolutionaries of her type in America. She saw governmental authority and small-town propriety as abstractions that had no right to control the actual pragmatic course of real people's lives. This fierce elevation of the actual is the bedrock theme of her literary celebration of the quintessential American spirit.

WORKS: *Art Smith's Story* (1915). *Henry Ford's Own Story* (1917). *Diverging Roads* (1919). *White Shadows in the South Seas* (1919). *The Making of Herbert Hoover* (1920). *The Dancers of Shamahka* (1923). *The Peaks of Shala* (1923). *He Was a Man* (1925). *Hill Billy* (1925). *Cindy* (1928). *Let the Hurricane Roar* (1933). *Old Home Town* (1935). *Give Me Liberty* (1936). *Free Land* (1938). *The Discovery of Freedom* (1943). *Woman's Day Book of American Needlework* (1963). *The Lady and the Tycoon* (1973).

BIBLIOGRAPHY: MacBride, R., ed., *The Lady and the Tycoon: Letters of Rose Wilder Lane and Jasper Crane* (1973). MacBride, R., *Rose Wilder Lane: Her Story* (1977). Weaver, H., *Mainspring, Based on the Discovery of Freedom* (1947).

For articles in reference works, see: *20thCA. 20thCAS.*
Other references: *NewR* (24 April 1944).

L. W. KOENGETER

Susanne Katherina Knauth Langer

B. 20 Dec. 1895, New York City
Writes under: Susanne K. Langer
D. of Antonio and Else Uhlich Knauth; m. William L. Langer, 1921

L. received her B.A., M.A., and Ph.D. degrees all from Radcliffe College. She studied for a year (1921–22) at the University of Vienna. L. served as a tutor in philosophy at her alma mater from 1927 to 1942 and taught at the University of Delaware in 1943 and at Columbia University from 1945 to 1950. She was professor of philosophy at Connecticut College for Women from 1954 to 1962. She has been the recipient of numerous research grants and honorary degrees.

L. has two sons. She was divorced in 1942. She now lives in Olde Lyme, Connecticut.

In her first major work, *The Practice of Philosophy* (1930), L. introduces many of the themes that engage her later thinking. Intended as an introduction to philosophy, the book defines philosophy as the search for the logical connections among meanings and contrasts it with science, which seeks the empirical connections among facts. The study of symbolic logic, the logic of relations, is therefore an indispensable preliminary to the study of the more engrossing problems of metaphysics, ethics, and aesthetics.

In *An Introduction to Symbolic Logic* (1937), L. sets out at length the system whose value she had proposed in *The Practice of Philosophy*.

Philosophy in a New Key: A Study in the Symbols of Reason, Rite, and Art (1942) is the explicit exposition of the theory of symbolism which had only been indicated in her two earlier works. The "new key" is the focus upon symbol-using as the essence of such diverse enterprises as mathematics, science, psychology, and art. L. does not claim to have been the first to strike this new key, but only to have recognized it and to have shown how some of the chief questions of philosophy have been transposed into it.

In *Feeling and Form: A Theory of Art Developed from Philosophy in a New Key* (1953), L. applies the theory of art proposed in the earlier book to the various major art forms. The arts are alike in that they all create forms symbolic of human feeling; they differ in that each creates a different "primary illusion."

All of the essays in *Philosophical Sketches* (1962) are preliminary studies for a complete philosophy of mind, which is attempted in *Mind: An Essay on Human Feeling* (1967, 1972). Her purpose here is to understand "the nature and origin of the veritable gulf that divides human from animal mentality, in a perfectly continuous course of development of life on earth that has no breaks." She develops the thesis that the departure of human from animal mentality "is a vast and special evolution of feeling in the hominid stock," a development so great that it adds up to a qualitative difference that sets human nature apart from the rest of the animal kingdom.

The fault she finds in most previous theories of mind is that they borrow their images from physics, and such images are inadequate to the richness of mental phenomena. L., in contrast, turns to works of art, which, as "images of the forms of feeling," can more adequately reveal the psychic life.

L.'s own works exhibit what she finds in the course of evolution: a process of growth in which there is no break in continuity from the beginning to the present and yet in which there is considerable development and enrichment. Her writings are from the earliest characterized by an exceptional sensitivity to both art and the dynamisms of the subjective life; she has combined with this sensitivity a familiarity with a broad range of scientific research.

L. has acknowledged the influence on her ideas of such diverse thinkers as Alfred North Whitehead, Bertrand Russell, Ludwig Wittgenstein, Sigmund Freud, and Ernst Cassirer; however, she is an original thinker whose insights have transformed what she has received from others. She has continued to present her insights within the framework of an overall empiricist philosophy, but even those who question this framework find much to value in her work. L.'s sensitivity to the life of feeling and her refusal to consign art (and myth, and ritual) to a place of less importance than that held by the discursive enterprises assure her a place of lasting influence among philosophers, art theorists, and the lay public.

WORKS: *The Cruise of the Little Dipper, and Other Fairy Tales* (1923; rev. ed., 1963). *The Practice of Philosophy* (1930). *An Introduction to Symbolic Logic* (1937; rev. eds., 1953, 1967). *Philosophy in a New Key: A Study in the Symbolism of Reason, Rite, and Art* (1942; rev. eds., 1951, 1957).

Language and Myth by E. Cassirer (translated by Langer, 1946). *Structure, Method, and Meaning: Essays in Honor of Henry M. Sheffer* (edited by Langer, with P. Henle and H. M. Kallen, 1951). *Feeling and Form: A Theory of Art Developed from Philosophy in a New Key* (1953). *Problems of Art: Ten Philosophical Lectures* (1957). *Reflections on Art: A Source Book of Writings by Artists, Critics, and Philosophers* (edited by Langer, 1958). *Philosophical Sketches* (1962). *Mind: An Essay on Human Feeling* (2 vols.; 1967, 1972).

BIBLIOGRAPHY: Liddy, R. M., *Art and Feeling: An Analysis and Critique of the Philosophy of Art of Susanne Katherina Langer* (1970).

For articles in reference works, see: *CA*, 41–44 (1974). *CB* (Nov. 1963). *20thCAS*.

Other references: *BJA* 8 (Oct. 1968). *Gregorianum* 53 (1972). *JAAC* (14, 1955–56; 27, 1968; 28, 1970; 29, 1970; 30, 1972; 31, 1972). *Personalist* 46 (1965). *Process Studies* 4 (Fall 1974). *Review of Metaphysics* (7, 1954; 16, 1962–63; 23, 1970).

HELENE DWYER POLAND

Lucy Larcom

B. 5 March 1824, Beverly, Massachusetts; d. 17 April 1893, Boston, Massachusetts
D. of Benjamin and Lois Barrett Larcom

L. grew up in the seaport town of Beverly. Her father was a retired shipmaster; her mother raised a family of ten children, of which L. was next to the youngest. The events and experiences of her early childhood are vividly described in her autobiography, *A New England Girlhood, Outlined from Memory* (1889).

This work remains one of our most important authentic descriptions of the daily experience of a young working woman in the 19th c. Remarkably unsentimental, L. captures the sights and sounds of a bustling port town and relates the reactions of a growing girl to her social environment.

When L. was nine years old, her father died; having no other means of support, her mother moved the family to the mill town of Lowell, Massachusetts, where even the children could earn enough to contribute to the family income. L.'s mother ran a boardinghouse for the factory girls, and L. herself went to work in the mills at the age of eleven, as a "bobbin girl," changing the bobbins on the spinning frames. The hours of work were from 5 A.M. to 7 P.M.

L. and her sister Emeline initiated a series of biweekly journals to which they and other women in their boardinghouse contributed creative pieces. L.'s own contributions were mainly poetical, following a bent she had developed in early childhood. By 1840 creative works of the mill women were being published in two literary magazines, the *Lowell Offering* and the *Operatives' Magazine*. In 1842 these merged as the *Lowell Offering*, edited by Harriet Farley and Harriot Curtiss. It continued until 1847 and at its height had a subscription list of four thousand. L. contributed regularly to this journal, which is now recognized as a unique literary expression of working-class women.

At age sixteen L. was transferred to the position of bookkeeper in the Lawrence Mills. There she had more time to study and to write. In 1846 L. moved with her sister Emeline's family to Illinois, where she graduated in 1852 from the Monticello Female Seminary in Alton. She then returned to the East and in 1854 began teaching at the Wheaton Seminary in Norton, Massachusettts. That year she published her first book, *Similitudes from the Ocean and the Prairie*, a series of prose parables, which she later dismissed as an immature work.

During this period she published poetry in newspapers and in the *Atlantic Monthly*. In 1862 she resigned her teaching position and in 1865 became, along with Gail Hamilton (Mary Abigail Dodge) and J. T. Trowbridge, an editor of *Our Young Folks*, a leading juvenile magazine. In 1868 she was named sole editor. L. never married, mainly because she wished to remain independent enough to pursue her career as a writer.

Her first collection of verse, *Poems* (1868), was reissued in 1885 in the popular "household edition." L.'s most important poetical work was *An Idyl of Work* (1875), a long poem in blank verse, which dealt with the Lowell factory women she had known in the 1840s.

L. edited several anthologies with her friend John Greenleaf Whittier. These included *Child Life* (1871), *Child Life in Prose* (1873), and *Songs of Three Centuries* (1875). These collections were all published under Whittier's name, but it is clear that she had the major hand in their creation from the fact that he split the royalties with her. In the preface to *Child Life in Prose*, Whittier acknowledges that L. did most of the work. Works by both L. and Whittier were included in these collections. She also herself compiled several popular books of collected poems.

L.'s reputation today rests not so much on the popular verse which brought her fame in her own day, but rather on the straightforward, unsentimental picture of her life and times she has given us in her prose works.

WORKS: *Similitudes from the Ocean and the Prairie* (1854). *Lottie's Thought-Book* (1858). *Ships in the Mist, and Other Stories* (1860). *Leila among the Mountains* (attributed to Larcom, 1861). *Breathings of a Better Life* (1866). *Poems* (1868). *Child Life* (edited by Larcom, with J. G. Whittier, 1871). *Child Life in Prose* (edited by Larcom, with J. G. Whittier, 1873). *Childhood Songs* (1875). *An Idyl of Work* (1875). *Songs of Three Centuries* (edited by Larcom, with J. G. Whittier, 1875). *Roadside Poems for Summer Travellers* (compiled by Larcom, 1876). *Hillside and Seaside in Poetry: A Companion to 'Roadside Poems'* (compiled by Larcom, 1877). *Snow Bloom, and Other Poems* (ca. 1880–82). *Wild Roses of Cape Ann, and Other Poems* (1881). *Wheaton Seminary: A Centennial Sketch* (1885). *The Cross and the Grail* (1887). *A New England Girlhood, Outlined from Memory* (1889). *Easter Gleams: Poems* (1890). *As It Is in Heaven* (1891). *At the Beautiful Gate, and Other Songs of Faith* (1892). *The Unseen Friend* (1892). *Lucy Larcom: Life, Letters, and Diary* (Ed. D. D. Addison, 1894). *Beckonings from Every Day: A Calendar of Thought* (1895). *Letters of Lucy Larcom to the Whittiers* (Ed. G. F. Shepard, 1930).

The papers of Lucy Larcom are at the Essex Institute, James Duncan Phillips Library, Salem, Massachusetts.

BIBLIOGRAPHY: Eisler, B., *The Lowell Offering* (1971). Robinson, H. H., *Loom and Spindle; or, Life among the Mill Girls* (1898). Ward, S. H., ed., *The Rushlight, Special Number in Memory of L. L.* (1894). Westbrook, P. D., *Acres of Flint, Writers of Rural New England 1870–1900* (1951).

For articles in reference works, see: *AA. AW. DAB*, V, 2. *FPA. NCAB*, 1. *NAW* (article by D. Baldwin).

Other references: *Women's Studies* I (1973).

JOSEPHINE DONOVAN

Elizabeth Wormeley Latimer

B. 26 July 1822, London, England; d. 4 Jan. 1904, Baltimore, Maryland
Wrote under: Elizabeth W. Latimer, Elizabeth Wormeley
D. of Ralph Randolph and Caroline Preble Wormeley; m. Randolph Brandt
   Latimer, 1856

L.'s family roots were planted in three soils: her father, although raised in England and a rear admiral in the British Navy, was of old-landed Virginia stock; her mother was the daughter of an East-India merchant of Boston. In her youth, L. lived in London, Paris, Boston, Newport, and Virginia. In London and Paris she attended the funeral of William IV and the reburial of Napoleon, saw Queen Victoria in coronation regalia, met William M. Thackeray, and attended Louis Philippe's balls. In Boston, in 1842, she met George Ticknor, William H. Prescott, and Julia Ward Howe, who encouraged her to write. Her first publication was a translation of a Mexican poem for the appendix of Prescott's *History of the Conquest of Mexico.*

In 1848, after witnessing the revolution in Paris and Chartist demonstrations in London, the Wormeley family moved back to New England. L. published several novels before marrying and moving to Maryland. She then spent twenty years rearing children and, during the Civil War, caring for wounded soldiers. Although her eyes were weak, she read assiduously and, during the last thirty years of her life, she published prolifically: novels, magazine articles, translations from French and Italian, and popular European histories that went through many editions.

L.'s best works are her histories, anecdotal in style. As a compiler and editor, she read copiously from magazines, newspapers, books, and private papers, then presented her information in lively, compact, confident prose. She did not claim to be a historian, but stated in her prefaces that she concentrated on the historical figures who interested her. She was fascinated by the adventures of royalty, explorers, and military people. Occasionally she inserted information from her family's experiences. In *France in the Nineteenth Century* (1892), for example, she wrote from personal observation, and in *Europe in Africa in the Nineteenth Century* (1898), L. mentioned some personal letters she had received from Liberians in 1854. In all the histories, one senses her desire to keep abreast of events in the world and, at the century's end, to sum up historic achievements.

Some of her novels are quite bad. *Salvage* (1880), for example, is largely a diatribe against easy divorce and in favor of long-suffering, dutiful love, especially of a wife towards her husband. The plot is wholly predictable, and the characters are flat.

Our Cousin Veronica (1855) is probably L.'s best novel. Its vividness of action and description derives from L.'s own experience in England and Virginia. At the novel's end, the female narrator marries a slave owner only after a serious discussion of abolition. He opposes freeing his slaves outright, for they would be harassed in their own state and unprotected if they moved north. Quoting Wilberforce, she impresses her husband with the responsibility they have as masters, not just for their slaves' physical needs, but for their souls. Husband and wife both hope for a general emancipation and in the meantime free and aid those of their slaves who are willing to emigrate to Liberia.

In her novels, L. is strongest when she is closest to historical anecdote. Her histories are valuable for the interest she generates in people and for her amassing of historic information often inaccessible to others.

WORKS: *Forest Hill: A Tale of Social Life in 1830–31* (1846). *Amabel: A Family History* (1853). *Our Cousin Veronica; or, Scenes and Adventures over the Blue Ridge* (1855). *Madame Gosselin* by L. Ulbach (translated by Latimer, 1878). *Recollections of Ralph Randolph Wormeley, Rear Admiral, R.N.; Written Down by His Three Daughters* (with A. R. W. Curtis, 1879). *Salvage* (1880). *My Wife and My Wife's Sister* (1881). *Princess Amelie: A Fragment of Autobiography* (1883). *Familiar Talks on Some of Shakespeare's Comedies* (1886). *The Steel Hammer: A Novel* by L. Ulbach (translated by Latimer, 1888). *For Fifteen Years: A Sequel to The Steel Hammer* by L. Ulbach (translated by Latimer, 1888). *History of the People of Israel* by E. Renan (translated by Latimer, with J. H. Allen, 1888–96). *A Chain of Errors* (1890). *Nanon* by G. Sand (translated by Latimer, 1890). *France in the Nineteenth Century, 1830–1890* (1892). *Russia and Turkey in the Nineteenth Century* (1893). *England in the Nineteenth Century* (1894). *My Scrap-book of the French Revolution* (edited by Latimer, 1894). *Italy in the Nineteenth Century and the Making of Austro-Hungary and Germany* (1896). *Spain in the Nineteenth Century* (1897). *Europe in Africa in the Nineteenth Century* (1898). *Judea from Cyrus to Titus, 537 B.C.–70 A.D.* (1899). *The Last Years of the Nineteenth Century* (1900). *The Italian Republics* by J. C. L. de Sismondi (translated by Latimer, 1901). *The Love Letters of Victor Hugo, 1820–1822* (translated by Latimer, 1901). *Men and Cities of Italy* (1901). *The Prince Incognito* (1902). *Talks of Napoleon at St. Helena with Gen. Baron Gourgaud, Together with the Journal Kept by Gourgaud on Their Journey from Waterloo to St. Helena* by G. Gourgaud (translated by Latimer, 1903).

BIBLIOGRAPHY: Hayden, H. E., *Virginia Genealogies* (1891). Logan, M. S., *The Part Taken by Women in American History* (1912). Preble, G. H., *Genealogical Sketch of the First Three Generations of Prebles in America* (1868).

For articles in reference works, see: *AA. AW. A Critical Dictionary of English Literature and British and American Authors*, S. A. Alibone (1872). *A Dictionary of American Authors*, Ed. O. F. Adams (1897). *DAB*, VI. *Index to Women of the World, from Ancient to Modern Times: Biographies and Portraits*, Ed. N. D. Ireland (1970). *NCAB*, 9.

Other references: Baltimore *American* (3, 4, 7 Jan. 1904). Baltimore *Sun* (4, 5 Jan. 1904). *Dial* (1 Feb. 1904). *Harper's* (Feb. 1856). London *Athenaeum* (1853). London *Literary Gazette* (1846). New England *Historical and Genealogical Register* (Oct. 1868). *NYT* (5 Jan. 1904). *Putnam's* (Feb. 1856).

KAREN B. STEELE

Emma Lazarus

B. *22 July 1849, New York City; d. 19 Nov. 1887, New York City*
D. *of Moses and Esther Nathan Lazarus*

L. was privately educated and revealed an early gift for poetry and languages. Although the family was part of the cultivated and fashionable New York society—her father was a wealthy industrialist—L. had little contact with literary groups until her twenties, when she met Ralph Waldo Emerson, who served as a sometime literary mentor. Trips to Europe brought her into contact with English writers and thinkers.

L.'s *Poems and Translations* (1867), published when she was just eighteen, contains translations of Hugo, Dumas, Schiller, and Heine, as well as original poems dealing with conventionally romantic subjects. The title poem in *Admetus, and Other Poems* (1871), dedicated to Emerson, retells in blank verse the myth of Alcestis, whose strength and courage saved her husband from death. In L.'s version, the heroic willingness of Alcestis to sacrifice herself as the substitute the Fates had demanded becomes the crucial incident, and the portrait is a significant advance in the depiction of women in romantic poetry. In another poem, "Epochs," L. personifies work as a woman. The maturity of L.'s thinking is reflected in "Heroes," which stresses the problems of the aftermath of war, rather than the presumed glory of the battlefield.

L.'s studies led her to an interest in Goethe; the novel *Alide* (1874) is based on an incident in his life. Turgenev praised the work, which considers the artist's quandary in choosing between ordinary life and the demands of his art.

Poems and Translations of Heinrich Heine (1881) is L.'s major achievement as a translator; in many instances her rendition is the definitive English version still in use today. Although translations of Heine's poems were among her earliest works, this volume contains for the first time Heine's poems on specifically Jewish subjects, on which L. worked in the 1870s. Particularly effective is her translation of the ironic "Donna Clara," in which the insouciant charm of the ballad form clashes with the mock revenge against the rabid anti-Semite.

The pogroms in Russia and the mass immigration of refugees to the U.S. mobilized L.'s energetic support of her people. *Songs of a Semite* (1882) was issued in an inexpensive edition so that it might reach as wide an audience as possible. Along with ballads, sonnets, and translations of Hebrew poets, it contains one of her finest works, *The Dance to Death*. In this verse drama L. tells the tragic events of a pogrom in the 14th c., and portrays a stirring affirmation of the life and spirit of the persecuted people: "Even as we die in honor, from our death / Shall bloom a myriad of heroic lives, / Brave through our bright example, virtuous / Lest our great memory fall in disrepute."

L. also relied on prose to explain the position of the Jewish people. While only a few selections are available in book form, these essays represent one of L.'s greatest accomplishments, explaining in sharp, incisive fashion the attainments of the Jewish people, their heroics and their contributions to the contemporary world, and—even at this early date—calling for the formation of a Jewish state.

L.'s essays on other topics are equally valuable, although they, too, are buried in the periodicals of the day. Her strong humanitarian spirit led her to readings in socialism, and a visit to William Morris's workshops in England is described in warm, affectionate terms. An essay on Longfellow, while pointing out the flaws in his work, calls for a specifically American literature, rather than one dependent on the English tradition.

The last few years of L.'s short life were wracked by cancer; she nonetheless produced *By the Waters of Babylon* (1887), a series of prose poems using the long, sweeping line reminiscent of Walt Whitman and full of prophetic fire.

L.'s fame today rests largely on the sonnet "The New Colossus," which was written to raise money for a base for the Statue of Liberty, and which, as James Russell Lowell said, gave it its spiritual basis. But consideration of her entire literary output leads to a more far-reaching appreciation. From a shy, sensitive girl writing on romantic topics in a stilted diction, she became a mature artist, an impassioned supporter of her people, of the downtrodden of all nations, and of her own country and its literary accomplishments.

WORKS: *Poems and Translations* (1867). *Admetus, and Other Poems* (1871). *Alide* (1874). *The Spagnoletto: a Drama in Verse* (1876). *Poems and Translations of Heinrich Heine* (1881). *Songs of a Semite* (1882). *By the Waters of Babylon* (1887). *The Poems of Emma Lazarus* (2 vols., 1889). *The Letters of Emma Lazarus, 1868–1885* (Ed. M. U. Schappes, 1949). *Emma Lazarus: Selections from Her Poetry and Prose* (Ed. M. U. Schappes, 3rd ed., 1967).

BIBLIOGRAPHY: Baym, M. I., *A Neglected Translator of Italian Poetry: Emma Lazarus* (1956). Harap, L., *The Image of the Jew in American Literature* (1974). Lazarus, J., Introduction to *The Poems of Emma Lazarus* (1889). Merriam, E., *Emma Lazarus* (1956). Rusk, R., *Letters of Emma Lazarus in the Columbia University Library* (1939).

For articles in reference works, see: *AA. AW. DAB*, IV, 1. *NAW* (article by S. J. Hurwitz). *NCAB*, 3.

Other references: *Poet Lore* (1893). *Publications of the American Jewish Historical Society* (Sept. 1952; June 1956).

CAROL B. SCHOEN

Ursula K. LeGuin

B. 21 Oct. 1929, Berkeley, California
D. of Alfred L. and Theodora K. Kroeber; m. Charles A. LeGuin, 1953

L. grew up in a stimulating environment; her father was an anthropologist and her mother, a writer. She studied at Radcliffe College and Columbia University. During a Fulbright year in France (1953) she married a historian. L. lives with him in Portland, Oregon; they have three children. L. is a member of Phi Beta Kappa and Science Fiction Writers of America.

L.'s first science-fiction novels were *Rocannon's World* (1966), *Planet of Exile* (1966), and *City of Illusions* (1967). They show an interest in anthropology and even in e.s.p., rather than in technology, which places them in the "New Wave" of science fiction. At the same time, their magical, romantic tone suggests a hint of "Sword and Sorcery."

These novels were followed by L.'s most unified work, the Earthsea trilogy, in which basic human problems are discussed in fairy-tale terms, complete with wizards and dragons. In *A Wizard of Earthsea* (1968), which won the Boston *Globe* Horn Book Award for excellence, she stresses the importance of coming to grips with the evil in one's own personality. In *The Tombs of Atuan* (1971), she shows a girl coming to trust a man whom she had seen as an intruder in her feminine world. And in *The Farthest Shore* (1972), which won the National Book Award for Children's Literature, she presents the fact that life is meaningless if one refuses to face the reality of death. But the relation of form to content is not that of the sugar helping the medicine go down: they are the same thing.

L. describes herself at times as a Taoist. This means that she feels that wholeness is reached through a dynamic balance of opposites. This philosophy is expressed most directly in *The Left Hand of Darkness* (1969), which won the Hugo and Nebula awards. In this novel the imaginary planet Gethen is peopled by "androgynes," who have a biologically regulated, almost guilt-free sex life and do not, as yet, wage war. L.'s aim is to show what it means to be simply human, working one's way through conflicts that are not based on sex roles. It is interesting to see that we are still left with love and faith, disappointment and betrayal, face saving, incest, religion, politics, and the weather.

Many of L.'s novels and short stories have won Hugo and Nebula awards. "The Word for World Is Forest" (1972), combines insight into dream states with a scathing satire on American involvement in Vietnam. *The Dispossessed* (1974) shows a physicist from an anarchist moon colony who is obliged to go to the capitalist mother planet in order to be able to continue his research. Finally he returns to his own society in the hopes of leading it back to its original free principles. *The New Atlantis* (1975), in contrast, depicts a repressive, bureaucratic U.S., which is destroyed by a visionary cataclysm out of Edgar Cayce. L. calls the stories in *The Wind's Twelve Quarters* (1975) "psychomyths."

Some of her most recent publications have been much closer to mainstream literature. *Orsinian Tales* (1976), a collection of stories about an imaginary East European country, is quite realistic. *Very Far Away from Anywhere Else* (1976), a novella for young adults, describes without any fantasy the pressures brought to bear on sensitive young Americans to force them into conformity.

On the whole, L. has shown a preference for science fiction and fantasy over the techniques of the mainstream novel. She has great faith in the creative imagination and wants it to be free; science fiction and fantasy give her the scope for this. Probably it is because she allows so much free play to the imagination that she is able to be concerned with moral issues without appearing moralistic and to discuss politics without being forced into other people's molds. Liberty, in short, is her watchword.

WORKS: *Planet of Exile* (1966). *Rocannon's World* (1966). *City of Illusions* (1967). *A Wizard of Earthsea* (1968). *The Left Hand of Darkness* (1969). *The Tombs of Atuan* (1971). *The Lathe of Heaven* (1971). *The Farthest Shore* (1972). *From Elfland to Poughkeepsie* (1973). *The Dispossessed* (1974). *Dreams Must Explain Themselves* (1975). *The New Atlantis* (1975). *Wild Angels* (1975). *The Wind's Twelve Quarters* (1975). *Orsinian Tales* (1976). *Very Far Away from Anywhere Else* (1976). *The Water Is Wide* (1976). *The Word for World Is Forest* (1976). *Leese Webster* (1979). *Malafrena* (1979). *The Language of the Night* (1979). *The Beginning Place* (1980). *Hard Words, and Other Poems* (1981).

BIBLIOGRAPHY: Bucknall, B., *Ursula K. LeGuin* (1981). LeGuin, U., "Is Gender Necessary?" in *Aurora, beyond Equality*, Eds. V. N. McIntyre and S. J. Anderson (1976). Scholes, R., "The Good Witch of the West," in *Structural Fabulation: An Essay on Fiction of the Future* (1975). Scholes, R., and E. S. Rabkin, "The Left Hand of Darkness," in *Science Fiction: History, Science, Vision* (1977). Slusser, G. E., *The Farthest Shores of Ursula LeGuin* (1976).

For articles in reference works, see: *CA*, 21–22 (1969).

Other references: *Extrapolation* (Dec. 1976). *Foundation* (July 1973). *QJLC* (April 1975). *RQ* (Feb. 1972). *SFS* (1, 1974; 2, 1975; 4, 1977).

BARBARA J. BUCKNALL

Madeleine L'Engle

B. 29 Nov. 1918, New York City
D. of Charles Wadsworth and Madeleine Barnett Camp; m. Hugh
Franklin, 1946

The only child of a foreign correspondent, playwright, and critic (her father) and a pianist (her mother), L. led a lonely, isolated city life until she was twelve, occupying her time with writing, drawing, and playing the piano. When her family moved to Europe, L. was put in an austere and strict English boarding school in Switzerland, where she learned to withdraw into the world of the imagination for solitude. After graduating from Smith College with honors, she published some magazine articles and then returned to New York City to work in the theater, taking the family name of L'Engle. After her marriage to an actor, L. gave up her stage career permanently for writing. Now parents (of three children) and grandparents, the Franklins live in an apartment in New York City in the winter and spend their summers in Connecticut at their two-hundred-year-old farmhouse.

L.'s earlier works, intended for adults, feature adolescent girls and grew out of her life as a child in New York City, in boarding schools, and later in the theater. Some of these early novels were rewritten for young people in the 1960s. Sensitive and perceptive, these books are important in showing the development of the author's style and philosophy.

The highly praised, family-centered fantasy *A Wrinkle in Time* (1962) was rejected by several publishers because it was so unusual for a children's book. It combines comedy and deep seriousness for exciting reading even though it suffers from a lack of unity and an overload of ideas. Adolescent Meg Murry "tesseracts"—takes a wrinkle in time—to go into space to rescue her scientist father from It, a disembodied brain. *A Wrinkle in Time* won the Newbery Medal. The complex and highly philosophical *A Wind in the Door* (1973) repeats the theme of the power of love with Meg rescuing her brother Charles Wallace. Although the highly imaginative and innovative *Wrinkle* has received the most critical acclaim, three later books about the conflict of good and bad (*The Arm of the Starfish,* 1965; *The Young Unicorns,* 1968; and *Dragons in the Waters,* 1976) are less didactic and contrived.

The witty verse-drama, *The Journey with Jonah* (1967), a retelling of the biblical story, stands out among the versatile L.'s other writings, as does her 1969 collection of intense, personal lyrics reflecting her experience and observation of life. Her autobiographical works for adults, *A Circle of Quiet* (1972), *The Summer of the Great-Grandmother* (1974), and *The Irrational Season* (1977), are not only thought-provoking and compelling as literature, they are essential for an understanding of her motivations and objectives as a writer.

Recurring themes in L.'s work are the conflict between good and evil and the problem of distinguishing one from the other, the nature of God, the dangers of conformity, and the necessity for giving love. A bold writer who dares to strike out in new directions and to challenge her readers, she obviously takes young people very seriously and regards them as being as worthy of intellectual stimulation as adults. In spite of her over-concern with ideas and her at-times uncontrolled virtuosity, L.'s ability to tell a good story has earned her a number of awards. She is regarded as one of today's outstanding writers for children and young people.

WORKS: *18 Washington Square* (1945). *The Small Rain* (1945). *Ilsa* (1946). *And Both Were Young* (1949). *Camilla Dickinson* (1951). *A Winter's Love* (1957). *Meet the Austins* (1960). *A Wrinkle in Time* (1962). *The Moon by Night* (1963). *The Twenty-four Days before Christmas* (1964). *The Arm of the Starfish* (1965). *Camilla* (1965). *The Love Letters* (1966). *The Journey with Jonah* (1967). *Prelude* (1968). *The Young Unicorns* (1968). *Dance in the Desert* (1969). *Lines Scribbled on an Envelope, and Other Poems* (1969). *The Other Side of the Sun* (1971). *A Circle of Quiet* (1972). *A Wind in the Door* (1973). *Everyday Prayers* (1974). *Prayers for Sunday* (1974). *The Summer of the Great-Grandmother* (1974). *Dragons in the Waters* (1976). *The Irrational Season* (1977). *A Swiftly Tilting Planet* (1978).

BIBLIOGRAPHY: Townsend, J. R., *A Sense of Story* (1971).
For articles in reference works, see: *CA,* 1–4 (1967). *More Books by More People,* L. B. Hopkins (1974). *More Junior Authors,* Ed. M. Fuller (1963). *Newbery and Caldecott Medal Books, 1956–1965,* Ed. L. Kingman (1965). *Something about the Author,* Ed. A. Commire (1971).
Other references: *Language Arts* 54 (1977).

ALETHEA K. HELBIG

Miriam Florence Folline Leslie

B. 5 June 1836, New Orleans, Louisiana; d. 18 Sept. 1914
Wrote under: Frank Leslie, Miriam Florence Folline Leslie, Miriam F. Squier
D. of Charles Follin and Susan Danforth; m. David Charles Peacock, 1854;
m. Ephraim George Squier, 1856; m. Frank Leslie, 1873; m. William C.
Kingsbury Wilde, 1891

L. changed her name, birth date, and the details of her parentage to suit her altered mood or circumstance. Although they probably never married, L.'s parents lived together as man and wife, and Susan used the Follin name. L. was educated at home by her father. The intellectual skills she honed at this time were matched by her seductive skills. Her first marriage, a shotgun marriage to a jeweler's assistant, was annulled after two years. L. then began a stage career, traveling with actress Lola Montez as her sister Minnie.

L. gave up acting in 1857 to marry Squier, an amateur archeologist. With him, she published a Spanish newspaper, *Noticias de Neuva York*. Through him, she met Frank Leslie, whom she married after divorcing Squier. Head of a successful publishing house, Leslie made L. the editor of his *Lady's Magazine*. L. also worked on *Frank Leslie's Chimney Corner* and *Frank Leslie's Lady's Journal*, and some said she was the power behind the Leslie throne. Financial mismanagement and the publisher's 1880 death nearly destroyed the business, but L. was a good manager and editor with sound news judgment and the ability to gauge the public's interests. Her decision to reduce the number of Leslie magazines and to concentrate on *Frank Leslie's Popular Monthly* displayed sound business sense.

L. also had a flair for personal publicity. She changed her name to Frank Leslie and lived extravagantly. Her every move made news. Her marriage to the brother of Oscar Wilde, sixteen years her junior, ended when she divorced him in 1893.

Tired of romance and work, L. sailed for Europe, leaving her publishing house in control of a syndicate. The group mismanaged the business, and L. was called home in 1898. Again she changed the Leslie fortunes;

and again she changed her name, to the Baroness de Bazus, after doubtful Huguenot ancestors. L. sold her business in 1903 for a half-million dollars. When she died, L. left nearly one million dollars to Carrie Chapman Catt, the suffrage leader, to mount the successful campaign for woman suffrage.

During the course of her colorful career, L. produced not only newspapers, but also newpaper columns and several books. She even wrote a play. *The Froth of Society*, L.'s translation of Dumas's *Demi-Monde*, opened in 1893 to terrible reviews. L.'s was the third adaptation of the work to be presented on the New York stage, and she had taken considerable liberties with the original play.

L.'s books of opinion and advice—*Rents in Our Robes* (1888), *Are Men Gay Deceivers?* (1893), and *A Social Mirage* (1899)—deal with essentially female interests: love, beauty, marriage, and sex. Dress is discussed extensively, L. believing that "fashion is not society—it is its genius."

The triumvirate of beauty, love, and fashion that L. said should motivate other women as it had motivated her is most evident in *Beautiful Woman of Twelve Epochs* (1890). This lavishly illustrated book begins with a picture of L. It describes, in flowery language, such generic females as the druidess, the Puritan maiden, and the Saxon maid, admiring them more for how they looked and who they loved than for what they did.

Written from the point of view of a grande dame, *California: A Pleasure Trip from Gotham to the Golden Gate* (1877) betrays intellectual snobbery and racial and regional elitism. The book, however, does present some graphic sketches of the West in 1877, and it excels in its portraiture, providing the reader with insights about Mormon women, American Indians, frontiersmen, Chinese immigrants, and especially about L. herself.

Rents in Our Robes warns women not to compete overzealously with men, not to become masculine, and *California* constantly alludes to the "feeble female mind." This attitude seems like a contradiction from the one woman of her time to run, and to run successfully, a major publishing house.

WORKS: *Travels in Central America* by A. Morelet (translated by Leslie, 1871). *California: A Pleasure Trip from Gotham to the Golden Gate* (1877). *Rents in Our Robes* (1888). *Beautiful Women of Twelve Epochs* (1890). *Are Men Gay Deceivers?* (1893). *A Social Mirage* (1899).

BIBLIOGRAPHY: Bird, C., *Enterprising Women* (1976). Ross, I., *Charmers and Cranks* (1965). Stern, M., *Purple Passage: The Life of Mrs. Frank Leslie* (1971).

For articles in reference works, see: *AA. DAB*, VI. 1. *NAW* (article by M. B. Stern). *NCAB*, 25.

Other references: Nevada *Daily Territorial Enterprise* (14 July 1878).

LYNNE MASEL-WALTERS

Meridel Le Sueur

B. 22 Feb. 1900, Murray, Iowa
D. of Marian Lucy Wharton Le Sueur and Winston Wharton

L.'s life and work are rooted in midwestern culture; she has often been referred to as the "Voice of the Prairie." Her mother was a militant feminist; her stepfather, Arthur Le Sueur, was a socialist lawyer. L.'s life-long association with artists of the radical left, Wobblies, Marxists, and prairie populists provides the rich backdrop for over fifty prolific years of prose, poetry, journalism, history, and philosophical writing.

L.'s social writing began during her teen-age years. In 1927, her short story, "Afternoon," was published in the *Dial* literary journal. During the 1930s, L. was a prominent figure on the "literary left"—writing and advocating a revolutionary aesthetic based on change in form, style, and content. L.'s work appeared in such varied journals and publications as the *Daily Worker, Partisan Review, New Masses, American Mercury, Pagany, Scribner's,* and the *Anvil.*

Salute to Spring (1940), a collection of L.'s short stories, reflects her deep commitment to the political struggles of the Depression, and the effects of the period's social trauma, especially on women, poor workers, and farmers in the Midwest. Included in the collection is perhaps her finest short story, "Annunciation." Celebrating the creative force, L. shares the intense feelings of an expectant mother as she meditates on her pregnancy and the impending birth. Speaking to the unknown child within her, the woman seeks to explain the world into which the child will be born. Rich in organic and transcendental imagery, "Annunciation" is representative of both the subject matter and style for which L. would become known. L. always sought to create outside the narrative form. "Annunciation" demonstrates her early success in creating a literary "moment" or reflection that stylistically integrates prose and poetry.

North Star Country (1945) is a lyrical history of the northern Mid-west. Rich in the language of the common man and woman, the book is a unique document for the folklorist. Early criticism rejected the book's rich oral data base, but contemporary historians have looked more appreciatively on the original oral and written material.

The McCarthy era was particularly harsh on L. Her literary outlet continued through such radical journals as *Masses and Mainstream*, but she was excluded from a wider audience through an informal blacklist. She turned to writing children's stories, primarily historical treatments of American cultural myths and heroes: Johnny Appleseed, Davey Crockett, Abraham Lincoln, and Nancy Hanks Lincoln. She also wrote a delightful cross-cultural book for children about an Indian and a white boy, *Sparrow Hawk* (1950).

In addition to the reissuing of many of her works, L. published two new collections in the 1970s. One, *Rites of Ancient Ripening* (1975), is a collection of poetry which reflects her militant feminism, and in which she articulates her Indian philosophy. In *Rites*, the mature writer emerges, integrating rhythms and imagery of the rich plurality of American culture.

The Girl, a novel written in 1939, was not published until 1978. Here L. sensitively and brilliantly portrays the "girl" in all of us. *The Girl* has a unique and powerful style. The rhythm of a woman's culture is shown in patterns rather than through narrative development. The girl is not a heroine so much as a counterpoint to the world through which she moves.

L.'s journals (over 125 volumes) are yet to be published. They contain L.'s original contribution to American political philosophy. Students of indigenous American Marxist-Anarchism, American Indian philosophies, radical feminism, and the aesthetics of the left will find the journals a rich mine for future inquiry.

WORKS: *Annunciation* (1935). *Worker Writers* (193?). *Salute to Spring* (1940). *North Star Country* (1945). *Little Brother of the Wilderness: The Story of Johnny Appleseed* (1947). *Nancy Hanks of Wilderness Road* (1949). *Sparrow Hawk* (1950). *Chanticleer of Wilderness Road: A Story of Davey Crockett* (1951). *The River Road: A Story of Abraham Lincoln* (1954). *Crusaders* (1955). *Corn Village* (1970). *Conquistadors* (1973). *The Mound Builders* (1974). *Rites of Ancient Ripening* (Ed. M. E. Shaw, 1975). *Harvest: Collected Stories* (1977). *Song for My Time* (1977). *The Girl* (1978). *Women on the Bread Lines* (1978). *Ripening: Selected Work, 1927–1980* (1982).

BIBLIOGRAPHY: Halpert, S., and R. Johns, eds., *A Return to Pagany 1929–32* (1969). Hart, H., ed., *American Writers' Congress* (1935). Yount, N. J.,

" 'America: Song We Sang without Knowing—' Meridel Le Sueur's America" (Ph.D. diss., Univ. of Minnesota, 1978).

For articles in reference works, see: *CA*, 49–52 (1975). *Minnesota Writers*, Ed. C. N. Richards (ca. 1961). *More Junior Authors*, Ed. M. Fuller (1963). Other references: Minnesota *Daily* (19 Nov. 1973). Minnesota *Leader* (10 Feb. 1975). *Moons and Lion Tailes* 11 (1976). *MS* (Aug. 1975). *North Country Anvil* (Feb.–March 1974; June–July 1977). *Sentinel* (28 Nov. 1954).

NEALA YOUNT SCHLEUNING

Denise Levertov

B. 24 Oct. 1923, Essex, England
D. of Paul Philip and Beatrice Spooner-Jones Levertoff; m. Mitchell
  Goodman, 1947

L. grew up in Ilford, Essex, England. The younger of two daughters of a Welsh mother and Russian Jewish father, who became a Church of England clergyman, L. was educated chiefly at home by her mother, the BBC Schools Programs, and private tutors for French, art, and piano. She became a nurse in World War II, married writer Mitchell Goodman in 1947 (she had one son and was later divorced), emigrated to the U.S. in 1948, and was naturalized a U.S. citizen in 1955. L. has taught at several American universities. She is currently professor of English at Tufts University and has also served as poetry editor of the *Nation*. L. has long been a political activist, especially against the Vietnam War, and has given antiwar readings and helped in student demonstrations from Maryland and Massachusetts to California. Her distinctions and awards are many.

L.'s eleven major books of poetry, published between 1946 and 1975, show consistency of theme, tone, and technical control, with only moderate changes in emphasis caused by increasing maturity and increasing concern with social justice. Her mood is intense, ranging from tenderness to ebullience or outrage. Her subject matter is feminine without being feminist, and ranges from the smallest sensory or personal detail of domestic life to international social and military atrocities, especially those which involve children.

Many of the poems concern the creative process. L.'s technique is determined by the strongly emotional impulses which generate her poems. She writes in the rhythms of speech, often excited, impulsive speech, and in open forms which often reflect physical movement. L. writes with great attention to accurate sensory detail, is very sparing in her use of prose connective tissue, and uses metaphor and allusion moderately. She employs a significant amount of direct, emotionally charged statement, which tends to make the meanings of her poems more linear than multilevel, more explicit than mysterious. At her most successful, the poem is a single swift stab of experience which implies felt idea; at her least successful (most often in the political poems), she becomes sentimental and expository.

L.'s movement from the first poems to the most recent seems to be toward a larger proportion of ideological poems in a reflective or angry mood and a smaller proportion of poems expressing joy in terms of physical sensation. More typical of her earlier poems are "One A.M.," "The Curve," and "Jacob's Ladder." More typical of her later poems are "Conversation in Moscow," "Bus," and "The Distance."

L.'s prose analyses of her own creative process (many of them collected in *The Poet in the World*, 1973) consistently explain what her poems demonstrate: a reverence for and cultivation of the initial subconscious emotional impulse and a rhythm dependent on "the cadence of the thinking-feeling process." Though L. has often been classified with Charles Olson and the Projectivist or Black Mountain poets, she partly rejects that classification because she has "never fully gone along with Charles Olson's idea of the use of the breath."

L. also favors a "semiconscious" creation of metaphor from literal details and a use of diction and reference which achieves "a fairly constant balance between the aesthetic and humane needs" of the writer and her readers, that is, a style neither "elitist" nor "popular." In other words, L. believes that "a poem *is* a sonic, sensuous event and not a statement or a string of ideas." Her best poems are such events, as is "The Curve," from *Relearning the Alphabet* (1970), in which L. describes a literal walk along a railroad track: "Along the tracks / counting / always the right foot awarded / the tie to step on / the left stumbling all the time in cinders . . ." By means of sequence, selection of detail, and rhythm, she makes the experience represent not only the faith-doubt and hope-surprise inherent in taking such a walk, but in discovering even wider universal meanings or creating a poem as well.

WORKS: *The Double Image* (1946). *Here and Now* (1957). *5 Poems* (1958).

Overland to the Islands (1958). *With Eyes at the Back of Our Heads* (1959). *The Jacob's Ladder* (1961). *City Psalm* (1964). *O Taste and See* (1964). *Poems Concerning the Castle* (1966). *Out of the War Shadow: An Anthology of Current Poetry* (edited by Levertov, 1967). *The Cold Spring, and Other Poems* (1968). *In Praise of Krishna: Songs from the Bengali* (translated and edited by Levertov, with E. C. Dimock, Jr., 1968). *In the Night: A Story* (1968). *A Marigold from North Vietnam* (1968). *The Sorrow Dance* (1968). *Three Poems* (1968). *A Tree Telling of Orpheus* (1968). *Embroideries* (1969). *Selected Poems of Guillevic* (translated by Levertov, 1969). *A New Year's Garland for My Students, MIT 1969–70* (1970). *Relearning the Alphabet* (1970). *Summer Poems 1969* (1970). *To Stay Alive* (1971). *Footprints* (1972). *The Poet in the World* (1973). *The Freeing of the Dust* (1975). *Modulations for Solo Voice* (1977). *Light up the Cave* (1981). *Pig Dreams: Scenes from the Life of Sylvia* (1981). *A Wanderer's Dream* (1981).

BIBLIOGRAPHY: Mersmann, J., *Out of the Vietnam Vortex* (1974). Wilson, R. A., *A Bibliography of D. L.* (1967).

For articles in reference works, see: *CA*, 1–4 (1967). *Contemporary Poets*, Ed. R. Murphie (1970). *Contemporary Poets*, Eds. J. Vinson and D. L. Kirkpatrick (1975). *WA*.

Other references: *CentR* 17 (1973). *DAI* 36 (1975). *Descant: The Texas Christian University Literary Journal* 19 (1974). *HudR* 27 (1974). *MQ* 16 (1975).

ALBERTA TURNER

Estelle Anna Robinson Lewis

B. April 1824, Baltimore, Maryland; d. 24 Nov. 1880, London, England
Wrote under: Estelle Anna Lewis, Estelle Anna Blanche Lewis,
  Estelle Anna Robinson Lewis, Stella
D. of John N. Robinson; m. Sylvanus D. Lewis, 1841

L. was the daughter of a wealthy, cultivated, and influential Cuban of English and Spanish parentage, who died in her childhood. She attended Emma Hart Willard's Female Seminary, where she studied "masculine" subjects including law. After leaving school in 1841, she continued a regimen of independent study in classical and modern languages, comparative literature, and history. She published her first poem at fourteen; married, at seventeen, a counsellor at law, of Brooklyn; and published a first book of poems, in 1844, at twenty. Sharing an enthusiasm for the work of Edgar Allan Poe with whom the husband began a friendship in 1845, the Lewises are remembered in accounts of the Poe circle. As Poe pointed out—however ironically in view of his own goaded imagination —the predominant trait of L.'s disposition was "a certain romantic sensibility, bordering upon melancholy, or even gloom."

Divorced in 1858, L. traveled in Europe, read at the Vatican Library and the Bibliothèque Imperiäle, and lived for the last decades of her life in London, where she took a house in Bedford Square and studied frequently at the British Museum. Having published occasional translations of Virgil, articles on travel and American art, stories and a play, as well as additional poetry, she then wrote her most ambitious work, a dramatization in verse of Sappho's life. Appearing in 1868, it was widely reviewed in England, the U.S., and France, translated into modern Greek, and staged in Athens. In the complexity of characterization, L. anticipates the Sappho later revealed by scholarly research as a woman with primitive passions, unappeasable longing, frailties of ego, and an imperious will, but L.'s awareness of the poet's keen intelligence, charms, and genius is not matched by the pedestrian verse.

L. is usually mentioned in Poe biographies as a scribbling woman given to immense sentimentality, but she is rather an expert in the histrionics of passion. The title of the first poems, *Records of the Heart* (1844), could serve for all of L.'s major work; the convulsive emotions and fickle vows of love resulting in "frightful wrecks of mutual ill" for both men and women are her most persistent themes. Although she relies on the exhausted conventions, language and meters of romantic poetry in her period, she has nevertheless a disciplined energy for her criticisms of life from a woman's point of view. She is a formidable scribbler.

L.'s imagination is perhaps at its best in "Laone," a history of adolescent conflict. The poem depicts the harsh consequences of a relationship between two young people who have been inseparable for five years. The boy develops sexually and emotionally much earlier than the shy girl he has protected since their childhood as a promise to her dying father. Neither youth is censured for the disparity in needs or the failure to perceive them until it is too late. A century before Robert Frost's comparable poem, "The Subverted Flower," for instance, L. confronts the subject with more equanimity than either Frost or a mere sentimentalist, in spite of the fact that she writes in the cadences, images, and metaphors of an age when natural expression was inhibited by scrupulous nicety or plain prudery.

The ambitions of L., it has been said, "were underwritten by her husband and Poe." While she benefited from their aid, she also received early commendation by poets as different as William Cullen Bryant and Lamartine. *Records of the Heart* was, moreover, in an eleventh edition, and *Sappho*, in a sixth edition at the time of her death. The rapid decline in L.'s reputation can be accounted for not only by the derivative manner of the verse but also by radical changes in taste.

WORKS: *Records of the Heart* (1844). *Child of the Sea, and Other Poems* (1848). *Myths of the Minstrel* (1852). *Poems by Estelle Anna Lewis* (1857). *Sappho: A Tragedy in Five Acts* (1868). *The King's Stratagem; or, The Pearl of Poland* (1869). *Minna Monte* (1872).

BIBLIOGRAPHY: Poe, E. A., *Complete Works of Poe XIII* (Ed. J. A. Harrison, 1902). Poe, E. A., *The Literati* (1850).

For articles in reference works, see: *AA. CAL. FPA. LSL. NCAB*, 10.
Other references: *The Athenaeum* (4 Dec. 1880). *SLM* (Sept. 1848).

ELIZABETH PHILLIPS

Janet Lewis

B. 17 Aug. 1899, Chicago, Illinois
D. of Edwin Herbert and Elizabeth Taylor Lewis; m. Yvor Winters, 1926

L. received a Bachelor of Philosophy degree from the University of Chicago. She then worked for a time at the American Consulate in Paris and, in Chicago, as a proofreader for *Redbook* and as a teacher. L. married the poet and critic Yvor Winters. They settled in Los Altos, California, and had two children. Winters died in 1968. She has taught at Stanford and at other universities and has received several awards.

L.'s first novel, *The Invasion* (1932), established her talent for historical fiction. It is an account of the Johnston family, whose American ancestry began shortly after the Revolution, when John Johnston, an Irishman, settled with an Ojibway Indian wife in northern Michigan. The effects of the gradual invasion by white settlers of Indian lands are background to the family history.

Two subsequent novels take their sources from historical accounts of trials L. first encountered in the 19th-c. *Famous Cases of Circumstantial Evidence*. In *The Trial of Sören Qvist* (1947), set in 17th-c. Denmark, Qvist is framed for murder, convicted, and executed. In *The Wife of Martin Guerre* (1941), the setting is 16th-c. France. This is a classic novella that tells the story of Bertrande de Rols, the child bride of Martin Guerre. When Bertrande's husband presumably returns from war, after long absence, her growing conviction that the returning soldier is an impostor leads to a climactic trial that became a famous case in French jurisprudence. By focusing upon Bertrande, a devout young woman tormented by her love for two men, L. transforms a legal record into a moving domestic tragedy. In 1958, L. wrote a libretto based on her novel.

In her most ambitious novel, *The Ghost of Monsieur Scarron* (1959), L. again deals with French history, during the reign of Louis XIV. Here two plots and two worlds interweave. The first plot concerns the discovery at the Court of Versailles of a libelous pamphlet against the King and the effort of the King's authorities to find the man responsible. The second plot deals with the life of a devout and simple Parisian bookbinder, Jean Larcher. When Larcher is convicted, upon circumstantial evidence, of the crime against the King, the two plots merge, and the story becomes one of a wife's infidelity and an ensuing tragedy of betrayal and revenge.

The mark of L.'s fiction is craftsmanship, evident in the precision of her style, her command of historical detail, and her rigorous control of her narratives. Her approach to history is essentially dramatic; history provides her with the plots and settings of tragedy. Her interest is not in great historical personages, but in forgotten, everyday lives where, as with high tragedy, evil motives and passions may also elude human justice and destroy the innocent as well as the guilty.

L.'s poetry is composed of short lyrics, usually in traditional forms, meticulously executed. In contrast to the darker themes of her fiction, L.'s poetry is strongly affirmative. Her subjects—unfashionable in contemporary poetry—center in the contentments of domestic life. Although limited in range, these are not poems of complacency. Many are shaded by the one inevitable grief, the death of loved ones. A more inclusive theme is the spiritual discipline necessary to "combine despair and joy / Into a stable whole," as she writes in "Morning Devotion." For L. this means a moral commitment to constancy, an adherence to rationally chosen, enduring values. The failure of such commitment, and its consequences, is the subject of one of her most moving poems,

"Helen Grown Old," in which Helen of Troy epitomizes a life "ruled by passion," the threat of which, in assessing her own experience, L. is aware. In "The Candle Flame," she acknowledges in her nature the variability that might turn loyalty into "a flickering vagrancy" that leaves "nothing certain." One of her finest love poems, "Old Love," is a tribute to an enduring marriage in which love eventually becomes "Love that is rooted deep, / Quiet as friendship seeming, / Secure as quiet sleep." The ultimate wisdom, L. implies in "White Oak," is to achieve a stability subject only to death. The human analogy for the metaphoric white oak, "Forever stirring in the air yet not / Forsaking this one spot," is that of living experience rooted in permanent values.

Although L. has an excellent reputation among a select audience—mainly writers and poets themselves—she has not had the critical recognition merited by the quality of her work. Perhaps this is because she has never been a follower of fashion, and, in poetry, her production has been relatively small.

WORKS: *Indians in the Woods* (1922). *Adventures of Ollie Ostrich* (1923). *The Wheel in Midsummer* (1927). *The Invasion* (1932). *The Wife of Martin Guerre* (1941; libretto, 1958). *Against a Darkening Sky* (1943). *Goodbye Son, and Other Stories* (1946). *The Trial of Sören Qvist* (1947). *Poems, 1924–1944* (1950). *The Ghost of Monsieur Scarron* (1959). *Keiko's Bubble* (1961). *The Last of the Mohicans* (libretto by Lewis, 1977). *The Birthday of the Infanta* (libretto by Lewis, 1977).

BIBLIOGRAPHY: For articles in reference works, see: *20thCAS*.

MARGARET PETERSON

Laura Jean Libbey

B. *22 March 1862, Brooklyn, New York; d. 25 Oct. 1925, New York City*
D. *of Thomas H. and Elizabeth Nelson Libbey; m. Van Mater Stilwell, 1898*

L. was one of this country's most prolific writers of fiction, publishing some eighty volumes in her thirty-year career as a popular novelist. Her fiction provided a formula for female escape literature which persists even into the present. Yet despite her productivity and popularity, L.'s current reputation is negligible and her biography obscure. Most of L.'s novels were printed serially in newspapers, magazines, and the weekly "story papers," and then reprinted in cheap paperbound editions. Few libraries kept these inexpensive copies of her once best-selling books.

The obscurity of her biography is partly owing to L.'s own sense that her private life was not the public's business. We do know that she lived most of her life in Brooklyn, although as an adult she traveled continually in order to promote her books. On most of these journeys, the author was accompanied by her mother, a strict, domineering woman who governed L.'s life and forbade her daughter to marry. L. disobeyed this command only after her mother's death in 1898. True to the heroines in her fiction, the popular novelist gave up her career upon marriage to a respectable husband. Only after nearly a decade of retirement could she be coaxed to work again.

L. was a leading practitioner of the so-called working-girl novel. These books about young, female proletarian protagonists netted the author over fifty thousand dollars a year, hardly a working-class income by any standard. All of the novels preached the same simple and not very original message: A young girl who remains virtuous (i.e., virginal) can ultimately expect to secure not only a husband and happiness, but a fortune too.

Not one of the novels can be singled out from the L. canon since each, invariably, tells the same story, shares the same plot, preaches the same moral, and portrays the same heroes, heroines, villains, and villainesses. The books all include compulsory scenes depicting the harshness of city life, thus echoing a standard theme in much popular fiction of the last decade of the 19th c. Named little Leafy, pretty Guelda, or poor Faynie, the heroine attempts to make her way alone in the cruel city. After having been cast out of her idyllic rural home, often by a wicked stepmother or selfish foster parent, she finds she now must support herself and frequently must support indigent siblings as well. In a backhanded and almost ludicrously sentimentalized fashion, this formulaic plot attests to a changing pattern in the American labor force after the Civil War, when women were finding employment in increasing numbers, frequently in low-paying factory jobs.

But L.'s novels do not focus much on the actual working conditions endured by the female protagonists. Instead, the heroine's energies are devoted to fending off often hostile masculine attentions. Only after a series of victimizations is the heroine finally rescued by the hero, a character both virtuous and prosperous. Their marriage presages happiness ever after and an end to both the threat of assault and the daily grind of a factory job. Although men are always the aggressors in these novels and the heroine's moral character is never even questioned, it is interesting to note that the heroine alone is responsible for maintaining her virtue.

The message of L.'s novels is a conservative one, and certainly one that ran counter to ideas endorsed by a growing number of feminists in late-19th-c. America; but the credo she preached is of interest to the social historian. What Horatio Alger did for American working-class men, L. did for female readers. Alger's heroes worked hard, took advantage of every opportunity, and, against all odds, realized the American dream. L.'s heroines worked hard too. But the 19th-c. business world held few opportunities for women. So real success for L.'s heroines came through successful marriage. L.'s socially conservative fables, however we might object to them, spoke to millions of working-class women who needed a fantasy of their own to take them away from the real grime of the sweatshops, the bookbinderies, and the cotton mills.

WORKS: This is a representative list of Libbey's novels, many of which are not even listed in the Library of Congress catalogues: *A Fatal Wooing* (1883). *All for Love of a Fair Face; or, A Broken Betrothal* (1885). *Madolin Rivers; or, The Little Beauty of Red Oak Seminary: A Love Story* (1885). *A Forbidden Marriage; or, In Love with a Handsome Spendthrift* (1888). *Miss Middleton's Lover; or, Parted on Their Bridal Tour* (1888). *Leonie Locke: The Romance of a Beautiful New York Working Girl* (1889). *Willful Gaynell; or, The Little Beauty of the Passaic Cotton Mills* (1890). *Little Leafy, the Cloakmaker's Beautiful Daughter: A Romantic Story of a Lovely Working Girl in the City of New York* (1891). *A Master Workman's Oath; or, Coralie the Unfortunate: A Love Story Portraying the Life, Romance, and Strange Fate of a Beautiful New York Working Girl* (1892). *Only a Mechanic's Daughter: A Charming Story of Love and Passion* (1892). *Parted at the Altar* (1893). *A Handsome Engineer's Flirtation; or, How He Won the Hearts of Girls* (190?). *Was She Sweetheart or Wife* (190?). *Wooden Wives: Is It a Story for Philandering Husbands?* (1923).

BIBLIOGRAPHY: Davidson, C. N., and A. E. Davidson, "Carrie's Sisters: The Popular Prototypes for Dreiser's Heroine," *MFS* (Autumn 1977). Noel, M., *Villains Galore: The Heyday of the Popular Story Weekly* (1954). Papashvily, H. W., *All the Happy Endings* (1956).

For articles in reference works, see: *NAW* (article by S. G. Walcutt). *NCAB*, 19.

Other references: *American Mercury* (Sept. 1931). *Historical Society of Michigan Chronicle* (4th quarter 1975).

CATHY N. DAVIDSON

Anne Morrow Lindbergh

B. 22 June 1906, Englewood, New Jersey
D. of Dwight and Elizabeth Cutter Morrow; m. Charles A. Lindbergh, 1929

Born into a family devoted to books and scholarship, L. learned to value education, self-discipline, and personal ambition from an early age. She acquired a sense of history firsthand from traveling with her parents throughout Europe. L. received a B.A. (1928) from Smith College, where she also earned recognition as a writer. With her marriage, the publicity engulfing Lindbergh extended to L., shattering the privacy she had treasured.

After her marriage L. learned to fly and operate radio, studied dead reckoning and celestial navigation, and became the first woman in America to obtain a glider-pilot's license. Between 1931 and 1933 L. assisted her husband in charting the international air routes later used for commercial air travel. For her work as copilot and radio operator in flights exceeding forty thousand miles over five continents, the National Geographic Society awarded her the Hubbard Gold Medal in 1934.

In the midst of these achievements the public curiosity haunting the Lindberghs reached frenzied levels with the kidnapping and murder of their twenty-month-old son in 1932. The tragedy and the prolonged investigation terminated with the conviction of Bruno Richard Hauptman. In December 1935, for protection and privacy, the Lindberghs left the U.S. for England, and later France; when World War II descended on Europe in 1939, the Lindberghs returned to the U.S. Since her husband's death in 1974, L. has continued to occupy the family home in Darien, Connecticut, while maintaining a residence on the Hawaiian island of Maui. Although her duties as celebrity and mother of a large family have drawn heavily on her energy, L. has never abandoned her writing career, producing both fiction and nonfiction throughout her life.

In *Gift from the Sea* (1955), originally conceived as a series of autobiographical essays, L. presents a microcosm of modern American womanhood as contemplated by a solitary figure in retreat at a seashore. With attention to the effects of marriage on woman's struggle for self-identity, L. traces the stages of marriage from the early self-contained relationship between man and woman, through the middle years weighed down with responsibilities, and finally to the mature marriage characterized by a newly acquired sense of freedom.

With the abandoned argonauta, one of several seashells used to symbolize the different stages of marriage, L. offers her view of the ideal relationship: "the meeting of two whole fully developed people as persons." Recognizing that the many demands of marriage hinder woman's growth, L. advocates as a counterbalance to these demands periods of solitude devoted to creativity. If practiced, such creativity would yield self-knowledge. Having reaffirmed her faith in the power of solitude, L. leaves the seashore, strengthened by her reflections, especially by her awareness of the dynamic nature of life. With her customary modesty, L. acknowledges that her answer to woman's predicament is not definitive, except in her assertion that the desire for self-identity will persist. Moreover, she admits new problems will appear just as certainly as the ebb and flow of the sea continues. With this, her most significant work, L. reveals not only her poetic sensitivity but her insight into the nature of womanhood as well.

L.'s single collection of poetry, *The Unicorn, and Other Poems* (1956), presents the spiritual odyssey of an individual pursuing personal freedom. Throughout the poems, L. identifies the demons obstructing this pursuit, all the while attempting to destroy them. Irregular lyric forms appropriately capture her meandering reflections, just as images drawn from winter effectively support passages dealing with spiritual isolation in contrast to the aerial images signaling hope and joy.

L. returns to the theme of marriage in her novel *Dearly Beloved* (1962). Writing in the tradition of the experimental novel, L. eschews simple narration in favor of the stream-of-consciousness technique as a means of revealing certain basic truths about marriage. Organized around the single event of a family wedding in a structure reminiscent of Virginia Woolf's *Mrs. Dalloway*, the novel examines the different attitudes towards marriage held by the wedding guests.

L.'s literary themes have their genesis in the five volumes of her letters and diaries. From these pages there emerges the figure of a sensitive individual with a penchant for writing, whose circumstances in life have plunged her into the maelstrom of public activity. The anxiety resulting from these conflicting forces and her determination to assert spiritual independence spill over into L.'s writing, making it all of one piece.

L.'s artistic forte lies in her ability to shape her themes into impressive forms. Since her themes are open-ended, her forms are appropriately organic: the lyric, the stream-of-consciousness novel, the familiar essay. L. manages aesthetic distance by objectifying nature. Seashells, barren trees, the sky, birds, and mountains are favorite images conveying her vision. L.'s astute handling of diverse forms and her instinct for selecting the near-perfect image have contributed to her reputation as a significant modern writer.

WORKS: *North to the Orient* (1935). *Listen! The Wind* (1938). *The Wave of the Future* (1940). *The Steep Ascent* (1944). *Gift from the Sea* (1955). *The Unicorn, and Other Poems: 1935–1955* (1956). *Dearly Beloved: A Theme and Variations* (1962). *Earth Shine* (1966). *Bring Me a Unicorn: Diaries and Letters of Anne Morrow Lindbergh, 1922–1928* (1971). *Hour of Gold, Hour of Lead* (1973). *Locked Rooms and Open Doors: Diaries and Letters of Anne Morrow Lindbergh, 1933–1935* (1974). *The Flower and the Nettle: Diaries and Letters, 1936–1939* (1976). *War Within and Without: Diaries and Letters, 1939–1944* (1980).

BIBLIOGRAPHY: For articles in reference works, see: *CA*, 17–20 (1976). *CB* (Nov. 1940; June 1976). *NCAB*, F. *20thCA. 20thCAS.*
  Other references: *America* (28 Feb. 1968). *NYT* (10 June 1962). *NYTBR* (20 March 1955; 27 Feb. 1972). *SR* (2 April 1955; 12 Jan. 1957).

ELSIE F. MAYER

Sara Jane Clarke Lippincott

B. 23 Sept. 1823, Pompey, New York; d. 20 April 1904, New Rochelle, New York
Wrote under: Sara J. Clarke, Grace Greenwood, Mrs. L. K. Lippincott
D. of Thaddeus and Deborah Baker Clarke; m. Leander K. Lippincott, 1853

The youngest daughter among eleven children of a physician and a great-granddaughter of Jonathan Edwards, L. spent her childhood near Syracuse, New York, and attended school for eight years in Rochester, New York. When she was nineteen, she moved with her family to New Brighton, Pennsylvania.

L.'s first poems appeared in Rochester papers, and in 1844 her verse was published in N. P. Willis's *New Mirror*. Soon she wrote prose and informal letters for the *Mirror* and *Home Journal* under the pseudonym "Grace Greenwood." Later she worked as a journalist and correspondent for *Godey's Lady's Book*, *Graham's*, *Sartain's*, the *Saturday Evening Post*, the abolitionist *National Era*, the *New York Times*, and the New York *Tribune*. Throughout her career, because of her Puritan heritage or her own staunch sense of right, L. spoke out strongly for such causes as abolition, woman suffrage, prison reform, and Colorado's right to state-hood and against capital punishment.

Her marriage was unhappy. She and Lippincott were coeditors of the early and highly popular juvenile magazine *The Little Pilgrim* (1853–75), but in 1876 Lippincott fled the country and disappeared after being indicted for embezzlement connected with his job at the Department of the Interior.

Greenwood Leaves (1850), L.'s first bestseller, epitomizes mid-19th-c. taste. It combines saccharine and sentimental tales and sketches ("Sly Peeps into the Heart Feminine," "A Spring Flower Faded") with a series of lively informal letters and parodies of Poe, Melville, Longfellow, and other authors. The letters, though often prolix and gushing, give promise of the journalism that would later be L.'s forte.

Haps and Mishaps of a Tour in Europe (1854) was another Greenwood bestseller and was still being reprinted in the 1890s. A lively and often humorous account of her journey alone to England, Scotland, Ireland, France, Germany, and Italy, it records visits to literary and historical sites, prisons, almshouses, and lunatic asylums and meetings with literary, artistic, and political lions. *Haps and Mishaps* mixes sentiment and gush, American chauvinism, and some of the dry Yankee wit later to be fully developed in Twain's *The Innocents Abroad*. As in the first and second series of *Greenwood Leaves*, the most interesting parts are the segments of straight reporting, especially L.'s impressions of people.

Merrie England (1855), like *Bonnie Scotland* (1861) and other juvenile works, first appeared in *The Little Pilgrim*. Linked with sites she visited on her first trip to Europe are "tales" or "historical sketches." Most of the history presented is highly suspect by modern standards and often seems comic in its invention and moralizing: "But the neighbors all shook their heads wisely, and said, 'Mrs. Shakespeare is spoiling that boy; he'll never make the man his father is.' I am sorry to say that, as he grew out of boyhood, the young poet fell into rather wild ways."

Much of L.'s best writing is in accounts of her travels in Europe during the 1870s and 1880s written for the *Independent*, after she stopped gushing. Her power and charm continued in letters from Washington, D.C., written through the 1890s and even into the 20th c.

Once-popular books by "Grace Greenwood" have now been largely forgotten, while the works of contemporaries she far outsold in her lifetime (e.g., Thoreau and Melville) have become American classics. L.'s poetry, sentimental tales and sketches, and children's books merit obscurity, but her strong-minded, firsthand reporting still deserves and rewards attention.

WORKS: *Greenwood Leaves* (1850). *History of My Pets* (1851). *Poems* (1851). *Greenwood Leaves, Second Series* (1852). *Recollections of My Childhood, and Other Stories* (1852). *Haps and Mishaps of a Tour in Europe* (1854). *Merrie England* (1855). *A Forest Tragedy* (1856). *Old Wonder-Eyes* (1857). *Stories and Legends of Travel and History* (1857). *Stories from Famous Ballads* (1859). *Bonnie Scotland* (1861). *Nelly, the Gypsy Girl* (1863). *Records of Five Years* (1867). *Stories and Sights of France and Italy* (1867). *Stories of Many Lands* (1867). *New Life in New Lands* (1873). *Heads and Tails: Studies and Stories of My Pets* (1874). *Emma Abbott, Prima Donna* (1878). *Treasures from Fairy Land* (with R. W. Raymond, 1879). *Queen Victoria: Her Girlhood and Womanhood* (1883). *Some of My Pets* (1884). *Stories for Home-Folks, Young and Old* (1884). *Stories and Sketches* (1892).

BIBLIOGRAPHY: Pattee, F. L., *The Feminine Fifties* (1940). Thorp, M. F., *Female Persuasion* (1949).

For articles in reference works, see: *AA. The American Female Poets*, Ed. C. May (1854). *American Literary Manuscripts*, Ed. J. A. Robbins. *AW. CAL. DAB*, VI, 1. *Eminent Women of the Age*, Eds. J. Parton et al. (1869). *FPA. The Female Prose Writers of America*, Ed. J. S. Hart (1857). *HWS. NAW* (article by B. Welter). *NCAB*, 4. *Woman's Record*, Ed. S. J. Hale (1853).

Other references: *AL* (Jan. 1938). *Atlantic* (June 1859; Sept. 1859). *NYT* (21 April 1904).

SUSAN SUTTON SMITH

Jane Erminia Starkweather Locke

B. 25 April 1805, Worthington, Massachusetts; d. 8 March 1859, Ashburnham, Massachusetts
Wrote under: Jane E. Locke
D. of Charles and Deborah Brown Starkweather; m. John Goodwin Locke, 1829

A deacon's daughter, L. reflects in her work the religious and patriotic idealism nurtured in her childhood home. Her uncle Ezra was a Massachusetts state senator and a member of the Constitutional Convention of 1820, as was L.'s father-in-law, John Locke. She was the youngest of ten children.

L. followed her husband to New York shortly after their marriage. The first of their seven children was born there; three of the children were to die in early childhood, and only one, Grace LeBaron Upham, was to survive to adulthood. The family settled in Lowell (1833) and in Boston (1849). While Locke pursued a career in business and government service, L. cared for the children and pursued her own literary interests.

L.'s first collection of poetry is *Miscellaneous Poems* (1842). In the preface, the author tells us that the poems were written "for the most part . . . to relieve the soul of what would cumber it unuttered. . . ." The poems range in subject from reminiscences of her childhood home to expressions of love and concern for husband and children, and beyond this family circle to acknowledgments of the genial accomplishments of others—mostly contemporaries.

One important aspect of L.'s poetry is the evidence of sincere personal concerns and beliefs pertaining to women. A poem entitled "To an Infant," dated 11 August 1837, commemorates the birth of her first daughter. However, rather than greet the child in cheerful language, L. bemoans the estate which the child inherits: the wearisome toil of woman's daily existence. Despite this pessimistic, recurrent theme, in other poems L. stresses in stronger, more positive language another aspect of woman's existence: motherhood.

Two of the most notable examples of this latter theme can be found in the poems "Mount Holyoke Seminary" and "A Poem Adapted to the Times." In the former, L. compares the glories of the school in Northampton to those of the Propylaea at Athens and says, "To learning's inner temple here / Pass *mothers* of the race. . . ." That L. believes generations of educated women will produce generations of enlightened men, implicit here, is explicit in the latter poem, which also reflects her sympathy with the abolitionist movement: "An influence benign she will exert . . . In childhood hearts, that, hence, *man's* common acts / Will be but deeds of charity and love, / And the forged bands of the dark slave fall off, Spontaneous and uninvoked."

L.'s firm, patriotic vision is set forth in a forty-six-page poem entitled *Boston: A Poem* (1846), dedicated "to the names of Appleton and Lawrence. . . ." In it, L. honors scientists, educators, and working men and women, as well as industrialists, all of whom, she believes, contributed to the economic and academic well-being of the "Athens of America."

In *Rachel; or, The Little Mourner* (1844) L. touches with astute sensitivity the problematic situation of the Christian who must try to reconcile joyful belief in eternal life with very real sorrow and pain at the earthly parting.

The Recalled, in Voices of the Past, and Poems of the Ideal (1854), is a collection of poetry that reflects the more mature mind at work. Rather than a random selection of poetry gathered almost at whim, L. arranges this volume in four sections. "Voices of the Past" commemorates public occasions, historic events, and the achievements of prominent personages and includes "Requiem for Edgar A. Poe," whom L. knew. The poems in "Passages from Life" are autobiographical, but L. is more selective than in *Miscellaneous Poems*. Love filtered through Christian belief is reflected in personal poems such as "One Thousandth Imitation of an Old Song," written for her husband, and "Proverbs," written to her son.

Throughout all of her work, L. alludes to the "ideal," which is also the subject of the third section, "Poems of the Ideal." "The Sisters of Avon," her most philosophical offering, suggests at least an acquaintance with Hermetic philosophy. The final section, a tribute to Daniel Webster consistent with L.'s political sympathies, was first published separately as *Daniel Webster: A Rhymed Eulogy* (1854).

Between 1850 and 1854, L. worked as a newspaper correspondent for the Boston *Journal* and the *Daily Atlas*.

In the same period, she also worked for the James Monroe Publishing Company, writing prefaces for the English publications which they reproduced in this country. L.'s writing, prose and poetry, is lucid and straightforward. Her poetry is representative of the popular poetry of the 19th c. in general, and of the varied interests of its women in particular.

WORKS: *Miscellaneous Poems* (1842). *Rachael; or, The Little Mourner* (1844). *Boston: A Poem* (1846). *The Recalled, in Voices of the Past, and Poems of the Ideal* (1854). *Daniel Webster: A Rhymed Eulogy* (1854). *Nothing Ever Happens* (1938).

BIBLIOGRAPHY: Baldwin, J. S., *Memories and Traditions* (1909). Locke, J. G., *Book of the Lockes* (1853). Starkweather, C. L., *A Brief Genealogical History of Robert Starkweather of Roxbury and Ipswich* (1904). Upham, G. L., *Contributions of the Old Residents' Historical Association, Lowell, Mass.* (1891).

For articles in reference works, see: *CAL.*

Other references: *Lowell Historical Society* (1940).

ROSALIE TUTELA RYAN

Mary Simmerson Cunningham Logan

B. *15 Aug. 1838, Petersburgh, Boone County, Missouri; d. 22 Feb. 1923, Washington, D.C.*
Wrote under: *Mrs. J. A. Logan*
D. *of Captain John M. and Elizabeth H. La Fontaine Cunningham; m. John Alexander Logan, 1855*

L. was born to parents of Irish-French ancestry. L.'s maternal grandfather, La Fontaine, owned many slaves and large tracts of land in Missouri, and her paternal grandfather was a slave owner in Tennessee. Shortly after her birth, L.'s parents moved to southern Illinois, where her father became registrar of the land office as well as an army officer.

L., the oldest of thirteen children, had little formal education except that provided by itinerant teachers. When L. was fifteen, she studied for a year at St. Vincent's Academy near Morganfield, Kentucky. After graduation, L. returned home to marry a friend of her father's. L. wrote in the preface of her autobiography, "To tell my own story is to tell that of my own famous husband, General John A. Logan. Our marriage was a real partnership for thirty-one happy years."

L. traveled with her husband and assisted him by drawing up the forms for indictments and helping draft briefs. When Logan ran for Congress, L. was by his side throughout the political campaign.

After the Civil War, both General Logan and L. were concerned about the welfare of returning veterans. They were enthusiastic participants in the development of the Grand Army of the Republic (GAR). L. was also closely associated with the women's auxiliary of the GAR: the Women's Relief Corps. The Logans were responsible for the establishment of Memorial Day as a national holiday. In 1868, L. noted that the graves of Confederate soldiers in a cemetery in Richmond, Virginia, were marked by small Confederate flags and flowers. As a Senator, Logan effected passage of legislation to perpetuate Memorial Day as a national holiday.

After the death of Logan, L. was forced to earn a living for herself and her two children. *The Home Magazine* was started especially for her to edit and was successful for seven years. However, L.'s political influence and good works were continued. President Harrison appointed her to the board of the Lady Managers of the Chicago World's Columbian Exposition. In 1919, four years before her death, L. received the Belgian medal of Queen Elizabeth for work during the First World War.

L.'s first book was *The Home Manual* (1889), which bore a direct relationship to L.'s magazine. A compendium of etiquette, nostrums, recipes, stories, and games, its focus was self-improvement and self-help. In one chapter, "Society Small Talk," L. writes, "It is true that the newcomer into society often discovers that his or her greatest difficulty lies in finding just the right thing to say at the right time."

Thirty Years in Washington (1901) and *Reminiscences of a Soldier's Wife* (1913) manifest L.'s pride in the city of Washington and in being the wife of a famous general and statesman. *Thirty Years* is composed of a series of vignettes that describe the many agencies and offices of the national government. L.'s descriptions of her privileged access to behind-the-scenes workings of the government make this work an interesting source of information. That there are inaccuracies in the work does not detract from the general interest provided by rich details and L.'s general enthusiasm.

This same enthusiasm is apparent throughout L.'s best work, the autobiographical *Reminiscences*. L.'s eyewitness narration of the Lincoln–Douglas debates, her husband's political campaigns, and battle scenes of the Civil War provide a moving, personal view of those well-known events.

Using the resources of the Library of Congress from 1902 to 1909, L. and her daughter, Mary Logan Tucker, prepared a compendium of biographies of American women. *The Part Taken by Women in American History* (1912) contains two thousand biographical sketches varying in length and organized under rubrics such as Aboriginal Women, Pioneers, Women of the Revolution, Suffragists, etc. Like many other compendiums of the time, effusive encomiums based on scant factual material abound. However, this work is valuable for its great number of biographies of worthy women.

Throughout her life, L. was accorded equal praise with her husband. However, she lived thirty-seven years longer than he, and forged a career of her own as an editor and writer. L.'s works, especially the autobiography, exhibit her enthusiastic appreciation of the historic times through which she lived.

WORKS: *The Home Manual* (prepared by Logan, 1889). *Thirty Years in Washington* (1901; reissued, with two additional chapters, as *Our National Government*, 1908). *The Part Taken by Women in American History* (1912). *Reminiscences of a Soldier's Wife* (1913).

The Logan family papers are in The Library of Congress.

BIBLIOGRAPHY: Busbey, K. G., "Concerning the Author, Mrs. John. A. Logan," in *The Part Taken by Women in American History* (1912).

For articles in reference works, see: *AW*. NCAB, 4. *NAW* (article by L. M. Young).

Other references: *American Historical Review* (Oct. 1902). *Independent* (14 June 1919). *NYT* (23 Feb. 1923).

DOROTHEA MOSLEY THOMPSON

Olive Logan

B. 22 April 1839, Elmira, New York; d. 27 April 1909, Banstead, England
Wrote under: Chroniqueuse, Olive Logan, Mrs. Wirt Sikes
D. of Cornelius Logan and Eliza Akeley; m. Henry A. DeLille, 1857;
  m. William Wirt Sikes, 1871; m. James O'Neill, 1892

L., the daughter of a theatrical couple, made her stage debut as a child
and continued acting in New York City and on tour throughout the
U.S. until about 1868. Her career was interrupted in the mid-fifties for
eight years during her first marriage. It was not for love of the theater
that L. returned briefly to the stage in her own play, *Eveleen*, in 1864.
The economic necessity brought on by her divorce from DeLille forced
her resumption of one career, acting, that she always despised and one,
writing, that she enjoyed. She had also by this time begun to make a name
for herself as a feminist lecturer. The exact date of her retirement is uncertain, but she seems to have entirely abandoned acting by 1868, continuing her connection with the theater as playwright only. Three plays,
Surf (1870), *Newport* (1879)—both mild satires of high society—and
Armadale (1866), a dramatization of Wilkie Collins's novel, were produced for the stage but not published. Her second marriage in 1872 to
William Wirt Sikes lasted until his death in 1883. Her third husband,
O'Neill, was twenty years her junior. L.'s literary productivity was particularly intense during those years when she was not being supported
by a husband. The poverty and insanity which haunted her for most of
her adult life became acute in old age and she died at the age of seventy
in an English home for the insane.

L.'s literary career began with lectures, articles, and a lengthy record
of "politics, art, fashion, and anecdote" in the Paris of 1862. *Photographs of
Paris Life* (1862) was first published under the pseudonym Chroniqueuse.
Chateau Frissac: Home Scenes in France (1865), L.'s first novel, attacked the evils in the French marriage of convenience. In the melodramatic style, love is temporarily thwarted by inadequate dowries, family disapproval, and arranged alliances. Another short novel followed in
1867; *John Morris' Money* is the story of a family of modest means who
take in a widowed aunt, entertain her with four tales of the triumph

of romantic love over greed, and finally, at the old woman's death, un-expectedly inherit her secret fortune.

In *Apropos of Women and the Theater* (1869), L. expounded upon a theme which often occupied her: the immorality of Lydia Thompson's "British Blondes," the lavish 1866 production of *The Black Crook*, both of which featured dancers in flesh-colored tights, and the subsequent seminudity which gave respectable actresses bad names. L.'s most im-pressive and longest work appeared in 1870 under the title *Before the Footlights and Behind the Scenes* and in 1871 as *The Mimic World*. This is one of the most informative but disorganized and often biased ac-counts of backstage life from the legitimate stage to the circus. It in-cludes biographical sketches and anecdotes, arguments for treating actors with respect, and attacks on stage nudity and the third tier.

Also published in 1870, "The Good Mr. Bagglethorpe," is a cinderella story about a poor, orphaned young actress appearing in "moral dramas" who is seen and loved by the well-heeled, Willie Gentry. To make the union between the two possible, she must be taken from the stage and educated for two years.

L. continued her interest in writing nonfiction with *Get Thee Behind Me, Satan: A Home-born Book of Home-Truths* (1872), a celebration of marriage and the home under attack by free love and loveless "mercan-tile" marriages. L. also warns women of the dangers in believing that marriage is the only existence that awaits them and in allowing them-selves to be treated as commodities. Portraits of several types of unhappy women underscore her thesis: one woman whose family is excessively eager to see her married, one considered only as a beautiful object, and one who is neglected by her husband.

They Met By Chance: A Society Novel (1873), L.'s last major work of published fiction, describes the life of the wealthy aristocrat in 19th-c. New York: the vacation spots, the entertainments, the matchmaking, and the petty games. As in her other novels of high society, much hangs on disguise, mistaken reports of a character's death, coincidence, and intrigue.

L.'s strengths lie, not in her imagination and creativity, but in her ob-servations of attitudes and details which help to characterize the 19th-c. life and mind.

WORKS: *Photographs of Paris Life* (1862). *Chateau Frissac: Home Scenes in France* (1865). *John Morris' Money* (1867). *Apropos of Women and the Theater* (1869). *Before the Footlights and Behind the Scenes* (1870; reprinted as *The Mimic World*, 1871). *Get Thee Behind Me, Satan: A Home-born*

Book of Home-Truths (1872). *They Met By Chance: A Society Novel* (1873). *The American Abroad* (1882).

BIBLIOGRAPHY: Brown, T. A., *History of the American Stage* (1903). Ireland, J. N., *Records of the New York Stage* (1866–67). Ludlow, N., *Dramatic Life as I Found It* (1913). Winter, W., *The Wallet of Time* (1913).

For articles in reference works, see: *AA. DAB*, VI, 1. *NAW* (article by A. E. Johnson). *NCAB* 6.

CLAUDIA D. JOHNSON

Anita Loos

B. 26 April 1893, Sissons, California; d. 18 Aug. 1981, New York City
D. of Richard Beers and Minnie Ellen Loos; m. Frank Pallma, Jr., 1915;
m. John Emerson, 1919

When L. was four, her family moved from Sissons (now Mount Shasta), California, to San Francisco's Barbary Coast, where her ne'er-do-well father engaged in a series of journalistic and theatrical schemes. L. became a child actress and the family's chief mainstay for many years. After a period in Los Angeles, where her father managed an early movie house, the family settled in San Diego. By this time a youthful correspondent for the New York *Morning Telegraph*, L. hit upon the idea of writing movie scenarios for the Biograph Company. *The New York Hat* (1912) was her first filmed scenario, and by 1915 she had sold D. W. Griffith over one hundred scripts.

Eager to leave her family behind, L. married in 1915. After one night she deserted her young husband and set out for Hollywood where Biograph quickly offered her a contract. (The marriage was later annulled.) It was L. who wrote the title cards for Griffith's epic, *Intolerance* (1916). Her wisecracking verbal humor seemed ill-suited to the silent screen, however, until the chance success of an early Douglas Fairbanks film proved that audiences were willing to read comic subtitles. For the next few years, L. worked closely with Fairbanks, with Constance Talmadge, and with the suave director John Emerson, whom she married in 1919. In collaboration with Emerson she wrote two books about the motion picture industry, *How to Write Photoplays* (1920) and *Breaking into the Movies* (1921), along with several Broadway plays.

Living in New York, L. became a friend of H. L. Mencken. As a spoof of his taste for dim-witted blondes, she wrote a comic diary which first appeared in *Harper's Bazaar* in 1925. *Gentlemen Prefer Blondes* (1925), featuring the irrepressible Lorelei Lee, was a runaway international success, gaining L. such celebrated admirers as Winston Churchill, George Santayana, Mussolini, and James Joyce.

As one of the first women who dared hike her hemlines and bob her hair, L. came to epitomize the flappers of the 1920s. But despite her earning power, she was not in all respects an independent modern woman. As a self-described pushover for rogues, she remained loyal to her husband even while he dated other women and tried to take credit for L.'s own achievements. When she returned to Hollywood as a highly-paid screenwriter under Irving Thalberg at MGM, she protected Emerson's fragile ego by finding him a sinecure at the studio. Seemingly proud of her financial ineptitude, she turned her entire income over to "Mr. E.", who put everything into his own name in a move that could have left her penniless upon his death. Emerson was ultimately diagnosed as a manic-depressive, and spent the last eighteen years of his life in a sanitarium. In her autobiographical *Kiss Hollywood Good-By* (1974), L. chronicles her strictly platonic relationships with several attractive men, among them "the love of her life," the gambler and con man Wilson Mizner.

L.'s Broadway successes include several musical versions of *Gentlemen Prefer Blondes*, two romantic comedies adapted from the works of Colette, and *Happy Birthday* (1947), written for her good friend Helen Hayes. Hayes, who had recently starred as Queen Victoria and Harriet Beecher Stowe, was "fed up with being noble," and L. obliged with a comic portrait of a drab librarian who blossoms in a barroom. With Hayes she has published *Twice Over Lightly* (1972), an exuberant tour of New York City, her adopted home.

In three play versions, a sequel, and such later works as *A Mouse Is Born* (1951), L. tried to repeat her triumph with *Gentlemen Prefer Blondes*, but she never again so artfully captured Lorelei's blend of innocence and avarice, nor her highly original gift of gab. Though L.'s later novels seem sadly dated, her gossipy Hollywood memoirs, *A Girl Like I* (1972) and *Kiss Hollywood Good-By*, are delightful souvenirs of a bygone age.

WORKS: *How to Write Photoplays* (with J. Emerson, 1920). *Breaking into the Movies* (with J. Emerson, 1921). *The Whole Town's Talking* (with J. Emerson, 1925). *Gentlemen Prefer Blondes* (1925; dramatized by Loos, with J. Emerson, 1926). *But—Gentlemen Marry Brunettes* (1928). *Happy Birthday*

(1947). *A Mouse Is Born* (1951). *Gigi* (dramatization of the story by Colette, 1951; revised, 1956). *Chéri* (dramatization of the novel by Colette, 1959). *No Mother to Guide Her* (1961). *A Girl Like I* (1966). *The King's Mare* (1967). *Twice Over Lightly: New York Then and Now* (with H. Hayes; 1972). *Kiss Hollywood Good-By* (1974). *Cast of Thousands* (1977).

BIBLIOGRAPHY: For articles in reference works, see: *CA*, 21–22 (1969). *CB* (Feb. 1974). *20thCA. 20thCAS.*

Other references: *Atlantic* (Oct. 1966). *Film Comment* (Winter 1970–71). *NewR* (10 Aug. 1974). *NY* (28 Dec. 1946). *NYT* (27 Dec. 1925). *NYTBR* (18 Aug. 1974). *SatR* (24 Sept. 1966).

BEVERLY GRAY BIENSTOCK

Harriet Mulford Stone Lothrop

B. 22 June 1844, New Haven, Connecticut; d. 2 Aug. 1924, Concord, Massachusetts
Wrote under: Margaret Sidney
D. of Sidney Mason and Harriet Mulford Stone; m. David Lothrop, 1881

L. grew up in a religious New England family whose ancestors included the Reverend Thomas Hooker and several distinguished colonial governors. L.'s father was a respected architect, and it was in deference to his disapproval of women writers that L. adopted the pen name of "Margaret Sidney." The disciplined atmosphere of learning and religion that pervaded L.'s childhood days is reflected in the tight moral tone dominating her many works.

In 1878, L. contributed a short story entitled "Polly Pepper's Chicken Pie" to *Wide Awake*, a children's magazine. Reader response was enthusiastic, and the editor requested that L. provide the magazine with twelve more installments. L. hesitated, unsure of her ability; but she succeeded in completing the requested chapters. They were later compiled into the best-selling children's book, *Five Little Peppers and How They Grew* (1881).

L. followed this first success with *Five Little Peppers Midway* (1890) and then proceeded to write ten more Pepper volumes, ending with *Our Davie Pepper* in 1916. The Pepper series traces the development of five energetic children from their early childhood days in the country, through their adolescent education in the big city, and on to the decisions of their adult lives. Although all the Pepper volumes were greeted with enthusiastic reviews, L.'s first volume remained the most popular, selling over two million copies by the time of her death.

Five Little Peppers and How They Grew opens in a little brown house in the country where five children and their recently widowed mother are struggling to survive through a bitter winter. L., herself from a well-to-do family, always wanted to live in a little brown house, and the picture she presents of impoverished country life is extremely romanticized. Despite their many misfortunes, the Peppers are never downcast and they meet all adversity with an amazing fortitude. They are intent on being good Christians, never giving in to petty emotions such as jealousy or conceit.

This moral tone does not get in the way of the narrative, however. The Pepper adventure is energetic and amusing, filled with mischief and practical joking. L. has a deep-rooted understanding of children and she provides the action as well as the repetition that her audience demands. Her language, although overworked, is effective and sincere. L. claimed that the Peppers lived independently in her imagination for years before she ever wrote about them, and this philosophy gives her narratives a natural fluidity.

In 1881, at the age of thirty-seven, L. married a Boston publisher of children's books, and they moved to Concord, Massachusetts. Here, L. gave birth to her only child, Margaret, and Lothrop bought the historic house, The Wayside, as a surprise for his wife. The Wayside had been the childhood residence of Louisa May Alcott, whose work L.'s so closely resembles. In Massachusetts, L. continued working on the Pepper narratives, as well as writing historical novels such as *A Little Maid of Concord Town* (1898) and *The Judges' Cave* (1900). L. had a strong interest in history and was a careful researcher, but she never succeeded in bringing life to these historical novels. Primarily written for an adult audience, they lack the spark and energy of the Pepper novels, while retaining their didactic overtones.

L. was always active in community life. She combined her interest in history with her interest in children by founding the national society of Children of the American Revolution. She belonged to innumerable clubs—women's, writers', and historical—but showed little interest in the woman suffrage movement. Shortly before her death at the age of eighty, she was still going strong, working on an article about Edgar Allan Poe.

WORKS: Five Little Peppers and How They Grew (1881). *So As By Fire* (1881). *The Pettibone Name* (1882). *Hester, and Other New England Stories* (1886). *The Minute Man* (1886). *A New Departure for Girls* (1886). *Dilly and the Captain* (1887). *How Tom and Dorothy Made and Kept a Christian House* (1888). *Five Little Peppers Midway* (1890). *Rob: A Story for Boys* (1891). *Five Little Peppers Grown Up* (1892). *Old Concord, Her Highways and Byways* (1893). *Whittier with the Children* (1893). *The Old Town Pump* (1895). *The Gingham Bag* (1896). *Phronsie Pepper* (1897). *A Little Maid of Concord Town* (1898). *The Stories Polly Pepper Told* (1899). *An Adirondack Cabin* (1900). *The Adventures of Joel Pepper* (1900). *The Judges' Cave* (1900). *Five Little Peppers Abroad* (1902). *Ben Pepper* (1903). *Sally, Mrs. Tubbs* (1903). *Five Little Peppers and Their Friends* (1904). *The Five Little Peppers at School* (1907). *Five Little Peppers in the Little Brown House* (1907). *A Little Maid from Boston Town* (1910). *Our Davie Pepper* (1916).

BIBLIOGRAPHY: Lothrop, M., *The Wayside: Home of Authors* (1940). Swayne, J. L., *The Story of Concord* (1906).

For articles in reference works, see: *AA. AW. DAB*, VI, 1. *NAW* (article by E. F. Hoxie). *NCAB*, 8.

Other References: *Book News Monthly* (Feb. 1910). *Boston Transcript* (4 Aug. 1924). *PW* (9 Aug. 1924).

CHRISTIANE BIRD

Amy Lowell

B. 9 Feb. 1874, Brookline, Massachusetts; d. 12 May 1925, Brookline, Massachusetts
D. of Augustus and Katherine Bigelow Lawrence Lowell

L., a descendant of a clan of cultivated New England intellectuals, was raised in a family of devout Episcopalians on a ten-acre estate (Sevenels); the stately brownstone mansion, with its high mansard roof and extravagant gardens, became her home on the death of her parents. Her life of opulence was reinforced by a full staff of servants and her secretary-companion, Ada Russell. L. disapproved of wasting time and money on frivolities, however, claiming she was "an old-fashioned Puritan," who "let each day pass, well ordered in its usefulness."

Following several years of solitary apprenticeship in the atmosphere of the seven-thousand-book–lined library at Sevenels, she became a student of verse, and finally, in 1902, settled into the serious business of being a poet. The image of the social *grand dame* was not easily overcome; however, L. was determined that she be recognized as a hardworking, serious poet. At the time her first serious poem, "Fixed Idea," appeared in *The Atlantic Monthly* (Aug. 1910) her recognition consisted of the admiration accorded the sister of an eminent astronomer and the president of Harvard.

Despite the uncharitable opinions of some of her relatives, the portly, liberated woman, who resembled the director of a girls' school in her mannish coat, stiff collar, and pince-nez, knew what she was about. For more than thirteen years, L. was an ardent and indefatigable campaigner for poetry, and her prominence in both social and literary circles, coupled with her histrionic presence, gave her easy access to poetry societies, publishing offices, and public platforms. As a self-appointed prophet, she felt her mission was to reconstruct the taste of the American public, whom she felt had little comprehension of contemporary poetry.

It was not until her meeting with the Imagists in London in 1913 that L. began to gain some recognition. Despite controversy with writers such as Ford Maddox Ford and Ezra Pound over the reconstructed version of Imagism she imported to America, L. successfully published three Imagist anthologies and continued unwavering in her determination to create a climate conducive to the creation of American poetry.

Together with her poetry, L. published two volumes of critical essays, *Six French Poets* (1915) and *Tendencies in Modern American Poetry* (1917), and numerous reviews, some of which reflected critical misjudgments particularly in the case of Pound, Eliot, and Marianne Moore.

Following the publication of her first volume of poems, *A Dome of Many-Colored Glass* (1912), highly conventional in subject and style, L. was more experimental, studiously noting in each of her prefaces the development of her own poetics, her experimentation with unrhymed cadence, fluctuating rhythm, and most notably "polyphonic verse," a flexible verse form which she first used in *Sword Blades and Poppy Seeds* (1914), and later in *Can Grande's Castle* (1918). Generally, L. was successful when she was on native ground; her lack of success is reflected in departures, such as her "oriental poems."

Occasionally a memorable poem ("Meeting-House Hill," "Patterns," "Lilacs") appears among the six hundred and fifty preserved in published volumes, but L. will not be memorialized for her poetry. She had unlimited faith in her own capacity and a shared concern with other poets for the enterprise of poetry; and until her death she was a tireless and dedicated impresario of modern poetry.

WORKS: *A Dome of Many-Colored Glass* (1912). *Sword Blades and Poppy Seeds* (1914). *Six French Poets* (1915). *Some Imagist Poets: An Annual Anthology* (1915–17). *Men, Women, and Ghosts* (1916). *Tendencies in Modern American Poetry* (1917). *Can Grande's Castle* (1918). *Pictures of the Floating World* (1919). *Fir-Flower Tablets* (translated by Lowell, with F. Ayscough, 1920). *Legends* (1921). *A Critical Fable* (1922). *John Keats* (1925). *What's O'Clock* (1925). *Eastwind* (1926). *Ballads for Sale* (1927). *Selected Poems* (1928). *Poetry and Poets* (1930). *Correspondence of a Friendship* (with F. Ayscough, 1946). *Complete Poetical Works of Amy Lowell* (Ed. L. Untemeyer, 1955).

BIBLIOGRAPHY: Damon, S. F., *Amy Lowell: A Chronicle, with Extracts from Her Correspondence* (1935). Gould, J., *Amy: The World of Amy Lowell and the Imagist Movement* (1963). Healey, C., "Amy Lowell Visits London," *NEQ* (Sept. 1970). Healey, C., "Some Imagist Essays: Amy Lowell," *NEQ* (March 1970). Ruihley, G. R., *The Thorn of a Rose: Amy Lowell Reconsidered* (1963). Scott, W. T., *Exiles and Fabrications* (1961).

For articles in reference works, see: *DAB*, VI, 1. *NAW* (article by W. Berthoff). *NCAB*, 19. *20thCA*. *20thCAS*.

Other references: *JML* 5 (1963). *TQ* 6 (1964).

CLAIRE HEALEY

Mina Loy

B. 27 Dec. 1882, London, England; d. 25 Sept. 1966, Aspen, Colorado
D. of Sigmund and Julia Brian Lowy; m. Stephen Haweis, 1903; m. Arthur
Cravan (Fabian Avenarius Lloyd), 1918

L. has always been considered an American modernist poet. Her modernist education began at seventeen with the study of painting in Munich, London, and Paris. She was elected to the Autumn Salon in 1906 and then left Paris for Florence. There she met the Futurists and incorporated their revolutionary theories of painting and literature into her early poetry. Her poems began appearing in the American little magazines in 1914, and she joined the New York avant-garde in 1916. L. shared the Americans' commitment to the rejuvenation of word and image and their search for new poetic forms, derived from modern painting, to depict the movement of consciousness. At the forefront of poetic experiment, L. earned notoriety for her structural innovations and her sexual subject matter. After 1925 she was largely forgotten, partly because she lacked the discipline to develop her early breakthroughs, and also because she gave much of her creative energy to painting.

L. was married twice: in 1903 to Stephen Haweis, an English painter; in 1918 to Dadaist Arthur Cravan. Of her four children, one died in infancy, one in adolescence. She lived in Paris from 1923 to 1936 and in New York from 1936 to 1954; she spent the remainder of her life with her daughters in Aspen, Colorado.

In her poetry, L. explores the self, "a covered entrance to infinity." Her main symbol is the eye; her enduring theme the necessity of persistent, self- and world-defining vision in a chaotic and indifferent universe. In poems written from 1914 to 1917, she analyzes a female self deformed by social mores that limit women to the roles of wife and mistress and make her success in the marriage market dependent on virginity and sexual ignorance. Educated on romantic love stories, the Italian matrons of "At the Door of the House" (1917) and "The Effectual Marriage" (1917) are soon disillusioned with marriage. The semiautobiographical *Anglo-Mongrels and the Rose* (first half, *Little Review*, 1923–24; second half, *Contact Collection of Contemporary Writers*, 1925) details the English version of the domestic drama. "Parturition" (1914) uses irregular typography to convey woman's physical pain and spiritual quest during childbirth. Her central work is the *Love Songs* (Poems I–IV, *Others*, 1915), or *Songs to Joannes* (Poems I–XXXIV, *Others*, 1917), thirty-four poems on the failure of romantic love, using irregular typography and a collage structure. Proto-surrealist images link sexuality and the psyche, and narrative blurs as the speaker is accosted by fragments of love that introduce her to a meaningless universe. L. retreats from nihilism in "Human Cylinders" (1917), "The Black Virginity" (1918), and "The Dead" (1920), where, recognizing the impossibility of attaining absolute answers to the cosmic mystery, she shifts her emphasis to the *act* of vision.

Lunar Baedeker (1923) contains early poems (thirteen *Love Songs* from 1914 and 1915) and new poems. The theme of the unique vision of the artist, who alone shapes chaos into divine Form, dominates the newer poems. L.'s heritage here is Art for Art's Sake as it developed through Baudelaire, Parnassianism, Laforgue, and the English 1890s. "Apology of Genius" (1922) stresses the artist's alienation from philistine society, the supremacy of art, and the importance of artistic craftsmanship. Other poems draw upon this heritage to defend abstract art. The title poem and "Crab-Angel" satirize the dishonest artist who abandons vision and treats art as a circus for self-display.

Lunar Baedeker reflects the development of L.'s imagery. Early poems alternate abstraction and image to depict the movement of consciousness between intellect and intuition. Later poems are series of vivid images, unified by the interplay of sounds (L.'s trademark), that unite abstraction and image in flashes of vision.

Lunar Baedeker & Time-Tables (1958) retraces former ground and includes a few later poems. In poems written during the 1940s and 1950s L. elaborates a minor early subject, the clownish bum who, as "in Hot Cross Bum," sidesteps vision to pursue false Nirvanas. His companions are other denizens of the metropolis who fabricate illusions in order to escape reality.

Since 1944 L. has been rediscovered by poets and critics who find in her, as in Gertrude Stein, Ezra Pound, and William Carlos Williams, elements of modernist poetry that feed the present. An innovative structuring of consciousness, honesty of subject, and deployment of radiant words and images are qualities that made L. a seminal modernist and connect her to the present.

WORKS: Auto-Facial Constructions (1919). *Psycho-Democracy* (1920). *Lunar Baedeker* (1923). *Lunar Baedeker & Time-Tables: Selected Poems of Mina Loy* (1958).

BIBLIOGRAPHY: Burke, G. G., in *Americans in Paris, 1920–1939* (Dictionary of Literary Biography, 1980). Burke, G. G., in *Women's Studies* (1980). Fields, K., "The Rhetoric of Artifice—Ezra Pound, T. S. Eliot, Wallace Stevens, Walter Conrad Arensberg, Donald Evans, Mina Loy, and Yvor Winters" (Ph.D. diss., 1967). Kouidis, V. M., *Mina Loy: American Modernist Poet* (1980). Kouidis, V. M., "Rediscovering Our Sources: An Introduction to the Poetry of Mina Loy," *Boundary 2* (Spring 1980).

For articles in reference works, see: *CB* (Oct. 1950).

Other references: *Circle* (1944). *ConL* (Spring-summer 1961). *Dial* (June 1926). *Little Review* (March 1918). *Nation* (May 1961). New York *Evening Sun* (13 Feb. 1917). *SoR* (July 1967).

VIRGINIA M. KOUIDIS

Clare Boothe Luce

B. 10 April 1903, New York City
Writes under: Clare Boothe, Clare Boothe Brokaw, Clare Boothe Luce
D. of William F. and Ann Clare Snyder Boothe; m. George Tuttle Brokaw,
1923; m. Henry R. Luce, 1935

L. has been a playwright, journalist, politician, diplomat, and feminist.
She planned a theatrical career, attending Clare Tree Major's School of
the Theater, but her direction was changed by a brief stint for the
woman suffrage movement and her marriage to George Brokaw in 1923.
Six years later when her marriage ended, she turned to journalism, serving in editorial posts for *Vogue* and then *Vanity Fair*. In 1931 she resigned, determined to write plays, and shortly thereafter married Henry
Luce, then president of Time Inc.

This second marriage did not interrupt her career. She wrote four
plays for Broadway, then devoted herself to journalism and politics. She
traveled and wrote for *Life*, campaigned for Wendell Willkie and later
for Eisenhower, served two terms as U.S. Congresswoman from Connecticut in the 1940s, and competed for a Republican senatorial nomina-
tion in the early 1950s. She lost the last race, but Eisenhower appointed
her Ambassador to Italy.

During these years, L. wrote and lectured, not only on politics but
also on Catholicism, to which she was converted in mid-life. After the
death of Henry Luce, she retired to Hawaii, where she still writes and
lectures on such diverse subjects as the women's movement, the Catholic
stance on abortion, and conservative Republicanism.

As a writer, L.'s most significant body of work is her plays. The first,
Abide with Me (1935), is a somber melodrama about a sadistic husband
who is finally shot by the faithful family servant. It ran for only thirty-six
performances. Fame came with *The Women* (1936), a vitriolic comedy
about wealthy ladies of leisure. The play centers on the struggles of a devoted wife to regain her husband while living amidst a jungle of catty
women nourished on gossip and the misfortunes of their acquaintances.
The play was filmed twice, in 1939 and 1956, and was revived on Broadway in 1973. In the light of the women's liberation movement of the
1960s and 70s, however, the play comes across as false and unworthy.

L. made Broadway again with *Kiss the Boys Good-Bye* (1938), a frivolous comedy about the much-ballyhooed Hollywood search for an unknown actress to play Scarlett O'Hara, which ran for 286 performances. L.'s last play, *Margin for Error*, a satiric melodrama with an anti-Nazi plot, was produced in 1939. All of her plays, except the first, were later filmed.

A review of L.'s journalistic writings reveals her personal development. Her first piece, *Stuffed Shirts* (1931), is a brittle series of sketches lampooning various New York characters, such as the newly rich dowager, the divorcee, and the Wall Street ladies' man. Later L.'s interests became more international. *Europe in the Spring* (1940) is a lively account of her European travels at the time of the great German offensive. After her seven years in politics, she wrote a series of articles for *McCall's* magazine (1947) describing her religious conversion. In 1952 she edited a volume of essays by American and British authors called *Saints for Now. Ladies' Home Journal* printed the essay "Growing Old Beautifully" in 1973.

Despite the more mellow works of her later years, L. is remembered best as a playwright with a heavy hand for sensationalism and sentimentality—two qualities with great appeal for audiences of the 1930s. Her plays are infused with social snobbery and a brisk but vituperative wit with which she characterized the wealthy, sophisticated class. It is a great irony that the hostile, unflattering portraits of her own sex, in plays such as *The Women* and *Kiss the Boys Good-Bye*, should overshadow the more constructive efforts of this feminist.

WORKS: *Stuffed Shirts* (1931). *Abide with Me* (1935). *The Women* (1936; film versions: *The Women*, 1939; *The Opposite Sex*, 1956). *Kiss the Boys Good-Bye* (1938; film version, 1941). *Margin for Error* (1940; film version, 1943). *Europe in the Spring* (1940). *Saints for Now* (edited by Luce, 1952).

BIBLIOGRAPHY: Betts, A. P., *Women in Congress* (1945). Gray, J., "Dream of Unfair Women," in *On Second Thought* (1946). Mersand, J., *American Drama 1930–1940* (1941).

For articles in reference works, see: *CA*, 45–48 (1974). *Catholic Authors: Contemporary Biographical Sketches, 1930–1947*, Ed. M. Hoehn (1952). *NCAB*, F. *20thCA. 20thCAS*.

Other references: *NewR* (11 May 1953). *Newsweek* (26 Nov. 1973). *Woman's Home Companion* (Nov. 1955; Dec. 1955; Jan. 1956).

LUCINA P. GABBARD

Mabel Ganson Dodge Luhan

B. 26 Feb. 1879, Buffalo, New York; d. 13 Aug. 1962, Taos, New Mexico
Wrote under: Mabel Dodge, Mabel Dodge Luhan
D. of Charles and Sarah Ganson; m. Karl Evans, 1900; m. Edwin Dodge,
  1905 (?); m. Maurice Sterne, 1917; m. Antonio Luhan, 1923

The only child of upper-class parents, L. had an economically and socially secure, but emotionally starved, childhood. Tended by nursemaids
and kept at a distance by an ineffectual father and a strong-willed, socialite mother, L. felt like an orphan who spent her life in search of a
community in which she could be "at home."

L. devoted her life to overcoming her anomie by directing her
energies to the discovery and creation of her identity. She identified herself with an enormous variety of aesthetic and political causes; constructed model communities she hoped would define her role and purpose
in modern society; collected famous artists and activists whose careers
she tried to shape and who, in turn, she hoped would give shape and
meaning to her life; spent twenty years in psychoanalysis while dabbling
in a number of mind-cure philosophies; and left twenty-four volumes of
autobiographical materials that bear witness to the multiple ways in
which she sought self-definition.

Although financially independent and sexually liberated, L. was crippled by her belief in woman's cultural subservience. Believing women
capable of only "secondary" forms of creativity, she played the role of
Muse to men of genius, attempting to achieve an identity by inspiring
their creativity. At the same time, she wished to create in her own right,
so her relationships with men often turned destructive and self-destruc-
tive. She was married four times; only in her last marriage to a full-
blooded Pueblo Indian did she achieve any sense of fulfillment. Among
the Pueblos, she found a culture in which individual, social, and religious
values were integrated by a unifying mythos that was organically related to a land in which she finally felt at home.

L. became a leading symbol of modernism, in fact and fiction. As a
spokeswoman for the avant-garde, L. was a published poet, book reviewer, essayist, biographer, and social critic. Her prose styles and subject matter were a melting pot of Americana, ranging from the banality of

the Dorothea Dix–type columns she wrote for the Hearst papers to superbly evocative descriptive prose on life in the Southwest.

L.'s major contribution to American literature is her book *Winter in Taos* (1935). While she sought for years to find writers (D. H. Lawrence and Robinson Jeffers were the two most famous) to publicize her southwestern paradise, she wrote its finest testament herself. *Winter in Taos* is a first-rank contribution to American regional literature, a work of intense lyrical beauty and metaphoric power that achieves a richly sustained integration of her emotional life with the landscape surrounding her.

L.'s discovery of the Indians as potential saviors for a declining white civilization led to the writing of her best-known works, *Intimate Memories* (4 vols., 1933–37). Begun in 1924 as part of an ongoing process of psychotherapy, L. presented her fragmented personality as a metaphor for a world she wished would die and be reborn, as she felt she had, through the grace offered by a prewestern tribal culture. Although L. was not a feminist, her self-portrait reveals the destructiveness of the feminine mystique of which she was both perpetrator and victim.

L.'s memoirs are a significant contribution to social, intellectual, and feminist history. In spite of her sometimes unreliable and self-serving observations, she is an insightful eyewitness to childrearing in Victorian America, the fin de siècle world of American expatriates in Europe, the major revolutionary movements of pre–World War I America, and the fascination of postwar intellectuals with "primitives."

WORKS: *Lorenzo in Taos* (1932). *Intimate Memories* (Vol. 1, *Background*, 1933; Vol. 2, *European Experiences*, 1935; Vol. 3, *Movers and Shakers*, 1936; Vol. 4, *Edge of the Taos Desert*, 1937). *Winter in Taos* (1935). *Taos and Its Artists* (1947).

BIBLIOGRAPHY: Crunden, R., *From Self to Society, 1919–1941* (1972). Hahn, E., *Mabel* (1978). Lasch, C., *The New Radicalism in America (1889–1963)* (1967). Rudnick, L. P., "The Unexpurgated Self: A Critical Biography of Mabel Dodge Luhan" (Ph.D. diss., Brown Univ., 1977).
For articles in reference works, see: *20thCA. 20thCAS.*

LOIS P. RUDNICK

Grace Lumpkin

B. 1903 (?), Milledgeville, Georgia

Raised and educated largely in South Carolina, L. later taught school in Georgia and worked as a home demonstration agent for the government, thereby coming into contact with the poverty of many southern farm families. Her sympathy for the poor was expanded by living and working among North Carolina mountain people and watching their migration to the cotton mills. She became a staunch anticapitalist and ardent supporter of industrial unionism.

L. went to New York when she was twenty-five and began to write short stories, becoming involved in liberal and radical politics. Her first story was published in *The New Masses,* and during the 1930s, like many young writers, she became a fellow traveler. During this period she wrote two proletarian novels, both about the southern poor. *A Sign for Cain* (1935) was the subject of a 1953 inquiry by the Senate Permanent Investigating Sub-Committee, at which L. testified that she had been forced to write communist propaganda into that novel, under threat of having her career "broken" by communist book reviewers. L., who lives now in Columbia, South Carolina, is said to be working at present on a new novel, *God and a Garden.*

L.'s first and best novel, *To Make My Bread* (1932), traces the movement of poor southern tenant farmers and sharecroppers from their rural homes to newly industrialized mill towns. It is a compassionate novel that uses the author's intimate knowledge of these people to explore the cultural shock and the disillusion that they encountered in the transition. While in the southern mountains, these people had endured a stable kind of poverty, ameliorated by the natural beauty of their surroundings, the intoxicating rituals of their fundamentalist religion, and the closeness of family and community ties. In the cotton mills, their large families became a burden, especially for the women who were needed as wage earners; their religion became a tool of the bosses who exploited and distorted its ideals of submissiveness; and the natural beauty was replaced by dreary industrial ugliness. L.'s heroine, Bonnie McClure, like many of the other women, is pushed, almost reluctantly, out of her traditional feminine role as childbearer by the economic exigencies of her life: sooner than watch children starve to death she will become a union organizer and strike leader. L.'s sympathies for factory women are strong, but she tends ultimately to see the resolution of their problems in a socialist transformation of society, despite the fact that their sufferings are markedly different in nature from those of their husbands and brothers.

In her second novel, *A Sign for Cain*, L. again attempts to demonstrate that the interests of all the poor are best served by communism, this time by exploring the potential power of a political alliance between black and white sharecroppers in the South. This novel has, as a kind of antiheroine, a rebellious bourgeois woman, Caroline Gault, who, modern and assertive in her sexual morality, is nevertheless condemned for trying to substitute a reactionary code of individualism for collective action. This novel proposes even more directly than the first that women should not seek sexual justice outside the framework of a socialist redistribution of society's resources.

L.'s third novel, *The Wedding* (1939) makes a movement away from political tendentiousness in favor of a rather sympathetic examination of a southern middle-class family in a state of personal crisis. Her last published work, *Full Circle* (1962), is a novel that has enhanced neither her political nor her literary reputation, dealing as it does with what one critic has called the overcultivated soil of international communist conspiracy.

It is in the first two novels that L. makes her most significant contribution to the literature of feminism. Both provide early examples of the continuing dialectical debate between the adherents of solidarity with other movements of oppressed groups and those who believe that no economic or social equality can ever exist without a prior radical revision of the relationships between men and women.

WORKS: *To Make My Bread* (1932; dramatization, *Let Freedom Ring* by A. Bein, 1936). *A Sign for Cain* (1935). *The Wedding* (1939). *Full Circle* (1962).

BIBLIOGRAPHY: Rideout, W. B., *The Radical Novel in the United States, 1900–1954: Some Interrelations of Literature and Society* (1956).

For articles in reference works, see: *20thCA. 20thCAS.*

Other references: *Books* (27 Oct. 1935). *Nation* (19 Oct. 1932). *NewR* (7 Dec. 1932; 23 Oct. 1935). *NYT* (26 Feb. 1939). *SatR* (9 Nov. 1935).

SYLVIA COOK

Alma Lutz

B. 2 March 1890, Jamestown, North Dakota; d. 31 Aug. 1973, Berlin, New York
D. of George and Matilda Bauer Lutz

L. was a free-lance writer, a journalist, and a contributing editor of *Equal Rights*, the official journal of the National Women's Party. She achieved her literary prominence primarily as the biographer of 19th-c. women leaders.

L.'s first work was *Emma Willard: Daughter of Democracy* (1929). For this narrative biography of the early 19th-c. educator, L. focuses particularly on Willard's early pioneering investigatory work to prove women's intellectual capacity and on Willard's achievements through her Troy, New York, school. L. later published a revised edition of this book entitled *Emma Willard, Pioneer Educator of American Women* (1964). This second version gives a tightened, more sharply honed study of Willard's mature thought and practice. L. portrays with sympathetic insight the consistency of Willard's views in the midst of changing circumstance.

In 1940 L. turned to the women's rights movement, publishing *Created Equal: A Biography of Elizabeth Cady Stanton*. L. gives relatively little attention to the formative experiences of Stanton's early life or even to her early career. She centers instead on the post-1860 years of Stanton's life, when she could devote nearly full-time attention to the women's rights cause as publicist, lecturer, and brilliant formulator of policy statements. L. places particular stress on Stanton as a "torchbearer for women," underscoring Stanton's broad-ranging concerns, the clarity of her perspective, and her role as pioneer anticipator of issues.

L. further extended the Stanton story by collaborating with Elizabeth's daughter, Harriot Stanton Blatch in Blatch's memoirs, *Challenging Years* (1940). The memoirs themselves deal largely with the women's-rights efforts of the late 19th and early 20th centuries.

In the work about Stanton, L. reveals a keen appreciation of the importance of the Stanton-Anthony collaboration. In 1959 Lutz published a significant biographical study of that second figure, *Susan B. Anthony: Rebel, Crusader, Humanitarian*. L. thoughtfully appraises the complementary nature of the two women's work and also traces with careful precision the separate line of Anthony's thought and action. She underscores the crucial importance of Anthony's organizing ability and the unflagging involvement which made her eventually the symbol of the woman-suffrage movement.

L.'s final work on 19th-c. women leaders was *Crusade for Freedom* (1968), a study of women's roles in the antislavery campaigns. In this collective biography L. evaluates the work of such varied personalities as the early antislavery writer, Elizabeth Chandler; the educator, Prudence Crandle; and the lecturer-writers, the Grimké sisters. She underscores the significance of the interwoven strands of antislavery efforts and the emerging women's-rights movement. L. sees this same interweaving of concerns reemerging as an important theme of the 1960s.

L. was essentially a narrative biographer, concerned primarily with the broad public record of 19th-c. women leaders. She developed a strong, dramatic style of writing and became a vivid portrayer of reform personalities. Though concerned with the ideas of the women's movement, L. focused primarily on the efforts to translate ideas into reality. She gave relatively little attention to intellectual history itself or to critical appraisal of the broad social context within which the women functioned. She excelled in the presentation of the individual personality and the detailed accounts of women's campaigns, rather than in analytical background studies.

L.'s studies of Willard and of Stanton in particular were pioneering works. The Stanton work was the first significant appraisal of that leader since the general *History of Woman Suffrage*. The Anthony biography and the study of antislavery women presented more familiar material and drew more on well-known sources. The works provided dramatic restatements of these women's roles.

L. wrote perceptively, lucidly, and with fervor about the 19th-c. struggles for women's rights. She had a strong, appreciative sense of what had been achieved, but also a personal concern for the unfinished tasks. In the years between the first and second women's movements, L. kept before the general public the sharply lit images of forceful women leaders of the past.

WORKS: *Emma Willard: Daughter of Democracy* (1929; rev. ed., *Emma Willard, Pioneer Educator of American Women,* 1964). *Mary Baker Eddy Historical House, Swampscott, Massachusetts: The Birthplace of Christian Science* (1935). *Challenging Years: The Memoirs of Harriot Stanton Blatch* (with H. S. Blatch, 1940). *Created Equal: A Biography of Elizabeth Cady Stanton, 1815–1902* (1940). *Mary Baker Eddy Historical House, Rumney Village, New Hampshire: The Rumney Years* (1940). *With Love, Jane: Letters of American*

Women on the War Fronts (1945). *Susan B. Anthony: Rebel, Crusader, Humanitarian* (1959). *Crusade for Freedom: Women of the Antislavery Movement* (1968).

BIBLIOGRAPHY: For articles in reference works, see: *CA*, 45–48 (1974); *Permanent Series* (1975).

   Other references: *AHR* (July 1959; Dec. 1968). *NewR* (29 July 1940). *NEQ* (Dec. 1959). *NYT* (9 June 1919; 1 Sept. 1973). *SatR* (7 March 1959).

                                                                INZER BYERS

Grace Livingston Hill Lutz

B. 15 April 1865, Wellsville, New York; d. 23 Feb. 1947, Swarthmore, Pennsylvania
Wrote under: Grace Livingston Hill, Grace Livingston Hill-Lutz, Grace Livingston, Marcia Macdonald
D. of Charles Montgomery and Marcia Macdonald Livingston; m. Frank Hill, 1892; m. Flavius J. Lutz, 1916

L.'s mother published four romances under the name of Mrs. C. M. Livingston, but devoted herself primarily to being a preacher's wife. Apparently in order to honor her mother as an individual, L. published three novels under her mother's given name, Marcia Macdonald. L.'s father, a Presbyterian minister, also did some writing, exclusively on theological topics. His influence is reflected in L.'s establishment and direction of a mission Sunday school in Swarthmore. Perhaps the strongest of all family influences was that of L.'s aunt, Isabella Macdonald ("Pansy") Alden, an author who not only encouraged L. to write but persuaded her own publisher to print the youngster's first effort, *The Esseltynes; or, Alphonso and Marguerite.*

   L.'s first husband, also a Presbyterian minister, died after seven years of marriage. L. was forced to publish enough to support herself and her two daughters. She began with Sunday-school lessons in a column syndicated by ten local newspapers, but soon turned to fiction. By 1904 she was successful enough to build herself a comfortable home in Swarthmore. L.'s second marriage was unhappy and soon led to separation, although L. remained adamant in her opposition to divorce. She was active as a writer until the end of her life, her final novel being completed by her daughter Ruth for posthumous publication.

L. worked in a wide range of genres, specializing in the adventure story and contemporary romance but also including fantasy (her first novel, *A Chautauqua Idyll*, 1887), nonfiction (*The War Romance of the Salvation Army*, 1919), historical romance (*Marcia Schuyler*, 1908), and mystery (*The Mystery of Mary*, 1912). She wrote 107 books, which sold over three million copies during her lifetime.

L. was especially successful at writing fast-paced adventures featuring intelligent and resourceful heroines. A good example is *The Red Signal* (1919), set during World War I. When the German truck farm where young Hilda Lessing works turns out to be swarming with German spy activity, Hilda shows herself to be both brave and lucky as she saves the U.S. from a major disaster and wins a presidential medal. She also wins the reward reserved for all of L.'s finest heroines—marriage with a handsome and affluent young man. Although the historical perspective is simplistic—World War I is explained as the result of Germany's "forgetting God"—and although the plot turns on some very unlikely coincidences, the narrative is compelling enough to have thrilled many a reader.

L.'s most popular books were contemporary romances, such as *Matched Pearls* (1933), *Beauty for Ashes* (1935), and *April Gold* (1936). The most widely read of all, *The Witness* (1917), brought her thousands of letters of gratitude. In it as in most of her books, L. utilizes one-dimensional characterization in which Christian believers are sincere, brave, and altruistic while unbelievers are selfish and corrupt. Paul Courtland is the typical L. hero: rich, handsome, popular, athletic, a Phi Beta Kappa man. A rich girl, who parallels the biblical "scarlet woman" by attempting to seduce Paul away from his faith, possesses a "nasty little chin" with "a Satanic point." She is contrasted with a poor orphan girl who, because of her modesty and integrity, wins the prize of marriage to the hero. L. manifests a lively sense of social justice by having Paul refuse a lucrative management position in a company that exploits its factory workers in unsafe conditions. The novel's theme is the actual presence of Christ in any life devoted to human concern and justice. As one character puts it, "It's heaven or hell, both now and hereafter."

L. knew how to wring human emotion and enlist current events to enliven her novels while she was making fairly overt attempts to convert her readers to Christ. For instance, a 1944 novel, *Time of the Singing of Birds*, features an attractive officer who returns wounded from World

War II. When he eventually marries the most deserving of his Christian girlfriends, an observer comments, "Heavens! If I thought I could have a marriage like that it would be worth-while trying to be a Christian."

Improbable coincidence, avoidance of moral ambiguity, unconscious sexism, and almost exclusive use of stock characters work together to keep L.'s fiction lightweight. But her fast-paced upbeat style has refreshed and relaxed many people. And there can be little doubt that L. provided a shining ideal for younger readers by featuring so many heroines of unshakable standards and determined, triumphant integrity.

WORKS: *A Chautauqua Idyll* (1887). *A Little Servant* (1890). *The Parkerstown Delegate* (1892). *Katharine's Yesterday, and Other Christian Endeavor Stories* (1895). *In the Way* (1897). *Lone Point; a Summer Outing* (1898). *A Daily Rate* (1900). *The Angel of His Presence* (1902). *An Unwilling Guest* (1902). *According to the Pattern* (1903). *The Story of a Whim* (1903). *Because of Stephen* (1904). *The Girl from Montana* (1908). *Marcia Schuyler* (1908). *Phoebe Deane* (1909). *Dawn of the Morning* (1910). *Aunt Crete's Emancipation* (1911). *The Mystery of Mary* (1912). *The Best Man* (1914). *The Man of the Desert* (1914). *Miranda* (1915). *The Finding of Jasper Holt* (1916). *A Voice in the Wilderness* (1916). *The Witness* (1917). *The Enchanted Barn* (1918). *The Red Signal* (1919). *The Search* (1919). *The War Romance of the Salvation Army* (with E. Booth, 1919). *Cloudy Jewel* (1920). *Exit Betty* (1920). *The Tryst* (1921). *The City of Fire* (1922). *The Big Blue Soldier* (1923). *Tomorrow About This Time* (1923). *Re-Creations* (1924). *Ariel Custer* (1925). *Not Under the Law* (1925). *Coming through the Rye* (1926). *A New Name* (1926). *The Honor Girl* (1927). *Job's Niece* (1927). *The White Flower* (1927). *Blue Ruin* (1928). *Crimson Roses* (1928). *Found Treasure* (1928). *Duskin* (1929). *An Interrupted Night* by I. M. Alden (introduction by Lutz, 1929). *Out of the Storm* (1929). *The Prodigal Girl* (1929). *The Gold Shoe* (1930). *Ladybird* (1930). *The White Lady* (1930). *The Chance of a Lifetime* (1931). *Kerry* (1931). *Memories of Yesterday* by I. M. Alden (edited by Lutz, 1931). *Silver Wings* (1931). *Beggarman* (1932). *The Challengers* (1932). *Happiness Hill* (1932). *Her Wedding Garment* (1932). *The House across the Hedge* (1932). *The Story of the Lost Star* (1932). *The Beloved Stranger* (1933). *Matched Pearls* (1933). *The Ransom* (1933). *Amorelle* (1934). *The Christmas Bride* (1934). *Rainbow Cottage* (1934). *Beauty for Ashes* (1935). *The Strange Proposal* (1935). *White Orchids* (1935). *April Gold* (1936). *Mystery Flowers* (1936). *The Substitute Guest* (1936). *Brentwood* (1937). *Daphne Deane* (1937). *Sunrise* (1937). *The Best Birthday* (1938). *The Divided Battle* (1938). *Dwelling* (1938). *Homing* (1938). *The Lost Message* (1938). *Maria* (1938). *Marigold* (1938). *The Minister's Son* (1938). *Patricia* (1939). *The Seventh Hour* (1939). *Stranger within the Gates* (1939). *Head of the House* (1940). *Partners* (1940). *Rose Galbraith* (1940). *Astra* (1941). *By Way of the Silverthorns* (1941). *In Tune with Wedding Bells* (1941). *Crimson Mountain* (1942). *The Girl of the Woods* (1942). *The Street of the City* (1942). *The Sound of the Trumpet* (1943). *The Spice Box* (1943).

Through These Fires (1943). *More than Conquerer* (1944). *Time of the Singing of Birds* (1944). *All through the Night* (1945). *A Girl to Come Home To* (1945). *Bright Arrows* (1946). *Where Two Ways Met* (1947). *Mary Arden* (completed by R. L. Hill, 1948).

BIBLIOGRAPHY: Karr, J., *Grace Livingston Hill: Her Story and Her Writings* (1948).

For articles in reference works, see: *DAB*, Suppl. 4. *NAW* (article on Grace Livingston Hill by P. S. Boyer). *Reader's Encyclopedia of American Literature*, Ed. M. J. Herzberg (1962). *20thCA*. *20thCAS*.

Other references: *Book News Monthly* (Oct. 1915).

VIRGINIA RAMEY MOLLENKOTT

Helen Merrell Lynd

B. *1896, La Grange, Illinois; d. 30 Jan. 1982, Warren, Ohio*
D. *of Edward Tracy and Mabel Waite Merrell; m. Robert S. Lynd, 1921*

Raised as a Congregationalist, L. shifted her religious orientation while at Wellesley College (B.A. 1919) to an explanation of the world based on Hegelian dialectics. She earned an M.A. (1922) and a Ph.D. (1944) in history from Columbia University; her teaching career centered around Sarah Lawrence College, where she taught from 1929 to 1964. L. shared with her husband a rich, full life as wife, mother of their two children, and professional colleague.

Middletown: A Study in Contemporary American Culture (1929) and the companion volume, *Middletown in Transition: A Study in Cultural Conflicts* (1935), written by L. and her husband, are well-documented studies outstanding in their comprehensiveness, accuracy, and interpretation of community life in the U.S. In 1924 and 1925, the Lynds and their research staff lived in the Middletown community and collected information from a variety of sources, as anthropologists study primitive tribes. The study is organized by an analysis of the major activities for community survival: getting a living, making a home, training the young, and engaging in religious practices and community activities. Although ending their first study on a cautious note recognizing the problems resulting from rapid social change, the prosperity and optimism of the community is evident.

The Lynds returned to Middletown during the Depression. Earning a living, staying healthy, and in general surviving the effects of financial collapse make life in 1935 starkly different from what it was in 1925. The ability of the city to recover and retain optimism is still striking though. Class privileges and strain are more apparent in the later study, yet a sense of worker solidarity is lacking. Radical social change did not occur as a result of radical changes in economics. Rather, the community adhered to "the American way," hoping for a better future.

These remarkable community studies provide a systematic view of an American city in times of stability and change. They also set a high standard of sociological expertise making them landmark studies of community development.

In *Field Work in College Education* (1945), L. studies student-teacher interaction and the application of social-science principles in everyday life. *England in the Eighteen-Eighties: Toward a Social Basis for Freedom* (1945) is a sweeping and powerful study, beautifully written, of the interaction between ideas, material changes, and social movements during a period of social ferment. In *On Shame and the Search for Identity* (1958), L. analyzed more contemporary problems arising from the relationship between the individual and society. The 1965 collection, *Toward Discovery*, serves as a brief overview of L.'s writings.

L.'s interests and skills cover a wide range of topics and disciplines. Always dedicated to the holistic approach to human behavior, her work reflects her standards of excellence and consistent probing for new insights into the human experience.

WORKS: Middletown: A Study in Contemporary American Culture (1929). *Middletown in Transition: A Study in Cultural Conflicts* (1935). *Field Work in College Education* (1945). *England in the Eighteen-Eighties: Toward a Social Basis for Freedom* (1945). *On Shame and the Search for Identity* (1958). *Toward Discovery* (Ed. B. J. Loewenberg, 1965).

BIBLIOGRAPHY: Loewenberg, B. J., Introduction to *Toward Discovery* (1965).
    For articles in reference works, see: *20thCA. 20thCAS.*

MARY JO DEEGAN